CLASSIC CAR
2012 PRICE GUIDE 1945-1990

Contents
5 Editorial
6 Introduction
10 Buying a classic

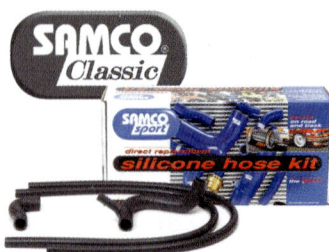

CLASSIC CAR
2012 PRICE GUIDE 1945-1990

Editorial office
Octane, 4 Tower Court, Irchester Road,
Wollaston, Northants NN29 7PJ, UK
Tel: +44 (0)20 7907 6585. Fax: +44 (0)1933 663367
Email: info@octane-magazine.com
Website: www.octane-magazine.com

Advertising office
Octane Media Advertising Dept, 19 Highfield Lane,
Maidenhead, Berkshire SL6 3AN, UK
Tel: +44 (0)1628 510080. Fax: +44 (0)1628 510090
Email: ads@octane-magazine.com

Octane editor	David Lillywhite
Price guide editor	Keith Adams
Production editor	Glen Waddington
Art editor	Mark Sommer
Designer	Rob Gould
Contributors	Richard Gunn
	Paul Hardiman
	Matthew Hayward
	Russ Smith
Advertising director	Sanjay Seetanah
Advertising sales	Rob Schulp
Advertising production	Anisha Mogra
Publishing director	Geoff Love
Digital production manager	Nicky Baker
MagBook publisher	Dharmesh Mistry
Operations director	Robin Ryan
Managing director of advertising	Julian Lloyd-Evans
Newstrade director	David Barker
Commercial and retail director	Martin Belson
COO	Brett Reynolds
Group finance director	Ian Leggett
CEO	James Tye
Chairman	Felix Dennis

Classic cars: safe port in a nasty economic storm

'If you buy the right car, it'll rise in value far faster than your building society balance'

CLASSIC CARS ARE great. Of course, you'd expect me to say that, but bear with me for a moment if you will. We've been enduring some tough economic times, and that means most of us are contemplating our spending decisions very closely indeed.

In these straitened times, there might be those who feel that classic cars are a frivolous pursuit. But they'd be wrong. Sure, everyone needs a little escapism and enjoyment, and what better than to experience the sights, sounds and smells of a bygone era in a classic car? But there's a strong financial argument, too: you'd be quite unlucky to lose money on many classic cars. And if you buy the right one, it'll rise in value far faster than your boring building society balance ever will.

So, now I've persuaded you (or more likely your partner) that it's a great time to buy a classic car, what are you waiting for? Enjoy these marque and model guides, along with the fully updated price listings.

I hope they inspire you to do the right thing.

Keith Adams

Classic Car Price Guide ISBN 1-907779-22-1

To license this product please contact Carlotta Serantoni on +44 (0)20 7907 6550 or email carlotta_serantoni@dennis.co.uk To syndicate content from this product please contact Anj Dosaj-Halai on +44 (0)20 7907 6132 or email anj_dosaj-halai@dennis.co.uk.

The *Classic Car Price Guide* is published under licence from Octane Media Ltd, a subsidiary company of Dennis Publishing Limited, United Kingdom. All rights in the licensed material belong to Felix Dennis, Octane Media or Dennis Publishing and may not be reproduced, whether in whole or in part, without their prior written consent. *Octane* is a registered trademark.

Repro by Octane Repro
Printed by BGP, Bicester, Oxfordshire
Distribution Seymour, 2 East Poultry Avenue, London EC1A 9PT. Tel: +44 (0)20 7429 4000

Periodicals Postage paid @ Emigsville, PA.
Postmaster: send address corrections to Octane Media c/o 3330 Pacific Ave, Suite 404, Virginia Beach, VA 23451

Contributors

ROB GOULD
Rob is now pushing forward with digital platforms for *Octane* and its sister magazine *Evo* – as well as finding time to design the *Classic Car Price Guide*. See it on your iPad soon too.

GLEN WADDINGTON
Octane's production editor has been busy revisiting every entry in this guide – as well as making suggestions for new ones. Good job he loves what he does and knows the market inside out.

MATTHEW HAYWARD
Staff writer for *Octane* magazine, and 1980s car guru Matthew has been ultra-busy sourcing new pictures, researching specification data and writing potted histories.

RUSS SMITH
A freelance contributor and former editor of several classic car magazines, Russ Smith has been writing about classics for 20 years, as well as driving them and getting his hands dirty too.

RICHARD DREDGE
The original 'data dad', for *Top Gear* magazine, and founder of Magic Car Pics, Richard's huge personal photo archive has been stretched putting together this price guide.

RICHARD GUNN
Writer and photographer Richard Gunn has several books to his credit. He is known for his soft spot for Volvos and British Leyland cars. Thankfully, he knows a lot about Aston Martins too.

CLASSICS IN 2012

Interest in the classic car scene is at an unprecedented high, your choice of events has never been wider, and values are on the rise, too. Here's to what promises to be a vintage year

More people than ever before are becoming interested in classic cars. It's an international hobby at the very vanguard of which is the UK, and it's one that looks certain for years to come. It's also a multi-billion-pound industry that employs thousands of people – and brings pleasure to many, many more. What's best about the classics movement is that it's all-inclusive – it doesn't matter if your budget is £500 or £5 million, there's bound to be a model that's for you.

Exactly why classic cars are on the march right now is interesting. The cult of nostalgia continues to grow, and

cars – as well as music, film and television – are central to this. As history becomes more accessible, people are finding more reasons to be fascinated by it. And there's a ready car market out there to sate the demand of those in love with the past. Currently, the 1970s and '80s are where interest is most acute – and because the vehicles from this era are increasingly durable, there are more to go around.

But it's not just nostalgia that's fuelling the rise in classics. More than ever, the social scene is improving – with more and more breakfast club-style arrive 'n' drive events popping up to

IT'S A GOOD NEWS STORY

Classic car values have been going through a revolution. Prices have consistently risen since 2008, fuelled by an escalation of demand – and a reduction in the supply of the very best automobiles. But unlike the classic boom of the late 1980s – and the subsequent bust in the early '90s – the rise has been steady, consistent, and focused on only blue-chip cars.

We've had auction record after auction record throughout the year – the Top Ten lists are constantly being rewritten. And it has been a stellar 12 months for top-end collector cars, with a world record price of $16,390,000 paid for the 1957 Ferrari Testa Rossa at the Gooding & Co auction at Pebble Beach last August.

The Historic Automobile Group International (HAGI), which monitors the upper echelons of the marketplace for *Octane* magazine, produced some fascinating figures in its year-end sum-up of 2011's market. 'Classic cars really are better than gold,' Dietrich Hatlapa, founder of HAGI says. 'Annual figures reveal that values in some segments of the classics market have advanced by more than 20%. By contrast, gold, the traditional safe haven in times of economic uncertainty, returned growth of just 9.93% in 2011.'

It is worth noting that HAGI currently tracks the auction and private transactions for what it calls its 'top' cars, as well as Porsche and Ferrari. The latter, certainly, has been on the march – with a 250GTO becoming the UK's most expensive automobile sale in early 2012, at around £20m. That same car was bought in 2008 for £15m – so you get an idea of the growth.

Yet the classic car scene isn't all about numbers and values, and we shouldn't get too fixated on them. As Hatlapa concludes: 'Historics are a tangible asset; once a model has become collectable it has never become uncollectable. And classic cars are fun to own and drive.'

But before you break out the champagne and congratulate yourself on your financial acumen by just owning the old car of your choice, it is worth saying right now that the classics market – and values in general – are diversifying. And not all are going up. Yes, there is growth and strength right at the top, but for the rest of us, and the real world in general, the rise has been far gentler.

The much-vaunted rise of the 'youngtimers' – or the cult cars from between 1980 and 2000 – has pretty much stalled. There's no lack of interest, but healthy survival rates and a depressed economy mean supply outstrips demand, and prices remain – on the whole – low. Exceptions to that include rare Japanese metal, such as the Toyota Corolla GT AE86 coupé; rarer RS-badged Fords, such as the Sierra Cosworth RS500 and Escort RS Turbo (first series); and limited-production specials, such as the Lancia Delta Integrale and Porsche 968 Clubsport. And static values are actually great news for keen enthusiasts looking to get onto the classic car ladder.

In the middle market, it's a case of steady growth and a widening gap between the best condition 1/concours cars

get people out and about in their cherished cars at the weekend. And it just wouldn't do to turn up in your company car. Beyond that, there are tours, drives, fun runs – and for those with a motorsport bent, classic rallying and regularity events. The only limitation is your imagination. And the depth of your pockets...

If you're new to our price guide, we hope that it fuels your dreams and provides a whole raft of fresh inspiration for you. The pleasure in this MagBook is that each page should provide new – and sometimes unexpected – classic car ideas that have you wondering: 'I could have one of those...'

and those that don't make the grade. Again, that means there are still plenty of opportunities to grab yourself a great classic car bargain, especially if you're handy with a spanner.

In 2011, the story was all about the Jaguar E-type, as it enjoyed its 50th birthday celebrations. But just as quickly as its stock rose at the start of the year, it fell back to original levels as fatigue set in. Expect more of the same in 2012 with the MGB and Lotus Elan; perhaps less with more esoteric anniversary cars, such as the Alfa Romeo Giulia and Ferrari 250GTO.

So, the story for 2012 is one of classic car growth fuelled by demand. Demand from private individuals is easily understood; it comes down to nostalgia or investment potential. A new phenomenon has been rise in the number of company-classic-car drivers – something that's on the rise, due to changes in taxation. It's a trend well worth keeping an eye on, especially as company owners trade in their Bentley Continental GTs and Aston Martin DB9s for 3 Litres and DB5s.

WHAT IS COVERED BY THIS GUIDE?

We're remaining within our 1945-1990 policy of inclusion. If you could buy it new during that period and it has a following today, it's allowed in. Even the youngest cars in the guide will be well over 20 years old in terms of design, while the oldest are usually rooted in the pre-war days, in spite of the 1945 threshold. There are a handful of new entries for 2012, and a complete set of marque guides – but the big news is the updated values, as the market volatility of the past 12 months has been fascinating.

For 2012, our unrivalled coverage of the headline classic marques has been bolstered significantly by the expansion of other manufacturers' line-ups, creating a more balanced guide to classic cars – and their values. And where, for instance, we would once have included only the hot versions of family cars, we now have entries for their bread-and-butter counterparts.

These revisions have led to a number of surprising additions to the listings and we hope you appreciate their inclusion. Areas we've concentrated on are the supercar sector, which has shown consistent and huge growth since 2008; Japanese cars, which continue to fascinate younger fans brought up on more than 15 years of PlayStation *Gran Turismo* gaming; and early post-war historic racers, which tend to be overlooked in other price guides.

Given the expansion of interest in the 1980-2000 performance car market, we look forward to compiling next year's price guide with eager anticipation. For now, please enjoy finding out about the state of play in 2012.

THE SPEC TABLES

Years produced: If a car was launched in the preceding year to start of production, it will be the latter date that's quoted. Often American cars are termed in model years, so a 1985 Pontiac Fiero, for instance, will have been launched in 1984. The figure in brackets following this refers to production numbers where known.

Performance: We have tried to obtain independent road test data from a number of sources, but where this has not been possible, we have quoted manufacturer data.

Engine: Plain English descriptions covering capacity, fuelling and cylinder count. Where there are several versions of the same model, we have identified which variation is described in the specification.

Power and torque: Quoted directly from the manufacturer in DIN standard. German (PS), American (SAE) and Japanese (JIS) figures have been converted to bhp wherever possible. Torque is quoted in UK-standard lb ft.

Drivetrain:
FWD: Front-wheel drive
RWD: Rear-wheel drive
AWD: All-wheel drive

Transmission:
The standard gearbox package, detailing the number of forward speeds and whether it's manual or automatic.

Structure:
The car's construction type, be it monocoque, separate chassis, backbone, or coachbuilt Superleggera. All descriptions are in plain English.

Weight:
Manufacturer-quoted dry weight in kg wherever possible although, throughout the years, car makers have changed the way they report weight, and some may include a full tank of fuel, or even the driver's weight. All figures, therefore, must be taken as a guide only.

PRICE GUIDE

Launch price:
The UK launch price wherever it is possible to quote. For model ranges, we have quoted the price of the entry-level car; therefore, for cars not officially imported into the UK, no price is applicable (N/A). In cases where cars were imported via a third party concessionaire and sold across the UK, theirs is the price we have quoted.

Excellent:
The value of a car in excellent all-round condition, where there is unlikely to be any expenditure required. Original factory-fresh condition, or the result of a high-standard restoration. Concours-condition cars, or those with specific historic significance, may be worth considerably more.

Good:
Sound, usable and presentable cars that you would be happy to drive on a regular basis. Not perfect, and may need some cosmetic or mechanical work, but a representative example of the breed, and one you would be happy to display at an owners' club meeting.

Average:
Running cars with plenty of issues that need sorting. Most will have MoTs, but might need some work to get through the next one. For newer cars, the average rating will refer to a reasonable car, but for anything built before 1975, the chances are it will need welding and other refurbishment.

Project:
This can cover a number of sins – either a car barn-stored over a long period of time, or one that has been well-used and needs a lot of work to get back on the road, or through its next MoT. Prices are very low but big expenditure awaits those not handy with a spanner or welding gear.

WHAT CLASSIC?

You've read the guide, dreamed a little and decided you need a classic in your life. Now it's time to buy one. Here's our handy guide to your main purchasing options...

CHOOSING AND BUYING your classic car is very much a case of heart versus head. The heart allows saccharin-coated nostalgia, an appreciation of beautiful styling and the all-round positive karma of owning an old car to take command of the senses far more than they ought to. When buying new, purchasers tend to be analytical, study the options and focus on buying the car that really suits their needs – but when buying a classic, all of that goes out of the window, and most people buy on looks, colour, smell and feel. Oh, and that old commodity 'gut feeling'.

And choosing the classic car to fill that beloved space in your garage *should* be all about feel and emotion. Only you know what it is that tugs your heartstrings, and rightly so. What these ten-point guides are all about is how to go about buying that car – the dos and don'ts of buying privately, at auction, from a dealer or online.

Gut feeling is good, but it works so much better when you follow a few basic rules.

BUYING AT AUCTION

This can be risky, although the potential benefits can be enormous. It's worth bearing in mind that, in the current market where dealers are struggling to secure good stock, you might find yourself in a competitive situation. So long as you're switched on, are hyper-aware of the speed at which an auction progresses, and stick to these ground rules, you shouldn't get your fingers burned.

1 DO YOUR HOMEWORK
Buy a catalogue and get a full description of the car you're interested in buying. Classic auction houses are excellent at providing historic information on the cars they're selling, but a call to the auctioneer in the days leading up to the sale can also be very revealing.

2 VIEW THE CAR AT YOUR LEISURE
Bear in mind that, on sale day, you might struggle to get a good look at the car as the auction hots up. So, if you can, try and turn up on preview day so you can have a good poke around. Do all those buying guide checks you're advised to and satisfy yourself that the car is exactly what you're looking for. At this point, decide the maximum you are prepared to pay for the car.

3 MAKE SURE YOU TAKE MONEY TO THE SALE
Sounds silly, but don't forget to take enough with you to cover at least the deposit on the car you're bidding on. Each auction house is slightly different in terms of what this is, so make sure you check for details in the catalogue.

4 HAVE A FRIEND WITH YOU
Taking a friend with you could be one of the most sensible things you do. They won't be as engaged as you, so will look at the situation more dispassionately. They may even spot faults with the car that you might miss. Most importantly, make sure they know how much you have – and that they are briefed to stop you making any rash bids.

5 BE PREPARED TO GET DIRTY
Wear old clothes so you don't feel reserved about looking underneath the car. Make sure you have a torch and magnet so you can look for underbody issues and check for thick layers of filler.

6 LISTEN AND WATCH
Once you're happy with the car you have in mind, and you've checked it the best you can, make sure you're close by when it's driven into the auction arena. Watch it being started, listen to the engine, make sure it sounds sweet and doesn't smoke – and, if you can, take a look at the gauges to ensure that vital signs, such as oil pressure, are healthy.

7 PAY ATTENTION TO THE AUCTIONEER
Before the bidding starts, the auctioneer will describe the car. Listen closely to this, as his words are legally binding. Then, before he starts the bidding, take a deep breath, compose yourself and focus on the maximum price you set yourself. This is very important, as once the bidding starts, the adrenaline can kick in, and it's very easy to run away with the bids.

8 MAKE YOUR INTENTIONS CLEAR
Make sure you're in full view of the auctioneer. Do not be tempted to raise your hand first – the auctioneer may suggest an opening bid, and usually it is on the high side. See who else is interested, watch around you, and don't get drawn straight away.

9 BID CONFIDENTLY...
...and don't worry about your intentions being misread (you can't buy a car on a sneeze or a wiped nose). You can tell the auctioneer to lower the bidding increments, and make sure you're actually bidding against someone, rather than just an auctioneer taking bids off the wall. All the time, consider your maximum figure, and make sure the adrenaline doesn't take over.

10 YOU WON!
If your bid is successful you will need to pay a deposit, followed by the balance within a short period (usually 24 hours). Delay and you may be charged storage. Now it's time to calm down, take stock, and remember that if you're taking the car home, to consider the MoT, tax and insurance situation. If in doubt, bring a trailer.

BUYING PRIVATELY

There are a lot of cars out there in the classified adverts, so you can afford to take your time and choose what's exactly right for you. As ever, stay on your toes and be sensible, and you should bag that classic car you've always hankered after.

1 STUDY THE ADVERT
Read the advert, and make sure you get an all-round feeling for what the seller is trying to say. Note down any questions you might have about the car or any points in the advert you're not sure about.

2 CHECK OUT THE SELLER
You've seen the pictures and read the description, and still like what you see – now it's time to get in touch. If there's an email address, don't be tempted to get in touch that way – always try and make the first contact via the phone. Is it a landline? If not, ask why.

3 FINDING OUT ABOUT THE CAR
You're talking to the seller. Always be polite, but firm – keep control of the conversation – ask how long he's owned the car; from there, ascertain how much work and care he's put in. Ask if he's in the owners' club, what sort of storage the car has, how often he uses it. Can you have an independent inspection? If any of the answers don't add up, it's time to back out.

4 MEETING THE SELLER
Always meet a private seller at their home address (or at a push, their workplace). Insist on going in – asking for a cup of tea or to use their facilities is a good excuse. Unless you know the seller, if they suggest a halfway point decline their kind offer. Be prepared to visit at a time to suit them – a day off work will cost you a lot less than the effects of buying a stolen car.

5 CHECKING THE OWNER
Get there a few minutes early, and make sure you have full access to the car. Do your research – get a buying guide for the model in question, and follow it closely. Check that the car is registered on the V5C Registration Certificate to that address and that you're talking to the registered keeper.

6 CHECKING THE CAR
Start the car from cold and look for exhaust smoke. Search for oil, air or water leaks. Are all the levels correct? Are all the tyres in good order with plenty of tread? Check their age and look for them going hard and cracking. Faulty tyres are a major issue that could get you in hot water on the drive home.

7 THE TEST DRIVE
Insist on driving the car, unless it's a project you're going to restore. Bring your insurance details and licence with you, and check that you are covered to take the car on a test drive. If the seller isn't keen, ask why, and reassure him that you're capable of driving his car. If he wants the sale, he will capitulate.

8 CHECK THE PAPERWORK
The drive went well, now it's time to examine the car's history. Check out the service record, and try to piece it together – if it has been restored, ask to see photos, as most people will keep such a record. See who's been doing the work; if it's a specialist, then that's a big positive. Finally, closely look at the legal documents – are they clean and unmolested? Check VIN and colour details, and cross-check against the documentation.

9 PAYING FOR IT
There are different ways you can pay for a vehicle – cash, cheque, banker's draft or bank transfer. An immediate bank transfer can be made using the CHAPS system for a nominal fee (£20-£30). Consider meeting the buyer at your bank and completing the transaction there.

10 DRIVE IT HOME
Make sure your insurer knows before you go anywhere, and that the car is taxed and MoT'd. Carry oil, water and a few tools – but if you've done your homework, you won't need them!

BUYING A CLASSIC

BUYING ONLINE

With the growth of online auction websites such as eBay, it has never been easier to buy the car of your dreams. However, treat an online sale as you would any other auction, do your homework properly, and you should bag yourself a bargain. But also remember that if a car looks too good to be true, it probably is.

1 STUDY THE ADVERT
Read the advert fully, and initially email any questions you may have. See if the seller has a 'Buy it Now' price, but don't even think of pressing that button until you've been in touch.

2 CHECK OUT THE SELLER
Check the seller's feedback, and their willingness to communicate about the car. If they are open and there are opportunities, try and arrange a viewing of the car.

3 FINDING OUT ABOUT THE CAR
Now you've arranged to meet the seller, go by the same rules as per private ads. Make sure the car is documented at the address, and to the person you're dealing with.

4 CHECKING THE CAR
Get to the seller's place a few minutes early, and give the car a thorough going over. Just because there's an auction running on it, there's no need to skimp on the examination.

5 THE TEST DRIVE
Unless it's not legal to do so (MoT, insurance, tax), give the car a decent test drive. Make sure it warms through properly and everything works as it should.

6 CHECK THE PAPERWORK
Thoroughly examine the history of the car, and if it is lacking then factor this into your offer. Remember that you're in the driving seat, so stay calm and polite.

7 MAKE AN OFFER
If you like the car, ask the seller if he is prepared to end the auction early. If he is, make an offer. But don't hand over any cash until he's ended the auction online. Remember that as the sale was made outside of the auction site, you may well lose your statutory rights regarding legal protection. So be confident in the car and the seller.

8 SEEING THE AUCTION THROUGH
If the seller insists on running the auction to its conclusion, consider your offer and place a bid on the auction when you get the opportunity. Do not be tempted to raise that in the heat of battle, and also be prepared to be 'sniped' by a last-minute bidder.

9 WINNING THE AUCTION
If you win, get in touch with the seller immediately. You're happy with the car and the seller, so when you pay, make sure it's through the auction site's official payment site, such as Paypal. If the seller prefers cash, try and leave a deposit electronically via the site, with the balance in cash when you collect the car. That way, you have a record of the transaction.

10 LEAVE FEEDBACK
Always leave feedback. If there are issues with the seller after the transaction is completed, then use the auction site's complaint procedures – and don't take issues into your own hands.

BUYING FROM A DEALER

It's probably still the most popular way of purchasing a classic car – and with good reason. Nothing beats the face-to-face deal, the banter and the flexibility of buying from a dealer.

1 STUDY THE ADVERT
Like what you see? Give the dealer a call and discuss the car. He is likely to know everything there is to know about it, especially if the car has been given a pre-sale service, so ask as many questions as you can.

2 VIEWING THE CAR
The great thing about buying from a dealer is that you get great access to the car and, in some cases, even a workshop. So make the most of these facilities – before you arrange to see the car, insist that you're the one who starts it from cold, and warn them that you'll be giving it a thorough going over. The chances are the dealer will be happy to see you're taking such an interest.

3 INSPECTING THE CAR: BODY
Check all the areas you've been advised to in the buying guides that you will have studied beforehand. Pay close attention to the bodywork and, if it has been restored, ask for details and pictures of the work that's been undertaken.

4 INSPECTING THE CAR: ENGINE
Leave the engine until you're completely satisfied with the condition of the bodywork. That way it will have cooled down if it's been run before you arrived. Listen to it start, check for fluid leaks, and watch that exhaust pipe.

5 INSPECTING THE CAR: INTERIOR
This is an often-overlooked cost in classic car ownership, but if the interior isn't perfect, and you want it to be, getting your car up to scratch inside could cost an arm and a leg. So don't gloss over that cracked veneer or damaged leather, as restoration and repair costs will rapidly mount up.

6 INSPECTING THE CAR: THE TEST DRIVE
Give the car a thorough test drive – feel the operation of the gearbox, brakes and steering; are they smooth? Does the car pull up in a straight line? Does it accelerate without hesitation? Drive at least 15 miles, and offer to put in petrol if the dealer says 'there's no fuel in it'. Listen carefully for anything unexpected, such as rattles, clonks or rumbles.

7 CHECK THE PAPERWORK
It's all about history these days, so make sure there's loads of it. Thoroughly examine the history of the car, and if it is lacking then factor this into your offer. If the dealer doesn't have everything to hand, try to find out all you can about the previous owner and get in touch with them.

8 MAKE AN OFFER
If all these boxes are ticked, then make an offer. Buying a classic car is very different to buying a merely secondhand one, and although there can be room for haggling in the sticker price, don't count on it, as it really depends on the car and the prevailing market conditions. If the dealer is confident someone will stump up the full asking price, he won't budge. But assess the situation, and aim to bring the price down – always be polite and firm as you attempt your negotiations.

9 SEALING THE DEAL
The dealer and you reach an agreement and shake on it. It's unlikely you'll be driving away in the car there and then, as he may want to prepare it to leave the garage – that should include a service and fresh MoT. If this is not mentioned, see if you can get these jobs done, and thrown in for the price you're paying. It never hurts to ask.

10 LIVING HAPPILY EVER AFTER
For the full ownership experience, join the clubs, get involved in the events, and get out and drive your car. It's your classic, now get the most from it!

ABARTH

FOUNDED as a hillclimb and sports car racing team in 1950, Carlo Abarth's company expanded into producing tuning equipment and engines for various Fiats alongside its own racing models. Such was the cachet of the name that Fiat was glad to have its products branded with the Abarth badge. Its best-known and arguably most fun creations were the tiny and giant-killing Fiat 500- and 600-based models. After a flirtation with Simca, Abarth was taken over by Fiat in 1971 and continued to denote performance models, although it became little more than a trim level during the 1990s and Noughties. It has recently been relaunched as a separate division by Fiat.

ABARTH
Fiat 750 Zagato

Carlo Abarth's 750 Zagato GT first appeared at the Geneva Motor Show in 1956 and immediately caused a storm. The pretty little coupé and roadster were based on the Fiat 500's running gear, but powered by a tuned version of the Abarth 747cc engine in high-compression form, delivering 44bhp. Later versions were available with a twin-cam head that made enough power to take the featherweight sports car to a top speed of 118mph and on to success in motor sport, including a class win on the Mille Miglia in 1957.

SPECIFICATIONS	
Years produced:	1957-1961
Performance:	0-60mph: 15.8sec
	Top speed: 95mph
Power & torque:	44bhp/44lb ft
Engine:	Normally aspirated 747cc four cylinder, petrol, carburettor, 8 valves
Drivetrain:	Rear-engine RWD
Structure:	Separate chassis
Transmission:	Four-speed manual
Weight:	535kg

PRICE GUIDE	
Launch price:	£2248
Excellent:	£47,500
Good:	£32,500
Average:	£20,000
Project:	£12,500

ABARTH
Fiat 850/1000

The Abarth-converted Fiat 850 and 1000 were front-running European Group one Touring Cars, winning the championship on several occasions. Their combination of grip, performance and low price made them highly desirable club-level competition cars, with the fastest TCR and Corsas easily topping 115mph. They remain popular with historic racers – and, appropriately, they are far better suited to the track than they are the road. Expensive and desirable today, but far from being the quickest track car for your money.

SPECIFICATIONS (1000TC Corsa)	
Years produced:	1960-1970
Performance:	0-60mph: 7.0sec
	Top speed: 118mph
Power & torque:	112bhp/65lb ft
Engine:	Normally aspirated 982cc four cylinder, petrol, carburettor, 8 valves
Drivetrain:	Rear-engine RWD
Structure:	Separate chassis
Transmission:	Four-speed manual
Weight:	583kg

PRICE GUIDE	
Launch price:	N/A in UK
Excellent:	£45,000
Good:	£22,500
Average:	£7500
Project:	£2500

ABARTH
Fiat 595/595SS/695SS

Carlo Abarth cut his performance car teeth on the rear-engined Fiat 500, producing some of Italy's finest pocket rockets. Although based on one of the slowest cars you could buy, the Abarth was every inch a Mini Cooper rival during the 1960s, with the bored-out 695 version packing a 40bhp punch. Abarths feature extrovert styling and, on the right road, will give much more powerful cars a real run for their money. Very rare and relatively valuable in the UK, and well worth seeking out if you like your thrills served on the raw side.

SPECIFICATIONS	
Years produced:	1963-1971
Performance:	0-60mph: N/A
	Top speed: N/A
Power & torque:	30bhp/33lb ft
Engine:	Normally aspirated 593cc twin, petrol, carburettor, 4 valves
Drivetrain:	Rear-engine RWD
Structure:	Separate chassis
Transmission:	Four-speed manual
Weight:	500kg

PRICE GUIDE	
Launch price:	N/A in UK
Excellent:	£37,500 (for £42,500 for 695SS)
Good:	£22,500
Average:	£7500
Project:	£2500

ABARTH
Fiat 124 Rally Spider

Homologation special based on 1800-engined 124 Spider. There's extra power from twin Weber carbs and new exhaust manifold – the last ones even being offered with an optional 16-valve head – and the stiffened shell was fitted with lightweight glassfibre bonnet and boot and alloy door skins. All got a rollcage and permanent hardtop. Independent rear suspension improved handling and one won the 1972 European rally Championship. 1013 were built, but pure road-going examples are almost impossible to find these days.

SPECIFICATIONS	
Years produced:	1972-1975 (1013 in total)
Performance:	0-60mph: 7.5sec
	Top speed: 118mph
Power & torque:	128bhp/117lb ft
Engine:	Normally aspirated 1756cc four cylinder, petrol, carburettor, 8 valves
Drivetrain:	Front-engine RWD
Structure:	Monocoque
Transmission:	Five-speed manual
Weight:	939kg

PRICE GUIDE	
Launch price:	N/A
Excellent:	£17,500
Good:	£13,000
Average:	£8500
Project:	£5000

AC

BRITAIN'S OLDEST independent car marque, AC – for Auto Carriers – built its first three-wheeled passenger vehicle in 1907. It gradually moved upmarket; four-wheeled vehicles appeared in 1913 and, after WW1, the company expanded into sports cars. It continued after the next war as a struggling specialist manufacturer, even going back to three-wheelers, until it hit paydirt with the Cobra in 1962, its Ace roadster fitted with Ford V8 engines by US racing god Carroll Shelby. The marque limped through the 1970s and '80s with models such as the unsuccessful ME3000 and remains active today, albeit building Cobra-influenced cars in tiny numbers in Germany and the USA.

AC
2-litre

After WW2 ended, AC resumed the building of low-volume quality cars with this gently sporting 2.0-litre saloon. A four-door was added to the range for 1953, by which time the already ageing triple-carb AC engine's output had risen from 74bhp to 85bhp. Bodies are aluminium over a wood frame and steel chassis; suspension also harks back to days past with solid axles and transverse leaf springs at each end of the car. At least the dampers are hydraulic: an AC first. Cable rear brakes are fitted to early cars, with an all-hydraulic system from 1951.

SPECIFICATIONS

Years produced:	1947-1958 (1284 in total)
Performance:	0-60mph: 19.9sec
	Top speed: 80mph
Power & torque:	74bhp/105lb ft
Engine:	Normally aspirated 1991cc straight six, petrol, carburettor, 12 valves
Drivetrain:	Front-engine RWD
Structure:	Separate chassis
Transmission:	Four-speed manual
Weight:	1222kg

PRICE GUIDE

Launch price:	£1277
Excellent:	£15,000
Good:	£10,000
Average:	£4500
Project:	£2000

AC
2-Litre DHC/Buckland

Straightforward drophead version of the saloon was only in production a year, so few were built and all went for export – though most were still right-hand drive. You are more likely to come across one of the Buckland tourers, whose bodies were built by a coachbuilder of that name. These were a lot prettier, with more rounded lines and a fold-flat windscreen. Later examples also got cutaway doors for an even more sporting look, though mechanically they were identical to the saloons. Quite hard to find, but not usually that expensive when you do.

SPECIFICATIONS

Years produced:	1949-1956
Performance:	0-60mph: 19.9sec
	Top speed: 80mph
Power & torque:	74bhp/100lb ft
Engine:	Normally aspirated 1991cc straight six, petrol, carburettor, 12 valves
Drivetrain:	Front-engine RWD
Structure:	Separate chassis
Transmission:	Four-speed manual
Weight:	1320kg

PRICE GUIDE

Launch price:	Not known
Excellent:	£25,000
Good:	£17,500
Average:	£12,000
Project:	£6000

AC
Ace (AC engine)

Designed to raise AC's post-war profile, and to tap into America's new-found enthusiasm for Brit sports cars. The simple but pretty aluminium body clothed a tube-frame chassis with all-independent suspension that gave excellent handling and stole a march over rivals like Jaguar – even if it was by transverse leaf springs. Finned aluminium drum brakes gradually gave way to discs around 1958. Only the engine disappointed. It was AC's own, but had been in production since the 1920s; output grew from 85bhp to 105bhp, but the car needed more.

SPECIFICATIONS

Years produced:	1951-1962 (223 in total)
Performance:	0-60mph: 9.5sec
	Top speed: 112mph
Power & torque:	85bhp/110lb ft
Engine:	Normally aspirated 1991cc straight six, petrol, carburettor, 12 valves
Drivetrain:	Front-engine RWD
Structure:	Separate chassis
Transmission:	Four-speed manual
Weight:	762kg

PRICE GUIDE

Launch price:	£1439
Excellent:	£150,000
Good:	£115,000
Average:	£90,000
Project:	£60,000

AC
Aceca-AC

Introduced for 1955, the Aceca was a grand touring coupé version of the Ace, offering more luxury than the roadster that fully justified its extra cost. The basic chassis followed the lines of the Ace, but with heavier-duty main rails, an extra crossmember and rubber mountings for the differential to reduce the amount of road noise transmitted to the cabin. For similar reasons, glassfibre front and rear bulkheads were used. Rather than the tubes of the Ace, doors and tailgate were wood-framed in the traditional manner. Only 151 examples were built.

SPECIFICATIONS

Years produced:	1954-1963 (151 in total)
Performance:	0-60mph: 13.4sec
	Top speed: 102mph
Power & torque:	85bhp/110lb ft
Engine:	Normally aspirated 1991cc straight six, petrol, carburettor, 12 valves
Drivetrain:	Front-engine RWD
Structure:	Separate chassis
Transmission:	Four-speed manual
Weight:	890kg

PRICE GUIDE

Launch price:	£1439
Excellent:	£70,000
Good:	£45,000
Average:	£22,500
Project:	£15,000

AC
Ace-Bristol

From 1956, all those who had criticised the Ace for its lack of power got an answer (though it was to be the first of many): Bristol's six-cylinder unit of similar capacity was bought in. Of slightly newer and more sophisticated design, most were supplied in 128bhp spec, though a few were delivered with 125 or even 105bhp. The better Bristol gearbox was also used, with overdrive a popular option. They were sold at a price premium alongside other Aces and one was driven to the 1959 Le Mans 24 Hours, winning the 2.0-litre class and finishing seventh overall.

SPECIFICATIONS

Years produced:	1956-1962 (463 in total)
Performance:	0-60mph: 9.1sec
	Top speed: 118mph
Power & torque:	125bhp/123lb ft
Engine:	Normally aspirated 1971cc straight six, petrol, carburettor, 12 valves
Drivetrain:	Front-engine RWD
Structure:	Separate chassis
Transmission:	Four-speed manual
Weight:	894kg

PRICE GUIDE

Launch price:	£2011
Excellent:	£225,000
Good:	£175,000
Average:	£115,000
Project:	£60,000

AC
Aceca-Bristol

In line with the Ace, a Bristol-engined version of the Aceca was added from 1956. Though markedly more expensive than the AC-engined car, it was a much better performer and outsold the lesser car, with 169 leaving the factory. As with all Acecas, you get details such as two rows of four louvres in the bonnet, burr walnut instrument surrounds and glovebox lid, and hinged rear side windows to aid ventilation. Though the car was directly related to the Ace, and had a similar nose and grille, no body panels are the same on both cars.

SPECIFICATIONS

Years produced:	1956-1963 (169 in total)
Performance:	0-60mph: 10.3sec
	Top speed: 115mph
Power & torque:	105bhp/123lb ft
Engine:	Normally aspirated 1971cc straight six, petrol, carburettor, 12 valves
Drivetrain:	Front-engine RWD
Structure:	Separate chassis
Transmission:	Four-speed manual
Weight:	895kg

PRICE GUIDE

Launch price:	£1722
Excellent:	£80,000
Good:	£55,000
Average:	£25,000
Project:	£17,500

AC
Greyhound

Stylish and dignified four-seat big brother to the Aceca, also panelled in aluminium and fitted with all the same engine choices, though in reality most ordered used the Bristol straight-six, either in 2.0- or 2.2-litre form. No more than three are thought to have received the Zephyr 2.6. Despite a change to coil springs for independent suspension, handling isn't a match for the Aceca and, although only a quarter as many were built as the smaller car, they have never set the market alight in the same way and can be bought for about half as much.

SPECIFICATIONS

Years produced:	1959-1963 (83 in total)
Performance:	0-60mph: 12.7sec
	Top speed: 104mph
Power & torque:	125bhp/132lb ft
Engine:	Normally aspirated 1971cc straight six, petrol, carburettor, 12 valves
Drivetrain:	Front-engine RWD
Structure:	Separate chassis
Transmission:	Four-speed manual
Weight:	991kg

PRICE GUIDE

Launch price:	£2891
Excellent:	£40,000
Good:	£20,000
Average:	£12,500
Project:	£7000

AC
Ace RS 2.6

Introduced in 1961 and originally a Ruddspeed conversion – hence the 'RS' – this used the cheap and cheerful 2.6-litre six-cylinder engine from a MkII Ford Zephyr. Depending on which state of tune the customer ordered, output could be up to 170bhp (Stage 3, with aluminium head and triple Webers). Even in that most potent form it was still cheaper then the Bristol-engined Ace. Now the most valuable Ace, only 37 were built and are recognised by a new nose and grille that would soon adorn Cobras – along with a further eight Aceca coupés.

SPECIFICATIONS

Years produced:	1961-1963 (37 in total)
Performance:	0-60mph: N/A
	Top speed: 120mph
Power & torque:	100bhp/133lb ft
Engine:	Normally aspirated 2553cc straight six, petrol, carburettor, 12 valves
Drivetrain:	Front-engine RWD
Structure:	Separate chassis
Transmission:	Four-speed manual
Weight:	813kg

PRICE GUIDE

Launch price:	Not known
Excellent:	£175,000
Good:	£130,000
Average:	£110,000
Project:	£60,000

AC
Cobra 260/289

Carroll Shelby's big idea outsold the Ace it was based on, with most sold the US and none in the UK until 1964. The first 75 used 4.2-litre Ford V8s; those and the next 51 4.7 versions had cam-and-peg steering; after that it was much improved rack-and-pinion. Ace chassis was beefed up to cope but, with all that power, handling can be entertaining. Standard smallblock Cobras have flat faces to their flared arches, though there were 27 AC 289s (no Cobra in name) built from mid-1966 with the big-arched Cobra 427 bodyshell and coil-sprung chassis.

SPECIFICATIONS

Years produced:	1961-1965 (673 in total)
Performance:	0-60mph: 5.5sec
	Top speed: 138mph
Power & torque:	271bhp/269lb ft
Engine:	Normally aspirated 4727cc V8, petrol, carburettor, 16 valves
Drivetrain:	Front-engine RWD
Structure:	Separate chassis
Transmission:	Four-speed manual
Weight:	952kg

PRICE GUIDE

Launch price:	£2454
Excellent:	£350,000
Good:	£250,000
Average:	£185,000
Project:	£150,000

AC
Cobra 427

A complete reworking of the Cobra's chassis was required for the installation of Ford's 'big block' 7.0-litre V8s, most of which were the 427ci in various states of tune, though some were sold with smaller-bore/longer-stroke 428ci engines. Chassis tubes were larger, with more crossmembers, and suspension was unequal-length wishbones with coil springs. The body changed, with bulging rear wings to cover much larger tyres, plus aggressively flared front wings. The 31 427 S/C (Semi Competition) models are particularly sought after and valuable.

SPECIFICATIONS

Years produced:	1965-1967 (413 in total)
Performance:	0-60mph: 4.2sec
	Top speed: 165mph
Power & torque:	410bhp/480lb ft
Engine:	Normally aspirated 6997cc V8, petrol, carburettor, 16 valves
Drivetrain:	Front-engine RWD
Structure:	Separate chassis
Transmission:	Four-speed manual
Weight:	1147kg

PRICE GUIDE

Launch price:	Not known
Excellent:	£600,000
Good:	£350,000
Average:	£250,000
Project:	£190,000

AC
428

Heavy-hitter from Thames Ditton uses a six-inch-extended Cobra chassis clothed in bodywork – steel this time – by Frua from Turin. Passing resemblance to Frua's Maserati Mistral, but only handles and door-glass frames are shared. Engine is the 7.0-litre Ford Galaxie V8 used in some Cobras, but the 428 was still no bargain. The cost of the bodies and shipping chassis to and from Italy meant prices were 20% higher than for Astons and Jensen Interceptors. The AC simply wasn't special enough to justify that and only 51 coupés were sold in six years.

SPECIFICATIONS

Years produced:	1967-1973 (51 in total)
Performance:	0-60mph: 5.4sec
	Top speed: 145mph
Power & torque:	345bhp/462lb ft
Engine:	Normally aspirated 7010cc V8, petrol, carburettor, 16 valves
Drivetrain:	Front-engine RWD
Structure:	Separate chassis
Transmission:	Three-speed automatic
Weight:	1483kg

PRICE GUIDE

Launch price:	£4250
Excellent:	£75,000
Good:	£45,000
Average:	£22,500
Project:	£15,000

AC
428 Convertible

Soft-top version of the Frua-styled Mistral lookalike is even rarer than the coupé with just 29 finding homes between 1969 and '73. A phenomenal performer, with sub-6.0sec 0-60mph times even in more popular auto form, it somehow yet manages to feel lazy too. Excellent chassis makes sure it is more than a dragster, with neutral handling, almost too much feedback from the rack-and-pinion steering, plus great stopping power from Girling discs and twin servos. Only the rather bland interior is likely to disappoint.

SPECIFICATIONS

Years produced:	1967-1973 (29 in total)
Performance:	0-60mph: 5.9sec
	Top speed: 145mph
Power & torque:	345bhp/462lb ft
Engine:	Normally aspirated 7010cc V8, petrol, carburettor, 16 valves
Drivetrain:	Front-engine RWD
Structure:	Separate chassis
Transmission:	Three-speed automatic
Weight:	1483kg

PRICE GUIDE

Launch price:	£4250
Excellent:	£140,000
Good:	£65,000
Average:	£27,500
Project:	£17,500

AC
3000ME

An attempt to lift sales by building something more affordable saw AC mid-mounting a Ford V6 transversely over a custom-made transmission. That was one problem: the engine's heavy weight and less-than-sporting output meant only 120mph. Delays in into production meant the 3000ME was pitched against the similarly-priced Lotus Esprit. Those volume sales never materialised, with only around 100 built, including a short-lived revival in 1984-85 when licensed to a Scottish factory. Good survival rate and a keen following.

SPECIFICATIONS

Years produced:	1979-1985 (100 approx in total)
Performance:	0-60mph: 8.5sec
	Top speed: 120mph
Power & torque:	138bhp/192lb ft
Engine:	Normally aspirated 2994cc V6, petrol, carburettor, 12 valves
Drivetrain:	Mid-engine RWD
Structure:	Glassfibre body/backbone chassis
Transmission:	Five-speed manual
Weight:	1128kg

PRICE GUIDE

Launch price:	£12,432
Excellent:	£14,000
Good:	£9000
Average:	£6500
Project:	£4250

AC
Cobra MkIV

The arrival of the Cobra MkIV heralded a new era for AC. The Hurlock family passed on the rights of the marque to Brian Angliss, who had been building Autokraft Cobra replicas for years, using much of the original '60s tooling. When they became ACs, these cars were lauded for their high levels of build quality and retention of the original's spirit. Most cars have subsequently had their '80s-era dashboards replaced by '60s replicas, and are well worth buying at current prices, especially considering the spiralling values of '60s examples.

SPECIFICATIONS

Years produced:	1983-1989
Performance:	0-60mph: 5.3sec
	Top speed: 134mph
Power & torque:	320bhp/385lb ft
Engine:	4942cc V8, petrol, electronic fuel injection, 16 valves
Drivetrain:	Front-engine RWD
Structure:	Separate chassis
Transmission:	Five-speed manual
Weight:	N/A

PRICE GUIDE

Launch price:	£25,000
Excellent:	£125,000
Good:	£75,000
Average:	£60,000
Project:	£35,000

ALFA ROMEO

WHAT STARTED life as Anonima Lombardo Fabbrica Automobili (ALFA) in 1910 in a factory bought from Darracq was taken over by Nicolo Romeo in 1915. Thus began one of the great marques in motoring history. Its glory days were the 1930s, when Alfa Romeos were among the best cars money could buy. Post-war survival drove them downmarket, but the spirit remained with fine ranges of coupés and spiders to complement the saloons. Sadly that wasn't enough and when financial losses piled too high in the '80s, Fiat headed off a bid from Ford to take control in 1987. These days, the marque retains some of its character, but with a lot of Fiat bits underneath.

ALFA ROMEO
Giulietta Sprint

Unusually it was the coupé version of the Giulietta line that appeared on the market first. The floorpan would prove adaptable, as the sheer number of variations that subsequently appeared bears testimony to, but for many, this remains the most desirable of the mainstream factory cars. From the beginning of its run, the Bertone-styled coupé was treated to a range of exciting twin-cams; even the original 1290cc version packed a respectable 65bhp, and enjoyed revving away. The later Veloce and SS versions boasted outputs up to 100bhp.

SPECIFICATIONS
Years produced: 1954-1962 (27,142 in total)
Performance: 0-60mph: 13.0sec
Top speed: 101mph
Power & torque: 80bhp/72lb ft
Engine: Normally aspirated 1290cc four cylinder, petrol, carburettor, 8 valves
Drivetrain: Front-engine RWD
Structure: Monocoque
Transmission: Four-speed manual
Weight: 860kg

PRICE GUIDE
Launch price: £2261
Excellent: £30,000
Good: £25,000
Average: £18,000
Project: £5000

ALFA ROMEO
Giulietta Spider

Like its coupé sister, the Spider's body was designed by Bertone, and was an object lesson in Italian style and understatement. It's still great to drive in all forms, and remains in demand today. As with the rest of the family, rust was (and is) a serious factor in its survival rate, and the condition of the bodywork and chassis are of paramount importance. There are problems with the engine, too (such as head gasket issues), but just about all the mechanical parts are readily available off-the-shelf, so they're not difficult to keep going.

SPECIFICATIONS
Years produced: 1955-1962 (17,096 in total)
Performance: 0-60mph: 11.8sec
Top speed: 113mph
Power & torque: 80bhp/72lb ft
Engine: Normally aspirated 1290cc four cylinder, petrol, carburettor, 8 valves
Drivetrain: Front-engine RWD
Structure: Monocoque
Transmission: Four-speed manual
Weight: 860kg

PRICE GUIDE
Launch price: £2116
Excellent: £35,000
Good: £25,000
Average: £20,000
Project: £6000

ALFA ROMEO
Giulietta Berlina

These saloons might have hit the market during the mid-1950s, but they enjoyed an advanced specification and were built with the sporting driver in mind. In typical Alfa style, the Berlina started out powered by a modest engine, but with each new season, or so it seemed, a more powerful variation was shoehorned in. The pick of the crop ended up being the 75bhp Ti version, which ticked all of the important sporting saloon boxes. Sadly, the survival rate is very low, with the main culprits being damp climates and rabid rust.

SPECIFICATIONS
Years produced: 1955-1963 (39,057 in total)
Performance: 0-60mph: 17.7sec
Top speed: 98mph
Power & torque: 63bhp/69lb ft
Engine: Normally aspirated 1290cc four cylinder, petrol, carburettor, 8 valves
Drivetrain: Front-engine RWD
Structure: Monocoque
Transmission: Four-speed manual
Weight: 870kg

PRICE GUIDE
Launch price: £1726
Excellent: £8000
Good: £5000
Average: £3000
Project: £800

ALFA ROMEO
Giulietta/Giulia Sprint Speciale

The Series 101 Giulietta was the first Alfa to be made available in Sprint Speciale form but, when the 105-Series Giulia followed on in 1962, these SS series Alfas really came into their own. With power from a 1570cc twin-cam, performance from these coupés was something rather special. The chances of finding an unrestored car these are quite slim, but when they do turn up, they still command strong values. Today, these are the Giulias, with the good looks that everyone wants, a fact reflected in their very strong values.

SPECIFICATIONS
Years produced: 1957-1962 (1366/1400 in total)
Performance: 0-60mph: 11.2sec
Top speed: 122mph
Power & torque: 106bhp/83lb ft
Engine: Normally aspirated 1290cc four cylinder, petrol, carburettor, 8 valves
Drivetrain: Front-engine RWD
Structure: Monocoque
Transmission: Five-speed manual
Weight: 785kg

PRICE GUIDE
Launch price: £2721
Excellent: £45,000
Good: £35,000
Average: £25,000
Project: £10,000

ALFA ROMEO
2000/2600 Spider

Although there's a strong family resemblance to the Giulietta, the six-cylinder 2000/2600 harks back to the previous-generation Alfa Romeo 1900. The elegant styling was by Touring and reflected its role as the grand tourer that sat at the top of the range – and its high price was justified by its 2+2 seating layout, detachable hardtop and five-speed gearbox. Performance was seriously improved with the arrival of the 2.6-litre version in 1962, with top speed now a impressive 125mph. Rare and expensive, too, but still desirable.

SPECIFICATIONS

Years produced:	1958-1965 (2255 in total)
Performance:	0-60mph: 10.9sec
	Top speed: 124mph
Power & torque:	145bhp/156lb ft
Engine:	Normally aspirated 2584cc straight six, petrol, carburettor, 12 valves
Drivetrain:	Front-engine RWD
Structure:	Monocoque
Transmission:	Five-speed manual
Weight:	1257kg

PRICE GUIDE

Launch price:	£2979
Excellent:	£40,000
Good:	£30,000
Average:	£22,000
Project:	£8000

ALFA ROMEO
Giulia Spider

Exquisite looks by Touring on a 101-series chassis shared with the Giulia Sprint coupé, though that bonnet scoop is a dummy. Its rarity today means your search will be long. Rust is a serious issue with these cars, and they suffer from it far more readily than the coupés and saloons. But engine and gearbox are strong with good support from a network of specialists. The last hurrah of the 101-series Alfas, but none the worse for that, and all versions are good to drive. Interest has increased in the wake of the Alfa Romeo centenary in 2010.

SPECIFICATIONS

Years produced:	1962-1965 (10,341 in total)
Performance:	0-60mph: 11.8sec
	Top speed: 106mph
Power & torque:	91bhp/80lb ft
Engine:	Normally aspirated 1570cc four cylinder, petrol, carburettor, 8 valves
Drivetrain:	Front-engine RWD
Structure:	Monocoque
Transmission:	Five-speed manual
Weight:	960kg

PRICE GUIDE

Launch price:	£1729
Excellent:	£30,000
Good:	£25,000
Average:	£18,000
Project:	£5000

ALFA ROMEO
2600 Sprint

The 2600 Sprint was the ultimate incarnation of the twin-cam straight six. Still considered very much a grand tourer, the coupé lacked the agility of its smaller cousins, despite its sports car looks. The torquey engine made this a car for covering continents – despite its prodigious straight-line pace. Significant because, along with the Gordon-Keeble GK1, this was one of Giorgetto Giugiaro's first designs, laying the foundations for a significant career ahead. Unlike more mainstream Alfas, parts for the 2600 Sprint are not so readily available.

SPECIFICATIONS

Years produced:	1962-1966 (700/6999 in total)
Performance:	11.7sec
	Top speed: 117mph
Power & torque:	145bhp/156lb ft
Engine:	Normally aspirated 2584cc straight six, petrol, carburettor, 12 valves
Drivetrain:	Front-engine RWD
Structure:	Monocoque
Transmission:	Five-speed manual
Weight:	1361kg

PRICE GUIDE

Launch price:	£2806
Excellent:	£15,000
Good:	£9500
Average:	£4500
Project:	£2250

ALFA ROMEO
Giulia Sprint GT/Veloce

A hot little number right now, the 'step front' Giulia coupé is very much in demand because of its good looks, driving experience and ease of tuning. Values have increased significantly in recent years, bolstered by the desirability of the GTA. When launched, the twin-cam 1600 versions were quick from the box, but subsequent versions (1750 and 2000) added even more excitement to the mix. The advice is to go for the example with the best body you can find and worry about the mechanics after that – as parts availability is excellent.

SPECIFICATIONS

Years produced:	1964-1967 (21,850 in total)
Performance:	0-60mph: 11.2sec
	Top speed: 107mph
Power & torque:	92bhp/87lb ft
Engine:	Normally aspirated 1570cc four cylinder, petrol, carburettor, 8 valves
Drivetrain:	Front-engine RWD
Structure:	Monocoque
Trans:	Five-speed manual
Weight:	905kg

PRICE GUIDE

Launch price:	£1650
Excellent:	£20,000
Good:	£15,000
Average:	£7000
Project:	£2500

ALFA ROMEO
Giulia 1300/1600 Ti/Super

The boxy 105-Series Giulia might not look like the most exciting saloon on the planet, but underneath that plain-Jane exterior beats the heart of a truly sporting saloon. Given the lusty twin-cam engines, five-speed gearbox and well set-up chassis, it's easy to see why Alfa Romeo was so annoyed by the way its cars were depicted being outrun by the Mini-Coopers in *The Italian Job*. Despite its rarity today, the Giulia was a massive success when new, with much of that founded on it being so good to drive. Well worth seeking out.

SPECIFICATIONS

Years produced:	1962-1971 (836,323 in total)
Performance:	0-60mph: 11.8sec
	Top speed: 117mph
Power & torque:	92bhp/108lb ft
Engine:	Normally aspirated 1570cc four cylinder, petrol, carburettor, 8 valves
Drivetrain:	Front-engine RWD
Structure:	Monocoque
Transmission:	Five-speed manual
Weight:	1016kg

PRICE GUIDE

Launch price:	£1659
Excellent:	£9000
Good:	£6000
Average:	£4000
Project:	£1500

ALFA ROMEO
Giulia TZ/TZ2

Created as a replacement for the gorgeous Giulietta SZ, the Zagato-styled TZ and TZ2 continued that car's glorious looks and race-bred handling. The TZ nomenclature stands for '*Tubolare Zagato*', denoting the car's tubular chassis. It was powered by Alfa's twin-cam with up to 170bhp, and its suspension was a sophisticated all-independent set-up – in other words, here was a true thoroughbred. The TZ was the first Alfa Romeo with a glassfibre body (ten were built that way), and the TZ2 (pictured left) had even more dramatic styling. Incredibly desirable now.

SPECIFICATIONS

Years produced:	1963-64/1965-66 (120/50 in total)
Performance:	0-60mph: 6.8sec
	Top speed: 152mph
Power & torque:	170bhp/122lb ft
Engine:	Normally aspirated 1570cc four cylinder, petrol, carburettor, 8 valves
Drivetrain:	Front-engine RWD
Structure:	Spaceframe
Transmission:	Five-speed manual
Weight:	630kg

PRICE GUIDE (TZ2)

Launch price:	N/A in UK
Excellent:	£2,000,000
Good:	£1,500,000
Average:	£1,250,000
Project:	N/A

ALFA ROMEO
Giulia Sprint GTA

The GTA might look like your standard Sprint GT, but it makes extensive use of aluminium body panels. The reason for this was simple – the GTA was built for racing and, wherever possible, weight-saving was applied. The A in its name means *Alleggerita*, Italian for 'lightened', and even the sump, camshaft cover, timing cover and clutch housing were replaced by featherweight magnesium alloy items, just to save a few extra kilos. For additional performance, the engine gained a new twin-plug cylinder head. A legend.

SPECIFICATIONS

Years produced:	1965-1969
Performance:	0-60mph: N/A
	Top speed: 115mph
Power & torque:	115bhp/105lb ft
Engine:	Normally aspirated 1570cc four cylinder, petrol, carburettor, 8 valves
Drivetrain:	Front-engine RWD
Structure:	Monocoque
Transmission:	Five-speed manual
Weight:	820kg

PRICE GUIDE

Launch price:	£2128
Excellent:	£90,000
Good:	£70,000
Average:	£60,000
Project:	£40,000

ALFA ROMEO
Spider 1600 Duetto

Forever associated with Dustin Hoffman in *The Graduate*, the stylish little Duetto didn't hang around for long at all. The pretty little Pininfarina-styled roadster appeared in 1966 as the final genuinely new variant on the 105-Series platform and was marked out by its enclosed headlamps and boat-tail rear end. Powered by the 1570cc twin-cam, it was a gem to drive with great handling, sharp steering and excellent all-round disc braking. It was also quicker than an MGB, although considerably more expensive in the UK.

SPECIFICATIONS

Years produced:	1966-1968 (6325 in total)
Performance:	0-60mph: 13.2sec
	Top speed: 102mph
Power & torque:	110bhp/101lb ft
Engine:	Normally aspirated 1570cc four cylinder, petrol, carburettor, 8 valves
Drivetrain:	Front-engine RWD
Structure:	Monocoque
Transmission:	Five-speed manual
Weight:	990kg

PRICE GUIDE

Launch price:	£1749
Excellent:	£20,000
Good:	£14,000
Average:	£9000
Project:	£4000

ALFA ROMEO
Giulia GT Junior

Due to the complexity of the 105-Series Giulia range the easiest way of relating to the GT Junior is to think of it as the entry-level model. That means it initially came with a 1300cc engine and simplified interior, and gave sporting Italians the chance to own a Giulia Sprint GT lookalike without the fiscal implications. Over time it was developed in parallel with the larger-engined cars and, in 1970, it lost its characteristic step-front. In 1972 a 1600cc Junior was introduced to close the gap in the range to the 2000cc GTV.

SPECIFICATIONS

Years produced:	1966-1977 (92,053 in total)
Performance:	0-60mph: 11.1sec
	Top speed: 109mph
Power & torque:	103bhp/104lb ft
Engine:	Normally aspirated 1290cc four cylinder, petrol, carburettor, 8 valves
Drivetrain:	Front-engine RWD
Structure:	Monocoque
Transmission:	Five-speed manual
Weight:	990kg

PRICE GUIDE

Launch price:	£1749
Excellent:	£12,000
Good:	£9000
Average:	£6000
Project:	£2000

ALFA ROMEO
Tipo 33 Stradale

As 1960s supercars go, the 33 Stradale is possibly the most special of all. Although its V8 displaced a 'mere' 2-litres, the lightly detuned racing engined pushed out an impressive 227bhp, giving the 700kg car an exceptionally healthy power-to-weight ratio. But the 33 Stradale is a racing car for the road. Its body was built by Franco Scaglione, the final assembly was by Autodelta and, with only 18 made, these cars take rare-and-exclusive to another level. Tipo 33s almost never come up for sale, so coming up with a definitive value is almost impossible.

SPECIFICATIONS

Years produced:	1967-1969 (18 in total)
Performance:	0-60mph: 6.5sec
	Top speed: 162mph
Power & torque:	227bhp/152lb ft
Engine:	Normally aspirated 1995cc V8, petrol, fuel injection, 16 valves
Drivetrain:	Mid-engine RWD
Structure:	Spaceframe
Transmission:	Six-speed manual
Weight:	700kg

PRICE GUIDE

Launch price:	N/A in UK
Excellent:	£2,000,000
Good:	£1,500,000
Average:	£1,250,000
Project:	N/A

ALFA ROMEO
1750/2000 GTV

To ally itself with the launch of the 1750 Berlina, the Giulia Sprint was facelifted to become the 1750 GTV coupé. It retained the original GT1300/GT Junior 1.6 bodyshell but gained a quad-headlight front end and cleaner external trim details (as well as losing the step-front). The revised interior was an ergonomic improvement, although purists prefer the older design. The 1779cc four cylinder was now the base power unit for the non-Junior line, meaning lusty performance. These later models are considered to be the easiest cars to live with.

SPECIFICATIONS

Years produced:	1967-1969 (44,269/37,459 in total)
Performance:	0-60mph: 11.2sec
	Top speed: 118mph
Power & torque:	122bhp/137lb ft
Engine:	Normally aspirated 1779cc four cylinder, petrol, carburettor, 8 valves
Drivetrain:	Front-engine RWD
Structure:	Monocoque
Trans/weight:	Five-speed manual/1040kg

PRICE GUIDE

Launch price:	£2248
Excellent:	£18,000
Good:	£14,000
Average:	£7000
Project:	£2500

ALFA ROMEO
Spider 1750 Veloce

After only 18 months in production, the gorgeous little Duetto was discontinued to make way for the 1750 Spider Veloce. The newer car wasn't a radical change and really just heralded the arrival of the more potent twin-carb engine and uprated suspension and braking set-up. New wheels and tyres, though, made this one a bit of a spotter's favourite. Although the Duetto name had been dropped in favour of the more traditional Spider moniker, it was very much a case of more of the same. The bigger changes would follow later.

SPECIFICATIONS

Years produced:	1967-1971 (8701 in total)
Performance:	9.2sec
	Top speed: 114mph
Power & torque:	114bhp/137lb ft
Engine:	Normally aspirated 1779cc four cylinder, petrol, carburettor, 8 valves
Drivetrain:	Front-engine RWD
Structure:	Monocoque
Trans/weight:	Five-speed manual/1040kg

PRICE GUIDE

Launch price:	£2199
Excellent:	£20,000
Good:	£14,000
Average:	£9000
Project:	£4000

ALFA ROMEO
1750/2000 Berlina

With Alfa Romeo's new model development concentrating on the 'Sud and Alfetta, the mid-range Giulia saloon was treated to a front and rear makeover and relaunched to become the 1750/2000 Berlina. Although the styling (by Pininfarina) was considered unimaginative, it retained the outgoing car's roomy interior and boot, as well as the driver's car credentials that made the original so appealing. An updated interior and dashboard made the car feel more modern. The top-of-the-range 2000cc version with 132bhp was a genuine sports saloon.

SPECIFICATIONS (1750)

Years produced:	1967-1977 (101,883 in total)
Performance:	0-60mph: 10.8sec
	Top speed: 116mph
Power & torque:	122bhp/139lb ft
Engine:	Normally aspirated 1779cc four cylinder, petrol, carburettor, 8 valves
Drivetrain:	Front-engine RWD
Structure:	Monocoque
Transmission:	Five-speed manual
Weight:	1110kg

PRICE GUIDE

Launch price:	£1898
Excellent:	£8000
Good:	£4000
Average:	£1850
Project:	£800

ALFA ROMEO
Spider 2000

Alfa Romeo couldn't leave its cars alone during the 1960s and '70s and, after just three years in production, revised the 1750 Spider Veloce to become the 2000 Spider. Unlike last time, when the beautiful Pininfarina styling was largely left alone, the 1970 restyle came with an exterior upgrade, as well as the fitment of the lustier 2000cc twin-cam. The boat-tail gave way to a much longer Kamm tail, while the front lost its plastic headlamp covers. The overall effect conspired to make the Spider look less streamlined but more modern.

SPECIFICATIONS

Years produced:	1969-1982 (22,059 in total)
Performance:	0-60mph: 8.8sec
	Top speed: 123mph
Power & torque:	131bhp/134lb ft
Engine:	Normally aspirated 1962cc four cylinder, petrol, carburettor, 8 valves
Drivetrain:	Front-engine RWD
Structure:	Monocoque
Transmission:	Five-speed manual/1040kg

PRICE GUIDE

Launch price:	£2439
Excellent:	£14,000
Good:	£9000
Average:	£6000
Project:	£1800

ALFA ROMEO
1300/1600 Junior Z

An appealing Italian 'bitza' that somehow transcends the sum of its parts. Created by Zagato using the chassis from the Spider and the five-speed gearbox from the Giulietta, the Junior Zagato was an arresting-looking coupé that added real variety to the Alfa Romeo line-up. The sloping front and Kamm tail were certainly a world apart from the well-crafted classicism of the rest of the Giulia-derived cars, but no less appealing for it. It was lighter and more aerodynamic than the standard cars so it was usefully quicker too.

SPECIFICATIONS

Years produced:	1970-1975 (1108/402 in total)
Performance:	0-60mph: 11.5sec
	Top speed: 118mph
Power & torque:	125bhp/115lb ft
Engine:	Normally aspirated 1570cc four cylinder, petrol, carburettor, 8 valves
Drivetrain:	Drivetrain: front-engine RWD
Structure:	Monocoque
Trans/weight:	Five-speed manual/950kg

PRICE GUIDE

Launch price:	Not known
Excellent:	£20,000
Good:	£14,000
Average:	£10,000
Project:	£5000

ALFA ROMEO
Montreal

Conceived as a junior-league supercar, the Montreal proved to be a commercial failure for Alfa Romeo. It originally appeared at Expo '67 in Montreal, Canada, (hence the name) as a concept car, and proved so popular that the company decided to turn it into a production reality. The small V8, despite being based on the Type 33 race car engine, wasn't potent enough and performance could not match its price rivals'. It remained in production throughout the worst of the 1970s, and today is viewed as a seriously desirable classic car.

SPECIFICATIONS

Years produced:	1970-1977 (3925 in total)
Performance:	7.6sec
	Top speed: 137mph
Power & torque:	200bhp/173lb ft
Engine:	Normally aspirated 2593cc V8, petrol, carburettor, 16 valves
Drivetrain:	Front-engine RWD
Structure:	Monocoque
Transmission:	Five-speed manual
Weight:	1267kg

PRICE GUIDE

Launch price:	£5077
Excellent:	£28,000
Good:	£18,000
Average:	£10,000
Project:	£5000

ALFA ROMEO
Alfetta

Alfa Romeo's first new big saloon of the '70s marked something of a departure from its predecessors. Boasting a new platform that would last for well over two decades, all the ingredients were there for a great sporting saloon: a range of twin-cam engines and a transaxle gearbox for perfect weight distribution. Build quality was variable, with the earliest cars the most solidly assembled, but a bigger problem was corrosion. Rare today, not fully understood, and perhaps more deserving of its own accolades than being known as the saloon that begat the GTV.

SPECIFICATIONS (2000)

Years produced:	1972-1984 (450,000 in total)
Performance:	0-60mph: 9.7sec
	Top speed: 115mph
Power & torque:	122bhp/129lb ft
Engine:	Normally aspirated 1962cc four cylinder, petrol, carburettor, 8 valves
Drivetrain:	Front-engine RWD
Structure:	Monocoque
Transmission:	Five-speed manual
Weight:	1080kg

PRICE GUIDE

Launch price:	£2649
Excellent:	£2500
Good:	£1200
Average:	£700
Project:	£150

ALFA ROMEO
Alfasud

When it went on sale in 1972, the Alfasud rewrote the small-car book. Given that Alfa Romeo had no experience of small, front-driven cars, the sheer dynamic excellence of the flat-four powered 'Sud came as a shock. However, Alfasud was also a government-led experiment in the redistribution of manufacturing (a new factory was built near Naples, where the workforce was hardly skilled in car-making). Customers found their new 'Suds would rust, or fall to pieces, overshadowing the great work done by the engineers. A flawed gem.

SPECIFICATIONS (1.5)

Years produced:	1972-1983 (387,734 in total excluding Ti)
Performance:	0-60mph: 11.8sec
	Top speed: 103mph
Power & torque:	93bhp/96lb ft
Engine:	Normally aspirated 1490cc flat four, petrol, carburettor, 8 valves
Drivetrain:	Front-engine FWD
Structure:	Monocoque
Transmission:	Five-speed manual
Weight:	885kg

PRICE GUIDE

Launch price:	£1399
Excellent:	£3000
Good:	£2500
Average:	£1250
Project:	£500

ALFA ROMEO
Alfetta GT 1.8/GTV 2000

It was left to Bertone to create a suitably handsome coupé from Alfetta underpinnings. It was originally launched as the Alfetta GT in 1779cc twin-cam form, and a 1.6GT joined the range in 1976 – along with the GTV 2000. With a full 2.0 litres under the bonnet, it delivered effortless performance, accompanied by the rorty soundtrack you would expect from an Alfa twin-cam. Buying a GTV now should be relatively painless given that the surviving examples should have been properly rebuilt. As ever, rust and flimsy build quality are the main enemies.

SPECIFICATIONS (GTV)

Years produced:	1973-1987 (31,267 in total)
Performance:	0-60mph: 9.7sec
	Top speed: 113mph
Power & torque:	122bhp/123lb ft
Engine:	Normally aspirated 1779cc four cylinder, petrol, carburettor, 8 valves
Drivetrain:	Front-engine RWD
Structure:	Monocoque
Transmission:	Five-speed manual
Weight:	Five-speed manual/1048kg

PRICE GUIDE

Launch price:	N/A
Excellent:	£6000
Good:	£3000
Average:	£1250
Project:	£800

ALFA ROMEO
Alfasud Sprint

The Italians have always been great at turning innocuous-looking family saloons into great sporting coupés. So when Alfa Romeo turned the rather good 'Sud into a usable small sporting car, the results were predictably sparkling. Styling was handled by Giugiaro, and to many the Sprint successfully eclipsed the already desirable GTV. It was especially rapid in twin-carb Veloce form, but any example will reward the enthusiastic driver. An iffy 1980s facelift did it no favours, though, and fans prefer the crisp original.

SPECIFICATIONS

Years produced:	1976-1990 (96,450 in total)
Performance:	0-60mph: 10.0sec
	Top speed: 105mph
Power & torque:	84bhp/89lb ft
Engine:	Normally aspirated 1490cc flat four, petrol, carburettor, 8 valves
Drivetrain:	Front-engine FWD
Structure:	Monocoque
Transmission:	Five-speed manual
Weight:	915kg

PRICE GUIDE

Launch price:	£3999
Excellent:	£4000
Good:	£3750
Average:	£1100
Project:	£275

ALFA ROMEO
Alfa Six

Strangely appealing today for those with a penchant for automotive losers, but the Alfa Six is a car the Arese company would rather choose to forget. It was ready for production by the mid-1970s, but the oil crisis and Alfa Romeo's enfeebled cashflow situation meant that the launch was continually delayed. When it arrived, the Six underwhelmed – its engine was magnificent, but the duff dynamics, narrow body and obvious Alfetta styling overtones let it down. Maybe a handful left in the UK now, so bask in its rarity if you find one, but don't pay over the odds.

SPECIFICATIONS

Years produced:	1979-1987 (12,070 in total)
Performance:	0-60mph: 9.8sec
	Top speed: 130mph
Power & torque:	160bhp/157lb ft
Engine:	Normally aspirated 2492cc V6, petrol, electronic fuel injection, 12 valves
Drivetrain:	Front-engine RWD
Structure:	Monocoque
Transmission:	Five-speed manual (opt. auto)
Weight:	1480kg

PRICE GUIDE

Launch price:	£11,900
Excellent:	£2000
Good:	£1250
Average:	£850
Project:	£500

ALFA ROMEO
Alfetta GTV6

As big Alfa saloons go the Six was not a huge success, but we owe the existence of one of the best-sounding Alfa Romeos to the failed executive saloon – and it donated its wonderful V6 engine to the Alfetta GTV. Running a new Bosch fuel injection system, the V6's power was up to 160bhp, giving the GTV6 a very useful power hike, as well as one of the most sublime soundtracks in motoring history. Like the Alfetta GT and GTV before it a good GTV6 was a phenomenally good car in the bends – especially as it finally had the power to exploit it.

SPECIFICATIONS

Years produced:	1980-1987 (279,821 in total)
Performance:	0-60mph: 8.8sec
	Top speed: 130mph
Power & torque:	160bhp/157lb ft
Engine:	Normally aspirated 2492cc V6, petrol, electronic fuel injection, 12 valves
Drivetrain:	Front-engine RWD
Structure:	Monocoque
Transmission:	Five-speed manual
Weight:	1210kg

PRICE GUIDE

Launch price:	£9495
Excellent:	£7000
Good:	£4000
Average:	£2000
Project:	£450

ALFA ROMEO
Alfa 33

Much was expected of the 33. It was supposed to build on the best bits of the Alfasud, to create a formidable new family car for the slick '80s. Instead, it failed to move on the game at all – even if the styling hinted that this was a much more upmarket offering. As it was, the wedge from Naples sold slowly and despite a welter of improvements throughout its life, stubbornly refused to realise its potential. As a driver's car, it's marred by a weird driving position but, for the family, it's an excellent proposition, thanks to its roomy cabin. Cheap and characterful now, but a 'Sud betters it.

SPECIFICATIONS (1.5)

Years produced:	1983-1994
Performance:	0-60mph: 11.8sec
	Top speed: 108mph
Power & torque:	85bhp/69lb ft
Engine:	Normally aspirated 1490cc flat four, petrol, carburettor, 8 valves
Drivetrain:	Front-engine FWD
Structure:	Monocoque
Transmission:	Five-speed manual
Weight:	890kg

PRICE GUIDE

Launch price:	£5690
Excellent:	£2000
Good:	£1000
Average:	£650
Project:	£350

ALFA ROMEO
Spider 2000 S3/S4

The final restyle of the Spider took place at the beginning of 1990 – and Pininfarina was given the honour of preparing the Spider for its final days. The car was rounded off with smoother bumpers and slimmer rear light clusters. By this point the Spider was almost 30 years old, but the new fuel-injected engines, along with power-assisted steering, prolonged its life for three years. North American sales of the S4 Spider remained strong right to the end, with more than 75% of the production run ending up in the USA.

SPECIFICATIONS

Years produced:	1982-1993 (18,456 in total)
Performance:	0-60mph: 9.2sec
	Top speed: 119mph
Power & torque:	120bhp/117lb ft
Engine:	Normally aspirated 1962cc four cylinder, petrol, electronic fuel injection, 8 valves
Drivetrain:	Front-engine RWD
Structure:	Monocoque
Transmission:	Five-speed manual
Weight:	1110kg

PRICE GUIDE (S4, for S3, deduct 25%)

Launch price:	£15,950
Excellent:	£7000
Good:	£5000
Average:	£4000
Project:	£2000

ALFA ROMEO
Alfa 90

Should have been an appealing one this: styling by Bertone; an Alfa Six engine and Alfetta running gear. In truth, it never really gelled, and managed to sell even more slowly than the two cars whose parts it combined in order to replace. There are some other redeeming features to this appealing 'bitza', such as the dash-mounted briefcase (try finding one now!) and a tacho that looked as if lifted straight from an '80s Japanese stack system. Not surprisingly, rust is the main issue with electrics a close second. Buy if you're brave – or admire from a safe distance.

SPECIFICATIONS

Years produced:	1984-1987
Performance:	0-60mph: 8.5sec
	Top speed: 126mph
Power & torque:	154bhp/155lb ft
Engine:	Normally aspirated 2492cc V6, petrol, mechanical fuel injection, 12 valves
Drivetrain:	Front-engine RWD
Structure:	Monocoque
Transmission:	Five-speed manual
Weight:	1170kg

PRICE GUIDE

Launch price:	£10,850
Excellent:	£2500
Good:	£1500
Average:	£750
Project:	£500

ALFA ROMEO
75 V6/3.0 V6

Launched on Alfa Romeo's 75th anniversary, the 75 was a mixture of Giulietta and Alfa 90. Alfa engineered the car to use a transaxle and this gave it almost perfect 50:50 weight distribution. That, coupled with the melodic V6 engine, made the 75 one of the most desirable sporting saloons of the 1980s. The styling was done in-house, following on from the Alfa 33, which had a similar square headlamp and grille arrangement. The 75 also came with a reasonable amount of equipment as standard, but power steering was extra.

SPECIFICATIONS (3.0)

Years produced:	1985-1992
Performance:	0-60mph: 7.5sec
	Top speed: 137mph
Power & torque:	187bhp/181lb ft
Engine:	Normally aspirated 2959cc V6, petrol, electronic fuel injection, 12 valves
Drivetrain:	Front-engine RWD
Structure:	Monocoque
Transmission:	Five-speed manual
Weight:	1160kg

PRICE GUIDE

Launch price:	£11,649
Excellent:	£2400
Good:	£1800
Average:	£850
Project:	£350

ALFA ROMEO
SZ/RZ

First conceived as a design study in 1987, the Sprint Zagato caused such a sensation that, in 1989, Alfa launched a production version at the Geneva Motor Show. Based on a heavily modified 75, the SZ had the performance (and sound) to back up its sporty yet unconventional looks. Its ability to hang on in bends really made the SZ special – it could generate 1.1g of cornering force. The RZ (Roadster Zagato) was produced from 1992 until the end of 1993. Only 284 were made, making it highly sought after – and more expensive than the SZ.

SPECIFICATIONS

Years produced:	1989-1994 (998 in total)
Performance:	0-60mph: 6.9sec
	Top speed: 153mph
Power & torque:	210bhp /181lb ft
Engine:	Normally aspirated 2959cc V6, petrol, electronic fuel injection, 24 valves
Drivetrain:	Front-engine RWD
Structure:	Monocoque
Transmission:	Five-speed manual
Weight:	1260kg

PRICE GUIDE

Launch price:	£40,000
Excellent:	£25,000
Good:	£18,000
Average:	£14,500
Project:	£12,000

ALLARD

SYDNEY ALLARD founded the marque that bore his name in 1936, with his first car being based on a Ford V8. The first bespoke Allards came along in 1945, still with Ford V8 engines but now with very distinctive long-nosed bodies.

Always competition-orientated, Allards remained rather idiosyncratic and dramatic-looking until the 1950s when a series of roadsters – the K3, Palm Beach and JR – came out, sporting four- and six-cylinder engines as well as

V8s. Demand plummeted as rivals produced cheaper, faster, better-looking alternatives. The firm ended up modifying Ford Anglias until 1966 when a fire destroyed the factory. Sydney Allard died at home the same night.

ALLARD
L/M

If you enjoy your Allard-shaped kicks with the kids in the back seats then the Allard L and M are just the ticket. Effectively just a K1 with a six-inch wheelbase stretch (to 112in) and a pair of occasional seats in the rear, the additional model in the Allard line-up proved surprisingly popular. The M added some civilities such as coil-sprung suspension (from 1949) and a column gearchange. Although most UK cars were fitted with Ford Pilot engines, many were shipped overseas without a powertrain, leaving the owner to chose a more suitable local engine.

SPECIFICATIONS

Years produced:	1946-1950 (191/500 in total)
Performance:	0-60mph: 15.2sec
	Top speed: 82mph
Power & torque:	85bhp/N/A
Engine:	Normally aspirated 3622cc V8, petrol, carburettor, 16 (side) valves
Drivetrain:	Front-engine RWD
Structure:	Separate chassis
Transmission:	Three-speed manual
Weight:	1396kg

PRICE GUIDE

Launch price:	£1151
Excellent:	£37,500
Good:	£30,000
Average:	£20,000
Project:	£11,000

ALLARD
K1/K2

Allard's first post-war sports car was a leap forward. Although it looked ungainly (a subsequent family trait) it was a great car to drive, proving very effective in competition. The technical make-up might have been simple, with a box-section frame, transverse leaf springs and a steel body, but careful chassis development was the key. The fitment of a powerful V8 engine (from the Ford Pilot) delivered plenty of effortless performance. The end result was a charismatic English sports car that has a loyal following to this day.

SPECIFICATIONS

Years produced:	1946-1951 (151/119 in total)
Performance:	0-60mph: 13.6sec
	Top speed: 102mph
Power & torque:	85bhp/150lb ft
Engine:	Normally aspirated 3622cc V8, petrol, carburettor, 16 valves
Drivetrain:	Front-engine RWD
Structure:	Separate chassis
Transmission:	Three-speed manual
Weight:	1118kg

PRICE GUIDE

Launch price:	£1277
Excellent:	£75,000
Good:	£50,000
Average:	£25,000
Project:	£15,000

ALLARD
P1

Derived from the M 'drophead coupé', the Allard P1 was a hard-topped two-door saloon that broke with tradition for the marque. Although marketed as something of a gentleman's carriage, the P1 couldn't disguise its competition roots, making it an appealing proposition for enthusiastic drivers. Sydney Allard drove one to victory in the 1952 Monte Carlo Rally, making him the only person in the history of the event to win the event in a car bearing his own name. Today, the P1 commands enviable market values.

SPECIFICATIONS

Years produced:	1949-1951 (559 in total)
Performance:	0-60mph: 15.2sec
	Top speed: 85mph
Power & torque:	85bhp/150lb ft
Engine:	Normally aspirated 3622cc V8, petrol, carburettor, 16 valves
Drivetrain:	Front-engine RWD
Structure:	Separate chassis
Transmission:	Three-speed manual
Weight:	1372kg

PRICE GUIDE

Launch price:	£1277
Excellent:	£27,500
Good:	£23,000
Average:	£18,500
Project:	£8500

ALLARD
J2/J2X

The most famous of all the Allard racers and, despite their rarity (just 83 were produced), the most likely to come onto the market. It was the J2X that introduced the new method of construction, which employed small chassis tubes and parallel side members attached together to create the chassis frame. It sounds rudimentary, but the results speak for themselves, with the J2 having a successful racing career on both sides of the Atlantic. Suspension was more sophisticated than the earlier cars', ensuring excellent handling.

SPECIFICATIONS

Years produced:	1950-1951 (173 total – 90 J2, 83 J2X)
Performance:	0-60mph: 7.4sec
	Top speed: 111mph
Power & torque:	120bhp/221lb ft
Engine:	Normally aspirated 4375cc V8, petrol, carburettor, 16 valves
Drivetrain:	Front-engine RWD
Structure:	Separate chassis
Transmission:	Three-speed manual
Weight:	914kg

PRICE GUIDE

Launch price:	£1277
Excellent:	£350,000
Good:	£250,000
Average:	£175,000
Project:	£100,000

ALLARD
K3

Altogether more sophisticated than its earlier relatives, the K3 was Allard's attempt at appealing to more sophisticated buyers with luxuries such as a one-piece bonnet and wide bench seat that was supposed to accommodate the entire family. This being Allard's supposedly softer option, Americans were the target. Problem was, Stateside buyers were looking for the exact opposite in their English sports cars, and so the K3's market failure was disappointing. But it was a pretty car, especially by Allard's standards.

SPECIFICATIONS

Years produced:	1952-1955 (62 in total)
Performance:	0-60mph: N/A
	Top speed: 85mph
Power & torque:	85bhp/150lb ft
Engine:	Normally aspirated 3622cc V8, petrol, carburettor, 16 valves
Drivetrain:	Front-engine RWD
Structure:	Separate chassis
Transmission:	Three-speed manual
Weight:	1181kg

PRICE GUIDE

Launch price:	£1713
Excellent:	£80,000
Good:	£60,000
Average:	£32,500
Project:	£22,500

ALPINE

SOCIÉTÉ ANONYME des Automobiles Alpine was born in 1954, the brainchild of competition driver Jean Rédélé. It used Renault underpinnings with attractive glassfibre coupé bodies on top, leading to 1962's definitive A110. It remained in production until 1977 and turned Alpine into France's leading sports car maker. Alpine was always closely tied with Renault, which took over in 1974. This era also saw the striking A310 model, intended to take on Porsche, which in time evolved into the GTA and A610. The last Alpine-badged car was built in 1994 and there are periodic hopes that the name will be revived. Alpine's Dieppe factory curently builds RenaultSport models instead.

ALPINE
A110

Rally driver and dealer Jean Rédélé branched out into producing competition-style cars based on Renault running gear in 1956 with the Alpine A106. The car proved so effective (winning its class in the 1956 Mille Miglia) that production blossomed as keen drivers clamoured to get hold of their own versions. By the time the A110 hit the market in 1962 the formula was pretty much perfected with a glassfibre body fixed to Renault 8 Gordini running gear, making for a seriously effective – and good-looking – rally weapon.

SPECIFICATIONS

Years produced:	1965-1973
Performance:	0-60mph: 6.3sec
	Top speed: 132mph
Power & torque:	138bhp/117lb ft
Engine:	Normally aspirated 1565cc four cylinder, petrol, carburettor, 8 valves
Drivetrain:	Rear-engine RWD
Structure:	Glassfibre body/backbone chassis
Transmission:	Five-speed manual
Weight:	625kg

PRICE GUIDE

Launch price:	N/A in UK
Excellent:	£42,500
Good:	£27,500
Average:	£10,000
Project:	£7000

ALPINE
A310

Bringing the Alpine family firmly into the 1970s, the A310 was developed from the rear-engined A110 GT4, but civilised to such an extent that it could be taken seriously as a day-to-day road car. The wedge-shaped styling was certainly striking, and the glassfibre body was as light and aerodynamic as Alpine tradition demanded. Powered by the Renault 17TS high-output 1605cc engine, it could easily top 125mph. Although never officially imported into the UK, many examples have crossed the Channel but they are expensive compared with rivals.

SPECIFICATIONS

Years produced:	1971-1976 (40,386 in total)
Performance:	0-60mph: 8.1sec
	Top speed: 131mph
Power & torque:	127bhp/108lb ft
Engine:	Normally aspirated 1605cc four cylinder, petrol, carburettor, 8 valves
Drivetrain:	Rear-engine RWD
Structure:	Glassfibre body/backbone chassis
Transmission:	Five-speed manual
Weight:	940kg

PRICE GUIDE

Launch price:	N/A in UK
Excellent:	£12,000
Good:	£7500
Average:	£3000
Project:	£2000

ALPINE
A310 V6

Alpine was rapidly moving upmarket and the scale of its ambition was reflected in the A310 V6. Introduced in 1976, it slotted in the range above the four cylinder car, which was discontinued shortly afterwards. Powered by the 2664cc Douvrin V6, co-developed by Renault and Peugeot, the latest Alpine developed 150bhp in the rortiest fashion possible. However, despite the excellent soundtrack, and the company's assertion that it was a credible Porsche 911 alternative, the car wasn't fast enough, nor did it have the right badge.

SPECIFICATIONS

Years produced:	1976-1980 (5970 in total)
Performance:	0-60mph: 7.6sec
	Top speed: 137mph
Power & torque:	150bhp/150lb ft
Engine:	Normally aspirated 2664cc V6, petrol, carburettor, 12 valves
Drivetrain:	Rear-engine RWD
Structure:	Glassfibre body/backbone chassis
Transmission:	Five-speed manual
Weight:	1016kg

PRICE GUIDE

Launch price:	£4300
Excellent:	£13,500
Good:	£7500
Average:	£5000
Project:	£3000

ALPINE
GTA

Known as the Alpine A610 in Europe, the GTA was a very effective update of the A310 V6. Although the basic layout was shared with the older car, the slippery new glassfibre body and expanded PRV V6 engine gave the standard model (which boasted 160bhp) a top speed of nearly 140mph. However, the GTA's main forte was its handling. Despite the overhung rear engine, it provided huge lateral grip and near-flat cornering. Sales in the UK were pitiful and as a marketing exercise for Renault it was a huge failure. Buy one today and enjoy the attention.

SPECIFICATIONS

Years produced:	1986-1991
Performance:	0-60mph: 7.5sec
	Top speed: 139mph
Power & torque:	157bhp/163lb ft
Engine:	Normally aspirated 2849cc V6, petrol, carburettor, 12 valves
Drivetrain:	Mid-engine RWD
Structure:	Glassfibre body/backbone chassis
Transmission:	Five-speed manual
Weight:	1140kg

PRICE GUIDE

Launch price:	£19,040
Excellent:	£7000
Good:	£5500
Average:	£3750
Project:	£2000

ALPINE
GTA V6 Turbo

When launched, the GTA Turbo became France's fastest-ever production car. With a power output of nearly 200bhp from its 2.5-litre V6 engine, shared with the Renault 25, its top speed pushed 150mph. Pricing in the UK was ambitious and the GTA went head-to-head with the Porsche 911 and Lotus Esprit. These more established cars continued to overshadow the French upstart, outselling it comfortably. Few original RHD cars remain in the UK (less than 40) but in recent years a number of left-hookers have been imported.

SPECIFICATIONS

Years produced:	1986-1991
Performance:	0-60mph: 6.3sec
	Top speed: 149mph
Power & torque:	197bhp/214lb ft
Engine:	Turbocharged 2458cc V6, petrol, fuel injection, 12 valves
Drivetrain:	Rear-engine RWD
Structure:	Glassfibre body/backbone chassis
Transmission:	Five-speed manual
Weight:	1180kg

PRICE GUIDE

Launch price:	£23,635
Excellent:	£10,000
Good:	£7250
Average:	£4250
Project:	£2500

ALVIS

FOUNDED in 1919, the Alvis name reputedly came from a design of piston: 'al' from 'aluminium' and 'vis' meaning 'strong' in Latin. Its 12/50 and 12/60 models were notable early designs and it was also a pioneer of front-wheel-drive during the 1920s. It built a range of imposing and progressive sports models during the 1930s but adopted a one-model policy after the war. In 1955, Swiss firm Graber penned a new and very handsome body and the TC108G, TD21 , TE21 and TF21 that followed were noted for their arresting appearance, especially the final stacked-headlamp cars. Competitor Rover took over the firm in 1965 and, from 1967, Alvis was confined to making military machines.

ALVIS
TA14

Despite the fact that the TA14 was merely a mildly modified version of the 1938 12/70, it was Alvis's post-war best-seller – explained by the traditional styling. It also means cart springs and mechanically operated brakes, though you get a slightly wider track and longer wheelbase. The engine was bored out by an extra 50cc, but extra weight means this high-quality car can manage only 75mph. There were quite a few special bodies about, and it's these – particularly the Tickford and Carbodies dropheads – that are most sought after.

SPECIFICATIONS
Years produced:	1946-1950 (3311 in total)
Performance:	0-60mph: 22.2sec
	Top speed: 74mph
Power & torque:	65bhp/95lb ft
Engine:	Normally aspirated 1892cc four cylinder, petrol, carburettor, 8 valves
Drivetrain:	Front-engine RWD
Structure:	Separate chassis
Transmission:	Four-speed manual
Weight:	1422kg

PRICE GUIDE
Launch price:	£893
Excellent:	£13,500
Good:	£11,000
Average:	£5250
Project:	£2500

ALVIS
TA21/TC21

The cabin was carried over from the TA14, but rounded wings with rear wheel covers and faired-in headlamps added a hint of modernity. Brakes are now hydraulic and there's independent coil-sprung front suspension, but the big change is under the bonnet. Alvis's all-new 3.0-litre engine – with twin carbs on all but the first few – is tough and torquey as well as smooth and quiet. By the time the TA evolved into the TC21/100 'Grey Lady' in 1953, with wire wheels and hidden hinges, higher compression meant 100bhp... and just about 100mph.

SPECIFICATIONS
Years produced:	1950-1955 (2074 in total)
Performance:	0-60mph: 16.5sec
	Top speed: 86mph
Power & torque:	90bhp/147lb ft
Engine:	Normally aspirated 2993cc straight six, petrol, carburettor, 12 valves
Drivetrain:	Front-engine RWD
Structure:	Separate chassis
Transmission:	Four-speed manual
Weight:	1518kg

PRICE GUIDE
Launch price:	£1598
Excellent:	£25,000
Good:	£20,000
Average:	£12,000
Project:	£7000

ALVIS
TA21/TC21 Convertible

Even though it looked distinctly pre-war, the TA21 was the first post-war Alvis to feature a brand new chassis. The coachwork was by Tickford, and it was heavily influenced by the earlier TA14 Cabriolet. The new chassis and 90bhp engine gave the car hugely improved dynamics and driveability. The updated TC21 was unveiled in 1953 and the addition of twin SU carburettors boosted the existing 2993cc engine to 100bhp. Both TA21 and TC21 featured independent front suspension and remained unchanged for years.

SPECIFICATIONS
Years produced:	1950-1955
Performance:	0-60mph: 16.5sec
	Top speed: 86mph
Power & torque:	90bhp/147lb ft
Engine:	Normally aspirated 2993cc straight six, petrol, carburettor, 12 valves
Drivetrain:	Front-engine RWD
Structure:	Separate chassis
Transmission:	Four-speed manual
Weight:	1448kg

PRICE GUIDE
Launch price:	£1822
Excellent:	£50,000
Good:	£35,000
Average:	£20,000
Project:	£10,000

ALVIS
TA14 Convertible

With a design that originated in the '30s, the TA14 was never intended to be break new ground, merely to re-start Alvis production following the war. The Cabriolet was introduced alongside the saloon, and two drophead bodies were offered from the start – one by Tickford and the other by Carbodies. All versions featured the same front-end treatment, and the interior had high-quality leather seats and a wooden dashboard. The single-carburettor pushrod engine wasn't powerful, but it was smooth, and suited the touring-car nature of the TA14.

SPECIFICATIONS
Years produced:	1946-1950
Performance:	0-60mph: 22.2sec
	Top speed: 74mph
Power & torque:	65bhp/95lb ft
Engine:	Normally aspirated 1892cc four cylinder, petrol, carburettor, 8 valves
Drivetrain:	Front-engine RWD
Structure:	Separate chassis
Transmission:	Four-speed manual
Weight:	1447kg

PRICE GUIDE
Launch price:	£893
Excellent:	£25,000
Good:	£20,000
Average:	£15,000
Project:	£7000

ALVIS
TB21

Alvis launched the TB21 to replace the TB14, which had been a huge commercial failure, but – unlike the TB14 – the new model had a much more conventional grille and was widely lauded as a great-looking sports car. The TB21 used the same chassis as the TA21, and AP Metalcraft modified its TB14 bodyshell to fit the upgraded chassis. The new car was also fitted with the TA21's 90bhp engine, giving it sprightly performance. However, it was expensive, being pitched at £1598. The result: a mere 31 cars were produced.

SPECIFICATIONS
Years produced:	1952 (31 in total)
Performance:	0-60mph: N/A
	Top speed: 95mph
Power & torque:	90bhp/150lb ft
Engine:	Normally aspirated 2993cc straight six, petrol, carburettor, 12 valves
Drivetrain:	Front-engine RWD
Structure:	Separate chassis
Transmission:	Four-speed manual
Weight:	1283kg

PRICE GUIDE
Launch price:	£1598
Excellent:	£50,000
Good:	£35,000
Average:	£20,000
Project:	£10,000

ALVIS
TD21

A completely new body was designed by Park Ward – based loosely on the 16 TC21s (designated TC108G) styled by Swiss coachbuilder Graber and built in Loughborough by bus maker Willowbrook from 1956-57. The TD, however, is larger and offers a lot more space for passengers and luggage. Front brakes are discs, and all but the first few TDs got an uprated 120bhp engine. A cheaper Austin-Healey gearbox was employed, but these cars got better during production. The Series II, from October '62, has all-wheel disc brakes and a ZF five-speed box.

SPECIFICATIONS
Years produced:	1956-1963 (1070 in total)
Performance:	0-60mph: 13.9sec
	Top speed: 104mph
Power & torque:	115bhp/152lb ft
Engine:	Normally aspirated 2993cc straight six, petrol, carburettor, 12 valves
Drivetrain:	Front-engine RWD
Structure:	Separate chassis
Transmission:	Four-speed manual
Weight:	1495kg

PRICE GUIDE (Convertible in brackets)
Launch price:	£2766
Excellent:	£22,500 (£50,000)
Good:	£18,500 (£35,000)
Average:	£10,000 (£20,000)
Project:	£4500 (£11,000)

ALVIS
TE/TF21

Easily distinguished from its TD predecessor by those stacked twin headlamps that were *so* fashionable in the early 1960s, the TE gained a new cylinder head that lifts power output to 130bhp. Both saloon and drophead were available, and it's the latter that makes serious money today. Power steering became a desirable option from 1965, but Alvis saved the best for last. Just 106 TFs were built, but they come with a triple-carb 150bhp engine, improved gearbox and uprated suspension. After 1967 Alvis concentrated on armoured vehicles.

SPECIFICATIONS
Years produced:	1963-1967
Performance:	0-60mph: 12.5sec
	Top speed: 112mph
Power & torque:	130bhp/172lb ft
Engine:	Normally aspirated 2993cc straight six, petrol, carburettor, 12 valves
Drivetrain:	Front-engine RWD
Structure:	Separate chassis
Transmission:	Four-speed manual
Weight:	1473kg

PRICE GUIDE (Convertible in brackets)
Launch price:	£2775
Excellent:	£25,000 (£55,000)
Good:	£45,000 (£35,000)
Average:	£40,000
Project:	£20,000

ARMSTRONG SIDDELEY

SIDDELEY was founded in 1902 and, after various partnerships, was taken over by the Armstrong Whitworth Development Company in 1919. The new Armstrong-Siddeley combine specialised in large luxury machines (although it did market a smaller 12hp model). In the week WW2 ended, it launched the patriotically-named Lancaster saloon and Hurricane drophead coupés, soon followed by the Typhoon and Whitley variants. The Sapphire 346 of 1952 brought power steering to British cars for the first time, but the smaller and awkwardly styles 234 and 236 models were a failure and contributed to the decision to end car production after a merger with Bristol in 1960.

ARMSTRONG SIDDELEY
Hurricane DHC

As part of a two-pronged attack on the world's car markets, Armstrong Siddeley introduced this stylish two-door drophead. Using the same chassis and running gear as the Lancaster, it was stodgy to drive, but the styling set it apart from its pre-war counterparts: flush-fitting headlights and faired-in front wings (from the Lancaster) were up-to-the-minute. The 70bhp 1991cc overhead-valve engine was carried over from the pre-war 16hp, but was rugged and torquey, offering easy 50mph cruising in those restrained times.

SPECIFICATIONS
Years produced:	1946-1949 (2606 in total)
Performance:	0-60mph: 29.9sec
	Top speed: 75mph
Power & torque:	75bhp/107lb ft
Engine:	Normally aspirated 2309cc straight six, petrol, carburettor, 12 valves
Drivetrain:	Front-engine RWD
Structure:	Separate chassis
Transmission:	Four-speed manual
Weight:	1412kg

PRICE GUIDE
Launch price:	£1151
Excellent:	£14,000
Good:	£11,000
Average:	£7500
Project:	£3250

ARMSTRONG SIDDELEY
Lancaster

It might have been the company's first post-war car, but underneath the Lancaster's skin beat the heart of a pre-war car. Despite that, it can justifiably be described as Britain's first all-new post-war car, appearing on the market the same week hostilities ceased in Europe. The 2.0-litre saloon was hardly groundbreaking but, with torsion bar suspension, hydromechanical brakes and a four-speed all-synchromesh gearbox, it was comfortable and easy to drive. Dignified and refined it might have been, but it suffered badly from rust.

SPECIFICATIONS
Years produced:	1946-1952 (3597 in total)
Performance:	0-60mph: 29.7sec
	Top speed: 75mph
Power & torque:	70bhp/N/A
Engine:	Normally aspirated 1991cc straight six, petrol, carburettor, 12 valves
Drivetrain:	Front-engine RWD
Structure:	Separate chassis
Transmission:	Four-speed manual
Weight:	1527kg

PRICE GUIDE
Launch price:	£1151
Excellent:	£10,000
Good:	£7500
Average:	£4500
Project:	£2250

ARMSTRONG SIDDELEY
Typhoon Coupé

The Typhoon is the entry-level version of the Hurricane, but that doesn't stop it having an appeal all of its own. Just like its Hurricane/Lancaster brethren it features a front suspension set-up of surprising sophistication: independent with longitudinal torsion bars, along with a more traditional rear set-up of a live axle and leaf springs. The driving experience is stately and dignified, befitting of its upright styling. But the steel-and-aluminium bodywork is corrosion-prone and tough to restore.

SPECIFICATIONS

Years produced:	1946-1953 (1701 in total)
Performance:	0-60mph: 29.7sec
	Top speed: 78mph
Power & torque:	70bhp/109lb ft
Engine:	Normally aspirated 1991cc straight six, petrol, carburettor, 12 valves
Drivetrain:	Front-engine RWD
Structure:	Separate chassis
Transmission:	Four-speed manual
Weight:	1351kg

PRICE GUIDE

Launch price:	£1214
Excellent:	£11,000
Good:	£8500
Average:	£5750
Project:	£2750

ARMSTRONG SIDDELEY
Whitley

Once the great export drive was under way, Armstrong Siddeley was instantly building a car that it considered more than suitable for the Colonies. More imposing styling was the key to its appeal, with an updated nose and roofline to distance it from the Lancaster. It wasn't the new recipe that the British car industry needed, although it did prove a big seller. Underneath it was a familiar story, powered by the familiar 2.3-litre straight six that saw service in the last of the previous generation of models. It was big and comfortable, too.

SPECIFICATIONS

Years produced:	1950-1954 (2582 in total)
Performance:	0-60mph: 19.0sec
	Top speed: 80mph
Power & torque:	75bhp/107lb ft
Engine:	Normally aspirated 2309cc straight six, petrol, carburettor, 12 valves
Drivetrain:	Front-engine RWD
Structure:	Separate chassis
Transmission:	Four-speed manual
Weight:	1430kg

PRICE GUIDE

Launch price:	£1247
Excellent:	£10,000
Good:	£7500
Average:	£4000
Project:	£1750

ARMSTRONG SIDDELEY
Sapphire 346

When it appeared, it could have been easy to conclude that the 346 was just another rebody of the pre-war models, such was the timidity of its design. However, it was entirely new underneath, featuring a fresh suspension set-up of coil springs at the front and leaf springs at the back. It received a new engine, too – a lusty 3.4-litre six that was powerful enough to push the the 346 to 95mph, a significant step forward. But compared with the opposition it was too unwieldy for mass appeal, and a downturn in Armstrong Siddeley's fortunes quickly followed.

SPECIFICATIONS

Years produced:	1952-1958 (8187 in total)
Performance:	0-60mph: 13sec
	Top speed: 100mph
Power & torque:	150bhp/185lb ft
Engine:	Normally aspirated 3435cc straight six, petrol, carburettor, 12 valves
Drivetrain:	Front-engine RWD
Structure:	Separate chassis
Transmission:	Four-speed manual
Weight:	1575kg

PRICE GUIDE

Launch price:	£1728
Excellent:	£12,000
Good:	£9000
Average:	£4750
Project:	£1750

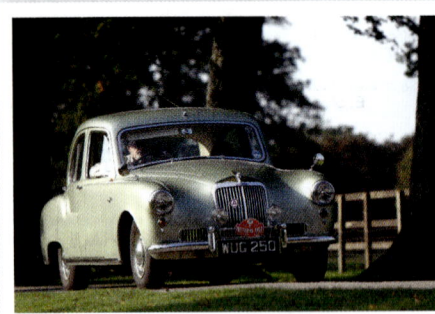

ARMSTRONG SIDDELEY
Sapphire 234/236

Despite sharing a name with the bigger 346, this Sapphire was less appealing thanks to the 236 being powered by a 2.3-litre engine previously seen on the Whitley and Lancaster/Hurricane, and the 234 by a smaller version of the 346's power unit. Both cars failed to make an impression on the market, selling disastrously – and you'll be hard-pressed to find one now, thanks to their relative lack of appeal compared with the 346 and the Star Sapphire. Best known for being a contributing factor in Armstrong Siddeley's closure.

SPECIFICATIONS

Years produced:	1955-1958 (803/603 in total)
Performance:	0-60mph: 15.5sec
	Top speed: 97mph
Power & torque:	120bhp/139lb ft
Engine:	Normally aspirated 2290cc four cylinder, petrol, carburettor, 8 valves
Drivetrain:	Front-engine RWD
Structure:	Separate chassis
Transmission:	Four-speed manual
Weight:	1360kg

PRICE GUIDE

Launch price:	£1599
Excellent:	£12,000
Good:	£7000
Average:	£3750
Project:	£1500

ARMSTRONG SIDDELEY
Star Sapphire

Star by name, star by nature. Although it looked rather similar to the Sapphire 346, the Star Sapphire was in an entirely different league as far as driving pleasure was concerned. It received a lusty 4.0-litre straight-six that could deliver genuine 100mph performance – and, finally, the four-speed all-synchromesh gearbox was joined by the option of a Rolls-Royce Hydramatic automatic transmission that made driving this swift saloon genuinely easy. Even today, a well-sorted Star Sapphire will surprise other people on the road.

SPECIFICATIONS

Years produced:	1958-1960 (980 in total)
Performance:	0-60mph: 15.7sec
	Top speed: 100mph
Power & torque:	145bhp/230lb ft
Engine:	Normally aspirated 3990cc straight six, petrol, carburettor, 12 valves
Drivetrain:	Front-engine RWD
Structure:	Separate chassis
Transmission:	Four-speed manual
Weight:	1778kg

PRICE GUIDE

Launch price:	£2646
Excellent:	£13,000
Good:	£10,000
Average:	£5500
Project:	£2500

ASTON MARTIN

LIONEL MARTIN and Robert Bamford built the first Aston Martin in 1914, the 'Aston' coming from the Aston Clinton hillclimb. From this small acorn grew one of Britain's best-loved sports car marques. The golden era for the manufacturer began in 1948 when industrialist David Brown took over; the iconic DB series cars were fast, beautiful, desirable and expensive. After Brown sold up in 1972, Aston Martin had a number of owners while the venerable V8 model kept the firm afloat. Ford's takeover in 1987 led to a new period of stability and expanded model range with cars such as the DB7 and Vanquish. In 2007, the struggling US giant sold Aston Martin to a British-led consortium.

ASTON MARTIN
DB2

While the 2-Litre of 1948 has become retrospectively known as the DB1, the DB2 of 1950 was the first officially to wear the initials of owner David Brown. The chassis was largely the same as for the 2-Litre, but the curvaceous fastback body with an imposingly long bonnet was fresh and graceful, and would inspire Aston's styling for two decades. The 2.6-litre twin-cam engine was a WO Bentley design for Lagonda and initially proved temperamental. It eventually settled down to give the DB2 impressive performance, especially in 121mph Vantage form from 1951.

SPECIFICATIONS
Years produced: 1950-1953 (411 in total)
Performance: 0-60mph: 11.2sec / Top speed: 116mph
Power & torque: 105bhp/125lb ft
Engine: Normally aspirated 2580cc straight six, petrol, carburettor, 12 valves
Drivetrain: Front-engine RWD
Structure: Superleggera
Transmission: Four-speed manual
Weight: 1207kg

PRICE GUIDE
Launch price: £1920
Excellent: £125,000
Good: £80,000
Average: £50,000
Project: £30,000

ASTON MARTIN
DB2 & 2/4 Convertible

A peculiar quirk of the marque is that it refers to its fixed-head coupés as saloons. No such confusion with the drophead coupés though. The DB2 appeared soon after the 'saloon' and, like its tin-top sibling, could be specified with three-abreast seating if a column shift was fitted. Only 102 were built. Open-top DB 2/4s were slightly more plentiful, at 132. However, most exclusive were the Spiders built by Bertone. Alfred Hitchcock featured a drophead coupé in The Birds – an early brush with fame for a marque that would soon become a cinema celebrity.

SPECIFICATIONS
Years produced: 1951-1957
Performance: 0-60mph: 11.2sec / Top speed: 116mph
Power & torque: 105bhp/125lb ft
Engine: Normally aspirated 2580cc straight six, petrol, carburettor, 12 valves
Drivetrain: Front-engine RWD
Structure: Superleggera
Transmission: Four-speed manual
Weight: 1207kg

PRICE GUIDE
Launch price: £2621
Excellent: £200,000
Good: £120,000
Average: £75,000
Project: £50,000

ASTON MARTIN
DB2/4

The '4' tacked onto the DB2's title denoted that this reworking of the theme could now fit four people... at a squeeze. The 2+2 seating was made more habitable by a higher roofline and opening rear screen – perhaps so those in the back could escape easily if it became too tight! However, the extra weight affected performance, so a boost to 3.0 litres in 1954 took power to 140bhp. The Mk2 of 1955 incorporated a rear-end restyle and a stronger rear axle, and also introduced the incredibly rare notchback hardtop version, of which just 34 were made.

SPECIFICATIONS
Years produced: 1953-1957 (764 in total)
Performance: 0-60mph: 10.5sec / Top speed: 119mph
Power & torque: 125bhp/139lb ft
Engine: Normally aspirated 2580cc straight six, petrol, carburettor, 12 valves
Drivetrain: Front-engine RWD
Structure: Superleggera
Transmission: Four-speed manual
Weight: 1257kg

PRICE GUIDE
Launch price: £2622
Excellent: £115,000
Good: £75,000
Average: £47,500
Project: £27,500

ASTON MARTIN
DB MkIII Coupé

Really the third series of DB2/4, but Aston dropped the 2/4 nomenclature for its 1957 to 1959 range of saloons and dropheads. The most noticeable change was a more tapering front end topped by a neater grille, there were vertical rear lights and the body was tidied. Mechanically, the engine rose marginally in capacity but was made a lot stronger and more powerful at 162bhp. Aston claimed 214bhp was possible with the competition-tuned triple-carb version, but this was probably exaggerated. Front discs standard from late 1957.

SPECIFICATIONS
Years produced: 1957-1959 (551 in total)
Performance: 0-60mph: 9.3sec / Top speed: 119mph
Power & torque: 162bhp/180lb ft
Engine: Normally aspirated 2922cc straight six, petrol, carburettor, 12 valves
Drivetrain: Front-engine RWD
Structure: Superleggera
Transmission: Four-speed manual
Weight: 1270kg

PRICE GUIDE
Launch price: £3076
Excellent: £125,000
Good: £80,000
Average: £50,000
Project: £30,000

ASTON MARTIN
DB4

The definitive and best-loved Aston Martin shape was born with the DB4 of 1958. It was massively over-engineered with a hefty chassis and new all-alloy 240bhp DOHC engine of 3.0 litres (but capable of being expanded well beyond if needed). But what really grabbed the headlines was the Superleggera body. Designed by Italian coachbuilder Touring, its stunning lines were formed of aluminium panels laid over a frame of steel tubes, making the car strong but also light. From 1958 to 1962, there were five series of DB4s.

SPECIFICATIONS	
Years produced:	1958-1963 (1113 in total)
Performance:	0-60mph: 8.5sec
	Top speed: 141mph
Power & torque:	240bhp/240lb ft
Engine:	Normally aspirated 3670cc straight six, petrol, carburettor, 12 valves
Drivetrain:	Front-engine RWD
Structure:	Superleggera
Transmission:	Four-speed manual with overdrive/auto
Weight:	1361kg

PRICE GUIDE	
Launch price:	£3980
Excellent:	£250,000
Good:	£175,000
Average:	£115,000
Project:	£80,000

ASTON MARTIN
DB4 GT

For some the standard DB4 just wasn't enough, so the DB4 GT was created. With its wheelbase shortened by five inches, it became one of the great racers of its era. Less length meant less weight and the twin-plug engine meant more power (302bhp), so it was a fast machine. Later versions had faired-in headlamps, adopted as standard on the succeeding DB5. Zagato built 19 versions with an even sleeker, sexier body and 314bhp, 0-60mph in 6.1sec and a top speed of over 150mph. Very exhilarating – but one of those will cost you four times the GT price.

SPECIFICATIONS	
Years produced:	1959-1961 (81 in total)
Performance:	0-60mph: 6.4sec
	Top speed: 152mph
Power & torque:	302bhp/278lb ft
Engine:	Normally aspirated 3670cc straight six, petrol, carburettor, 12 valves
Drivetrain:	Front-engine RWD
Structure:	Superleggera
Transmission:	Four-speed manual
Weight:	1277kg

PRICE GUIDE	
Launch price:	£4534
Excellent:	£1,250,000
Good:	£750,000
Average:	£600,000
Project:	£450,000

ASTON MARTIN
DB4 drophead

While DB4 saloons are special enough, even more prized are the scarce and beautiful drophead coupés. Production didn't begin until 1961, three years after the enclosed cars arrived. Just 70 emerged, of which 38 had the standard 240bhp engine and 32 were endowed with the 266bhp of the Vantage engine. In addition to the hood, a hard-top was available; when fitted, it made the British car look much like a Maserati 3500 coupé from behind. It's not surprising that Touring of Milan was responsible for the looks of both.

SPECIFICATIONS	
Years produced:	1961-1963 (70 in total)
Performance:	0-60mph: 8.5sec
	Top speed: 141mph
Power & torque:	240bhp/240lb ft
Engine:	Normally aspirated 3670cc straight six, petrol, carburettor, 12 valves
Drivetrain:	Front-engine RWD
Structure:	Superleggera
Transmission:	Four-speed manual
Weight:	1352kg

PRICE GUIDE	
Launch price:	£3980
Excellent:	£500,000
Good:	£300,000
Average:	£250,000
Project:	£185,000

ASTON MARTIN
DB5

Had not a certain James Bond turned the DB5 into the most famous car in the world, this DB4 evolution might have gone largely unnoticed; originally, it was just going to be called the DB4 Series 6. However, *Goldfinger* and *Thunderball* made stars of both the car and its maker. Four litres of potent power – 282bhp as standard, 314bhp for the Vantage – and long, lean looks meant the legend was largely justified. Disc brakes were now on each wheel, and all but the very earliest cars had five gears – less entertaining were the autos. Licensed to thrill.

SPECIFICATIONS	
Years produced:	1963-1965 (1063 in total)
Performance:	0-60mph: 8.1sec
	Top speed: 141mph
Power & torque:	282bhp/288lb ft
Engine:	Normally aspirated 3995cc straight six, petrol, carburettor, 12 valves
Drivetrain:	Front-engine RWD
Structure:	Superleggera
Transmission:	Four/five-speed manual
Weight:	1346kg

PRICE GUIDE	
Launch price:	£4249
Excellent:	£400,000
Good:	£200,000
Average:	£160,000
Project:	£80,000

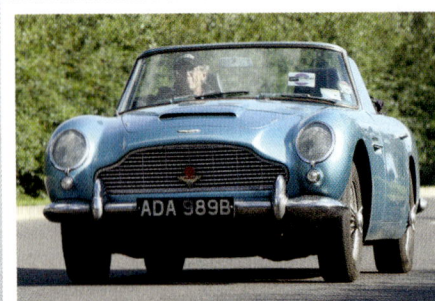

ASTON MARTIN
DB5 convertible

As well as the rare Radford DB5 'shooting brake' estates, those seeking an out-of-the-ordinary DB5 could plump for the drophead coupé. Extra bracing compensated for the lack of a roof, although the huge chassis meant the DB5 could cope well with some of its original strength removed. Production of the saloon finished in 1965 but 37 convertibles were built afterwards. Aston would subsequently use the Volante name to describe all its soft-tops. The Superleggera construction is as the DB5 saloon's and the styling was carried over to the DB6 Volante.

SPECIFICATIONS	
Years produced:	1963-1966 (123 in total)
Performance:	0-60mph: 8.1sec
	Top speed: 141mph
Power & torque:	282bhp/288lb ft
Engine:	Normally aspirated 3995cc straight six, petrol, carburettor, 12 valves
Drivetrain:	Front-engine RWD
Structure:	Superleggera
Transmission:	Five-speed manual
Weight:	1465kg

PRICE GUIDE	
Launch price:	£4249
Excellent:	£575,000
Good:	£375,000
Average:	£260,000
Project:	£150,000

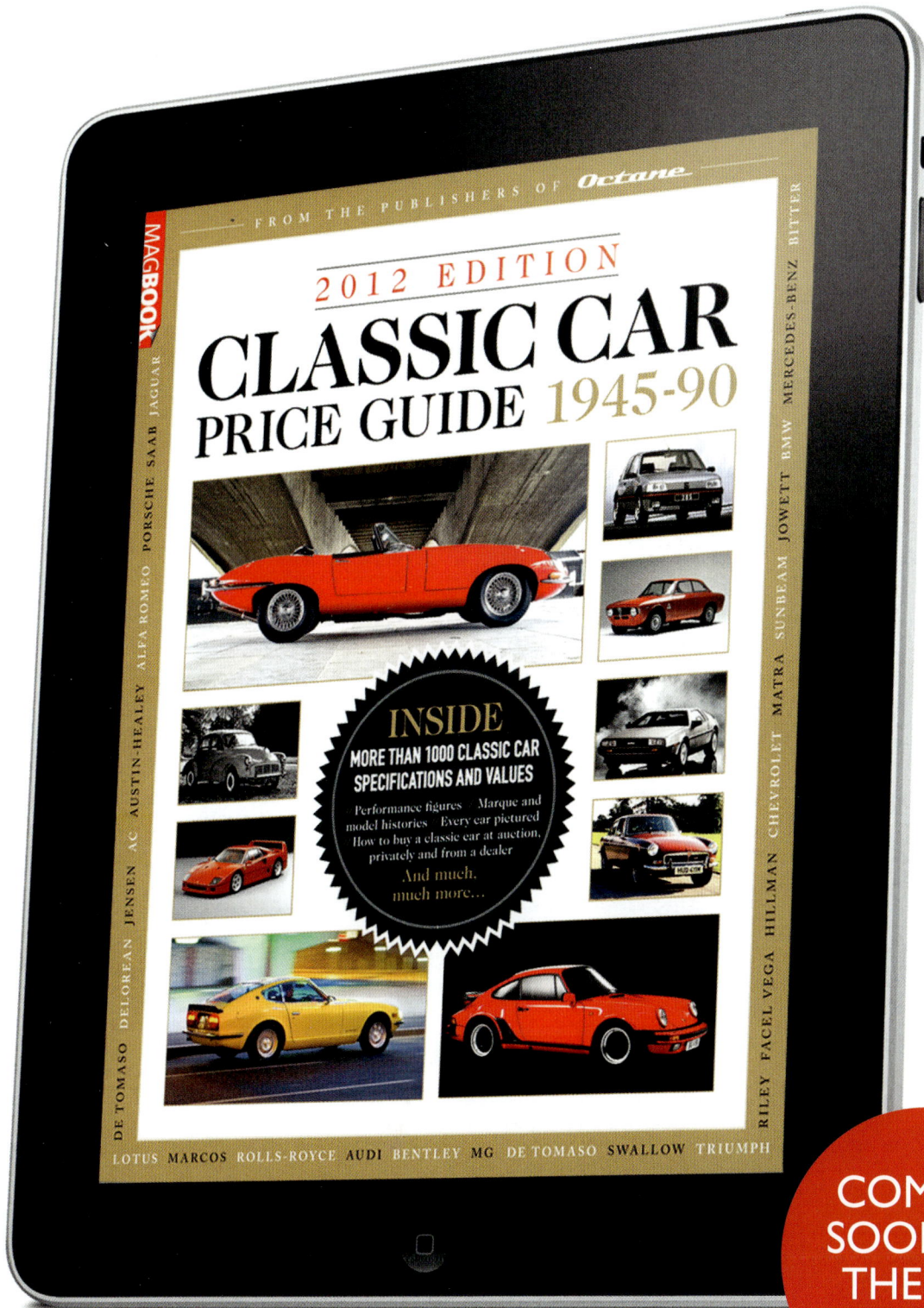

ASTON MARTIN
DB6

The 'proper' DB series reached a graceful end with the DB6. A longer wheelbase meant it could seat four people, although only the two up-front would have any real comfort. The higher roofline, split bumpers and more aerodynamic Kamm tail were the main identifying points. Extra civilisation was offered in the form of power steering, air-con and a limited-slip diff and, as was the Aston way, there was a more powerful Vantage version boasting 325bhp. The Mk2 appeared in 1969, characterised by flared arches and optional fuel injection.

SPECIFICATIONS

Years produced:	1965-1970 (1567 in total)
Performance:	0-60mph: 6.5sec
	Top speed: 148mph
Power & torque:	325bhp/290lb ft
Engine:	Normally aspirated 3995cc straight six, petrol, carburettor, 12 valves
Drivetrain:	Front-engine RWD
Structure:	Spaceframe
Transmission:	Five-speed manual/three-speed auto
Weight:	1474kg

PRICE GUIDE

Launch price:	£4998
Excellent:	£150,000
Good:	£100,000
Average:	£75,000
Project:	£50,000

ASTON MARTIN
DB6 Volante

Although the first 37 Volantes – Aston speak for convertibles – were built on the shorter DB5 chassis, genuine DB6s started to appear from October 1966. The time-consuming Superleggera construction was dropped; although aluminium was still used for the panels, the steel tubing underneath was replaced by folded metal. 140 Mk1 Volantes were constructed before the debut of the Mk2 in July 1969: its much shorter run meant that only 38 of these could be fitted in before the DB6 Volante reached the end of its road in November 1970.

SPECIFICATIONS

Years produced:	1965-1970 (215 in total)
Performance:	0-60mph: 6.5sec
	Top speed: 140mph
Power & torque:	282bhp/288lb ft
Engine:	Normally aspirated 3995cc straight six, petrol, carburettor, 12 valves
Drivetrain:	Front-engine RWD
Structure:	Spaceframe
Transmission:	Five-speed manual
Weight:	1466kg

PRICE GUIDE

Launch price:	£4998
Excellent:	£400,000
Good:	£350,000
Average:	£250,000
Project:	£180,000

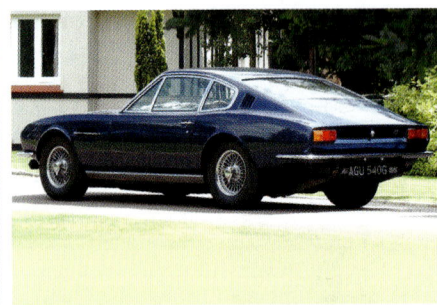

ASTON MARTIN
DBS

A new stylist – William Towns – meant a completely new look for Aston, with the DBS shifting focus from Italy to America with its arresting muscle-car stance. The four-passenger DBS was designed for a V8, but Aston's eight-pot wasn't ready in time so the car used the DB6's 4.0-litre engine with an uprated Vantage option. However, all that extra weight knocked performance back; a DBS could offer only the same kind of speeds as a DB4. Although the V8 model was available from 1969, the six-cylinder continued until 1973 as the entry-level Aston.

SPECIFICATIONS

Years produced:	1967-1973 (899 in total)
Performance:	0-60mph: 7.8sec
	Top speed: 140mph
Power & torque:	282bhp/288lb ft
Engine:	Normally aspirated 3995cc straight six, petrol, carburettor, 12 valves
Drivetrain:	Front-engine RWD
Structure:	Monocoque
Transmission:	Five-speed manual/three-speed auto
Weight:	1705kg

PRICE GUIDE

Launch price:	£5500
Excellent:	£70,000
Good:	£45,000
Average:	£22,500
Project:	£12,000

ASTON MARTIN
DBS-V8

Two years after the 1967 launch of the DBS, the car finally gained the engine it had always been destined for; Tadek Marek's sparkling new quad-cam fuel-injected 5340cc V8. However, the model's size and weight made it more grand tourer than out-and-out sports car. Externally, there was little difference to the DBS save for the alloy wheels – where the DBS had wires – and a front air dam. The Hillman Hunter rear lights remained the same, though, proving that even the most prestigious machines have some touches of the real world about them.

SPECIFICATIONS

Years produced:	1969-1972 (402 in total)
Performance:	0-60mph: 6.0sec
	Top speed: 162mph
Power & torque:	315bhp/400lb ft
Engine:	Normally aspirated 5340cc V8, petrol, fuel injection, 16 valves
Drivetrain:	Front-engine RWD
Structure:	Monocoque
Transmission:	Five-speed manual/three-speed auto
Weight:	1724kg

PRICE GUIDE

Launch price:	£6897
Excellent:	£75,000
Good:	£47,500
Average:	£32,500
Project:	£17,000

ASTON MARTIN
V8

If the 1960s was Aston's golden era, the glow faded in the '70s. David Brown sold the firm in 1972, resulting in the DB initials being dropped and the V8's front end being restyled with single lights, a smaller grille and a few more curves. The engine's troublesome fuel injection was soon dropped in favour of four Weber carbs, plus a bonnet bulge to clear them. A lack of cash meant the V8 would have a long existence; with many detail changes and updates, it survived until 1990, an unprecedented lifespan for a top-flight luxury sports car's engine.

SPECIFICATIONS

Years produced:	1972-1990 (2012 in total)
Performance:	0-60mph: 7.2sec
	Top speed: 146mph
Power & torque:	320bhp/360lb ft
Engine:	Normally aspirated 5340cc V8, petrol, carburettor, 16 valves
Drivetrain:	Front-engine RWD
Structure:	Monocoque
Transmission:	Five-speed manual/three-speed auto
Weight:	1814kg

PRICE GUIDE

Launch price:	N/A
Excellent:	£50,000
Good:	£30,000
Average:	£15,000
Project:	£10,000

ASTON MARTIN
V8 Vantage

With 1977 the Queen's Silver Jubilee year, Britain seemed keen to celebrate all that was best about itself. So what better time for the V8 Vantage to be launched? Hailed as 'Britain's first supercar,' its 5.3-litre V8 unleashed an incredible 438bhp. The dash to 60mph took just 5.4sec; top speed was 170mph. Visually, the car could be distinguished by a blanked-off grille and bonnet scoop. 1978's Oscar India variant adopted a small boot spoiler and a smoother bonnet, the car continuing in this form until 1990. The rich man's Ford Capri!

SPECIFICATIONS
Years produced:	1977-1989 (313 in total)
Performance:	0-60mph: 5.4sec
	Top speed: 170mph
Power & torque:	438bhp/400lb ft
Engine:	Normally aspirated 5340cc V8, petrol, fuel injection, 16 valves
Drivetrain:	Front-engine RWD
Structure:	Monocoque
Transmission:	Five-speed manual
Weight:	1818kg

PRICE GUIDE
Launch price:	£20,000
Excellent:	£60,000
Good:	£50,000
Average:	£30,000
Project:	£20,000

ASTON MARTIN
Lagonda

Even Aston Martin wasn't immune to the craziness of the 1970s: behold the strangely glorious Lagonda, launched in 1977. Outside, the car – on a stretched V8 chassis – was an uncompromisingly razor-edged wedge shape by William Towns; inside it was a technological tour de force of touch-sensitive switches, digital displays and futuristic gizmos. These proved its Achilles heel, for the Lagonda soon became known for its unreliability. Simplification followed and the wedge stayed in production until 1990. Utterly mad, yet endearingly British.

SPECIFICATIONS
Years produced:	1977-1990 (645 in total)
Performance:	0-60mph: 8.8sec
	Top speed: 143mph
Power & torque:	280bhp/302lb ft
Engine:	Normally aspirated 5340cc V8, petrol, fuel injection, 16 valves
Drivetrain:	Front-engine RWD
Structure:	Monocoque
Transmission:	Three-speed automatic
Weight:	2023kg

PRICE GUIDE
Launch price:	£24,570
Excellent:	£35,000
Good:	£20,000
Average:	£12,500
Project:	£10,000

ASTON MARTIN
V8 Volante

Aston held out until June 1978 to slice the roof off its V8, a surprising length of time (as the saloon could trace its origins back to 1967) for a car with so much sales potential. But the firm's more optimistic outlook of the late 1970s finally gave rise to the marriage of open-top enjoyment with V8 performance. A fully-lined power hood, and new burr walnut dash and door cappings cosseted the occupants. Up until 1981, every Volante was exported to North America; the rest of the world had to wait until March of that year to see what all the fuss was about.

SPECIFICATIONS
Years produced:	1978-1990 (562 in total)
Performance:	0-60mph: 7.7sec
	Top speed: 140mph
Power & torque:	N/A/N/A
Engine:	Normally aspirated 5340cc V8, petrol, fuel injection, 16 valves
Drivetrain:	Front-engine RWD
Structure:	Monocoque
Transmission:	Five-speed manual/three-speed auto
Weight:	1794kg

PRICE GUIDE
Launch price:	£33,864
Excellent:	£70,000
Good:	£40,000
Average:	£20,000
Project:	£12,000

ASTON MARTIN
V8 Vantage Volante

Alongside the Vantage saloon, 'Britain's first supercar' could be had as a steroid-enhanced convertible. It came with the same luxuries as the 'ordinary' Volante, but also trumpeted the 5.3-litre Vantage-spec engine. The USA was desperate for a new high-performance drophead coupé – Aston hadn't built one since 1970 – so this breeze machine was keenly received there. And it's where the vast majority ended up, making them a rare sight in Europe and their homeland... although James Bond managed to get hold of one for 1987's The Living Daylights.

SPECIFICATIONS
Years produced:	1986-1989 (116 in total)
Performance:	0-60mph: 5.4sec
	Top speed: 165mph
Power & torque:	438bhp/400lb ft
Engine:	Normally aspirated 5340cc V8, petrol, fuel injection, 16 valves
Drivetrain:	Front-engine RWD
Structure:	Monocoque
Transmission:	Five-speed manual/three-speed auto
Weight:	1650kg

PRICE GUIDE
Launch price:	£87,000
Excellent:	£100,000
Good:	£75,000
Average:	£60,000
Project:	£35,000

ASTON MARTIN
Zagato

Looking to reignite a successful past relationship, Aston asked Italian coachbuilder Zagato to think up an exotic body which could be fitted to a lightened, shortened chassis. The result divided opinion, gone were the luscious curves of Zagato's Aston revamps of the 1960s and in their place were brutal straight lines and angled edges, with an extensive use of flush-fitting glass. Critics found it hard to get over the resemblance to contemporary Japanese sports coupés but, with only 83 ever built, they are surprisingly valuable today.

SPECIFICATIONS
Years produced:	1986-1989 (83 in total)
Performance:	0-60mph: 5.0sec
	Top speed: 186mph
Power & torque:	432bhp/395lb ft
Engine:	Normally aspirated 5340cc V8, petrol, fuel injection, 16 valves
Drivetrain:	Front-engine RWD
Structure:	Monocoque
Transmission:	Five-speed manual
Weight:	1650kg

PRICE GUIDE
Launch price:	£87,000
Excellent:	£150,000
Good:	£80,000
Average:	£40,000
Project:	£22,500

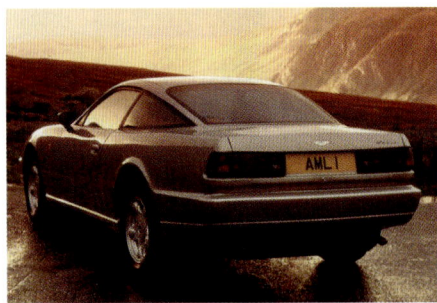

ASTON MARTIN
Virage

After 20 years of the V8 saloon, even Aston was forced to concede that it was time for a change – the Virage, the final blast of the original V8 concept. A bold and imposing new body was designed by Royal College of Art tutors John Heffernan and Ken Greenley, and slotted over the existing V8 chassis. Despite the old-fashioned underpinnings, the car still looked sufficiently sleek and modern to revitalise Aston Martin for the 1990s. From 1992, Aston Martin introduced a service to convert the Virage engine to a 500bhp 6.3-litre.

SPECIFICATIONS
Years produced:	1989-1995 (365 in total)
Performance:	0-60mph: 6.8sec
	Top speed: 157mph
Power & torque:	330bhp/350lb ft
Engine:	Normally aspirated 5340cc V8, petrol, electronic fuel injection, 32 valves
Drivetrain:	Front-engine RWD
Structure:	Monocoque
Transmission:	Five-speed manual/three-speed auto
Weight:	1948kg

PRICE GUIDE
Launch price:	£120,000
Excellent:	£32,000
Good:	£27,000
Average:	£20,000
Project:	£13,000

AUDI

AUGUST HORCH chose Audi as a name for his 1909 company because 'Horch' in German means 'hark', which equates to 'Audi' in Latin. Audi became best-known for its luxurious and sporting big-engined cars, joining with the Wanderer, DKW and Horch firms to form Auto Union in 1932, leading to the four-ring logo. Largely dormant after the war because its factories were in East Germany, Auto Union was bought by Volkswagen in 1964 and relaunched the Audi brand, building FWD cars. The marque came into its own in the 1980s with advanced models such as the AWD Quattro. It is now pitched as a prestige manufacturer, up against BMW and Mercedes-Benz.

AUDI
100 Coupé S

The 100 saloon was a bit like the school swot; useful to know but ultimately quite dull to be around. However, when shorn of its sensible suit and clothed in an Aston DBS-like coupé bodyshell, it suddenly started to look a little more interesting. Although never a massive seller when new, the 100S Coupé is one of those cars that has become more desirable with the passage of time, as classic car enthusiasts warm to its love-me styling combined with thorough German engineering. And that's turned it into something of a cult car.

SPECIFICATIONS
Years produced:	1970-1976 (30,687 in total)
Performance:	0-60mph: 10.8sec
	Top speed: 118mph
Power & torque:	112bhp/118lb ft
Engine:	Normally aspirated 1871cc four cylinder, petrol, carburettor, 8 valves
Drivetrain:	Front-engine RWD
Structure:	Monocoque
Transmission:	Four-speed manual
Weight:	1082kg

PRICE GUIDE
Launch price:	£2418
Excellent:	£4000
Good:	£2750
Average:	£1400
Project:	£500

AUDI
80 (B1)

Audi's first 80 was a bold step into the '70s, even if much of the engineering that underpinned it looked rather familiar. FWD was hardly new to a company rooted in DKW and NSU, but the EA827 engine that powered the 80 was nothing short of revolutionary – and it would live on well into the 21st century. The 80 was light and efficient, and wore a sharp Gandini-penned suit. Owner Volkswagen benefited from Audi by badge-engineering the 80 to become the Passat – the car that made Wolfsburg's long wished-for move away from its air-cooled past.

SPECIFICATIONS
Years produced:	1972-1978 (1,103,766 in total)
Performance:	0-60mph: 11.0sec
	Top speed: 104mph
Power & torque:	75bhp/70lb ft
Engine:	Normally aspirated 1588cc four cylinder, petrol, carburettor, 8 valves
Drivetrain:	Front-engine FWD
Structure:	Monocoque
Transmission:	Four-speed manual
Weight:	855kg

PRICE GUIDE
Launch price:	£1275
Excellent:	£2000
Good:	£1000
Average:	£500
Project:	£350

AUDI
80/Quattro (B2)

When it came to facelifting the 80, it was up to Giugiaro to make it look like a more substantial car. He did such a good job that it became difficult to tell it apart from the 100. Like its predecessor, the 80 was light and efficient so, when it was fitted with a 1.6-litre fuel-injection engine, it was transformed into a genuinely quick sporting saloon. It was facelifted again in 1984, with smoother styling and a posher interior – and the five-cylinder cars became 90s. Getting sought after now, and values are on the up – especially for the quick ones.

SPECIFICATIONS
Years produced:	1978-1986 (1,680,146 in total)
Performance:	0-60mph: 12.1sec
	Top speed: 104mph
Power & torque:	85bhp/86lb ft
Engine:	Normally aspirated 1588cc four cylinder, petrol, carburettor, 8 valves
Drivetrain:	Front-engine FWD/AWD
Structure:	Monocoque
Trans./weight:	Five-speed manual/910kg

PRICE GUIDE
Launch price:	£4650
Excellent:	£2500
Good:	£1200
Average:	£500
Project:	£300

AUDI
200

Audi continued its habit of producing new model designations by upping the power and equipment levels on a cooking model – in this case by adding a turbocharger to the 100 to create the 200. The new model was priced to compete with the BMW 528i and could easily outgun what was considered the pacesetter of the class. And it wasn't restrained – its quad headlamps looked brutal, while the chintzy velour-clad interior took some getting used to. A rare beast, but far more characterful than the car it was based on.

SPECIFICATIONS
Years produced: 1979-1982
Performance: 0-60mph: 7.5sec
Top speed: 125mph
Power & torque: 170bhp/195lb ft
Engine: Turbocharged 2144cc five cylinder, petrol, electronic fuel injection, 10 valves
Drivetrain: Front-engine FWD
Structure: Monocoque
Transmission: Five-speed manual
Weight: 1260kg

PRICE GUIDE
Launch price: £12,500
Excellent: £2000
Good: £1200
Average: £900
Project: £500

AUDI
Quattro

Developed as a low-volume homologation special – and no-one could have predicted just how big an impact the Quattro would have on the motoring industry. With four-wheel drive and 200bhp of turbocharged power, the new coupé ook the world by storm, and the rest of the industry struggled to catch up. But despite being a competition-bred machine, the Quattro was always civilised on the road. These early cars are now the rarest and are easily identifiable thanks to their chrome-rimmed quad headlamps.

SPECIFICATIONS
Years produced: 1980-1983
Performance: 0-60mph: 7.1sec
Top speed: 137mph
Power & torque: 200bhp/210lb ft
Engine: Turbocharged 2144cc five cylinder, petrol, electronic fuel injection, 10 valves
Drivetrain: Front-engine AWD
Structure: Monocoque
Transmission: Five-speed manual
Weight: 1300kg

PRICE GUIDE
Launch price: £14,500
Excellent: £12,000
Good: £8500
Average: £4500
Project: £2250

AUDI
Coupé

Six months after the Quattro burst onto the scene, Audi launched its lower-powered FWD sister car onto the market. Although the Coupé shared its doors and basic body with the Quattro, its slimline wheelarches and slimmer wheels meant that no-one was going to confuse the pair. A facelift in 1984 saw the Coupé's square-rigged styling softened with the arrival of wrap-around bumpers and plastic sill extensions. Solid, dependable, and desirable in top condition, with plenty of retro kudos. Parts getting hard to come by, and Quattro drivetrain components pricey.

SPECIFICATIONS
Years produced: 1980-1989 (174,687 in total)
Performance: 0-60mph: 9.1sec
Top speed: 122mph
Power & torque: 136bhp/126lb ft
Engine: Normally aspirated 2144/2226cc five cylinder, petrol, mechanical fuel injection
Drivetrain: Front-engine FWD/AWD
Structure: Monocoque
Transmission: Five-speed manual
Weight: 1050kg

PRICE GUIDE
Launch price: £7475
Excellent: £3500
Good: £1750
Average: £600
Project: £450

AUDI
100/200/Quattro (C3)

The trouble with the Audi 100 is that it looks too modern for its own good. It's hard to believe that the cigar-shaped executive dates back to 1982 but, then, it redrew the map when it arrived on the scene. Pioneering use of flush glass and an aerodynamic shape meant that the 2.2-litre version could outpace a Rover 3500 but use 30% less fuel. The 100 is still reasonably common thanks to tough build and a galvanised shell from 1985, but the 200 is endangered – a shame given its 140mph potential. Still not regarded as 'classic' enough, so values remain low.

SPECIFICATIONS (200 Turbo)
Years produced: 1982-1991 (1,078,443 in total)
Performance: 0-60mph: 7.4sec
Top speed: 143mph
Power & torque: 182bhp/186lb ft
Engine: Turbocharged 2226cc five cylinder, petrol, fuel injection, 10 valves
Drivetrain: Front-engine FWD/AWD
Structure: Monocoque
Transmission: Five-speed manual
Weight: 1410kg

PRICE GUIDE
Launch price: £8772
Excellent: £2500
Good: £1500
Average: £850
Project: £500

AUDI
Quattro

Not one to sit on its laurels, Audi continued to develop the Quattro (which is now retrospectively known as the ur-Quattro). Big rectangular headlamps, RHD and a slightly larger engine came in 1983, with the controversial digital dashboard (which you'll either love or hate) arriving the following year. But despite that, the basic recipe remained the same throughout the 1980s and drivers continued to love the grippy handling and that warbling five-cylinder soundtrack. Values have steadily risen on the back of 2010's TV stardom.

SPECIFICATIONS
Years produced: 1983-1989
Performance: 0-60mph: 7.3sec
Top speed: 137mph
Power & torque: 200bhp/210lb ft
Engine: Turbocharged 2226cc five cylinder, petrol, fuel injection, 10 valves
Drivetrain: Front-engine AWD
Structure: Monocoque
Transmission: Five-speed manual
Weight: 1290kg

PRICE GUIDE
Launch price: £29,445
Excellent: £13,000
Good: £11,000
Average: £7500
Project: £3500

AUDI
90/Quattro

The 90 was proof positive that, as the '80s progressed, Audi was becoming increasingly ambitious. Despite being a facelift of a six-year-old car, this rebadged 80 was considered by Audi to be a credible rival to the BMW 3-Series and Mercedes-Benz 190 – and it was *just* good enough thanks to its warbling five-pot and grippy four-wheel drive handling. Plush interiors and Coupé-style bodykits certainly differentiated the 90 from its Plain Jane sister car, but whether that justified premium pricing was a different matter. Rare now, but the 90 has a small following.

SPECIFICATIONS

Years produced:	1984-1987
Performance:	0-60mph: 9.7sec
	Top speed: 122mph
Power & torque:	136bhp/137lb ft
Engine:	Normally aspirated 2226cc five cylinder, petrol, electronic fuel injection, 10 valves
Drivetrain:	Front-engine FWD/AWD
Structure:	Monocoque
Transmission:	Five-speed manual
Weight:	1150kg

PRICE GUIDE

Launch price:	£12,500
Excellent:	£2000
Good:	£1500
Average:	£700
Project:	£500

AUDI
Sport Quattro

By 1984, the Quattro's best Group B rallying days were behind it. It was simply too big and heavy to compete with the flighty new Peugeot 205T16 – so, as a riposte, Audi lopped 20cm from the original car's wheelbase, and installed a 20-valve head on its turbo five. The rally cars met with moderate success, while the road versions proved quick if costly. They're rare and valuable now though, and on the crest of a Group B revival, but there are many fakes out there, so make sure you're looking at a real one. The upright Audi 80 windscreen is a giveaway.

SPECIFICATIONS

Years produced:	1983-1985 (200 in total)
Performance:	0-60mph: 4.8sec
	Top speed: 155mph
Power & torque:	302bhp/243lb ft
Engine:	Turbocharged 2133cc five cylinder, petrol, mechanical fuel injection, 20 valves
Drivetrain:	Front-engine AWD
Structure:	Monocoque
Transmission:	Five-speed manual
Weight:	1000kg

PRICE GUIDE

Launch price:	N/A in UK
Excellent:	£150,000
Good:	£90,000
Average:	£75,000
Project:	N/A

AUDI
V8

Audi was all about being upwardly mobile during the '80s, and no car it produced better embodied its ambition than the V8. Although clearly based on the 100/200, it was powered by an all-new 3.6-litre V8 and underpinned by a capable quattro drivetrain. Typically, it was also crammed with all the technology that Audi could stuff in – much of which caused problems for hapless owners down the line. It was an admirable first go at a top-line motor, but the V8 wasn't a success, and that makes it a rarity – yet one worth seeking out if you like your barges lesser-spotted.

SPECIFICATIONS

Years produced:	1988-1993 (21,564 in total)
Performance:	0-60mph: 7.6sec
	Top speed: 152mph
Power & torque:	247bhp/251lb ft
Engine:	Normally aspirated 3562cc V8, petrol, electronic fuel injection, 32 valves
Drivetrain:	Front-engine AWD
Structure:	Monocoque
Transmission:	Five/six-speed manual
Weight:	1710kg

PRICE GUIDE

Launch price:	£40,334
Excellent:	£3000
Good:	£2000
Average:	£1200
Project:	£750

AUDI
Quattro 20v

The Audi quattro was supposed to fade quietly out of production in 1988. However massive demand – especially from the UK – ensured that the old favourite remained in production long after the 80/90/Coupé from which it was derived had disappeared from the scene. To celebrate its stay of execution, Audi shoehorned in the 20-valve five-cylinder engine from the 200 and upped the output to a more-than-useful 220bhp. Of all the quattros, these last-of-line 20v examples are by far the best to drive – and quickest to boot.

SPECIFICATIONS

Years produced:	1989-1991 (931 in total)
Performance:	0-60mph: 6.3sec
	Top speed: 141mph
Power & torque:	220bhp/228lb ft
Engine:	Turbocharged 2226cc five cylinder, petrol, electronic fuel injection, 20 valves
Drivetrain:	Front-engine AWD
Structure:	Monocoque
Transmission:	Five-speed manual
Weight:	1300kg

PRICE GUIDE

Launch price:	£32,995
Excellent:	£23,000
Good:	£15,000
Average:	£8000
Project:	£6000

Austin AUSTIN

FOUNDED IN Longbridge, Birmingham in 1905, Herbert Austin's car company grew to become one of Britain's industrial powerhouses. Its early, troubled years came to an end with the hugely-popular Austin Seven of 1922, arguably the UK's first people's car. After WW2, Austin became the dominant partner in BMC, and the successful and forward-thinking models continued; not least the best-selling Mini. Economic conditions saw BMC becoming part of British Leyland in 1968 and led to troubled times symbolised by such models as the Maxi and Allegro. The 1980 Metro was a much-needed sales triumph, but the Austin name was dropped in 1987 by the then Rover Group.

AUSTIN
A40 Devon/Dorset

Austin's first step into the brave new world of flush-mounted headlamps and front-hinged doors was a raging success, with over a quarter of a million built. It's also notable for first using what would come to be known as the BMC B-series engine, here in its smallest capacity. There's still a separate chassis with hydro-mechanical brakes, but independent front suspension makes it a decent drive. Dorset is merely a two-door version of the Devon, nearly all of which went for export. More hot-rodded than standard examples survive in the UK.

SPECIFICATIONS

Years produced:	1947-1952 (289,897 in total)
Performance:	0-60mph: 34.8sec
	Top speed: 67mph
Power & torque:	40bhp/57lb ft
Engine:	Normally aspirated 1200cc four cylinder, petrol, carburettor, 8 valves
Drivetrain:	Front-engine RWD
Structure:	Separate chassis
Transmission:	Four-speed manual
Weight:	965kg

PRICE GUIDE

Launch price:	£403
Excellent:	£4000
Good:	£3200
Average:	£1600
Project:	£600

AUSTIN
A125/A135

The Sheerline was Austin's first post-war flagship car, even if its design dated back to the 1930s. The first model, designated A110, was powered by a 3.5-litre straight six, but this was soon upgraded to four litres to become the A125 – the iconic luxury car without the price. Offered in both saloon and limousine versions, these big bruisers became synonymous with the undertaking world, as well as a mainstay on mayoral fleets. Not sophisticated, nor good to drive, but effective and surprisingly popular on the classic car scene.

SPECIFICATIONS

Years produced:	1947-1956 (9000/1910 in total)
Performance:	0-60mph: 19.4sec
	Top speed: 81mph
Power & torque:	125bhp/N/A
Engine:	Normally aspirated 3990cc straight six, petrol, carburettor, 12 valves
Drivetrain:	Front-engine RWD
Structure:	Separate chassis
Transmission:	Four-speed manual
Weight:	2000kg

PRICE GUIDE

Launch price:	£1277
Excellent:	£7750
Good:	£6500
Average:	£4000
Project:	£1750

AUSTIN
A70 Hampshire

Just like an Austin Devon, only larger (the easiest way to tell them apart is the Hampshire's rear 'skirts'). It's a tall car, designed for people who wore hats, and you can seat three abreast on both front and rear seats, making it just the thing for those extended family trips to Goodwood. The 2.2-litre engine is an overhead-valve unit carried over from the Austin 16 – strong on torque but short on gearing, so they fly up hills but run out of steam above 60mph. Probably as well – the steering's not great and half-mechanical brakes need careful setting up.

SPECIFICATIONS

Years produced:	1948-1950 (35,261 in total)
Performance:	0-60mph: 21.5sec
	Top speed: 82mph
Power & torque:	64bhp/96lb ft
Engine:	Normally aspirated 2199cc four cylinder, petrol, carburettor, 8 valves
Drivetrain:	Front-engine RWD
Structure:	Separate chassis
Transmission:	Four-speed manual
Weight:	1270kg

PRICE GUIDE

Launch price:	£608
Excellent:	£5000
Good:	£4200
Average:	£2250
Project:	£750

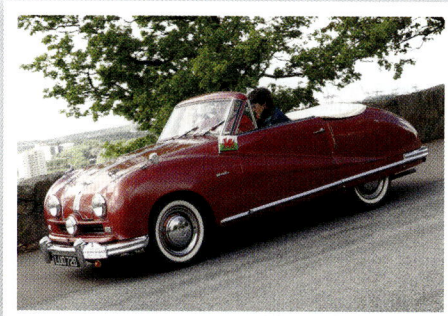

AUSTIN
A90 Atlantic

Quirky styling that looks more interesting now than it did to Americans in 1948. That was the car's target market but the US had cheaper options with bigger engines, and a row of chrome strips down the bonnet fooled nobody into thinking it was a Pontiac. At least the Atlantic's big four-pot found fame a little later in the Austin-Healey 100. Convertible version (add 60% for their values) was launched before fabric-topped coupé, but stayed in production for only two years. By the end, in 1952, Austin had managed to shift slightly less than 8000 of them.

SPECIFICATIONS

Years produced:	1948-1952 (7981 in total)
Performance:	0-60mph: 16.6sec
	Top speed: 91mph
Power & torque:	88bhp/140lb ft
Engine:	Normally aspirated 2660cc four cylinder, petrol, carburettor, 8 valves
Drivetrain:	front-engine RWD
Structure:	Separate chassis
Transmission:	Four-speed manual
Weight:	1359kg

PRICE GUIDE (Convertible in rackets)

Launch price:	£953	
Excellent:	£11,500	(£17,500)
Good:	£7500	(£12,500)
Average:	£4000	(£7500)
Project:	£1500	(£4000)

AUSTIN
A40 Sports

The aluminium body is by Jensen and mounted to an Austin Devon chassis. Fun as these soft-tops are, 'Sports' is maybe pushing the idea a little too far. Still, with the help of twin carbs and larger inlet valves, the Devon engine's power was raised from 40bhp to 46bhp, so a genuine 80mph was possible. Also, to lend credibility, one was driven to victory in the 1956 RAC Rally Ladies' Cup, beating various Fords and an MGA in the process. Column-shift gearchange from 1952 is less desirable, and despite low build numbers there are still quite a few about.

SPECIFICATIONS

Years produced:	1950-1953 (4011 in total)
Performance:	0-60mph: 25.6sec
	Top speed: 80mph
Power & torque:	46bhp/61lb ft
Engine:	Normally aspirated 1200cc four cylinder, petrol, carburettor, 8 valves
Drivetrain:	Front-engine RWD
Structure:	Separate chassis
Transmission:	Four-speed manual
Weight:	695kg

PRICE GUIDE

Launch price:	£818
Excellent:	£7500
Good:	£6000
Average:	£3500
Project:	£1750

AUSTIN
A70 Hereford

This was the Hampshire's replacement, and in keeping with Austin's styling policy it's very much an inflated Somerset. Indeed, it can be difficult to tell those two cars apart when they're not side-by-side: they even share the same doors and rear wings. For at-a-glance recognition look out for the raised pressing around the front wheelarches and the full-width 'whiskers' below the grille. There's an improvement in power, but 68bhp is still disappointing from 2.2 litres. They are also quite thirsty, and you don't buy one for its handling.

SPECIFICATIONS

Years produced:	1950-1954 (50,421 in total)
Performance:	0-60mph: 21.4sec
	Top speed: 81mph
Power & torque:	68bhp/116lb ft
Engine:	Normally aspirated 2199cc four cylinder, petrol, carburettor, 8 valves
Drivetrain:	Front-engine RWD
Structure:	Separate chassis
Transmission:	Four-speed manual
Weight:	1280kg

PRICE GUIDE

Launch price:	£687
Excellent:	£5000
Good:	£3900
Average:	£2200
Project:	£700

AUSTIN
A30/A35

Austin's answer to the Morris Minor was lighter and more compact, but with a steering box and part-hydraulic, part-rod brakes, it doesn't feel as advanced. At first A30s came with an 803cc engine and four doors. A two-door was added in late 1953. The more usable A35 replaced it in 1956, armed with more power from the 948cc A-series engine. Visually the changes included a painted grille and a much larger rear window. Saloon production ceased in 1959, but the van went on as late as 1968, with 1098cc, then 848cc, powerplants.

SPECIFICATIONS

Years produced:	1951-1968 (527,000 in total)
Performance:	0-60mph: 30.1sec
	Top speed: 72mph
Power & torque:	34bhp/50lb ft
Engine:	Normally aspirated 948cc four cylinder, petrol, carburettor, 8 valves
Drivetrain:	Front-engine RWD
Structure:	Monocoque
Transmission:	Four-speed manual
Weight:	685kg

PRICE GUIDE

Launch price:	£507
Excellent:	£4000
Good:	£2500
Average:	£1350
Project:	£500

AUSTIN
A40 Somerset

The successor to the Devon ensured Austin kept on churning out large numbers of quality saloons for the masses. The styling is more bulbous, but the separate chassis is much the same as before, though this time the brakes are low-maintenance hydraulics. There's another couple of bhp from the 1200cc engine, though they still won't quite hit the national speed limit. Not particularly collectible, except for the convertible version: rare in any condition, the good ones keep commanding ever-higher prices – currently double those of saloons.

SPECIFICATIONS

Years produced:	1952-1954 (173,306 in total)
Performance:	0-60mph: 31.6sec
	Top speed: 69mph
Power & torque:	42bhp/62lb ft
Engine:	Normally aspirated 1200cc four cylinder, petrol, carburettor, 8 valves
Drivetrain:	Front-engine RWD
Structure:	Separate chassis
Transmission:	Four-speed manual
Weight:	1000kg

PRICE GUIDE

Launch price:	£728
Excellent:	£3750
Good:	£2900
Average:	£1400
Project:	£500

AUSTIN
A40/A50/A55 Cambridge

Austin took a big step forward with its 1954 Cambridge saloons, finally adopting monocoque construction for its mid-sized cars. Bottom of the pile was the A40, which used the 1200cc 42bhp engine from the Somerset, while the A50 had the newly-enlarged 1489cc B-series unit and 50bhp. Customers spending the extra money for the Deluxe version were treated to additional chrome and leather. The A55 succeeded both types in 1957, with a bigger boot, fledgling fins and a larger back window. In van and pick-up form, these models lasted until 1971.

SPECIFICATIONS

Years produced:	1954-1958 (299,500 in total)
Performance:	0-60mph: 28.8sec
	Top speed: 74mph
Power & torque:	50bhp/74lb ft
Engine:	Normally aspirated 1489cc four cylinder, petrol, carburettor, 8 valves
Drivetrain:	Front-engine, RWD
Structure:	Monocoque
Transmission:	Four-speed manual
Weight:	1118kg

PRICE GUIDE

Launch price:	£650
Excellent:	£3250
Good:	£2500
Average:	£1000
Project:	£300

AUSTIN
A90/A95/A105 Westminster

Although it looked like a glammed-up version of the Cambridge, it shared only the same doors as its smaller sibling. The 2.6-litre C-series put out a mere 85bhp, meaning performance was leisurely. This was addressed with the A95 and A105 of 1956, the former getting 92bhp, the latter 102bhp. Together with its lower suspension, standard overdrive and two-tone paint, the A105 was almost sporty, with a top speed approaching 100mph. For the ultimate in Westminster appeal, there was a Vanden Plas version, dripping with leather.

SPECIFICATIONS

Years produced:	1954-1959 (60,367 in total)
Performance:	0-60mph: 19.8sec
	Top speed: 90mph
Power & torque:	92bhp/130lb ft
Engine:	Normally aspirated 2639cc straight six, petrol, carburettor, 12 valves
Drivetrain:	Front-engine RWD
Structure:	Monocoque
Transmission:	Four-speed manual
Weight:	1100kg

PRICE GUIDE

Launch price:	£792
Excellent:	£4000
Good:	£3000
Average:	£1350
Project:	£500

AUSTIN
Metropolitan

Never actually badged an Austin, the Metropolitan was originally made solely for Nash in America, which wanted a small car but had no experience of building one. This explains the bumper-car-like American styling. On sale in the UK from 1957, the car had by then been given the 1489cc B-series in place of the original 1200. One strange quirk is the three-speed gearbox, an A50 four-speed with the slot for first blanked off. Both hardtop and convertible versions were made, and about equal numbers of each survive in the UK.

SPECIFICATIONS	
Years produced:	1954-1956
Performance:	0-60mph: 22.4sec
	Top speed: 70mph
Power & torque:	42bhp/58lb ft
Engine:	Normally aspirated 1200cc four cylinder, petrol, carburettor, 8 valves
Drivetrain:	Front-engine RWD
Structure:	Monocoque
Transmission:	Three-speed manual
Weight:	810kg

PRICE GUIDE (Add £1000 for convertible)

Launch price:	N/A
Excellent:	£6500
Good:	£5000
Average:	£2500
Project:	£750

AUSTIN
A30/35 Countryman

Introduced in September 1954 – so you won't find many A30 versions – the Countryman is a tiny estate created by fitting back seats, a full headlining and two-piece sliding rear side windows to the A30 van. Many vans have since been converted to look like a Countryman (an okay alternative, but don't pay the Countryman premium for one of these). As a giveaway, many conversions use fixed side windows and fail to remove the van's vent roof. Also, only the A30 and early A35 versions have van-style indent pressings in the doors.

SPECIFICATIONS	
Years produced:	1954-1962
Performance:	0-60mph: 31.0sec
	Top speed: 73mph
Power & torque:	34bhp/50lb ft
Engine:	Normally aspirated 948cc four cylinder, petrol, carburettor, 8 valves
Drivetrain:	Front-engine RWD
Structure:	Monocoque
Transmission:	Four-speed manual
Weight:	749kg

PRICE GUIDE

Launch price:	£541
Excellent:	£4000
Good:	£3000
Average:	£1500
Project:	£700

AUSTIN
A40 Farina

The unassuming Austin A40 Farina is one of the marque's most significant models ever. Why? Well it was the first Pininfarina-styled BMC car, the first 'two-box' design and, in Countryman estate form with a split tailgate, has a claim to fame as one of the first hatchbacks. The 1958 car that would inform so many future models was mainly Austin A35 underneath its Italian suit, even down to the inferior hydro-mechanical brakes. Fortunately, these were changed to hydraulic on the 1961 MkII, while 1962 saw a 1098cc A-series slotted in.

SPECIFICATIONS	
Years produced:	1958-1967 (364,064 in total)
Performance:	0-60mph: 27.1sec
	Top speed: 82mph
Power & torque:	48bhp/60lb ft
Engine:	Normally aspirated 948cc four cylinder, petrol, carburettor, 8 valves
Drivetrain:	Front-engine RWD
Structure:	Monocoque
Transmission:	Four-speed manual
Weight:	761kg

PRICE GUIDE

Launch price:	£639
Excellent:	£3250
Good:	£2200
Average:	£1000
Project:	£350

AUSTIN
Gipsy

The failure of the Champ might have been ringing in its ears, but that didn't stop Austin having another go at building a Land Rover beater. The second time around, it produced a car that many casual observers thought was Solihull's latest product. The Gipsy was available with a petrol or diesel engine and offered with two wheelbases. It had an all-steel body, and innovative Moulton Flexitor suspension, but these weren't big enough advantages to tempt people out of their Land Rovers. Rust claimed many examples, but not that rare... or valuable.

SPECIFICATIONS	
Years produced:	1958-1968 (21,208 in total)
Performance:	0-60mph: N/A
	Top speed: 65mph
Power & torque:	62bhp/102lb ft
Engine:	Normally aspirated 2199cc four cylinder, petrol, carburettor, 8 valves
Drivetrain:	Front-engine AWD
Structure:	Separate chassis
Transmission:	Four-speed manual
Weight:	1010kg

PRICE GUIDE

Launch price:	N/A
Excellent:	£5000
Good:	£2500
Average:	£1200
Project:	£800

AUSTIN
A99/A110 Westminster

Pininfarina's finest BMC moment was the 1959-'68 Westminster series; the larger canvas suited the angular lines and resulted in a suitably prestigious machine. A twin-carb C-series engine pumped up to 3 litres coupled with a three-speed transmission allowed stately progress with reasonable haste if pushed. Servo-assisted front disc brakes added to the enjoyment. 1961's A110 was even better, but the ultimate Westminster was the MkII of 1964, which gained four gears for the model's final four years of production.

SPECIFICATIONS	
Years produced:	1959-1968 (41,250 in total)
Performance:	0-60mph: 14.4sec
	Top speed: 98mph
Power & torque:	103bhp/165lb ft
Engine:	Normally aspirated 2912cc straight six, petrol, carburettor, 12 valves
Drivetrain:	Front-engine RWD
Structure:	Monocoque
Transmission:	Four-speed manual/three-speed auto
Weight:	1530kg

PRICE GUIDE

Launch price:	£1149
Excellent:	£6000
Good:	£3500
Average:	£1400
Project:	£550

AUSTIN/MORRIS
Cambridge/Oxford

Pininfarina styled the Austin Cambridge A55/A60 and Morris Oxford V/VI for the 1960s and turned in a smart job. As fins were fashionable, the Farina twins wore them, but their underpinnings were much the same as with the previous Cambridge. The 1489cc motors struggled to shift these heavy models but, in 1961, the engine was enlarged to 1622cc for the A60 and Oxford VI. BMC badge engineering was at its height, and resulted in Wolseley, Riley and MG versions, too. Values for Morris and Austin very similar, although the former lived two years longer.

SPECIFICATIONS (A55)

Years produced:	1959-1969/1971 (426,500/296,255 total)
Performance:	0-60mph: 23.0sec
	Top speed: 78mph
Power & torque:	52bhp/82lb ft
Engine:	Normally aspirated 1489cc four cylinder, petrol, carburettor, 8 valves
Drivetrain:	Front-engine RWD
Structure:	Monocoque
Transmission:	Four-speed manual
Weight:	1118/1054kg

PRICE GUIDE

Launch price:	£802
Excellent:	£3500
Good:	£2200
Average:	£1000
Project:	£300

AUSTIN/MORRIS
1100/1300

BMC badge engineering ran rampant with the 1100/1300 range, Alec Issigonis' extension of his Mini concept using front-wheel drive, front disc brakes, interconnected Hydrolastic fluid suspension and a Tardis-like interior. Performance was lively thanks to the A-series engines, in 1098cc and (from 1967) 1275cc sizes, and handling came close to Mini standards. Much cleverer than their Ford, Vauxhall and Rootes rivals, these cars consistently topped British sales charts but rusted ferociously. Great to drive, but 1100s are undergeared for the motorway.

SPECIFICATIONS (1300)

Years produced:	1963/1962-1974 (1,119,800 in total)
Performance:	0-60mph: 17.3sec
	Top speed: 87mph
Power & torque:	60bhp/69lb ft
Engine:	Normally aspirated 1275cc four cylinder, petrol, carburettor, 8 valves
Drivetrain:	Front-engine FWD
Structure:	Monocoque
Transmission:	Four-speed manual
Weight:	776kg

PRICE GUIDE

Launch price:	£593
Excellent:	£2500
Good:	£1500
Average:	£750
Project:	£200

AUSTIN/MORRIS
1300GT

British Leyland's attempt at injecting some entertainment and passion into the 1300 was quite successful. Imagine a Mini-Cooper grown plump on pies, and you have some idea of what this racy 1300 was like. The twin-carb engine was tuned to MG/Riley spec and lairy colours such as orange and yellow were offered, complemented by that essential black vinyl roof. 58bhp was the norm for an Austin 1300, the GT had 70bhp and a thoroughly entertaining 93mph capability. A cult following these days is proof that Minis don't have all the fun!

SPECIFICATIONS

Years produced:	1969-1974 (52,107 in total)
Performance:	0-60mph: 15.6sec
	Top speed: 93mph
Power & torque:	70bhp/74lb ft
Engine:	Normally aspirated 1275cc four cylinder, petrol, carburettor, 8 valves
Drivetrain:	Front-engine FWD
Structure:	Monocoque
Transmission:	Four-speed manual
Weight:	855kg

PRICE GUIDE

Launch price:	£910
Excellent:	£3500
Good:	£2250
Average:	£1100
Project:	£450

AUSTIN/MORRIS
1800/2200

After the Mini and 1100/1300 range, the 1800/2200 models were expected to complete Alec Issigonis' successful hat-trick of BMC front-wheel-drive cars. But they didn't – and that was down to building the new car around the MGB-tune B-series engine, which Issigonis exploited to make a larger car than was necessary. Despite the 1800 winning the Car of the Year award in 1964, sales were disappointing. Over-engineered and with Hydrolastic suspension, the ungainly looks and austere interior counted against them. Best had with power steering.

SPECIFICATIONS (1800)

Years produced:	1964-1975/1966-1975 (315,000 in total)
Performance:	0-60mph: 17.1sec
	Top speed: 90mph
Power & torque:	85bhp/90lb ft
Engine:	Normally aspirated 1798cc four cylinder, petrol, carburettor, 8 valves
Drivetrain:	Front-engine FWD
Structure:	Monocoque
Transmission:	Four-speed manual
Weight:	1200kg

PRICE GUIDE

Launch price:	£769
Excellent:	£2500
Good:	£1600
Average:	£800
Project:	£200

AUSTIN
3-Litre

After the handsome Westminster, the 3-Litre – its 1967 replacement – was a big disappointment. Big was the operative word, but being saddled with the centre section of the 1800/2200 with a long bonnet and boot tacked on either end did not make it attractive. The cabin was massive, but at the expense of much of the usual luxury and traditional design that buyers expected in a car of this class. Rear-wheel drive and a 2.9-litre engine shared with the MGC gave reasonable performance, yet prestige was lacking... thus, so were sales.

SPECIFICATIONS

Years produced:	1968-1971 (9992 in total)
Performance:	0-60mph: 15.7sec
	Top speed: 100mph
Power & torque:	124bhp/163lb ft
Engine:	Normally aspirated 2912cc straight six, petrol, carburettor, 12 valves
Drivetrain:	Front-engine RWD
Structure:	Monocoque
Transmission:	Four-speed manual
Weight:	1524kg

PRICE GUIDE

Launch price:	£1418
Excellent:	£3500
Good:	£2000
Average:	£1000
Project:	£350

AUSTIN
Maxi

BMC became British Leyland in 1968, and one of its first products was the Austin Maxi. It was essentially a good car with some innovative ideas, but the finer details and lack of quality let the Maxi down – traits that would come to characterise BL. Britain's first real hatchback had plenty of space and seats that folded down into a double bed, yet taking the centre section from the 1800/2200 range meant looks were bland. Hydrolastic (and later Hydragas) suspension and five gears were its good points, but the gearchange itself was memorably bad.

SPECIFICATIONS	
Years produced:	1969-1981 (472,098 in total)
Performance:	0-60mph: 13.2sec
	Top speed: 97mph
Power & torque:	91bhp/104lb ft
Engine:	Normally aspirated 1485cc four cylinder, petrol, carburettor, 8 valves
Drivetrain:	Front-engine FWD
Structure:	Monocoque
Transmission:	Five-speed manual
Weight:	979kg

PRICE GUIDE	
Launch price:	£979
Excellent:	£1750
Good:	£1000
Average:	£500
Project:	£300

AUSTIN
Allegro

The Allegro stands for all that was wrong with Britain's car industry in the 1970s. Strange looks, lack of build quality, reliability issues and that infamous quartic steering wheel meant that what good touches it did have (a wide choice of engines from 1.0-litre through to 1750cc, compliant Hydragas suspension, five gears and a distinctive character) were overlooked. Some cult appeal nowadays as the ideal starter classic for the impecunious. 1979 Equipe special edition worth double the money of its standard counterpart.

SPECIFICATIONS (1500)	
Years produced:	1973-1982 (642,340 in total)
Performance:	0-60mph: 13.6sec
	Top speed: 91mph
Power & torque:	69bhp/77lb ft
Engine:	Normally aspirated 1485cc four cylinder, petrol, carburettor, 8 valves
Drivetrain:	Front-engine FWD
Structure:	Monocoque
Transmission:	Five-speed manual
Weight:	850kg

PRICE GUIDE	
Launch price:	£974
Excellent:	£1350
Good:	£900
Average:	£550
Project:	£250

AUSTIN/LEYLAND
Princess

The Princess couldn't have looked more different from the 1800/2200 series it replaced, even though it kept the same four- and six-cylinder engines and front-wheel drive. Originally badged as Austins, Morrises and Wolseleys, the individual marques were soon dropped and all types became collectively known as Princess. Lack of build quality and reliability let down an innovative design, although if a hatchback had been incorporated right from the start it might well have done better. More appreciated now than when current.

SPECIFICATIONS	
Years produced:	1975-1982 (224,942 in total)
Performance:	0-60mph: 13.1sec
	Top speed: 99mph
Power & torque:	93bhp/112lb ft
Engine:	Normally aspirated 1994cc four cylinder, petrol, carburettor, 8 valves
Drivetrain:	Front-engine FWD
Structure:	Monocoque
Transmission:	Five-speed manual
Weight:	1089kg

PRICE GUIDE	
Launch price:	£2237
Excellent:	£1500
Good:	£950
Average:	£450
Project:	£100

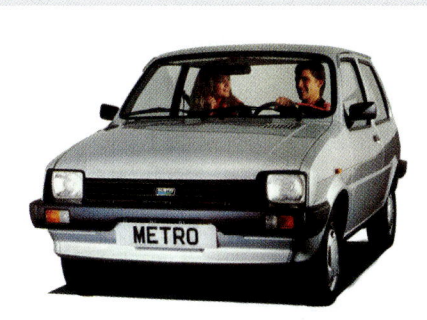

AUSTIN
Metro

Billed as the 'British car to beat the world' when it was launched amid a barrage of flag-waving patriotism in 1980, the Metro initially sold like hot cakes, and seemed like the light at the end of a very long tunnel for BL. In fact, it was more like a grown-up Mini than a brave new start, but the older car's charm added to the Metro's homespun appeal. Survival rate is low due to rust, apathy and its suitability as an engine donor for Minis, and values are still laughably low for all but the mintest examples. Not the best small car of its era, but certainly one of the most intriguing.

SPECIFICATIONS	
Years produced:	1980-1991 (1,518,932 in total)
Performance:	0-60mph: 18.9sec
	Top speed: 84mph
Power & torque:	44bhp/52lb ft
Engine:	Normally aspirated 998cc four cylinder, petrol, carburettor, 8 valves
Drivetrain:	Front-engine FWD
Structure:	Monocoque
Transmission:	Four-speed manual
Weight:	743kg

PRICE GUIDE	
Launch price:	£3095
Excellent:	£1000
Good:	£600
Average:	£400
Project:	£200

AUSTIN
Ambassador

BL's £29m facelift of the Princess gave it the one thing it was crying out for from day one: a hatchback. Sadly, in becoming the Ambassador, the quirky full-sized Brit also seemed to lose a great deal of its individuality. But as well as being more practical than its predecessor, the Ambassador also rode even more smoothly, making it an uncannily comfortable cruiser. Lacks the offbeat appeal of the Princess, and can be picked up for pennies; a rusty reminder of when BL's back was firmly against the wall. Choice model is the velour-lined 100bhp Vanden Plas.

SPECIFICATIONS	
Years produced:	1982-1984 (43,500 in total)
Performance:	0-60mph: 14.3sec
	Top speed: 100mph
Power & torque:	92bhp/114lb ft
Engine:	Normally aspirated 1994cc four cylinder, petrol, carburettor, 8 valves
Drivetrain:	Front-engine FWD
Structure:	Monocoque
Transmission:	Four-speed manual
Weight:	1263kg

PRICE GUIDE	
Launch price:	£5105
Excellent:	£1000
Good:	£600
Average:	£350
Project:	£200

AUSTIN
Maestro

Following hard on the heels of the Metro, the Maestro was supposed to return BL to profitability in the '80s. It reality, it hit the market five years too late, and lacked the showroom appeal of the sharp-suited Ford Escort and Vauxhall Astra. It racked up even poorer sales figures than the Allegro despite being considerably more capable. Engines and (VW-sourced) gearboxes were a disappointment, and rust continues to be a real problem. Talking-dash Vanden Plas is interesting, as is the ultra-economical HLE version – and probably the ones to have in coming years.

SPECIFICATIONS (1.3 HLE)

Years produced:	1983-1994 (605,410 in total)
Performance:	0-60mph: 12.8sec
	Top speed: 96mph
Power & torque:	68bhp/73lb ft
Engine:	Normally aspirated 1275cc four cylinder, petrol, carburettor, 8 valves
Drivetrain:	Front-engine FWD
Structure:	Monocoque
Transmission:	Four-speed manual
Weight:	875kg

PRICE GUIDE

Launch price:	£4955
Excellent:	£1500
Good:	£750
Average:	£400
Project:	£200

AUSTIN
Montego

Considering the Montego is so closely based on the Maestro, it looks refreshingly different. Hardly handsome, but certainly a departure. Built to capture the hearts and minds of the UK's company car drivers, the Montego performed exceedingly well considering its less-than-inspired underpinnings. Wide range of engines (from 1.3 to 2 litres) and trim levels make this a car for all people, and as it's currently unloved, it's a bargain buy. Seven-seat Countryman estate is a cheap people carrier – just make sure those sills aren't too rusty and the engine is leak-free.

SPECIFICATIONS

Years produced:	1984-1995 (571,457 in total)
Performance:	0-60mph: 11.5sec
	Top speed: 103mph
Power & torque:	86bhp/91lb ft
Engine:	Normally aspirated 1598cc four cylinder, petrol, carburettor, 8 valves
Drivetrain:	Front-engine FWD
Structure:	Monocoque
Transmission:	Five-speed manual
Weight:	1020kg

PRICE GUIDE

Launch price:	£5281
Excellent:	£1250
Good:	£600
Average:	£400
Project:	£250

AUSTIN·HEALEY

RACER AND engineer Donald Healey built cars from 1945 onwards, but real success eluded him until his Healey 100 of 1952 was noticed by Austin boss Leonard Lord. Austin agreed to build the Healey, using its mechanical parts and, thus, Austin-Healey as a marque was formed, intended as a sort of Austin-centric version of MG. The 'Big' Healeys – the 100, 100/6 and 3000 models – were later joined by the smaller Austin-Healey Sprite, a small, cheap and cheerful roadster. Things soured with the formation of British Leyland in 1968; the 3000 came to an end the same year and the Sprite continued until 1971, when the Austin and Healey deal was finally cancelled.

AUSTIN-HEALEY
100

What was originally the Healey 100 became the Austin-Healey 100 overnight when Leonard Lord of BMC saw it at the 1952 London Motor Show and liked it enough to offer to build it. The brusque, low-slung looks hid running gear plucked from the Austin parts bin, including the four-cylinder 2660cc engine from the A90 Atlantic. The USA took the 100 to its heart, and the car was an instant success there. Racing improved the breed, leading to the legendary 100S of 1954, with light aluminium panels and a higher-output engine.

SPECIFICATIONS

Years produced:	1953-1956 (14,634 in total)
Performance:	0-60mph: 10.3sec
	Top speed: 103mph
Power & torque:	90bhp/144lb ft
Engine:	Normally aspirated 2660cc four cylinder, petrol, carburettor, 8 valves
Drivetrain:	Front-engine RWD
Structure:	Separate chassis
Transmission:	Three-speed with overdrive
Weight:	975kg

PRICE GUIDE

Launch price:	£1064
Excellent:	£50,000
Good:	£36,500
Average:	£22,000
Project:	£17,000

AUSTIN-HEALEY
100S

Created so the marque could be seen motor racing more widely than the works cars could cover, 50 examples of the 100S were built, although only six stayed in the UK. The 'S' actually refers to the Sebring 12-hour race in Florida, where a prototype finished a surprise third in 1954. Based on the 100, the 100S had a stiffer chassis and more aluminium body panels. Brakes were discs front and rear. The engines had the same capacity but a different block casting and aluminium Weslake head. Larger SU carburettors were fitted and the result was 132bhp.

SPECIFICATIONS

Years produced:	1954-1955 (50 in total)
Performance:	0-60mph: 7.8sec
	Top speed: 119mph
Power & torque:	132bhp/168lb ft
Engine:	Normally aspirated 2660cc four cylinder, petrol, carburettor, 8 valves
Drivetrain:	Front-engine RWD
Structure:	Separate chassis
Transmission:	Four-speed manual
Weight:	873kg

PRICE GUIDE

Launch price:	Special order only
Excellent:	£350,000
Good:	£200,000
Average:	£150,000
Project:	£100,000

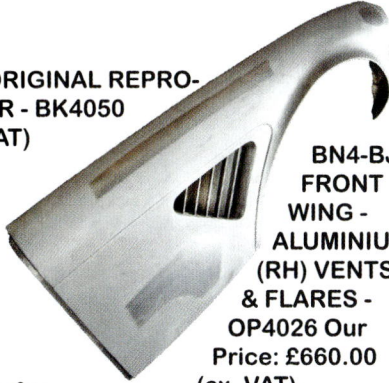

AUSTIN-HEALEY
100M

The potent abilities of the 100 meant that many owners wanted to take their cars racing, so the factory put together an upgrade kit that could either be retro-fitted or specified from new. If the latter option was chosen, the car became known as the 100M, the letter standing for 'Modified.' In 1955, the 100M became a model in its own right. Its engine – tuned to Le Mans specification – boasted 110bhp, the strapped-down bonnet had louvres in it to help keep things cool, and there was stiffer suspension and an anti-roll bar: 1159 were made.

SPECIFICATIONS
Years produced:	1955-1956 (1159 in total)
Performance:	0-60mph: 10.3sec
	Top speed: 103mph
Power & torque:	110bhp/144lb ft
Engine:	Normally aspirated 2660cc four cylinder, petrol, carburettor, 8 valves
Drivetrain:	Front-engine RWD
Structure:	Separate chassis
Transmission:	Four-speed manual with overdrive
Weight:	1041kg

PRICE GUIDE
Launch price:	Special order only
Excellent:	£75,000
Good:	£40,000
Average:	£30,000
Project:	£20,000

AUSTIN-HEALEY
100/6

The runaway success of the 100 convinced BMC it had a bright future, but the Austin four-cylinder engine was due to cease manufacture in 1956. No problem: the Westminster's 2639cc straight six took its place. Actually, this didn't automatically make the 100 a better car, as the heavier engine sapped performance until a new cylinder head and manifolds boosted power to 117bhp. Other changes included an oval grille and 2+2 seating, although the latter was a needless alteration that was dispensed with after just two years.

SPECIFICATIONS
Years produced:	1956-1959 (14,436 in total)
Performance:	0-60mph: 12.9sec
	Top speed: 103mph
Power & torque:	102bhp/142lb ft
Engine:	Normally aspirated 2639cc straight six, petrol, carburettor, 12 valves
Drivetrain:	Front-engine RWD
Structure:	Separate chassis
Transmission:	Four-speed with overdrive
Weight:	1105kg

PRICE GUIDE
Launch price:	£1144
Excellent:	£35,000
Good:	£22,000
Average:	£15,000
Project:	£10,000

AUSTIN-HEALEY
3000 MkI

The first generation of the 'Big' Healey arrived in 1959, when the C-series engine from the 100/6 was upgraded to three litres, for use in the new Westminster saloons. Although there was no change of styling (except new badges), the mechanical alterations – more power, a better gearbox and disc brakes on the front – were thought significant enough to merit the change of model designation. And there was the return of a 2+2 format, available alongside the two-seat roadster. The MkI continued without change until 1961.

SPECIFICATIONS
Years produced:	1959-1961 (17.712 in total)
Performance:	0-60mph: 11.2sec
	Top speed: 111mph
Power & torque:	117bhp/149lb ft
Engine:	Normally aspirated 2912cc straight six, petrol, carburettor, 8 valves
Drivetrain:	Front-engine RWD
Structure:	Separate chassis
Transmission:	Four-speed manual with overdrive
Weight:	1143kg

PRICE GUIDE
Launch price:	£1159
Excellent:	£45,000
Good:	£23,000
Average:	£13,500
Project:	£8000

AUSTIN-HEALEY
Sprite MkI

The original Sprite was a cheap and cheerful mass-produced sporting convertible that was also tremendous fun. Cheeky looks – those 'frogeye' headlamps were initially planned to be retractable until it was realised that would put the price up – distracted from the fact that underneath the skin the car was mainly a blend of Austin A35 and Morris Minor. However, that still meant entertaining performance. Prices today are out of all proportion to the budget origins; these are now dear machines in more ways than one.

SPECIFICATIONS
Years produced:	1958-1961 (48,987 in total)
Performance:	0-60mph: 20.5sec
	Top speed: 86mph
Power & torque:	43bhp/52lb ft
Engine:	Normally aspirated 948cc four cylinder, petrol, carburettor, 8 valves
Drivetrain:	Front-engine RWD
Structure:	Monocoque
Transmission:	Four-speed manual
Weight:	602kg

PRICE GUIDE
Launch price:	£669
Excellent:	£12,500
Good:	£8250
Average:	£4500
Project:	£2250

AUSTIN-HEALEY
3000 MkII

In theory, the move to triple carburettors for the 3000 MkII was a good one. In practice, the set-up proved difficult to keep in tune resulting in probably the least popular of the Big Healeys. Many owners found themselves spending more time fiddling with the engine rather than driving the car. The arrangement was dropped after a year, when the 3000 MkIIa Convertible went back to just two carburettors plus featured a curved front windscreen, wind-up windows, a more user-friendly hood and 2+2 seating as standard.

SPECIFICATIONS
Years produced:	1961-1962 (11,564 in total)
Performance:	0-60mph: 11.5sec
	Top speed: 112mph
Power & torque:	132bhp/167lb ft
Engine:	Normally aspirated 2912cc straight six, petrol, carburettor, 12 valves
Drivetrain:	Front-engine RWD
Structure:	Separate chassis
Transmission:	Four-speed manual with overdrive
Weight:	1158kg

PRICE GUIDE
Launch price:	£1159
Excellent:	£45,000
Good:	£24,000
Average:	£15,000
Project:	£9000

AUSTIN-HEALEY
Sprite MkII/III

The 1961 MkII was an effort to modernise the Sprite and make it more practical. Unfortunately, it also took away much of the car's character and novelty. However, it was still affordable and enjoyable, and at least passengers now had an opening boot to put a limited amount of luggage in. Gone were the upright headlamps, the light units now sitting conventionally each side of the grille. From 1962, there was a bigger 1098cc engine plus front disc brakes, but buyers had to wait until the MkIII of 1964 for door handles and winding windows.

SPECIFICATIONS
Years produced:	1961-1966 (31,665/25,905 in total)
Performance:	0-60mph: 20.0sec
	Top speed: 85mph
Power & torque:	46bhp/53lb ft
Engine:	Normally aspirated 948cc four cylinder, petrol, carburettor, 8 valves
Drivetrain:	Front-engine RWD
Structure:	Monocoque
Transmission:	Four-speed manual
Weight:	700kg

PRICE GUIDE
Launch price:	£670
Excellent:	£5000
Good:	£4000
Average:	£2250
Project:	£950

AUSTIN-HEALEY
3000 MkIII

The final genesis of the Big Healey appeared in 1964. Although the looks remained largely the same this was the most powerful Austin-Healey ever, its 148bhp output making for a top speed of 121mph. The Phase 2 versions had revised rear suspension which improved handling. However, the end was nigh for the Healey and the final car was built in March 1968. Many mourned its passing, and its replacement, the MGC, failed to impress buyers in the same way. MkIIIs fetch the best Big Healey money these days.

SPECIFICATIONS
Years produced:	1964-1968 (17,712 in total)
Performance:	0-60mph: 9.8sec
	Top speed: 121mph
Power & torque:	148bhp/165lb ft
Engine:	Normally aspirated 2912cc straight six, petrol, carburettor, 12 valves
Drivetrain:	Front-engine RWD
Structure:	Separate chassis
Transmission:	Four-speed manual with overdrive
Weight:	1180kg

PRICE GUIDE
Launch price:	£1108
Excellent:	£50,000
Good:	£30,000
Average:	£17,000
Project:	£12,500

AUSTIN-HEALEY
Sprite MkIV/Austin Sprite

In 1966 BMC upped the Sprite's game with the MkIV. Improvements included a 1275cc engine giving 65bhp and near-100mph potential. A proper hood improved things still further. The 1969 styling update saw the introduction of rather fetching black sills and Rostyle wheels, but the Sprite was sadly not long for this world: the end of BMC's arrangement with Healey in 1971 meant the final few cars were badged Austin Sprite. Its sibling, the MG Midget, soldiered on until 1979, though, so at least the type endured if not the name.

SPECIFICATIONS
Years produced:	1966-1971 (21,768/1022 in total)
Performance:	0-60mph: 14.6sec
	Top speed: 94mph
Power & torque:	65bhp/72lb ft
Engine:	Normally aspirated 1275cc four cylinder, petrol, carburettor, 8 valves
Drivetrain:	Front-engine RWD
Structure:	Monocoque
Transmission:	Four-speed manual
Weight:	714kg

PRICE GUIDE
Launch price:	£672
Excellent:	£5500
Good:	£4000
Average:	£2500
Project:	£1000

AUTOBIANCHI

BIANCHI WAS founded by Edoardo Bianchi in 1885, and initially built bicycles before moving into luxury car manufacture in 1899. However, the company's factory in Abruzzi was destroyed by bombing during WW2, and then its founder died in 1946, leaving Autobianchi in the hands of his son, Giuseppe. He wanted to restart production, but the new investment required was expensive, and so he turned to Fiat and Pirelli to form the Autobianchi partnership. Fiat-based cars were Autobianchi's main fare, and it was inevitable that the larger company would end up taking control, which it did in 1968. New models dried up, and the pioneering A112 supermini ended up being replaced by the Lancia Y10.

AUTOBIANCHI
Bianchina

As befitting the Fiat ownership, the Bianchina family of small cars was based heavily on the 500. The car was available as a saloon, estate, convertible and an appealing roll-top coupé, and although they allegedly had four seats, they were really designed for very friendly couples. Autobianchi Bianchinas were sold at a premium over their Fiat cousins, but offered more design flair. The Panoramica estate was based on the 500 Giardinera platform and made a useful family hold-all. Virtually unknown in the UK, but with a strong European following.

SPECIFICATIONS
Years produced:	1957-1968 (c.280,000 in total)
Performance:	N/A
	Top speed: 59mph
Power & torque:	21bhp/27lb ft
Engine:	Normally aspirated 499cc twin cylinder, petrol, carburettor, 4 valves
Drivetrain:	Rear-engine RWD
Structure:	Separate chassis
Transmission:	Four-speed manual
Weight:	517kg

PRICE GUIDE (Trasformabile)
Launch price:	N/A in UK
Excellent:	£7500
Good:	£5000
Average:	£2500
Project:	£1500

AUTOBIANCHI
Primula

The Autobianchi Primula was a front-wheel-drive hatchback pioneer. Long before the Renault 16 came along, and a decade before the VW Golf, Fiat's experiment in the future as engineered by Dante Giacosa paved the way for the opposition. Appealing styling had distinct BMC 1100 overtones, but the engineering was closer to the modern norm, boasting a transverse engine and end-on gearbox. Once Autobianchi had paved the way, Giacosa further developed the idea with new engines and independent suspension for the Fiat 128.

SPECIFICATIONS	
Years produced:	1964-1970
Performance:	Top speed: 85mph
	0-60mph: 15.1sec
Power & torque:	61bhp/69lb ft
Engine:	Normally aspirated 1221cc four cylinder, petrol, carburettor, 8 valves
Drivetrain:	Front-engine FWD
Structure:	Monocoque
Transmission:	Four-speed manual
Weight:	818kg
PRICE GUIDE	
Launch price:	N/A in UK
Excellent:	£2000
Good:	£1500
Average:	£1200
Project:	£1000

AUTOBIANCHI
A112

Once again, Fiat used Autobianchi to test the market waters for its upcoming products. So when it came to producing a small front-wheel-drive hatchback to replace the 600/850, it started from scratch. That meant a transverse engine with end-on gearbox as before. Originally powered by the 850 Sport engine, the A112 went on to use the 127's ohc units. With the A111 cancelled in 1972, the A112 battled on alone as Autobianchi's only production car. Abarth versions were fun and quick, and have a strong following in Italy and France.

SPECIFICATIONS (Abarth)	
Years produced:	1969-1986 (1,254,978 in total)
Performance:	Top speed: 99mph
	0-60mph: 11.6sec
Power & torque:	70bhp/63lb ft
Engine:	Normally aspirated 1050cc four cylinder, petrol, carburettor, 8 valves
Drivetrain:	Front-engine FWD
Structure:	Monocoque
Transmission:	Four-speed manual
Weight:	700kg
PRICE GUIDE	
Launch price:	N/A in UK
Excellent:	£3500
Good:	£2800
Average:	£1900
Project:	£1000

BENTLEY

THE FIRST Bentley appeared at the 1919 London Motor Show and, within a few years, the cars had become the darlings of rich playboys who delighted in taking them racing. Brooklands and Le Mans were two of the famous venues dominated by the marque. But in 1931, Bentley was bought by Rolls-Royce and its sporting glories started to fade. Although there were glorious moments such as the 1952-1955 R-type Continental, eventually the cars became nothing more than badge-engineered RRs. In the 1980s, though, the marque re-emerged from the shadow of its parent, with more emphasis on performance. Now owned by VW, Bentleys are once again sporting and individualistic machines.

BENTLEY
MkVI

The first of the postwar Bentleys was also the first with a steel body as standard, although many buyers still took the coachbuilding route. Its chassis was quite advanced for the time, with independent front suspension, servo brakes, a four-speed gearbox and the very useful centralised chassis lubrication system. The 4526cc (4566cc from 1951) straight six gained a reputation for sturdiness; not so the standard body which, despite its painstaking handbuilt construction, showed an unfortunate tendency to rust.

SPECIFICATIONS	
Years produced:	1946-1955 (5201 in total)
Performance:	0-60mph: 15.2sec
	Top speed: 100mph
Power & torque:	N/Q/N/Q
Engine:	Normally aspirated 4526cc straight six, petrol, carburettor, 12 valves
Drivetrain:	Front-engine RWD
Structure:	Separate chassis
Transmission:	Four-speed manual
Weight:	1816kg
PRICE GUIDE	
Launch price:	£2997
Excellent:	£25,000
Good:	£19,000
Average:	£10,000
Project:	£5500

BENTLEY
R-Type

With the standard steel body fitted, the 1952-1955 R-Type looked a lot like the MkVI – something the marque's traditional customers no doubt approved of. However, there was extra grace to the design thanks to the more flowing lines and a capacious boot. The same 4566cc straight-six engine as on the MkVI continued, but with the option of a four-speed automatic transmission from 1952. For 1953 there was a dashboard revamp, but the most exciting developments with the R-Type were saved for the Continental models.

SPECIFICATIONS	
Years produced:	1952-1955 (2320 in total)
Performance:	0-60mph: 15.0sec
	Top speed: 101mph
Power & torque:	N/Q/N/Q
Engine:	Normally aspirated 4566cc straight six, petrol, carburettor, 12 valves
Drivetrain:	Front-engine RWD
Structure:	Separate chassis
Transmission:	Four-speed manual/three-speed auto
Weight:	1816kg
PRICE GUIDE	
Launch price:	£4474
Excellent:	£27,500
Good:	£20,000
Average:	£11,000
Project:	£6500

BENTLEY
R-Type Continental

HJ Mulliner's Bentley Continental variant of the R-Type was pure automotive art. Looking far more modern than its 1952 origins, the sublime fastback shape, with the back wheels concealed by the curvaceous rear wings, was constructed from light alloy. This allowed a top speed of nigh-on 120mph; far faster than the saloon versions but the streamlined shape also helped the performance considerably, as did the 4887cc engine that found its way into the final cars. Hugely expensive now but every penny is worth it.

SPECIFICATIONS

Years produced:	1952-1955 (208 in total)
Performance:	0-60mph: 13.8sec
	Top speed: 117mph
Power & torque:	N/Q/N/Q
Engine:	Normally aspirated 4566cc straight six, petrol, carburettor, 12 valves
Drivetrain:	Front-engine RWD
Structure:	Separate chassis
Transmission:	Four-speed manual/three-speed auto
Weight:	1651kg

PRICE GUIDE

Launch price:	£7608
Excellent:	£500,000
Good:	£325,000
Average:	£275,000
Project:	£200,000

BENTLEY
S1 saloon

As striking as the S1 certainly was, it was also the Rolls-Royce Silver Cloud with different badges. However, gone were the traditional pre-war looks as in came a very sleek integrated body built out of alloy. The straight-six engine was now enlarged to 4887cc and improved brakes and front suspension were adopted, followed by a power-steering option available from 1956. Bentleys outsold their Rolls-Royce counterparts, so these more numerous Winged B models are generally cheaper than their Spirit of Ecstasy cousins.

SPECIFICATIONS

Years produced:	1955-1959 (3072 in total)
Performance:	0-60mph: 14.2sec
	Top speed: 101mph
Power & torque:	N/Q/N/Q
Engine:	Normally aspirated 4887cc straight six, petrol, carburettor, 8 valves
Drivetrain:	Front-engine RWD
Structure:	Separate chassis
Transmission:	Four-speed manual/three-speed auto
Weight:	1880kg

PRICE GUIDE

Launch price:	£4669
Excellent:	£35,000
Good:	£22,000
Average:	£11,000
Project:	£6500

BENTLEY
S1 Continental

While there was nothing that scaled the heights of the R, the Continental S-Types – constructed by a variety of different builders – were almost universally elegant. Most special are the 151 fastbacks by HJ Mulliner, followed by the 99 Park Ward coupés, and both Mulliner and James Young weighed in with four-door versions. Special permission needed to be obtained from Rolls-Royce for these to be built. The most innovative S1s were made by Hooper, and Franay and Graber did one each. A small number of dropheads accompanied the coupés.

SPECIFICATIONS

Years produced:	1955-1959 (431 in total)
Performance:	0-60mph: 12.9sec
	Top speed: 119mph
Power & torque:	N/Q/N/Q
Engine:	Normally aspirated 4887cc straight six, petrol, carburettor, 12 valves
Drivetrain:	Front-engine RWD
Structure:	Separate chassis
Transmission:	Three-speed auto/four-speed manual
Weight:	1930kg

PRICE GUIDE

Launch price:	£6127
Excellent:	£225,000-300,000 depending on body
Good:	£150,000
Average:	£125,000
Project:	£100,000

BENTLEY
S2 saloon

By 1959 it was time to replace the Rolls-Royce/Bentley straight-six inlet-over-exhaust-valve engines, and what better than a chunky V8 for a company with its eyes on the American market? The 6230cc unit installed in the S2 was smoothly powerful and transformed the Bentley into a silky grand tourer that could waft around all day. Power-steering and automatic transmission were standard fitments, but there was very little to distinguish an S2 from an S1 visually. Drophead coupé and Continental versions were also built.

SPECIFICATIONS

Years produced:	1959-1962 (1863 in total)
Performance:	0-60mph: 11.5sec
	Top speed: 113mph
Power & torque:	N/Q/N/Q
Engine:	Normally aspirated 6230cc V8, petrol, carburettor, 16 valves
Drivetrain:	Front-engine RWD
Structure:	Separate chassis
Transmission:	Three-speed auto/four-speed manual
Weight:	1981kg

PRICE GUIDE

Launch price:	£5661
Excellent:	£35,000
Good:	£22,500
Average:	£11,500
Project:	£6500

BENTLEY
S2/S3 Flying Spur

Continental chassis were intended just for two-door Bentleys but, in 1957, HJ Mulliner was given special dispensation to build variations with four doors. These graceful cars were christened Flying Spurs and featured bigger boots than their more racy-looking two-door counterparts. The same changes made to the S2 and S3 saloons were also applied to the Flying Spur, so in 1959 there came the 6230cc V8 engine and, for 1962, twin headlamps were adopted. These final cars were considered the most handsome of the bunch.

SPECIFICATIONS

Years produced:	1959-1965
Performance:	0-60mph: 12.3sec
	Top speed: 120mph
Power & torque:	N/Q/N/Q
Engine:	Normally aspirated 6230cc V8, petrol, carburettor, 16 valves
Drivetrain:	Front-engine RWD
Structure:	Separate chassis
Transmission:	Three-speed automatic
Weight:	1981kg

PRICE GUIDE

Launch price:	£6127
Excellent:	£100,000
Good:	£70,000
Average:	£45,000
Project:	£25,000

BENTLEY
S3 saloon

Hullabaloo surrounded the Bentley S3 of 1962-'65 because of its twin headlamps. There were other, less revolutionary touches as well in the form of restyled front wings, a lower bonnet line and improved appointments inside. Mechanically, some of the criticisms were answered with a higher-compression V8 engine and more effective power-steering. Alongside the saloons were the usual long-wheelbase version, a drophead coupé and some startling Continental creations which made intriguing use of the double light units.

SPECIFICATIONS

Years produced:	1962-1965 (1286 in total)
Performance:	0-60mph: 11.5sec
	Top speed: 113mph
Power & torque:	N/Q/N/Q
Engine:	Normally aspirated 6230cc V8, petrol, carburettor, 16 valves
Drivetrain:	Front-engine RWD
Structure:	Separate chassis
Transmission:	Three-speed automatic
Weight:	2077kg

PRICE GUIDE

Launch price:	£6127
Excellent:	£35,000
Good:	£25,000
Average:	£13,000
Project:	£10,000

BENTLEY
T1/T2

1965's T-series was another badge-engineering exercise in that the Bentleys were exactly the same as the Rolls-Royce Silver Shadows save for some minute details. This was the first of the marque to have unitary construction, which made it more difficult for coachbuilders to magic up alternative versions. Disc brakes featured on all wheels, as did self-levelling suspension. The V8 engine increased to 6750cc in 1970, while the T2 of 1977 had plastic bumpers, a revised dashboard and sharper rack-and-pinion steering.

SPECIFICATIONS

Years produced:	1965-1980 (1712 in total)
Performance:	0-60mph: 10.9sec
	Top speed: 115mph
Power & torque:	N/Q/N/Q
Engine:	Normally aspirated 6230cc V8, petrol, carburettor, 16 valves
Drivetrain:	Front-engine RWD
Structure:	Monocoque
Transmission:	Three-speed automatic
Weight:	2113kg

PRICE GUIDE

Launch price:	£6496
Excellent:	£17,500
Good:	£13,500
Average:	£6500
Project:	£2250

BENTLEY
Mulsanne/Eight Saloon

Rolls-Royce continued to build Bentleys as badge-engineered models with the Mulsanne of 1980. Named after the famous Le Mans straight, its alterations over the Silver Spirit included a black radiator insert and sports seats. The Eight, of 1984, departed further from the Rolls' appearance, though. The single rectangular headlamps were replaced by twin circular ones, and a mesh radiator grille was fitted along with a front spoiler. It was enough to set the car apart from the Rolls-Royce and help kick start a revival of interest in Bentley.

SPECIFICATIONS

Years produced:	1980-1992 (2039 in total)
Performance:	0-60mph: 9.6sec
	Top speed: 119mph
Power & torque:	N/Q/N/Q
Engine:	Normally aspirated 6750cc V8, petrol, carburettor, 16 valves
Drivetrain:	Front-engine RWD
Structure:	Monocoque
Transmission:	Three-speed automatic
Weight:	2226kg

PRICE GUIDE

Launch price:	£49,629
Excellent:	£14,000
Good:	£12,000
Average:	£7000
Project:	£4000

BENTLEY
Mulsanne Turbo

Sales of Bentleys had fallen so low during the T-series era that Rolls-Royce considered axing the marque. Fortunately, the decision was taken to make the Winged B cars stand out instead. The renaissance started with the Mulsanne Turbo of 1982. While the looks didn't differ much from the equivalent Rolls, attached to the 6750cc V8 engine was a Garrett AiResearch turbocharger which increased power by 50%. Being Rolls-Royce, of course, what this figure really was wasn't actually announced officially.

SPECIFICATIONS

Years produced:	1982-1986
Performance:	0-60mph: 7.0sec
	Top speed: 135mph
Power & torque:	298bhp/450lb ft
Engine:	Turbocharged 6750cc V8, petrol, carburettor, 16 valves
Drivetrain:	Front-engine RWD
Structure:	Monocoque
Transmission:	Three-speed automatic
Weight:	2250kg

PRICE GUIDE

Launch price:	£58,613
Excellent:	£17,500
Good:	£13,000
Average:	£7500
Project:	£4250

BENTLEY
Turbo R Saloon

In 1985, the Mulsanne Turbo theme was made more extreme with the Turbo R. The new Blower Bentley used the turbocharger and V8 engine of its previous incarnation but complemented it with Bosch MK-Motronic fuel injection. This put power up to 328bhp – not that the discreet Rolls-Royce would ever admit it – and gave a top speed of 135mph; this velocity had to be limited because of concerns that the tyres wouldn't cope with the weight of the car combined with unfettered high-speed running. A conspicuous bargain in today's market.

SPECIFICATIONS

Years produced:	1985-1995 (4815 in total)
Performance:	0-60mph: 6.7sec
	Top speed: 135mph
Power & torque:	328bhp/350lb ft
Engine:	Turbocharged 6750cc V8, petrol, electronic fuel injection, 16 valves
Drivetrain:	Front-engine RWD
Structure:	Monocoque
Transmission:	Four-speed automatic
Weight:	2234kg

PRICE GUIDE

Launch price:	£79,397
Excellent:	£20,000
Good:	£14,000
Average:	£8500
Project:	£5000

BERKELEY

BERKELEY WAS a caravan manufacturer until it diversified into tiny glassfibre sportscars designed by Lawrence Bond (of Bond car fame). Twin-cylinder motorcycle engines provided more than enough power for these very lightweight machines; the 50bhp B105 of 1959 could top 100mph. The most successful was the three-wheeled T60, of which 1830 were built between 1959 and 1960. However, the lure to customers of rivals like the Austin-Healey Sprite meant that the firm went bankrupt in 1961, although a new incarnation of it built a handful of T60s in the 1990s, using motorcycle engines. Meanwhile, the original Berkeley factory found employment making women's underwear...

BERKELEY
SA322/SE328

Sporting cars don't come much more minimalist than this – an Anzani two-stroke twin powered this glassfibre-bodied two-seater to a top speed of 65mph. Not fast, but certainly fun, and surprisingly popular during the boomtime 1950s. When seen away from other cars, the 322 and 328 look well-proportioned and ahead of their time, but the tiny size makes them a singular choice for the adventurous fans in real life. Cheap to fuel, cheap to buy, and easy to work on, these Berkeleys make great sense, and have a real following today.

SPECIFICATIONS

Years produced:	1956-1958 (146/1272 in total)
Performance:	0-60mph: 38.3sec
	Top speed: 65mph
Power & torque:	15bhp/16lb ft
Engine:	Normally aspirated 322cc twin cylinder, petrol, carburettor
Drivetrain:	Front-engine FWD
Structure:	Monocoque
Transmission:	Three-speed manual
Weight:	280kg

PRICE GUIDE

Launch price:	£575
Excellent:	£5000
Good:	£4000
Average:	£2200
Project:	£1100

BERKELEY
Sport SE492

First real update to the series saw power boosted by the fitment of a three-cylinder Excelsior motorcycle engine. The car was now considerably quicker, topping out at 80mph, a feat proved in motor sport when Giovanni Lurani found success running a team of three (with his own design of hardtop) in the Italian 750cc GT class of racing. The pinnacle of Berkeley's success was when Lorenzo Bandini scored a win in the 1958 Monza 12-hour race. A Foursome four-seater was also introduced, proving the flexibility of Lawrie Bond's original design.

SPECIFICATIONS

Years produced:	1957-1959 (666 in total)
Performance:	0-60mph: 21.8sec
	Top speed: 80mph
Power & torque:	30bhp/36lb ft
Engine:	Normally aspirated 492cc three cylinder, petrol, carburettor
Drivetrain:	Front-engine FWD
Structure:	Monocoque
Transmission:	Four-speed manual
Weight:	318kg

PRICE GUIDE

Launch price:	£650
Excellent:	£5500
Good:	£4500
Average:	£2400
Project:	£1250

BERKELEY
T60

Lop a wheel off the 322/328 and you're left with the T60 – a three-seat microcar that is just as much fun to drive as its four-wheel counterparts. Designed by Lawrie Bond, who went on to build cars under his own name, the three-wheeler lightweight was incredibly fun to drive in the right circumstances, and remains so to this day. Berkeley even managed to squeeze a rear seat into some of the last models off the line, and had it not been for the collapse of the parent company, many more than 1830 might have been built.

SPECIFICATIONS

Years produced:	1959-1960 (1830 in total)
Performance:	0-60mph: N/A
	Top speed: 60mph
Power & torque:	18bhp/22lb ft
Engine:	Normally aspirated 328cc twin cylinder, petrol, carburettor
Drivetrain:	Front-engine FWD
Structure:	Monocoque
Transmission:	Four-speed manual
Weight:	280kg

PRICE GUIDE

Launch price:	£400
Excellent:	£5000
Good:	£3000
Average:	£1750
Project:	£1000

BERKELEY
B95/B105

The evolution of the Berkeley was rapid and unabated, with the B95 and B105 the ultimate examples of the breed. Power was from a high-compression Royal Enfield Constellation parallel-twin, putting out 50bhp and pushing the car to a top speed of more than 100mph on the 105 model. Roadholding was excellent, as the chassis was easily capable of handling the extra power. However, as sound as the concept was, the Berkeley twins lost out in the market compared with the Austin-Healey Sprite and ended up selling disappointingly.

SPECIFICATIONS

Years produced:	1959-1961 (200 in total)
Performance:	0-60mph: 17.2sec
	Top speed: 105mph
Power & torque:	50bhp/45lb ft
Engine:	Normally aspirated 692cc twin cylinder, petrol, carburettor, 4 valves
Drivetrain:	Front-engine FWD
Structure:	Monocoque
Transmission:	Four-speed manual
Weight:	363kg

PRICE GUIDE

Launch price:	£628
Excellent:	£5750
Good:	£4750
Average:	£2500
Project:	£1350

BITTER

RACING DRIVER and car importer Erich Bitter was intrigued by a 1969 Opel concept he saw at the Frankfurt Motor Show. A deal was struck with Opel, and Bitter GMBH was formed, with Erich Bitter's reinterpretation of the Opel CD as its main product. The cars were actually constructed by Baur. After 395 had been built, the firm switched its attention to the more affordable SC in 1979, which was again Opel-based but had a coupé body designed by Bitter himself (although it did look awfully like the Ferrari 365 GT4 2+2). Convertibles and saloons followed, but Bitter failed in 1989. In 2007, though, Erich Bitter announced a comeback, with a new car he dubbed the Vero.

BITTER
CD

The Bitter CD started life as a styling study by Opel shown at the Frankfurt Motor Show in 1969 – and it was so well received that the company considered putting the Diplomat-engined coupé into production. However, it was down to former racing driver Erich Bitter to turn it into production reality in 1973 – just in time for the oil crisis. Despite the unpromising Opel platform and Chevrolet V8, the CD is a great car to drive, and an excellent long-distance tourer. The Baur-built bodies are prone to rusting, but many of the 395 cars built survive in the hands of enthusiastic owners.

SPECIFICATIONS
Years produced:	1973-1979 (395 in total)
Performance:	0-60mph: 9.4sec
	Top speed: 130mph
Power & torque:	230bhp/314lb ft
Engine:	Normally aspirated 5354cc V8, petrol, carburettor, 16 valves
Drivetrain:	Front-engine RWD
Structure:	Monocoque
Transmission:	Three-speed automatic
Weight:	1724kg

PRICE GUIDE
Launch price:	N/A in UK
Excellent:	£20,000
Good:	£15,000
Average:	£9000
Project:	£6000

BITTER
SC

The SC is said to offer the best of both worlds – rugged and capable GM engineering (this time the Opel Senator's platform) combined with glamorous Italianate styling. Initially the bodies were built by OCRA, but production was switched to ILCA after just 79 SCs were completed. Power didn't initially match the looks, but an upgraded 3.9-litre engine righted the situation. Rust was the enemy with these cars, and sadly sales weren't great, and by the late 1980s the SC's failure almost bankrupted Erich Bitter. Values now rising sharply for the underrated German tourer.

SPECIFICATIONS
Years produced:	1979-1989 (458 in total)
Performance:	0-60mph: 7.4sec
	Top speed: 142mph
Power & torque:	210bhp/257lb ft
Engine:	Normally aspirated 3848cc straight six, petrol, carburettor, 12 valves
Drivetrain:	Front-engine RWD
Structure:	Monocoque
Transmission:	Three-speed automatic
Weight:	1350kg

PRICE GUIDE
Launch price:	£26,950
Excellent:	£8000
Good:	£6000
Average:	£3000
Project:	£2500

BIZZARRINI

SPORTS CARS FOR the connoisseur, these were the creation of Giotto Bizzarrini, a former Alfa Romeo and Ferrari engineer who was heavily involved in the latter's legendary 250GTO. After leaving Ferrari in 1961, he worked on the Lamborghini V12 engine and Iso's Grifo project. In 1964, Bizzarrini SpA was formed, its first car being launched two years later. Based on the competition Grifo A3C, it was called the 5300 Strada. The firm's most famous design was the P538S, which raced at Le Mans. Only around 160 Bizzarrinis were built before production ceased in 1969. Giotto continued working as a consultant, producing prototypes and building replica P538s.

BIZZARRINI
GT Strada 5300

Taking the vast wealth of experience gained at Alfa Romeo and, more importantly, Ferrari, Giotto Bizzarrini set about creating the delectable GT Strada. Effectively a modified lightweight Iso Grifo clothed in a stunning and extremely low-line Giugiaro-styled set of clothes, this was a fully paid-up member of the supercar elite. As is the case with the Iso Grifo, the GT Strada is powered by a Chevrolet V8, which endows it with a very favourable power-to-weight ratio. A challenging car for gifted drivers, offered with glassfibre or aluminium body.

SPECIFICATIONS
Years produced:	1965-1969 (149 in total)
Performance:	0-60mph: 6.4sec
	Top speed: 165mph
Power & torque:	365bhp/376lb ft
Engine:	Normally aspirated 5354cc V8, petrol, carburettor, 16 valves
Drivetrain:	Front-engine RWD
Structure:	Separate chassis
Transmission:	Four-speed manual
Weight:	1252kg

PRICE GUIDE
Launch price:	N/A
Excellent:	£150,000
Good:	£100,000
Average:	£70,000
Project:	N/A

BMW

BAYERISCHE MOTOREN Werke was an aviation manufacturer banned from building aircraft after World War One. So, it turned to motorcycles and cars; its first automobile was an Austin Seven copy named the Dixi. From that,

BMW moved onto its own very fine sports and touring cars including the lovely 328. Turbulent times followed the end of World War Two, with BMW coming close to bankruptcy and turning to Isetta and 600 bubble cars to help

sustain it. The 'Neue Klasse' models from 1961 saved the firm, while 1973's 2002 Turbo was the very first turbocharged road car to be made in Europe. Today's BMW 'Series' cars are highly respected and capable machines.

BMW
501

Starting from near enough the ground up, BMW worked quickly to design, develop and launch the brand new 501 from its new factory in Munich. But what an impressive fresh beginning – the saloon and roadsters were impressively styled (hence the nickname 'Baroque Angel'), refined, expensive and luxurious. Initially powered by pre-war 326 engine, upgraded to 2.1 litres in 1955. Considering Germany was recovering from the effects of WW2, it was probably a case of too much, too soon, but these grand cars put BMW firmly on the map.

SPECIFICATIONS

Years produced:	1952-1958 (8936 in total)
Performance:	0-60mph: 17.2sec
	Top speed: 95mph
Power & torque:	73bhp/80lb ft
Engine:	Normally aspirated 1971cc straight six, petrol, carburettor, 16 valves
Drivetrain:	Front-engine RWD
Structure:	Separate chassis
Transmission:	Four-speed manual
Weight:	1270kg

PRICE GUIDE

Launch price:	N/A
Excellent:	£25,000
Good:	£17,500
Average:	£10,000
Project:	£5000

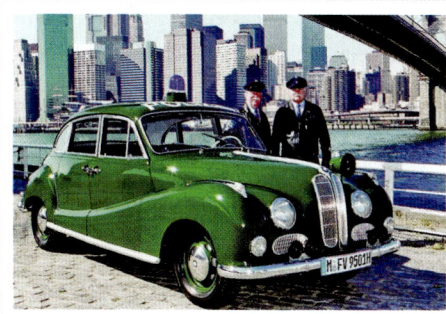

BMW
501 V8/502/2600/3200

Even during the 1950s, BMW had cottoned on to the creation of more desirable models simply by adding larger engines. It was a policy that would serve the company well for generations to come. Just like its six-cylinder counterpart, the V8 was available in saloon, coupé and cabriolet forms. As the years passed, and sales success evaded the ambitious car, the engine was expanded to its ultimate 3.2-litre form, which developed an impressive 160bhp. But in cash-starved '50s and early '60s Germany, few buyers stumped up and bought a BMW.

SPECIFICATIONS

Years produced:	1954-1963 (13,044 in total)
Performance:	0-60mph: 15.2sec
	Top speed: 103mph
Power & torque:	105bhp/95lb ft
Engine:	Normally aspirated 2581cc V8, petrol, carburettor, 16 valves
Drivetrain:	Front-engine RWD
Structure:	Separate chassis
Transmission:	Four-speed manual
Weight:	1334kg

PRICE GUIDE

Launch price:	N/A
Excellent:	£27,500
Good:	£20,000
Average:	£12,000
Project:	£7500

BMW
503

Based on the impressive 501, BMW's 503 coupé sported an exciting new bodystyle penned by Albrecht Goertz. It introduced a new era of modernism for the marque, but at a hefty price that few could afford. It drove as well as it looked, too, with a top speed of nearly 120mph. The 503 coupé was designed primarily for the American market, but sadly, it was far too expensive to take off, and a mere 412 were built. The outcome was disastrous for BMW, which teetered on the edge of bankruptcy by the end of the 1950s.

SPECIFICATIONS

Years produced:	1955-1959 (412 in total)
Performance:	0-60mph: 10sec
	Top speed: 118mph
Power & torque:	162bhp/163lb ft
Engine:	Normally aspirated 3168cc V8, petrol, carburettor, 16 valves
Drivetrain:	Front-engine RWD
Structure:	Separate chassis
Transmission:	Four-speed manual
Weight:	1501kg

PRICE GUIDE

Launch price:	£4801
Excellent:	£100,000
Good:	£75,000
Average:	£50,000
Project:	£25,000

BMW ISETTA
250/300

Although universally admired, BMW's luxury cars were selling slowly. So the decision to acquire the licence to build the Isetta proved to be an inspired piece of lateral thinking by the company's management. The Isetta was just what was needed, and as the effects of the Suez crisis started to hit, and petrol became a rare commodity, suddenly the motorcycle-engined car that could achieve 50mpg all day long made a great deal of sense. Front-hinged door and three-wheeled handling were questionable, but buyers loved them... for a while.

SPECIFICATIONS

Years produced:	1955-1965 (161,728 in total)
Performance:	0-60mph: N/A
	Top speed: 60mph
Power & torque:	13bhp/11lb ft
Engine:	Normally aspirated 297cc twin cylinder, petrol, carburettor, 4 valves
Drivetrain:	Rear-engine RWD
Structure:	Separate chassis
Transmission:	Four-speed manual
Weight:	350kg

PRICE GUIDE

Launch price:	£415
Excellent:	£8500
Good:	£6000
Average:	£3000
Project:	£1600

BMW
507

When it was launched alongside the 503 Coupé in 1956, the 507 was possibly the most beautiful convertible in the world. Whereas its hard-topped sister was slightly awkward to look at from some angles, the 507 came close to perfection. The aluminium-bodied roadster was built on a shortened 502 chassis and powered by the same V8 engine, which produced 150bhp and gave the 507 a fair turn of speed. Despite its beauty, high price and lack of an established image hampered sales – a mere 252 were made, at a significant loss.

SPECIFICATIONS

Years produced:	1956-1959 (252 in total)
Performance:	0-60mph: 9.5sec
	Top speed: 124mph
Power & torque:	150bhp/174lb ft
Engine:	Normally aspirated 3168cc V8, petrol, carburettor, 16 valves
Drivetrain:	Front-engine RWD
Structure:	Separate chassis
Transmission:	Four-speed manual
Weight:	1330kg

PRICE GUIDE

Launch price:	£4201
Excellent:	£600,000
Good:	£500,000
Average:	£250,000
Project:	£150,000

BMW
600

Following on from the original Isetta, the BMW 600 was a logical upward extension of the theme to capture buyers who'd grown out of their original bubble cars. The front-opening door remained in place, but the new car was larger, with an extra side door for rear passengers, a more powerful 582cc BMW flat-twin motorcycle engine and – most importantly – four wheels. It was usefully quicker than the original Isetta, but still crude for the price tag, being only marginally cheaper than a Beetle. Sales were unimpressive.

SPECIFICATIONS

Years produced:	1957-1959 (34,813 in total)
Performance:	0-60mph: N/A
	Top speed: 63mph
Power & torque:	19.5bhp/29lb ft
Engine:	Normally aspirated 582cc twin cylinder, petrol, carburettor, 4 valves
Drivetrain:	Rear-engine RWD
Structure:	Separate chassis
Transmission:	Four-speed manual
Weight:	510kg

PRICE GUIDE

Launch price:	£676
Excellent:	£6500
Good:	£4500
Average:	£2650
Project:	£1000

BMW
700 coupé/cabriolet

The 700 actually first appeared in coupé form, and although it looked a little awkward thanks to its sloping roofline, it proved just the right product for BMW. As the company's first unitary construction car, the 700's technical significance is oft-overlooked thanks to its rear-engined layout. The Sports model gained 10bhp thanks to twin carburettors and a high-compression engine, and it's these ones that buyers really want today. Open-topped cabriolet is often overlooked, but is just as much fun as its coupé counterpart.

SPECIFICATIONS

Years produced:	1959-1965 (11,166/2592 in total)
Performance:	0-60mph: 33.7sec
	Top speed: 75mph
Power & torque:	32bhp/37lb ft
Engine:	Normally aspirated 697cc twin cylinder, petrol, carburettor, 4 valves
Drivetrain:	Rear-engine RWD
Structure:	Monocoque
Transmission:	Four-speed manual
Weight:	640kg

PRICE GUIDE

Launch price:	N/A
Excellent:	£8000
Good:	£4500
Average:	£2500
Project:	£1500

BMW
1500/1600/1800/1800ti

Another pivotal model in BMW's history. The 700 might have saved the company from bankruptcy, but the 'Neue Klasse' 1500 came from nowhere and struck a chord with West Germany's emerging middle class, selling hugely and returning BMW to profitability. Under the well-judged Michelotti skin, the 1500 boasted an up-to-the-minute specification, including unitary construction, disc brakes, independent suspension and a smooth 1.5-litre overhead-cam engine. Continually upgraded, transforming into the 2000 in 1966.

SPECIFICATIONS (1500)

Years produced:	1961-1972 (c.200,000 in total)
Performance:	0-60mph: 13.1sec
	Top speed: 93mph
Power & torque:	80bhp/87lb ft
Engine:	Normally aspirated 1499cc four cylinder, petrol, carburettor, 8 valves
Drivetrain:	Front-engine RWD
Structure:	Monocoque
Transmission:	Four-speed manual
Weight:	1043kg

PRICE GUIDE (ti in brackets)

Launch price:	N/A
Excellent:	£8000 (£20,000)
Good:	£4000 (£15,000)
Average:	£2500 (£8000)
Project:	£1000 (£1000)

BMW
2000/2000ti/2000tii

The 2000 was the ultimate evolution of the 1500/1800cc saloon car line. The medium-sized model seemed its most appealing with the bored-out four cylinder under the bonnet, especially in fuel-injection Tii form, which packed a useful 135bhp. Interesting to drive and a bit of a handful in the wet, the 2000 set the tone for the next generations of BMW's mid-sized saloons – sporting and satisfying. Survival rate in the UK is low although they are still fairly commonplace in Germany, so that would be your first place to look when buying.

SPECIFICATIONS

Years produced:	1966-1972 (113,074 in total)
Performance:	0-60mph: 12.4sec
	Top speed: 104mph
Power & torque:	100bhp/116lb ft
Engine:	Normally aspirated 1990cc four cylinder, petrol, carburettor, 8 valves
Drivetrain:	Front-engine RWD
Structure:	Monocoque
Transmission:	Four-speed manual
Weight:	1130kg

PRICE GUIDE (ti/tii in brackets)

Launch price:	£1777
Excellent:	£8000 (£20,000)
Good:	£4000 (£15,000)
Average:	£2500 (£8000)
Project:	£1000 (£1000)

BMW
2000C/CS

BMW's 'Neue Klasse' range had proved an instant and substantial hit in Germany; and just as the Rover and Triumph 2000s had revolutionised the executive class here in the UK, the BMW equivalent changed the face of the market there. Easily the most appealing was the CS version, a pillarless coupé by Wilhelm Hofmeister. The Karmann-built bodies were pretty, but weren't immune to rust, and have now almost disappeared from the scene. Find a good one and cherish it – BMW's future success was mapped out here.

SPECIFICATIONS
Years produced:	1966-1969 (11,720 in total)
Performance:	0-60mph: 12.0sec
	Top speed: 110mph
Power & torque:	120bhp/123lb ft
Engine:	Normally aspirated 1990cc four cylinder, petrol, carburettor, 8 valves
Drivetrain:	Front-engine RWD
Structure:	Monocoque
Transmission:	Four-speed manual
Weight:	1150kg

PRICE GUIDE
Launch price:	£2950
Excellent:	£9000
Good:	£7000
Average:	£4000
Project:	£1650

BMW
1602/1502

With the 'Neue Klasse' doing the business in the executive market, BMW repeated the trick in the small saloon sector with its '02 series models. Despite their relatively high prices the smaller-engined cars in the '02 range were popular entry-level models, turning on a generation of drivers to BMW ownership – and today, they still enjoy a healthy following. Overshadowed somewhat by the pocket-rocket 2002, in many ways the 1502/1602 are better balanced and more satisfying to own – if you can find one that isn't riddled with rust.

SPECIFICATIONS
Years produced:	1966-1977 (324,320 in total)
Performance:	0-60mph: 14.5sec
	Top speed: 96mph
Power & torque:	85bhp/91lb ft
Engine:	Normally aspirated 1574cc four cylinder, petrol, carburettor, 8 valves
Drivetrain:	Front-engine RWD
Structure:	Monocoque
Transmission:	Four-speed manual
Weight:	920kg

PRICE GUIDE
Launch price:	£1298
Excellent:	£6000
Good:	£4000
Average:	£2500
Project:	£1000

BMW
1602/2002 cabriolet

The Baur-built 1600 cabriolet appeared on the market a year after the popular saloon, and looked like another sure-fire hit for BMW. But the four-seater was sold at a significant price premium over its tin-top counterpart, and lacked body rigidity, blunting its driver appeal considerably. However, those ills were put right by the 2002, which featured a beefed-up structure, with roll-over bar and targa panels. The addition of the potent 1990cc hemi-headed unit no doubt helped the driving experience, and today, both cars have a healthy following.

SPECIFICATIONS
Years produced:	1967-1975 (1682/2272 in total)
Performance:	0-60mph: 12.0sec
	Top speed: 107mph
Power & torque:	100bhp/116lb ft
Engine:	Normally aspirated 1990cc four cylinder, petrol, carburettor, 8 valves
Drivetrain:	Front-engine RWD
Structure:	Monocoque
Transmission:	Four-speed manual
Weight:	1040kg

PRICE GUIDE
Launch price:	£1948
Excellent:	£12,000
Good:	£9000
Average:	£5000
Project:	£2000

BMW
2800 CS/CSA

With a straight six under the bonnet and tidied-up front-end styling, the BMW CS coupé had finally come of age. The 2.8-litre engine developed 150bhp and that was enough to give the handsome CS a maximum speed of 120mph – more in the up-gunned CSA. But speed wasn't this car's major trick, and neither was its elegant styling – the firm and well-controlled suspension settings blessed it with first-rate handling and long-distance comfort. Mercedes-Benz had met its match, and BMW was now considered a key player in the luxury car market.

SPECIFICATIONS (CSA)
Years produced:	1968-1975 (9399 in total)
Performance:	0-60mph: 8.3sec
	Top speed: 124mph
Power & torque:	168bhp/173lb ft
Engine:	Normally aspirated 2788cc straight six, petrol, carburettor, 12 valves
Drivetrain:	Front-engine RWD
Structure:	Monocoque
Transmission:	Four-speed manual
Weight:	1290kg

PRICE GUIDE
Launch price:	£4997
Excellent:	£9000
Good:	£6000
Average:	£4000
Project:	£2000

BMW
2500/2800/3.0/3.3

With the compact and executive saloon markets now cornered, BMW turned its attention to the luxury car sector and came up with the 2500. It looked like an upscaled version of the '02 Series, but that was no bad thing considering the strong identity Wilhelm Hofmeister had carved out for the niche. On the road, the 2500 and its larger-engined derivatives were also true to the marque, with all the power and poise you could need in a full-sized saloon. Despite huge sales (relatively speaking), few survive, thanks to widespread corrosion.

SPECIFICATIONS
Years produced:	1968-1977 (217,635 in total)
Performance:	0-60mph: 9.0sec
	Top speed: 127mph
Power & torque:	180bhp/255lb ft
Engine:	Normally aspirated 2494cc straight six, petrol, carburettor, 12 valves
Drivetrain:	Front-engine RWD
Structure:	Monocoque
Transmission:	Four-speed manual
Weight:	1295kg

PRICE GUIDE
Launch price:	£2197
Excellent:	£6000
Good:	£4000
Average:	£1750
Project:	£1000

BMW
2002/2002ti saloon

The 2002 was introduced a couple of years after the 1502/1602 and ended up cementing the series' reputation as the car to beat in the sporting saloon sector. The 2-litre M10-series engine was essentially a bored-out version of the old 1.8-litre unit, producing 100bhp in standard form and proving an absolute gem. With 120bhp, the twin-carburettor Ti version was far more exciting, proving a real handful on challenging roads. Possibly one of the most sensible ways of owning an early-'70s sporting saloon.

SPECIFICATIONS
Years produced:	1971-1975 (2517 in total)
Performance:	0-60mph: 12.0sec
	Top speed: 107mph
Power & torque:	100bhp/116lb ft
Engine:	Normally aspirated 1990cc four cylinder, petrol, carburettor, 8 valves
Drivetrain:	Front-engine RWD
Structure:	Monocoque
Transmission:	Four-speed manual
Weight:	1040kg

PRICE GUIDE (ti in brackets)
Launch price:	£1948
Excellent:	£6000 (£10,000)
Good:	£4000 (£7000)
Average:	£2500 (£4000)
Project:	£1000 (£1500)

BMW
2002tii

One of Europe's finest Q-cars of its era, the fuel-injection 2002Tii could crack 120mph on the autobahn and drive sideways on the merest whiff of throttle. Retaining all the strengths of the rest of the '02 series cars, the Tii has justifiably gone on to become a legend. However, like all '02s, it can suffer from extensive corrosion, which undermines the quality and ruggedness of the rest of the package. Cult following means these cars are in demand and command a healthy premium over their less-glamorous counterparts.

SPECIFICATIONS
Years produced:	1971-1975 (38,701 in total)
Performance:	0-60mph: 10.0sec
	Top speed: 120mph
Power & torque:	130bhp/131lb ft
Engine:	Normally aspirated 1990cc four cylinder, petrol, mechanical fuel injection, 8 valves
Drivetrain:	Front-engine RWD
Structure:	Monocoque
Transmission:	Four-speed manual; Five-speed optional
Weight:	1010kg

PRICE GUIDE
Launch price:	£2299
Excellent:	£10,000
Good:	£7000
Average:	£4000
Project:	£1500

BMW
3.0CS/CSi

Although outwardly similar to the 2800, the 1971 3.0CS was a major step forwards thanks to an uprated chassis and braking set-up first seen in the saloon range. The excellent roadholding of the former model was easily surpassed, and unlike the smaller cars in the range, snap-oversteer was rare. The fuel-injection CSi passed the 200bhp mark, making it a paid-up member of the performance car elite, with a top speed of 139mph and 0-60mph time of less than eight seconds. Still considered by many to be the most desirable BMW coupé of them all.

SPECIFICATIONS
Years produced:	1971-1975 (19,207 in total)
Performance:	0-60mph: 7.5sec
	Top speed: 139mph
Power & torque:	200bhp/200lb ft
Engine:	Normally aspirated 2986cc straight six, petrol, electronic fuel injection, 12 valves
Drivetrain:	Front-engine RWD
Structure:	Monocoque
Transmission:	Four-speed manual
Weight:	1270kg

PRICE GUIDE
Launch price:	£6199
Excellent:	£20,000
Good:	£14,000
Average:	£6000
Project:	£2500

BMW
3.0CSL

As homologation specials go, the BMW CSL is perhaps the most memorable. Featuring lightweight aluminium panels, a spartan interior and Plexiglas side windows, the CSL was as effective on the track as its vanilla brother was on the road. UK models retained the luxury interior of the standard cars, taking away some of the raw appeal – but buyers loved them. The most famous of all, the Batmobile, of which only 39 were made, sported extraordinary aerodynamic appendages, and are now worth serious money for a BMW of this era.

SPECIFICATIONS
Years produced:	1972-1975 (1096 in total)
Performance:	0-60mph: 7.5sec
	Top speed: 138mph
Power & torque:	206bhp/195lb ft
Engine:	Normally aspirated 3153cc straight six, petrol, mechanical fuel injection, 12 valves
Drivetrain:	Front-engine RWD
Structure:	Monocoque
Transmission:	Four-speed manual
Weight:	1270kg

PRICE GUIDE
Launch price:	£6399
Excellent:	£35,000
Good:	£22,500
Average:	£12,000
Project:	£5000

BMW
2002 Turbo

For those thrill-seekers who wanted real excitement in their lives, and who could afford one, the BMW 2002 Turbo really was the ultimate driving machine. It was Europe's first turbocharged production model, and like all the earliest cars to sport a blower, the 2002 Turbo was prodigiously powerful and suffered from massive turbo lag. But keep the revs up, and anticipate when the turbo would start spinning, and there were few saloons in the world that could keep up. Only 1672 were built, making them rare and expensive today – but what a laugh for the money...

SPECIFICATIONS
Years produced:	1973-1974 (1672 in total)
Performance:	0-60mph: 8.0sec
	Top speed: 130mph
Power & torque:	170bhp/177lb ft
Engine:	Turbocharged 1990cc four cylinder, petrol, mechanical fuel injection, 8 valves
Drivetrain:	Front-engine RWD
Structure:	Monocoque
Transmission:	Four-speed manual/five-speed manual
Weight:	1080kg

PRICE GUIDE
Launch price:	£2433
Excellent:	£30,000
Good:	£18,500
Average:	£10,000
Project:	£5000

BMW
3-Series (E21)

The BMW 3-Series became the performance saloon to beat the moment it exploded onto the market in 1975. Four-cylinder M10-powered versions weren't quick, but were dependable. However, the straight-six cars with fuel injection were electrifying, especially in the wet. Build quality was impeccable, and the interior ergonomics were superb, making this a very satisfying car to own. Again, corrosion has been a constant factor, meaning survival rate is low – although many 323is ended up doing some inadvertent off-roading. Rare now, and prices are on the up.

SPECIFICATIONS
Years produced:	1975-1983 (1,364,039 in total)
Performance:	0-60mph: 12.9sec
	Top speed: 100mph
Power & torque:	90bhp/90lb ft
Engine:	Normally aspirated 1574cc four cylinder, petrol, carburettor, 8 valves
Drivetrain:	Front-engine RWD
Structure:	Monocoque
Transmission:	Four-speed manual
Weight:	1020kg

PRICE GUIDE
Launch price:	£2799
Excellent:	£5000
Good:	£3000
Average:	£1500
Project:	£500

BMW
633/628CSi

Like the CS before it, the 6-Series coupé was closely related to the luxury saloon in the BMW range. The key BMW selling points of sharp steering, keen dynamics and strong performance were all intact, but many customers bemoaned the styling of the new car, which was far less pretty. Conceived as more of a grand tourer than the CS, the 6-Series was easier to live with – and as a classic, it makes far more sense thanks to its commodious interior and improved reliability and rust resistance. The later 628CSi was a far more polished all-rounder.

SPECIFICATIONS
Years produced:	1976-1987 (29,382 in total)
Performance:	0-60mph: 8.5sec
	Top speed: 134mph
Power & torque:	197bhp/210lb ft
Engine:	Normally aspirated 3210cc straight six, petrol, electronic fuel injection, 12 valves
Drivetrain:	Front-engine RWD
Structure:	Monocoque
Transmission:	Five-speed manual
Weight:	1495kg

PRICE GUIDE
Launch price:	£13,980
Excellent:	£8000
Good:	£6000
Average:	£3000
Project:	£1000

BMW
7-Series (E23)

BMW's second attempt at a luxury saloon was more polished, yet less appealing than its predecessor. It bristled with up-to-the-second technology such as a check computer and fuel injection in the top models, but some of the driving immediacy of the previous model was lost thanks to ballooning dimensions. Treated to a mid-life facelift that standardised engine management and improved efficiency and driveability, it still lacked warmth. Few remain today, but one to look out for is the Europe-only 745i model, powered by a 3.2-litre turbocharged straight six.

SPECIFICATIONS
Years produced:	1977-1986 (285,029 in total)
Performance:	0-60mph: 9.3sec
	Top speed: 135mph
Power & torque:	181bhp/177lb ft
Engine:	Normally aspirated 2788cc straight six, petrol, fuel injection, 12 valves
Drivetrain:	Front-engine RWD
Structure:	Monocoque
Transmission:	Five-speed manual
Weight:	1470kg

PRICE GUIDE
Launch price:	£8950
Excellent:	£3500
Good:	£2500
Average:	£1250
Project:	£750

BMW
M1

The original M car, and easily the most exciting. The M1 was created for Group Five racing, but thanks to delays during development which led to BMW taking control of body production (when partner, Lamborghini, couldn't deliver its side of the bargain), it arrived late and never fulfilled its obvious racing potential. The styling by Giugiaro was spot on, as was its chassis and race-bred 24-valve engine, and BMW was justifiably proud of its new supercar. But after a run of 456, production of the era's most drivable supercar came to a halt. Revered today.

SPECIFICATIONS
Years produced:	1979-1980 (456 in total)
Performance:	0-60mph: 6.5sec
	Top speed: 163mph
Power & torque:	277bhp/243lb ft
Engine:	Normally aspirated 3453cc straight six, petrol, mechanical fuel injection, 24 valves
Drivetrain:	Mid-engine RWD
Structure:	Spaceframe
Transmission:	Five-speed manual
Weight:	1300kg

PRICE GUIDE
Launch price:	£37,570
Excellent:	£125,000
Good:	£100,000
Average:	£75,000
Project:	£50,000

BMW
M535i (E12)

Although not strictly an M5, the BMW Motorsport division's first sporting 5-Series was a template for the legendary Q-car. Shoehorning the 635CSi's engine into the compact 5-Series shell resulted in a seriously rapid sports saloon, although thanks to the Alpina-inspired chin spoiler and stripes, the world knew all about it. The M535i was offered with a limited-slip diff, and close-ratio gearbox, and shared its pin-sharp steering with the rest of the range – making it a driver's delight. Project cars can be had for a song, and many ended up being donors.

SPECIFICATIONS
Years produced:	1979-1981 (1410 in total)
Performance:	0-60mph: 8.0sec
	Top speed: 140mph
Power & torque:	218bhp/229lb ft
Engine:	Normally aspirated 3453cc straight six, petrol, electronic fuel injection, 12 valves
Drivetrain:	Front-engine RWD
Structure:	Monocoque
Transmission:	Five-speed manual
Weight:	1465kg

PRICE GUIDE
Launch price:	£13,705
Excellent:	£6500
Good:	£4500
Average:	£2500
Project:	£1500

BMW
635CSi

The earliest 6-Series cars never seemed quite as satisfying as they should have been. The heavier body stunted performance, and the big coupé just didn't seem quite as sporting as it once did. But the 635CSi went a long way to redressing the balance thanks to its crisp new engine and altered chassis settings. Throughout its life the CSi continued to be improved, thanks to further running changes. When it was replaced by the 850 in 1989, commentators bemoaned the fact that the new car wasn't as instantly appealing as the old – sound familiar?

SPECIFICATIONS
Years produced: 1978-1989
Performance: 0-60mph: 8.0sec
Top speed: 138mph
Power & torque: 218bhp/228lb ft
Engine: Normally aspirated 3453cc straight six, petrol, electronic fuel injection, 12 valves
Drivetrain: Front-engine RWD
Structure: Monocoque
Transmission: Five-speed manual
Weight: 1475kg

PRICE GUIDE
Launch price: £16,499
Excellent: £12,000
Good: £6000
Average: £3000
Project: £1000

BMW
3-Series Baur cabriolet

The Baur cabriolet, introduced in 1979, further extended the appeal of the 3-Series range, even if its bulky roll-over bar marred the open-air feel. Yet there were positive benefits – it felt solid and had ample crash protection. Lower-powered versions were almost sluggish thanks to a weighty body, but the 323i retained much of the amusement that the closed car had. Sales were slow, though, no doubt because of the high purchase price. Rare today, after many examples fell prey to the effects of corrosion and neglect.

SPECIFICATIONS
Years produced: 1979-1982
Performance: 0-60mph: 9.5sec
Top speed: 116mph
Power & torque: 123bhp/125lb ft
Engine: Normally aspirated 1991cc straight six, petrol, electronic fuel injection, 12 valves
Drivetrain: Front-engine RWD
Structure: Monocoque
Transmission: Five-speed manual
Weight: 1104kg

PRICE GUIDE
Launch price: N/A in UK
Excellent: £6000
Good: £4500
Average: £2500
Project: £1000

BMW
5-Series (E28)

This was BMW at its conservative best. The blink-and-you'll-miss-it rebody of the original E12 gave the impression that the new car was no such thing at all. But under the skin, the fresh 5-Series was cutting-edge, featuring standardised engine management plus a seriously uprated chassis and interior. Engine range was impressive spanning 1.8 to 3.5 litres, as well as, for the first time in BMW's history, a diesel. One curiosity was the 525e, which was powered by a 2.7-litre six, tuned for maximum economy. It was certainly relaxing to drive – a BMW first...

SPECIFICATIONS (525i)
Years produced: 1981-1988 (722,328 in total)
Performance: 0-60mph: 9.6sec
Top speed: 122mph
Power & torque: 148bhp/159lb ft
Engine: Normally aspirated 2495cc straight six, petrol, electronic fuel injection, 12 valves
Drivetrain: Front-engine RWD
Structure: Monocoque
Transmission: Five-speed manual
Weight: 1280kg

PRICE GUIDE
Launch price: £7595
Excellent: £3500
Good: £2000
Average: £1000
Project: £500

BMW
3-Series (E30)

Following on from the conservative and well-engineered E28-generation 5-Series, BMW gave its customers more of the same with the E30, and in doing so, created one of the most iconic cars of the '80s. But the E30 was bang up to date, and its mix of M40 four pots and M20 straight sixes was rather familiar, and such was the depth of the engineering that any 3-Series rewarded its owner with an immense sense of well-being. And that's why they sold over two million – many of which seem to be still in use, and performing brilliantly!

SPECIFICATIONS (318i)
Years produced: 1982-1991 (2,339,520 in total)
Performance: 0-60mph: 10.9sec
Top speed: 114mph
Power & torque: 103bhp/107lb ft
Engine: Normally aspirated 1766cc four cylinder, petrol, electronic fuel injection, 8 valves
Drivetrain: Front-engine RWD
Structure: Monocoque
Transmission: Five-speed manual
Weight: 1000kg

PRICE GUIDE
Launch price: N/A
Excellent: £2500
Good: £1750
Average: £1000
Project: £500

BMW
M535i (E28)

The second-generation M535i followed the same formula as the original. Created by installing the 218bhp 635CSi engine into the 5-Series body, it remained an astounding Q-car but was far more polished. The deep front spoiler remained, which was at odds with the unadorned (and more powerful) M5. Recaro seats and a limited-slip differential remained options, and just like the original many have now rusted away. The remaining cars are far too cheap, possibly because they are overshadowed by the M5.

SPECIFICATIONS
Years produced: 1984-1987 (45,655 in total)
Performance: 0-60mph: 6.9sec
Top speed: 143mph
Power & torque: 218bhp/224lb ft
Engine: Normally aspirated 3430cc straight six, petrol, electronic fuel injection, 12 valves
Drivetrain: Front-engine RWD
Structure: Monocoque
Transmission: Five-speed manual
Weight: 1391kg

PRICE GUIDE
Launch price: £13,745
Excellent: £7000
Good: £5000
Average: £3000
Project: £1250

BMW
M5 (E28)

The first M-Sport 5-Series was another case of following the formula to stuff a powerful engine under the bonnet of the well-proportioned 5-Series. This time around, the full-fat 24-valve 286bhp M1 engine created a super-saloon par excellence, and unlike the first car – which looked every bit the road car racer – the M5 was discreet to the point of anonymity. Canny owners debadged their examples and went supercar baiting. After years in the doldrums, the E28 is beginning to gain recognition as an '80s icon, and values are rising sharply.

SPECIFICATIONS
Years produced:	1984-1987 (2145 in total)
Performance:	0-60mph: 7.0sec
	Top speed: 156mph
Power & torque:	286bhp/251lb ft
Engine:	Normally aspirated 3452cc straight six, petrol, electronic fuel injection, 24 valves
Drivetrain:	Front-engine RWD
Structure:	Monocoque
Transmission:	Five-speed manual
Weight:	1250kg

PRICE GUIDE
Launch price:	£21,805
Excellent:	£16,000
Good:	£10,000
Average:	£6000
Project:	£3000

BMW
M635CSi

A 1980s sporting classic was created in 1984 when BMW hit on the bright idea of fitting the 286bhp M-Power engine from the mid-engined M1 into the 635CSi body. With stiffened suspension and improved damping, as well as a standard limited-slip differential, the full-sized coupé became a sublime package, with masses of all-round ability. Values remain significantly higher than for non-M-Sport coupés. Keep an eye out for fakes, and remember that the M-Sport engine costs significantly more to fix when it goes wrong.

SPECIFICATIONS
Years produced:	1984-1989 (5803 in total)
Performance:	0-60mph: 6.5sec
	Top speed: 158mph
Power & torque:	286bhp/246lb ft
Engine:	Normally aspirated 3453cc straight six, petrol, electronic fuel injection, 24 valves
Drivetrain:	Front-engine RWD
Structure:	Monocoque
Transmission:	Five-speed manual
Weight:	1505kg

PRICE GUIDE
Launch price:	£32,195
Excellent:	£16,000
Good:	£10,000
Average:	£6000
Project:	£3000

BMW
3-Series convertible (E30)

After the Baur cabriolets with their bulky roll-over structures, the in-house 3-Series convertible – which used a strengthened windscreen surround instead – looked an incredibly clean design. And in a marketplace dominated by cluttered-looking convertibles, the E30 soft-top did very well indeed. It was available with a variety of engine options; the 318i version was the most popular in the UK, although the 325i came a close second. Rapidly disappearing from the UK's roads, so grab a good one now – values are alreay on the up.

SPECIFICATIONS
Years produced:	1985-1993 (143,425 in total)
Performance:	0-60mph: 8.4sec
	Top speed: 135mph
Power & torque:	169bhp/167lb ft
Engine:	Normally aspirated 2494cc straight six, petrol, electronic fuel injection, 12 valves
Drivetrain:	Front-engine RWD
Structure:	Monocoque
Transmission:	Five-speed manual
Weight:	1090kg

PRICE GUIDE
Launch price:	£11,590
Excellent:	£6500
Good:	£5000
Average:	£3000
Project:	£1000

BMW
M3 (E30)

The M3 was conceived to compete in Group A Touring Cars, and was one of a rare breed of BMW homologation specials, as most M-Sport cars were designed solely for the road. The 2.3-litre S14 engine was loosely based on the venerable M10 four cylinder and it produced 192bhp straight from the box. However, it was developed throughout its life, and late Evo and Sport versions were pushing out 238bhp – a remarkable figure considering the lack of forced induction. In short, a brilliant sports saloon, and proof that racing improves the breed.

SPECIFICATIONS (Evo Sport)
Years produced:	1986-1990 (17,184 in total)
Performance:	0-60mph: 6.5sec
	Top speed: 154mph
Power & torque:	238bhp/177lb ft
Engine:	Normally aspirated 2467cc four cylinder, petrol, electronic fuel injection, 16 valves
Drivetrain:	Front-engine RWD
Structure:	Monocoque
Transmission:	Five-speed manual
Weight:	1200kg

PRICE GUIDE (Evo Sport in brackets)
Launch price:	£22,750
Excellent:	£20,000 (£30,000)
Good:	£15,000 (£22,000)
Average:	£12,500 (£17,000)
Project:	£6000 (£9000)

BMW
Z1

The Z1 was initially a concept at the 1987 Frankfurt Motor Show, but buyers were soon clamouring to buy one, leaving BMW rushing to get the innovative little roadster into production. Most notable for its doors, which drop into the sills, the Z1 bristled with advanced design features and weight-saving touches. Powered by the same engine as the 325i, it was no ball of fire considering its high price. Rapidly diminishing interest from buyers saw BMW halt production after 8000 were built. Only 50 official UK imports, but more have been shipped in.

SPECIFICATIONS
Years produced:	1988-1991 (8000 in total)
Performance:	0-60mph: 9.0sec
	Top speed: 136mph
Power & torque:	170bhp/164lb ft
Engine:	Normally aspirated 2494cc straight six, petrol, electronic fuel injection, 12 valves
Drivetrain:	Front-engine RWD
Structure:	Steel tub/plastic panels
Transmission:	Five-speed manual
Weight:	1290kg

PRICE GUIDE
Launch price:	£36,925
Excellent:	£23,000
Good:	£20,000
Average:	£15,000
Project:	£10,000

BMW
5-Series (E34)

The arrival of the C2-generation Audi 100 caught BMW napping. Suddenly, its beautifully engineered car looked old-hat thanks to its upright styling. The 1987 5-Series certainly put that right, not only modernising the mid-line saloons, but creating a look that would remain with BMW until into the 21st century. The same wide range of engines was used as before, although VANOS and 24-valve heads became standard fare for the sixes. Balanced, poised, and the benchmark when new, yet curiously underrated and overlooked now. Their time will come.

SPECIFICATIONS
Years produced:	1987-1996 (1,333,412 in total)
Performance:	0-60mph: 9.5sec
	Top speed: 137mph
Power & torque:	168bhp/164lb ft
Engine:	Normally aspirated 2494cc straight six, petrol, electronic fuel injection, 12 valves
Drivetrain:	Front-engine RWD
Structure:	Monocoque
Transmission:	Five-speed manual
Weight:	1450kg

PRICE GUIDE
Launch price:	£16,450
Excellent:	£3500
Good:	£2500
Average:	£1500
Project:	£750

BMW
M5 (E34)

The E34 generation took the M5 squarely into the 1990s, thanks to substantially-modernised styling and a smooth new interior. The fabulous straight six received various modifications to boost power to 315bhp, pushing the top speed to a limited 155mph. King of the hill from the moment it was launched, the M5's intimacy, balance and pace were something rivals struggled to match. Further improved in 1994, when the 3.5-litre engine's output was raised to 340bhp – although top speed remained the same unless the owner removed the limiter.

SPECIFICATIONS
Years produced:	1988-1995 (11,098 in total)
Performance:	0-60mph: 6.5sec
	Top speed: 155mph
Power & torque:	315bhp/265lb ft
Engine:	Normally aspirated 3535cc straight six, petrol, electronic fuel injection, 24 valves
Drivetrain:	Front-engine RWD
Structure:	Monocoque
Transmission:	Five-speed manual
Weight:	1720kg

PRICE GUIDE
Launch price:	£31,295
Excellent:	£12,000
Good:	£8000
Average:	£5000
Project:	£3500

BMW
325i Sport (E30)

The E30 is another '80s icon, regarded as a yuppie's plaything at the time, but now seen as the ultimate evolution of Hofmeister's seminal designs of the '60s. BMW's small saloon lent itself well to every engine installed, but the ultimate 2.5-litre straight six offered the biggest dose of thrills. The Sport model's slightly out-of-place bodykit lessened its Q-car appeal but that wailing engine, controllable rear-biased handling and all-round quality made this the sports saloon to beat. Today, it's seen as an inexpensive road to RWD fun, and shabby examples are still cheap.

SPECIFICATIONS
Years produced:	1989-1991
Performance:	0-60mph: 7.5sec
	Top speed: 140mph
Power & torque:	169bhp/195lb ft
Engine:	Normally aspirated 2494cc straight six, petrol, electronic fuel injection, 12 valves
Drivetrain:	Front-engine RWD
Structure:	Monocoque
Transmission:	Five-speed manual
Weight:	1147kg

PRICE GUIDE
Launch price:	£17,250
Excellent:	£7500
Good:	£6000
Average:	£3500
Project:	£2000

BMW
325i Touring (E30)

No-one who bought a BMW 3-Series Touring did so thinking this 'estate' was a practical hold-all. What they were getting was a stylish and driveable alternative to a hot hatchback – one that just happened to have 195bhp and rear-wheel drive. A 325iX four-wheel-drive version was also offered, but only in left-hand-drive form – and as a consequence, few made it into the UK. Of all the 'cooking' E30s, the Touring has the most timeless appeal, and still commands a healthy premium over the saloons. As with all '80s BMWs, there is a huge gulf between the values of excellent and shabby examples.

SPECIFICATIONS
Years produced:	1989-1991
Performance:	0-60mph: 8.5sec
	Top speed: 140mph
Power & torque:	195bhp/170lb ft
Engine:	Normally aspirated 2693cc straight six, petrol, electronic fuel injection, 12 valves
Drivetrain:	Front-engine RWD
Structure:	Monocoque
Transmission:	Five-speed manual
Weight:	1200kg

PRICE GUIDE
Launch price:	£17,250
Excellent:	£5000
Good:	£3000
Average:	£2000
Project:	£750

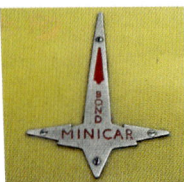

BOND

BOND STARTED life in 1948 with very spartan three-wheeler Minicars, the brainchild of founder Lawrie Bond. Although the Minicar continued until 1966, Bond diversified into more mature machines such as the 875 – three wheels and glassfibre bodywork – and the GT, which was a four-wheeled sports coupé using parts from the Herald bin. When Triumph moved on to the more powerful Vitesse, so did Bond, with the less visually appealing Equipe 2-Litre. The takeover by Reliant in 1970 killed off all these models, but the Bond name continued on the wacky Bug, a wedge-shaped three-wheeler designed purely for fun. Which is why it came only in bright tangerine...

BOND
Minicar three-wheeler

At the end of WW2 cars were at a premium, so engineer Lawrie Bond came up with a budget three-wheeler Britain could afford. The Bond Minicar was poverty motoring in the extreme: no roof, no doors, brakes only at the rear and precious little suspension. Its single-cylinder two-stroke 122cc motorcycle engine started life with just 5bhp, but gave 40mph and a claimed 104mpg. Minicars gradually became more refined and powerful, until production ended in 1966. The final Mark G had a roof, doors and hydraulic brakes.

SPECIFICATIONS

Years produced:	1948-1966 (24,484 in total)
Performance:	0-60mph: N/A
	Top speed: 50mph
Power & torque:	5-12bhp/N/A
Engine:	Normally aspirated 122cc, single cylinder two-stroke, petrol, carburettor
Drivetrain:	Front-engine FWD
Structure:	Monocoque, then separate chassis
Transmission:	Chain drive
Weight:	140kg

PRICE GUIDE

Launch price:	£199
Excellent:	£3750
Good:	£3000
Average:	£1500
Project:	£700

BOND
GT 2+2/GT4S

In 1963, Bond expanded into the world of specialist sportscars – with four wheels. But the full quotient of wheels still didn't fulfil the firm's claims that this was 'the most beautiful car in the world', although this glassfibre coupé on a Triumph Herald chassis was a neat enough effort. Initially the engine was the 1147cc from the Triumph Spitfire, which rose to 1296cc in 1967 when the Spitfire expanded. The improved GT4S of 1964 had four headlamps, a boot that actually opened and greater headroom that helped to up comfort levels.

SPECIFICATIONS

Years produced:	1963-1970 (2949 in total)
Performance:	0-60mph: 20.0sec
	Top speed: 91mph
Power & torque:	67bhp/67lb ft
Engine:	Normally aspirated 1147cc four cylinder, petrol, carburettor, 8 valves
Drivetrain:	Front-engine RWD
Structure:	Separate chassis
Transmission:	Four-speed manual
Weight:	737kg

PRICE GUIDE

Launch price:	£822
Excellent:	£3500
Good:	£2200
Average:	£1400
Project:	£400

BOND
Equipe 2-litre

Having built a Herald-based sports coupé, it was only logical that Bond would try something similar with the Vitesse chassis. The result, in 1967, was the Equipe GT, also known as the 2-Litre. The styling of the glassfibre/steel-panelled vehicle was totally different to Bond's previous version; more square-rigged and heavier. However, the extra weight didn't matter too much, as the additional power of the Triumph straight six (95bhp at first, 104bhp from 1968) gave this specialist sportscar adequate performance, with 100mph eventually obtainable.

SPECIFICATIONS

Years produced:	1967-1970 (1432 in total)
Performance:	0-60mph: 10.7sec
	Top speed: 102mph
Power & torque:	95bhp/117lb ft
Engine:	Normally aspirated 1998cc straight six, petrol, carburettor, 12 valves
Drivetrain:	Front-engine RWD
Structure:	Separate chassis
Transmission:	Four-speed manual
Weight:	914kg

PRICE GUIDE

Launch price:	£1096
Excellent:	£5000
Good:	£2750
Average:	£1500
Project:	£450

BOND
Bug 700E

This funky and fun three-wheeler was built for pure entertainment purposes by Reliant, Bond's new owner. A cheesy car for a cheesy decade, its Ogle Design-styled wedge shape gave the two passengers access via the pull-forward canopy. The only colour officially available was a very vibrant tangerine. The engines were Reliant: a 700cc unit offering 29bhp, and 31bhp on the ES model, followed by a 748cc offering 32bhp in 1973. Utterly mad, but the classic car world is all the richer for bizarre machines such as these.

SPECIFICATIONS

Years produced:	1970-1974 (2270 in total)
Performance:	0-60mph: 23.2sec
	Top speed: 76mph
Power & torque:	29bhp/35lb ft
Engine:	Normally aspirated 700cc four cylinder, petrol, carburettor, 8 valves
Drivetrain:	Front-engine FWD
Structure:	Separate chassis
Transmission:	Four-speed manual
Weight:	394kg

PRICE GUIDE

Launch price:	£629
Excellent:	£6000
Good:	£3250
Average:	£1750
Project:	£1000

BORGWARD

IN 1929, car radiator manufacturer Carl Borgward became a director of Hansa Lloyd AG; gradually this company became just Borgward. Its stylish models were typified by the large and sleek-looking 2400, which was the first European car to have its own automatic transmission, and the pretty Isabella, of 1954 to 1961, which was named after the founder's wife. Well over 200,000 were sold, thanks to the looks and the car's reputation for being almost bulletproof. Problems elsewhere in the conglomerate that Borgward was a part of led to bankruptcy in 1961, even though the company itself was still making money. Borgward himself died just two years later.

BORGWARD
Isabella TS saloon

A superbly-engineered car that was a revelation in its day. Alloy-head 1500 engine puts out an impressive 75bhp, which Ford only just surpassed eight years later with the Cortina GT, and no Cortina ever enjoyed the Isabella's independent rear suspension. Before he became a Vauxhall tuning guru, Bill Blydenstein successfully raced one in the 1950s. Brakes are another strong point and even the four-speed column change is a delight to use. Thanks to a strong following in the car's native Germany, parts supply is almost total.

SPECIFICATIONS

Years produced:	1954-1961 (202,862 in total)
Performance:	0-60mph: 16.0sec
	Top speed: 95mph
Power & torque:	75bhp/85lb ft
Engine:	Normally aspirated 1493cc four cylinder, petrol, carburettor, 8 valves
Drivetrain:	Front-engine RWD
Structure:	Separate chassis
Transmission:	Four-speed manual
Weight:	1080kg

PRICE GUIDE

Launch price:	£1124
Excellent:	£7500
Good:	£6000
Average:	£3000
Project:	£1000

BORGWARD
Isabella coupé

Generally considered to be Carl Borgward's masterpiece, the Isabella coupé was initially conceived as an image booster for the firm. The 2+2 oozes class, has a decent turn of speed and handles tidily with its all-independent coil-sprung suspension and rear swing axles. The unburstable engines even run happily on unleaded fuel without any alteration. A cabriolet version was also built, but these are much rarer. However, the drop-tops are very highly thought of in Germany, and can easily fetch twice the price of a coupé.

SPECIFICATIONS

Years produced:	1955-1961
Performance:	0-60mph: 16.9sec
	Top speed: 81mph
Power & torque:	60bhp/79lb ft
Engine:	Normally aspirated 1493cc four cylinder, petrol, carburettor, 8 valves
Drivetrain:	Front-engine RWD
Structure:	Separate chassis
Transmission:	Four-speed manual
Weight:	1080kg

PRICE GUIDE

Launch price:	£1874
Excellent:	£13,500
Good:	£10,000
Average:	£5500
Project:	£1750

BRICKLIN

MALCOLM BRICKLIN had a continuing relationship with the automotive industry, starting out as an importer for the Subaru 360. That didn't work out, and he turned his hands to thoughts of building his own 'safety sports car'. The Bricklin Vehicle Corporation was set-up in St John, New Brunswick in Canada – taking advantage of government enterprise loans to help support an area of high unemployment. Production costs caused by material wastage and general body-fit problems amounted to $6300 per car, and production rapidly wound up. Bricklin returned to the industry in the 1980s, joining forces with Zastava to import the Yugo 45 into the USA.

BRICKLIN
SV-1

Safety cars were all the rage in the early 1970s, and Malcolm Bricklin's attempt at building a 'safety sports car' looked promising it its early days. The gullwing design was wedgy and edgy, although performance didn't quite live up to the looks. Early cars were powered by an AMC engine before being replaced by a Ford V8 the following year. Gullwing doors suffered from quality issues, and hampered sales. Canadian government stumped up $23m to assist the company, but lost out when the venture failed. Insert DeLorean comparisons here…

SPECIFICATIONS

Years produced:	1974-1975 (2891 in total)
Performance:	0-60mph: 9.0sec
	Top speed: 120mph
Power & torque:	175bhp/254lb ft
Engine:	Normally aspirated 5766cc V8, petrol, carburettor, 16 valves
Drivetrain:	Front-engine RWD
Structure:	Monocoque
Transmission:	Three-speed automatic
Weight:	1574kg

PRICE GUIDE

Launch price:	N/A
Excellent:	£20,000
Good:	£15,000
Average:	£10,000
Project:	£5500

BRISTOL

WITH SPARE production capacity after the end of the war, the Bristol Aeroplane Company decided to enter the car-making business and acquired the rights to the various pre-war BMW models. It was soon building the streamlined, fast and luxurious 403 using aviation principles of construction. The prestige machines continued thereafter, being expensively handmade in small numbers for well-heeled customers. Chrysler V8 engines were introduced with the 407 of 1961. 1970s, '80s and '90s saw less new model development, although the 200mph Fighter made up for it in 2007. Rescued from administration by Frazer-Nash Engineering group in 2011 – new models to come.

BRISTOL
400

Bristol Cars was formed when the Bristol Aeroplane Company joined forces with Frazer-Nash's parent company, AFN. Before the war, AFN was the concessionaire for BMW in the UK, so after Bristol took possession of BMW's designs, AFN was the natural choice for a build partner. The 400 was the first fruit of the combined companies' efforts, and was clearly based on a mixture of the pre-war BMW 326 (chassis) and 327/80 (body). Many changes were made – and aeroplane levels of build quality were a clear benefit.

SPECIFICATIONS

Years produced:	1947-1950 (700 in total)
Performance:	0-60mph: 14.7sec
	Top speed: 94mph
Power & torque:	80bhp/96lb ft
Engine:	Normally aspirated 1971cc straight six, petrol, carburettor, 12 valves
Drivetrain:	Front-engine RWD
Structure:	Separate chassis
Transmission:	Four-speed manual
Weight:	1118kg

PRICE GUIDE

Launch price:	£2374
Excellent:	£55,000
Good:	£40,000
Average:	£20,000
Project:	£12,500

BRISTOL
401/403

Putting right the 400's main failing – its ungainly body – the 401 was introduced initially for export markets only. Its handsome styling was the result of extensive wind tunnel work, after a basic design was submitted by Superleggera Touring. It was a look way ahead of its time, merely let down by a lack of power. This shortcoming was put right five years later, with the appearance of the 403 – and a welcome upgrade to 100bhp. Bristols were expensive and well crafted – the latter trait keeps them surprisingly usable today.

SPECIFICATIONS

Years produced:	1949-1955 (950 in total)
Performance:	0-60mph: 15.1sec
	Top speed: 97mph
Power & torque:	85bhp/107lb ft
Engine:	Normally aspirated 1971cc straight six, petrol, carburettor, 12 valves
Drivetrain:	Front-engine RWD
Structure:	Separate chassis
Transmission:	Four-speed manual
Weight:	1224kg

PRICE GUIDE

Launch price:	£3214
Excellent:	£42,500
Good:	£19,000
Average:	£9500
Project:	£7500

BRISTOL
404

Essentially, the 404 was a short-wheelbase Arnolt-Bristol chassis married to an exquisitely styled two-door coupé bodyshell. But it was not without problems. There was the small issue of price (it cost twice as much as a Jaguar XK120) and a lack of ultimate power compared with its Coventry rival. There were problems with the construction, too, and the aluminium body and pitch pine frame have caused problems for owners in later years. But for all its issues, the 404 looks at least allowed it to break away from its Teutonic forebears.

SPECIFICATIONS

Years produced:	1953-1955 (52 in total)
Performance:	0-60mph: N/A
	Top speed: 110mph
Power & torque:	105bhp/123lb ft
Engine:	Normally aspirated 1971cc straight six, petrol, carburettor, 12 valves
Drivetrain:	Front-engine RWD
Structure:	Separate chassis
Transmission:	Four-speed manual
Weight:	1039kg

PRICE GUIDE

Launch price:	£3543
Excellent:	£75,000
Good:	£32,500
Average:	£20,000
Project:	£10,000

BRISTOL
405

This saloon was effectively a long-wheelbase version of the 404 (it had four doors). It went on to score significantly more commercial success, and was the first car produced by Bristol to have an opening bootlid. Unlike the 404, which, through its extensive use of wood in its construction, has a low survival rate, the 405 has fared much better over the years. That's mainly because most of the wood in the body is *above* the waistline – a boon in damp climes. It was a pretty four-door GT that was crying out for more power.

SPECIFICATIONS

Years produced:	1954-1956 (340 in total)
Performance:	0-60mph: N/A
	Top speed: 110mph
Power & torque:	105bhp/123lb ft
Engine:	Normally aspirated 1971cc straight six, petrol, carburettor, 12 valves
Drivetrain:	Front-engine RWD
Structure:	Separate chassis
Transmission:	Four-speed manual with overdrive
Weight:	1230kg

PRICE GUIDE (Convertible in brackets)

Launch price:	£3189
Excellent:	£35,000 (£75,000)
Good:	£24,000 (£50,000)
Average:	£17000 (£40,000)
Project:	£9000 (£30,000)

BRISTOL
406

The 406 ended up being the last Bristol to be powered by the BMW-derived straight six, but the first of a long line of cars that would use essentially the same body, with a series of running updates. In terms of power, the 406 had no more than the 405, despite its engine being enlarged to 2.2 litres, and performance with this large body was predictably leisurely. The brakes were improved, though, featuring discs front and rear, and the back suspension got a Watt linkage. More would come with the arrival of the V8-powered cars.

SPECIFICATIONS

Years produced:	1958-1961 (292 in total)
Performance:	0-60mph: N/A
	Top speed: 106mph
Power & torque:	105bhp/129lb ft
Engine:	Normally aspirated 2216cc straight six, petrol, carburettor, 12 valves
Drivetrain:	Front-engine RWD
Structure:	Separate chassis
Transmission:	Four-speed manual with overdrive
Weight:	1365kg

PRICE GUIDE

Launch price:	£4494
Excellent:	£30,000
Good:	£13,500
Average:	£10,000
Project:	£5000

BRISTOL
407/408/409/410

Changes in the ownership of Bristol Cars meant that it was now a separate entity to the aeroplane manufacturer. Although that wouldn't make much difference to the high-quality cars produced, it marked the point when the Chrysler V8 was finally installed under the long bonnet of the 406, giving the elegant sporting saloon the performance to match its looks. With a top speed of over 125mph, the Bristol became a credible alternative to Aston Martin and Jaguar. American muscle under the bonnet also meant improved parts and support.

SPECIFICATIONS
Years produced: 1961-1969 (88/83/74/79 in total)
Performance: 0-60mph: 8.8sec
Top speed: 130mph
Power & torque: 250bhp/340lb ft
Engine: Normally aspirated 5211cc V8, petrol, carburettor, 16 valves
Drivetrain: Front-engine RWD
Structure: Separate chassis
Transmission: Three-speed automatic
Weight: 1600kg

PRICE GUIDE
Launch price: £4848
Excellent: £30,000
Good: £15,000
Average: £8500
Project: £3500

BRISTOL
411

Considered by Bristol aficionados to be the best of the V8-powered 400 Series cars, the 411 appeared at the end of the 1960s, still looking understated and elegant. This version sported a 6.3-litre version of the Chrysler Type B V8 engine and could effortlessly top 140mph after sprinting from 0-60mph in seven seconds. It might not have been the ideal power unit during the oil crisis of the early '70s, but Bristol continued to sell cars to its loyal customer base while those around went under – and continues to do so against the odds today.

SPECIFICATIONS
Years produced: 1969-1976 (600 in total)
Performance: 0-60mph: 7.0sec
Top speed: 140mph
Power & torque: 335bhp/335lb ft
Engine: Normally aspirated 6556cc V8, petrol, carburettor, 16 valves
Drivetrain: Front-engine RWD
Structure: Separate chassis
Transmission: Three-speed automatic
Weight: 1712kg

PRICE GUIDE
Launch price: £8793
Excellent: £32,500
Good: £17,000
Average: £9500
Project: £4000

BRISTOL
412

Even maestros have a bad day. That could explain the square-looking Zagato styling of the 412. But despite being launched during the blackest days of the '70s with a gigantic V8 engine, the 412 continued to sell for Bristol, even building up a modest waiting list. The quality was as deep rooted as ever, and the chassis was straight from the tried-and-tested 411, although the targa roof panel was a genuine innovation for the company. The 6.6-litre V8 was downsized to 5.9 litres in the late '70s, but the grunt remained intact.

SPECIFICATIONS
Years produced: 1975-1980
Performance: 0-60mph: 7.4sec
Top speed: 140mph
Power & torque: 335bhp/N/A
Engine: Normally aspirated 6556cc V8, petrol, carburettor, 16 valves
Drivetrain: Front-engine RWD
Structure: Separate chassis
Transmission: Three-speed automatic
Weight: 1715kg

PRICE GUIDE
Launch price: £14,584
Excellent: £26,000
Good: £11,500
Average: £6000
Project: £2800

BRISTOL
603/Britannia

In the late 1970s, Bristol started offering a two-model range: the 412 for those looking for open-topped motoring, and the 603, an elegantly-styled fastback with saloon levels of interior accommodation. It was an interesting mix, and one that ensured the firm's survival into the '80s. Under that new aluminium body lay the same basic separate chassis found in the 412 (and its predecessors), and it was none the worse for this. By now, Bristol was positively delighted with its image of exclusivity, and had a number of high-profile fans – notably writer LJK Setright – in its ranks.

SPECIFICATIONS
Years produced: 1976-1982
Performance: 0-60mph: 8.6sec
Top speed: 140mph
Power & torque: 335bhp/270lb ft
Engine: Normally aspirated 5898cc V8, petrol, carburettor, 16 valves
Drivetrain: Front-engine RWD
Structure: Separate chassis
Transmission: Three-speed automatic
Weight: 1783kg

PRICE GUIDE
Launch price: £19,661
Excellent: £30,000
Good: £17,500
Average: £12,000
Project: £7500

BRISTOL
Beaufighter convertible

An interesting one, this, as although it was yet another revision of the continuously-evolving model line, the Beaufighter had rather more (undisclosed) power than the 412 it was based upon. The secret was, of course, turbocharging – which by the time the Beaufighter appeared, everyone was getting in on. Although Bristol was coy about power figures, or lending out test cars, the performance had leapt forwards – 0-60mph in 5.9 seconds with a top speed of 150mph. But importantly, this fine car remains rather less obvious than a Bentley Turbo R.

SPECIFICATIONS
Years produced: 1980-1993
Performance: 0-60mph: 5.9sec
Top speed: 150mph
Power & torque: c.400bhp/N/A
Engine: Turbocharged 5898cc V8, petrol, carburettor, 16 valves
Drivetrain: Front-engine RWD
Structure: Separate chassis
Transmission: Three-speed automatic
Weight: 1746kg

PRICE GUIDE
Launch price: £37,999
Excellent: £27,500
Good: £11,500
Average: £6000
Project: £2800

BRISTOL
Brigand

It was inevitable the turbocharged version of the Chrysler V8 that was so praised by Beaufighter customers would find its way into the Britannia. And just as it did with the targa-topped car's upgrade, Bristol re-named its coupé, launching the freshly-boosted Britannia as a brand new car. Considering the chassis and suspension set-up originated from the late 1940s – albeit with countless changes – it's remarkable the car remained unchanged when given an additional 20% of power. Specialist help is readily available, most notably from Bristol itself.

SPECIFICATIONS
Years produced:	1982-1993
Performance:	0-60mph: 5.9sec
	Top speed: 150mph
Power & torque:	N/A/N/A
Engine:	Turbocharged 5898cc V8, petrol, carburettor, 16 valves
Drivetrain:	Front-engine RWD
Structure:	Separate chassis
Transmission:	Three-speed automatic
Weight:	1746kg

PRICE GUIDE
Launch price:	£46,843
Excellent:	£30,000
Good:	£17,500
Average:	£12,000
Project:	£7500

CADILLAC

ORIGINALLY THE Henry Ford Company, the American equivalent of Rolls-Royce changed name in 1902 (after Ford left) to that of the founder of Detroit. It became part of the General Motors group in 1909 and served as the conglomerate's high-status brand. Cadillacs were all about visual impression, luxury and power; during the 1930s the marque even offered V16 models as well as V12s. After the war, Caddys grew ever more excessive, as personified by the 1959 cars with their towering fins and rocketship styling. Things calmed down during the following decades, although there was always an element of over-the-top excess to Cadillac that persists to this day.

CADILLAC
Eldorado Biarritz

The popularity of the 1959 Eldorado Biarritz has been enduring in the UK. It's probably because of the over-the-top styling, which for many represents the absolute zenith of US car design thanks to the stylised fins and rocket-shaped lights. The range-topping convertible boasted huge levels of equipment – and the Eldorado also came in Seville coupe and Brougham limo guise. Masses of room and all the wafty road presence you'll ever need make these cars surprisingly easy to live with. As long as you have space... and a thick skin.

SPECIFICATIONS
Years produced:	1959
Performance:	0-60mph: 12.0sec
	Top speed: 115mph
Power & torque:	345bhp/435lb ft
Engine:	Normally aspirated 6832cc V8, petrol, carburettor, 16 valves
Drivetrain:	Front-engine RWD
Structure:	Separate chassis
Transmission:	Three-speed automatic
Weight:	2295kg

PRICE GUIDE
Launch price:	N/A
Excellent:	£40,000
Good:	£30,000
Average:	£18,500
Project:	£8000

CATERHAM

WHEN LOTUS stopped building its basic Seven sportscar in 1973, the rights were acquired by Caterham Cars, a Lotus dealer. The Kent firm has now built the Seven for far longer than the 16 years the model's creator stuck with it for. The original 1950s styling may be sacred, but elsewhere the car has been comprehensively updated with Vauxhall, Ford and Rover mechanicals. Caterham dabbled with something different to the Seven only once; the C21, with its expanded bodywork, proved not to be a success and only 48 were built between 1995 and 1999. The company has stuck doggedly with the Seven ever since, and seems likely to do so for many more years to come.

CATERHAM
Super Seven S3

Thank Colin Chapman for the fact you can still buy the Seven today. Taking Lotus upmarket in the early 1970s, he sold the lucrative model to dealer Caterham Cars, which quickly returned the sporting icon to production and has never looked back. The tubular steel chassis, bodied in aluminium, has remained almost unchanged since, although engines have been updated to reflect improvements in technology. Prices depend on condition and spec rather than age and mileage, so decide how much performance you want before going shopping.

SPECIFICATIONS
Years produced:	1974-1995
Performance:	0-60mph: 7.7sec
	Top speed: 99mph
Power & torque:	84bhp/96lb ft
Engine:	Normally aspirated 1598cc four cylinder, petrol, carburettor, 8 valves
Drivetrain:	Front-engine RWD
Structure:	Spaceframe
Transmission:	Four/five-speed manual
Weight:	518kg

PRICE GUIDE
Launch price:	£2887
Excellent:	£12,500
Good:	£10,000
Average:	£7000
Project:	£4500

CHEVROLET

ONE OF the great American marques, often immortalised in song, Chevrolet was founded in 1911 by Billy Durant and Louis Chevrolet. Profits from the firm allowed Durant to buy General Motors in 1917, and thus Chevy became a major constituent of GM. It was soon the US's best-selling brand, building over a million cars annually by 1927. Designs in the 1950s were futuristic and powerful, with Chevy V8s becoming a legend in their own right. The glassfibre Corvette sportscar made a similar name for itself – as did the later Corvair, but for all the wrong, safety-related reasons. Recent times have been turbulent, but Chevrolet still remains the archetypical American car maker.

CHEVROLET
Corvette C1

Conceived as an image-builder, the Corvette was built in glassfibre because that was the quickest and cheapest way to get it into production. Only 300 were completed in 1953, all hand-built; these now command almost double the prices quoted here for '54/55 'Vettes. Most of this first series of Corvettes used a 3.8-litre straight six, and all but seven of the paltry 700 built in 1955 had a new 4.3-litre V8. The low numbers were because GM still had plenty of '54 Corvettes left to sell and nearly pulled the plug. Now, of course, these models are very collectible.

SPECIFICATIONS

Years produced:	1953-1955 (4640 in total)
Performance:	0-60mph: 11.0sec
	Top speed: 107mph
Power & torque:	150bhp/172lb ft
Engine:	Normally aspirated 3859cc straight six, petrol, carburettor, 12 valves
Drivetrain:	Front-engine RWD
Structure:	Separate chassis
Transmission:	Two-speed automatic
Weight:	1227kg

PRICE GUIDE

Launch price:	N/A
Excellent:	£100,000
Good:	£75,500
Average:	£50,000
Project:	£27,500

CHEVROLET
Bel Air coupe

These are the cars that best encapsulate the optimistic era of '50s America, the dawn of rock 'n' roll, and any number of roadside diners. The Bel Air tag generically attached to them is actually the range-topping trim level – there was also the One-Fifty and Two-Ten. A radical departure from previous dull and dumpy Chevrolets, the models' body styling was updated each year with ever-growing fins, and this was the car that introduced the small-block Chevy V8 engine, in 1955. Straight-six versions were also available.

SPECIFICATIONS

Years produced:	1955-1957
Performance:	0-60mph: 9.7sec
	Top speed: 105mph
Power & torque:	180bhp/260lb ft
Engine:	Normally aspirated 4344cc V8, petrol, carburettor, 16 valves
Drivetrain:	Front-engine RWD
Structure:	Separate chassis
Transmission:	Three-speed automatic
Weight:	1515kg

PRICE GUIDE

Launch price:	£2326
Excellent:	£20,000
Good:	£15,000
Average:	£10,000
Project:	£5000

CHEVROLET
Bel Air convertible

As ever, it's the soft-top in the range that brings in the big money. Added to that, all the 1955-1957 convertibles were sold in range-topping Bel Air trim. Of the three years – which has led to devotees referring to these cars as 'Tri-Chevys' – the 1957 incarnation is the most popular, and therefore most expensive. Not only do you get more chrome and bigger fins, but there was a larger V8, with tuning options all the way up to fuel injection as used in the Corvette. Although never officially marketed in the UK, plenty have found their way here over the years.

SPECIFICATIONS

Years produced:	1955-1957
Performance:	0-60mph: 9.7sec
	Top speed: 106mph
Power & torque:	180bhp/260lb ft
Engine:	Normally aspirated 4638cc V8, petrol, carburettor, 16 valves
Drivetrain:	Front-engine RWD
Structure:	Separate chassis
Transmission:	Three-speed automatic
Weight:	1550kg

PRICE GUIDE

Launch price:	N/A
Excellent:	£30,000
Good:	£25,000
Average:	£18,000
Project:	£10,000

CHEVROLET
Corvette C1

This is the version that started the Corvette legend, thanks to the input of two men. Bill Mitchell turned it from good-looking into gorgeous and Zora Arkus-Duntov added power. By early '57 even the carburetted version (now 4.7 litres) was up from 195bhp to as high as 270bhp. In place of the old two-speed auto, a manual gearbox was now standard. Sales rose five-fold, just don't ask about the handling. The optional Rochester fuel-injection 'Fuelie' versions introduced in 1957 attract a 20-25% premium on the prices shown here.

SPECIFICATIONS

Years produced:	1956-1957 (9806 in total)
Performance:	0-60mph: N/A
	Top speed: 119mph
Power & torque:	195bhp/260lb ft
Engine:	Normally aspirated 4344cc V8, petrol, carburettor, 16 valves
Drivetrain:	Front-engine RWD
Structure:	Separate chassis
Transmission:	Four-speed manual
Weight:	1227kg

PRICE GUIDE

Launch price:	N/A
Excellent:	£42,500
Good:	£36,500
Average:	£20,000
Project:	£12,500

CHEVROLET
Corvette C1

Evolved styling provides a more aggressive face, along with more efficient (and trendy) twin headlamps. Power rose again, with even base models getting 230bhp, although a golden rule for Corvettes (then and now) is the higher the quoted power output, the more you pay. To this might be added: and the more you wonder about the wisdom of trying to control up to 290bhp on 5.5in crossply tyres. The 1961 model brought new ducktail rear styling, and the following year engine capacity increased to 5.4 litres/327ci, with up to 360bhp.

SPECIFICATIONS
Years produced:	1958-1962 (54,569 in total)
Performance:	0-60mph: 5.9sec
	Top speed: 131mph
Power & torque:	270bhp/285lb ft
Engine:	Normally aspirated 4638cc V8, petrol, carburettor, 16 valves
Drivetrain:	Front-engine RWD
Structure:	Separate chassis
Transmission:	Four-speed manual
Weight:	1397kg

PRICE GUIDE
Launch price:	N/A
Excellent:	£40,000
Good:	£34,000
Average:	£21,000
Project:	£15,000

CHEVROLET
Corvair

The Corvair was conceived as General Motors' answer to the rising tide of imports flowing into the USA by the late-'50s. The characterful rear-engined air-cooled saloon was as far removed from the Detroit norm as it comes, and for its brief production run, the first-generation model sold very well indeed. However, its unpredictable handling and rearward weight bias incurred the wrath of safety campaigner Ralph Nader, who declared it 'Unsafe at any speed'. The two-door coupé has a cult following, and the Monza turbo (1962-1964) is now quite collectible.

SPECIFICATIONS
Years produced:	1960-1964 (1,271,089 in total)
Performance:	0-60mph: 14.4sec
	Top speed: 101mph
Power & torque:	80bhp/125lb ft
Engine:	Normally aspirated 2296cc flat six, petrol, carburettor, 12 valves
Drivetrain:	Rear-engine RWD
Structure:	Separate chassis
Transmission:	Four-speed manual
Weight:	1095kg

PRICE GUIDE
Launch price:	N/A
Excellent:	£7500
Good:	£5000
Average:	£3000
Project:	£2000

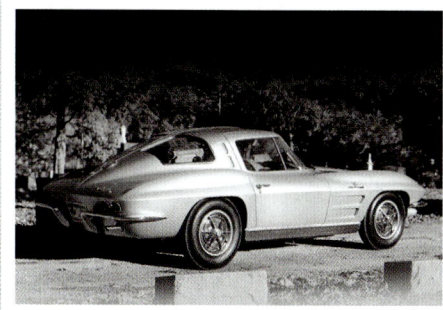

CHEVROLET
Corvette Sting Ray C2

Everything but the engine and box were changed for this new version of the 'Vette, power steering and independent rear suspension were useful advances and the Corvette now came as a coupé or convertible. More of the latter were sold, and prices are now roughly the same as for coupés. Sting Rays from 1964 are worth around 20% less than quoted, thanks to not having the '63 coupés' split rear window, or the later cars' disc brakes. From 1965 a 'big-block' 6.5-litre V8 was added; these, and fuel-injection cars, attract 30-50% more than quoted.

SPECIFICATIONS
Years produced:	1963-1967 (117,966 in total)
Performance:	0-60mph: 6.2sec
	Top speed: 142mph
Power & torque:	360bhp/352lb ft
Engine:	Normally aspirated 5354cc V8, petrol, carburettor, 16 valves
Drivetrain:	Front-engine RWD
Structure:	Separate chassis
Transmission:	Three/four-speed manual
Weight:	1377kg

PRICE GUIDE
Launch price:	£3323
Excellent:	£42,500
Good:	£35,000
Average:	£18,500
Project:	£10,000

CHEVROLET
Camaro

The Camaro was General Motors' response to the success of the Ford Mustang, and a very good response it was, too. The 'Coke bottle' styling of the coupé body for this first generation of Camaros was spot-on for the time, yet still looks good today, and this was the perfect home for exploiting Chevrolet's range of ever-more-powerful V8 engines. You'll need to pay more than quoted for any that come with an 'SS' performance upgrade package, and really big amounts for those with the initials 'Z28' attached. These excite the serious collectors.

SPECIFICATIONS
Years produced:	1967-1969
Performance:	0-60mph: 9.1sec
	Top speed: 125mph
Power & torque:	325bhp/410lb ft
Engine:	Normally aspirated 6478cc V8, petrol, carburettor, 16 valves
Drivetrain:	Front-engine RWD
Structure:	Separate chassis
Transmission:	Two/three-speed auto/four-speed manual
Weight:	1403kg

PRICE GUIDE
Launch price:	N/A
Excellent:	£17,500
Good:	£14,000
Average:	£9000
Project:	£5000

CHEVROLET
Corvette Stingray C3

Based on the Mako Shark II concept, the Corvette's late-'60s makeover is largely defined by its long, pointed nose and fat tyres – at 8in wide for 1969, they were the largest on any car at the time. Coupés started to outsell convertibles, so the latter are now worth around 25% more. Once again, engines come in a variety of small- and big-block options, with outputs ranging from 300-435bhp. Our prices are for the former – expect double for the latter and fill the gap with anything in between. Emissions regulations put the squeeze on power from 1971.

SPECIFICATIONS
Years produced:	1968-1972 (133,449 in total)
Performance:	0-60mph: 7.2sec
	Top speed: 135mph
Power & torque:	370bhp/370lb ft
Engine:	Normally aspirated 5733cc V8, petrol, carburettor, 16 valves
Drivetrain:	Front-engine RWD
Structure:	Separate chassis
Transmission:	Four-speed manual
Weight:	1402kg

PRICE GUIDE
Launch price:	£3432
Excellent:	£20,000
Good:	£15,000
Average:	£9500
Project:	£5000

CHEVROLET
Camaro

For 1970, a brand new monocoque body saw the car become an independent model line in its own right. It was offered with four-, six- and V8 engines spanning 95-375bhp, so there really was a Camaro for every American. As the 1970s progressed, the car became fatter, slower and weighed down with anti-smog equipment. The Z28 was the top of the heap, and is the most collectable of all Camaros – but not exactly rare, with 250,000 built. Badge-engineered Pontiac Firebird was more widely known in Europe thanks to numerous film appearances.

SPECIFICATIONS

Years produced:	1970-1981 (1,811,973 in total)
Performance:	0-60mph: 7.5sec
	Top speed: 125mph
Power & torque:	360bhp/360lb ft
Engine:	Normally aspirated 6573cc V8, petrol, carburettor, 16 valves
Drivetrain:	Front-engine RWD
Structure:	Monocoque
Transmission:	Four-speed manual
Weight:	1617kg

PRICE GUIDE (Z28 in brackets)

Launch price:	N/A
Excellent:	£8000
Good:	£6000
Average:	£4000
Project:	£2000

CHEVROLET
Corvette Stingray C3

Corvettes from this era might still look the part, but are more for your ageing rock star. By 1975 output of the base model's 5.7-litre V8 had fallen as low as 165bhp (though weight had gone up significantly) and the 7.5-litre big-block had been consigned to the dustbin. A year later the poor-selling convertible joined it. That of course means a big-block or convertible (or both) 'Vette from this era is worth more than a small-block coupé. Strangely, despite all this, sales of Corvettes continued to rise, which also contributes to their bargain prices now.

SPECIFICATIONS

Years produced:	1973-1977 (202,202 in total)
Performance:	0-60mph: 7.4sec
	Top speed: 124mph
Power & torque:	250bhp/285lb ft
Engine:	Normally aspirated 7440cc V8, petrol, carburettor, 16 valves
Drivetrain:	Front-engine RWD
Structure:	Separate chassis
Transmission:	Four-speed manual
Weight:	1600kg

PRICE GUIDE

Launch price:	N/A
Excellent:	£15,000
Good:	£12,000
Average:	£7000
Project:	£3500

CHEVROLET
Corvette C3

The main change for the Corvette's 25th anniversary year was the adoption of fastback styling for the coupé – no convertibles were built in these years and the Stingray name was gone. The only engine size offered was Chevrolet's ubiquitous 350ci/5.7-litre small-block, though at least its output had risen over its predecessor's. Base models from 1978-80 offer 185-195bhp, with the preferable L82 option ranging from 220-230bhp (also add 30-35% to the price tag). For 1981 and '82, only a single version was offered, with 190-200bhp.

SPECIFICATIONS

Years produced:	1978-1982 (182,219 in total)
Performance:	0-60mph: 7.7sec
	Top speed: 130mph
Power & torque:	190bhp/280lb ft
Engine:	Normally aspirated 5733cc V8, petrol, carburettor, 16 valves
Drivetrain:	Front-engine RWD
Structure:	Separate chassis
Transmission:	Three-speed automatic
Weight:	1677kg

PRICE GUIDE

Launch price:	N/A
Excellent:	£14,000
Good:	£10,000
Average:	£6000
Project:	£2750

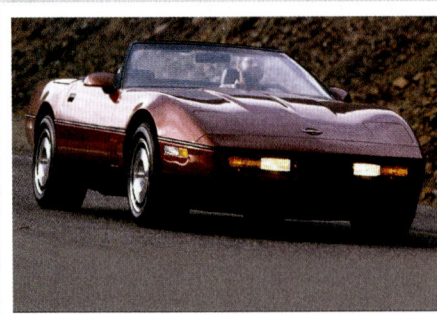

CHEVROLET
Corvette C4

After taking a year out to solve production problems, Chevrolet came back with an all-new and vastly improved Corvette in 1984. Sadly, the 'Vette's image was blunted by styling which – when compared with what had gone before – was clean and tidy rather than wild and rebellious. Fans welcomed the return of a convertible version in 1986, now worth around 40% more than a coupé. The real collectible arrived in 1990, though, in the shape of the ZR-1 coupé. Lotus was involved in developing the aluminium four-cam V8 and the handling settings.

SPECIFICATIONS

Years produced:	1984-1996 (366,227 in total)
Performance:	0-60mph: 6.0sec
	Top speed: 155mph
Power & torque:	245bhp/340lb ft
Engine:	Normally aspirated 5733cc V8, petrol, electronic fuel injection, 16 valves
Drivetrain:	Front-engine RWD
Structure:	Chassis and glassfibre body
Transmission:	Six-speed manual
Weight:	1523kg

PRICE GUIDE

Launch price:	£28,757
Excellent:	£15,000
Good:	£12,000
Average:	£9500
Project:	£7500

CHRYSLER UK

THE AMERICAN giant Chrysler took over the Rootes Group in 1967 and added Simca to the mix. It didn't actually use the Chrysler badge on cars until the 180 of 1970, and it was another six years before the name replaced Hillman on the Avenger. The Alpine and Horizon were produced in conjunction with Chrysler France, and the Sunbeam (see Talbot) was an emergency development of the Avenger, but the Americans soon had enough and sold out to Peugeot in 1978. It in turn applied Talbot badges to most of the range the following year, leaving the final European car to wear a Chrysler badge as the 2-Litre, a development of the Chrysler 180 that had started the game. That continued until 1980.

CHRYSLER
180/2-Litre

When it arrived in 1970, the 180 suffered from an identity crisis. Known as the Simca 1610 in France, and the Chrysler 180 in the UK, the car was seen as 'foreign' in both 'home' markets. Vaguely handsome styling and a capable chassis were never going to be enough to save the car marketed as 'an American in Paris', and as its ten-year life went on, sales slowed to a trickle. Rare and almost impossible to find now (rust, apathy...), especially the Spanish-built Barreiros diesel-engined model. The model to have (if you must) is the 2-litre in automatic form.

SPECIFICATIONS	
Years produced:	1970-1980
Performance:	0-60mph: 13.6sec
	Top speed: 99mph
Power & torque:	97bhp/106lb ft
Engine:	Normally aspirated 1812cc four cylinder, petrol, carburettor, 8 valves
Drivetrain:	Front-engine RWD
Structure:	Monocoque
Transmission:	Four-speed manual/three-speed auto
Weight:	1095kg

PRICE GUIDE	
Launch price:	£1498
Excellent:	£1500
Good:	£1000
Average:	£750
Project:	£500

CHRYSLER
Alpine

Chrysler had huge ambition for its European division during the early 1970s – and using the diverse Rootes and Simca ranges as a starting point, drew up a modern-looking range of FWD hatchbacks. First off the blocks was the Alpine in 1975, which was good enough to win the European Car of The Year award. It looked smart and of the moment, but the politics of its maker took over, and when the Americans pulled out in 1978, the Chryslers became Talbots. Should have been more successful, but the rusty, tappety Alpine really was less than the sum of its parts.

SPECIFICATIONS (LS)	
Years produced:	1975-1986 (185,827 in UK)
Performance:	0-60mph: 14.6sec
	Top speed: 96mph
Power & torque:	68bhp/79lb ft
Engine:	Normally aspirated 1294cc four cylinder, petrol, carburettor, 8 valves
Drivetrain:	Front-engine FWD
Structure:	Monocoque
Transmission:	Five-speed manual
Weight:	1040kg

PRICE GUIDE	
Launch price:	£3872
Excellent:	£1200
Good:	£700
Average:	£400
Project:	£250

CHRYSLER
Sunbeam/1600Ti

In 1977, and thanks to a UK government bailout, Chrysler UK introduced the Sunbeam. Although it was little more than a shortened Avenger with a stylish new liftback body, it sold enough to sustain the company's Linwood factory for another five years. Most were dull to drive, but the 1600Ti version was an interesting proposition, as it was effectively a shortened Avenger Tiger. Performance was rapid thanks to the 100bhp 1.6-litre running twin Weber carburettors, and proved a popular entrant in club-level rallying. See Talbot for the Sunbeam Lotus.

SPECIFICATIONS	
Years produced:	1977-1981 (10,113 in total)
Performance:	0-60mph: 10.7sec
	Top speed: 107mph
Power & torque:	100bhp/96lb ft
Engine:	Normally aspirated 1598cc four cylinder, petrol, carburettor, 8 valves
Drivetrain:	Front-engine RWD
Structure:	Monocoque
Transmission:	Four-speed manual
Weight:	920kg

PRICE GUIDE	
Launch price:	£3779
Excellent:	£5000
Good:	£3250
Average:	£1500
Project:	£750

CHRYSLER
Horizon

In 1978, Chrysler produced this stylish Volkswagen Golf rival based on the Simca 1100. In the showroom it looked great, but on the road the Horizon struggled against its agile German rival. Like the Alpine, the model bagged the European Car of The Year award in an admittedly slow year. Available with a selection of ex-Simca engines, they were all distinguished by tappet rattle and excellent fuel economy. The Horizon became a Talbot in the summer of 1979 and, thanks to Peugeot, inherited the excellent XUD diesel in 1982. Rusty, and rare, but virtually worthless.

SPECIFICATIONS	
Years produced:	1978-1985 (53,320 in UK)
Performance:	0-60mph: 13.6sec
	Top speed: 95mph
Power & torque:	64bhp/87lb ft
Engine:	Normally aspirated 1442cc four cylinder, petrol, carburettor, 8 valves
Drivetrain:	Front-engine FWD
Structure:	Monocoque
Transmission:	Four-speed manual
Weight:	990kg

PRICE GUIDE	
Launch price:	£3320
Excellent:	£1000
Good:	£700
Average:	£400
Project:	£250

CHRYSLER USA

THIS MARQUE was founded by Walter Chrysler in 1925 out of the remnants of the Maxwell Motor Company, and had already overseen the launch of the well-received six-cylinder Chrysler automobile the previous year. The new company soon became associated with good-value products, and flourished during the 1930s when such things mattered. The firm was grown along the lines of GM, and soon incorporated Dodge, Plymouth, De Soto, Fargo and – after the war – Valiant and Imperial. It hit trouble in the 1970s, biting off more than it could chew in Europe, before being rescued by the Minivan in 1984. More woes going into the 2010s, but remains with us – against the odds.

CHRYSLER
C-300

Currently going through an image renaissance, the 'Letter-series Chryslers' are as desirable now as they were when new. The C-300 hardtop is where the phenomenon began, and where the US musclecar race began, thanks to the installation of a 300bhp Hemi (it's here where the C-300 got its name from). Virgil Exner styled the model magnificently, with few of the excesses of later US musclecars. The development of the C-300 is reputed to have been $100 million, which is a lot for such a short production run, but worth every penny as a halo product.

SPECIFICATIONS	
Years produced:	1955 (3825 in total)
Performance:	0-60mph: 9.0sec
	Top speed: 125mph
Power & torque:	300bhp/400lb ft
Engine:	Normally aspirated 5426cc V8, petrol, carburettor, 16 valves
Drivetrain:	Front-engine RWD
Structure:	Separate chassis
Transmission:	Three-speed automatic
Weight:	1921kg

PRICE GUIDE	
Launch price:	N/A
Excellent:	£50,000
Good:	£35,000
Average:	£22,500
Project:	£15,000

CHRYSLER
300F

Five years on from the C-300, and the musclecar wars were in full flight. And once again, Chrysler continued to set the pace with its 'Wedge' engine pushing out 375bhp, making the 300 the king of quarter-mile strip. As well as the three-speed auto, the 300F buyer could also specify a four-speed manual as supplied by Pont-à-Mousson, for even quicker getaways. Well equipped, plush and surprisingly advanced – with a unitary body. Available as a coupe or convertible, and extremely popular as a club racer back then, it is now revered as one of the most desirable of all musclecars.

SPECIFICATIONS	
Years produced:	1960 (964/248 in total)
Performance:	0-60mph: 7.0sec
	Top speed: 135mph
Power & torque:	375bhp/450lb ft
Engine:	Normally aspirated 6746cc V8, petrol, carburettor, 16 valves
Drivetrain:	Front-engine RWD
Structure:	Monocoque
Transmission:	Three-speed automatic
Weight:	2201kg

PRICE GUIDE	
Launch price:	N/A
Excellent:	£75,000
Good:	£50,000
Average:	£35,000
Project:	£22,500

CHRYSLER
Dodge Caravan

The Minivan was game changer. Not just for Chrysler, because it saved the company; but also for the motor industry as a whole, because it popularised the MPV in the USA. Lee Iaccoca had originally tried developing the concept at Ford, but it never happened; instead, he developed it at Chrysler. The Minivan was launched six months before the Renault Espace in Europe, but both were epoch-making. The Dodge Caravan (and later Chrysler Voyager) was a clever machine, based on the K-Car platform (itself an extended Horizon), with adaptable interiors and a lofty driving position.

SPECIFICATIONS	
Years produced:	1984-1990
Performance:	0-60mph: 12.9sec
	Top speed: 103mph
Power & torque:	102bhp/101lb ft
Engine:	Normally aspirated 2213cc four cylinder, petrol, fuel injection, 8 valves
Drivetrain:	Front-engine FWD
Structure:	Monocoque
Transmission:	Three-speed automatic
Weight:	1921kg

PRICE GUIDE	
Launch price:	N/A
Excellent:	£2000
Good:	£1200
Average:	£900
Project:	£750

CITROËN

CITROËN STARTED life in 1919 as a builder of worthy but ultimately dull machines. And then came the revolutionary Traction Avant in 1934 with front-wheel drive and svelte modern styling. That established Citroën as a free-thinking radical and the firm lived up to the hype with subsequent creations such as the utilitarian 2CV and the Hydropneumatic wonders that were the Goddess-like DS, the Maserati-engined SM, the futuristic CX and the novel GS.

A takeover by Peugeot in 1975 killed off some of Citroën's quirkiness – although 1989's XM was in the marque's best mad traditions – but individuality and daring have returned again in recent years... thankfully!

CITROËN
Traction Avant

Before the Traction Avant, Citroën was just another European manufacturer of worthy but dull cars. The Traction's arrival in 1934 changed all that. It was a revolutionary machine, Europe's first mass-produced front-wheel-drive car of monocoque construction. Independent suspension and some very sleek bodies were also part of its chic cocktail; there was simply nothing like it at the time and its rivals wouldn't catch up for years. Initial cars had 1303cc engines and the range gradually expanded to include the popular 1911cc.

SPECIFICATIONS	
Years produced:	1934-1957 (760,000 in total)
Performance:	0-60mph: 23.4sec
	Top speed: 72mph
Power & torque:	56bhp/91lb ft
Engine:	Normally aspirated 1911cc four cylinder, petrol, carburettor, 8 valves
Drivetrain:	Front-engine FWD
Structure:	Monocoque
Transmission:	Three-speed manual
Weight:	1143kg

PRICE GUIDE	
Launch price:	£573
Excellent:	£12,500
Good:	£9000
Average:	£5000
Project:	£2500

CITROËN
2CV

Envisaged as a car to motorise the French peasant population, the 2CV went on to become a true world car. The deceptively simple appearance belied a car that was very clever, with interconnected suspension and a tough air-cooled twin-cylinder engine. The simply-constructed body was considered ugly when the car was launched in 1948, leading to nicknames such as Tin Snail and Duck. But it was that endearingly quirky styling that helped win the 2CV a legion of followers, and it stayed in production for 42 years.

SPECIFICATIONS

Years produced:	1948-1960
Performance:	0-60mph: N/A
	Top speed: 49mph
Power & torque:	9bhp/17lb ft
Engine:	Normally aspirated 375cc twin, petrol, carburettor, 4 valves
Drivetrain:	Front-engine FWD
Structure:	Separate chassis
Transmission:	Four-speed manual
Weight:	682kg

PRICE GUIDE

Launch price:	£565
Excellent:	£6000
Good:	£3500
Average:	£2000
Project:	£1000

CITROËN
DS19/ID19

The Citroën DS is one of the most extraordinary cars ever created. Its 'goddess' name – 'Déesse' in French – was entirely justified because it looked like it was from another world. The beautiful shape was like nothing else, while Hydropneumatics controlled the self-levelling suspension, brakes, clutch and power steering, with the ride height adjustable from inside the car. Only the old 1911cc engine was carried over from the Traction Avant. The budget-conscious ID19 appeared a year after the DS19 and featured conventional brakes and steering.

SPECIFICATIONS

Years produced:	1955-1975
Performance:	0-60mph: 22.1sec
	Top speed: 88mph
Power & torque:	75bhp/101lb ft
Engine:	Normally aspirated 1911cc four cylinder, petrol, carburettor, 8 valves
Drivetrain:	Front-engine FWD
Structure:	Monocoque
Transmission:	Four-speed manual
Weight:	1237kg

PRICE GUIDE

Launch price:	£1486
Excellent:	£12,500
Good:	£8000
Average:	£3000
Project:	£900

CITROËN
DS Décapotable

While a few European coachbuilders decapitated DSs, it was the guillotine work of Henri Chapron that was considered the most stylish and elegant – so much so that Citroën added his cars to its catalogue in 1961. The mechanics and any improvements mirrored those of the saloons but the looks were far more eye-catching, with the open-top, two-door format and long, sloping tail giving a characteristically elegant look – at twice the price of the saloon, the cabriolet needed to be special. Only 1365 were officially built.

SPECIFICATIONS

Years produced:	1958-1973 (1365 in total)
Performance:	0-60mph: 15.5sec
	Top speed: 100mph
Power & torque:	83bhp/98lb ft
Engine:	Normally aspirated 1911cc four cylinder, petrol, carburettor, 8 valves
Drivetrain:	Front-engine FWD
Structure:	Monocoque
Transmission:	Four-speed manual
Weight:	1235kg

PRICE GUIDE

Launch price:	Special order only
Excellent:	£150,000
Good:	£90,000
Average:	£75,000
Project:	£50,000

CITROËN
DS19 Safari

The Citroën DS Safari, introduced in 1958, was one of the most competent estate cars ever produced. As well as swallowing luggage it was also a seven-seater in ordinary form, but the Familiale version had three rows of seats and could accommodate eight. The Hydropneumatic suspension came into its own on the load-lugging DS as, however much you packed in the back, the car would always stay level. Safaris followed IDs, but offered all engine options of the DS saloons and adopted the same shark-like front end as its siblings in 1967.

SPECIFICATIONS

Years produced:	1959-1975
Performance:	0-60mph: 19.4sec
	Top speed: 88mph
Power & torque:	66bhp/98lb ft
Engine:	Normally aspirated 1911cc four cylinder, petrol, carburettor, 8 valves
Drivetrain:	Front-engine FWD
Structure:	Monocoque
Transmission:	Four-speed maual
Weight:	1260kg

PRICE GUIDE

Launch price:	£1745
Excellent:	£10,000
Good:	£7000
Average:	£3250
Project:	£1500

CITROËN
Ami 6/8/Super

Citroën produced several 2CV-based cars, with the Ami being one of the more fascinating. The styling was strange even by French standards, especially the original 6 model, which had a reverse-rake window emulating the Ford Anglia 105E. A 602cc 20bhp engine provided reasonable performance and the Ami was better appointed inside than the 2CV. A redesign in 1969 brought the Ami 8, with a more conventional (and more boring) slope to the rear window. The ultimate Ami was the Super of 1972, with the GS's flat four.

SPECIFICATIONS

Years produced:	1961-1978 (1,840,159 in total)
Performance:	0-60mph: 17.1sec
	Top speed: 88mph
Power & torque:	26bhp/31lb ft
Engine:	Normally aspirated 602cc twin, petrol, carburettor, 4 valves
Drivetrain:	Front-engine FWD
Structure:	Separate chassis
Transmission:	Four-speed manual
Weight:	673kg

PRICE GUIDE

Launch price:	£824
Excellent:	£3500
Good:	£1900
Average:	£900
Project:	£400

CITROËN
DS 20/21/23

The DS deserved better engines than those that had been used in the Traction Avant before the war and, from 1965, it started to get them. In that year, the Citroën DS21 was launched with a 2175cc engine offering 109bhp. After a very successful restyle in 1967 – with swivelling headlamps within a shark-like nose – the DS19 was replaced by the DS20 (1985cc and 90bhp). But it was in the 1970s that the Goddess reached its ultimate evolution, with a 2347cc engine, to create the DS23. Subsequently with fuel injection, it pumped out 141bhp.

SPECIFICATIONS
Years produced:	1966-1974
Performance:	0-60mph: 10.4sec
	Top speed: 120mph
Power & torque:	100bhp/121lb ft
Engine:	Normally aspirated 2175cc four cylinder, petrol, carburettor, 8 valves
Drivetrain:	Front-engine FWD
Structure:	Monocoque
Transmission:	Four-speed manual
Weight:	1280kg

PRICE GUIDE
Launch price:	£1977
Excellent:	£20,000
Good:	£12,000
Average:	£5000
Project:	£2500

CITROËN
Dyane 4/6

The Dyane was intended to replace the 2CV... but the Tin Snail was too much of a survivor. So this upgraded and restyled 2CV went on sale alongside the model it was designed to supersede. The chassis was the same with a 425cc twin for the 4 and a 602cc powerhouse for the 6, and the more angular looks were still closely 2CV-related, even down to the full-length canvas sunroof. The Dyane was clearly an update of the original design, with the addition of a hatchback, but it was dropped five years before the car it was meant to oust.

SPECIFICATIONS
Years produced:	1967-1985 (1,443,583 in total)
Performance:	0-60mph: 30.8sec
	Top speed: 70mph
Power & torque:	32bhp/31lb ft
Engine:	Normally aspirated 602cc twin, petrol, carburettor, 4 valves
Drivetrain:	Front-engine FWD
Structure:	Separate chassis
Transmission:	Four-speed manual
Weight:	600kg

PRICE GUIDE
Launch price:	£549
Excellent:	£2750
Good:	£1750
Average:	£800
Project:	£300

CITROËN
SM

The 1968 marriage of Citroën and Maserati led to the birth of a highly individualistic coupé. The SM took DS technology, threw in a Maserati V6 and was finished off with a swooping body that was uniquely Citroën, but also looked prestigious. Utterly original and technologically advanced, this idiosyncratic French car demanded care and developed a reputation for fragility, which harmed sales. When Citroën was taken over by Peugeot in 1975 the SM was one of the first casualties, despite late production being shunted to Ligier.

SPECIFICATIONS
Years produced:	1970-1975 (12,920 in total)
Performance:	0-60mph: 8.8sec
	Top speed: 135mph
Power & torque:	168bhp/170lb ft
Engine:	Normally aspirated 2670cc V6, petrol, fuel injection, 12 valves
Drivetrain:	Front-engine FWD
Structure:	Monocoque
Transmission:	Five-speed manual
Weight:	1450kg

PRICE GUIDE
Launch price:	£5480
Excellent:	£35,000
Good:	£17,500
Average:	£12,000
Project:	£6000

CITROËN
SM Chapron Mylord

The DS Décapotable by Chapron has entered into the realms of super-valuedom yet, with 1365 built, it's positively common compared with his next Citroën-based open-top: the SM Mylord. This curiously named car (which was obviously inspired by the British gentry) was only available to special order and, due to its high cost, a mere seven were built in total. But what a fantastic looking convertible! Thanks to the SM's inherent strength, it's taken to the conversion very well indeed. Highly desirable with values to match.

SPECIFICATIONS
Years produced:	1970-1975 (7 in total)
Performance:	0-60mph: 8.8sec
	Top speed: 135mph
Power & torque:	168bhp/170lb ft
Engine:	Normally aspirated 2670cc V6, petrol, fuel injection, 12 valves
Drivetrain:	Front-engine FWD
Structure:	Monocoque
Transmission:	Five-speed manual
Weight:	N/A

PRICE GUIDE
Launch price:	N/A
Excellent:	£125,000
Good:	£75,000
Average:	£50,000
Project:	N/A

CITROËN
SM Chapron Opéra

Making a saloon out of one of Europe's sleekest coupés might have seemed like an odd undertaking for Chapron, but it's one that worked remarkably well. The long nose of the donor car is balanced well by the lengthened rear end although, by contemporary standards, it resulted in a huge car, well over five metres in length. The work undertaken on the Opéra and Mylord was put to good use in the 1972 Presidential limousine – a hugely lengthened open-topped SM. It was so good that it remained in service well into the 1990s.

SPECIFICATIONS
Years produced:	1970-1975 (8 in total)
Performance:	0-60mph: 8.8sec
	Top speed: 135mph
Power & torque:	168bhp/170lb ft
Engine:	Normally aspirated 2670cc V6, petrol, fuel injection, 12 valves
Drivetrain:	Front-engine FWD
Structure:	Monocoque
Transmission:	Five-speed manual
Weight:	N/A

PRICE GUIDE
Launch price:	N/A
Excellent:	£150,000
Good:	£85,000
Average:	£50,000
Project:	N/A

CITROËN
GS

Citroën brought its big-car Hydropneumatic technology to the small-car market with 1970's GS. It looked like a scaled-down blend of DS and SM, with motive power from a 1015cc air-cooled flat-four engine. The interior looked like it had borrowed its controls from a spaceship and, naturally, there was self-levelling suspension. The car became a hatchback as the GSA in 1979, but in the process gained ugly plasic bumpers and a 1980s-generic dashboard. All models love being driven hard, but get thirsty when they are. Rare and on the rise now.

SPECIFICATIONS (GS Club)

Years produced:	1970-1979/1985 (2,473,150 GS and GSA)
Performance:	0-60mph: 16.2sec
	Top speed: 92mph
Power & torque:	55bhp/52lb ft
Engine:	Normally aspirated 1015cc flat four, petrol, carburettor, 8 valves
Drivetrain:	Front-engine FWD
Structure:	Monocoque
Transmission:	Four-speed manual
Weight:	880kg

PRICE GUIDE

Launch price:	£1001
Excellent:	£3500
Good:	£1850
Average:	£850
Project:	£250

CITROËN
Birotor

In for a penny, in for a pound seemed to be Citroën's mantra in the early '70s. If the act of producing advanced cars for bread-and-butter money wasn't enough, the company decided that Wankel engines were its future. A twin-rotor Comotor 624 unit, also used in the NSU Ro80, was installed in the GS to produce a fast and effortless saloon in 1973. However, it was too expensive (more than a DS) and thirsty, and failed to sell. Within months of Peugeot's takeover, the car was withdrawn and the company attempted to buy back all 847 cars to save face. A few survive.

SPECIFICATIONS

Years produced:	1973 only (847 in total)
Performance:	0-60mph: 14.0sec
	Top speed: 109mph
Power & torque:	106bhp/101lb ft
Engine:	Normally aspirated 1990cc (equivalent) twin-rotor Wankel, petrol, carburettor
Drivetrain:	Front-engine FWD
Structure:	Monocoque
Transmission:	Three-speed semi-auto
Weight:	1140kg

PRICE GUIDE

Launch price:	N/A in UK
Excellent:	£10,000
Good:	£8000
Average:	£5000
Project:	N/A

CITROËN
CX

Enthusiasts generally refer to 1974's CX as the last of the true Citroëns because it was the final model launched before Peugeot took over. A technological tour de force with typically innovative and individualistic sleek looks, the CX featured the usual hydraulics controlling many aspects of the car plus Varipower self-centring steering, which took a little getting used to. The interior was simply mad, although from 1985, Series 2 cars had traditional instrumentation and colour-coded bumpers. Engines extended from 2.0-litre petrol to 2.5-litre diesel.

SPECIFICATIONS (2200)

Years produced:	1974-1990 (1,034,489 in total)
Performance:	0-60mph: 9.7sec
	Top speed: 114mph
Power & torque:	115bhp/131lb ft
Engine:	Normally aspirated 2165cc four cylinder, petrol, carburettor, 8 valves
Drivetrain:	Front-engine FWD
Structure:	Monocoque
Transmission:	Five-speed manual
Weight:	1245kg

PRICE GUIDE

Launch price:	£3195
Excellent:	£4000
Good:	£2250
Average:	£900
Project:	£300

CITROËN
2CV6

Although probably the world's best minimalist car, the 2CV became increasingly luxurious. These terms are relative, of course, and additions to the car that motorised a generation of French farmers included improved interior trim and a slightly uprated engine. The best features remained – the loping ride, comfortable seats and pull-back roof – and that helped maintain sales for what had become a cult car even during its production run. Finally laid to rest in 1990, the Citroën 2CV's place in society is assured – as are its values, which continue to rise.

SPECIFICATIONS

Years produced:	1978-1990
Performance:	0-60mph: 32.4sec
	Top speed: 71mph
Power & torque:	26bhp/29lb ft
Engine:	Normally aspirated 602cc twin, petrol, carburettor, 4 valves
Drivetrain:	Front-engine FWD
Structure:	Separate chassis
Transmission:	Four-speed manual
Weight:	560kg

PRICE GUIDE

Launch price:	£899
Excellent:	£4500
Good:	£2750
Average:	£1000
Project:	£350

CITROËN
GSA

Despite being well into its ninth year of production, the GS still looked contemporary, and drove well. But its lack of a hatchback seriously dented its practicality especially compared with the latest generation of small hatchbacks, such as the Renault 14 and Peugeot 104. Citroën's GSA put right this failing, adding a wide opening tailgate, and using the opportunity to facelift the interior with a friendlier-looking dashboard, and the exterior with chunky plastic bumpers. The GSA continued to sell well, despite the arrival of the BX in 1982.

SPECIFICATIONS

Years produced:	1979-1987
Performance:	0-60mph: 13.1sec
	Top speed: 101mph
Power & torque:	65bhp/69lb ft
Engine:	Normally aspirated 1015cc flat four, petrol, carburettor, 8 valves
Drivetrain:	Front-engine FWD
Structure:	Monocoque
Transmission:	Five-speed manual
Weight:	920kg

PRICE GUIDE

Launch price:	£3299
Excellent:	£3500
Good:	£1850
Average:	£850
Project:	£250

CITROËN
BX

Launched under the Eiffel Tower at the end of 1982, the BX was a clever fusion of Peugeot rationalism and Citroën individualism. Despite being idiosyncratically styled by Marcello Gandini and blessed with drum dials and paddle switchgear, the BX was sold on the back of an advertising campaign that played on its easy-to-service nature. Sales started slowly but, following the arrival of facelifted models (and round dials) in 1986, then the turbodiesels and GTi model, they picked up massively. Survivors have thinned out, and banger status will soon be behind the BX.

SPECIFICATIONS (16TRS)
Years produced: 1982-1994 (2,315,739 in total)
Performance: 0-60mph: 10.8sec
Top speed: 109mph
Power & torque: 94bhp/101lb ft
Engine: Normally aspirated 1580cc four cylinder, petrol, carburettor, 8 valves
Drivetrain: Front-engine FWD
Structure: Monocoque
Transmission: Five-speed manual
Weight: 960kg

PRICE GUIDE
Launch price: £4790
Excellent: £1000
Good: £750
Average: £500
Project: £250

CITROËN
Visa Cabriolet

Four-door cabriolets don't come along very often, so when the Visa made an appearance in 1984, certain members of the press proclaimed it as the modern-day successor to the Morris Minor Convertible. Citroën's cheap rag-top was converted by Heuliez, and sold as a mainstream model, although it was based on the low-powered 11RE version – no doubt to avoid internal PSA competition with the recently-launched Talbot Samba cabriolet. Rare when new – it failed to take off in the UK – and almost extinct now due to horrendous corrosion.

SPECIFICATIONS
Years produced: 1984-1988
Performance: 0-60mph: 15.1sec
Top speed: 87mph
Power & torque: 57bhp/59lb ft
Engine: Normally aspirated 1124cc twin, petrol, carburettor, 4 valves
Drivetrain: Front-engine FWD
Structure: Monocoque
Transmission: Four-speed manual
Weight: 850kg

PRICE GUIDE
Launch price: £4850
Excellent: £3000
Good: £1750
Average: £900
Project: £600

CITROËN
CX GTi/GTi Turbo

Finally matching high performance to dramatic looks, 1977's CX GTi was Citroën's return to grand touring after the demise of the SM. Using the DS23's fuel-injected 2347cc engine gave 128bhp and a 120mph top speed, while the cars could be identified by their special alloy wheels, blacked-out trim and more sports-orientated interiors. In 1984 Citroën made things even more frantic with the CX GTi Turbo, rated at 168bhp. A long time in the shadow of the DS, the CX is now being recognised as one of the great Citroëns.

SPECIFICATIONS
Years produced: 1984-1989
Performance: 0-60mph: 8.2sec
Top speed: 129mph
Power & torque: 166bhp/217lb ft
Engine: Turbocharged 2499cc four cylinder, petrol, electronic fuel injection, 8 valves
Drivetrain: Front-engine FWD
Structure: Monocoque
Transmission: Five-speed manual
Weight: 1490kg

PRICE GUIDE
Launch price: £6530
Excellent: £5000
Good: £3600
Average: £1500
Project: £750

CITROËN
BX 4TC

Group B has a lot to answer for. And although we all remember the amazing Audi Quattros, Peugeot 205T16s and Ford RS200s, cursiosities like the Citroën BX 4TC have been almost forgotten. This apathy is mainly down to Peugeot's decision to downgrade the 4TC project before its first competitive rallying season in 1986. In its first events, the 4TC proved less than competitive, hampered by its poor weight distribution and unreliability. 200 were built, but the company bought back as many as it could, making this one of the rarest Group B cars.

SPECIFICATIONS
Years produced: 1985-1986 (200 in total)
Performance: 0-60mph: 7.1sec
Top speed: 138mph
Power & torque: 200bhp/217lb ft
Engine: Normally aspirated 2141cc four cylinder, petrol, electronic fuel injection, 16 valves
Drivetrain: Front-engine AWD
Structure: Monocoque
Transmission: Five-speed manual
Weight: 1280kg

PRICE GUIDE
Launch price: N/A
Excellent: £60,000
Good: £30,000
Average: £27,500
Project: N/A

CITROËN
Visa GTi

As unlikely hot hatches go, the Visa GTi is probably top of the list. When the original Visa appeared in 1978, it married odd styling with rational Peugeot underpinnings to create a spacious, comfortable and totally conventional small 'big' car. Sporting it was not. Yet the boys from Citroën decided it would be good for them to install the hot little 1.6-litre from the 205GTi. The resulting car was quick, comfortable and surprisingly capable. Early models had 105bhp, upgunned to 115 in 1988. Quad headlamps look cool, too. If you can find one, snap it up, cosset it and enjoy.

SPECIFICATIONS
Years produced: 1985-1988
Performance: 0-60mph: 9.1sec
Top speed: 109mph
Power & torque: 105bhp/99lb ft
Engine: Normally aspirated 1580cc four cylinder, petrol, mechanical fuel injection, 8 valves
Drivetrain: Front-engine FWD
Structure: Monocoque
Transmission: Five-speed manual
Weight: 890kg

PRICE GUIDE
Launch price: £5899
Excellent: £2500
Good: £1200
Average: £650
Project: £400

CITROËN
AX GT/GT5

The lightweight AX was transformed into a latter-day Mini-Cooper when given the sporting treatment. 'Rocky Marciano' was how the advertisers described it, and they had a point: it was a featherweight that packed a giant-killing punch. Despite being powered by a carb-fed 1.4-litre packing a mere 85bhp, the GT could sprint to 60mph in 8.4 seconds, and stay with the hot hatch grandees on the twisty stuff. Flimsy interior was a bit of a turn-off for some, but a constant source of delight for others. Now gaining a bit of a following after years in the doldrums.

SPECIFICATIONS

Years produced:	1987-1993
Performance:	0-60mph: 8.4sec
	Top speed: 110mph
Power & torque:	85bhp/86lb ft
Engine:	Normally aspirated 1360cc four cylinder, petrol, carburettor, 8 valves
Drivetrain:	Front-engine FWD
Structure:	Monocoque
Transmission:	Five-speed manual
Weight:	722kg

PRICE GUIDE

Launch price:	£7914
Excellent:	£1200
Good:	£600
Average:	£350
Project:	£200

CITROËN
BX 16 Valve

Perhaps one of the performance car surprises of the '80s, given the base car's utter lack of go-faster pretension. But when Citroën slotted in an all-aluminium engine pumping out 160bhp, beefed up the suspension and tacked on a bodykit, a sporting express was created. With a top speed of 135mph and 0-60mph in comfortably under 8sec, the BX could trade punches with far more expensive cars, but despite being relatively good value, sales were disappointing after an initial flurry. Most have gone, having fallen prey to the engine-swap brigade.

SPECIFICATIONS

Years produced:	1987-1993 (15,440 in total)
Performance:	0-60mph: 7.4sec
	Top speed: 135mph
Power & torque:	160bhp/133lb ft
Engine:	Normally aspirated 1905cc four cylinder, petrol, electronic fuel injection, 16 valves
Drivetrain:	Front-engine FWD
Structure:	Monocoque
Transmission:	Five-speed manual
Weight:	1070kg

PRICE GUIDE

Launch price:	£12,300
Excellent:	£1800
Good:	£1000
Average:	£750
Project:	£500

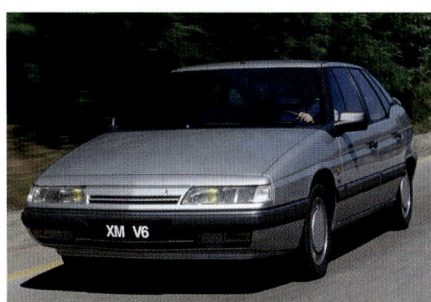

CITROËN
XM

Pity the XM: it had so much to live up to, following on from the DS and CX. In an age of PSA rationality, infusing it with the individuality of its forebears was always going to be challenging. Yet the fluid-suspended, computer-controlled XM managed that arduous task with considerable aplomb. Firmer-riding than Citroëns of old, the XM was still a magic carpet compared with executive class rivals. A wide range of normally aspirated and turbo petrols and diesels was offered during its ten-year life, and the XM is at its most realistic as a turbodiesel.

SPECIFICATIONS (V6 24v)

Years produced:	1989-2000 (333,775 in total)
Performance:	0-60mph: 7.5sec
	Top speed: 146mph
Power & torque:	200bhp/192lb ft
Engine:	Normally aspirated 2975cc V6, petrol, electronic fuel injection, 24 valves
Drivetrain:	Front-engine FWD
Transmission:	Five-speed manual
Weight:	1475kg

PRICE GUIDE

Launch price:	£14,499
Excellent:	£4000
Good:	£2500
Average:	£1250
Project:	£400

CLAN

CLAN WAS created by Paul Haussauer after leaving Lotus in 1970. The factory was set-up in his former employer's stamping ground of Norfolk and, joined by Lotus man John Frayling, the team designed a composite-bodied sports car that would run on Hillman Imp power. The all-aluminium engine was light, and parent company Chrysler guaranteed continued supplies. Production started slowly, because of component supply problems – a shame because press reveiws were ecstatic about the car's performance and efficiency. Died in 1974 (along with most of the UK kit-car industry, due to taxation changes), only to make a brief return in the mid-80s.

CLAN
Crusader

So much more than a kit car, the Clan Crusader was an exercise in lightness and efficiency, while proving that the Hillman Imp's Coventry Climax engine really was something special. It was a classic '70s British sports car – glassfibre body, off-the-shelf engine and gearbox, all clothed in a wedge-shaped body. It was pricey, at 40% more than an MG Midget, but the Crusader was electric to drive, and the material choice for the bodywork means the survival rate is rather good. The engine is well-supported in the tuning community, too.

SPECIFICATIONS

Years produced:	1971-1974 (315 in total)
Performance:	0-60mph: 12.5sec
	Top speed: 100mph
Power & torque:	51bhp/52lb ft
Engine:	Normally aspirated 875cc four cylinder, petrol, carburettor, 8 valves
Drivetrain:	Rear-engine RWD
Structure:	Glassfibre body/backbone chassis
Transmission:	Four-speed manual
Weight:	578kg

PRICE GUIDE

Launch price:	£1399
Excellent:	£4500
Good:	£3250
Average:	£1650
Project:	£650

DAF

DAF WAS A Dutch truck and trailer maker that decided to branch out into car design with its two-cylinder 600cc Daffodil of 1958. This was considered innovative because of its Variomatic belt-drive transmission, which meant it was just as fast in reverse as it was forwards. Good sales led to more powerful variants as well as the Michelotti-penned 44 of 1966; four-cylinder engines followed in 1967 as did rather cute-looking coupés. Volvo, which had been buying shares since the 1970s, took over fully in 1975, badged the current DAF 66 as one of its own models and went onto launch the belt-drive Volvo 300 series in 1976, which had initially been conceived as a DAF.

DAF
600/750/Daffodil/33

The Van Doorne brothers had enjoyed good times building trucks, and concluded that they could do the same in the car industry. Their first car, the 600 – with its air-cooled two-cylinder engine – looked like an unexceptional addition to the mini-car market. But there was technical novelty in the transmission, a continuously variable automatic device that relied on V-section rubber bands to match engine and road speed. And that meant the driver had the choice of two gears, forward and reverse. How easy was that?

SPECIFICATIONS (33 De Luxe)	
Years produced:	1959-1975 (312,367 in total)
Performance:	0-60mph: 28.5sec
	Top speed: 70mph
Power & torque:	32bhp/42lb ft
Engine:	Normally aspirated 746cc twin, petrol, carburettor, 4 valves
Drivetrain:	Front-engine RWD
Structure:	Monocoque
Transmission:	CVT automatic
Weight:	670kg

PRICE GUIDE	
Launch price:	N/A
Excellent:	£2250
Good:	£1650
Average:	£750
Project:	£300

DAF
44/46/55/66/Volvo 66

With the DAF car business off to a flying start, the company decided to launch a larger stablemate to the 33. The Michelotti-styled 44 had its wheelbase extended by 8in and, the following year, it received the four-cylinder Renault power unit to become the 55, the company's largest-engined product yet. Continuously evolved during its life, but always exclusively offered with the CVT gearbox; received a chunkier front end in 1973, and it was in this form that the 66 was re-badged a Volvo in 1975. Remained in production as a Volvo until 1980.

SPECIFICATIONS (33 De Luxe)	
Years produced:	1966-1975 (510,786 in total)
Performance:	0-60mph: 14.9sec
	Top speed: 87mph
Power & torque:	43bhp/62lb ft
Engine:	Normally aspirated 1108cc four cylinder, petrol, carburettor, 8 valves
Drivetrain:	Front-engine RWD
Structure:	Monocoque
Transmission:	CVT automatic
Weight:	787kg

PRICE GUIDE	
Launch price:	N/A
Excellent:	£2000
Good:	£1500
Average:	£750
Project:	£300

DAF
Marathon

The 55 was a big step forward for the Dutch firm. It used a Renault water-cooled four-cylinder engine that offered a huge improvement in performance, even if the characteristic hum of the older model was gone. To celebrate its success in the London-Sydney Marathon, DAF introduced a Marathon upgrade kit, boosting power, handling and roadholding. It was an immediate success and soon became a fully-fledged production model. Renault parts commonality means that availability is good, and the club has excellent back-up.

SPECIFICATIONS	
Years produced:	1968-1972
Performance:	19.4sec
	Top speed: 90mph
Power & torque:	63bhp/63lb ft
Engine:	Normally aspirated 1108cc four cylinder, petrol, carburettor, 8 valves
Drivetrain:	Front-engine RWD
Structure:	Monocoque
Transmission:	CVT automatic
Weight:	810kg

PRICE GUIDE	
Launch price:	£1050
Excellent:	£3250
Good:	£1650
Average:	£750
Project:	£300

DAIMLER

THE BRITISH DAIMLER is unrelated to the German one; it was founded in 1897 after obtaining a licence to use Gottlieb Daimler's name. Royal patronage gave its early models an enviable reputation, with the marque specialising in luxury machines. It merged with BSA in 1910, leading to some incredibly flamboyant and imposing machines when Sir Bernard and Lady Docker were in overall charge. However, after World War Two, Daimler found itself struggling and was taken over by rival company Jaguar in 1960. While some individuality was retained for a while, eventually the Daimler name became little more than a trim level to distinguish top-flight Jags.

DAIMLER
DB18/Consort

Daimler started moving towards smaller, more sporty cars before World War Two, with its DB18 proving quite successful in rallies. The war caused a hiatus in production, but the car returned afterwards largely unchanged as a saloon or drophead coupé. A 2522cc six-cylinder engine gave 70bhp and reasonable performance. Things moved forwards with the 1949 Consort, an update of the design with headlamps blended into the wings, the grille and bumpers developed curves, and hydromechanical brakes were fitted.

SPECIFICATIONS
Years produced:	1938-1953 (8223 in total)
Performance:	28.3sec
	Top speed: 72mph
Power & torque:	70bhp/N/A
Engine:	Normally aspirated 2522cc six cylinder, petrol, carburettor, 12 valves
Drivetrain:	Front-engine RWD
Structure:	Separate chassis
Transmission:	Four-speed manual
Weight:	1650kg

PRICE GUIDE
Launch price:	£1183
Excellent:	£6750
Good:	£5000
Average:	£2500
Project:	£700

DAIMLER
DB18 Sports Special

With the DB18 saloons and convertibles representing the sportier side of Daimler, the 1948 Sports Special version of the type was a step closer to the wild side. Twin carburettors helped squeeze 85bhp from the 2522cc six-cylinder engine. Barker was responsible for most of the bodies and its design featured a rear passenger seat facing sideways, thus making the car a three-seater. Hooper weighed in with the heavier 'Empress' saloon style, although alloy-on-ash construction for both machines helped keep performance up.

SPECIFICATIONS
Years produced:	1948-1953 (608 in total)
Performance:	0-60mph: 23.3sec
	Top speed: 84mph
Power & torque:	85bhp/N/A
Engine:	Normally aspirated 2522cc six cylinder, petrol, carburettor, 12 valves
Drivetrain:	Front-engine RWD
Structure:	Separate chassis
Transmission:	Four-speed manual
Weight:	1650kg

PRICE GUIDE
Launch price:	£2560
Excellent:	£20,000
Good:	£16,500
Average:	£9000
Project:	£4000

DAIMLER
Regency

The Regency took the Consort chassis, fitted it with a new 3.0-litre engine and topped it all off with a larger, more flowing and graceful body. Introduced in 1951, just 50 were built before production stalled in 1952. Reincarnation came in 1954 with the Regency Mk2, this time with a longer, lower body and a more powerful 3.5-litre engine. Offshoots were the Hooper-built Empress saloon and the more exciting Sportsman, which had a 140bhp alloy-head engine and offered good performance for its size and the era.

SPECIFICATIONS
Years produced:	1951-1956 (452 in total)
Performance:	19.1sec
	Top speed: 83mph
Power & torque:	90bhp/N/A
Engine:	Normally aspirated 3468cc six cylinder, petrol, carburettor, 12 valves
Drivetrain:	Front-engine RWD
Structure:	Separate chassis
Transmission:	Four-speed manual
Weight:	1721kg

PRICE GUIDE
Launch price:	£2335
Excellent:	£7000
Good:	£5250
Average:	£3500
Project:	£950

DAIMLER
Conquest Roadster

Daimler's first attempt at an out-and-out sports car was the Conquest-based, aluminium-bodied Roadster of 1953. Much sleeker and lower than any previous car from the company it was a somewhat bizarre-looking creation; this was thanks to Daimler trying to retain the style of the big saloons, which didn't lend itself to the hunkered-down format. After 65 had been made from 1953 to 1955, it was dropped, but then came back from 1956 to 1957. Only another 54 managed to find homes second time around.

SPECIFICATIONS
Years produced:	1953-1957 (119 in total)
Performance:	0-60mph: 14.5sec
	Top speed: 101mph
Power & torque:	100bhp/N/A
Engine:	Normally aspirated 2443cc six cylinder, petrol, carburettor, 12 valves
Drivetrain:	Front-engine RWD
Structure:	Separate chassis
Transmission:	Four-speed manual
Weight:	1219kg

PRICE GUIDE
Launch price:	£1673
Excellent:	£16,500
Good:	£12,500
Average:	£8000
Project:	£3500

DAIMLER
Conquest/Century

The Consort gave way to the Conquest in 1953. Well, it actually gave way to Daimler's badge-engineered version of the Lanchester 14, which was what the Conquest actually was. The Daimler was an improvement on its sister model though – thanks to a bigger engine with two extra cylinders – while its compact size gave it pleasing performance and handling. But for those who wanted a little more performance there was the Century drophead coupé, so called because of the 100bhp afforded by its alloy-head twin-carb engine.

SPECIFICATIONS
Years produced:	1953-1958 (9620 in total)
Performance:	0-60mph: 24.3sec
	Top speed: 82mph
Power & torque:	75bhp/N/A
Engine:	Normally aspirated 2433cc six cylinder, petrol, carburettor, 12 valves
Drivetrain:	Front-engine RWD
Structure:	Separate chassis
Transmission:	Four-speed manual
Weight:	1397kg

PRICE GUIDE
Launch price:	£1511
Excellent:	£6250
Good:	£4500
Average:	£2200
Project:	£700

DAIMLER
104/Majestic

Although the 1954 Daimler 104 looked very much like the Regency it replaced, the structure was bulked up, the brakes were improved and the 3468cc six-pot engine was granted more power. A special version was the Lady's Model, with a more 'feminine' interior including walnut veneer, satin chrome, picnic gear and, of all things, a gold-propelling pencil! 50 customers bought one. In 1958, the body put on considerable weight to become the Majestic. The bigger 3794cc engine pitched it directly against Jaguar.

SPECIFICATIONS

Years produced:	1955-1962 (1399 in total)
Performance:	0-60mph: 15.4sec
	Top speed: 100mph
Power & torque:	137bhp/N/A
Engine:	Normally aspirated 3468cc six cylinder, petrol, carburettor, 12 valves
Drivetrain:	Front-engine RWD
Structure:	Separate chassis
Transmission:	Four-speed manual
Weight:	1880kg

PRICE GUIDE

Launch price:	£2672
Excellent:	£7500
Good:	£5250
Average:	£3000
Project:	£750

DAIMLER
SP250

The final all-new sports car to be offered by Daimler, and the most interesting of all. With its glassfibre body and 2.5-litre V8 engine, the SP250 was quick and agile. It was originally called 'Dart', but Chrysler forced Daimler to drop the name. There were problems – the glassfibre used to crack, and the handling wasn't as good as it should have been – and, following Jaguar's takeover of Daimler, the appealing roadster was on borrowed time, as it was considered a rival to the E-type. Numbers are low, and that helps to keep values up.

SPECIFICATIONS

Years produced:	1959-1964 (2650 in total)
Performance:	0-60mph: 10.2sec
	Top speed: 121mph
Power & torque:	140bhp/155 ft
Engine:	Normally aspirated 2548cc V8, petrol, carburettor, 16 valves
Drivetrain:	Front-engine RWD
Structure:	Glassfibre body/separate chassis
Transmission:	Four-speed manual
Weight:	940kg

PRICE GUIDE

Launch price:	£1395
Excellent:	£25,000
Good:	£15,000
Average:	£8000
Project:	£3000

DAIMLER
Majestic Major

What was most majestic and major about 1960's Majestic Major was its engine... Daimler's new 4561cc V8 with hemispherical combustion heads, designed by Edward Turner. An impressive 220bhp gave a top speed of 120mph, making the Majestic Major a superb luxury express and one that was easy to drive thanks to automatic transmission and power steering. The bodywork remained largely unchanged from the standard Majestic, save for a longer boot. For 1961 there was a two-ton limousine version, which was dubbed a '120mph funeral taxi'.

SPECIFICATIONS

Years produced:	1960-1968 (1180 in total)
Performance:	0-60mph: 10.3sec
	Top speed: 119mph
Power & torque:	220bhp/283lb ft
Engine:	Normally aspirated 4561cc V8, petrol, carburettor, 16 valves
Drivetrain:	Front-engine RWD
Structure:	Separate chassis
Transmission:	Four-speed manual
Weight:	1778kg

PRICE GUIDE

Launch price:	£2995
Excellent:	£9250
Good:	£7250
Average:	£3750
Project:	£800

DAIMLER
2.5-litre/V8250

1959's Mk2 was the archetypal Jaguar saloon of the era; Daimler's version dropped the 2548cc V8 from the SP250 roadster under the bonnet. The two suited each other well with the handsome and curvaceous body complemented by the smooth and sophisticated power source. Arguably, the Daimler was a nicer car to drive than the Jaguar thanks to the engine's light weight and the eight cylinders endowing it with silky flexibility. Just imagine what it would have been like with the 4561cc version of the V8 instead...

SPECIFICATIONS

Years produced:	1962-1969 (17,620 in total)
Performance:	0-60mph: 13.8sec
	Top speed: 112mph
Power & torque:	140bhp/155lb ft
Engine:	Normally aspirated 2548cc V8, petrol, carburettor, 16 valves
Drivetrain:	Front-engine RWD
Structure:	Monocoque
Transmission:	Four-speed manual
Weight:	1473kg

PRICE GUIDE

Launch price:	£1786
Excellent:	£15,000
Good:	£11,000
Average:	£5250
Project:	£2500

DAIMLER
Sovereign

There was probably a very good case for the 1966-69 Sovereign – the badge-engineered version of Jaguar's big 420 – making use of the existing 4.5-litre Daimler V8 engine to power it. Unfortunately, Jaguar didn't hear it, and so the Sovereign came out with the same 4235cc six-cylinder XK engine as the 420. Not that this made it a bad car, but it took away some Daimler distinctiveness as the only different touches were a fluted grille, the 'D' bonnet mascot, 'Daimler' on the cam cover and assorted badges.

SPECIFICATIONS

Years produced:	1966-1969 (5700 in total)
Performance:	0-60mph: 9.9sec
	Top speed: 123mph
Power & torque:	245bhp/283lb ft
Engine:	Normally aspirated 4235cc straight six, petrol, carburettor, 12 valves
Drivetrain:	Front-engine RWD
Structure:	Monocoque
Transmission:	Four-speed manual
Weight:	1575kg

PRICE GUIDE

Launch price:	£2121
Excellent:	£10,000
Good:	£8000
Average:	£4000
Project:	£1250

DAIMLER
Sovereign SI-SIII

The Sovereign name was re-used for the Daimler version of the XJ6, introduced in 1969. As with the original Sovereign, any 'Daimlerisations' were confined to the most minor of details; the traditional fluted grille and Daimler badges here, there and everywhere. The original engine options were either the 2.8-litre or 4.2-litre XK six; by now Daimler's wonderful V8 engine – which might have suited the Sovereign so well – had ceased production. The Sovereign name continued through the Series 2 and 3 versions of the XJ until 1987.

SPECIFICATIONS
Years produced:	1969-1987 (55,435 in total)
Performance:	0-60mph: 8.8sec
	Top speed: 124mph
Power & torque:	173bhp/227lb ft
Engine:	Normally aspirated 2792cc six cylinder, petrol, carburettor, 12 valves
Drivetrain:	Front-engine RWD
Structure:	Monocoque
Transmission:	Four-speed (+O/D)/Three-speed auto
Weight:	1537kg

PRICE GUIDE
Launch price:	£2356
Excellent:	£6500
Good:	£5000
Average:	£2200
Project:	£750

DAIMLER
Double Six SI-III saloon

Jaguar took its XJ saloon to new heights with its new and exciting V12 engine from 1972. The Daimler variant revived a title that had last been used from 1926 to 1938, that of the Double Six. This created one of the better luxury cruisers of the era, a worthy rival for BMW, Mercedes-Benz and even Rolls-Royce, although build quality was often patchy. The 5343cc V12 engine may have been terribly thirsty, but it was also terribly fast and refined too. Vanden Plas versions had even more opulence, including better interiors and a vinyl roof.

SPECIFICATIONS
Years produced:	1972-1979 (16,608 in total)
Performance:	0-60mph: 7.4sec
	Top speed: 146mph
Power & torque:	265/285bhp to 304/350lb ft
Engine:	Normally aspirated 5343cc V12, petrol, carburettor, 24 valves
Drivetrain:	Front-engine RWD
Structure:	Monocoque
Transmission:	Three-speed auto
Weight:	1760kg

PRICE GUIDE
Launch price:	£3849
Excellent:	£8500
Good:	£6000
Average:	£2200
Project:	£1000

DAIMLER
4.2 Coupé

Announced in 1973, the Daimler Coupé – a short-wheelbase, pillarless variation on the XJ6/Sovereign saloon theme – seemed to have a lot going for it. The lines were even more handsome than those of the standard saloons and the truncated length added a sporty aura. However, when the Coupé finally made it into production in 1975, as a Series 2 model, it had a difficult life. Build quality was poor and the black vinyl roofs sported by each model were allegedly there to hide imperfections. Just 1598 were made before a halt was called in 1977.

SPECIFICATIONS
Years produced:	1975-1977 (399 in total)
Performance:	0-60mph: 8.8sec
	Top speed: 124mph
Power & torque:	173bhp/227lb ft
Engine:	Normally aspirated 4235cc six cylinder, petrol, carburettor, 12 valves
Drivetrain:	Front-engine RWD
Structure:	Monocoque
Transmission:	Four-speed manual/three-speed auto
Weight:	1689kg

PRICE GUIDE
Launch price:	£5590
Excellent:	£10,250
Good:	£8250
Average:	£4000
Project:	£1200

DAIMLER
Double Six Coupé

As with the Sovereign saloons, Jaguar's V12 engine also made its way into the Daimler-badged Coupés. One of the rarest of all Daimlers – just 407 were made from 1975 to 1977 – this 285bhp 5343cc pillarless and shortened sophisticate had wonderful looks with a top speed of nearly 150mph. Unfortunately, all this couldn't quite make up for the supply and quality problems that bedevilled it during its short life. This was a model that deserved a fate better than befell it. Rarity makes them even more exclusive than the 1855 Jaguar versions made.

SPECIFICATIONS
Years produced:	1975-1977 (407 in total)
Performance:	0-60mph: 7.6sec
	Top speed: 148mph
Power & torque:	285bhp/301lb ft
Engine:	Normally aspirated 5343cc V12, petrol, carburettor, 24 valves
Drivetrain:	Front-engine RWD
Structure:	Monocoque
Transmission:	three-speed auto
Weight:	1835kg

PRICE GUIDE
Launch price:	£6959
Excellent:	£9250
Good:	£7000
Average:	£3250
Project:	£1200

DATSUN/NISSAN

JAPANESE CAR-MAKER DAT was founded by the team of Den, Aoyama and Takeuchi in 1914. In 1931, one of its smaller cars was christened the Datson; when the Nissan conglomerate took over in 1933, it tweaked the name to Datsun, to honour the sun on the Japanese flag. Some of its early cars were copies of British Austins – including the Seven – but in the 1950s and '60s it started building its own designs. Much attention in the USA and Europe was garnered by its sporty Fairlady and 240Z models, and Datsuns came to sell strongly across the world. However, in 1986, the badge was dropped in those export markets and all the cars became known as Nissans instead.

DATSUN
Fairlady

The Sports Fairlady, to give the car its export name, was proof that the fledgling Japanese motor industry was willing to follow Western design themes. The sports car closely resembled an MGB, but it was underpinned by a crude ladder-frame chassis, and had leaf springs at the rear. It might not sound that promising, but the Fairlady looked good and sold well in the USA – and it's from there that most of the UK and European examples have originated. The best model to have is the 2.0-litre five-speed version. If you can find one.

SPECIFICATIONS

Years produced:	1962-1969
Performance:	0-60mph: 8.3sec
	Top speed: 125mph
Power & torque:	150bhp/138lb ft
Engine:	Normally aspirated 1982cc four cylinder, petrol, carburettor, 12 valves
Drivetrain:	Front-engine RWD
Structure:	Separate chassis
Transmission:	Five-speed manual
Weight:	910kg

PRICE GUIDE

Launch price:	N/A in UK
Excellent:	£10,000
Good:	£7500
Average:	£4000
Project:	N/A

DATSUN
240Z

Here's where it all began. The first in what has become the world's best sports car line, the Datsun 240Z had success written all over it from day one. The looks were spot on, thanks to styling input from Albrecht Goertz, and performance from its rorty straight six was ample. Being a Datsun, reliability was a given, but the agile, tail-happy handling was a pleasant surprise. During its five-year run, over 150,000 were produced, but survivors are now seriously appreciating. Rust has been its main enemy, so be careful when buying.

SPECIFICATIONS

Years produced:	1969-1974 (622,649 inc 260Z in total)
Performance:	0-60mph: 8.3sec
	Top speed: 125mph
Power & torque:	161bhp/198lb ft
Engine:	Normally aspirated 2393cc six cylinder, petrol, carburettor, 12 valves
Drivetrain:	Front-engine RWD
Structure:	Monocoque
Transmission:	Five-speed manual
Weight:	1025kg

PRICE GUIDE

Launch price:	£2288
Excellent:	£15,000
Good:	£9000
Average:	£5000
Project:	£2000

DATSUN
Cherry (E10/F10)

With the Cherry, Nissan was one of the first entrants in what became known as the supermini sector. The E10 models featured all-independent suspension, front-wheel drive, BMC-inspired A-series engine and appealing Transatlantic styling. When they first arrived in Europe in 1973, it didn't take buyers long to cotton on to how good these reliable little cars were. The Cherry matured into the second series a couple of years later, known as the F11 in the UK, and became a top-ten seller. Rare now, and the few that have survived the ravages of rust have a following.

SPECIFICATIONS (E10 100A)

Years produced:	1970-1978 (389,807/668,038 in total)
Performance:	0-60mph: 16.8sec
	Top speed: 86mph
Power & torque:	59bhp/60lb ft
Engine:	Normally aspirated 988cc four cylinder, petrol, carburettor, 8 valves
Drivetrain:	Front-engine FWD
Structure:	Monocoque
Transmission:	Four-speed manual
Weight:	645kg

PRICE GUIDE

Launch price:	£766/£1242
Excellent:	£3000
Good:	£1200
Average:	£750
Project:	£350

DATSUN
Cedric 260C

The large and conventionally engineered Cedric 260C was Datsun's first foray into the UK executive sector when it arrived here in 1973. Given that the brash and Transatlantic-looking saloon was up against Rover and Triumph's 2000 models, it's no surprise that the 260C (as it was called here) failed to catch on. Its main selling points were generous equipment, given reliability and a low list price. Today, the 260C and imported Glorias have gained quite a following, Japanese car enthusiasts can't get enough of them, and they're prepared to pay well.

SPECIFICATIONS (260C)

Years produced:	1971-1976
Performance:	0-60mph: 11.3sec
	Top speed: 109mph
Power & torque:	151bhp/188lb ft
Engine:	Normally aspirated 2565cc six cylinder, petrol, carburettor, valves
Drivetrain:	Front-engine RWD
Structure:	Monocoque
Transmission:	Five-speed manual
Weight:	1350kg

PRICE GUIDE

Launch price:	N/A
Excellent:	£6000
Good:	£2500
Average:	£1200
Project:	£750

DATSUN
Sunny 120Y/Coupé

For many 1970s drivers, fed up with being let down by their British cars, the reliable and well-equipped Sunny was an indoctrination into Japanese car ownership. And although road-testers tended to look down their noses at the underdamped, under-geared 120Y, buyers loved them. The coupé, especially, picked up quite a following thanks to its swoopy styling and unmistakable 'pie-dish' hub caps. Most were driven into scrapyards in the 1980s, healthy engines pulling their rotten shells to their doom, but those that survive are loved and cherished.

SPECIFICATIONS

Years produced:	1973-1978 (2,360,670 in total)
Performance:	0-60mph: 16.0sec
	Top speed: 90mph
Power & torque:	53bhp/70lb ft
Engine:	Normally aspirated 1171cc four cylinder, petrol, carburettor, 8 valves
Drivetrain:	Front-engine RWD
Structure:	Monocoque
Transmission:	Four-speed manual
Weight:	810kg

PRICE GUIDE

Launch price:	£1049
Excellent:	£2500
Good:	£1500
Average:	£650
Project:	£350

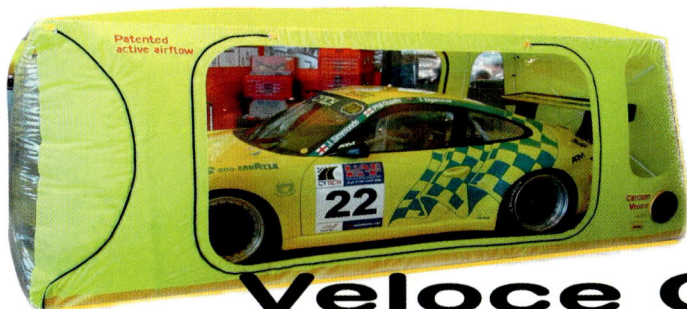

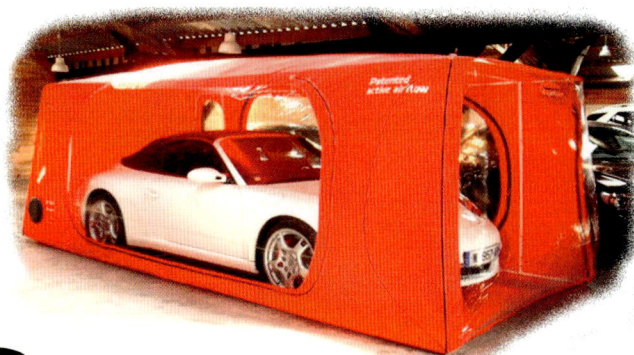

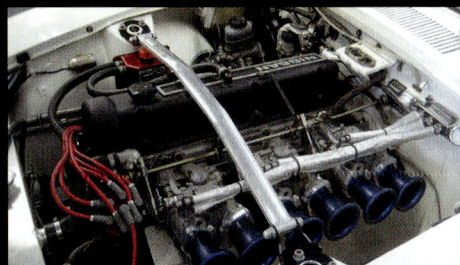

DATSUN
260Z

Despite adding power and equipment to the mix, the Datsun 260Z has always lived in the shadow of its older brother. Two-seat models looked as good as the original, but the introduction of the 2+2 with a 12-inch longer wheelbase and reprofiled roofline diluted appeal despite being a lot more useful. Performance for the two-seater car is similar to the 240Z's and, because prices are lower, they are excellent value. Sold half as many as the first Z-car, and survival rate is shocking in the UK – mainly because, like all '70s Datsuns, it rusted appallingly.

SPECIFICATIONS

Years produced:	1974-1978 (total: see 240Z)
Performance:	0-60mph: 8.8sec
	Top speed: 127mph
Power & torque:	162bhp/152lb ft
Engine:	Normally aspirated 2565cc six cylinder, petrol, carburettor, 12 valves
Drivetrain:	Front-engine RWD
Structure:	Monocoque
Transmission:	Five-speed manual
Weight:	1164kg

PRICE GUIDE

Launch price:	£2896
Excellent:	£10,000
Good:	£7000
Average:	£3500
Project:	£1500

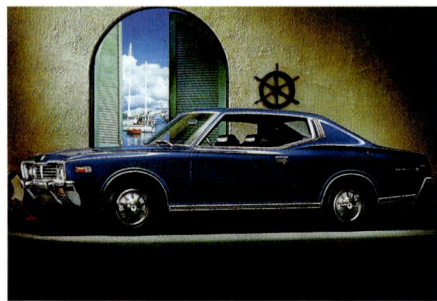

DATSUN
Cedric 260C (330)

Large Datsuns failed to capture the imagination of British executive car buyers during the 1970s. It was hoped that the 1976 260C would turn the tide, but a combination of duff dynamics and tacky image (and interiors) saw the 260C continue to be a showroom ornament through the strife-torn '70s. The facelift gave the 260C more style, even if it looked too American – but it certainly looks good now. The pillarless coupé was never imported into the UK new, but a few have subsequently been imported, and are popular with those who like '70s Orientals.

SPECIFICATIONS (260C)

Years produced:	1976-1979
Performance:	0-60mph: 11.3sec
	Top speed: 109mph
Power & torque:	151bhp/188lb ft
Engine:	Normally aspirated 2565cc six cylinder, petrol, carburettor, 12 valves
Drivetrain:	Front-engine RWD
Structure:	Monocoque
Transmission:	Five-speed manual/three-speed auto
Weight:	1350kg

PRICE GUIDE

Launch price:	N/A
Excellent:	£7000
Good:	£2500
Average:	£1200
Project:	£750

DATSUN
Bluebird 160/180B

The Bluebird 710 series rode on the crest of Datsun's big push into the UK, and its follow-up, the 810 or 180B, really sold well. Although the road-testers did their best to disparage the 180B for its vague damping and steering, customers loved its keen pricing and standard-fit radio/cassette. The 180B SSS Coupé suffered, like all Datsuns of the time, from fussy styling, and failed to attract Capri and Manta buyers. But today, it's the pillarless two-door rather than the four-door saloon that people want – and examples continue to be imported into the UK.

SPECIFICATIONS (180B Coupé)

Years produced:	1976-1979
Performance:	0-60mph: 10.9sec
	Top speed: 106mph
Power & torque:	95bhp/103lb ft
Engine:	Normally aspirated 1770cc four cylinder, petrol, carburettor, valves
Drivetrain:	Front-engine RWD
Structure:	Monocoque
Transmission:	Five-speed manual
Weight:	1035kg

PRICE GUIDE

Launch price:	N/A
Excellent:	£4500
Good:	£2500
Average:	£1200
Project:	£750

DATSUN
240K Skyline

Although the Skyline had been around in Japan since 1957, when it was introduced by defunct manufacturer Prince, the UK had to wait until the '70s to see what had become Datsun's big GT. When unveiled in 1978, the straight six-powered 240K was distinguished by its American-inspired styling but, following a series of damning road tests that criticised its sloppy handling and excessive thirst, it failed to sell. Datsun quietly pulled the plug, and few remain as a result. A number have since been imported, riding high on the Skyline GT-R cult and vibrant scene for Japanese classics.

SPECIFICATIONS

Years produced:	1978-1981 (576,797 in total)
Performance:	0-60mph: 11.0sec
	Top speed: 109mph
Power & torque:	127bhp/132lb ft
Engine:	Normally aspirated 2393cc six cylinder, petrol, mechanical fuel injection, 12 valves
Drivetrain:	Front-engine RWD
Structure:	Monocoque
Transmission:	Five-speed manual
Weight:	1266kg

PRICE GUIDE

Launch price:	£6001
Excellent:	£3000
Good:	£1500
Average:	£650
Project:	£500

DATSUN/NISSAN
280ZX

Symbolic of the Z-car's descent into middle-aged spread, the 280ZX was far less appealing than the car it replaced. Longer, wider, heavier and uglier, the new 2.8-litre car was very much a boulevardier rather than a full-blooded sports car. Equipment levels were lavish, and power steering, all-round disc brakes and semi-trailing arm rear suspension were further refinements that cast the Z-car very much in the luxury car sector. Despite being panned when new, it sold well in the USA and is still very much in demand as a modern, useable classic car.

SPECIFICATIONS

Years produced:	1978-1983 (414,358 in total)
Performance:	0-60mph: 8.3sec
	Top speed: 117mph
Power & torque:	140bhp/149lb ft
Engine:	Normally aspirated 2753cc six cylinder, petrol, electronic fuel injection, 12 valves
Drivetrain:	Front-engine RWD
Structure:	Monocoque
Transmission:	Five-speed manual
Weight:	1272kg

PRICE GUIDE

Launch price:	£8103
Excellent:	£4250
Good:	£3000
Average:	£1750
Project:	£800

NISSAN
Silvia

The Silvia name was familiar to North American and Asian buyers, but was new to Britain in 1984. And when it was launched, the Silvia was a breath of fresh air in a stagnating coupé market. With a turbocharged 1.8-litre engine and RWD, it was huge fun to drive thanks to its keen, direct steering and firm, well-controlled suspension. Considering the 1984 300ZX was such a disappointment, this was a welcome return to form for Nissan. Not many left in the UK as most succumbed to rust, but those that remain are cherished.

SPECIFICATIONS

Years produced:	1984-1989
Performance:	0-60mph: 8.1sec
	Top speed: 125mph
Power & torque:	133bhp/141lb ft
Engine:	Turbocharged 1809cc four cylinder, petrol, electronic fuel injection, 8 valves
Drivetrain:	Front-engine RWD
Structure:	Monocoque
Transmission:	Five-speed manual
Weight:	1150kg

PRICE GUIDE

Launch price:	£11,870
Excellent:	£4000
Good:	£2600
Average:	£1000
Project:	£600

NISSAN
300ZX Turbo

A sharp new look for the 1984 Nissan 300ZX failed to add any excitement to the Z-car line, despite it being all-new under the skin, and the first in the line to feature a V6 engine. The familiar-looking styling was more aerodynamic than before, boasting a drag co-efficient of just 0.30. In the UK, it was the first to be fitted with a turbo, which delivered lots of straight-line pace if not finesse. Handling was firmer than the Datsun 280ZX's, but still not good enough for the 300ZX to be considered a sports car in the traditional sense of the word.

SPECIFICATIONS

Years produced:	1984-1989
Performance:	0-60mph: 7.1sec
	Top speed: 147mph
Power & torque:	226bhp/246lb ft
Engine:	Turbocharged 2960cc V6, petrol, electronic fuel injection, 12 valves
Drivetrain:	Front-engine RWD
Structure:	Monocoque
Transmission:	Five-speed manual
Weight:	1324kg

PRICE GUIDE

Launch price:	£16,996
Excellent:	£3600
Good:	£4000
Average:	£2000
Project:	£800

NISSAN
Sunny ZX Turbo

Nissan's 1986 Sunny range was hardly a memorable addition to the Escort class. Known as the Pulsar just about everywhere else in the world, the competent FWD hatchback became a driving school favourite, because it was so easy to operate. The ZX coupé had one distinction over the car it was based on: it was a head-turner. Sadly, the looks were deceiving, because that promising styling wasn't realised on the road. Poor ride and handling could be forgiven on the low-powered version, but the turbocharged car with 135bhp could be a real handful.

SPECIFICATIONS

Years produced:	1987-1991 (1,900,000 in total)
Performance:	0-60mph: 8.3sec
	Top speed: 128mph
Power & torque:	135bhp/141lb ft
Engine:	Turbocharged 1809cc four cylinder, petrol, fuel injection, 8 valves
Drivetrain:	Front-engine FWD
Structure:	Monocoque
Transmission:	Five-speed manual
Weight:	1070kg

PRICE GUIDE

Launch price:	£11,696
Excellent:	£1800
Good:	£1250
Average:	£750
Project:	£350

NISSAN
Skyline GT-R (R32)

When the GT-R came to Europe, it made serious waves. Capable of lapping the Nürburgring faster than a Porsche 928GTS, this triumph of technology over breeding created a new breed of cult Japanese sports cars. The car was conceived for Group A racing, and featured four-wheel drive, four-wheel steering and a turbocharged RB20 straight six. In Europe, the Skyline GT-R failed to sell in huge numbers, but gained a giant-killing reputation that subsequent generations have maintained. Affordable today, but unmodified versions are few and far between.

SPECIFICATIONS

Years produced:	1989-1994 (43,706 in total)
Performance:	0-60mph: 5.6sec
	Top speed: 156mph
Power & torque:	276bhp/260lb ft
Engine:	Twin turbocharged 2569cc straight six, petrol, fuel injection, 8 valves
Drivetrain:	Front-engine FWD
Structure:	Monocoque
Transmission:	Five-speed manual
Weight:	1430kg

PRICE GUIDE

Launch price:	N/A in UK
Excellent:	£12,000
Good:	£7500
Average:	£5000
Project:	£2500

NISSAN
Silvia 200SX

When the 200SX arrived on the scene in 1989 it seemed that Nissan had rediscovered its sports car mojo, which was apparently lost at the end of the 260Z production run in 1978. With 197bhp on tap and an exploitable RWD chassis, it was an excellent driver's car – and thanks to old-fashioned good looks, it was also desirable in the showroom. Nissan had no trouble selling all it could import, and it remained popular until it went out of production. Has gone on to enjoy a successful afterlife thanks to the drifting scene, and unmolested examples are now rare.

SPECIFICATIONS

Years produced:	1989-1996 (1,081,200 in total)
Performance:	0-60mph: 7.0sec
	Top speed: 146mph
Power & torque:	197bhp/195lb ft
Engine:	Turbocharged 1998cc four cylinder, petrol, fuel injection, 16 valves
Drivetrain:	Front-engine RWD
Structure:	Monocoque
Transmission:	Five-speed manual
Weight:	1270kg

PRICE GUIDE

Launch price:	£16,996
Excellent:	£4000
Good:	£2600
Average:	£1000
Project:	£600

NISSAN
Pao

Not too many people remember the Pao today, as it's been overshadowed by the 1991 Figaro. But the 1989 Pao was Nissan's first stab at a retro-styled pastiche, perfectly judged for the boom in classic car interest in Japan. Corrugated sides and hinged side windows hinted at the Renault 4 and Citroën 2CV, while the frontal styling and general cuddliness shouted Mini. But underneath, the Pao was a Micra, and that meant reliability and a nice and easy drive. The Pao was the second of a series of three retro-cars (following Be-1) and sold out in three months.

SPECIFICATIONS

Years produced:	1989
Performance:	0-60mph: 14.1sec
	Top speed: 85mph
Power & torque:	51bhp/55lb ft
Engine:	Normally aspirated 988cc four cylinder, petrol, carburettor, 8 valves
Drivetrain:	Front-engine FWD
Structure:	Monocoque
Transmission:	Five-speed manual
Weight:	720kg

PRICE GUIDE

Launch price:	N/A in UK
Excellent:	£4000
Good:	£3000
Average:	£2500
Project:	N/A

NISSAN
S-Cargo

Nissan's cutely named Pike factory, which also saw Be-1, Pao and Figaro production, was responsible for the S-Cargo. Clearly the success of the Citroën 2CV had a big impact on Nissan, and its S-Cargo ('Escargot', get it?) was heavily influenced by the French car. Stand-out points are the bug headlamps and slab sides, but the single-spoke steering wheel must have been a welcoming touch for Citroënistes. The S-Cargo is popular around the world as a grey import, where its funky looks make for a great promotional tool.

SPECIFICATIONS

Years produced:	1989-1991 (c.12,000 in total)
Performance:	0-60mph: 14.1sec
	Top speed: 85mph
Power & torque:	72bhp/86lb ft
Engine:	Normally aspirated 1487cc four cylinder, petrol, carburettor, 8 valves
Drivetrain:	Front-engine FWD
Structure:	Monocoque
Transmission:	Three-speed automatic
Weight:	950kg

PRICE GUIDE

Launch price:	N/A in UK
Excellent:	£3500
Good:	£3000
Average:	£2000
Project:	N/A

DELOREAN

JOHN Z DELOREAN was an all-American high-flying car industry hero. At General Motors he'd made it to the sixth floor at a famously young age, thanks to the success of his GTO muscle car. However, he wanted to produce top-flight sports cars, and that ambition eventually forced him to cut loose. In the early '70s, he started work on a new gullwing sports car and, thanks to Italdesign, Lotus and the British government, managed to get the DMC-12 into production in Dunmurry, Northern Ireland, in 1981. However, the car sold poorly, and the company went bankrupt the following year – following allegations that DeLorean was selling drugs, a charge of which he was acquitted in court.

DELOREAN
DMC-12

John DeLorean set out to build his own vision of a sports car in the late 1970s and, on paper, it must have looked amazing. It featured a low-slung and pointy Giugiaro design, brushed steel outer skin, gullwing doors and a fuel-injection 2849cc V6 engine mounted 911-style at the rear. Unfortunately, the 1981 reality turned out to be less stimulating. The car was so heavy that the V6 struggled to offer sporty performance and the handling remained dodgy even after Lotus engineers had done their best. The company collapsed amid scandal in 1982.

SPECIFICATIONS

Years produced:	1981-1982 (c10,000 in total)
Performance:	0-60mph: 9.6sec
	Top speed: 130mph
Power & torque:	130bhp/153lb ft
Engine:	Normally aspirated 2849cc V6, petrol, electronic fuel injection, 12 valves
Drivetrain:	Rear-engine RWD
Structure:	Backbone chassis/glassfibre core
Transmission:	Five-speed manual
Weight:	1244kg

PRICE GUIDE

Launch price:	£10,674
Excellent:	£25,000
Good:	£17,000
Average:	£12,000
Project:	£8000

DE TOMASO

ARGENTINEAN FORMER racing driver Alejandro de Tomaso moved to Italy in the late '50s and started to build racing cars. In 1967, De Tomaso branched out into production cars with the Mangusta. Like most subsequent models this was powered by a Ford V8 engine. The company's staple product, the Pantera, followed in 1970, and was soon joined by the Deauville and Longchamps. In the '70s De Tomaso acquired Maserati and Innocenti, which ended selling the Mini across Europe, though the former was sold off in 1993. Production in fits and starts since, including V8-powered Guarà and Bigua, and relaunched in 2011 with a luxury saloon/crossover.

DE TOMASO
Vallelunga

First displayed at the 1964 Turin Show, the De Tomaso Vallelunga was a mid-engineered pioneer. It was a racer for the road, powered by a Ford Cortina engine with a Hewland transaxle, the glorious-looking was shaped in aluminium at the Fissore coachworks. Only three were were built before De Tomaso transferred the contract to Ghia, and these later cars were finished in glassfibre. Torsional rigidity was lacking, and that compromised handling and refinement. After a run of 50, the sweet little Vallelunga was dropped in favour of the Magusta.

SPECIFICATIONS

Years produced:	1964-1968 (55 in total)
Performance:	0-60mph: 6.0sec
	Top speed: 155mph
Power & torque:	135bhp/112lb ft
Engine:	Normally aspirated 1498cc four cylinder, petrol, carburettor, 16 valves
Drivetrain:	Mid-engine RWD
Structure:	Separate chassis
Transmission:	Five-speed manual
Weight:	500kg

PRICE GUIDE

Launch price:	N/A in UK
Excellent:	£125,000
Good:	£80,000
Average:	£65,000
Project:	N/A

DE TOMASO
Mangusta

De Tomaso married the cancelled Ford 70P racing car programme with a rejected Iso design proposal by Giugiaro to create the Mangusta – the company's very first supercar. Essentially a racing car for the road with svelte styling, it ended up being too hard to handle, and extremely difficult to live with. But that doesn't stop it being great today – and although values seriously lag behind those of the supercar opposition, don't imagine that the Mangusta isn't a desirable car with prices that are bound to rise. It's a real stunner.

SPECIFICATIONS

Years produced:	1967-1972 (400 in total)
Performance:	0-60mph: 6.0sec
	Top speed: 155mph
Power & torque:	305bhp/392lb ft
Engine:	Normally aspirated 4727cc V8, petrol, carburettor, 16 valves
Drivetrain:	Mid-engine RWD
Structure:	Separate chassis
Transmission:	Five-speed manual
Weight:	1322kg

PRICE GUIDE

Launch price:	Special order only
Excellent:	£75,000
Good:	£45,000
Average:	£30,000
Project:	£17,500

DE TOMASO
Deauville

It seemed like a good idea at the time, and had there been any justice, more Deauvilles might have found their way into owners' hands. As it was, it was a big failure. De Tomaso set out to create its own XJ6, but without the complexity. So in went the Pantera's Detroit V8, and had BL not been in dire straits itself, the company's lawyers may have been well knocking on the door over the matter of the Deauville's styling. Despite the market not wanting it then, it's an interesting classic today, and well worth a look, should the opportunity arise.

SPECIFICATIONS

Years produced:	1970-1989 (355 in total)
Performance:	0-60mph: 6.4sec
	Top speed: 143mph
Power & torque:	330bhp/325lb ft
Engine:	Normally aspirated 5763cc V8, petrol, carburettor, 16 valves
Drivetrain:	Front-engine RWD
Structure:	Monocoque
Transmission:	Five-speed manual/three-speed auto
Weight:	1814kg

PRICE GUIDE

Launch price:	£8992
Excellent:	£15,000
Good:	£10,000
Average:	£5000
Project:	£2000

DE TOMASO
Pantera

De Tomaso learned a lot of lessons with the Mangusta, so when it came to creating a new supercar for Ford to sell in the USA, it made sure the car was a lot more habitable. The reworked chassis ensured there was a lot less rearward weight bias and, therefore, snap oversteer wasn't an inevitable consequence of a bungled corner. The interior was roomier, and had standard air conditioning. However, quality and reliability were poor and, when Ford withdrew its support, De Tomaso had to go it alone with the Pantera.

SPECIFICATIONS

Years produced:	1971-1985
Performance:	0-60mph: 6.2sec
	Top speed: 159mph
Power & torque:	330bhp/325lb ft
Engine:	Normally aspirated 5763cc V8, petrol, carburettor, 16 valves
Drivetrain:	Mid-engine RWD
Structure:	Monocoque
Transmission:	Five-speed manual
Weight:	1411kg

PRICE GUIDE

Launch price:	£6996
Excellent:	£45,000
Good:	£30,000
Average:	£15,000
Project:	£9000

DE TOMASO
Longchamp

Having failed with the Deauville, De Tomaso went and repeated the concept with its Longchamp. Again, it was a case of producing an Italian version of another manufacturer s car – this time, the Mercedes-Benz 450SLC – going down the same road to do so. Again, sales were non-existent, mainly because there was simply no demand, and the quality just wasn't there. Once De Tomaso took a controlling interest in Maserati, it tried again with the car, rebadging it the Kyalami (complete with Maserati V8). Similar apathy ensued.

SPECIFICATIONS

Years produced:	1972-1989 (409 in total)
Performance:	0-60mph: 6.4sec
	Top speed: 149mph
Power & torque:	330bhp/325lb ft
Engine:	Normally aspirated 5763cc V8, petrol, carburettor, 16 valves
Drivetrain:	Front-engine RWD
Structure:	Monocoque
Transmission:	Five-speed manual/three-speed auto
Weight:	1814kg

PRICE GUIDE

Launch price:	£9945
Excellent:	£25,000
Good:	£15,000
Average:	£7500
Project:	£4500

DE TOMASO
Pantera GT5/GT5S

De Tomaso didn't give up on the Pantera. The firm toughened it up, offered a 300bhp entry model, and rejigged the Tom Tjaarda styling with flared arches and wider wheels wearing Pirelli P7s to give it near-Countach levels of road presence. The days of big sales were gone, but somehow the Pantera survived like this into the 1990s by receiving a number of facelifts along the way. Its survival and subsequent appreciation are a credit to the original design, and testament to the effectiveness of an Italian supercar powered by Detroit muscle.

SPECIFICATIONS

Years produced:	1985-1991 (10,000 approx in total)
Performance:	0-60mph: 5.2sec
	Top speed: 146mph
Power & torque:	350bhp/330lb ft
Engine:	Normally aspirated 5763cc V8, petrol, carburettor, 16 valves
Drivetrain:	Mid-engine RWD
Structure:	Monocoque
Transmission:	Five-speed manual
Weight:	1491kg

PRICE GUIDE

Launch price:	£41,410
Excellent:	£40,000
Good:	£30,000
Average:	£20,000
Project:	£12,000

ELVA

ELVA STARTED out as a specials manufacturer set-up by Frank Nichols and based in Bexhill, Sussex. Its first car was completed in 1955, based on a combination of Ford power, Standard suspension and a hand-fabricated chassis, and known as the Mk1. It soon established itself as quite a force in club level competition. The Mk1 was subsequently developed with more sophisticated suspension set-ups and esoteric (Coventry Climax) engines, and sold well in the USA.

Unfortunately, financial problems beset Elva in 1961, when the government refused to support the company's proposed growth plans. Although it continued until 1965, Nichols meanwhile sold the operation to Ken Sheppard.

ELVA
Courier

Created by Frank Nichols for racing, the Courier was a quintessential English specialist car that married low weight, great handling and excellent performance in a low-cost package. However, Nichols sold the project to Trojan, which introduced an improved version in 1962. In MkIII form, the Courier received a number of small changes to its chassis as well as a roomier cockpit. Sales dried up following the Trojan takeover and production ceased in 1968 after a final fling with a stylish coupé version,

SPECIFICATIONS

Years produced:	1958-1961 (500 in total)
Performance:	0-60mph: 12.7sec
	Top speed: 98mph
Power & torque:	72bhp/77lb ft
Engine:	Normally aspirated 1489cc four cylinder, petrol, carburettor, 8 valves
Drivetrain:	Front-engine RWD
Structure:	Glassfibre body/separate chassis
Transmission:	Four-speed manual
Weight:	453kg

PRICE GUIDE

Launch price:	£725
Excellent:	£10,000
Good:	£8000
Average:	£5000
Project:	£2500

ELVA
Elva-BMW GT160

The GT160 marked a massive change in direction for Elva when it was launched in 1964 – and it had the ingredients for success, had events not overtaken it. Trojan, Elva's parent company, was pulling out of car manufacture and, even though the Trevor Fiore-styled GT160 looked promising, a mere three were built. It was built on a Mk7S racing chassis and, with the prototype pushing out 182bhp, performance was impressive. One was entered at the Le Mans 24 Hours in 1965, where it proved to be the fastest British car.

SPECIFICATIONS

Years produced:	1964 (3 in total)
Performance:	0-60mph: 6.9sec
	Top speed: 140mph
Power & torque:	185bhp/150lb ft
Engine:	Normally aspirated 1991cc four cylinder, petrol, carburettor, 8 valves
Drivetrain:	Front-engine RWD
Structure:	Glassfibre body/separate chassis
Transmission:	Four-speed manual
Weight:	559kg

PRICE GUIDE

Launch price:	N/A
Excellent:	Currently too rare to value
Good:	N/A
Average:	N/A
Project:	N/A

FACEL VEGA

FACEL VEGA – handily shortened from the cumbersome 'Forges et Ateliers de Construction de l'Eure et Loire' – was a French coachbuilder before, in 1954, it branched out into cars. The company only existed for ten years but, in that decade, it built some extraordinary machines with lashings of luxury and powerful Chrysler V8 engines. They were also expensive so, in 1959, the company attempted something more competitively priced in the form of the four-cylinder Facellia. It was unreliable and even Volvo P1800 and Austin-Healey 3000 engines couldn't save the car or the company. Facel Vega went bust in 1964, toppled by the many warranty claims against it.

FACEL VEGA
FV/FVS

Facel started out by building bodies for other manufacturers before going it alone in 1954 with a De Soto-engined car called the Vega. Once the car became established the company rebranded itself Facel Vega, and the car became the FVS. From the original 4.5-litre V8, the FVS moved to 5.4-litre Chrysler power – and the tubular-framed chassis car boasted 330bhp. To rein in all that power, a brake servo was fitted in 1957, and disc brakes were an option the following year. It was a simple recipe and the quality was there, as was the driving experience.

SPECIFICATIONS
Years produced: 1954-1958 (352 in total)
Performance: 0-60mph: 9.6sec
Top speed: 134mph
Power & torque: 330bhp/430lb ft
Engine: Normally aspirated 5801cc V8, petrol, carburettor, 16 valves
Drivetrain: Front-engine RWD
Structure: Separate chassis
Transmission: Two-speed auto/four-speed manual
Weight: 1863kg

PRICE GUIDE
Launch price: £4726
Excellent: £75,000
Good: £60,000
Average: £45,000
Project: £30,000

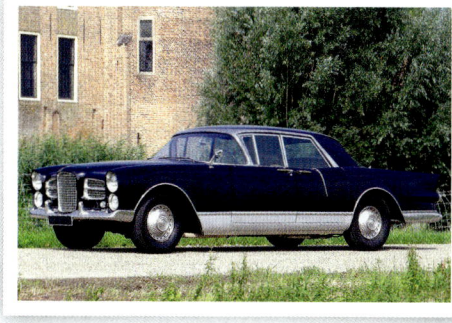

FACEL VEGA
Excellence

It was France's flagship limousine for six glorious years, and although the Excellence was far from perfect, it oozed charisma. Facel Vega created the Excellence by extending the FVS wheelbase by 20in and creating an all-new body. It was a fantastic-looking limousine, with clap-hands doors and panoramic windscreen, but the lack of a B-pillar caused structural issues in later life. Once again, Chrysler V8 power ensured ample performance (and thirst), and simpler restorations. A desirable prestige saloon, not just for Francophiles.

SPECIFICATIONS
Years produced: 1958-1964 (152 in total)
Performance: 0-60mph: 11.0sec
Top speed: 120mph
Power & torque: 335bhp/380lb ft
Engine: Normally aspirated 5905cc V8, petrol, carburettor, 16 valves
Drivetrain: Front-engine RWD
Structure: Separate chassis
Transmission: Three-speed auto
Weight: 1956kg

PRICE GUIDE
Launch price: N/A
Excellent: £100,000
Good: £75,000
Average: £45,000
Project: £15,000

FACEL VEGA
HK500

The FVS was uprated in 1959 with a 360bhp 6.3-litre engine, making it one of the most powerful cars in Europe. Even with the power boost, the all-drum brake set-up was standard kit on the HK500 – not what you would necessarily want in a car with such prodigious straight-line performance. Despite that, it was a perfect flagship for the French car industry, even if the overall dynamics of the HK500 lagged behind the styling and straight-line performance. Chrysler power, steering and transmissions mean that parts supply is good. Rare, expensive and hard to find now.

SPECIFICATIONS
Years produced: 1958-1961 (490 in total)
Performance: 0-60mph: 9.7sec
Top speed: 130mph
Power & torque: 360bhp/400lb ft
Engine: Normally aspirated 5905cc V8, petrol, carburettor, 16 valves
Drivetrain: Front-engine RWD
Structure: Separate chassis
Transmission: Four-speed manual
Weight: 1829kg

PRICE GUIDE
Launch price: £4726
Excellent: £65,000
Good: £30,000
Average: £20,000
Project: £10,000

FACEL VEGA
Facellia

Facel Vega needed to up its production volumes to make up the shortfall in its third-party body supply business. As the 'affordable' second model, the Facellia was to help the firm expand while allowing it to continue producing V8-powered supercars. The 1.6-litre twin-cam engine had an impressive specification, but the 115bhp it made wasn't enough for anything other than average performance, and it wasn't reliable enough either. A great concept marred in the execution, with gorgeous HK500-like styling and still prized by enthusiasts today.

SPECIFICATIONS
Years produced: 1960-1964 (1767 in total)
Performance: 0-60mph: 11.9sec
Top speed: 106mph
Power & torque: 115bhp/106lb ft
Engine: Normally aspirated 1647cc four cylinder, petrol, carburettor, 8 valves
Drivetrain: Front-engine RWD
Structure: Separate chassis
Transmission: Four-speed manual
Weight: 1153kg

PRICE GUIDE
Launch price: £2582
Excellent: £25,000
Good: £14,000
Average: £8000
Project: £3250

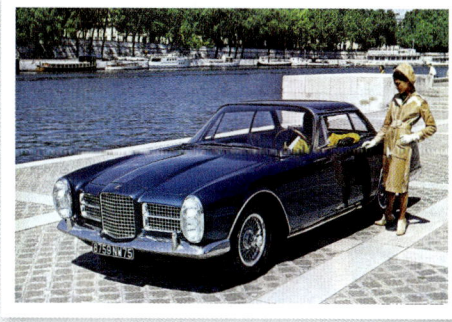

FACEL VEGA
Facel II

Continuing Facel Vega's policy of regular updates, the HK500 remained in production for only two years, moving over for the Facel II. The new car featured sharper styling and an even more powerful Chrysler V8, now offerng 390bhp and finally allowing the French supercar to top a genuine 150mph. However, the chassis and steering were simply not good enough to control all this power, marring what was an extremely appealing package. Despite all that, a very cool car today, especially as it's the last in the line of big V8 Facel Vegas.

SPECIFICATIONS
Years produced: 1961-1964 (183 in total)
Performance: 0-60mph: 8.4sec
Top speed: 129mph
Power & torque: 355bhp/380lb ft
Engine: Normally aspirated 6286cc V8, petrol, carburettor, 16 valves
Drivetrain: Front-engine RWD
Structure: Separate chassis
Transmission: Four-speed manual
Weight: 1842kg

PRICE GUIDE
Launch price: £4879
Excellent: £110,000
Good: £80,500
Average: £50,000
Project: £35,000

FACEL VEGA
Facel III

Amazingly, when it came to replacing the Facel II, the idea of increasing power and opulence was thrown out of the window as the company adopted a clean-sheet policy for its new car. The Facel III was powered by a 1780cc Volvo engine, and delivered the sort of performance that was ample for most drivers. It sold well too, as it managed to retain all the dignity and style of the V8 cars in a more manageable package. However, the company was already in trouble when it launched and, despite its relative success, it failed to halt the inevitable.

SPECIFICATIONS

Years produced:	1963-1964
Performance:	0-60mph: N/A
	Top speed: N/A
Power & torque:	108bhp/N/A
Engine:	Normally aspirated 1780cc four cylinder, petrol, carburettor, 8 valves
Drivetrain:	Front-engine RWD
Structure:	Separate chassis
Transmission:	Four-speed manual
Weight:	1089kg

PRICE GUIDE

Launch price:	N/A
Excellent:	£25,000
Good:	£16,000
Average:	£9000
Project:	£4000

FERRARI

Maranello
CLASSIC PARTS

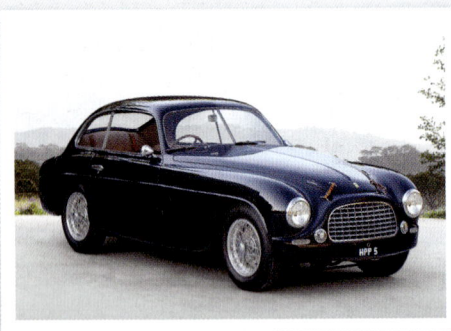

ONE OF MOTORING'S great legends, Enzo Ferrari left Alfa Romeo in 1938 to build his own racing cars. To help finance these he turned to road car production in 1947 with the V12-powered 166. Many still only consider V12 cars to be 'real' Ferraris, and they are revered by collectors. Years of domination in F1, sports cars and road-car desirability followed. In 1969 the company joined the Fiat empire, but retained control of its pedigree, rarely even dipping far into Fiat's parts bin. Enzo stepped down in 1971, retaining influence until his death in 1988, aged 90. The legacy of the company he created remains in safe hands, still racing in F1, and still creating hugely desirable road cars.

FERRARI
166

Although Enzo Ferrari set up his own car company in 1940, it wasn't until 1947 that he launched the racing 125. Subsequently available with Touring bodies, they proved to be wonderful machines when partnered with Gioacchino Colombo's jewel-like V12 engine. The 125s were 1.5-litres, while the true road-going 166 was introduced with a 2.0-litre. Available with Pinin Farina, Bertone, Ghia, Vignale and Allemano bodies to complement the most widely known by Touring. Racing credentials were thoroughly proven at Le Mans, where it won in 1949.

SPECIFICATIONS

Years produced:	1947-1953 (71 in total)
Performance:	0-60mph: 9.5sec
	Top speed: 106mph
Power & torque:	110bhp/120lb ft
Engine:	Normally aspirated 1995cc V12, petrol, carburettor, 24 valves
Drivetrain:	Front-engine RWD
Structure:	Tubular frame
Transmission:	Four-speed manual
Weight:	980kg

PRICE GUIDE (Barchetta worth more)

Launch price:	N/A
Excellent:	£350,000
Good:	£220,000
Average:	£175,000
Project:	£125,000

FERRARI
195

A logical and useful update of the 166 that cemented Ferrari's position at the pinnacle of motor sport and road car production. The V12 had been bored out and, in the hottest versions with a trio of carburettors, was capable of delivering 180bhp. The Inter model was the car you bought for the road, while the Sport was the one you raced. As with the 166, the 195 was available with a number of coachbuilt bodies, all in aluminium. The most popular were by Ghia and Vignale, but Pinin Farina, Touring and Ghia-Aigle were also available.

SPECIFICATIONS (195 Inter)

Years produced:	1950-1952 (27 in total)
Performance:	0-60mph: 8.0sec
	Top speed: 115mph
Power & torque:	130bhp/130lb ft
Engine:	Normally aspirated 2341cc V12, petrol, carburettor, 24 valves
Drivetrain:	Front-engine RWD
Structure:	Tubular frame
Transmission:	Four-speed manual
Weight:	950kg

PRICE GUIDE (Barchetta worth more)

Launch price:	N/A
Excellent:	£400,000
Good:	£250,000
Average:	£175,000
Project:	£125,000

FERRARI
212

The 195's V12 was once again bored out, this time to 2562cc – or 212cc per cylinder, hence the name. Power and torque were improved, most notably to improve all-round flexibility. Ferrari's reputation continued to rise as the 212's competition victories were racked up. The 212 was an important Ferrari in the USA, where the Export model sold well. Also available in 212 Inter form, which meant road spec, and these cars received a lengthened 98.5in wheelbase. Still essentially based on the Type 166 and available with a myriad of coachbuilt bodies.

SPECIFICATIONS

Years produced:	1951-1953 (106 in total)
Performance:	0-60mph: 8.1sec
	Top speed: 120mph
Power & torque:	140bhp/162lb ft
Engine:	Normally aspirated 2562cc V12, petrol, carburettor, 24 valves
Drivetrain:	Front-engine RWD
Structure:	Tubular frame
Transmission:	Four-speed manual
Weight:	923kg

PRICE GUIDE (Barchetta worth more)

Launch price:	N/A
Excellent:	£500,000
Good:	£350,000
Average:	£275,000
Project:	£200,000

FERRARI
340/342/375 America

The 340 was the final flowering of the 166 chassis. As for the V12, a long-block version had been designed by Aurelio Lampredi, and also used in Ferrari's Formula 1 cars. The combination was exciting, and a fitting finale for the 166, especially as the ultimate Mexico developed 280bhp, almost three times the original car's power. 340 and 342 shared the 4.1-litre engine; the 375 had no less than 4.5-litres, and was available in road and competition car form. Values are at least double those of the 166, although they vary hugely due to provenance.

SPECIFICATIONS (340 Mexico)

Years produced:	1950-1955 (41 in total)
Performance:	0-60mph: 6.0sec
	Top speed: 142mph
Power & torque:	280bhp/228lb ft
Engine:	Normally aspirated 4102cc V12, petrol, carburettor, 24 valves
Drivetrain:	Front-engine RWD
Structure:	Tubular frame
Transmission:	Four-speed manual
Weight:	1000kg

PRICE GUIDE (Spider worth more)

Launch price:	N/A
Excellent:	£500,000
Good:	£350,000
Average:	£275,000
Project:	£200,000

FERRARI
250GT Boano/Ellena

The strange name comes from the coachbuilding firm that bodied the cars for Ferrari. Although designed by Pininfarina, it was erecting a new plant and didn't have capacity to build them. The work was given to former employee Mario Boano, then, after around 80 were built, the contract was passed to his son-in-law Ezio Ellena, who assembled another 50. Early cars put out 220bhp from their 3.0-litre V12 engines, but this rose to 240bhp. Despite independent double wishbone front suspension, the chassis is fairly crude.

SPECIFICATIONS

Years produced:	1956-1959 (130 in total)
Performance:	0-60mph: 7.1sec
	Top speed: 126mph
Power & torque:	260bhp/232lb ft
Engine:	Normally aspirated 2953cc V12, petrol, carburettor, 24 valves
Drivetrain:	Front-engine RWD
Structure:	Tubular frame
Transmission:	Four-speed manual
Weight:	1315kg

PRICE GUIDE

Launch price:	N/A
Excellent:	£300,000
Good:	£220,000
Average:	£175,000
Project:	£125,000

FERRARI
250 California Spider

Largely built for the American market, California Spiders were that bit more sporting than the 250 GT Cabriolets they were based on. By 1960, just under 50 long-wheelbase versions were built with 240bhp engines. The wheelbase was then chopped by 8in to create the short wheelbase (SWB) version. Power went up to 280bhp and another 50 of these were sold over the next three years. They can be worth around 25% more than the LWB cars, but the rare alloy-bodied versions of either (just 12 built) can hit the £5m mark.

SPECIFICATIONS

Years produced:	1958-1962 (100 approx in total)
Performance:	0-60mph: 7.2sec
	Top speed: 137mph
Power & torque:	240bhp/181lb ft
Engine:	Normally aspirated 2953cc V12, petrol, carburettor, 24 valves
Drivetrain:	Front-engine RWD
Structure:	Tubular frame
Transmission:	Four-speed manual
Weight:	1277kg

PRICE GUIDE (long wheelbase in brackets)

Launch price:	N/A
Excellent:	£3,500,000 (£2,000,000)
Good:	£3,000,000 (£1,750,000)
Average:	£2,500,000 (£1,500,000)
Project:	£2,000,000 (£1,250,000)

FERRARI
250GT SWB

Seriously collectable Ferraris, not least due to the fact that only just over 150 were built and almost half were competition cars. The racers reigned supreme in the GT classes and one was driven in period by Stirling Moss; such exploits rub off on the desirability and value of road cars. History and provenance can have almost as much effect on an individual SWB's price as condition. All came with 3.0-litre V12s and power can range from 220/240bhp in road cars to 280bhp from competition-specification engines.

SPECIFICATIONS

Years produced:	1959-1962 (167 in total)
Performance:	0-60mph: 6.4sec
	Top speed: 167mph
Power & torque:	280bhp/203lb ft
Engine:	Normally aspirated 2953cc V12, petrol, carburettor, 24 valves
Drivetrain:	Front-engine RWD
Structure:	Tubular frame
Transmission:	Four-speed manual
Weight:	1180kg

PRICE GUIDE (add 25% for alloy cars)

Launch price:	N/A
Excellent:	£2,500,000
Good:	£2,000,000
Average:	£1,500,000
Project:	£1,000,000

FERRARI
250GT Cabriolet S2

Well-appointed and suitably expensive in its day, the GT Cabriolet was very much an open version of the 250 Coupé – less sporting and more sober-looking than the Spyders they were sold alongside. The giveaway is that Cabriolets had small quarterlights in the doors; you'd have to see the cars side-by-side to see they also had a taller windscreen. Under the bonnet, however, you'll find the same engine as in the LWB Spyder so, with little performance difference between them, the Cabriolet looks quite a bargain in comparison.

SPECIFICATIONS

Years produced:	1960-1962 (200 in total)
Performance:	0-60mph: 7.1sec
	Top speed: 161mph
Power & torque:	240bhp/N/A
Engine:	Normally aspirated 2953cc V12, petrol, carburettor, 24 valves
Drivetrain:	Front-engine RWD
Structure:	Tubular frame
Transmission:	Four-speed manual
Weight:	1200kg

PRICE GUIDE

Launch price:	N/A
Excellent:	£450,000
Good:	£275,000
Average:	£175,000
Project:	£135,000

FERRARI
250GTE 2+2

Built with the clear intention of taking a slice of the premium four-seater market, this was Ferrari's first production 2+2. It was powered by the same 3.0-litre V12 used in the 250 Coupés, but moved forward eight inches in the chassis to help create interior space without making the car look too long. The GTE's success is evident in the 955 examples sold over three years. The collectors' market, of course, doesn't appreciate big numbers like that – or Ferrari's with extra seats – so they are relatively cheap to buy, though hard to find in top condition.

SPECIFICATIONS

Years produced:	1960-1963 (955 in total)
Performance:	0-60mph: 8.0sec
	Top speed: 136mph
Power & torque:	240bhp/181lb ft
Engine:	Normally aspirated 2953cc V12, petrol, carburettor, 24 valves
Drivetrain:	Front-engine RWD
Structure:	Tubular frame
Transmission:	Four-speed manual with overdrive
Weight:	1406kg

PRICE GUIDE

Launch price:	£6326
Excellent:	£140,000
Good:	£90,000
Average:	£70,000
Project:	£60,000

FERRARI
400 Superamerica

The Ferrari tradition of naming its cars after the displacement of a single cylinder should have seen this called the 330, but it chose 400 instead, referring to the 4.0-litre capacity, perhaps as the model was very much headed for the land where more is better. Aimed at the super-rich, numbers were low with just 47 built over four years. Most of these were 'Aerodynamica' coupés, but Pininfarina also built 11 quite exquisite and imposing cabriolets that fetch roughly 50% more than the coupé. Hugely collectable.

SPECIFICATIONS

Years produced:	1960-1964 (58 in total)
Performance:	0-60mph: 9.2sec
	Top speed: 160mph
Power & torque:	340bhp/235lb ft
Engine:	Normally aspirated 3967cc V12, petrol, carburettor, 24 valves
Drivetrain:	Front-engine RWD
Structure:	Tubular frame
Transmission:	Five-speed manual
Weight:	1363kg

PRICE GUIDE (Cabrio in brackets)

Launch price:	N/A
Excellent:	£900,000 (£1,250,000)
Good:	£750,000 (£800,000)
Average:	£400,000
Project:	£300,000

FERRARI
250GT Berlinetta Lusso

Last of the 250 GT line, the Lusso is also on many an aficionado's list of all-time best-looking Ferraris. On a chassis derived from the 250GTO, but with the engine moved forward to improve cabin space, the Lusso has a steel shell with all the opening panels, floor and firewall in aluminium – a fact that can add to the cost and complication of restoration. The engine is the familiar 3.0-litre V12 with three twin-choke Webers and 250bhp. Bucket seats add to the sporting feel, though still manage to be comfortable.

SPECIFICATIONS

Years produced:	1962-1964 (350 in total)
Performance:	0-60mph: 8.0sec
	Top speed: 149mph
Power & torque:	250bhp/217lb ft
Engine:	Normally aspirated 2953cc V12, petrol, carburettor, 24 valves
Drivetrain:	Front-engine RWD
Structure:	Tubular frame
Transmission:	Four-speed manual
Weight:	1020kg

PRICE GUIDE

Launch price:	£5607
Excellent:	£500,000
Good:	£400,000
Average:	£275,000
Project:	£200,000

FERRARI
250LM

The 'LM', if you haven't already worked it out, stands for Le Mans, the spiritual home of competition Ferraris and where these cars did indeed race. They weren't the planned success, however, as the FIA wouldn't homologate them as a replacement for the 250GTO in the GT class, so they had to compete against the more powerful Prototypes. That said, the 250LM still stands as Ferrari's first series production mid-engined car and many of the 32 built racked up good competition careers in the hands of privateers.

SPECIFICATIONS

Years produced:	1964-1966 (32 in total)
Performance:	0-60mph: N/A
	Top speed: 183mph
Power & torque:	320bhp/231lb ft
Engine:	Normally aspirated 3285cc V12, petrol, carburettor, 24 valves
Drivetrain:	Mid-engine RWD
Structure:	Spaceframe
Transmission:	Five-speed manual
Weight:	850kg

PRICE GUIDE

Launch price:	N/A
Excellent:	£4,000,000
Good:	£2,500,000
Average:	£2,000,000
Project:	N/A

FERRARI
275GTS

The Spyder version shared the new 3.3-litre V12 and all the advances of its GTB brother, but this was far from just a soft-topped version of the coupé. Their bodies – though both styled by Pininfarina – were totally different, with the softer, less aggressive-looking GTS staying much closer to the lines of previous 250GTs. It is perhaps this factor that has resulted in the unusual situation of a convertible being worth less than its coupé equivalent, a fact that looks even more surprising when you consider twice as many coupés were sold.

SPECIFICATIONS

Years produced:	1964-1966 (200 in total)
Performance:	0-60mph: 7.2sec
	Top speed: 150mph
Power & torque:	280bhp/188lb ft
Engine:	Normally aspirated 3286cc V12, petrol, carburettor, 24 valves
Drivetrain:	Front-engine RWD
Structure:	Tubular frame
Transmission:	Five-speed manual
Weight:	1152kg

PRICE GUIDE

Launch price:	£5973
Excellent:	£400,000
Good:	£300,000
Average:	£225,000
Project:	£175,000

FERRARI
500 Superfast

Evolved from the 400 Superamerica, the 500 Superfast had a slightly longer wheelbase and only came in aerodynamic coupé form, with the 400's styling tidied up and improved upon. Surprisingly, the market says they're actually worth a lot less than those 400s, despite only 36 Superfasts being built. Some of that may be down to fear of the mighty 5.0-litre V12 engine. Despite the low build numbers, much of its construction was unique to this model, so you wouldn't want to break one. Eight were built with right-hand drive.

SPECIFICATIONS
Years produced:	1964-1966 (36 in total)
Performance:	0-60mph: 7.8sec
	Top speed: 174mph
Power & torque:	400bhp/350lb ft
Engine:	Normally aspirated 4963cc V12, petrol, carburettor, 24 valves
Drivetrain:	Front-engine RWD
Structure:	Tubular frame
Transmission:	Five-speed manual
Weight:	1400kg

PRICE GUIDE
Launch price:	£11,519
Excellent:	£750,000
Good:	£450,000
Average:	£250,000
Project:	£175,000

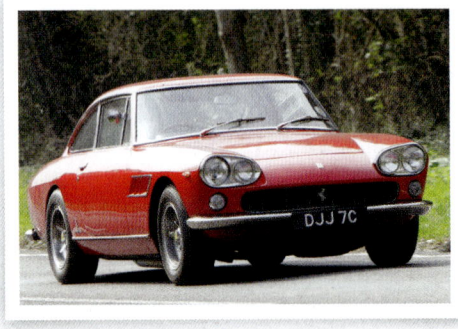

FERRARI
330GT 2+2

Taking over from the commercially very successful 250GTE as Ferrari's four-seater option, the 330GT came with a litre more engine capacity for vastly improved performance figures – top speed was raised by 10mph over the older car. Unfortunately the 330GT also came with an awkward twin-headlamp arrangement that, in polite terms, received mixed reviews. Thankfully the Series II, introduced halfway through production, reverted to a prettier single-headlamp arrangement, and it's these cars the market prefers.

SPECIFICATIONS
Years produced:	1964-1967 (1075 in total)
Performance:	0-60mph: 6.3sec
	Top speed: 152mph
Power & torque:	300bhp/288lb ft
Engine:	Normally aspirated 3967cc V12, petrol, carburettor, 24 valves
Drivetrain:	Front-engine RWD
Structure:	Tubular frame
Transmission:	Five-speed manual
Weight:	1442kg

PRICE GUIDE
Launch price:	£6522
Excellent:	£85,000
Good:	£55,000
Average:	£35,000
Project:	£20,000

FERRARI
275GTB/GTB4

Though the body was a gentle evolution from what had gone before, underneath the 275 is special and significant, as Ferrari finally introduced long-overdue advances in chassis technology. All-independent suspension, a disc brake at every corner, and a five-speed transaxle brought it into the modern era. Bodies were built in steel or alloy – with the latter being worth up to 50% more. Power from the 3.3-litre V12 could be 250bhp, or 275bhp with the optional six-carb set-up. This was raised to 300bhp for the four-cam GTB/4.

SPECIFICATIONS
Years produced:	1964-1968 (730 in total)
Performance:	0-60mph: 6.0sec
	Top speed: 162mph
Power & torque:	280bhp/188lb ft
Engine:	Normally aspirated 3286cc V12, petrol, carburettor, 24 valves
Drivetrain:	Front-engine RWD
Structure:	Tubular frame
Transmission:	Five-speed manual
Weight:	1098kg

PRICE GUIDE
Launch price:	£5973
Excellent:	£800,000 (£1,100,000 for alloy car)
Good:	£600,000
Average:	£300,000
Project:	£250,000

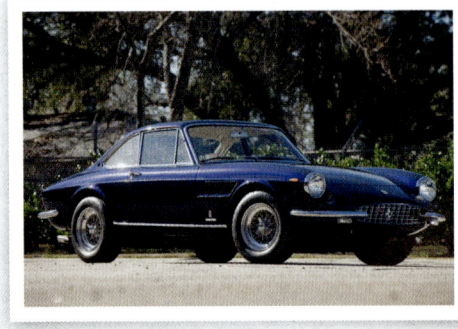

FERRARI
330GTC

Looking like a coupé version of the 275GTS with the nose of a 500 Superfast, the 330GTC lacks the styling purity of the coupés either side of it in the Ferrari family tree. It's a lot better from some angles than others and that is reflected in their values, though they are by no means cheap – even by Ferrari collectors' standards. They certainly suffer no shortfall in the performance department, the 4.0-litre V12's 300bhp offering up genuine 150mph capability. Continued use of a five-speed rear transaxle ensures good handling and cruising.

SPECIFICATIONS
Years produced:	1966-1968 (600 in total)
Performance:	0-60mph: 6.8sec
	Top speed: 152mph
Power & torque:	300bhp/288lb ft
Engine:	Normally aspirated 3967cc V12, petrol, carburettor, 24 valves
Drivetrain:	Front-engine RWD
Structure:	Tubular frame
Transmission:	Five-speed manual
Weight:	1433kg

PRICE GUIDE
Launch price:	£6515
Excellent:	£175,000
Good:	£110,000
Average:	£80,000
Project:	£55,000

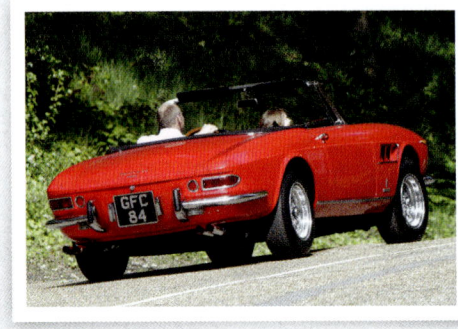

FERRARI
330GTS

In something of a break with Ferrari tradition, the 330 Spyder was simply the coupé 330GTC with the roof lopped off. Then again, given how much better the topless car looks, it's very likely that the Spyder was designed first and had the roof added. Buyers certainly value the Spyder significantly higher than the coupé, and that difference isn't all to do with the lack of a roof and only 100 being built compared with six times as many GTCs. The GTS really is that far ahead in style and bragging rights. Remarkably friendly to drive despite its 300bhp.

SPECIFICATIONS
Years produced:	1966-1968 (100 in total)
Performance:	0-60mph: 6.9sec
	Top speed: 146mph
Power & torque:	300bhp/288lb ft
Engine:	Normally aspirated 3967cc V12, petrol, carburettor, 24 valves
Drivetrain:	Front-engine RWD
Structure:	Tubular frame
Transmission:	Five-speed manual
Weight:	1297kg

PRICE GUIDE
Launch price:	£6515
Excellent:	£500,000
Good:	£250,000
Average:	£160,000
Project:	£100,000

FERRARI
365GTC/GTS

These were stop-gap models, little more than the 330GTC and GTS with the V12 bored out by 400cc to 4.4 litres. Visually the only way to tell them apart is that the row of three outlet vents on each front wing has vanished, to be replaced by a pair of flush-fit grilles to the rear of the bonnet. Mechanically the cars were identical to their predecessors with the exception of the braking system, which was switched from Dunlop/Girling to ATE. The GTS was shortlived, being dropped after just a year with just 20 completed. GTCs numbered 150.

SPECIFICATIONS
Years produced:	1968-1970 (150/20 in total)
Performance:	0-60mph: 6.3sec
	Top speed: 152mph
Power & torque:	320bhp/268lb ft
Engine:	Normally aspirated 4390cc V12, petrol, carburettor, 24 valves
Drivetrain:	Front-engine RWD
Structure:	Tubular frame
Transmission:	Five-speed manual
Weight:	1451kg

PRICE GUIDE
Launch price:	£7909
Excellent:	£185,000 (£600,000 for GTS)
Good:	£120,000
Average:	£80,000
Project:	£55,000

FERRARI
365GT 2+2

Replacement for the 330GT, the 365 was Ferrari's first 2+2 to have independent rear suspension – a Koni self-levelling system to boot. It's a big car, once dubbed 'the Queen Mother of Ferraris' by *Road & Track*, but the sleek lines are more successful than the 330's, especially at the front. With the V12 bored out to 4.4 litres it's not short of performance, grip is good and the standard power steering helps make it feel smaller from the driver's seat. 800 of them were built and it's never really caught on with collectors.

SPECIFICATIONS
Years produced:	1968-1970 (800 in total)
Performance:	0-60mph: 7.1sec
	Top speed: 125mph
Power & torque:	320bhp/268lb ft
Engine:	Normally aspirated 4390cc V12, petrol, carburettor, 24 valves
Drivetrain:	Front-engine RWD
Structure:	Tubular frame
Transmission:	Five-speed manual
Weight:	1462kg

PRICE GUIDE
Launch price:	£7500
Excellent:	£60,000
Good:	£50,000
Average:	£35,000
Project:	£20,000

FERRARI
365GTB/4 Daytona

One of the legendary Ferraris, not least because it held the title of World's Fastest Production Car for some time at 174mph. That was all made possible by the quad-cam 4.4-litre V12 with its bank of six twin-choke Weber carbs – good for 352bhp in street trim. And though it was built as a road car, privateers were still racing them successfully as late as 1979. Headlamps were initially fixed behind a Perspex nose, changed after complaints to pop-up lights in 1970. Nearly 1400 were built – a lot for a top-end Ferrari.

SPECIFICATIONS
Years produced:	1968-1973 (1284 in total)
Performance:	0-60mph: 5.9sec
	Top speed: 174mph
Power & torque:	352bhp/318lb ft
Engine:	Normally aspirated 4390cc V12, petrol, carburettor, 24 valves
Drivetrain:	Front-engine RWD
Structure:	Tubular frame
Transmission:	Five-speed manual
Weight:	1197kg

PRICE GUIDE
Launch price:	£8750
Excellent:	£220,000
Good:	£155,000
Average:	£140,000
Project:	£120,000

DINO
206/246GT

Undeniably pretty, and with a mid-mounted V6 in an alloy body, but a 2.0-litre wasn't quite enough for Ferrari's move into a volume market and only around 150 206GTs were built before it was replaced by the real-deal 246GT. OK, these were built in steel, with an iron (rather than alloy) engine block, but the four-cam 2.4-litre V6 would take it all the way to 150mph. The public snapped them up and they continue to feature on many an enthusiast's wish list. Though only tiny numbers of 206s were built, all LHD, almost 2500 246 GTs were built.

SPECIFICATIONS
Years produced:	1969-1974 (152/2487 produced)
Performance:	0-60mph: 7.1sec
	Top speed: 145mph
Power & torque:	195bhp/166lb ft
Engine:	Normally aspirated 2418cc V6, petrol, carburettor, 12 valves
Drivetrain:	Mid-engine RWD
Structure:	Spaceframe
Transmission:	Five-speed manual
Weight:	1077kg

PRICE GUIDE (246GT in brackets)
Launch price:	£5486
Excellent:	£100,000 (£120,000)
Good:	£80,000 (£100,000)
Average:	£55,000 (£75,000)
Project:	£55,000 (£60,000)

FERRARI
365GTC/4

Sharing its four-cam V12, though in a slightly lower state of tune and with six sidedraft (rather than downdraft) Webers, the GTC/4 was sold alongside the Daytona – notching up 500 sales in 10 short months. It sports a similar profile to the Daytona too, though there's just about room to squeeze two kids into the back of the GTC/4. It compares favourably to the Daytona in two ways: with its power steering, softer suspension and hydraulic clutch the GTC/4 is nice to drive. It also happens to cost about a third of what you need for a Daytona.

SPECIFICATIONS
Years produced:	1971-1972 (500 in total)
Performance:	0-60mph: 6.2sec
	Top speed: 163mph
Power & torque:	340bhp/312lb ft
Engine:	Normally aspirated 4390cc V12, petrol, carburettor, 24 valves
Drivetrain:	Front-engine RWD
Structure:	Tubular frame
Transmission:	Five-speed manual
Weight:	1450kg

PRICE GUIDE
Launch price:	£10,251
Excellent:	£80,000
Good:	£60,000
Average:	£50,000
Project:	£25,000

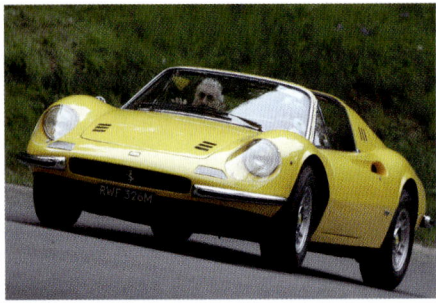

DINO
246GTS

The Targa-roofed spin on the Dino theme arrived in 1972, setting a trend for the fresh air option in mid-engined Ferraris that soon became the norm. As well as the lift-out roof panels, the other big change was deletion of the rear side windows. Not a big deal to many, but it is felt by some to detract ever so slightly from the fine balance of the original design. It's still one of the most beautiful cars ever built and would surely be worth even more if Ferrari hadn't managed to sell so many. Figures for the GTS are lower than for the GT.

SPECIFICATIONS

Years produced:	1972-1974 (1274 in total)
Performance:	0-60mph: 7.1sec
	Top speed: 146mph
Power & torque:	195bhp/166lb ft
Engine:	Normally aspirated 2418cc V6, petrol, carburettor, 12 valves
Drivetrain:	Mid-engine RWD
Structure:	Tubular frame
Transmission:	Five-speed manual
Weight:	1100kg

PRICE GUIDE

Launch price:	£5486
Excellent:	£150,000
Good:	£110,000
Average:	£85,000
Project:	£75,000

FERRARI
365GT4 2+2/400/412i

Aimed at the family man of style and substance. Allow for number changes around the same bodyshell and this is the longest-running Ferrari of all time at 17 years. The 365s started with a 4.4-litre V12, but this grew to 4.8 litres (400) and finally five litres (412i) by 1986. Quick and fine-handling despite their size, the penalty comes at the pumps, where you can expect 10-12mpg. Prices quoted are for the 412i; 365s are a little more and 400s cost a little less. Most came with a General Motors-sourced automatic gearbox.

SPECIFICATIONS

Years produced:	1972-1989 (525/1810/576 in total)
Performance:	0-60mph: 6.7sec
	Top speed: 147mph
Power & torque:	340bhp/333lb ft
Engine:	Normally aspirated 4390cc V12, petrol, carburettor, 24 valves
Drivetrain:	Front-engine RWD
Structure:	Monocoque
Transmission:	Five-speed manual/three-speed auto
Weight:	1884kg

PRICE GUIDE

Launch price:	£12,783
Excellent:	£25,000
Good:	£17,500
Average:	£13,500
Project:	£9000

FERRARI
365 Berlinetta Boxer

Having experimented with a small, mid-engined road car in the shape of the Dino, Ferrari went the whole hog with the Daytona's replacement – the Berlinetta Boxer. The Boxer bit refers to the new engine's flat-12 layout; all it shared with the outgoing V12 was its 4.4-litre capacity. Keeping with its race car image, the whole tail section lifts to reveal the bare bones of the chassis and the engine which, thanks to its low profile, sits above the transmission. For the first time in a road-going Ferrari the camshafts were belt-driven.

SPECIFICATIONS

Years produced:	1973-1976 (387 in total)
Performance:	0-60mph: 6.5sec
	Top speed: 176mph
Power & torque:	380bhp/302lb ft
Engine:	Normally aspirated 4390cc V12, petrol, carburettor, 24 valves
Drivetrain:	Mid-engine RWD
Structure:	Semi-monocoque
Transmission:	Five-speed manual
Weight:	1235kg

PRICE GUIDE

Launch price:	£15,492
Excellent:	£125,000
Good:	£65,000
Average:	£45,000
Project:	£30,000

FERRARI
Dino 308GT4

The 308 GT4 has the rare distinction of being designed by Bertone, making it the first Ferrari for nearly 20 years that wasn't styled by Pininfarina. It also contained the company's first production V8 engine – effectively two-thirds of a 365's V12 – and was its first mid-engined 2+2. None of these facts have helped endear it to latter-day Ferrari buyers, though it stayed in production for seven years and racked up almost 3000 sales. A competent and quick car, though of course they rust; find a good one and it makes a fine first Ferrari.

SPECIFICATIONS

Years produced:	1974-1980 (2826 in total)
Performance:	0-60mph: 6.7sec
	Top speed: 147mph
Power & torque:	255bhp/209lb ft
Engine:	Normally aspirated 2927cc V8, petrol, carburettor, 16 valves
Drivetrain:	Mid-engine RWD
Structure:	Monocoque
Transmission:	Five-speed manual
Weight:	1265kg

PRICE GUIDE

Launch price:	£7699
Excellent:	£25,000
Good:	£15,000
Average:	£10,000
Project:	£5500

FERRARI
308GTB (glassfibre)

Blessed with the V8 from the recently-launched 308GT4, this was Ferrari's first ever glassfibre car, though that bold move fizzled out after less than two years and 712 examples. Quite simply it was cheaper and quicker to build in steel, and demand for the 308 was high. The steel cars were also heavier, and when you add that lot together, it makes the original GRP cars much more collectible and expensive than their successors. You have fewer rust issues to worry about as well, though only with regard to the outer panels.

SPECIFICATIONS

Years produced:	1975-1977 (712 in total)
Performance:	0-60mph: 6.7sec
	Top speed: 152mph
Power & torque:	255bhp/209lb ft
Engine:	Normally aspirated 2927cc V8, petrol, carburettor, 16 valves
Drivetrain:	Mid-engine RWD
Structure:	Spaceframe
Transmission:	Five-speed manual
Weight:	1265kg

PRICE GUIDE

Launch price:	£11,992
Excellent:	£50,000
Good:	£37,500
Average:	£27,500
Project:	£15,000

FERRARI
512BB/BBi

Took over from the 365BB as Ferrari's 12-cylinder range-topper and stayed there for over a decade. Similar to its predecessor, little was changed apart from the lower nose with integrated spoiler to reduce front-end lift. The 5.0-litre flat-12 was treated to Bosch fuel injection from 1981, which added another 20bhp and gave a little assistance to economy. Probably a better bet than a 365 BB, but the fact that four times as many 512 Berlinetta Boxers were built makes them a little cheaper to put in your garage.

SPECIFICATIONS
Years produced:	1976-1985 (1936 in total)
Performance:	0-60mph: 5.9sec
	Top speed: 188mph
Power & torque:	360bhp/332lb ft
Engine:	Normally aspirated 4942cc V12, petrol, electronic fuel injection, 24 valves
Drivetrain:	Mid-engine RWD
Structure:	Monocoque
Transmission:	Five-speed manual
Weight:	1515kg

PRICE GUIDE
Launch price:	£26,000
Excellent:	£100,000
Good:	£60,000
Average:	£40,000
Project:	£27,500

FERRARI
308GTB/GTS (steel)

One of the company's great success stories and still regarded as one of the best ways to introduce yourself to Ferrari ownership. Early cars are the most powerful, with the 1980-on Bosch fuel-injection models (signified by an 'i' suffix) losing 40bhp to emission controls. Much of this was restored two years later with the four-valves-per-cylinder qv models, identified by cooling slats in the front bonnet. Perhaps the best buys are those built after January 1984, thanks to corrosion-reducing Zincrox coating on the steel panels.

SPECIFICATIONS
Years produced:	1977-1985
Performance:	0-60mph: 7.3sec
	Top speed: 145mph
Power & torque:	240bhp/209lb ft
Engine:	Normally aspirated 2926cc V8, petrol, carburettor, 16 valves
Drivetrain:	Mid-engine RWD
Structure:	Spaceframe
Transmission:	Five-speed manual
Weight:	1265kg

PRICE GUIDE
Launch price:	£16,499
Excellent:	£35,000
Good:	£20,000
Average:	£14,000
Project:	£8500

FERRARI
Mondial/QV

A cheaper four-seater alternative to Ferrari's 400i, the Mondial was built around 308GTB running gear. As such, it shared that car's mechanical upgrades: four valves per cylinder from 1982, 3.2 litres from 1985, then 3.4 litres from a longitudinal engine and transverse gearbox for the Mondial t from 1989. Those four seats, along with less than striking looks (for a Ferrari, at any rate), combine to make this the cheapest ticket to the Prancing Horse ball, though not all have been well cared for. A cabriolet version joined the coupé in 1984.

SPECIFICATIONS
Years produced:	1980-1994 (4274 in total)
Performance:	0-60mph: 7.1sec
	Top speed: 145mph
Power & torque:	240bhp/213lb ft
Engine:	Normally aspirated 2927cc V8, petrol, electronic fuel injection, 16 valves
Drivetrain:	Mid-engine RWD
Structure:	Spaceframe
Transmission:	Five-speed manual
Weight:	1446kg

PRICE GUIDE
Launch price:	£24,488
Excellent:	£20,000
Good:	£14,000
Average:	£9000
Project:	£6000

FERRARI
288GTO

The revival of that legendary GTO badge on a car whose looks obviously derive from the ageing 308GTB could easily have been a travesty. It wasn't. Let's start with the lightweight glassfibre and Kevlar bodyshell, on a revised chassis with a 4in wheelbase stretch over the 308's. That was done to accommodate longitudinal mounting of the twin-turbocharged 2.9-litre engine. The result is electrifying performance that helped make the GTO an almost-instant collector's item. The low build number ensures superstar status and prices.

SPECIFICATIONS
Years produced:	1984-1987 (272 in total)
Performance:	0-60mph: 4.8sec
	Top speed: 190mph
Power & torque:	400bhp/366lb ft
Engine:	Twin-turbocharged 2855cc V8, petrol, electronic fuel injection, 32 valves
Drivetrain:	Mid-engine RWD
Structure:	Spaceframe
Transmission:	Five-speed manual
Weight:	1160kg

PRICE GUIDE
Launch price:	Special order only
Excellent:	£500,000
Good:	£340,000
Average:	£300,000
Project:	N/A

FERRARI
Testarossa

Perhaps the ultimate automotive status symbol to emerge from the 'greed is good' decade. The Testarossa's imposing size and in-your-face attitude tend to hide the fact that here we have a remarkably user-friendly supercar; mighty performance delivered in a smooth manner by a sweet and free-revving flat-12. It also has windows you can actually see out of. That Testarossa remains so comparatively cheap to buy partly because of the stigma of '80s excess, but mostly thanks to the huge numbers built.

SPECIFICATIONS
Years produced:	1984-1992 (7177 in total)
Performance:	0-60mph: 5.2sec
	Top speed: 180mph
Power & torque:	390bhp/361lb ft
Engine:	Normally aspirated 4942cc flat 12, petrol, electronic fuel injection, 48 valves
Drivetrain:	Mid-engine RWD
Structure:	Monocoque
Transmission:	Five-speed manual
Weight:	1506kg

PRICE GUIDE
Launch price:	£62,666
Excellent:	£60,000
Good:	£45,000
Average:	£30,000
Project:	£20,000

FERRARI
328GTB/GTS

Not wanting to risk its golden goose, changes from the 308 were kept to a minimum and even then justified as improvements to aerodynamics and stability. Front and rear panels below bumper level were deepened, a larger grille fitted, and some lights changed. There's the same glorious howl from the mid-mounted quad-cam V8 but, in the 328, it uses an extra 200cc to provide 30bhp more than its predecessor along with a lot more torque. The only downside is the interior, which employs Fiat-issue switchgear.

SPECIFICATIONS
Years produced:	1985-1988 (1344/6068 in total)
Performance:	0-60mph: 6.0sec
	Top speed: 163mph
Power & torque:	270bhp/224lb ft
Engine:	Normally aspirated 3186cc V8, petrol, electronic fuel injection, 32 valves
Drivetrain:	Mid-engine RWD
Structure:	Spaceframe
Transmission:	Five-speed manual
Weight:	1263kg

PRICE GUIDE
Launch price:	£32,220
Excellent:	£35,000
Good:	£25,000
Average:	£18,000
Project:	£11,000

FERRARI
F40

Built to celebrate Ferrari's 40th birthday, the F40 is just the car for anyone who finds the 288GTO a bit on the tame side. The spec of the two cars carries a similarity too: twin-turbocharged V8 engine and a composite body mounted on a spaceframe chassis. The difference is that the F40 has an extra 78bhp from its slightly larger engine, and in the search for lightness it offers even less in the way of content – not even carpets or door panels. But buyers loved it and Ferrari built almost three times as many as originally intended.

SPECIFICATIONS
Years produced:	1987-1992 (1315 in total)
Performance:	0-60mph: 3.9sec
	Top speed: 201mph
Power & torque:	478bhp/426lb ft
Engine:	Twin-turbocharged 2936cc V8, petrol, electronic fuel injection, 32 valves
Drivetrain:	Mid-engine RWD
Structure:	Spaceframe
Transmission:	Five-speed manual
Weight:	1100kg

PRICE GUIDE
Launch price:	£193,000
Excellent:	£400,000
Good:	£300,000
Average:	£200,000
Project:	N/A

FERRARI
348tb/ts

In many ways the 348 is more closely related to its big brother Testarossa than the 328 it replaced. The V8 engine is still there, but it's been much revised, upped to 3.4 litres with an extra 30bhp, and turned 90 degrees to be mounted longitudinally and set lower in the chassis. Only the gearbox is transverse this time. Great strides were made with aerodynamics, and the side strakes and black grille over the tail-lights are straight out of the Testarossa design book, as is the relatively spacious cockpit. It is more nervous to drive than a 328 though.

SPECIFICATIONS
Years produced:	1989-1995 (8844 in total)
Performance:	0-60mph: 5.6sec
	Top speed: 170mph
Power & torque:	300bhp/237lb ft
Engine:	Normally aspirated 3405cc V8, petrol, electronic fuel injection, 32 valves
Drivetrain:	Mid-engine RWD
Structure:	Monocoque
Transmission:	Five-speed manual
Weight:	1393kg

PRICE GUIDE
Launch price:	£67,499
Excellent:	£28,000
Good:	£25,000
Average:	£20,000
Project:	£15,000

FIAT

ONE OF the few car-makers to have survived unscathed through over 100 years of production, Fabbrica Italiana Automobili Torino debuted with a rear-engined two-cylinder machine in 1899. This was the same layout used for the iconic Fiat 500 (launched 58 years later) that the company will always be best remembered for. Even today no Italian cityscape is complete without them, though they are quickly being replaced by the 'new' 500. Various licensing deals mean Fiat's products are built worldwide. Along the way, the company has swallowed up Ferrari, Lancia, Alfa Romeo and the tuning firm Abarth, whose name still graces its more sporting models.

FIAT
500/500B

The tiny Topolino two-seater was launched in 1936 but after the war it came back in restyled 500B and 500C form; the only post-war version that came to the UK, and even then imports didn't begin until 1954. Earlier cars like the one pictured have found their way here since. Nearly all of the post-war series were roll-back cabriolets, but there is the odd estate version around and even a woody – expect to pay a premium for either. The little four-cylinder engines are quite perky but still very economical.

SPECIFICATIONS
Years produced:	1948-1955 (143,836 in total)
Performance:	Top speed: 55mph
	0-60mph: N/A
Power & torque:	13bhp/N/A
Engine:	Normally aspirated 569cc four cylinder, petrol, carburettor, 8 valves
Drivetrain:	Front-engine RWD
Structure:	Separate chassis
Transmission:	Four-speed manual
Weight:	740kg

PRICE GUIDE
Launch price:	£582
Excellent:	£6500
Good:	£5250
Average:	£2750
Project:	£1250

FIAT
8V

The Fiat 8V was the spectacular project developed by Dante Giacosa that bore fruit in 1952. With its bespoke V8 engine and tubular spaceframe chassis, it owed nothing to the rest of the Fiat range – which was undergoing reinvention at the time. It packed advanced features such as all-round independent suspension and an all-synchro gearbox, and proved to be a very effective sports car. 34 were bodied by Carozzeria Speciale FIAT, with the rest being split between Zagato, Ghia and Vignale. A mixture of coupés and spiders, all are exceptionally desirable.

SPECIFICATIONS

Years produced:	1952-1954 (114 in total)
Performance:	Top speed: 118mph
	0-60mph: 9.5sec
Power & torque:	105bhp/110lb ft
Engine:	Normally aspirated 1996cc V8, petrol, carburettor, 8 valves
Drivetrain:	Front-engine RWD
Structure:	Spaceframe
Transmission:	Four-speed manual
Weight:	930kg

PRICE GUIDE (depending on coachwork)

Launch price:	N/A
Excellent:	£350,000
Good:	£290,000
Average:	£220,000
Project:	£175,000

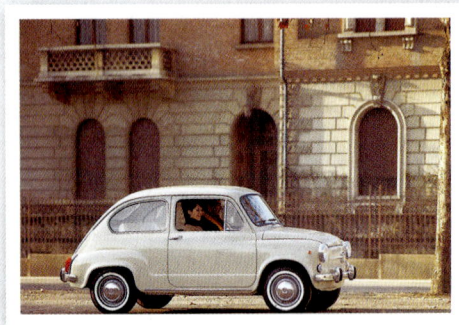

FIAT
600/600D

No, this wasn't merely a big-engined version of the Fiat 500. Though they share a strong family resemblance, the 600 was launched first and has the benefit of a water-cooled four-cylinder engine. That started out at 633cc, but grew to 767cc for 1960's revamped Fiat 600D. Being a direct competitor to the Mini spoiled things for the 600 in the UK, but there's a school of thought that says it's a better bet than the smaller, less practical 500. And you may never tire of telling people that this was the best-selling car of the 1960s... in Argentina.

SPECIFICATIONS

Years produced:	1955-1970 (891,107 in total)
Performance:	Top speed: 66mph
Power & torque:	29bhp/40lb ft
Engine:	Normally aspirated 767cc four cylinder, petrol, carburettor, 8 valves
Drivetrain:	Rear-engine RWD
Structure:	Monocoque
Transmission:	Four-speed manual
Weight:	585kg

PRICE GUIDE

Launch price:	£585
Excellent:	£5000
Good:	£4000
Average:	£2000
Project:	£850

FIAT
600 Multipla

This is the version of the 600 that most classic car enthusiasts are more familiar with. It's also probably the world's smallest minibus, with six-seat capacity despite being under 12ft long. A highly sought-after collectable in its own right, recent price rises have made their restoration a more sensible proposition. They share the same engines as the 600, but their progress has never been more than sedate. However, if originality is not at issue, these engines were developed into the 903cc unit and used in the Uno and Cinquecento.

SPECIFICATIONS

Years produced:	1955-1960 (130,000 in total)
Performance:	Top speed: 59mph
Power & torque:	29bhp/40lb ft
Engine:	Normally aspirated 767cc four cylinder, petrol, carburettor, 8 valves
Drivetrain:	Rear-engine RWD
Structure:	Monocoque
Transmission:	Four-speed manual
Weight:	700kg

PRICE GUIDE

Launch price:	£799
Excellent:	£9500
Good:	£7500
Average:	£4000
Project:	£2000

FIAT
500

Cheap to run and, with excellent spares support, the diminutive Fiat 500 makes the ideal classic for city dwellers. In fact darting around busy city streets is what it has always done best. Pre-1965 cars had suicide doors and never more than 18bhp, except in the rare 500 Sport. The later 500F and 500L are a better bet, especially if you want to drive any distance, and have conventional front-hinged doors. Last model, the 500R has a detuned 594cc Fiat 126 engine; a point not lost on many Fiat 500 owners, who commonly fit the full-strength 126 engine.

SPECIFICATIONS

Years produced:	1957-1975 (3,427,648 in total)
Performance:	Top speed: 59mph
Power & torque:	18bhp/N/A
Engine:	Normally aspirated 499cc twin, petrol, carburettor, 4 valves
Drivetrain:	Rear-engine RWD
Structure:	Separate chassis
Transmission:	Four-speed manual
Weight:	500kg

PRICE GUIDE

Launch price:	£556
Excellent:	£7000
Good:	£5500
Average:	£3000
Project:	£1250

FIAT
1800/2100/2300

Fiat's tidy and elegant middle-class saloon employed Pininfarina's generic styling scheme of the day, looking almost identical to the Peugeot 404 and Austin Cambridge. The centrepiece of the 1800 series was Lampredi's impressive new six-cylinder engine, which was powerful and smooth. Improved through its life, with the leaf-suspended rear end being replaced by coils and the drum brakes replaced by discs. An excellent and understated saloon that enjoys a low-profile, but faithful, following in the UK. Good value at current prices.

SPECIFICATIONS (1800)

Years produced:	1959-1968 (c185,000 in total)
Performance:	0-60mph: 15.0sec
	Top speed: 95mph
Power & torque:	76bhp/93lb ft
Engine:	Normally aspirated 1796cc six cylinder, petrol, carburettor, 8 valves
Drivetrain:	Front-engine RWD
Structure:	Monocoque
Transmission:	Four-speed manual
Weight:	1215kg

PRICE GUIDE

Launch price:	N/A
Excellent:	£7000
Good:	£5000
Average:	£3500
Project:	£2000

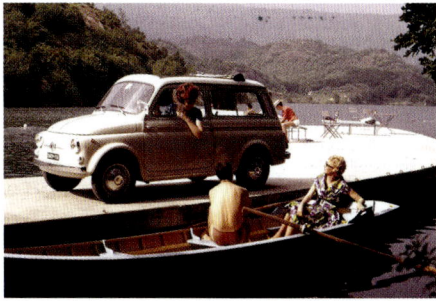

FIAT
500 Giardiniera

Fiat's effectiveness at squeezing the most out of its platforms was never more evident than in the 500 and 600. To create an estate version of the 500, the wheelbase was extended by 4in and the vertical-twin engine mounted under the boot on its side. The loadbay was surprisingly large for a 10ft 5in car, and accessed by a wide-opening side-hinged tailgate. An appealing and practical small car that in many ways previewed upcoming generations of hatchbacks. It was built and badged by Autobianchi from 1968, and is rare and desirable in the UK in any form.

SPECIFICATIONS
Years produced:	1960-1977 (c327,000 in total)
Performance:	Top speed: 59mph
Power & torque:	18bhp/N/A
Engine:	Normally aspirated 499cc twin, petrol, carburettor, 4 valve
Drivetrain:	Rear-engine RWD
Structure:	Separate chassis
Transmission:	Four-speed manual
Weight:	500kg

PRICE GUIDE
Launch price:	£556
Excellent:	£7500
Good:	£5500
Average:	£3000
Project:	£1250

FIAT
1500 Cabriolet

Predecessor to the better-known Fiat Spider, the 1500 cabriolet was also only available in left-hand drive. That and prices that were grossly inflated by import duty meant that few reached UK shores. No reason why you couldn't import from Europe though, where their numbers are much greater. Styling was by Pininfarina, which explains their passing resemblance to the Ferrari 275GTS, only smaller, and much cheaper. Advanced for its time with a five-speed gearbox and disc brakes. Engines are tough and reliable.

SPECIFICATIONS
Years produced:	1960-1967 (c34,000 inc 1500S in total)
Performance:	0-60mph: 14.8sec
	Top speed: 100mph
Power & torque:	72bhp/82lb ft
Engine:	Normally aspirated 1481cc four cylinder, petrol, carburettor, 8 valves
Drivetrain:	Front-engine RWD
Structure:	Monocoque
Transmission:	Five-speed manual
Weight:	970kg

PRICE GUIDE
Launch price:	£1197
Excellent:	£6000
Good:	£4750
Average:	£2500
Project:	£1000

FIAT
2300S Coupé

Fiat's large-car efforts have tended to lack commercial success, and sometimes it's difficult to understand why. While the Dino and 130 had obvious failings, the 2300S Coupé looked like the right product for its time. Styled by Ghia, the 2300S Coupé was very much a grand tourer, even featuring electric windows. Its 2.3-litre six-cylinder engine delivered plenty of power and was further boosted by twin carburettors. However, true to form, the 2300S wasn't a big seller, and remains one of the lost cousins of Fiat history.

SPECIFICATIONS
Years produced:	1961-1968 (N/A total)
Performance:	0-60mph: 11.6sec
	Top speed: 121mph
Power & torque:	136bhp/145lb ft
Engine:	Normally aspirated 2279cc six cylinder, petrol, carburettor, 12 valves
Drivetrain:	Front-engine RWD
Structure:	Monocoque
Transmission:	Four-speed manual
Weight:	1266kg

PRICE GUIDE
Launch price:	£2610
Excellent:	£7000
Good:	£5000
Average:	£2750
Project:	£1000

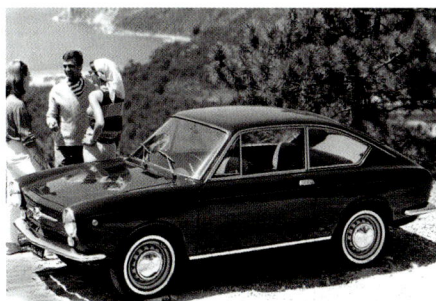

FIAT
850 Coupé

Based on the slightly dull and dumpy 850 saloon, the Coupé thankfully bore no resemblance to it, being more in the fashion of a scaled-down Dino. It had a perkier version of the saloon's 843cc engine too, which was upgraded to 903cc from 1968. Rear-mounted and water-cooled, it gives the baby coupé a decent turn of speed and its light weight contributes to the car's excellent handling abilities. It sold well in the UK, but our climate has wiped out most of them now. Survivors are reasonably priced, or you could sniff out a left-hooker to import.

SPECIFICATIONS
Years produced:	1965-1973 (342,873 in total)
Performance:	0-60mph: 15.6sec
	Top speed: 84mph
Power & torque:	47bhp/45lb ft
Engine:	Normally aspirated 843cc four cylinder, petrol, carburettor, 8 valves
Drivetrain:	Rear-engine RWD
Structure:	Monocoque
Transmission:	Four-speed manual
Weight:	690kg

PRICE GUIDE
Launch price:	£850
Excellent:	£4000
Good:	£2500
Average:	£1250
Project:	£500

FIAT
850 Spider

A small, pretty and nippy but rust-prone roadster. We could be talking about a Midget, but this is an Italian job with styling beautifully executed by Bertone. It includes a hood that neatly stows away beneath the rear deck. As with all the 850 range it's rear-engined, initially with 843cc, but receiving the more powerful and just as rev-happy 903cc unit in 1968. At the same time the original sloping headlamps were replaced by more efficient upright units. Most 850s went to America and, once again, none were built with right-hand-drive.

SPECIFICATIONS
Years produced:	1965-1973 (124,660 in total)
Performance:	0-60mph: 18.2sec
	Top speed: 87mph
Power & torque:	47bhp/45lb ft
Engine:	Normally aspirated 843cc four cylinder, petrol, carburettor, 8 valves
Drivetrain:	Rear-engine RWD
Structure:	Monocoque
Transmission:	Four-speed manual
Weight:	735kg

PRICE GUIDE
Launch price:	£1000
Excellent:	£7000
Good:	£4250
Average:	£2200
Project:	£1000

FIAT
124

Advanced saloon that outshone and outsold the Ford Escort MkI. With disc brakes all round and a well-located rear axle on coil springs, it's a capable driver. Has suffered in classic terms from the usual Fiat rust problems, but mostly by growing up to become the long-running heart of the Lada range. Revvy overhead-valve engines are even impressive in base 1200 form, but the Special T is the one to have. Available in the UK from 1971 with a 1438cc twin-cam engine, which was upgraded to 1592cc from 1973.

SPECIFICATIONS

Years produced:	1966-1974 (1,543,000 in total)
Performance:	0-60mph: 11.8sec
	Top speed: 102mph
Power & torque:	80bhp/80lb ft
Engine:	Normally aspirated 1438cc four cylinder, petrol, carburettor, 8 valves
Drivetrain:	Front-engine RWD
Structure:	Monocoque
Transmission:	Four-speed manual
Weight:	950kg

PRICE GUIDE

Launch price:	£774
Excellent:	£2200
Good:	£1500
Average:	£750
Project:	£150

FIAT
124 Coupé

A thin-pillared beauty from Fiat's own design team, blessed with real ability thanks to twin-cam engines and all-wheel disc brakes. Favoured models include the 1967-69 'AC', which is prettier with its single headlamps and lower bonnet line, and lighter so it handles better. The 1974-75 final 'CC' models also get snapped up as their 1800cc engine is the most powerful offered. A small thumbs-down for the BC-series cars that arrived in 1970 with softer suspension and twin headlamps. Sadly all 124 Coupés suffered badly from corrosion.

SPECIFICATIONS

Years produced:	1966-1975 (279,672 in total)
Performance:	0-60mph: 10.5sec
	Top speed: 115mph
Power & torque:	118bhp/113lb ft
Engine:	Normally aspirated 1438cc four cylinder, petrol, carburettor, 8 valves
Drivetrain:	Front-engine RWD
Structure:	Monocoque
Transmission:	Four-speed manual
Weight:	980kg

PRICE GUIDE

Launch price:	£1298
Excellent:	£5000
Good:	£4000
Average:	£1750
Project:	£500

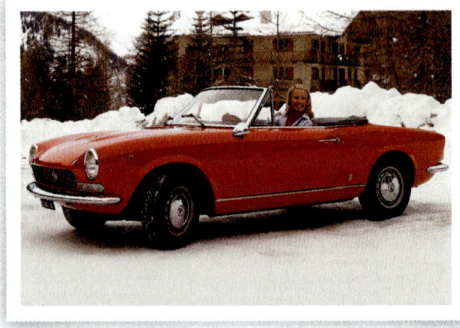

FIAT
124 Spider

Pininfarina designed and built the bodies for these pretty sports cars, using any number of Ferrari styling cues and Fiat's excellent twin-cam engines. All are left-hand drive and around 85% of them were sold in America, although upwards of 1500 have since been imported into the UK. As with the 124 Coupé, the first and last cars are most popular with collectors: pre-1975 cars had lower suspension and prettier slimline bumpers, 1979-on Spiders received 2.0-litre Bosch fuel-injection engines. From 1982-85 complete production passed to Pininfarina.

SPECIFICATIONS

Years produced:	1966-1985 (178,439 in total)
Performance:	0-60mph: 10.9sec
	Top speed: 109mph
Power & torque:	102bhp/110lb ft
Engine:	Normally aspirated 1438cc four cylinder, petrol, carburettor, 8 valves
Drivetrain:	Front-engine RWD
Structure:	Separate chassis
Transmission:	Five-speed manual
Weight:	945kg

PRICE GUIDE

Launch price:	Special order
Excellent:	£9000
Good:	£6250
Average:	£3000
Project:	£1250

FIAT
Dino Spider

Fancy a cheap convertible Ferrari? This is about as close as you'll get without having the actual Prancing Horse badge on the nose. Styled by Pininfarina and using the same engines that powered the Dino GT, they have rarity on their side as far as collectibility goes. Early models had an all-alloy 2.0-litre engine and a live axle on leaf springs. In 1969 it was all change to an iron-block 2.4-litre V6 with another 15bhp, and the rear suspension was changed to independent coil springs. Mechanical and body parts still in good supply.

SPECIFICATIONS

Years produced:	1967-1973 (1583 in total)
Performance:	0-60mph: 8.0sec
	Top speed: 124mph
Power & torque:	160bhp/127lb ft
Engine:	Normally aspirated 1987cc V6, petrol, carburettor, 12 valves
Drivetrain:	Front-engine RWD
Structure:	Monocoque
Transmission:	Five-speed manual
Weight:	1222kg

PRICE GUIDE

Launch price:	Special order
Excellent:	£35,000
Good:	£25,000
Average:	£13,000
Project:	£6500

FIAT
Dino Coupé 2000/2400

Though mechanically identical to the closely related Dino Spiders, the Coupé has a completely different body, designed by Bertone. The same changes were made in 1969, from 2.0 to a 2.4-litre quad-cam V6, along with a tougher ZF five-speed gearbox and the independent rear suspension swiped from underneath Fiat's 130 saloon. The 2000 and 2400 bodies look identical at first sight, but changes in grille, badge and vent arrangements mean that only the bootlid is a straight swap between cars. The 2400 was assembled at the Ferrari factory.

SPECIFICATIONS

Years produced:	1967-1973 (6068 in total)
Performance:	0-60mph: 8.1sec
	Top speed: 124mph
Power & torque:	160bhp/127lb ft
Engine:	Normally aspirated 1987cc V6, petrol, carburettor, 12 valves
Drivetrain:	Front-engine RWD
Structure:	Monocoque
Transmission:	Five-speed manual
Weight:	1220kg

PRICE GUIDE

Launch price:	£3493
Excellent:	£20,000
Good:	£15,000
Average:	£6500
Project:	£3000

FIAT
130

Fiat had no history of building big saloon cars before it surprised everyone with the technologically advanced, Mercedes-baiting, 130 – the world was bound to treat it with caution. But what a car. The styling may lack flair, but underneath we find all-independent suspension, passive rear steering and four disc brakes. Not bad for 1969. Capacity of the quad-cam V6 went up from 2.8 litres to 3.2 in 1971, and UK imports started in '72. Worth seeking out. Enzo Ferrari drove one every day: do you need any greater recommendation than that?

SPECIFICATIONS
Years produced:	1969-1976 (15,000 in total)
Performance:	0-60mph: 11.4sec
	Top speed: 118mph
Power & torque:	165bhp/184lb ft
Engine:	3235cc V6, petrol, carburettor, 12 valves
Drivetrain:	Front-engine RWD
Structure:	Monocoque
Transmission:	Five-speed manual
Weight:	1615kg

PRICE GUIDE
Launch price:	£3818
Excellent:	£4000
Good:	£3000
Average:	£1500
Project:	£500

FIAT
128

Although its simple styling hinted at an update of the 124, what nestled under the skin makes this one of the most important cars of the 1960s. The 128 remains a Dante Giacosa masterpiece – powered by a transverse OHC engine and driven by the front wheels via an end-on gearbox. It's the recipe for a technical orthodoxy that has since been adopted by the entire industry. Despite that, and being a great car to drive, shoddy build and horrendous rust mean few survive, and it's still rather unloved. But its sheer rarity in the UK guarantees that values are heading the right way.

SPECIFICATIONS
Years produced:	1969-1984 (2,776,000 in total)
Performance:	0-60mph: 14.8sec
	Top speed: 87mph
Power & torque:	55bhp/57lb ft
Engine:	Normally aspirated 1116cc four cylinder, petrol, carburettor, 8 valves
Drivetrain:	Front-engine FWD
Structure:	Monocoque
Transmission:	Four-speed manual
Weight:	815kg

PRICE GUIDE
Launch price:	£871
Excellent:	£2200
Good:	£1200
Average:	£800
Project:	£500

FIAT
127

The 128 might have been the car that created Fiat's template for modern motoring, but it was the 127 that truly exploited it in 1971. The 127 used the 850's engine installed 128-style, and packaged in a stylish two-door 'shell. A hatchback was added a couple of years later, and the true Italian supermini was born. The 127 was a huge success, and over four million were built before the Uno replaced it – but it carried on in Brazil and Argentina. To find one today isn't the work of a moment, especially an early car, but if you do, you'll find Mini-stye fun and a little extra space.

SPECIFICATIONS (127 Sport)
Years produced:	1971-1983 (3,730,000 in total)
Performance:	0-60mph: 14.0sec
	Top speed: 100mph
Power & torque:	70bhp/61lb ft
Engine:	Normally aspirated 1049cc four cylinder, petrol, carburettor, 8 valves
Drivetrain:	Front-engine FWD
Structure:	Monocoque
Transmission:	Four-speed manual
Weight:	775kg

PRICE GUIDE
Launch price:	£799
Excellent:	£2000
Good:	£1000
Average:	£600
Project:	£400

FIAT
130 Coupé

With straight-edged styling from Pininfarina's Rolls-Camargue/Lancia Gamma Coupé school, the 130 Coupé has a vast and elegant but almost intimidating presence. Arriving a couple of years later than the 130 saloon, the Coupés only ever came with the larger 3.2-litre four-cam V6, so there's plenty of performance to go with the tidy handling and, thankfully, this isn't spoilt by the light power steering. Many came with a three-speed automatic, but enough were specified with the ZF five-speed manual.

SPECIFICATIONS
Years produced:	1972-1976 (4491 in total)
Performance:	0-60mph: 10.6sec
	Top speed: 123mph
Power & torque:	165bhp/184lb ft
Engine:	3235cc V6, petrol, carburettor, 12 valves
Drivetrain:	Front-engine RWD
Structure:	Monocoque
Transmission:	Five-speed manual/three-speed auto
Weight:	1559kg

PRICE GUIDE
Launch price:	£6165
Excellent:	£8000
Good:	£5500
Average:	£2650
Project:	£900

FIAT
X1/9 1300

There's a lot to be said for a compact mid-engined two-seater with a targa top, not least in the handling department. So it seems unfair that, although the X1/9 was launched in Europe in 1972, the UK had to wait five years before right-hand-drive examples became available. Those early cars had 1.3-litre engines and four-speed gearboxes, and were considered somewhat underpowered compared with rivals such as the Triumph TR7. But the X1/9 had balance, poise and style that British sports car buyers could only dream about.

SPECIFICATIONS
Years produced:	1972-1982 (141,108 inc 1500 in total)
Performance:	0-60mph: 12.7sec
	Top speed: 99mph
Power & torque:	75bhp/72lb ft
Engine:	Normally aspirated 1290cc four cylinder, petrol, carburettor, 8 valves
Drivetrain:	Mid-engine RWD
Structure:	Monocoque
Transmission:	Four/five-speed manual
Weight:	912kg

PRICE GUIDE
Launch price:	£2997
Excellent:	£4500
Good:	£3000
Average:	£1000
Project:	£700

FIAT
126

Continuing the appealing boxy styling established by the 127, Fiat's baby replacement for the 500 looked just the ticket to motorise a generation of trendy young Italians. The air-cooled two-cylinder engine stubbornly remained slung out to the rear, despite Fiat's move to FWD elsewhere in the range, and performance was leisurely in the extreme. But it's cheap as chips to run today and, thanks to a long production run in Italy and then Poland, there's still a plentiful supply of cars and parts. The usual story of rust and unreliability keeps its image low-key.

SPECIFICATIONS

Years produced:	1975-1978 (1,970,000)
Performance:	0-60mph: 42.3sec
	Top speed: 63mph
Power & torque:	23bhp/29lb ft
Engine:	Normally aspirated 594cc twin, petrol, carburettor, 4 valves
Drivetrain:	Rear-engine RWD
Structure:	Monocoque
Transmission:	Four-speed manual
Weight:	580kg

PRICE GUIDE

Launch price:	£698
Excellent:	£1500
Good:	£1000
Average:	£600
Project:	£300

FIAT
128 Coupé/3P

A car that lurks somewhere in that grey area between coupé and hatchback that was popularised by the VW Scirocco a year earlier. In fact '3P' stands for *tre porte* – Italian for three-door. With that cleared up, it's time to point out just how under-rated these cars are. Though they have long had a cult following, most in the UK lost the battle against corrosion years ago, though you can still find fair numbers in Italy and Greece. There's decent performance from the overhead-cam 1300, and entertaining handling too.

SPECIFICATIONS

Years produced:	1975-1978 (330,897 in total)
Performance:	0-60mph: 11.7sec
	Top speed: 93mph
Power & torque:	64bhp/61lb ft
Engine:	Normally aspirated, 1116cc four cylinder, petrol, carburettor, 8 valves
Drivetrain:	Front-engine RWD
Structure:	Monocoque
Transmission:	Four-speed manual
Weight:	820kg

PRICE GUIDE

Launch price:	£1398
Excellent:	£5000
Good:	£4000
Average:	£2000
Project:	£500

FIAT
132/Argenta

Italy's reputation for being unable to build good big cars was founded by the 132. It should have had the world at its feet thanks to eager engines, five-speed 'boxes, crisp styling and decades of sporting saloon experience. But thanks to uninspiring road manners and a distinct lack of showroom appeal, the 132 remains less than the sum of its parts. It was offered in the UK only in luxury versions, so we were spared the 1.6-litre base version that sold well in Italy. Twin-cam quad-headlamp version was no BMW-beater, but black Bellini special edition still looks good.

SPECIFICATIONS (1600 GLS)

Years produced:	1972-1984 (975,970 in total)
Performance:	0-60mph: 11.6sec
	Top speed: 102mph
Power & torque:	98bhp/97lb ft
Engine:	Normally aspirated 1592cc four cylinder, petrol, carburettor, 8 valves
Drivetrain:	Front-engine RWD
Structure:	Monocoque
Transmission:	Five-speed manual
Weight:	1095kg

PRICE GUIDE

Launch price:	£2276
Excellent:	£2250
Good:	£1500
Average:	£650
Project:	£250

FIAT
131/Mirafiori

Well-engineered replacement for the 124 was built at Fiat's Mirafiori factory, hence the name it adopted in export markets. Conventionally engineered with rear-wheel drive and a range of single- and twin-cam engines, the 131 was perfectly conceived for the Cortina/Cavalier market. As ever, a huge seller in Italy and mainly overlooked elsewhere. The most memorable version is the twin-cam Supermirafiori model that hit the market in 1978 – although it was not the caged tiger the adverts hinted at – but most have succumbed to rust and as engine donors.

SPECIFICATIONS (1300 L)

Years produced:	1974-1984 (1,850,000 in total)
Performance:	0-60mph: 16.1sec
	Top speed: 91mph
Power & torque:	64bhp/75lb ft
Engine:	Normally aspirated 1297cc four cylinder, petrol, carburettor, 8 valves
Drivetrain:	Front-engine RWD
Structure:	Monocoque
Transmission:	Four-speed manual
Weight:	965kg

PRICE GUIDE

Launch price:	£1619
Excellent:	£1800
Good:	£1500
Average:	£650
Project:	£250

FIAT
131TC/Sport

Based on a two-door Mirafiori shell, the 131 Sport was, in effect, an Italian equivalent to the Escort RS2000 that was launched at the same time. Both have 2.0-litre engines with the Fiat's twin-cam efficiency compensating for the 131 Sport's extra weight. Both were pure road cars being sold on the back of rally successes. These days, however, the Fiat is substantially cheaper to buy than the Ford. They were only sold in black, orange, silver or grey and have plastic wheelarch lips and a spoiler built into the front bumper.

SPECIFICATIONS

Years produced:	1978-1984 (N/A total)
Performance:	0-60mph: 10.1sec
	Top speed: 112mph
Power & torque:	115bhp/123lb ft
Engine:	Normally aspirated, 1995cc four cylinder, petrol, carburettor, 8 valves
Drivetrain:	Front-engine RWD
Structure:	Monocoque
Transmission:	Five-speed manual
Weight:	1020kg

PRICE GUIDE

Launch price:	£4636
Excellent:	£4000
Good:	£3000
Average:	£1500
Project:	£500

FIAT
X1/9 1500

Everyone who drove an X1/9 1300 felt that it was crying out for more power. It had the looks of a 308GT4 or Urraco, wth road manners to match, yet struggled to crack 100mph. The answers to many of these criticisms came in 1978, when the X1/9 received an uprated 1.5-litre engine and five-speed gearbox. Sadly, it also gained US-spec impact absorbing bumpers that took away a great deal of the original car's delicate style. Still cruelly undervalued compared with more conventional sports cars, the X1/9 is a genuine scale-model supercar.

SPECIFICATIONS
Years produced:	1978-1989 (141,108 inc 1500 in total)
Performance:	0-60mph: 10.8sec
	Top speed: 110mph
Power & torque:	85bhp/87lb ft
Engine:	Normally aspirated 1498cc four cylinder, petrol, carburettor, 8 valves
Drivetrain:	Mid-engine RWD
Structure:	Monocoque
Transmission:	Five-speed manual
Weight:	914kg

PRICE GUIDE
Launch price:	£4575
Excellent:	£3500
Good:	£2000
Average:	£1000
Project:	£700

FIAT
Strada

Fiat's entrant in the Golf sector, and eventual replacement for the 128, was the Strada. Its major appeal now lies in its oddball styling and vivacious driving experience, but when new it was trumpeted in a memorable advertising campaign for being 'handbuilt by Robots'. The Strada's interior was a perfect example of form over function, while build quality was lax at best. 1982's Super Strada was an improvement, while the facelift models (which lost the appealing styling details) of '83 were better still. Prices are still low despite utter rarity.

SPECIFICATIONS (75 L)
Years produced:	1978-1988 (1,790,000 in total)
Performance:	0-60mph: 13.3sec
	Top speed: 95mph
Power & torque:	75bhp/87lb ft
Engine:	Normally aspirated 1498cc four cylinder, petrol, carburettor, 8 valves
Drivetrain:	Front-engine FWD
Structure:	Monocoque
Transmission:	Five-speed manual
Weight:	850kg

PRICE GUIDE
Launch price:	£3990
Excellent:	£1500
Good:	£900
Average:	£650
Project:	£300

FIAT
Panda

Fiat's attempt at a new entry-level people's car that harked back to the Renault 4 or Citroën 2CV made quite a first impression, almost winning the 1981 Car of the Year award. The plastic-clad exterior and flat glass smacked of minimalism, and the interior, with its deckchair seats and functional dashboard, was utterly utilitarian. The Panda worked because Italdesign made it look appealing. Panda II of 1986 ws slightly plusher, and remained a top-ten seller in Italy until 2003. Interesting Steyr-Puch 4x4 version still popular in mountainous Europe. Tough to find now.

SPECIFICATIONS
Years produced:	1980-2003 (4,500,000 in total)
Performance:	0-60mph: 17.9sec
	Top speed: 85mph
Power & torque:	45bhp/49lb ft
Engine:	Normally aspirated 903cc four cylinder, petrol, carburettor, 8 valves
Drivetrain:	Front-engine FWD
Structure:	Monocoque
Transmission:	Four-speed manual
Weight:	680kg

PRICE GUIDE
Launch price:	£2995
Excellent:	£1300
Good:	£900
Average:	£650
Project:	£300

FIAT
Strada Abarth 130TC

Built to bloody some noses in the escalating hot-hatch wars of the '80s, the Abarth 130TC was a real drivers' car that posted better performance figures than even the omnipresent Golf GTI for a year or so. Surprisingly, in a world where fuel injection was now king, Fiat did it the old-fashioned way with a pair of Weber carburettors feeding its 2-litre twin-cam. Unfortunately the car found more friends among the motoring press than it did in showrooms, so they have always been quite exclusive. Prices have been on the up as word has got out.

SPECIFICATIONS
Years produced:	1984-1987 (N/A in total)
Performance:	0-60mph: 7.9sec
	Top speed: 122mph
Power & torque:	128bhp/130lb ft
Engine:	Normally aspirated 1995cc four cylinder, petrol, carburettor, 8 valves
Drivetrain:	Front-engine FWD
Structure:	Monocoque
Transmission:	Five-speed manual
Weight:	950kg

PRICE GUIDE
Launch price:	£7800
Excellent:	£5000
Good:	£3000
Average:	£1500
Project:	£600

FIAT
Uno Turbo ie

In the mid-1980s the hot hatch ruled, and without one Fiat would have missed a great opportunity. Like Renault with the 5, the company went down the route of forced induction and the Uno Turbo i.e. was born. Fiat cleverly decided to price the Turbo to directly compete with the 205 GTi, but straight-line speed alone was not enough to take sales from the mighty lion, and the Uno lacked overall finesse in the chassis department when put up against its rivals. The car received a mild facelift in 1989, when power was increased from 105 to 118bhp.

SPECIFICATIONS
Years produced:	1985-1994 (N/A in total)
Performance:	0-60mph: 8.3sec
	Top speed: 122mph
Power & torque:	105bhp/108lb ft
Engine:	Turbocharged 1299cc four cylinder, petrol, fuel injection, 8 valves
Drivetrain:	Front-engine FWD
Structure:	Monocoque
Transmission:	Five-speed manual
Weight:	845kg

PRICE GUIDE
Launch price:	£6889
Excellent:	£4000
Good:	£1750
Average:	£700
Project:	£250

FIAT
Croma

The Croma was another famous 'nearly car' from Fiat. Based on the Type 4 platform that also sired the Lancia Thema, Saab 9000 and Alfa Romeo 164, it had all the ingredients for major commercial success, but outside of Italy sales were seriously lacking. Given its clean Giugiaro styling and close resemblance to the more expensive stablemates, the Croma should have boasted serious showroom appeal. Standard models were capable, roomy and quck, but the Turbo version was a seriously rapid express that helped define the term 'torque steer' for the motoring press.

SPECIFICATIONS (2.0ie Turbo)
Years produced:	1985-1996 (N/A in total)
Performance:	0-60mph: 8.0sec
	Top speed: 130mph
Power & torque:	153bhp/173lb ft
Engine:	Turbocharged 1995cc four cylinder, petrol, electronic fuel injection, 8 valves
Drivetrain:	Front-engine FWD
Structure:	Monocoque
Transmission:	Five-speed manual
Weight:	1180kg

PRICE GUIDE
Launch price:	£8849
Excellent:	£1500
Good:	£1100
Average:	£500
Project:	£400

FIAT
Tipo

Replacing and improving on the Strada wasn't going to take the work of a genius given how the opposition had left it far behind, but the Tipo's excellence was a surprise. The boxy body was galvanised, too, making this the first mid-line Fiat not to rust away in front of it's owner's eyes. But its main contribution to car history was that it lent its platform to a bewildering array of Fiat Group products topped by the Alfa Romeo 155 V6. Never won the hearts of buyers in the UK, despite appealing *sedicivalvole* coming on stream in the early '90s, and still epitomises the term 'banger'.

SPECIFICATIONS (1.1 FIRE)
Years produced:	1989-1995 (N/A in total)
Performance:	0-60mph: 17.2sec
	Top speed: 93mph
Power & torque:	55bhp/66lb ft
Engine:	Normally aspirated 1108cc four cylinder, petrol, carburettor, 8 valves
Drivetrain:	Front-engine FWD
Structure:	Monocoque
Transmission:	Five-speed manual
Weight:	905kg

PRICE GUIDE
Launch price:	£7150
Excellent:	£700
Good:	£500
Average:	£350
Project:	£200

FORD (UK)

It was in Manchester, England, in 1911 that the first Ford factory outside the USA opened, assembling Model Ts. Fords designed specifically for the British market started in 1932 with the Model Y, and a European-minded range evolved with the subsequent Zephyr, Zodiac, radically-styled Anglia and best-selling Cortina. In the late-'60s, the UK arm merged with its German counterpart to produce cars intended to be sold all over the continent; models such as the Mustang-like Capri and the Escort were phenomenally successful. Later products such as the Sierra and Focus have helped cement the company's position as one of Europe's biggest automotive players.

FORD
Pilot V8

The V8 Pilot was the British Ford flagship immediately post-war. In essence it was an amalgam of the pre-war V8-62 body with a new 2.5-litre engine. This proved not quite up to the task of propelling such a large lump of metal around, so the old and lazy 3622cc V8 that Ford used in so many wartime military vehicles came out of retirement. Despite the size of its engine, its power was just 85bhp, giving this lumbering but bulletproof beast a top speed of 83mph. Despite this, it proved popular as a police car.

SPECIFICATIONS
Years produced:	1947-1951 (21,487 in total)
Performance:	0-60mph: 20.5sec
	Top speed: 83mph
Power & torque:	85bhp/140lb ft
Engine:	Normally aspirated 3622cc V8, petrol, carburettor, 16 valves
Drivetrain:	Front-engine RWD
Structure:	Separate chassis
Transmission:	Three-speed manual
Weight:	1473kg

PRICE GUIDE
Launch price:	£585
Excellent:	£11,000
Good:	£9000
Average:	£6000
Project:	£3000

FORD
Consul MkI

Ford UK adopted unitary construction for its all-new Consul of 1950, the entry-level model in the new EOTA range that also included the Zephyr and Zephyr Zodiac. The Consul 'made do' with a 1508cc four-cylinder overhead valve engine of 48hp plus a three-speed transmission, although its MacPherson strut front suspension and fully hydraulic brakes meant that what performance there was could be made the most of. The slab-sided styling was very American in appearance, but suited the convertibles very well.

SPECIFICATIONS
Years produced:	1950-1956 (231,481 in total)
Performance:	0-60mph: 27.7sec
	Top speed: 75mph
Power & torque:	47bhp/72lb ft
Engine:	Normally aspirated 1508cc four cylinder, petrol, carburettor, 8 valves
Drivetrain:	Front-engine RWD
Structure:	Monocoque
Transmission:	Three-speed manual
Weight:	1041kg

PRICE GUIDE
Launch price:	£544
Excellent:	£3850
Good:	£3000
Average:	£1500
Project:	£500

FORD
Zephyr/Zodiac Mk I

The next step up from the Mk I Consul was the Zephyr, distinguished by its different grille, longer wheelbase and 2262cc six-cylinder engine of 68bhp giving better, smoother performance. Unveiled in 1951, the range was further complemented by the Zephyr Zodiac of 1953, with a high compression (71bhp) engine, leather, fog lamps and, just so everybody knew it was special, two-tone paint and gold-coloured badges. As well as the coachbuilt estates, there was the convertible with its power-operated hood.

SPECIFICATIONS
Years produced:	1950-1956 (152,677 in total)
Performance:	0-60mph: 20.1sec
	Top speed: 84mph
Power & torque:	68bhp/112lb ft
Engine:	Normally aspirated, 2262cc six cylinder, petrol, carburettor, 12 valves
Drivetrain:	Front-engine RWD
Structure:	Monocoque
Transmission:	Three-speed manual
Weight:	1181kg

PRICE GUIDE
Launch price:	£684
Excellent:	£5000
Good:	£4000
Average:	£1900
Project:	£650

FORD
Pop/Anglia/Prefect 100E

Unitary construction reached small Fords in 1953 with the 100E models. Looking like scaled-down Consuls and Zephyrs, 100Es came in basic two-door Anglia form or as the higher-spec Prefect, with four doors. Sidevalve engine technology persisted – the all-new 1172cc engine just happened to be exactly the same capacity as that in the old Anglias and Prefects. When the 105E Anglia was launched in 1959 the 100E became the Popular, a no-nonsense, low-budget machine intended to lure customers away from the Mini.

SPECIFICATIONS
Years produced:	1953-1962 (572,510 in total)
Performance:	0-60mph: 33.2sec
	Top speed: 68mph
Power & torque:	36bhp/52lb ft
Engine:	Normally aspirated 1172cc four cylinder, petrol, carburettor, 8 valves
Drivetrain:	Front-engine RWD
Structure:	Monocoque
Transmission:	Three-speed manual
Weight:	749kg

PRICE GUIDE
Launch price:	£348
Excellent:	£2250
Good:	£1750
Average:	£800
Project:	£300

FORD
Consul MkII

The first of the 'Three Graces' – the advertising slogan Ford used for this MkII family – was the Consul. It was the cheapest of the bunch, with four cylinders rather than the six found in the Zephyr and Zodiac, and a lesser level of trim. Convertibles had manually operated hoods and estates were only available as special coachbuilt orders. Ford also introduced a future industry standard by having a combined key-operated ignition and starter. The Consul Deluxe of 1957 was equipped almost to Zodiac level and had two-tone paintwork.

SPECIFICATIONS
Years produced:	1956-1962 (290,951 in total)
Performance:	0-60mph: 23.2sec
	Top speed: 79mph
Power & torque:	59bhp/91lb ft
Engine:	Normally aspirated 1702cc four cylinder, petrol, carburettor, 8 valves
Drivetrain:	Front-engine RWD
Structure:	Monocoque
Transmission:	Three-speed manual
Weight:	1143kg

PRICE GUIDE
Launch price:	£520
Excellent:	£4750
Good:	£3750
Average:	£1600
Project:	£550

FORD
Prefect 107E

The exciting new Anglia 105E of 1959 brought a revolution to small Fords... but not, unfortunately, four doors. So, for those who wanted the practicality of a four-door car and the innovation of an overhead valve engine but weren't that bothered about fashion-conscious looks, there was the Prefect 107E. In effect, this was the four-door 100E shape fitted with the 105E's overhead-valve engine and four-speed transmission, plus some plusher touches than had been the case on previous 100Es. Two-tone paintwork was standard.

SPECIFICATIONS
Years produced:	1959-1961 (38,154 in total)
Performance:	0-60mph: 27.2sec
	Top speed: 73mph
Power & torque:	39bhp/52.5lb ft
Engine:	Normally aspirated 996cc four cylinder, petrol, carburettor, 8 valves
Drivetrain:	Front-engine RWD
Structure:	Monocoque
Transmission:	Four-speed manual
Weight:	800kg

PRICE GUIDE
Launch price:	£622
Excellent:	£2500
Good:	£1900
Average:	£950
Project:	£350

FORD
Anglia 105E/123E

One of the most significant Fords ever, the Anglia 105E brought new levels of sophistication to the company's British arm. At last, here was an eager overhead-valve engine and nifty handling. These alone might have made the Anglia a family favourite, but allied to this was the eye-catching mini-Ford Thunderbird fins 'n' chrome styling and that infamous reverse-rake rear window, which was like nothing seen in Britain before. Estate versions arrived in 1961, closely followed by the 123E Super the following year.

SPECIFICATIONS
Years produced:	1959-1967 (1,083,960 in total)
Performance:	0-60mph: 26.9sec
	Top speed: 77mph
Power & torque:	39bhp/52lb ft
Engine:	Normally aspirated 997cc four cylinder, petrol, carburettor, 8 valves
Drivetrain:	Front-engine RWD
Structure:	Monocoque
Transmission:	Four-speed manual
Weight:	786kg

PRICE GUIDE
Launch price:	£610
Excellent:	£3500
Good:	£2750
Average:	£1400
Project:	£700

FORD
Consul Capri/GT

The Consul Classic was one of the prettiest cars ever built by Ford in the UK. While the saloon just looked clumsy and fussy, the coupé was svelte and elegant. Unfortunately, performance didn't live up to the looks, although the Capri GT of 1963 managed to squeeze 78bhp from its twin-carburettor 1498cc engine, meaning 95mph flat-out. Out of the total production run of 18,716, a mere 2002 were GTs. Ford would revive the Capri name in 1969, with much more successful results, but these original Capris are now highly sought after.

SPECIFICATIONS

Years produced:	1961-1963 (18,716 in total)
Performance:	0-60mph: 14.1sec
	Top speed: 93.3mph
Power & torque:	78bhp/91lb ft
Engine:	Normally aspirated 1498cc four cylinder, petrol, carburettor, 8 valves
Drivetrain:	Front-engine RWD
Structure:	Monocoque
Transmission:	Four-speed manual
Weight:	950kg

PRICE GUIDE

Launch price:	£916
Excellent:	£6750
Good:	£5000
Average:	£3000
Project:	£1000

FORD
Consul Classic

Seeking to repeat the success of the Anglia, Ford launched the similarly-styled Consul Classic in 1961. The reverse-rake window was back but the larger canvas gave Ford the opportunity to really go to town with the Transatlantic touches. But it proved a little too much for conservative British tastes, especially once the Cortina arrived to occupy a similar niche. The original 1340cc engine was replaced by a 1498cc unit in 1962. After only two years the car was dropped. The looks make it an interesting classic today though.

SPECIFICATIONS

Years produced:	1961-1963 (109,045 in total)
Performance:	0-60mph: 20.1sec
	Top speed: 80mph
Power & torque:	59bhp/79lb ft
Engine:	Normally aspirated 1340cc four cylinder, petrol, carburettor 8 valves
Drivetrain:	Front-engine RWD
Structure:	Monocoque
Transmission:	Four-speed manual
Weight:	930kg

PRICE GUIDE

Launch price:	£767
Excellent:	£3500
Good:	£2500
Average:	£1200
Project:	£500

FORD
Zephyr/Zodiac MkIII

For their 1962 MkIII incarnation Ford's Zephyrs put on considerable weight and adopted a razor-sharp style with prominent fins framing the wide, capacious boot and huge bonnet. As the Consul name was now being used elsewhere, the four-cylinder version – using the same 1703cc engine as on the MkII, albeit giving an extra 5bhp to give 65bhp – became known as the Zephyr 4; those blessed with an additional two cylinders were dubbed Zephyr 6. Externally the 6s had a different split grille and other dashes of affluence.

SPECIFICATIONS

Years produced:	1962-1966 (79,285/229,450 in total)
Performance:	0-60mph: 17.5sec
	Top speed: 87mph
Power & torque:	98bhp/134lb ft
Engine:	Normally aspirated 2553cc six cylinder, petrol, carburettor, 12 valves
Drivetrain:	Front-engine RWD
Structure:	Monocoque
Transmission:	Four-speed manual
Weight:	1242kg

PRICE GUIDE

Launch price:	£772
Excellent:	£4000
Good:	£3200
Average:	£1750
Project:	£500

FORD
Lotus Cortina MkI

Dropping the 105bhp twin-cam into Ford's lightweight Cortina bodyshell created a saloon car legend. Almost all came in white with the green side flashes, and their minimalist quarter-bumpers became de riguer for several generations of Ford tuners. The first year's production came with aluminium doors, bonnet and bootlid, along with an A-frame for the rear axle location. This is prone to cracking its mounts and was changed for leaf springs, but those earlier cars still command something like a 20% price premium.

SPECIFICATIONS

Years produced:	1963-1966 (3301 in total)
Performance:	0-60mph: 13.8sec
	Top speed: 108mph
Power & torque:	115bhp/108lb ft
Engine:	Normally aspirated 1558cc four cylinder, petrol, carburettor, 8 valves
Drivetrain:	Front-engine RWD
Structure:	Monocoque
Transmission:	Four-speed manual
Weight:	842kg

PRICE GUIDE

Launch price:	£1100
Excellent:	£40,000
Good:	£20,000
Average:	£14,000
Project:	£5000

FORD
Corsair

In the 1960s the Corsair was introduced to plug the void between Cortina and Zephyr. The handsome looks suggested Ford's Thunderbird reduced in size to British proportions. After two years the original 1498cc engine was replaced by a 1662cc V4 which, while it may have given more oomph, wasn't noted for its smoothness or sophistication. In 1967, capacity went up again, this time to 1996cc. This led to one of Ford's 'E' offshoots, the 2000E, which justified its Executive status with a different grille, wooden dash and a black vinyl roof.

SPECIFICATIONS

Years produced:	1963-1970 (294,591 in total)
Performance:	0-60mph: 13.5sec
	Top speed: 97mph
Power & torque:	88bhp/116lb ft
Engine:	Normally aspirated 1663cc V4, petrol, carburettor, 8 valves
Drivetrain:	Front-engine RWD
Structure:	Monocoque
Transmission:	Four-speed manual
Weight:	995kg

PRICE GUIDE

Launch price:	£650
Excellent:	£3300
Good:	£2500
Average:	£1250
Project:	£500

FORD
Cortina MkII/1600E

While the MkII Cortina used much of the old MkI for its underpinnings, its well-proportioned and boxy body was all new, helping to spearhead the move in the UK towards less curvaceous looks for cars during the tail end of the 1960s. Appreciative customers were given a multitude of different trim and engine options from 1297cc to 1599cc and quite austere saloons and estates through to sporty and posh Executive versions. The legendary 1600E had Lotus suspension, Rostyle wheels, a plush interior and black grille – add £1000 on to 1600 values.

SPECIFICATIONS (1600E)
Years produced: 1966-1970 (963,750 in total)
Performance: 0-60mph: 11.8sec
Top speed: 96mph
Power & torque: 88bhp/96lb ft
Engine: Normally aspirated 1599cc four cylinder, petrol, carburettor, 8 valves
Drivetrain: Front-engine RWD
Structure: Monocoque
Transmission: Four-speed manual
Weight: 924kg

PRICE GUIDE
Launch price: £799
Excellent: £5250
Good: £4250
Average: £2250
Project: £750

FORD
Cortina-Lotus

Comes with slightly more power than the MkI, but to some extent the moment had passed and it was quickly overshadowed by the Escort Twin Cam that was launched the following year. Less successful in competition than the Lotus Cortina MkI too, and built in higher numbers, so values fall well shy of their predecessors', and will remain that way. Still a handy tool, even if 109.5bhp doesn't feel as fast as it used to. Beware of fakes as rust and the unscrupulous mean more than a few have been created from Cortina GT bodyshells over the years.

SPECIFICATIONS
Years produced: 1966-1970 (4032 in total)
Performance: 0-60mph: 9.9sec
Top speed: 102mph
Power & torque: 110bhp/107lb ft
Engine: Normally aspirated 1558cc four cylinder, petrol, carburettor, 8 valves
Drivetrain: Front-engine RWD
Structure: Monocoque
Transmission: Four-speed manual
Weight: 905kg

PRICE GUIDE
Launch price: £1068
Excellent: £15,000
Good: £8500
Average: £5000
Project: £2500

FORD
Zephyr/Zodiac MkIV

The Zephyr and Zodiac range had grown consistently with every new reincarnation but, for the MkIV, things just went over the top. With their enormously long bonnets and short, stubby ends, the 1966-72 range looked like aircraft carriers on wheels... and handled in a similar way. V-configuration engines featured throughout; the Zephyr 4 had a 1996cc V4, the Zephyr 6 had a 2495cc V6, and the meaty Zodiac weighed in with a 2994cc V6. Top of the range was the Jaguar wannabe Executive model, loaded with occupant-pampering goodies and gadgets.

SPECIFICATIONS
Years produced: 1966-1972 (149,263 in total)
Performance: 0-60mph: 17.1sec
Top speed: 95mph
Power & torque: 88bhp/123lb ft
Engine: Normally aspirated 1996cc V4, petrol, carburettor, 8 valves
Drivetrain: Front-engine RWD
Structure: Monocoque
Transmission: Four-speed manual
Weight: 1250kg

PRICE GUIDE
Launch price: £933
Excellent: £4000
Good: £2750
Average: £1100
Project: £500

FORD
Escort MkI

Originally intended to be the new Anglia, the Escort name was adopted instead for the fresh small Ford after the formation of Ford of Europe in 1967. With less distinctive styling than the Anglia, it proved to be a huge hit, for its simplicity, neat appearance and good performance endeared it to millions. Even the basic 1098cc version proved surprisingly sporty, thanks to rack-and-pinion steering and effective MacPherson strut front suspension, while some of the higher-powered 'specialist' models were effectively rally machines for the road.

SPECIFICATIONS
Years produced: 1968-1975 (895,873 in total)
Performance: 0-60mph: 20.6sec
Top speed: 83mph
Power & torque: 58bhp/72lb ft
Engine: Normally aspirated 1098cc four cylinder, petrol, carburettor, 8 valves
Drivetrain: Front-engine RWD
Structure: Monocoque
Transmission: Four-speed manual
Weight: 745kg

PRICE GUIDE
Launch price: £635
Excellent: £5000
Good: £2500
Average: £1250
Project: £650

FORD
Escort Twin Cam

The word 'Lotus' was silently attached to the Escort Twin Cam, for this model was basically the Lotus Cortina engine and running gear clothed in the lighter two-door Escort bodyshell; something which made it even more of a wolf in sheepish clothing. Available from the start of MkI production in 1968, this 1558cc-engined machine had a very usable 106bhp – more than double that of the standard Escort 1100 – and a top speed of around 113mph. Constructed in limited numbers for homologation purposes. Production ended in 1971.

SPECIFICATIONS
Years produced: 1968-1971 (1263 in total)
Performance: 0-60mph: 8.7sec
Top speed: 113mph
Power & torque: 109bhp/106lb ft
Engine: Normally aspirated 1558cc four cylinder, petrol, carburettor, 8 valves
Drivetrain: Front-engine RWD
Structure: Monocoque
Transmission: Four-speed manual
Weight: 785kg

PRICE GUIDE
Launch price: £1263
Excellent: £30,000
Good: £19,000
Average: £13,500
Project: £9000

FORD
Capri MkI

According to Ford, this was 'The car you always promised yourself'. And, for 1.2 million customers, they were telling the truth, such was the sales success of this Mustang wannabe. The Capri was inspired by its American cousin and nobody cared that much that it was simply a Cortina in a party frock. The long bonnet swallowed up the four-cylinder 1300s and 1600s and even the V4 1996cc and V6 2994cc engines fitted with space to spare. GT badging was used to distinguish between 1300, 1600 and 2000 models.

SPECIFICATIONS

Years produced:	1968-1973 (1,172,900 in total)
Performance:	0-60mph: 13sec
	Top speed: 100mph
Power & torque:	72bhp/70lb ft
Engine:	Normally aspirated 1598cc four cylinder, petrol, carburettor, 8 valves
Drivetrain:	Front-engine RWD
Structure:	Monocoque
Transmission:	Four-speed manual
Weight:	920kg

PRICE GUIDE

Launch price:	£1041
Excellent:	£3500
Good:	£2500
Average:	£1250
Project:	£600

FORD
Capri MkI 3000

The big daddies of the mainstream MkI Capri range were the 3000 models, available as the performance-orientated 3000GT, the more luxury-focused 3000E and (from 1972) the flagship 3000GXL. Trumpeted as Ford's fastest ever production line cars, with a maximum velocity around the 120mph mark, these big bruisers of the Capri world could be distinguished by their bonnet bulges... at least until the smaller-engined models also adopted the same posing pouches in 1972. Shame they had nothing to fill them.

SPECIFICATIONS

Years produced:	1968-1973 (347,700 in total)
Performance:	0-60mph: 9.2sec
	Top speed: 114mph
Power & torque:	128bhp/173lb ft
Engine:	Normally aspirated 2994cc V6, petrol, carburettor, 12 valves
Drivetrain:	Front-engine RWD
Structure:	Monocoque
Transmission:	Four-speed manual
Weight:	1057kg

PRICE GUIDE

Launch price:	£1087
Excellent:	£6500
Good:	£4000
Average:	£2250
Project:	£900

FORD
Escort RS1600

Ford set up its Advanced Vehicle Operations in Essex in 1970 and first-born was the RS1600. This was an extension of the Escort Twin Cam, fitted with the new 16-valve Cosworth BDA twin-cam. The engine was developed from a Formula 2 racing unit and, even in detuned state, it made the Escort a furious machine, with the potential to hit almost 120mph. Most buyers ended up tuning them back up again and using them for competition. The RS1600 demanded a lot of care and attention beyond the means of most 'ordinary' owners.

SPECIFICATIONS

Years produced:	1970-1973 (1200 in total)
Performance:	0-60mph: 8.3sec
	Top speed: 114mph
Power & torque:	120bhp/112lb ft
Engine:	Normally aspirated, 1599cc four cylinder, petrol, carburettor, 8 valves
Drivetrain:	Front-engine RWD
Structure:	Monocoque
Transmission:	Four-speed manual
Weight:	785kg

PRICE GUIDE

Launch price:	£1447
Excellent:	£30,000
Good:	£21,000
Average:	£15,000
Project:	£9500

FORD
Escort Mexico/RS2000

Ford's victory in the tough and demanding 1970 World Cup Rally to Mexico gave the perfect excuse to unleash another 'hotted up' Escort upon an unsuspecting public. Based on the RS1600, the Mexico forwent the specialist twin-cam engine of that car and opted for a simpler – and therefore more reliable – 1598cc Kent overhead valve engine instead. 2.0-litre Pinto power (first seen in the MkIII Cortina) arrived in 1973 to create the RS2000 out of essentially the same platform. All look the part with lairy colours, decals and stripes.

SPECIFICATIONS

Years produced:	1970-1975 (9382/4324 in total)
Performance:	0-60mph: 9.0sec
	Top speed: 108mph
Power & torque:	100bhp/108lb ft
Engine:	Normally aspirated, 1993cc four cylinder, petrol, carburettor, 8 valves
Drivetrain:	Front-engine RWD
Structure:	Monocoque
Transmission:	Four-speed manual
Weight:	915kg

PRICE GUIDE

Launch price:	£1150/1586
Excellent:	£18,500
Good:	£10,000
Average:	£5000
Project:	£3000

FORD
Cortina MkIII

A new Cortina for a new decade, the MkIII was ideal for the more flamboyant and funky era that was the '70s. The 'Coke bottle' styling had overtones of American Fords and there was a mass of different options: X, XL, GT or GXL anyone? And would Sir like that with a 1300, 1600 or 2000 engine in his two-door or four-door saloon or estate? In all, there were 35 variants of Cortina at its launch. While its predecessor had been a MkI makeover, the MkIII was completely fresh, with new coil-and-wishbone suspension. Slick.

SPECIFICATIONS

Years produced:	1970-1976 (1,126,559 in total)
Performance:	0-60mph: 12.9sec
	Top speed: 104mph
Power & torque:	98bhp/111lb ft
Engine:	Normally aspirated, 1993cc four cylinder, petrol, carburettor, 8 valves
Drivetrain:	Front-engine RWD
Structure:	Monocoque
Transmission:	Four-speed manual
Weight:	1000kg

PRICE GUIDE

Launch price:	£700
Excellent:	£4000
Good:	£3000
Average:	£1500
Project:	£600

FORD
Consul/Granada

Forever immortalised by *The Sweeney*, the 1972-77 Consul and Granada series was Ford's return to reality after the excesses of the previous Zephyr/ Zodiac range. The Consuls served as the entry level models – with 1996cc V4 and 2495cc of 2994cc V6 engines – while the Granadas were the better-equipped and more expensive choice. Ford's recent purchase of Italian coachbuilder Ghia resulted in the luxurious Granada Ghia in 1974, soon joined by the Ghia Coupé. Consuls were discontinued in 1975 after which more basic Granadas filled the void.

SPECIFICATIONS
Years produced:	1972-1977 (50,747 in total)
Performance:	0-60mph: 10.4sec
	Top speed: 109mph
Power & torque:	120bhp/132lb ft
Engine:	Normally aspirated, 2495cc V6, petrol, carburettor, 12 valves
Drivetrain:	Front-engine RWD
Structure:	Monocoque
Transmission:	Four-speed manual
Weight:	1270kg

PRICE GUIDE
Launch price:	£1416
Excellent:	£6500
Good:	£2750
Average:	£1500
Project:	£500

FORD
Capri MkII

Falling sales caused Ford to have a rethink for the MkII Capri, launched in 1974. Some of the primitive raucousness of the original was taken away and replaced with more sophisticated practicality, and a hatchback instead of a boot. The body was also smoothed out, although not enough to make the car particularly aerodynamic. Still, it was better to drive than the original Capri, with a more civilised interior too. Currently less valuable than the MkI and MkIII, making this the thinking man's Capri – 3000S and Midnight Special are the ones to have.

SPECIFICATIONS (1600S)
Years produced:	1974-1977 (727,657 in total)
Performance:	0-60mph: 11.4sec
	Top speed: 104mph
Power & torque:	88bhp/93lb ft
Engine:	Normally aspirated 1593cc four cylinder, petrol, carburettor, 8 valves
Drivetrain:	Front-engine RWD
Structure:	Monocoque
Transmission:	Four-speed manual
Weight:	1023kg

PRICE GUIDE
Launch price:	£1336
Excellent:	£5000
Good:	£2250
Average:	£1500
Project:	£1000

FORD
Escort MkII

In 1975, the MkII Escort came along and, like the Cortina before it, lost many of the curves of the original in favour of a square-cut look that many considered bland. However, bland often sells well if the rest of the package is good, and the MkII proved this, with around two million sold during its five-year life. Underneath the boxy body, everything was much the same as on the MkI model, albeit with the addition of a 1599cc engine to complement the existing 1098cc and 1298cc ones. Trim levels were just as varied as before.

SPECIFICATIONS
Years produced:	1975-1980 (960,000 in total)
Performance:	0-60mph: 20.8sec
	Top speed: 79mph
Power & torque:	41bhp/52lb ft
Engine:	Normally aspirated 1097cc four cylinder, petrol, carburettor, 8 valves
Drivetrain:	Front-engine RWD
Structure:	Monocoque
Transmission:	Four-speed manual
Weight:	875kg

PRICE GUIDE
Launch price:	£1299
Excellent:	£4000
Good:	£3000
Average:	£2000
Project:	£1000

FORD
Escort MkII Sport/RS Mexico

Ford continued to offer sporty Escorts for both the masses and more focused drivers. Intended for more general consumption were the Sport and Mexico. The Sport used a 1599cc engine with 84bhp extracted from it, just enough to make it capable of the ton. However, to give the impression that it was capable of more, it had special wheels, spotlamps perched above its split front bumpers and pinstriping with '1600 Sport' branding. The Mexico, sold from 1976-78, did similar with its looks, but added touches from the RS2000.

SPECIFICATIONS (Mexico)
Years produced:	1975-1980
Performance:	0-60mph: 10.5sec
	Top speed: 107mph
Power & torque:	95bhp/92lb ft
Engine:	Normally aspirated, 1593cc four cylinder, petrol, carburettor, 8 valves
Drivetrain:	Front-engine RWD
Structure:	Monocoque
Transmission:	Four-speed manual
Weight:	903kg

PRICE GUIDE
Launch price:	£2978
Excellent:	£7500
Good:	£4500
Average:	£2500
Project:	£1000

FORD
Escort MkII RS2000

When the Escort MkII was launched, the RS name continued with the Cosworth-engined RS1800, produced in tiny numbers. More widespread Rallye Sport production was initiated with the RS2000 of 1976, which substituted the diva-ish Cosworth unit for a sturdier 2.0-litre Pinto engine. However, the real talking point about the RS2000 was its polyurethane 'droop snoot' front end and air dam, a modification that clearly distinguished it from any other Escort. Even so, poor sales led to a revamped version in 1978.

SPECIFICATIONS
Years produced:	1976-1980 (10,039 in total)
Performance:	0-60mph: 8.5sec
	Top speed: 108mph
Power & torque:	110bhp/119lb ft
Engine:	Normally aspirated, 1993cc four cylinder, petrol, carburettor, 8 valves
Drivetrain:	Front-engine RWD
Structure:	Monocoque
Transmission:	Four-speed manual
Weight:	925kg

PRICE GUIDE
Launch price:	£2857
Excellent:	£15,000
Good:	£9000
Average:	£4750
Project:	£2500

FORD
Cortina MkIV

The 1976 MkIV marked the convergence of Germany's Taunus and the UK's Cortina and, from that point on, a pan-European model strategy. Under the skin it was similar to the MkIII, but the range now included a Cologne V6 for the top-of-the-line Ghia models. The MkIV was a UK best-seller every month it was on sale, and that success was all about being able to offer its demanding customer base exactly everything it wanted. Today, it lacks the '70s retro appeal of the MkIII despite being longer lived and more successful. German-made cars have lasted far better.

SPECIFICATIONS (2.3 Ghia)

Years produced:	1976-1979
Performance:	0-60mph: 12.2sec
	Top speed: 99mph
Power & torque:	108bhp/130lb ft
Engine:	Normally aspirated 2293cc V6, petrol, carburettor, 12 valves
Drivetrain:	Front-engine RWD
Structure:	Monocoque
Transmission:	Three-speed automatic
Weight:	1128kg

PRICE GUIDE

Launch price:	£1950
Excellent:	£3500
Good:	£1750
Average:	£500
Project:	£300

FORD
Granada MkII

Granada MkIIs adopted Ford's new family appearance of squared-off lines. The angular appearance worked especially well with the larger proportions, cunningly disguising that what was underneath was mainly MkI. Fresh V6 engines were added in 2293cc and 2792cc capacities plus, for those who prized economy over performance, a 2112cc diesel. Trim levels of L, GL, S and Ghia covered all bases and there were limited edition versions such as the Sapphire and Chasseur. The 1981 facelift cars were a big improvement.

SPECIFICATIONS

Years produced:	1977-1985 (918,969 in total)
Performance:	0-60mph: 8.9sec
	Top speed: 117mph
Power & torque:	160bhp/163lb ft
Engine:	Normally aspirated 2792cc V6, petrol, mechanical fuel injection, 12 valves
Drivetrain:	Front-engine RWD
Structure:	Monocoque
Transmission:	Five-speed manual
Weight:	1455kg

PRICE GUIDE

Launch price:	£5913
Excellent:	£5500
Good:	£2250
Average:	£950
Project:	£300

FORD
Capri MkIII

As exciting as the MkII was rational, the Capri MkIII was one of the industry's most effective facelifts. Quad headlights, wrap-around bumpers and a plethora of TV star appearances restored the Capri's mojo. The Essex-powered 3000S and Ghia were replaced by the 2792cc Cologne V6-powered 2.8 Injection in 1981 and gave the flagship model a 127mph maximum speed – Porsche 944 performance for two-thirds the price. Best of all was the Brooklands Green 280, the last Capri of them all – a mere 1038 of which were made.

SPECIFICATIONS (2.8 Injection)

Years produced:	1978-1987
Performance:	0-60mph: 7.7sec
	Top speed: 127mph
Power & torque:	160bhp/163lb ft
Engine:	Normally aspirated 2994cc V6, petrol, mechanical fuel injection, 12 valves
Drivetrain:	Front-engine RWD
Structure:	Monocoque
Transmission:	Five-speed manual
Weight:	1230kg

PRICE GUIDE

Launch price:	£7995
Excellent:	£7500
Good:	£4000
Average:	£2000
Project:	£750

FORD
Cortina 80

At first glance the Cortina 80 didn't look much different to the MkIV, but it received a huge number of improvements that kept it on top until the arrival of the Sierra in 1982. A bigger glass area and lamp clusters, wrap-around bumpers and an aeroflow radiator grille are immediate identifiers. Build quality and rust resistance improved over the MkIV, and that means survival rate is increased. The most prized models are the wood-trimmed Ghia and the run-out Crusader, which buyers clamoured for in 1982, in preference to buying a new Sierra.

SPECIFICATIONS (Cortina 1.3L)

Years produced:	1979-1982
Performance:	0-60mph: 16.1sec
	Top speed: 87mph
Power & torque:	61bhp/68lb ft
Engine:	Normally aspirated 1297cc four cylinder, petrol, carburettor, 8 valves
Drivetrain:	Front-engine RWD
Structure:	Monocoque
Transmission:	Four-speed manual
Weight:	965kg

PRICE GUIDE

Launch price:	£3475
Excellent:	£3000
Good:	£1750
Average:	£500
Project:	£300

FORD
Escort XR3/XR3i

With cars such as the Volkswagen Golf stealing sales, 1980's Escort MkIII moved to a front-wheel-drive hatchback configuration to compete. The XR3 had the Golf GTI firmly as its target. A tuned 1597cc CVH engine produced 96bhp thanks to a twin-choke carburettor, while front and rear spoilers and blacked-out trim made it visually appealing to '80s eyes. Better was to come though with the fuel-injection XR3i of 1983. Boy racers soon fell in love with the XRs, in the same way their fathers had with the old rear-wheel-drive Escorts.

SPECIFICATIONS

Years produced:	1981-1986
Performance:	0-60mph: 9.7sec
	Top speed: 113mph
Power & torque:	94bhp/97lb ft
Engine:	Normally aspirated 1598cc four cylinder, petrol, carburettor, 8 valves
Drivetrain:	Front-engine FWD
Structure:	Monocoque
Transmission:	Five-speed manual
Weight:	970kg

PRICE GUIDE

Launch price:	£5750
Excellent:	£5000
Good:	£2500
Average:	£1000
Project:	£300

FORD
Fiesta XR2

Ford finally entered the mini-car market in 1976 with the Fiesta; an unqualified success right from the word go. Surprisingly, it took nearly six years before a genuine performance version was added to the range, in the neat and tidy form of the XR2, with a larger, more powerful engine than any other Fiesta. Black plastic trim decorated the interior and exterior, there were alloy wheels, and large circular driving lamps were added. Ford's 'Cooper clone' continued through the MkII and MkIII versions of the Fiesta, until dropped in 1994.

SPECIFICATIONS
Years produced:	1981-1989
Performance:	0-60mph: 9.4sec
	Top speed: 106mph
Power & torque:	94bhp/97lb ft
Engine:	Normally aspirated 1597cc four cylinder, petrol, carburettor, 8 valves
Drivetrain:	Front-engine FWD
Structure:	Monocoque
Transmission:	Five-speed manual
Weight:	840kg

PRICE GUIDE
Launch price:	£5713
Excellent:	£4000
Good:	£2500
Average:	£1250
Project:	£400

FORD
Sierra

The Sierra was a brave replacement for the Cortina, and slightly surprising. The aerodynamic body, penned by Patrick Le Quément, clothed conventional engineering – Pinto engines, RWD, and Granada-style rear suspension. Sales were slow as buyers baulked at buying a 'jellymould', but Ford stuck with the concept. In 1987, it was facelifted and a Sapphire saloon version was added, and success soon followed. It isn't long ago that every street was littered with Sierras, but most have now disappeared. Appealing for its '80s bravura; less so for the driving experience.

SPECIFICATIONS
Years produced:	1982-1992 (3,444,229 in total)
Performance:	0-60mph: 10.5sec
	Top speed: 118mph
Power & torque:	114bhp/130lb ft
Engine:	Normally aspirated 2294cc V6, petrol, carburettor, 12 valves
Drivetrain:	Front-engine RWD
Structure:	Monocoque
Transmission:	Four-speed manual
Weight:	1115kg

PRICE GUIDE
Launch price:	£4783
Excellent:	£1750
Good:	£1250
Average:	£650
Project:	£150

FORD
Escort RS Turbo

With the XR3i and homologation-special RS1600i very close in both looks and performance, Ford decided to make the volume-production Escort RS line a little more enticing with 1985's RS Turbo. Mechanically, the car took the best features from the XR3i and RS1600i then bolted a Garrett T3 turbocharger onto the 1597cc CVH engine to increase power to a laggy 132bhp for a 125mph top speed. Seven-spoke alloys, a bodykit and aerodynamic aids marked out the RS Turbo as the '80s boy racer's favourite.

SPECIFICATIONS
Years produced:	1984-1990 (8604 in total)
Performance:	0-60mph: 8.2sec
	Top speed: 125mph
Power & torque:	132bhp/133lb ft
Engine:	Turbocharged 1597cc four cylinder, petrol, fuel injection, 8 valves
Drivetrain:	Front-engine FWD
Structure:	Monocoque
Transmission:	Five-speed manual
Weight:	940kg

PRICE GUIDE (Series 1)
Launch price:	£9951
Excellent:	£10,000
Good:	£4500
Average:	£2850
Project:	£800

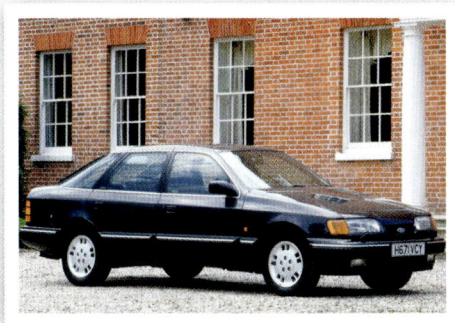

FORD
Granada/Scorpio

Even though the Sierra had proved slow-selling, Ford pressed-on with the similarly styled Granada Mk3. In Europe, the all-new car received an all-new name – Scorpio – but in the UK Ford didn't want to risk further alienating existing customers with its new hatchback. The Granada was memorable not only for its radical styling, but also for its standardisation of anti-lock brakes, a European first. Four-pot versions were underpowered, but V6s were capable. Later Cosworth models are genuine future classics, while the 1990s saloon and estate are mini-cabbers' favourites.

SPECIFICATIONS (2.4i Ghia)
Years produced:	1985-1994 (755,037 in total)
Performance:	0-60mph: 9.5sec
	Top speed: 120mph
Power & torque:	128bhp/150lb ft
Engine:	Normally aspirated 2395cc V6, petrol, electronic fuel injection, 12 valves
Drivetrain:	Front-engine RWD
Structure:	Monocoque
Transmission:	Five-speed manual
Weight:	1306kg

PRICE GUIDE
Launch price:	£8514
Excellent:	£1500
Good:	£800
Average:	£450
Project:	£250

FORD
Sierra RS Cosworth

As if the grandiosity of the bespoilered Sierra XR4i wasn't enough, Ford went even more extreme with the Sierra RS Cosworth. Launched in 1986, it used a 1993cc double-overhead camshaft engine, with the now requisite turbocharger attached, to give an output of 204bhp. Just 5545 were built, and insurance premiums were astronomical. It didn't help, of course, that a Cosworth Sierra was very obvious even from long distance, thanks to its massive whale-tail spoiler positioned halfway down the rear window.

SPECIFICATIONS
Years produced:	1985-1987 (5545 in total)
Performance:	0-60mph: 6.2sec
	Top speed: 142mph
Power & torque:	204bhp/203lb ft
Engine:	Turbocharged 1993cc four cylinder, petrol, electronic fuel injection, 16 valves
Drivetrain:	Front-engine RWD
Structure:	Monocoque
Transmission:	Five-speed manual
Weight:	1240kg

PRICE GUIDE
Launch price:	£15,950
Excellent:	£15,000
Good:	£10,000
Average:	£7000
Project:	£4250

FORD
Sierra Cosworth RS500

Why RS500? Ford chose the name to indicate that only 500 of this 1987 evolution of the original RS Cosworth would be built. It was constructed for motor sport homologation purposes, and put together by Aston Martin subsidiary Tickford. Mechanical modifications increased power to 224bhp. As well as uprated brakes and a modified front end, the RS500 signified the zenith of Ford's spoiler obsession, with a second small one now hiding beneath the existing whale-tail contrivance at the rear.

SPECIFICATIONS
Years produced:	1987-1987 (500 in total)
Performance:	0-60mph: 6.1sec
	Top speed: 154mph
Power & torque:	224bhp/204lb ft
Engine:	Turbocharged 1993cc four cylinder, petrol, electronic fuel injection, 16 valves
Drivetrain:	Front-engine RWD
Structure:	Monocoque
Transmission:	Five-speed manual
Weight:	1240kg

PRICE GUIDE
Launch price:	£19,995
Excellent:	£35,000
Good:	£18,000
Average:	£13,000
Project:	£10,000

FORD
Sapphire RS Cosworth

Things calmed down with the launch of the Sapphire Cosworth in 1988, which was much more discreet and down-to-earth than previous Sierra Cosworths. As its name suggests, it was based on the Sapphire saloon version of the Sierra and used the existing 1993cc Cosworth twin-cam turbo. Perhaps wisely, now missing were the flashy spoilers, replaced by just a small and subtle one on the bootlid. Even the two available colours were sensible too; white or grey. 11,000 were made before the Sapphire RS Cosworth 4x4 replaced it in 1990.

SPECIFICATIONS
Years produced:	1987-1992 (20,250 in total)
Performance:	0-60mph: 6.5sec
	Top speed: 151mph
Power & torque:	204bhp/203lb ft
Engine:	Turbocharged 1993cc four cylinder, petrol, electronic fuel injection, 16 valves
Drivetrain:	Front-engine RWD
Structure:	Monocoque
Transmission:	Five-speed manual
Weight:	1250kg

PRICE GUIDE
Launch price:	£19,500
Excellent:	£10,000
Good:	£6500
Average:	£4000
Project:	£2000

FORD (USA)

THE FORD Motor Company was founded by Henry Ford in Dearborn near Detroit in June 1903. The company made its fortune by introducing methods for large-scale manufacturing of cars and large-scale management of an industrial workforce using elaborately engineered manufacturing sequences typified by moving assembly lines. Henry Ford's methods came to be known around the world as Fordism by 1914. The first mass-produced Ford was the Model T, which motorised the USA before going on to sell 15 million copies worldwide. The company remains a huge player, and is currently the USA's second-largest car manufacturer behind General Motors.

FORD
Mustang

The original Mustang was exactly the right car at the right time and thus this sports car for the masses sold a million in less than two years. Available as a notchback coupé, convertible or, from 1965, a fastback coupé, the array of trim and engine options meant that there was a 'Stang to satisfy anyone... although it was in powerful V8 form that this fast Ford was most fulfilling. While handling was soft compared with Europe's best, the Mustang's other attractions meant rival manufacturers were soon rushing to offer their own 'Pony Car' pretenders.

SPECIFICATIONS
Years produced:	1964-1968 (2,204,038 in total)
Performance:	0-60mph: 10sec
	Top speed: 115mph
Power & torque:	225bhp/305lb ft
Engine:	Normally aspirated 4728cc V8, petrol, carburettor, 16 valves
Drivetrain:	Front-engine RWD
Structure:	Monocoque
Transmission:	Four-speed manual
Weight:	1450kg

PRICE GUIDE
Launch price:	£1925
Excellent:	£20,000
Good:	£15,000
Average:	£12,000
Project:	£10,000

FORD
Mustang (1969-1973)

After four massive years of sales success, the Mustang received its first major facelift. The new car grew in all directions and gained bulging flanks at the expense of the earlier car's sculpted look, and sales began to fall off a cliff. It wasn't only the mid-life changes that blunted the Mustang's appeal; that was just as much down to changing times. The ultimates were the Mach 1 and Boss, which Ford produced to fight the Shelby cars in the showrooms. These cars had up to 375bhp and could sprint to 60mph in under six seconds. They are valued accordingly.

SPECIFICATIONS
Years produced:	1969-1973 (900,909 in total)
Performance:	0-60mph: N/A
	Top speed: 115mph
Power & torque:	177bhp/284lb ft
Engine:	Normally aspirated 5753cc V8, petrol, carburettor, 16 valves
Drivetrain:	Front-engine RWD
Structure:	Monocoque
Transmission:	3/4-speed manual/three-speed auto
Weight:	1527kg

PRICE GUIDE
Launch price:	Not sold in UK
Excellent:	£15,000
Good:	£12,000
Average:	£10,000
Project:	£8000

FRAZER NASH

FRAZER NASH STARTED out in 1924 building idiosyncratic chain-driven sports cars, but was taken over in 1929 and began importing BMWs instead, thus allowing it to use BMW mechanicals – such as the 2.0-litre 328 engine – in its competition-orientated machines. Spartan bodywork gradually expanded into more elegant lines and more power came along courtesy of BMW's 3.2-litre V6 engine. Frazer Nash named several of its models after events and venues in which it had achieved sporting success, such as Le Mans, Sebring, Mille Miglia and Targa Florio. In 1960, the company decided to retreat from car production and concentrate on other engineering disciplines.

FRAZER NASH
Le Mans Replica

Following the privateer success for Frazer Nash in the 1949 Le Mans 24 Hour race, the company produced its own version following on from the tradition first started with the 1932 TT Replica. The Le Mans was powered by a 1971cc BMW straight six delivering a healthy 120bhp and, with the lightweight 'High Speed' body, proved prodigiously quick. Like all Nashes the Le Mans Replica was completely handbuilt, with the customer getting the final say on engine configuration and suspension set-up.

SPECIFICATIONS	
Years produced:	1948-1953 (34 in total)
Performance:	0-60mph: 8.8sec
	Top speed: 110mph
Power & torque:	125bhp/N/A
Engine:	Normally aspirated 1971cc straight six, petrol, carburettor, 12 valves
Drivetrain:	Front-engine RWD
Structure:	Separate chassis
Transmission:	Four-speed
Weight:	635kg
PRICE GUIDE	
Launch price:	£3074
Excellent:	£400,000
Good:	£275,000
Average:	£140,000
Project:	£100,000

FRAZER NASH
Fast Roadster/Mille Miglia

A roadgoing sports car with direct competition heritage – the Fast Roadster, Cabriolet and Mille Miglia were Frazer Nash's attempts to widen the appeal of its product line. But under the skin, it was almost pure Le Mans Replica. The full-width body certainly looked the part, even if housing the spare wheel Bristol-style caused an odd-looking bulge in the front wing. The Cabriolet runs on a lengthened wheelbase. Rare and fabulously valuable, but a wonderful driver's tool especially in 125bhp Mille Miglia specification.

SPECIFICATIONS	
Years produced:	1949-1953 (12 in total)
Performance:	0-60mph: 9.3sec
	Top speed: 110mph
Power & torque:	125bhp/N/A
Engine:	Normally aspirated 1971cc straight six, petrol, carburettor, 12 valves
Drivetrain:	Front-engine RWD
Structure:	Separate chassis
Transmission:	Four-speed
Weight:	735kg
PRICE GUIDE	
Launch price:	N/A
Excellent:	£200,000
Good:	£175,000
Average:	£140,000
Project:	£100,000

GILBERN

THE ONLY TRULY Welsh car manufacturer, Gilbern is also one of the few firms to graduate from kit-cars to completed production vehicles, though all used the same production method of a glassfibre body over a steel tube chassis. The Gilbern name is a combination of its two founders, Giles Smith and Bernard Friese. Early GTs were based on BMC mechanical parts, but over the years the company used more and more parts from the cheaper source of Ford, starting with its V6 engines for the Genie and Invader models. By the Invader III all mechanical parts were stamped with the Ford logo. The energy crisis and VAT changes (which upped the prices of kit cars) killed the company off in 1974.

GILBERN
GT

Good looking little 2+2 from Wales, with a glassfibre body over a tube frame. To some degree or other the 277 built were sold as kit-cars to avoid purchase tax, so parts and spec can vary a little between cars. They were initially offered with A-series or MGA engines, but most survivors you'll find will have MGB power, along with front suspension from the same source. Thanks to an enthusiastic club parts sourcing is much better than you might expect, right down to reproduction bodies and chassis if necessary.

SPECIFICATIONS	
Years produced:	1959-1967 (277 in total)
Performance:	0-60mph: 12.0sec
	Top speed: 111mph
Power & torque:	95bhp/110lb ft
Engine:	Normally aspirated 1798cc four cylinder, petrol, carburettor, 8 valves
Drivetrain:	Front-engine RWD
Structure:	Glassfibre body/tubular chassis
Transmission:	Four-speed manual
Weight:	813kg
PRICE GUIDE	
Launch price:	£748
Excellent:	£7000
Good:	£5000
Average:	£2900
Project:	£1000

GILBERN
Genie

Gilbern's move upmarket to full GT status. Larger, more angular body now contains a Ford Zephyr V6, mostly in 3.0 capacity, though some were sold with 2.5s. Another big change was that you could buy a Genie factory-built as well as in component form. The first 30 or so came with MGB front suspension and rear axle, then these were upgraded to MGC spec. Somewhere close to 200 were built. Overdrive was an option worth finding now, and some even came with electric windows. Twin fuel tanks add to their kudos.

SPECIFICATIONS

Years produced:	1966-1970 (197 in total)
Performance:	0-60mph: 10.7sec
	Top speed: 115mph
Power & torque:	141bhp/181lb ft
Engine:	Normally aspirated 2994cc V6, petrol, carburettor, 12 valves
Drivetrain:	Front-engine RWD
Structure:	Glassfibre body/tubular chassis
Transmission:	Four-speed manual
Weight:	965kg

PRICE GUIDE

Launch price:	£1752
Excellent:	£6000
Good:	£4750
Average:	£2750
Project:	£1000

GILBERN
Invader

The MkI and II Invaders differed visually only in detail from the Genie they replaced. Flush-fitting doorhandles and rear pillar vents are the biggest giveaways. Underneath, the front suspension is still MGC-based, but with double wishbones and coil-overs replacing the MG's lever-arm dampers. For 1971-72 there was also an estate version, of which 105 were built. MkIII uses the same 3.0-litre engine, but a switch to Cortina MkIII axles and suspension brings the need for flared wheelarches. A full-width grille adds further distinction.

SPECIFICATIONS

Years produced:	1969-1974 (603 in total)
Performance:	0-60mph: 10.7sec
	Top speed: 115mph
Power & torque:	141bhp/181lb ft
Engine:	Normally aspirated 2994cc V6, petrol, carburettor, 12 valves
Drivetrain:	Front-engine RWD
Structure:	Glassfibre body/tubular chassis
Transmission:	Four-speed manual
Weight:	903kg

PRICE GUIDE

Launch price:	N/A
Excellent:	£7000
Good:	£5000
Average:	£2750
Project:	£1000

GINETTA

The four car-mad Walklett brothers – Bob, Ivor, Trevor and Douglas – of Essex founded Ginetta and built their first car the first Ginetta was built in 1958. The company built both competition and road cars, all using glassfibre bodies and steel frames, until the going got tough in the mid-1970s, after which they kept going by refurbishing existing Ginettas, and eventually reintroducing the popular G4. After the Walkletts retired in 1989, Ginetta was sold to a Sheffield consortium and production moved north, where the new G20 and G32 were launched. In 2005 the company was acquired by LNT Automotive and production moved to Leeds. New model launches are planned.

GINETTA
G15

As the more obviously road-focused model it's clear why the G15 became Ginetta's best-selling model. Powered by the excellent Coventry Climax based Hillman Imp engine, mid-mounted in the lightweight glassfibre 'shell, weight distribution was near-perfect and handling predictably good as a result. The suspension set-up was a mixture of Triumph and Hillman and used to great effect. A more powerful G15S was launched and pushed the top speed up to 115mph – but sadly the G15 was taken out of production in 1973.

SPECIFICATIONS

Years produced:	1968-1974 (800 in total)
Performance:	0-60mph: 12.9sec
	Top speed: 94mph
Power & torque:	50bhp/49lb ft
Engine:	Normally aspirated 875cc four cylinder, petrol, carburettor, 8 valves
Drivetrain:	Rear engine RWD
Structure:	Glassfibre body/tubular chassis
Transmission:	Four-speed manual
Weight:	501kg

PRICE GUIDE

Launch price:	£1024
Excellent:	£8500
Good:	£6500
Average:	£3500
Project:	£1500

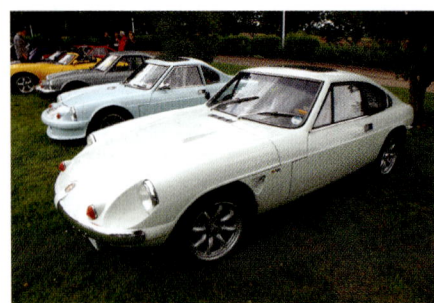

GINETTA
G21

The more upmarket G21 reflected Ginetta's ambitions in the wake of the collapse of the kit-car market. Its sleek glassfibre body was fitted over a new tubular steel chassis and a choice of Sunbeam Rapier H120 or Ford V6 engines meant that there was real power on tap. The two-seat coupé wasn't offered with an opening rear door and, in the wake of the MGB and Ford Capri, this seemed like an oversight – but despite this, most of the 170 built were sold as complete cars, and not in kit form.

SPECIFICATIONS

Years produced:	1973-1978 (180 in total)
Performance:	0-60mph: 9.7sec
	Top speed: 112mph
Power & torque:	85bhp/91lb ft
Engine:	Normally aspirated 1725cc four cylinder, petrol, carburettor, 8 valves
Drivetrain:	Front-engine RWD
Structure:	Glassfibre body/tubular chassis
Transmission:	Four-speed manual
Weight:	737kg

PRICE GUIDE

Launch price:	£1875
Excellent:	£8000
Good:	£6000
Average:	£3250
Project:	£1500

GINETTA
G32

A new look for the 1980s saw Ginetta going for the Toyota MR2 with its Ford-based mid-engined G32. Again, suspension was an off-the-shelf set-up taken from Ford, while the XR2 engine in the middle gave plenty of performance. After being in the business for so long, Ginetta had perfected getting a high quality finish from its glassfibre bodies, although the cunning use of the Fiesta's doors no doubt added to the feeling of solidity. Rare and unusual now, but satisfying if you can find the right one – and easy to keep on the road.

SPECIFICATIONS
Years produced:	1989-1992
Performance:	0-60mph: N/A
	Top speed: N/A
Power & torque:	90bhp/98lb ft
Engine:	Normally aspirated 1597cc four cylinder, petrol, carburettor, 8 valves
Drivetrain:	Mid-engine RWD
Structure:	Glassfibre body/tubular chassis
Transmission:	Five-speed manual
Weight:	753kg

PRICE GUIDE
Launch price:	£10,490
Excellent:	£5000
Good:	£4000
Average:	£3000
Project:	£1750

GINETTA
G33 V8

The G33 saw the return of 'back to basics' at Ginetta. Its body was a development of the curvaceous G27's (which harked back to the G4), and a Rover V8 engine shoehorned into the front provided TVR-rivalling thrills and soundtrack. But, being a Ginetta it was more track-focused than its Blackpool rival, making it a harder-edged alternative. The chassis was galvanised and holding it up was a fully independent suspension set-up featuring double wishbones all-round and front and rear anti-roll bars.

SPECIFICATIONS
Years produced:	1990-1996
Performance:	0-60mph: 5.3sec
	Top speed: 137mph
Power & torque:	198bhp/220lb ft
Engine:	Normally aspirated 3946cc V8, petrol, electronic fuel injection, 16 valves
Drivetrain:	Front-engine RWD
Structure:	Glassfibre body/tubular chassis
Transmission:	Five-speed manual
Weight:	874kg

PRICE GUIDE
Launch price:	£18,187
Excellent:	£12,500
Good:	£10,000
Average:	£7500
Project:	£5000

GLAS

HANS GLAS Isaria Maschinenfabrik was formed in 1883 as a maker of agricultural machinery. In 1951 it branched into car manufacture with a 246cc motor scooter. A range of microcars followed, but it wasn't until 1957 that the first *proper* car – the 1004 – arrived wearing the Glas nameplate. A range of increasingly pretty (Frua-styled) and technically advanced cars were subsequently introduced, culminating with the 2.6-litre V8 coupé. Unfortunately the company hit financial troubles in 1965, and BMW bought-out the operation, continuing production of the 1700 in South Africa as one of its own cars. The old Glas factory in Dingolfing, Germany, continues today.

GLAS
2600 V8/3000

The final flowering of the Glas marque was by far its most impressive. The underpinnings were sound enough, being based on the older 1700 saloon's, but the DOHC V8 up front had been created from a pair of 1300GT fours joined together. It was a delight to drive, and comfortable too, thanks to a well engineered de Dion rear axle with self-levelling. The Frua styling was glamorous, and probably influenced the company that ended up taking over Glas – BMW. Rare and desirable now and, as a marque swansong, few better the Glas V8. Replaced by the BMW 2800CS.

SPECIFICATIONS
Years produced:	1966-1968
Performance:	0-60mph: 10.5sec
	Top speed: 124mph
Power & torque:	138bhp/152lb ft
Engine:	Normally aspirated 2580cc V8, petrol, carburettor, 16 valves
Drivetrain:	Front-engine RWD
Structure:	Monocoque
Transmission:	Four-speed manual
Weight:	1127kg

PRICE GUIDE
Launch price:	N/A in UK
Excellent:	£15,000
Good:	£9000
Average:	£6500
Project:	£N/A

GORDON-KEEBLE

THE COMPANY may have been shortlived, but the car it produced was a stunner. John Gordon (previously behind the Peerless GT) and Jim Keeble used a beautiful glassfibre Giugiaro-styled 2+2 body and the Corvette V8 engine to produce a 135mph super coupé that was as good to drive as look at. But a price 40% higher than a Jaguar E-type's meant buyers were hard to find and the money ran out in 1965 after just 90 had been built. The company was bought by Geoffrey West and Harold Smith, who built another nine before giving up the following year. An amazing 90% of the cars produced have survived thanks to enthusiasts, and they remain utterly desirable.

GORDON-KEEBLE
GK1

With achingly pretty Giugiaro styling and the vocal accompaniment of a Corvette V8, you'd never know these were lovingly assembled in a large shed near Southampton. Just 99 were built before the company folded for the second and last time, but enthusiastic support and a glassfibre body over a square tube chassis means that almost all of the cars survive. Commonly found (and much better to drive) with a power-assisted rack-and-pinion steering conversion. Easy to drive fast and simple to look after.

SPECIFICATIONS

Years produced:	1964-1966 (99 in total)
Performance:	0-60mph: 7.5sec
	Top speed: 136mph
Power & torque:	300bhp/360lb ft
Engine:	Normally aspirated 5354cc V8, petrol, carburettor, 16 valves
Drivetrain:	Front-engine RWD
Structure:	Glassfibre body/tubular chassis
Transmission:	Four-speed manual
Weight:	1436kg

PRICE GUIDE

Launch price:	£2798
Excellent:	£40,000
Good:	£32,000
Average:	£24,000
Project:	£14,000

HEALEY

ENGINEER AND racer Donald Healey made a name for himself at Triumph before the war; after it, he formed his own motor company to build curvaceous roadsters and coupés using Riley parts. No British four-seater was faster than his Westland and Elliot models when launched. In 1949 came the Silverstone, a sleek and light sports car with stripped-down styling, aimed at weekend racers. An alliance with American firm Nash resulted in an attempt to sell cars in the USA, but little came of this endeavour. Healey then designed his iconic 100 sports car which so bewitched the British Motor Corporation that it agreed to build in under the Austin-Healey name from 1954.

HEALEY
Elliott

Formerly Triumph's technical director, Donald Healey started building his own cars in 1946, and the Elliott saloon was an important step in the development of his company. Considered to be the fastest closed four-seater available, these were thinly disguised racing cars, lightened with almost obsessive ruthlessness. At the Mille Miglia in 1948, Johnny Lurani and Giuglelmo Sandri won the production touring class in an Elliott, while Healey with his son, Geoffrey, finished ninth overall in a Westland Roadster.

SPECIFICATIONS

Years produced:	1948-1950 (64 in total)
Performance:	0-60mph: 12.3sec
	Top speed: 102mph
Power & torque:	104bhp/132lb ft
Engine:	Normally aspirated 2443cc four cylinder, petrol, carburettor, 8 valves
Drivetrain:	Front-engine RWD
Structure:	Separate chassis
Transmission:	Four-speed manual
Weight:	1143kg

PRICE GUIDE

Launch price:	£1566
Excellent:	£30,000
Good:	£12,000
Average:	£9000
Project:	£5000

HEALEY
Silverstone

The Silverstone showed just how far Healey had come in such a short time – it was an excellent road- or competition-car, and proved itself more than capable of living with much more expensive machinery. The short-framed car had an anti-roll bar and tenacious handling on the circuit. It was stylish too, and Healey easily sold every car built. However, this promising roadster was prematurely taken out of production when the deal between Nash and Healey to produce the Nash-Healey was concluded.

SPECIFICATIONS

Years produced:	1949-1950 (105 in total)
Performance:	0-60mph: 11.0sec
	Top speed: 105mph
Power & torque:	104bhp/132lb ft
Engine:	Normally aspirated 2443cc four cylinder, petrol, carburettor, 8 valves
Drivetrain:	Front-engine RWD
Structure:	Separate chassis
Transmission:	Four-speed manual
Weight:	940kg

PRICE GUIDE

Launch price:	£1246
Excellent:	£125,000
Good:	£37,500
Average:	£20,000
Project:	£12,500

HEALEY
Abbott

The Westland Roadster was Healey's first production car, and although it was capable of great things in competition it wasn't ideal as a road car. It might have enjoyed the benefits of a stiff box section chassis, all-round coil springs and the Riley engine helped it to a 105mph top speed but it lacked creature comforts. The Abbott drophead coupé was introduced to put that right with sharper style, a more compliant ride and lower gearing to improve tractability. It may have been slower but it was a more accomplished all-rounder.

SPECIFICATIONS

Years produced:	1950-1954 (77 in total)
Performance:	0-60mph: 14.6sec
	Top speed: 104mph
Power & torque:	106bhp/136lb ft
Engine:	Normally aspirated 2443cc four cylinder, petrol, carburettor, 8 valves
Drivetrain:	Front-engine RWD
Structure:	Separate chassis
Transmission:	Four-speed manual
Weight:	1143kg

PRICE GUIDE

Launch price:	£1854
Excellent:	£25,000
Good:	£17,000
Average:	£10,500
Project:	£6000

HEALEY
Tickford

Based on the Elliott, but more stylishly executed, the Healey Tickford is far cleaner-looking and more appealing than the original, perhaps taking the car away from its competition roots and into more exalted territory. Dynamically, it lost out to the Elliott, thanks to additional weight and a loss of agility. In dynamism's place it received a proper boot and glass (instead of Perspex) side windows. In the end, it outsold the original by two-to-one, proving that Healey's designs were good enough to warrant the premium they carried.

SPECIFICATIONS
Years produced:	1950-1954 (224 in total)
Performance:	0-60mph: 14.6sec
	Top speed: 104mph
Power & torque:	104bhp/132lb ft
Engine:	Normally aspirated 2443cc four cylinder, petrol, carburettor, 8 valves
Drivetrain:	Front-engine RWD
Structure:	Separate chassis
Transmission:	Four-speed manual
Weight:	1546kg

PRICE GUIDE
Launch price:	£1854
Excellent:	£20,000
Good:	£12,500
Average:	£9500
Project:	£5000

HEINKEL

DURING THE WAR, Heinkel had made military aircraft but, banned from doing this, it turned to bicycles and scooters instead. In 1956, it expanded into building bubblecars (following the path of BMW with its Isetta), both in three- and four-wheeled form. The quirky Heinkels were somewhat more sophisticated and spacious, however, than the closely-related Isetta. German production stopped in 1958, but continued under licence in Ireland and the UK (under the Trojan name) as well as in Argentina. Unfortunately for Hainkel, the impact of compact cars such as the Mini decimated bubblecar sales during the early 1960s and, by 1965, production had ceased worldwide.

HEINKEL/TROJAN
Cabin Cruiser/200

The archetypal bubblecar, the Heinkel was also produced in the UK by Trojan from 1961 as the Cabin Cruiser. Given its 197cc engine, cruiser was hardly an apt title for this economy special. As bubblecars go, the Heinkel was certainly an improvement over the BMW it was based on – it had space (just) for four people, was lighter, and could cruise happily at up to 50mph. Survival rate of these cars is exceptionally high, and that is down simply to their great build quality – as well as excellent club and specialist support.

SPECIFICATIONS
Years produced:	1956-1965 (23,000 in total)
Performance:	0-60mph: N/A
	Top speed: 53mph
Power & torque:	9.2bhp/N/A
Engine:	Normally aspirated 174cc single cylinder, petrol, carburettor, 2 valves
Drivetrain:	Rear-engine RWD
Structure:	Monocoque
Transmission:	Four-speed manual
Weight:	279kg

PRICE GUIDE
Launch price:	N/A
Excellent:	£8000
Good:	£5000
Average:	£2500
Project:	£2000

HILLMAN

FOUNDED IN 1907 by bicycle manufacturer William Hillman, the Hillman brand became successful despite – or perhaps because of – its range of frankly quite dull cars. After Hillman's death in 1921 the company passed to his son-in-laws John Black and Spencer Wilks, who respectively would later run Standard and Rover. Their moves were precipitated by a takeover from Humber in 1928, soon after which both companies were sucked into the Rootes Group. Hillman became the badge applied to Rootes' entry-level vehicles, with a succession of friendly-family cars such as the mainstay Minxes and later the Hunter, continuing until Chrysler killed off the name in 1976.

HILLMAN
Minx Phase I/II

While its upright looks were very traditional, the Hillman Minx Phase I was actually quite novel in some of its body design. Not only was there half-unitary construction but also a rear-hinged bonnet rather than the then-usual cumbersome side-opening panels. Introduced in 1939, the car continued to be built for armed forces use during the war, returning to the civilian arena in 1945. The 1185cc 35bhp sidevalve engine and conventional suspension were little to get excited about, although the Phase II of 1947 added hydraulic brakes.

SPECIFICATIONS
Years produced:	1939-1948 (60,000 in total)
Performance:	0-60mph: N/A
	Top speed: 59mph
Power & torque:	35bhp/N/A
Engine:	Normally aspirated 1185cc four cylinder, petrol, carburettor, 8 valves
Drivetrain:	Front-engine RWD
Structure:	Separate chassis
Transmission:	Four-speed manual
Weight:	876kg

PRICE GUIDE
Launch price:	£397
Excellent:	£3500
Good:	£2250
Average:	£900
Project:	£400

HILLMAN
Minx Phase III-VIIIA

The pre-war looks of the Minx were revamped with the Phase III cars of 1948, which switched to 'full-width' styling, completely unitary construction and coil-and-wishbone independent front suspension. After that, Hillman continued with its process of annual improvements, enlarging engines to give more power, upgrading the suspension, and tweaking the bodywork to keep it fresh. The alterations were subtle, but ensured that the breed kept up with its rivals until it was replaced by the Series Minxes of 1956.

SPECIFICATIONS	
Years produced:	1948-1957 (378,785 in total)
Performance:	0-60mph: 29.7sec
	Top speed: 73mph
Power & torque:	35bhp/N/A
Engine:	Normally aspirated 1185cc four cylinder, petrol, carburettor, 8 valves
Drivetrain:	Front-engine RWD
Structure:	Monocoque
Transmission:	Four-speed manual
Weight:	933kg

PRICE GUIDE	
Launch price:	£505
Excellent:	£2650
Good:	£2000
Average:	£900
Project:	£400

HILLMAN
Minx Californian

The USA was always a big target for British car firms, and Hillman had a head start on its competitors thanks to Studebaker-inspired styling by American Raymond Loewy. As its name suggested the Californian coupé was blatantly aimed across the Atlantic, where style was often much more important than substance. In essence, it was a 1953 Minx drophead coupé with a permanent hardtop attached. And what a roof, for the split three-piece rear screen was very eye-catching and the roof's contrasting paint made the car stand out.

SPECIFICATIONS	
Years produced:	1953-1956
Performance:	0-60mph: 34.7sec
	Top speed: 69mph
Power & torque:	37bhp/58lb ft
Engine:	Normally aspirated 875cc four cylinder, petrol, carburettor, 8 valves
Drivetrain:	Front-engine RWD
Structure:	Monocoque
Transmission:	Four-speed manual
Weight:	990kg

PRICE GUIDE	
Launch price:	£681
Excellent:	£4250
Good:	£2500
Average:	£1300
Project:	£500

HILLMAN
Minx Series I-IIIc

Hillman's new generation of family cars had smart and nicely-rounded styling, inspired by contemporary American trends. Sunbeam Rapiers and Singer Gazelles also used the same basic shell and body, but it was the Minx for the masses that was the big seller of course. With better performance and handling, plus more space inside, the Series cars were a significant step forward. Rootes fiddled with the formula almost every year; major changes included the 1390cc overhead valve engine rising to 1494cc with the Series III of 1958.

SPECIFICATIONS	
Years produced:	1956-1963 (341,681 in total)
Performance:	0-60mph: 27.7sec
	Top speed: 77mph
Power & torque:	48bhp/N/A
Engine:	Normally aspirated 1390cc four cylinder, petrol, carburettor, 8 valves
Drivetrain:	Front-engine RWD
Structure:	Monocoque
Transmission:	Four-speed manual
Weight:	965kg

PRICE GUIDE	
Launch price:	£748
Excellent:	£2500
Good:	£1850
Average:	£925
Project:	£350

HILLMAN
Super Minx

What had been planned as the new Minx eventually appeared in 1961 as the Hillman Super Minx. As it was bigger, heavier and (therefore) more expensive, Rootes had decided to release it as a separate model, with 'Super' added to highlight its improvements over the standard Minx. The bodyshell kept the family resemblance; underneath the mechanicals were mainly Minx. As well as the saloon and estate, there was a rather becoming four-seater convertible from 1962 (now worth twice saloon prices).

SPECIFICATIONS	
Years produced:	1961-1967
Performance:	0-60mph: 22.5sec
	Top speed: 83mph
Power & torque:	58bhp/86lb ft
Engine:	Normally aspirated 1592cc four cylinder, petrol, carburettor, 8 valves
Drivetrain:	Front-engine RWD
Structure:	Monocoque
Transmission:	Four-speed manual
Weight:	1069kg

PRICE GUIDE	
Launch price:	£856
Excellent:	£2000
Good:	£1500
Average:	£800
Project:	£250

HILLMAN
Minx Series V/VI

In 1963, the Minx received a facelift to make it look less 1950s. Although the changes weren't that sweeping, they succeeded in making the car look more like one from the decade it lived in. The rear fins were greatly reduced, the roof was flattened, the wrap-around rear screen replaced and a new windscreen and grille added. From today's viewpoint it was a less handsome vehicle but, back then, something needed to be done to boost the ageing Minx's appeal. The 1965 Series VI injected a bit more temptation with its 1725cc engine.

SPECIFICATIONS	
Years produced:	1963-1967
Performance:	0-60mph: 18.6sec
	Top speed: 80mph
Power & torque:	58bhp/87lb ft
Engine:	Normally aspirated 1592cc four cylinder, petrol, carburettor, 8 valves
Drivetrain:	Front-engine RWD
Structure:	Monocoque
Transmission:	Four-speed manual
Weight:	998kg

PRICE GUIDE	
Launch price:	£635
Excellent:	£2100
Good:	£1600
Average:	£800
Project:	£250

HILLMAN
Imp

A heroic failure for Rootes, the 1963 Imp was the company's attempt to tackle the Mini. And it was a great little machine, with a 37bhp alloy 875cc Coventry Climax engine mounted in the back. The all-independent suspension made it nimble on bends and the opening rear screen added practicality. Had it come along before the Mini, it might have been the big little star instead of BMC's baby. However, reliability issues and suspicion about its unusual nature robbed it of sales and it never recovered, despite being available until 1976.

SPECIFICATIONS
Years produced:	1963-1976 (440,032 in total)
Performance:	0-60mph: 18.5sec
	Top speed: 81mph
Power & torque:	39bhp/52lb ft
Engine:	Normally aspirated 875cc four cylinder, petrol, carburettor, 8 valves
Drivetrain:	Rear-engine RWD
Structure:	Monocoque
Transmission:	Four-speed manual
Weight:	694kg

PRICE GUIDE
Launch price:	£508
Excellent:	£2500
Good:	£1500
Average:	£850
Project:	£275

HILLMAN
Minx/Hunter

Hillman turned its back on the past with the Hunter. The angular looks were penned with the help of noted stylist William Towns and were neat but hardly stirred the blood. The 1725cc engine was the only real link with Rootes history and, with MacPherson strut front suspension, front disc brakes and overdrive, the Hunter gave a good account of itself. The Minx variant was more downmarket, with a 1496cc engine, but the old name disappeared in 1970. The Hunter soldiered on, largely unloved, with the 88bhp GT and 93bhp GLSs its most exhilarating versions.

SPECIFICATIONS
Years produced:	1966-1977 (470,000 in total)
Performance:	0-60mph: 13.9sec
	Top speed: 83mph
Power & torque:	79bhp/91lb ft
Engine:	Normally aspirated 1725cc four cylinder, petrol, carburettor, 8 valves
Drivetrain:	Front-engine RWD
Structure:	Monocoque
Transmission:	Four-speed manual
Weight:	953kg

PRICE GUIDE
Launch price:	£838
Excellent:	£1750
Good:	£1350
Average:	£650
Project:	£250

HILLMAN
Avenger

This 1970 Hillman was a car Rootes/Chrysler intended to sell to the world... and did, to some extent, for it was also available in the USA as a Plymouth. However, although its styling was more appealing than the Hunter's and the fresh range of OHV engines – 1248cc and 1498cc from launch, 1295cc and 1598cc in 1973 – were lively enough, the Avenger never really captured the public's imagination. It was rebadged a Chrysler in 1976 and then a Talbot in 1979, and remained in production until 1981 when the Linwood factory was closed.

SPECIFICATIONS
Years produced:	1970-1976 (638,631 in total)
Performance:	0-60mph: 19.8sec
	Top speed: 81mph
Power & torque:	58bhp/66lb ft
Engine:	Normally aspirated 1248cc four cylinder, petrol, carburettor, 8 valves
Drivetrain:	Front-engine RWD
Structure:	Monocoque
Transmission:	Four-speed manual
Weight:	830kg

PRICE GUIDE
Launch price:	£822
Excellent:	£2500
Good:	£1500
Average:	£600
Project:	£250

HILLMAN
Avenger Tiger

The Avenger seemed to go out of fashion really quickly. So much so that it has almost zero classic appeal. Except that in 1973, Hillman produced the Avenger Tiger, intended for club level competition. Its twin-caburettor engine was easily tuned, with upgrades available off the shelf. Tiger I and Tiger II models were produced, and it was the latter that lasted longer. All models were available in lairy colours with aerodynamic upgrades. Fun, but no Escort RS – and, although few were made, the car lived on in the form of the Chrysler Sunbeam Ti.

SPECIFICATIONS
Years produced:	1972-1973
Performance:	0-60mph: 11.8sec
	Top speed: 100mph
Power & torque:	78bhp/86lb ft
Engine:	Normally aspirated 1598cc four cylinder, petrol, carburettor, 8 valves
Drivetrain:	Front-engine RWD
Structure:	Monocoque
Transmission:	Four-speed manual
Weight:	880kg

PRICE GUIDE
Launch price:	£1302
Excellent:	£7500
Good:	£3500
Average:	£2500
Project:	£1000

HONDA

As a maker of bicycles and motorbikes, it was almost inevitable that Honda would branch out as the Japanese automobile industry expanded. It unveiled its first car in 1962 and for the first few years concentrated on building small models. As the range grew, so did the cars, with the long-running Civic becoming a common model worldwide. The Accord and Prelude also helped to establish Honda's global reputation, while its mid-engined NSX was a would-be Ferrari. Honda was one of the first mainstream manufacturers to market a hybrid electric vehicle, with its Insight, and is probably the most respected and prestigious of Japanese auto manufacturers.

HONDA
S800

In true Honda tradition the S800's party piece was under the bonnet. Only Honda would create a 791cc engine capable of producing 70bhp at 8000rpm, giving the car an impressive top speed of over 100mph. This impressive performance was not at the cost of fuel economy, which came in at 35mpg. Available as a coupé or a roadster, the car was loved by many but, with a shade over 10,000 sales worldwide, it was not massively successful. The S800 was the last Honda to wear the S badge until the S2000 in 1999.

SPECIFICATIONS

Years produced:	1966-1971 (25,853 in total)
Performance:	0-60mph: 13.4sec
	Top speed: 101mph
Power & torque:	70bhp/49lb ft
Engine:	Normally aspirated 791cc four cylinder, petrol, carburettor, 8 valves
Drivetrain:	Front-engine RWD
Structure:	Monocoque
Transmission:	Four-speed manual
Weight:	771kg

PRICE GUIDE (Convertible in brackets)

Launch price:	£779
Excellent:	£10,000 (£13,000)
Good:	£6000 (£9000)
Average:	£3500
Project:	£2500

HONDA
N360/N600

Honda's first car designed to compete in Japan's Kei-Class was a fair attempt at bettering Issigonis's Mini. It was launched in 360cc form in 1966 and featured an advanced specification that allowed it to punch well above its weight – its 354cc air-cooled OHC two-cylinder engine pushed out 31bhp, and it handled tidily thanks to a well-engineered FWD layout. In 1968, N360 was upgraded to N600 and blessed with an impressive 85mph top speed. Despite being a technical miracle, it failed to sell in big numbers in Europe – but it's prized today by collectors.

SPECIFICATIONS (N360)

Years produced:	1967-1972 (1,165,441 in total)
Performance:	0-60mph: 29.3sec
	Top speed: 72mph
Power & torque:	27bhp/24lb ft
Engine:	Normally aspirated 354cc twin, petrol, carburettor, 4 valves
Drivetrain:	Front-engine FWD
Structure:	Monocoque
Transmission:	Four-speed manual
Weight:	508kg

PRICE GUIDE

Launch price:	£536
Excellent:	£3000
Good:	£2250
Average:	£1650
Project:	£350

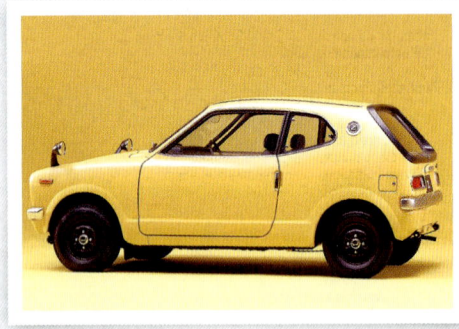

HONDA
Z600 Coupé

In Japan, the most important sector of the market is the Kei-class category. If your car falls within its stringent size, engine capacity and weight restrictions, you pay drastically reduced tax and insurance rates. Many Japanese car manufacturers embraced the Kei car and Honda was one of them. The Z600 pushed the limits of the Kei car regulations but, despite its limitations, the Z600 had no problem keeping up with traffic. All UK Z600s were painted orange, with a 'Starsky and Hutch' style black stripe running along the flanks.

SPECIFICATIONS

Years produced:	1973-1974 (40,586 in total)
Performance:	0-60mph: 32.6sec
	Top speed: 78mph
Power & torque:	32bhp/32lb ft
Engine:	Normally aspirated 599cc twin, petrol, carburettor, 4 valves
Drivetrain:	Front-engine FWD
Structure:	Monocoque
Transmission:	Four-speed manual
Weight:	580kg

PRICE GUIDE

Launch price:	£755
Excellent:	£3500
Good:	£2750
Average:	£1650
Project:	£350

HONDA
Civic I/II

Honda stuck to the N600's technical package when it came to creating the Civic, but scaled it up usefully to add global appeal. It arrived on the scene in 1972, making the Civic one of the first superminis to hit the market. Sales in the USA came just in time for Honda to capitalise on the demand for Japanese imports and more economical cars, and became a huge hit Stateside as a result. Sweet engines and a stylish interior stood the Civic apart from the opposition, and paved the way for Honda's huge success. The second generation was the basis of the Triumph Acclaim.

SPECIFICATIONS (1300 De Luxe)

Years produced:	1972-1983
Performance:	0-60mph: 13.5sec
	Top speed: 90mph
Power & torque:	68bhp/72lb ft
Engine:	Normally aspirated 1335cc four cylinder, petrol, carburettor, 12 valves
Drivetrain:	Front-engine FWD
Structure:	Monocoque
Transmission:	Four-speed manual
Weight:	735kg

PRICE GUIDE

Launch price:	£999
Excellent:	£2000
Good:	£1000
Average:	£550
Project:	£300

HONDA
Prelude I

Based on the second-generation Civic but powered by the Accord's free-spinning 1.6-litre engine, the Prelude was a sweet little coupé that sold steadily and paved the way for the company's gradual move upmarket. It was cramped and had an interior that could charitably be described as eccentric, and in the UK it was also rather expensive, all of which limited the Prelude's appeal in comparison with talented players such as the VW Scirocco and Alfasud Sprint. Well-kept examples fetch good money today, and are even being imported from Japan.

SPECIFICATIONS

Years produced:	1979-1982 (264,842 in total)
Performance:	0-60mph: 11.3sec
	Top speed: 98mph
Power & torque:	80bhp/93lb ft
Engine:	Normally aspirated 1602cc four cylinder, petrol, carburettor, 8 valves
Drivetrain:	Front-engine FWD
Structure:	Monocoque
Transmission:	Five-speed manual
Weight:	920kg

PRICE GUIDE

Launch price:	£4950
Excellent:	£3000
Good:	£1500
Average:	£750
Project:	£350

HONDA
CRX 1.6i/VTEC

One of the important lessons learned from the early CRX was that cars destined for Europe need a lot more rust protection than they do in Japan. Barely any Series 1 CRXs survive today, as many of them lost their battle with rust many years ago. Honda took this on board with the second incarnation of the CRX and, with a line-up of more powerful engines, it became a big hit in Europe. The 1.6 VTEC engine was a real firecracker that, like most Honda engines, delivered all of its power near to its 7600rpm rev-limit.

SPECIFICATIONS

Years produced:	1984-1991
Performance:	0-60mph: 8.0sec
	Top speed: 132mph
Power & torque:	158bhp/111lb ft
Engine:	Normally aspirated 1595cc four cylinder, petrol, electronic fuel injection, 16 valves
Drivetrain:	Front-engine FWD
Structure:	Monocoque
Transmission:	Five-speed manual
Weight:	1105kg

PRICE GUIDE

Launch price:	£6950
Excellent:	£3600
Good:	£2850
Average:	£1500
Project:	£500

HUMBER

ESTABLISHED IN Coventry in 1868 as a bicycle business, Thomas Humber's company had moved on to cars by 1898. Between the wars, its products became known for being well-engineered and rugged. When the Rootes Group took over

in 1930, it set up Humber as the luxury arm of its operation; the Royal family, Winston Churchill and Field Marshall Montgomery were all customers. Big Humbers continued after the war but, not long after Chrysler took over the

struggling Rootes concern in 1964, these larger cars were dropped and the smaller-proportioned Sceptre flew the flag for Humber until the demise of the marque in 1976, when the Anglo-French Chrysler 180 took over as flagship.

HUMBER
Super Snipe/Pullman II-IV

A curious blend of the old-style Super Snipes/Pullmans and the freshly-redesigned Hawks. The cabin and rear end weren't touched, but the front was given a Raymond Loewy makeover, with headlamps now incorporated into the wings. And running boards, which had been dropped in 1940, enjoyed a surprise revival. Dropheads were offered until 1950, and these can fetch up to double the quoted prices. Subtle improvements continued until 1952 and the MkIV model, which finally adopted the complete Hawk body style.

SPECIFICATIONS

Years produced:	1948-1957 (56,935 in total)
Performance:	0-60mph: 20.6sec
	Top speed: 81mph
Power & torque:	100bhp/N/A
Engine:	Normally aspirated 4086cc straight six, petrol, carburettor, 12 valves
Drivetrain:	Front-engine RWD
Structure:	Separate chassis
Transmission:	Four-speed manual
Weight:	1247kg

PRICE GUIDE

Launch price:	£1144
Excellent:	£7750
Good:	£6000
Average:	£2500
Project:	£800

HUMBER
Hawk MkIII-VIA

For the new Humber Hawk, the Rootes Group turned to legendary American stylist Raymond Loewy, who created an American-flavoured and modern design with a very imposing and elongated front end. The look endured to include the MkVIA version until this was dropped in 1957. Although the first MkIII cars used the same 1944cc four-cylinder sidevalve engine and gearbox as previous Hawks, independent front suspension was introduced. Further changes included a bigger engine for the 1950s MkIV.

SPECIFICATIONS

Years produced:	1949-1957 (59,282 in total)
Performance:	0-60mph: 30.7sec
	Top speed: 71mph
Power & torque:	56bhp/N/A
Engine:	Normally aspirated 1944cc four cylinder, petrol, carburettor, 8 valves
Drivetrain:	Front-engine RWD
Structure:	Separate chassis
Transmission:	Four-speed manual
Weight:	1247kg

PRICE GUIDE

Launch price:	£799
Excellent:	£4500
Good:	£3500
Average:	£1750
Project:	£500

HUMBER
Hawk I-IV

Unitary construction reached Humber with the Hawk Series 1 of 1957. Trumpeted as the largest bodyshell being built in the UK at the time, its size was due to Transatlantic styling: a big dollop of Detroit converted to Coventry dimensions. The 2267cc overhead valve engine from the previous generation of Hawk, giving 83mph from its 73bhp, was retained until the final MkIVA model. Series II cars had disc brakes, but the biggest change to the family came with the MkIV of 1964, when the cabin changed to a sleeker profile with more glass.

SPECIFICATIONS

Years produced:	1957-1967 (41,191 in total)
Performance:	0-60mph: 20.6sec
	Top speed: 83mph
Power & torque:	73bhp/N/A
Engine:	Normally aspirated 2267cc four cylinder, petrol, carburettor, 8 valves
Drivetrain:	Front-engine RWD
Structure:	Monocoque
Transmission:	Four-speed manual
Weight:	1433kg

PRICE GUIDE

Launch price:	£1261
Excellent:	£4000
Good:	£3000
Average:	£1500
Project:	£475

HUMBER
Super Snipe I-VA

As was Rootes' way, the final generation of Humber Super Snipe continued with the practice of using the less powerful, less luxurious Hawk as its basis, but giving it more power (and two more cylinders) plus some extra class-conscious touches. The original 1958 Series Super Snipes had a 2651cc six-cylinder engine, which rose to 2965cc the following year. For 1960 the nose was smartly restyled with quad-headlamps, one of the first British cars to have this arrangement and something never bestowed upon the Hawk. The final Super Snipes were built in 1967.

SPECIFICATIONS
Years produced:	1958-1967 (30,031 in total)
Performance:	0-60mph: 19.0sec
	Top speed: 92mph
Power & torque:	105bhp/N/A
Engine:	Normally aspirated 2651cc straight six, petrol, carburettor, 12 valves
Drivetrain:	Front-engine RWD
Structure:	Monocoque
Transmission:	Three-speed manual with overdrive
Weight:	1492kg

PRICE GUIDE
Launch price:	£1494
Excellent:	£5000
Good:	£4000
Average:	£1800
Project:	£500

HUMBER
Sceptre SI-II

Rootes introduced a new range of mid-sized cars in the early 1960s. At the top of this badge engineering tree, which also comprised the Hillman Super Minx and Singer Vogue, was the Humber Sceptre. More sporty than usual for a Humber – originally, the Sceptre was to be the new Sunbeam Rapier – the bodyshell was considerably altered from the other offshoots with a wraparound screen, quad-headlamps and a lowered roofline. The Series II of 1965 saw Rootes' well-liked 1725cc engine adopted, albeit with a cheaper Hillman-influenced nose.

SPECIFICATIONS
Years produced:	1963-1967 (28,996 in total)
Performance:	0-60mph: 17.1sec
	Top speed: 90mph
Power & torque:	80bhp/91lb ft
Engine:	Normally aspirated 1592cc four cylinder, petrol, carburettor, 8 valves
Drivetrain:	Front-engine RWD
Structure:	Monocoque
Transmission:	Four-speed manual
Weight:	1124kg

PRICE GUIDE
Launch price:	£977
Excellent:	£3250
Good:	£2500
Average:	£1200
Project:	£450

HUMBER
Sceptre SIII

Rootes, by now owned by the American Chrysler Corporation, swept away all its old models in 1966 and 1967 and replaced them with the Arrow range, personified by the Hillman Hunter. The Series III Sceptre was an upmarket Hunter, with a quad-headlamp nose, vinyl roof, fancy wheeltrims and a side order of wood veneer inside. Coupled with this was an uprated 1725cc engine of 88bhp with overdrive as standard. It may have been badge engineering, but the additional touches did much to make the Humber desirable.

SPECIFICATIONS
Years produced:	1967-1976 (43,951 in total)
Performance:	0-60mph: 13.1sec
	Top speed: 98mph
Power & torque:	79bhp/91lb ft
Engine:	Normally aspirated 1725cc four cylinder, petrol, carburettor, 8 valves
Drivetrain:	Front-engine RWD
Structure:	Monocoque
Transmission:	Four-speed manual with overdrive
Weight:	992kg

PRICE GUIDE
Launch price:	£1139
Excellent:	£2500
Good:	£1850
Average:	£1000
Project:	£300

INNOCENTI

INNOCENTI MADE ITS name making Lambretta scooters during the 1950s, and made the logical move into car manufacture in 1961, initially building Italian versions of the Austin A40 (but with a proper hatchback) and Austin-Healey Sprite. It became a successful business during the 1960s building Minis and BMC 1100s, before being purchased by an acquisitive British Leyland in 1972. That wasn't a happy marriage, and although the rebodied hatchback Mini of 1973 was a success, the local version of the Allegro (called Regent) was not. The partnership dissolved in 1975 as BL disintegrated, and Innocenti was picked up by Alejandro de Tomaso the following year. The marque died in 1997.

INNOCENTI
Spider/Coupé

Lambretta manufacturer Innocenti established itself as a car manufacturer capable of taking BMC products and making them look a whole lot more appealing. Although the company's first attempt following its licence-built Austin A40 was based on the Austin-Healey Sprite – itself a handsome little car – the Tom Tjaada-styled Spider and its Coupé sister managed to look more appealing and Euro-chic. Few were exported, and even fewer made it to the UK, where its high price compared with BMC's car made it a non-starter. Exclusive and fun if you can find one.

SPECIFICATIONS
Years produced:	1961-1970 (7651 in total)
Performance:	0-60mph: 20.5sec
	Top speed: 86mph
Power & torque:	43bhp/52lb ft
Engine:	Normally aspirated 948cc four cylinder, petrol, carburettor, 8 valves
Drivetrain:	Front-engine RWD
Structure:	Monocoque
Transmission:	Four-speed manual
Weight:	602kg

PRICE GUIDE
Launch price:	N/A in UK
Excellent:	£10,000
Good:	£6500
Average:	£3000
Project:	N/A

INNOCENTI
Mini 90/120

By the 1970s, everyone knew that the Mini needed a hatchback. But with BL firefighting elsewhere, it was a project that was prioritised behind more profitable models. However, Innocenti couldn't wait and commissioned Bertone to style a new hatchback body for its Mini, which was losing out against the Fiat 127 on the Italian market. The resulting car was stylish and had many people asking why BL couldn't do the same. A few made it to the UK, but rust was a major problem. The sporting De Tomaso version was a striking and apt replacement for the Mini-Cooper.

SPECIFICATIONS
Years produced:	1974-1983
Performance:	0-60mph: 11.9sec
	Top speed: 90mph
Power & torque:	65bhp/72lb ft
Engine:	Normally aspirated 1275cc four cylinder, petrol, carburettor, 8 valves
Drivetrain:	Front-engine FWD
Structure:	Monocoque
Transmission:	Four-speed manual
Weight:	715kg

PRICE GUIDE
Launch price:	N/A in UK
Excellent:	£4000
Good:	£2500
Average:	£1250
Project:	£1000

ISO

AFTER TRYING its hand at producing fridges, scooters, air-conditioning and the Isetta bubblecar, Iso turned its attention to the luxury car market in 1962 with the Rivolta, a steel-bodied car with more than a passing resemblance to the Gordon-Keeble GK1. Like all subsequent Isos it was powered by an American V8 engine. The car Iso is best remembered for, the Grifo, created by Giotto Bizzarrini, was launched the following year and stayed in production until Iso closed its doors in 1974. With a range of cars that had reached their sell-by date, the final nail was driven into the company's coffin by the oil crisis, and huge downward pressure on speed limits.

ISO
Rivolta

The Rivolta was an example of the Italo-American breed that proved popular during the 1960s and '70s and which allowed drivers to sample Ferrari-style glamour and performance without the price. The Rivolta had all the credentials to deliver the goods: Giugiaro styling; Bizzarini chassis and a 140mph top speed from its General Motors-sourced V8. Under the skin its box-section frame with de Dion rear suspension was a recipe for success and, indeed, the Rivolta sold nearly 800 examples during its eight-year production run.

SPECIFICATIONS
Years produced:	1962-1970 (797 in total)
Performance:	0-60mph: 7.8sec
	Top speed: 135mph
Power & torque:	300bhp/360lb ft
Engine:	Normally aspirated 5354cc V8, petrol, carburettor, 16 valves
Drivetrain:	Front-engine RWD
Structure:	Spaceframe
Transmission:	Four-speed manual
Weight:	1549kg

PRICE GUIDE
Launch price:	£3999
Excellent:	£35,000
Good:	£20,000
Average:	£14,000
Project:	£9000

ISO
Grifo

Continuing the Iso formula, the Grifo was another appealing 'bitza' that transcended the sum of its parts to become something of a supercar pacesetter. The Corvette power unit was good for 300bhp and gave the sleek Bertone-bodied grand tourer a 150mph-plus top speed with acceleration to match. Considered very much a rich playboy's supercar, the Grifo had the handling and poise to cut it against Ferrari, Maserati and Lamborghini's finest. Survival rate is reasonably good, although you'll struggle to find an unrestored car.

SPECIFICATIONS
Years produced:	1963-1974 (322 in total)
Performance:	0-60mph: 7.0sec
	Top speed: 143mph
Power & torque:	300bhp/360lb ft
Engine:	Normally aspirated 5354cc V8, petrol, carburettor, 16 valves
Drivetrain:	Front-engine RWD
Structure:	Spaceframe
Transmission:	Four-speed manual
Weight:	1450kg

PRICE GUIDE
Launch price:	£5950
Excellent:	£100,000
Good:	£60,000
Average:	£45,000
Project:	£30,000

ISO
Fidia

The gorgeous Giugiaro-styled Fidia started out as the Rivolta S4 when it was launched at the 1967 Frankfurt motor show, but with such an arresting style it seemed only right to have its own name in 1969. Initially promoted as '*le quattro poltrone piu veloci del mondo*' ('the world's fastest four-seater'), the Fidia picked up a degree of celebrity kudos (John Lennon had one), but sales were never strong enough to sustain the company as the crises of the 1970s deepened. Few come up for sale these days; despite mixed pedigree, they command top prices.

SPECIFICATIONS
Years produced:	1967-1975 (192 in total)
Performance:	0-60mph: 8.0sec
	Top speed: 137mph
Power & torque:	300bhp/360lb ft
Engine:	Normally aspirated 5354cc V8, petrol, carburettor, 16 valves
Drivetrain:	Front-engine RWD
Structure:	Spaceframe
Transmission:	Four-speed manual
Weight:	1500kg

PRICE GUIDE
Launch price:	£7225
Excellent:	£75,000
Good:	£60,000
Average:	£45,000
Project:	£30,000

ISO
Grifo 7-Litre

Although it was no slouch, Iso decided that the standard Grifo needed a shot of additional power to get on terms with the Ferrari Daytona and Maserati Ghibli. This was duly delivered thanks to a 7.0-litre (427ci) engine delivering no less than 390bhp. By 1968 supercar standards this was serious stuff and pushed Iso to the head of the pack. Top speed was a claimed 170mph and 0-60mph was around six seconds – quick even by today's standards. The Grifo disappeared off the new car price lists when Iso went out of business in 1974.

SPECIFICATIONS

Years produced:	1969-1974 (90 in total)
Performance:	0-60mph: 6.1sec
	Top speed: 171mph
Power & torque:	390bhp/460lb ft
Engine:	Normally aspirated 6999cc V8, petrol, carburettor, 16 valves
Drivetrain:	Front-engine RWD
Structure:	Spaceframe
Transmission:	Four-speed manual
Weight:	1410kg

PRICE GUIDE

Launch price:	£8700
Excellent:	£125,000
Good:	£75,000
Average:	£50,000
Project:	£35,000

ISO
Lele

Iso believed in platform sharing so it's understandable that the underpinnings used for the Grifo and Fidia were also put to good use when concocting a replacement for the Rivolta. Unlike the original car, the Lele failed to impress buyers who were turned off by the clumsy Gandini-styled coupé. Given that the 1973 oil crisis killed supercar sales stone dead, struggling Iso didn't have enough in the cupboard to ride the storm, and disappeared in 1974. The last few Leles were powered by a Ford V8 and offered with automatic transmission.

SPECIFICATIONS

Years produced:	1969-1974 (317 in total)
Performance:	0-60mph: 7.3sec
	Top speed: 155mph
Power & torque:	350bhp/361lb ft
Engine:	Normally aspirated 5358cc V8, petrol, carburettor, 16 valves
Drivetrain:	Front-engine RWD
Structure:	Spaceframe
Transmission:	Four-speed manual
Weight:	1640kg

PRICE GUIDE

Launch price:	£7725
Excellent:	£20,000
Good:	£15,000
Average:	£10,000
Project:	£5000

ISUZU

THE TOKYO Ishikawajima Shipuilding and Engineering Co started out by making licence-built Wolseleys between 1918 and 1927. With valuable experience gained, the company turned its attention to making its own US-inspired cars until the onset of World War Two. Various mergers and acquistions later, Isuzu Motors was born in 1949. Its first self-designed production car, the Bellel, arrived in 1961, and was built alongside Isuzu's own version of the Hillman Minx. In 1971, General Motors took a stake in the company, and all subsequent Isuzus were based upon its platforms, including the Gemini – a version of the GM T-Car that lent itself to became the basis of the Piazza.

ISUZU
117 Coupé

During its formative years, the Japanese car industry leaned on European designers to inject a sense of style into its cars. For the sporting version of Isuzu's forgettable Florian saloon, Giorgetto Giugiaro (while at Ghia) was commissioned to come up with a suitably export-friendly design. The Isuzu 117 Coupé was the result and, for the class of '68, it was very impressive indeed. It also hung around for a very long time, remaining in production until 1981. Engines were almost exclusively twin-cams with the exception of the original 1.6 and – unusually – a 2.2-litre diesel.

SPECIFICATIONS (1800)

Years produced:	1968-1981
Performance:	0-60mph: 9.5sec
	Top speed: 112mph
Power & torque:	115bhp/112lb ft
Engine:	Normally aspirated 1818cc four cylinder, petrol, carburettor, 8 valves
Drivetrain:	Front-engine RWD
Structure:	Monocoque
Transmission:	Four-speed manual
Weight:	1070kg

PRICE GUIDE

Launch price:	N/A in UK
Excellent:	£6000
Good:	£3500
Average:	£1250
Project:	N/A

ISUZU
Piazza

When it came to replacing the 117, Isuzu once again turned to Giugiaro (now running Italdesign) – this time adopting his Ace of Clubs design. Humble saloon mechanicals again formed the basis for a coupé, this time from the Gemini (closely related to the Vauxhall Chevette). The rudimentary suspension layout struggled to harness the power of its 2.0-litre turbo engine, so the company turned to Lotus. The Norfolk engineers did a good job, but not enough to save the Piazza in the UK. It's now a popular retro classic, thanks to its exploitable RWD chassis.

SPECIFICATIONS (Turbo)

Years produced:	1980-1990 (114,000 in total)
Performance:	0-60mph: 8.4sec
	Top speed: 130mph
Power & torque:	150bhp/166lb ft
Engine:	Turbocharged 1994cc four cylinder, petrol, electronic fuel injection, 8 valves
Drivetrain:	Front-engine RWD
Structure:	Monocoque
Transmission:	Five-speed manual
Weight:	1247kg

PRICE GUIDE

Launch price:	£11,950
Excellent:	£2750
Good:	£1500
Average:	£950
Project:	£550

JAGUAR

FOUNDED BY William Lyons in 1922 as Swallow Sidecars (SS), 'Jaguar' was used as one of the firm's model designations in 1935. Following the war – when SS had very unfortunate connotations – the whole business simply became

Jaguar instead. The newly christened company made a name for itself with such desirable cars as the XK and the Mk2 saloons. It will forever be known for the legendary and beautiful E-type (1961 to 1975), while the XJ6 saloon

was the mainstay of the British Leyland years from 1968 to 1984. After a period in the private sector, Jaguar was sold to Ford in 1989 and has recently ended up in the hands of the Indian tea/steel/cars conglomerate Tata.

JAGUAR
1.5 Litre Saloon

This is the entry-level model in a threesome of elegant saloons that went a very long way towards cementing Jaguar's position as the pre-eminent producer of sporting four-doors. Despite its modest engine capacity, the 1.5 Litre was quick enough to justify its styling. Introduced on the eve of World War Two, and brought back shortly afterwards, its technical specification didn't look that advanced (a rigid axle was no great shakes by 1945), but the whole exceeded the sum of the parts. Values are modest considering its place in Jaguar's history.

SPECIFICATIONS

Years produced:	1938-1949 (13,046 in total)
Performance:	0-60mph: 25.1sec
	Top speed: 72mph
Power & torque:	65bhp/97lb ft
Engine:	Normally aspirated 1776cc four cylinder, petrol, carburettor, 8 valves
Drivetrain:	Front-engine RWD
Structure:	Separate chassis
Transmission:	Four-speed manual
Weight:	1346kg

PRICE GUIDE

Launch price:	£684
Excellent:	£20,000
Good:	£12,500
Average:	£7500
Project:	£3500

JAGUAR
3.5 Litre Saloon/DHC

Rather like the 1.5 Litre Jaguar, but with rather a lot more power on tap, the 3.5 really was the first of the new-generation Jaguar saloons with the pace to back up its looks. The performance was impressive for a saloon car, especially for a pre-war car, thanks in no small part to the 125bhp it pushed out. Most of them ended up being exported and, as a result, are now scarce in the UK. Despite this, values lag behind the more illustrious sports cars – although the beautiful drophead version has been steadily rising in recent years.

SPECIFICATIONS

Years produced:	1938-1951 (14,215 in total)
Performance:	0-60mph: 14.7sec
	Top speed: 92mph
Power & torque:	125bhp/136lb ft
Engine:	Normally aspirated 3485cc straight six, petrol, carburettor, 12 valves
Drivetrain:	Front-engine RWD
Structure:	Separate chassis
Transmission:	Four-speed manual
Weight:	1626kg

PRICE GUIDE

Launch price:	£889
Excellent:	£35,000
Good:	£18,000
Average:	£11,500
Project:	£6000

JAGUAR
2.5 Litre/MkV

The first properly post-war Jaguar saloon was actually a bit of a stop-gap between the pre-war cars and the all-new metal on the horizon. The sweeping bodywork was all-new, but quite similar to what had come before, while the chassis would go on to underpin all of Jaguar's '50s saloons. Independent front suspension finally made an appearance, bringing the MkV into line with its rivals, and improving road manners. The limited production run – especially of the drophead – means finding the right one takes time.

SPECIFICATIONS

Years produced:	1946-1951 (8905 in total)
Performance:	0-60mph: 17sec
	Top speed: 87mph
Power & torque:	125bhp/N/A
Engine:	Normally aspirated 2663cc straight six, petrol, carburettor, 12 valves
Drivetrain:	Front-engine RWD
Structure:	Separate chassis
Transmission:	Four-speed manual
Weight:	1676kg

PRICE GUIDE

Launch price:	£1189
Excellent:	£25,000
Good:	£15,000
Average:	£8500
Project:	£4250

JAGUAR
XK120

Quite simply, the XK120 was the sports car that elevated Jaguar into the big time. Introduced at the 1948 Earls Court Motor Show, it featured an all-new twin-overhead camshaft straight six that lived well into the 1980s. And it was fast: the 120mph maximum speed was the reason for its name. Yet the XK120's real forté was its sheer all-round driving pleasure for such a low price. The earliest aluminium roadsters are easily the most valuable, with SEs commanding a premium, and the later Drophead Coupés not far behind.

SPECIFICATIONS

Years produced:	1948-1954 (7612 in total)
Performance:	0-60mph: 10.1sec
	Top speed: 120mph
Power & torque:	190bhp/200lb ft
Engine:	Normally aspirated 3442cc straight six, petrol, carburettor, 12 valves
Drivetrain:	Front-engine RWD
Structure:	Separate chassis
Transmission:	Four-speed manual
Weight:	1346kg

PRICE GUIDE (Alloy car in brackets)

Launch price:	£1263
Excellent:	£85,000 (£150,000)
Good:	£40,000 (£120,000)
Average:	£22,500 (£80,000)
Project:	£12,750

JAGUAR
XK120 Coupé

Once Jaguar had caught up with XK120 Roadster demand and production of steel-bodied examples was running smoothly, it developed the coupé to widen appeal. Aside from the obvious addition of a roof, the biggest difference between this and the Roadster is the use of a mostly steel floorpan, in place of plywood. As with all XK120s there was an SE option, which added 20bhp through the use of high-lift cams, uprated valve springs and a lightened flywheel. Wire wheels were fitted to SEs, and were a popular retro-fit on non-SE models.

SPECIFICATIONS
Years produced: 1951-1954 (2678 in total)
Performance: 0-60mph: 9.9sec
Top speed: 120mph
Power & torque: 160bhp/195lb ft
Engine: Normally aspirated 3442cc straight six, petrol, carburettor, 12 valves
Drivetrain: Front-engine RWD
Structure: Separate chassis
Transmission: Four-speed manual
Weight: 1143kg

PRICE GUIDE
Launch price: £1389
Excellent: £65,000
Good: £77,500
Average: £35,000
Project: £16,000

JAGUAR
C-type

Based on the XK120, the C-type actually started life being referred to as the 120C, but the quickly applied nickname stuck. The body, crafted by Malcolm Sayer, is completely different to the 120's, and considerably lighter thanks to its spaceframe chassis. Suspension featured torsion bars front and rear, the steering was by rack and pinion, and brakes were discs. The C-type's competition successes are legendary, particularly its two victories at Le Mans (1951 and 1953). C-types rarely come up for sale, and attract huge interest.

SPECIFICATIONS
Years produced: 1951-1953 (54 in total)
Performance: 0-60mph: 8.1sec
Top speed: 150mph
Power & torque: 200bhp/220lb ft
Engine: Normally aspirated 3442cc straight six, petrol, carburettor, 12 valves
Drivetrain: Front engine RWD
Structure: Spaceframe
Transmission: Four-speed manual
Weight: 939kg

PRICE GUIDE
Launch price: £2327
Excellent: £3,000,000
Good: £2,000,000
Average: £1,500,000
Project: £750,000

JAGUAR
MkVII-IX

Jaguar's post-war run of desirable and capable large saloons was truly kickstarted with the arrival of the MkVII in 1950. Although similar under the skin to the outgoing MkV, the newer car's forward-looking styling and use of the XK engine (first seen in the XK120) made it a genuine 100mph proposition. Subsequent revisions refined the big saloon and added even more power into the mix. Easy to find now, and not excessively expensive, the MkVII-IX saloons lack the cult following of later cars but drive just as well.

SPECIFICATIONS
Years produced: 1951-1961 (47,190 in total)
Performance: 0-60mph: 13.6sec
Top speed: 104mph
Power & torque: 160bhp/195lb ft
Engine: Normally aspirated 3442cc straight six, petrol, carburettor, 12 valves
Drivetrain: Front engine RWD
Structure: Separate chassis
Transmission: Four-speed manual/three-speed auto
Weight: 1753kg

PRICE GUIDE
Launch price: £1276
Excellent: £27,500
Good: £15,000
Average: £10,000
Project: £3500

JAGUAR
XK140 FHC

Introduced as a replacement to the XK120, the XK140 was slightly bigger and heavier, but more powerful. These characteristics changed the whole driving experience and, rather than being an uncompromised sports car, it was a much more comfortable and relaxed long distance cruiser – unless you were in the coupé's tight rear seats. Upgrades included the standard fitment of rack and pinion steering (from the C-type) as well as optional power-assisted steering. Coupés are worth less than roadsters, but are still very satisfying to drive.

SPECIFICATIONS
Years produced: 1954-57 (2808 in total)
Performance: 0-60mph: 8.4sec
Top speed: 121mph
Power & torque: 210bhp/213lb ft
Engine: Normally aspirated 3442cc straight six, petrol, carburettor, 12 valves
Drivetrain: Front-engine RWD
Structure: Separate chassis
Transmission: Four-speed manual with overdrive
Weight: 1422kg

PRICE GUIDE
Launch price: £1616
Excellent: £60,000
Good: £40,000
Average: £25,000
Project: £15,000

JAGUAR
XK140 Roadster

The additional weight of the XK140 over the XK120 was most evident in the Roadster version. The older car was an unashamed sports car, while its replacement was softer and much more refined – no doubt a deliberate ploy to appeal to American customers. Some sold in Special Equipment form with C-type cylinder head and 210bhp, turning this car into a much more sporting prospect, and the perfect fast-lane weapon for Britain's new motorway age. Worth rather less than the XK120, but the more intelligent choice for aficionados.

SPECIFICATIONS
Years produced: 1954-1957 (3354 in total)
Performance: 0-60mph: 8.4sec
Top speed: 125mph
Power & torque: 190bhp/210lb ft
Engine: Normally aspirated 3442cc straight six, petrol, carburettor, 12 valves
Drivetrain: Front-engine RWD
Structure: Separate chassis
Transmission: Four-speed manual with overdrive
Weight: 1422kg

PRICE GUIDE
Launch price: £1598
Excellent: £70,000
Good: £42,500
Average: £25,000
Project: £16,000

JAGUAR
XK140 DHC

Though similar in appearance to its predecessors, the XK140 came with a lot of small but significant differences. It's easily distinguished by a new seven-bar grille and one-piece bumpers. The Drophead Coupé added a pair of rear seats, although they were of little use for anything other than bags or small children. Even so, the DHC had been intelligently re-packaged: the battery was relocated behind the front wing, and the cockpit was shifted three inches forward. Today it's well-priced compared with other XK soft-tops.

SPECIFICATIONS
Years produced:	1954-1957 (2889 in total)
Performance:	0-60mph: 11.0sec
	Top speed: 129mph
Power & torque:	190bhp/207lb ft
Engine:	Normally aspirated 3442cc straight six, petrol, carburettor, 12 valves
Drivetrain:	Front-engine RWD
Structure:	Separate chassis
Transmission:	Four-speed manual
Weight:	1346kg

PRICE GUIDE
Launch price:	£1609
Excellent:	£65,000
Good:	£36,000
Average:	£21,000
Project:	£12,000

JAGUAR
MkI 2.4

The starting point in Jaguar's move into the compact sporting saloon market, even if from behind the wheel of an original 2.4 you'd be hard pushed to believe it, thanks to sluggish performance. Just like the D-type, the 2.4 featured unitary construction – it was the first roadgoing Jaguar to do so. The detuned, short-stroke 2.4-litre XK engine didn't tax the independent suspension set-up much, but was a restful cruiser with overdrive. All-disc brakes and automatic transmission were offered in 1957, but today the 2.4 is still seen as the runt of the litter.

SPECIFICATIONS
Years produced:	1955-1959 (19,992 in total)
Performance:	0-60mph: 14.4sec
	Top speed: 102mph
Power & torque:	112bhp/140lb ft
Engine:	Normally aspirated 2483cc straight six, petrol, carburettor, 12 valves
Drivetrain:	Front-engine RWD
Structure:	Monocoque
Transmission:	Four-speed manual/three-speed auto
Weight:	1372kg

PRICE GUIDE
Launch price:	£1344
Excellent:	£12,500
Good:	£9500
Average:	£5000
Project:	£2250

JAGUAR
MkI 3.4

Although the 2.4 was a significant car in Jaguar's evolution, the compact sporting saloon concept really came to life when the Coventry engineers crammed in the 3.4-litre engine from the XK140. Despite the MkI's curvaceous styling and reasonably commodious interior, its potent 3.4-litre engine delivered performance previously reserved for the sports car sector. The 3.4 was launched as a sister car to the 2.4 and featured a wider grille and cut-away spats. Despite a higher price, the 3.4 sold nearly as many examples during its two-year run.

SPECIFICATIONS
Years produced:	1957-1959 (17,405 in total)
Performance:	0-60mph: 9.1sec
	Top speed: 120mph
Power & torque:	210bhp/216lb ft
Engine:	Normally aspirated 3442cc straight six, petrol, carburettor, 12 valves
Drivetrain:	Front-engine RWD
Structure:	Monocoque
Transmission:	Four-speed manual/three-speed auto
Weight:	1448kg

PRICE GUIDE
Launch price:	£1672
Excellent:	£20,000
Good:	£12,000
Average:	£7000
Project:	£2750

JAGUAR
XK150 3.4 FHC

At 1364kg, the XK150 was not the lightweight sports car the XK120 had once been. Certain aluminium panels were added to try to reduce the overall weight, but it still tipped the scales at 50kg more than the XK140. It was the first Jaguar available with all-round disc brakes. In 1958, the XK150S was launched. The uprated car came with an impressive 250bhp at first, then 265bhp a year later when the capacity increased to 3.8 litres. A limited-slip differential was needed to handle the extra power. A 3.4S is worth an extra 15%.

SPECIFICATIONS
Years produced:	1957-1961 (4450 in total)
Performance:	0-60mph: 8.5sec
	Top speed: 124mph
Power & torque:	250bhp/240lb ft
Engine:	Normally aspirated 3442cc straight six, petrol, carburettor, 12 valves
Drivetrain:	Front-engine RWD
Structure:	Monocoque
Transmission:	Four-speed manual with overdrive
Weight:	1447kg

PRICE GUIDE
Launch price:	£1764
Excellent:	£65,000
Good:	£40,000
Average:	£23,500
Project:	£20,000

JAGUAR
XK150 Roadster

The Roadster differs from previous such XKs in having wind-up windows, though the hood is still quite rudimentary compared with the Drophead's. There's also a significant difference between these and other XK150s: the deletion of rear seats allowed the cockpit to be moved back four inches, so the Roadster has a correspondingly longer bonnet. Most came with 3.4-litre engines, but the 3.8 was added in 1959. Both had 'S' performance versions with an extra carburettor among other upgrades. Add 12% for 3.4S prices and 30% for a 3.8S.

SPECIFICATIONS
Years produced:	1958-1960 (2263 in total)
Performance:	0-60mph: 7.9sec
	Top speed: 136mph
Power & torque:	250bhp/237lb ft
Engine:	Normally aspirated 3442cc straight six, petrol, carburettor, 12 valves
Drivetrain:	Front-engine RWD
Structure:	Separate chassis
Transmission:	Four-speed manual
Weight:	1432kg

PRICE GUIDE
Launch price:	£1764
Excellent:	£65,000
Good:	£45,000
Average:	£26,000
Project:	£16,000

JAGUAR
Mk2 2.4

Generally speaking, facelifted cars don't look as good as those they are intended to replace. But Jaguar tore up the form book with its compact saloon which, thanks to William Lyons, was transformed by the fitment of revised upper door pressings, a deeper windscreen and wider rear track. The effect was to brighten the interior and update the overall style and, in doing so, to create the most iconic '60s saloon of them all. The 2.4 was still a modest performer, despite an additional 8bhp over the (retrospectively named) MkI.

SPECIFICATIONS

Years produced:	1959-1967 (83,976 of all Mk2s)
Performance:	0-60mph: 17.3sec
	Top speed: 96mph
Power & torque:	120bhp/144lb ft
Engine:	Normally aspirated 2483cc straight six, petrol, carburettor, 12 valves
Drivetrain:	Front-engine RWD
Structure:	Monocoque
Transmission:	Four-speed manual
Weight:	1448kg

PRICE GUIDE

Launch price:	£1534
Excellent:	£15,000
Good:	£11,000
Average:	£6500
Project:	£2500

JAGUAR
Mk2 3.4

Previously the 3.4-litre XK engine had been enough to top the compact saloon range, but all that changed with the arrival of the Mk2. For 1959, the mid-range car had been significantly improved, thanks to a raft of small but significant improvements. With more than enough power on board, the adoption of a wider front and rear track improved road manners, optimising a car that was hardly lacking in the first place. Heavier than before so the Mk2's performance was slightly blunted, but that was addressed by the arrival of the 3.8.

SPECIFICATIONS

Years produced:	1959-1967
Performance:	0-60mph: 11.9sec
	Top speed: 120mph
Power & torque:	210bhp/216lb ft
Engine:	Normally aspirated 3442cc straight six, petrol, carburettor, 12 valves
Drivetrain:	Front-engine RWD
Structure:	Monocoque
Transmission:	Four-speed manual, overdrive optional
Weight:	1499kg

PRICE GUIDE

Launch price:	£1669
Excellent:	£25,000
Good:	£17,000
Average:	£9000
Project:	£4000

JAGUAR
Mk2 3.8

The new flagship in the mid-sized saloon line-up certainly proved popular and profitable for Jaguar. But with a 125mph top speed and throttle-adjustable handling, the 3.8 became *the* car of choice for enthusiastic drivers. A limited-slip differential improved traction and controllability, while power-assisted steering (a standard fitment from 1960) further improved the way the car drove. Considered the best of all Mk2s and market values reflect this, but some would argue that it's too high a premium for what is, in effect, a 10bhp upgrade.

SPECIFICATIONS

Years produced:	1959-1967
Performance:	0-60mph: 8.5sec
	Top speed: 125mph
Power & torque:	220bhp/240lb ft
Engine:	Normally aspirated 3781cc straight six, petrol, carburettor, 12 valves
Drivetrain:	Front-engine RWD
Structure:	Monocoque
Transmission:	Four-speed manual/three-speed auto
Weight:	1499kg

PRICE GUIDE

Launch price:	£1779
Excellent:	£30,000
Good:	£20,000
Average:	£10,500
Project:	£6000

JAGUAR
MkX/420G

Jaguar really went for it when devising a flagship to replace its MkIX saloon. Physically huge and easily capable of seating six, the MkX was far more agile than its corpulent footprint implied, especially in 3.8-litre manual form. All cars had power-assisted steering as standard and disc brakes all-round with servo assistance. The torquier 4.2-litre engine arrived in 1964 and made the MkX even more effortless; then it became the 420G in 1966. A few limousines were built, and the car lived on to form the basis of the DS420 limousine, favoured by mayors all over Britain.

SPECIFICATIONS (3.8)

Years produced:	1961-1970 (18,519/5763 in total)
Performance:	0-60mph: 12.1sec
	Top speed: 120mph
Power & torque:	265bhp/260lb ft
Engine:	Normally aspirated 3781cc straight six, petrol, carburettor, 12 valves
Drivetrain:	Front-engine RWD
Structure:	Monocoque
Transmission:	Four-speed manual
Weight:	1791kg

PRICE GUIDE

Launch price:	£2393
Excellent:	£22,000
Good:	£12,000
Average:	£5000
Project:	£2000

JAGUAR
E-type 3.8 FHC

When it exploded onto the automotive landscape in 1961, the E-type redefined the way in which we all viewed sports cars, and how much you could expect for your money. Although the famous 150mph runs in pre-production models were never replicated by owners, the E-type was still fast enough to send sports car manufacturers back to their drawing boards. The recipe was simple enough: a 3.8-litre XK engine married to a beautiful and aerodynamic body designed by Malcolm Sayer, underpinned by all-independent suspension.

SPECIFICATIONS

Years produced:	1961-1964 (46,300 in total)
Performance:	0-60mph: 7.1sec
	Top speed: 149mph
Power & torque:	265bhp/260lb ft
Engine:	Normally aspirated 3781cc straight six, petrol, carburettor, 12 valves
Drivetrain:	Front-engine RWD
Structure:	Monocoque
Transmission:	Four-speed manual
Weight:	1219kg

PRICE GUIDE

Launch price:	£2098
Excellent:	£60,000
Good:	£29,500
Average:	£17,500
Project:	£15,000

JAGUAR
E-type 3.8 Roadster

Although the E-type coupé was the fastest and most useful of the breed, it's the Roadster that attracts by far the most attention these days. The underpinnings were well-considered and stiff enough to stave off the worst effects of scuttle shake, and that meant it was just as effective to drive as the Coupé. Hugely popular in the USA as well as Europe, and a high survival rate means that there are still plenty around – which keeps values lower than they would be had the badge on the bonnet been Italian or German.

SPECIFICATIONS

Years produced:	1961-1974 (46,300 in total)
Performance:	0-60mph: 7.1sec
	Top speed: 149mph
Power & torque:	265bhp/260lb ft
Engine:	Normally aspirated 3781cc straight six, petrol, carburettor, 12 valves
Drivetrain:	Front-engine RWD
Structure:	Monocoque
Transmission:	Four-speed manual
Weight:	1206kg

PRICE GUIDE

Launch price:	£2098
Excellent:	£80,000
Good:	£46,000
Average:	£26,000
Project:	£20,000

JAGUAR
S-type

Because the XJ6 was still years away from production, Jaguar decided that it needed an intermediate model to plug the gap between the Mk2 and the enormous MkX. Using the Mk2 as a starting point, the company created the S-type by adding the MkX's independent rear suspension and extended rear end, as well as improving its interior. The end result was a luxury sports saloon that actually drives better than the car it was based upon, usefully extending the life (and profitability) of the Mk2 platform.

SPECIFICATIONS

Years produced:	1963-1968 (24,900 in total)
Performance:	0-60mph: 14.2sec
	Top speed: 114mph
Power & torque:	210bhp/216lb ft
Engine:	Normally aspirated 3442cc straight six, petrol, carburettor, 12 valves
Drivetrain:	Front-engine RWD
Structure:	Monocoque
Transmission:	Four-speed manual/three-speed auto
Weight:	1626kg

PRICE GUIDE

Launch price:	£1669
Excellent:	£17,000
Good:	£10,000
Average:	£4500
Project:	£1500

JAGUAR
E-type S1 4.2 Roadster

Never one to sit on its laurels, Jaguar continued to develop the E-type throughout its life. The first results of this programme of improvements came in 1964, when the newly-enlarged XK engine was installed under the E-type's bonnet. Although the maximum power output remained unchanged at 265bhp, torque was usefully increased, improving driveability. Other improvements included the arrival of a fully-synchronised Moss gearbox. Worth slightly more than the 3.8-litre Roadsters because of the improvements.

SPECIFICATIONS

Years produced:	1964-1968 (46,300 in total)
Performance:	0-60mph: 7.4sec
	Top speed: 139mph
Power & torque:	265bhp/283lb ft
Engine:	Normally aspirated 4235cc straight six, petrol, carburettor, 12 valves
Drivetrain:	Front-engine RWD
Structure:	Monocoque
Transmission:	Four-speed manual
Weight:	1295kg

PRICE GUIDE

Launch price:	£1896
Excellent:	£70,000
Good:	£45,000
Average:	£25,000
Project:	£20,000

JAGUAR
E-type S1 4.2 Coupé

More torque from the 4.2-litre XK engine, yet 150mph remained an elusive target for those owners with access to derestricted motorways. Though limited to a top speed of 'only' 149mph, the E-type in 4.2-litre form remained a long way ahead of the opposition – cars that could match its speed were far more expensive, while similarly priced sports cars wouldn't have seen which way it went. The 4.2 actually felt more grown-up to drive, thanks to its lower red line and greater low-down pull, prompting some to say the zest had gone.

SPECIFICATIONS

Years produced:	1964-1968 (10,930 in total)
Performance:	0-60mph: 7.4sec
	Top speed: 149mph
Power & torque:	265bhp/283lb ft
Engine:	Normally aspirated 4235cc straight six, petrol, carburettor, 12 valves
Drivetrain:	Front-engine RWD
Structure:	Monocoque
Transmission:	Four-speed manual
Weight:	1410kg

PRICE GUIDE

Launch price:	£2245
Excellent:	£55,000
Good:	£35,000
Average:	£17,500
Project:	£10,500

JAGUAR
E-type S1 2+2

Despite its global success and accolades, Jaguar knew that E-type sales were being held back by the limitations of a two-seater. Enter the 2+2, created by extending the wheelbase and cabin by nine inches to make room for kids in the back. There's also a taller, more upright windscreen. And unlike some other two-plus-twos, you can actually get people with legs in there, as long as the driver isn't tall. The car was an instant sales success, outselling the fixed-head coupé from day one. Not as pretty, so it's a more affordable way into E-type ownership.

SPECIFICATIONS

Years produced:	1966-1967 (5600 in total)
Performance:	0-60mph: 8.9sec
	Top speed: 136mph
Power & torque:	256bhp/280lb ft
Engine:	Normally aspirated 4325cc straight six, petrol, carburettor, 12 valves
Drivetrain:	Front-engine RWD
Structure:	Monocoque
Transmission:	Four-speed manual
Weight:	1401kg

PRICE GUIDE

Launch price:	£2245
Excellent:	£27,500
Good:	£18,000
Average:	£13,000
Project:	£7500

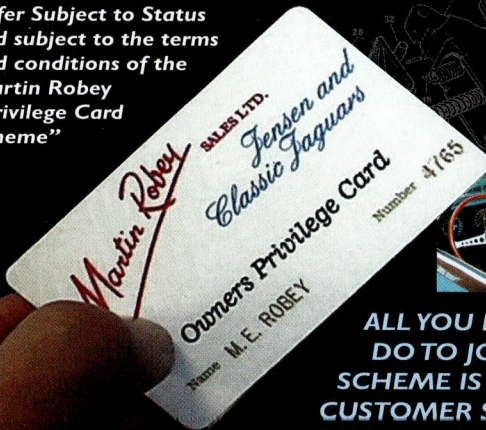

JAGUAR
420

The Jaguar 420 was basically an S-type fitted with the 4.2-litre version of the XK engine. The front end was completely restyled, previewing the upcoming XJ6 (as well as aping the 420G) and, although it looked slightly unbalanced, there was no question over the way the 420 went. By the time of its launch in 1968, the MkI/Mk2 platform had been stretched as far as possible in an attempt to maintain sales. The interior was further improved with the arrival of a padded fascia top, the first move towards the safety-led designs that followed.

SPECIFICATIONS

Years produced:	1966-1968 (9600 in total)
Performance:	0-60mph: 9.9sec
	Top speed: 123mph
Power & torque:	245bhp/283lb ft
Engine:	Normally aspirated 4235cc straight six, petrol, carburettor, 12 valves
Drivetrain:	Front-engine RWD
Structure:	Monocoque
Transmission:	Four-speed manual/three-speed auto
Weight:	1676kg

PRICE GUIDE

Launch price:	£1930
Excellent:	£12,000
Good:	£8500
Average:	£4000
Project:	£1400

JAGUAR
240

After a good innings, the Mk2 was finally facelifted in 1967 to become the 240/340. These models were priced below the outgoing cars, and evidence of cost-cutting was most notable inside where leather gave way to man-made Ambla. Despite its popularity in the Mk2, power-assisted steering wasn't even offered as an option on the 240, making the car feel a lot more ponderous than it might. The engine was upgraded with a 4.2-style cylinder head, and that finally gave it enough power to break the 100mph barrier.

SPECIFICATIONS

Years produced:	1967-1969 (6840 in total)
Performance:	0-60mph: 12.5sec
	Top speed: 106mph
Power & torque:	133bhp/146lb ft
Engine:	Normally aspirated 2483cc straight six, petrol, carburettor, 12 valves
Drivetrain:	Front-engine RWD
Structure:	Monocoque
Transmission:	Four-speed manual/three-speed auto
Weight:	1448kg

PRICE GUIDE

Launch price:	£1365
Excellent:	£12,500
Good:	£9500
Average:	£5000
Project:	£2500

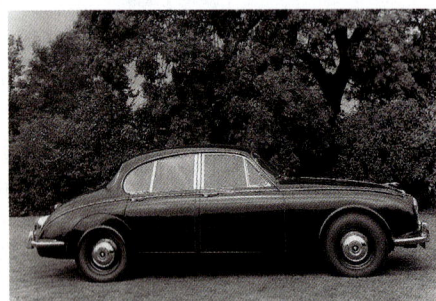

JAGUAR
340

With the XJ6 still a couple of years from production, the 240/340 ended up serving run-out duties for the Mk2 line for longer than anyone in Coventry would have hoped. But despite its advancing years, the 340 was still a car of great ability and proved a hit with buyers. With the same 210bhp engine as before, all of the performance that attracted buyers to the 3.4-litre Mk2 was there, but in a lower-priced package. Today, values lag behind the earlier cars because of their cost-constrained interiors, so the 340 is a great purchase for canny buyers.

SPECIFICATIONS

Years produced:	1967-1969 (6840 in total)
Performance:	0-60mph: 8.8sec
	Top speed: 115mph
Power & torque:	210bhp/216lb ft
Engine:	Normally aspirated 3442cc straight six, petrol, carburettor, 12 valves
Drivetrain:	Front-engine RWD
Structure:	Monocoque
Transmission:	Four-speed manual/three-speed auto
Weight:	1524kg

PRICE GUIDE

Launch price:	£1442
Excellent:	£16,500
Good:	£13,000
Average:	£6500
Project:	£3500

JAGUAR
E-type S1½/2 Roadster

The Series 1½ was, as the name suggests, a bridge between the SI and S2. Only current for a year, its main role seems to have been to introduce new-style headlamps with no covers but more chrome trim. They may not have looked so good but they worked better. The S2 brought more significant changes, like the larger grille opening, heavier front bumpers and bigger lamps. Mechanical changes were limited to an improved cooling system and (thank goodness!) better brakes, changed from Lockheed to Girling. Power steering was an option.

SPECIFICATIONS

Years produced:	1967-1970 (8630 in total)
Performance:	0-60mph: 7.4sec
	Top speed: 149mph
Power & torque:	265bhp/283lb ft
Engine:	Normally aspirated 4235cc straight six, petrol, carburettor, 12 valves
Drivetrain:	Front-engine RWD
Structure:	Monocoque
Transmission:	Four-speed manual
Weight:	1295kg

PRICE GUIDE

Launch price:	£2117
Excellent:	£55,000
Good:	£35,000
Average:	£20,000
Project:	£11,000

JAGUAR
E-type S1½/2 2+2

With their uncovered headlamps and less desirable body shape, these 2+2s are now the entry-level E-type – one you can buy for MGA money. And it has been pointed out that, while it doesn't match up to Jaguar's coupé or roadster, it may still be the 'third best looking car in the world'. One significant change over the previous 2+2 model was a new windscreen. Its base had been moved as far as the bulkhead would allow to increase the rake, improving aerodynamics. Because of its greater weight the 2+2 was fitted with stiffer front torsion bars.

SPECIFICATIONS

Years produced:	1968-1970 (5330 in total)
Performance:	0-60mph: 8.9sec
	Top speed: 137mph
Power & torque:	265bhp/280lb ft
Engine:	Normally aspirated 4235cc straight six, petrol, carburettor, 12 valves
Drivetrain:	Front-engine RWD
Structure:	Monocoque
Transmission:	Four-speed manual
Weight:	1401kg

PRICE GUIDE

Launch price:	£2284
Excellent:	£25,000
Good:	£17,500
Average:	£12,000
Project:	£7000

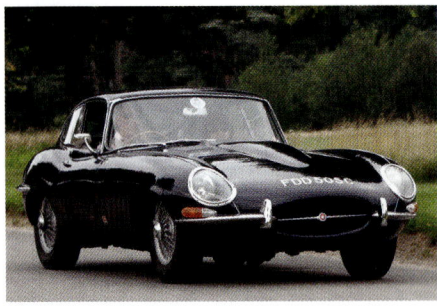

JAGUAR
E-type S1½/2 Coupé

Featuring all the changes made to the Roadsters, the main point of note about this series of coupés is that they are the rarest of all the E-types. Yet that doesn't them any more valuable. Having lost sales to the 2+2, fewer than 5000 were built, and the writing was on the wall for the shorter-wheelbase coupé bodystyle. The wire wheel locating nuts lost their 'ears' from March 1969 for safety legislation reasons, though as they are more aesthetically pleasing, you may find that eared spinners have been substituted at some point.

SPECIFICATIONS

Years produced:	1968-1970 (4860 in total)
Performance:	0-60mph: 7.1sec
	Top speed: 150mph
Power & torque:	265bhp/280lb ft
Engine:	Normally aspirated 4235cc straight six, petrol, carburettor, 12 valves
Drivetrain:	Front-engine RWD
Structure:	Monocoque
Transmission:	Four-speed manual
Weight:	1407kg

PRICE GUIDE

Launch price:	£2117
Excellent:	£40,000
Good:	£25,000
Average:	£15,000
Project:	£10,000

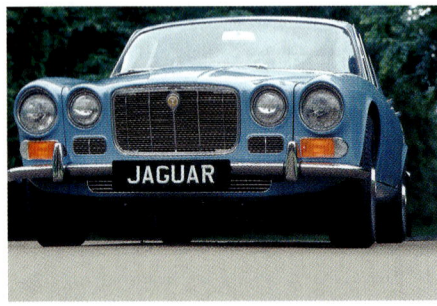

JAGUAR
XJ6 SI 2.8

This was the first generation of the very successful XJ model range, and introduced a new platform strategy that saw a single range replace the mixed bag of previous models. The Series I XJ6 was not an entirely new car, but it was designed to reinvent the Jaguar brand, echoing the important values of previous models while moving forwards. The XJ came with fully independent suspension all-round for a world-beating ride/handling combination, as well as the well-travelled XK engine though, in 2.8-litre form, it lacked urge and reliability.

SPECIFICATIONS

Years produced:	1968-1973
Performance:	0-60mph: 11.3sec
	Top speed: 117mph
Power & torque:	140bhp/150lb ft
Engine:	Normally aspirated 2792cc straight six, petrol, carburettor, 12 valves
Drivetrain:	Front-engine RWD
Structure:	Monocoque
Transmission:	Four-speed manual/three-speed auto
Weight:	1537kg

PRICE GUIDE

Launch price:	£1797
Excellent:	£6500
Good:	£4000
Average:	£1750
Project:	£600

JAGUAR
XJ6 SI 4.2

The optimum Jaguar XJ came with the XK engine in 4.2-litre form, and once again proved that Browns Lane was capable of producing the best mid-market saloon in the world. Unlike the 2.8-litre version, of which few survive, the 4.2-litre XJ in Series I form was popular with buyers and has a good survival rate today. It's easy to see why, as the ride quality and interior comfort are astounding, while roadholding is tenacious. Rust is a significant issue, though, and few unrestored cars remain. The best examples are now appreciating rapidly.

SPECIFICATIONS

Years produced:	1968-1973 (59,077 in total)
Performance:	0-60mph: 8.8sec
	Top speed: 124mph
Power & torque:	245bhp/280lb ft
Engine:	Normally aspirated 4235cc straight six, petrol, carburettor, 12 valves
Drivetrain:	Front-engine RWD
Structure:	Monocoque
Transmission:	Four-speed manual/three-speed auto
Weight:	1537kg

PRICE GUIDE

Launch price:	£1797
Excellent:	£7250
Good:	£5500
Average:	£2250
Project:	£750

JAGUAR
E-type S3 V12 2+2

Walter Hassan, one of Britain's pre-eminent post-war engineers and mastermind behind the Coventry Climax Formula 1 engines, worked with Harry Mundy to produce an all-new V12. It was Jaguar's first production V12, designed for maximum smoothness with single overhead camshafts. When fitted in the E-type, the turbine-smooth V12 was hailed an immediate success, especially in the USA – which market it was aimed at. Maximum speed was still shy of 150mph though, and fuel consumption was attrocious.

SPECIFICATIONS

Years produced:	1971-1975 (10,930 in total)
Performance:	0-60mph: 7.4sec
	Top speed: 139mph
Power & torque:	276bhp/304lb ft
Engine:	Normally aspirated 5343cc V12, petrol, carburettor, 32 valves
Drivetrain:	Front-engine RWD
Structure:	Monocoque
Transmission:	Four-speed manual/three-speed auto
Weight:	1410kg

PRICE GUIDE

Launch price:	£2245
Excellent:	£45,000
Good:	£21,000
Average:	£11,500
Project:	£10,000

JAGUAR
E-type S3 V12 Roadster

Although it's been criticised for being too much of a tourer and not enough of a sports car, the E-type Series III still has massive appeal. The front-end styling with its prominent chrome grille lacks the grace of the earlier cars', and the suspension was softer too, but as Jaguar was looking towards the American market, these changes were inevitable. The V12 was only 36kg heavier than the straight six, and handling balance wasn't too drastically affected. In Europe it became unsaleable overnight in the aftermath of the 1973 energy crisis.

SPECIFICATIONS

Years produced:	1971-1975 (15,290 in total)
Performance:	0-60mph: 6.4sec
	Top speed: 146mph
Power & torque:	276bhp/304lb ft
Engine:	Normally aspirated 5343cc V12, petrol, carburettor, 24 valves
Drivetrain:	Front-engine RWD
Structure:	Monocoque
Transmission:	Four-speed manual/three-speed auto
Weight:	1499kg

PRICE GUIDE

Launch price:	£3123
Excellent:	£65,000
Good:	£40,000
Average:	£30,000
Project:	£15,000

JAGUAR
XJ12 SI-III

Although the Hassan-designed V12 impressed in the E-type Series III, it found its true home in the larger XJ bodyshell. With up to 300bhp in the later versions, it offered dominant performance and up to 150mph in the right circumstances. The XJ12's mechanical smoothness could be its undoing as age and unreliability took hold – engines would drop a cylinder or two without being too noticeable, while the complex suspension set-up could break the odd bush here or there without the driver feeling a thing. Engine and body restorations are expensive.

SPECIFICATIONS
Years produced:	1972-1993 (42,461 in total)
Performance:	0-60mph: 7.4sec
	Top speed: 146mph
Power & torque:	265bhp/304lb ft
Engine:	Normally aspirated 5343cc V12, petrol, carburettor, 24 valves
Drivetrain:	Front-engine RWD
Structure:	Monocoque
Transmission:	Automatic
Weight:	1760kg

PRICE GUIDE
Launch price:	£3726
Excellent:	£7500
Good:	£5250
Average:	£2200
Project:	£750

JAGUAR
XJ 5.3C

Prematurely announced in the summer of 1973, it would be a further two years before the two-door XJ finally went on sale. The timing wasn't exactly great, though, as the world had been pushed into the midst of a fuel crisis and then recession, all of which took the best part of a decade to be overcome. A vinyl roof was fitted as standard to all models, and the frameless windows (which caused much trouble during development) were noisy at speed and often leaked. Fuel injection was added later, and caused further problems.

SPECIFICATIONS
Years produced:	1973-1977
Performance:	0-60mph: 7.6sec
	Top speed: 148mph
Power & torque:	285bhp/294lb ft
Engine:	Normally aspirated 5343cc V12, petrol, carburettor, 24 valves
Drivetrain:	Front-engine RWD
Structure:	Monocoque
Transmission:	Three-speed automatic
Weight:	1762kg

PRICE GUIDE
Launch price:	£6850
Excellent:	£11,000
Good:	£9000
Average:	£5000
Project:	£1250

JAGUAR
XJ6 Coupé

The V12-powered XJ 5.3C might have stolen all of the glamour at the launch of the two-door XJ, but the 4.2-litre version comfortably sold the most. With a 20kg weight advantage over the four-door XJ, acceleration was slightly improved, but cruising really was this car's forté. Sales never met management's expectations, mainly because of the recession, but also because of a rapidly deteriorating reputation on the back of poor build quality during the 1970s. Never made it into Series III form, which hints at unfulfilled potential.

SPECIFICATIONS
Years produced:	1973-1977 (8378 in total)
Performance:	0-60mph: 8.8sec
	Top speed: 124mph
Power & torque:	173bhp/227lb ft
Engine:	Normally aspirated 4235cc straight six, petrol, carburettor, 12 valves
Drivetrain:	Front-engine RWD
Structure:	Monocoque
Transmission:	Four-speed manual/three-speed auto
Weight:	1689kg

PRICE GUIDE
Launch price:	£5480
Excellent:	£10,000
Good:	£8000
Average:	£4000
Project:	£1000

JAGUAR
XJ6 S2/S3

Jaguar made many detail improvements to the Jaguar XJ to create the Series II. The new heating and ventilation system was welcome, as was the improved fuel economy thanks to an updated engine. The interior received a substantial update, but the only visual differences externally were the smaller grille and raised bumpers, to help the XJ meet US safety regulations. Unfortunately, the Series II was plagued with poor build quality and reliability issues, and that hit Jaguar's hard-earned reputation for quality.

SPECIFICATIONS
Years produced:	1973-1986
Performance:	0-60mph: 8.8sec
	Top speed: 124mph
Power & torque:	167bhp/230lb ft
Engine:	Normally aspirated 4235cc straight six, petrol, carburettor, 12 valves
Drivetrain:	Front-engine RWD
Structure:	Monocoque
Transmission:	Four-speed manual/three-speed auto
Weight:	1680kg

PRICE GUIDE
Launch price:	£2253
Excellent:	£6000
Good:	£4000
Average:	£1900
Project:	£650

JAGUAR
XJ-S

Based on a shortened XJ6 chassis, the XJ-S was the long awaited E-type replacement and ended up missing the mark by several miles, even if it successfully continued in the spirit of the Series III. The new car was not a sporting drive in the way the earlier E-types were, but a more sedate grand tourer, with over-light power-assisted steering. The XJ-S remained in production for more than 20 years – the longest run of any Jaguar – and went on to become a financial success for the company, with the last car coming off the line in 1996.

SPECIFICATIONS
Years produced:	1975-1981
Performance:	0-60mph: 6.9sec
	Top speed: 153mph
Power & torque:	285bhp/294lb ft
Engine:	Normally aspirated 5343cc V12, petrol, electronic fuel injection, 12 valves
Drivetrain:	Front-engine RWD
Structure:	Monocoque
Transmission:	Four-speed manual/three-speed auto
Weight:	1770kg

PRICE GUIDE
Launch price:	£8900
Excellent:	£6000
Good:	£4000
Average:	£2000
Project:	£1000

JAGUAR
MAINTAIN THE PRESTIGE

JAGUAR
XJ-SC 3.6 Cabriolet

The launch of a new Jaguar engine isn't exactly a common event, and is usually executed in stages. As is the case when the first V12s were fitted to the E-type sports car, when Jaguar finished its slant-six AJ6 engine in 1983, it installed it in the XJ-S before making it available to saloon car buyers three years later. The Cabriolet version of the XJ-S was a halfway house to full open-topped motoring, as it retained a heavy (and ugly) roll-over structure and the coupé's passenger doors. It paved the way for a full convertible in later years.

SPECIFICATIONS

Years produced:	1983-1987
Performance:	0-60mph: 8.7sec
	Top speed: 136mph
Power & torque:	223bhp/277lb ft
Engine:	Normally aspirated 3980cc straight six, petrol, electronic fuel injection, 24 valves
Drivetrain:	Front-engine RWD
Structure:	Monocoque
Transmission:	Five-speed manual/three-speed auto
Weight:	1611kg

PRICE GUIDE

Launch price:	£33,400
Excellent:	£7500
Good:	£6000
Average:	£3500
Project:	£1200

JAGUAR
XJ-S 3.6

As well as ushering in the Cabriolet bodyshell, the arrival of the AJ6 engine gave Jaguar the chance to refocus the car's marketing. Although it lacked the ultimate grunt of the V12, the new engine and manual transmission package added sporting appeal into the mix and, although it shouldn't have worked, the six-cylinder XJ-S actually went on to sell rather well. Sport versions were introduced to reflect the tastes of the 1980s, as well as a range of questionable body kits and trim options, which diluted the original car's appeal.

SPECIFICATIONS

Years produced:	1983-1991 (92,750 in total)
Performance:	0-60mph: 7.4sec
	Top speed: 142mph
Power & torque:	225bhp/240lb ft
Engine:	Normally aspirated 3690cc straight six, petrol, electronic fuel injection, 24 valves
Drivetrain:	Front-engine RWD
Structure:	Monocoque
Transmission:	Five-speed manual/three-speed auto
Weight:	1660kg

PRICE GUIDE

Launch price:	£19,249
Excellent:	£6000
Good:	£4250
Average:	£2400
Project:	£700

JAGUAR
XJ-S 5.3 Cabriolet

Like the six-cylinder XJ-SC, the V12 Cabriolet wasn't open-topped Jaguar motoring at its best. The roll-over structure engineered by Tickford cluttered the styling, even if it helped retain the structural integrity of such a large car. As with the coupé version, V12 power resulted in effortless performance and magnificent long-distance touring ability, hampered only by the car's great thirst. Despite retaining the closed coupé's interior, the rear seats were dropped, and turned into a neat little storage area with lidded bins.

SPECIFICATIONS

Years produced:	1985-1988 (16.790 in total)
Performance:	0-60mph: 7.6sec
	Top speed: 161mph
Power & torque:	295bhp/355lb ft
Engine:	Normally aspirated 5994cc V12, petrol, electronic fuel injection, 24 valves
Drivetrain:	Front-engine RWD
Structure:	Monocoque
Transmission:	Three-speed automatic
Weight:	1985kg

PRICE GUIDE

Launch price:	£45,100
Excellent:	£7500
Good:	£6000
Average:	£3500
Project:	£1500

JAGUAR
XJ6 2.9/3.2 (XJ40)

Development work on the XJ40 started back in 1973, and led to a protracted gestation period of more than 15 years. The long wait was down to the 1973 fuel crisis, then a lack of funding and management direction from BL. The project was continually delayed until it finally made its debut in 1986, by which time its styling had dated badly. Despite its elderly looks the XJ40 was great to drive, although the single-cam straight six was breathless and lacked power. Later 3.2-litre versions were vastly improved and have genuine classic appeal.

SPECIFICATIONS

Years produced:	1986-1994 (204,474 in total)
Performance:	0-60mph: 9.8sec
	Top speed: 117mph
Power & torque:	165bhp/176lb ft
Engine:	Normally aspirated 2919cc straight six, petrol, electronic fuel injection, 12 valves
Drivetrain:	Front-engine RWD
Structure:	Monocoque
Transmission:	Five-speed manual/four-speed auto
Weight:	1720kg

PRICE GUIDE

Launch price:	£16,495
Excellent:	£3000
Good:	£2200
Average:	£1100
Project:	£500

JAGUAR
XJ6 3.6/4.0 (XJ40)

The larger six-cylinder XJ40s were an entertaining mixture of old-school styling and cutting edge dynamics. The earliest 3.6-litre cars with their 'Tokyo-by-night' dashboards were riddled with electrical niggles that ended up frustrating their hapless owners. But following Ford's takeover and a significant injection of cash, the much-improved 4.0-litre cars appeared in 1990. They featured conventional instrumentation, uprated electrics and a much more torque, which made them easier to drive and even more refined.

SPECIFICATIONS

Years produced:	1986-1994
Performance:	0-60mph: 8.2sec
	Top speed: 141mph
Power & torque:	223bhp/278lb ft
Engine:	Normally aspirated 3980cc straight six, petrol, electronic fuel injection, 24 valves
Drivetrain:	Front-engine RWD
Structure:	Monocoque
Transmission:	Five-speed manual/four-speed auto
Weight:	1810kg

PRICE GUIDE

Launch price:	£25,200
Excellent:	£3500
Good:	£2500
Average:	£1200
Project:	£500

JAGUAR
XJ-S V12 Convertible

This is the best of the XJ-S range, a full convertible this time, with an electrically operated hood that incorporates a heated glass rear window. And as if to confirm its status, the XJ-S Convertible was only available with the V12 engine and an automatic gearbox. To make up for the loss of the Cabriolet's strengthening roof supports, there's a new subframe at the front to brace the body, though they are still not completely free of scuttle shake. The V12 Convertible made a comeback from 1993-95 with a 6.0-litre engine and 2+2 seating.

SPECIFICATIONS
Years produced:	1988-1991 (7420 in total)
Performance:	0-60mph: 8.0sec
	Top speed: 150mph
Power & torque:	285bhp/309lb ft
Engine:	Normally aspirated 5343cc V12, petrol, electronic fuel injection, 24 valves
Drivetrain:	Front-engine RWD
Structure:	Monocoque
Transmission:	Three-speed automatic
Weight:	1900kg

PRICE GUIDE
Launch price:	£36,000
Excellent:	£10,000
Good:	£8000
Average:	£6000
Project:	£3750

JENSEN

BROTHERS RICHARD and Alan Jensen started the family firm as a coachbuilder in 1934, but had built their own car by 1936, using Ford V8 engines. Post-war Jensens were large and impressive machines with the emphasis on grand touring. After experimenting with glassfibre-bodied cars (the 541 and individualistic CV8), Jensen suddenly leapt to fame and some fortune with the handsome and powerful Interceptor, powered by a Chrysler V8. It also built a less-successful but revolutionary four-wheel-drive and ABS-braked version, dubbed FF, but it couldn't repeat the success of the Interceptor, despite a 1970s tie-up with Healey to build sports cars, and bankruptcy struck in 1976.

JENSEN
541

Although the aerodynamically-styled 541 was launched in 1953, Jensen didn't manage to get it into production until 1955, by which time the decision had been taken to use glassfibre for its body. Most of the running gear came courtesy of Austin, with the hefty 3993cc six-cylinder engine borrowed from the Princess. In the 541's lighter grand tourer body, it gave a much better account of itself than in BMC's big limos. 1957's 541R had more power, while 1960's 541S was longer and wider for greater space inside. Unusual, characterful and likable.

SPECIFICATIONS
Years produced:	1954-1962 (549 in total)
Performance:	0-60mph: 9.2sec
	Top speed: 116mph
Power & torque:	130bhp
Engine:	Normally aspirated 3990cc straight six, petrol, carburettor, 12 valves
Drivetrain:	Front-engine RWD
Structure:	Glassfibre body/separate chassis
Transmission:	Four-speed manual
Weight:	1422kg

PRICE GUIDE
Launch price:	£2147
Excellent:	£30,000
Good:	£16,500
Average:	£9000
Project:	£3750

JENSEN
C-V8

Jensen furthered its knowledge of glassfibre construction with 1962's CV-8, a striking-looking machine characterised by slanting quad headlamps. This time round an enormous 5916cc Chrysler V8 replaced the Austin engine. Mated to an automatic transmission it was capable of pushing the C-V8 to 130mph, but this wasn't enough for Jensen so, in 1964, in went a 335bhp 6276cc. This raised potential speed to 140mph but also meant horrendous fuel consumption. 1965's MkIII saw further tweaks to those front lights.

SPECIFICATIONS
Years produced:	1962-1965 (499 in total)
Performance:	0-60mph: 8.4sec
	Top speed: 129mph
Power & torque:	305bhp/N/A
Engine:	Normally aspirated 5916cc V8, petrol, carburettor, 16 valves
Drivetrain:	Front-engine RWD
Structure:	Glassfibre body/separate chassis
Transmission:	Three-speed manual
Weight:	1517kg

PRICE GUIDE
Launch price:	£3861
Excellent:	£25,000
Good:	£15,000
Average:	£8000
Project:	£4250

JENSEN
Interceptor

One of the biggest and best British bruisers of the luxury GT world, 1966's Interceptor propelled Jensen into the limelight. The handsome lines were styled by Touring of Milan and, initially, the bodies (steel instead of glassfibre) were built by Vignale in Italy before Jensen switched production to the UK. The standard car's most distinctive feature was a curved glass hatchback but, even without this, it would still have been a very eye-catching and imposing creation, as the accompanying convertibles and notchback coupé proved.

SPECIFICATIONS
Years produced:	1966-1974 (6175 in total)
Performance:	0-60mph: 7.3sec
	Top speed: 133mph
Power & torque:	325bhp/425lb ft
Engine:	Normally aspirated 6286cc V8, petrol, carburettor, 16 valves
Drivetrain:	Front-engine RWD
Structure:	Monocoque
Transmission:	Three-speed automatic
Weight:	1768kg

PRICE GUIDE
Launch price:	£5334
Excellent:	£22,500
Good:	£12,000
Average:	£6250
Project:	£3250

JENSEN
Interceptor Convertible

Cutting the roof off the Interceptor resulted in a surprisingly stylish machine, despite the loss of the car's trademark curved glass hatchback. Conceived as a flagship to boost Jensen sales in the USA, the convertible was mechanically the same as the tin-top cars – the 7212cc Chrysler V8 with TorqueFlite automatic transmission – but changes to the body (aside from the obvious missing roof) included strengthening around the sills and the windscreen pillars, plus a spacious boot. Production ended in mid-1976 after 508 cars.

SPECIFICATIONS	
Years produced:	1966-1976 (508 in total)
Performance:	0-60mph: 7.3sec
	Top speed: 135mph
Power & torque:	300bhp/410lb ft
Engine:	Normally aspirated 6286cc V8, petrol, carburettor, 16 valves
Drivetrain:	Front-engine RWD
Structure:	Monocoque
Transmission:	Three-speed automatic
Weight:	1788kg

PRICE GUIDE	
Launch price:	£6744
Excellent:	£50,000
Good:	£27,000
Average:	£16,500
Project:	£10,000

JENSEN
FF

The advanced and forward-thinking Jensen FF was the world's first performance car with permanent four-wheel drive and anti-lock brakes. Introduced in 1966, alongside the Interceptor, it was closely related to that car but had a longer wheelbase, twin vents in the front wings and a bonnet scoop. Mechanically it was very different of course, although the same Chrysler 6276cc V8 did the business under the bonnet. FF stood for Ferguson Formula, the tractor company behind the all-wheel drive system, while the ABS was by Dunlop.

SPECIFICATIONS	
Years produced:	1968-1971 (320 in total)
Performance:	0-60mph: 8.4sec
	Top speed: 130mph
Power & torque:	325bhp/425lb ft
Engine:	Normally aspirated 6276cc V8, petrol, carburettor, 16 valves
Drivetrain:	Front-engine AWD
Structure:	Monocoque
Transmission:	Three-speed automatic
Weight:	1828kg

PRICE GUIDE	
Launch price:	£5340
Excellent:	£28,000
Good:	£16,500
Average:	£11,000
Project:	£5000

JENSEN
Interceptor SP

'SP' stood for 'Six-Pack' and denoted that these 1971-1973 Jensen Interceptors were rather special, with Chrysler V8 engines sporting three twin-barrel Holley carburettors in a 'six-pack' configuration. The designation also hinted at a macho and hairy-chested nature, for the SP was the most powerful Jensen ever built. That 7212cc powerhouses peaked at 385bhp, which meant a speed of 150mph was attainable. However, the SP didn't shout about its capabilities in the same way that many other 1970s high-performance cars did.

SPECIFICATIONS	
Years produced:	1971-1973 (232 in total)
Performance:	0-60mph: 6.4sec
	Top speed: 137mph
Power & torque:	330bhp/425lb ft
Engine:	Normally aspirated 7212cc V8, petrol, carburettor, 16 valves
Drivetrain:	Front-engine RWD
Structure:	Monocoque
Transmission:	Three-speed automatic
Weight:	1649kg

PRICE GUIDE	
Launch price:	£6744
Excellent:	£27,500
Good:	£13,000
Average:	£7500
Project:	£3750

JENSEN
Jensen-Healey

After British Leyland dropped its range of Austin-Healey sports cars, Donald and Geoffrey Healey joined Jensen to develop a successor. They came up with the body design for the 1972 convertible sports car simply known as the Jensen-Healey, using a mix of different parts from other manufacturers. The 1973cc twin-cam 16-valve engine was from Lotus, the suspension and steering from the Vauxhall Viva and the gearbox was a Sunbeam item. The mix never quite gelled, so this 'Healey remains far more affordable than its Austin predecessors.

SPECIFICATIONS	
Years produced:	1972-1976 (10,504 in total)
Performance:	0-60mph: 7.8sec
	Top speed: 119mph
Power & torque:	144bhp/134lb ft
Engine:	Normally aspirated 1973cc four cylinder, petrol, carburettor, 8 valves
Drivetrain:	Front-engine RWD
Structure:	Monocoque
Transmission:	Four-speed manual
Weight:	1061kg

PRICE GUIDE	
Launch price:	£1810
Excellent:	£7500
Good:	£5000
Average:	£3250
Project:	£1000

JENSEN
GT

With Healey's connection with Jensen now ended, the 1975 sporting estate that grew out of the Jensen-Healey convertible in 1975 was simply known as the Jensen GT. It used the same mechanicals – a 1973cc Lotus twin-cam engine mated to a Getrag five-speed gearbox – that, by then, was reliable. But grafting a fixed roof onto what was basically a convertible body still failed to produce a great car, despite the extra practicality and luxurious touches such as a walnut dashboard and electric windows.

SPECIFICATIONS	
Years produced:	1975-1976 (473 in total)
Performance:	0-60mph: 8.7sec
	Top speed: 119mph
Power & torque:	144bhp/134lb ft
Engine:	Normally aspirated 1973cc four cylinder, petrol, carburettor, 8 valves
Drivetrain:	Front-engine RWD
Structure:	Monocoque
Transmission:	Five-speed manual
Weight:	1096kg

PRICE GUIDE	
Launch price:	£4178
Excellent:	£7500
Good:	£4750
Average:	£3000
Project:	£1000

JOWETT

AFTER YEARS of experimentation, brothers William and Benjamin Jowett produced their first cars in Bradford in 1910, powered by the lightweight flat-twin engine that would still be used in their Bradford van after WW2. The cars gained a steady reputation for humble durability, and a four-cylinder version was finally added to the range in 1937. Post war, the company moved upmarket with the Javelin 'executive' saloon and Jupiter sports car, which raced with surprising success at Le Mans. The unreliability of early versions hurt Jowett, but this highly innovative company was ultimately killed off when its body supplier, Briggs, was taken over by Ford in 1953.

JOWETT
Javelin

A brave attempt by this small British manufacturer, and technologically advanced for the immediate post-war period. The Javelin was designed by Gerald Palmer to give sporting performance and handling, good aerodynamics and comfortable seating for five. It succeeded on all fronts and they were snapped up by professionals. Innovative and well-built, with torsion bar suspension and lightweight flat-four engine, they still feel surprisingly good to drive today and cruise happily at 65-70mph .

SPECIFICATIONS

Years produced:	1947-1953 (23,307 in total)
Performance:	0-60mph: 22.2sec
	Top speed: 78mph
Power & torque:	50bhp/N/A
Engine:	Normally aspirated 1486cc flat four, petrol, carburettor, 8 valves
Drivetrain:	Front-engine RWD
Structure:	Separate chassis
Transmission:	Four-speed manual
Weight:	1003kg

PRICE GUIDE

Launch price:	£819
Excellent:	£7000
Good:	£6000
Average:	£3250
Project:	£1600

JOWETT
Jupiter

This was Jowett's only sports car and was created by using Javelin mechanical bits in a tubular spaceframe. Though no beauty in the conventional sense, with its high nose and low tail, the body is at least distinctive and was created from a mixture of steel and aluminium panels. The whole front hinges upwards to give superb engine access. The MkIA from 1952 has a larger boot, with a bootlid this time. Three class wins at Le Mans and one in the Monte Carlo Rally proved the Jupiter's worth and attracted enthusiast buyers.

SPECIFICATIONS

Years produced:	1950-1953 (825 in total)
Performance:	0-60mph: 16.8sec
	Top speed: 84mph
Power & torque:	60bhp/N/A
Engine:	Normally aspirated 1486cc flat four, petrol, carburettor, 8 valves
Drivetrain:	Front-engine RWD
Structure:	Spaceframe
Transmission:	Four-speed manual
Weight:	1003kg

PRICE GUIDE

Launch price:	£1017
Excellent:	£20,000
Good:	£13,000
Average:	£9500
Project:	£5500

LADA

AFTER FIAT SIGNED a deal with the USSR in 1966 to supply expertise for a massive new car factory at Togliatti, AvtoVAZ stared building a model based on the Fiat 124 from 1969. When exported, the cars were badged as Ladas. They were crude, cheap, and gained a following with those who wanted a new car but couldn't afford capitalist prices. The Niva – a dependable 4x4 – joined the catalogue in 1979. However, financial difficulties as a result of lack of quality and constant jokes about Lada quality prompted AvtoVAZ to withdraw from most European markets in 1997, although it still builds and sells cars in its homeland, including the venerable old Niva.

LADA
1200/1300/1500/1600ES

The Soviet government inked a deal with Fiat to assist setting up a new factory to build its then-current 124. The factory that was set-up in Togliatti ended up being the largest in Europe, and the VAZ 2100-series it churned out became the Soviet Union's best-seller by a country mile. They were rechristened Lada for export markets, and soon picked up a decent market share thanks to low prices and high equipment levels. Stodgier than the Fiat to drive, but blessed with the best toolkit in the business, Ladas have their fans despite being laughed at by most sane people.

SPECIFICATIONS

Years produced:	1970-1984
Performance:	0-60mph: 14.7sec
	Top speed: 90mph
Power & torque:	62bhp/64lb ft
Engine:	Normally aspirated 1198cc four cylinder, petrol, carburettor, 8 valves
Drivetrain:	Front-engine RWD
Structure:	Monocoque
Transmission:	Four-speed manual
Weight:	945kg

PRICE GUIDE

Launch price:	£981
Excellent:	£1500
Good:	£600
Average:	£450
Project:	£250

LAGONDA

FROM TINY ACORNS... American Wilbur Gunn built his first twin-cylinder tri-car in his greenhouse in Staines, England in 1906. In the 1920s, his Lagonda marque moved into sports car production and by 1935 it had won at Le Mans. Before the war, WO Bentley was brought in as technical director and designed a V12 engine for use in the firm's products. In 1947, Lagonda was sold to David Brown and paired up with Aston Martin. Lagonda stole all the headlines in 1976 with its astonishing (and astonishingly complicated) saloon with ultra-sharp wedge-shaped styling. The badge has lain dormant since 1987, but Aston Martin recently revived it for a monstrous off-road concept car.

LAGONDA
2.6/2.9

Lagonda's 2.6 was introduced in 1946, just before David Brown took the company over to combine it with Aston Martin. It was a smaller car than pre-war Lagondas, and WO Bentley designed its engine and chassis. The latter was advanced for the time, with all-independent suspension. Bodies were saloon or drophead coupé, the latter now worth more than twice the quoted saloon prices. It metamorphosed into a 2.9-litre in 1953, with the same chassis, a larger-bore engine (well-proven in competition), and a body penned by Tickford.

SPECIFICATIONS

Years produced:	1948-1957 (780 in total)
Performance:	0-60mph: 18.8sec
	Top speed: 100mph
Power & torque:	105bhp/133lb ft
Engine:	Normally aspirated 2580cc straight six, petrol, carburettor, 12 valves
Drivetrain:	Front-engine RWD
Structure:	Separate chassis
Transmission:	Four-speed manual
Weight:	1471kg

PRICE GUIDE

Launch price:	£3110
Excellent:	£40,000
Good:	£25,000
Average:	£17,500
Project:	£10,000

LAGONDA
Rapide

From the front wheels back, Lagonda's 1961 to 1964 Rapide was a handsome and dignified machine. Ahead of that it was rather more challenging thanks to a sloped quad-headlamp nose and outlandish grilles. Given that it was designed by Touring this look was a big disappointment and no doubt contributed to the fact that only 54 were built. The car used an elongated DB4 chassis with suspension tweaks, and a 236bhp 4-litre six-cylinder engine that wouldn't graduate to Aston Martin until the DB5 three years later.

SPECIFICATIONS

Years produced:	1961-1964 (55 in total)
Performance:	0-60mph: N/A
	Top speed: 130mph
Power & torque:	236bhp/265lb ft
Engine:	Normally aspirated 3995cc straight six, petrol, carburettor, 12 valves
Drivetrain:	Front-engine RWD
Structure:	Superleggera
Transmission:	Three-speed auto/four-speed manual
Weight:	1715kg

PRICE GUIDE

Launch price:	£4950
Excellent:	£37,500
Good:	£25,000
Average:	£16,000
Project:	£10,000

LAMBORGHINI

WEALTHY TRACTOR magnate Ferruccio Lamborghini started building cars after falling out with Enzo Ferrari over how a supercar should be built. Aiming to outdo the Prancing Horse, Lamborghini adopted a rampant bull logo and launched the V12 350GT in 1963. But what really made the company's name was the mid-engined Miura three years later. Its subsequent run of over-the-top supercars continues to this day, though it's been a rocky road as the company passed first to a Swiss syndicate in 1972, was declared bankrupt in 1977 (but continued production), then went to Chrysler in 1987, and to Audi (via two other owners) in 1998. Audi has added reliability to the mix.

LAMBORGHINI
350GT

Here's where it all began, allegedly because Ferruccio Lamborghini was unhappy with the level of service he received from Enzo Ferrari when a car he bought from the Scuderia went wrong. When Lamborghini started his sports car company, he poached a number of Ferrari engineers to help create his first car – most notably Giotto Bizzarrini, who created the V12 engine, and Giampaolo Dallara, who sorted out the chassis. When the Touring-bodied 350GT arrived on the scene, it made a huge impact that resonated across Italy – and, from that moment on, Enzo took Ferruccio seriously.

SPECIFICATIONS

Years produced:	1964-1966 (120 in total)
Performance:	0-60mph: 6.8sec
	Top speed: 155mph
Power & torque:	320bhp/241lb ft
Engine:	Normally aspirated 3464cc V12, petrol, carburettor, 24 valves
Drivetrain:	Front-engine RWD
Structure:	Spaceframe
Transmission:	Five-speed manual
Weight:	1200kg

PRICE GUIDE

Launch price:	£6950
Excellent:	£225,000
Good:	£160,000
Average:	£120,000
Project:	£100,000

LAMBORGHINI
400GT 2+2

Lamborghini commissioned Touring to extend the 350GT. The coachbuilder came up with an all-new body based on a lengthened wheelbase that managed to incorporate a pair of occasional rear seats – it may have looked almost identical to the smaller car, but every panel was changed. To keep keen drivers happy, the newly developed 4.0-litre version of Bizzarni's V12 was installed, maintaining supercar-style performance. Although the 400 is actually the more accomplished car, values favour the 350GT.

SPECIFICATIONS	
Years produced:	1966-1968 (242 in total)
Performance:	0-60mph: 7.5sec
	Top speed: 155mph
Power & torque:	320bhp/276lb ft
Engine:	Normally aspirated 3929cc V12, petrol, carburettor, 24 valves
Drivetrain:	Front-engine RWD
Structure:	Spaceframe
Transmission:	Five-speed manual
Weight:	1380kg

PRICE GUIDE	
Launch price:	£7995
Excellent:	£175,000
Good:	£125,000
Average:	£80,000
Project:	£55,000

LAMBORGHINI
Miura P400/P400S

The Miura made its first appearance in chassis form at the 1965 Turin show, attracting orders and deposits before the body itself was even designed. That box chassis (full of holes for lightness) housed an engine and transmission placed transversely just ahead of the rear wheels. The V12 engine sat on top of the gearbox with the two sharing the same oil. Nothing like it had been seen before and it captured the imaginations of many. Every coachbuilder in Italy clamoured for the opportunity to clothe the spectacular chassis. Bertone was chosen. A legend was born.

SPECIFICATIONS (P400S)	
Years produced:	1966-1968 (475 in total)
Performance:	0-60mph: 5.5sec
	Top speed: 177mph
Power & torque:	370bhp/286lb ft
Engine:	Normally aspirated 3939cc V12, petrol, carburettor, 24 valves
Drivetrain:	Mid-engine RWD
Structure:	Spaceframe
Transmission:	Five-speed manual
Weight:	1040kg

PRICE GUIDE (S in brackets)	
Launch price:	£10,860
Excellent:	£250,000 (£350,000)
Good:	£225,000 (£250,000)
Average:	£175,000 (£200,000)
Project:	£110,000 (£175,000)

LAMBORGHINI
Islero

The Islero was introduced to the public at the 1968 Geneva Motor Show. It was not as aggressive as the Espada or Miura, catering more for the grand touring crowd. However, it offered luxurious benefits such as air conditioning and a more spacious interior, and was designed with one eye on the American market. An S version followed in 1969 which was shortlived, with only 100 being produced. The Islero is named after a fighting bull that killed the famous matador Manuel Rodriguez in August of 1947.

SPECIFICATIONS	
Years produced:	1968-1970 (125 in total)
Performance:	0-60mph: 6.2sec
	Top speed: 165mph
Power & torque:	350bhp/290lb ft
Engine:	Normally aspirated 3929cc V12, petrol, carburettor, 24 valves
Drivetrain:	Front-engine RWD
Structure:	Spaceframe
Transmission:	Five-speed manual
Weight:	1460kg

PRICE GUIDE	
Launch price:	£7950
Excellent:	£85,000
Good:	£60,000
Average:	£40,000
Project:	£22,500

LAMBORGHINI
Miura P400 SV

If the 350/400GTs paved the way for Lamborghini to become a major player in the supercar scene, the trendsetting Miura left Ferrari floundering in its wake. At a time when mid-engined cars were very much for competition and niche cars, Lamborghini embraced the layout for its range-topping sports car. The ultimate series-production Miura was the SV, which had its power boosted to a claimed 385bhp (the SVJ and Jota were specials), and a top speed of around 180mph if you were brave. The loss of the eyelashes was a minus point, but perhaps the only one.

SPECIFICATIONS	
Years produced:	1968-1971 (140 in total)
Performance:	0-60mph: 5.0sec
	Top speed: 180mph
Power & torque:	385bhp/286lb ft
Engine:	Normally aspirated 3939cc V12, petrol, carburettor, 24 valves
Drivetrain:	Mid-engine RWD
Structure:	Spaceframe
Transmission:	Five-speed manual
Weight:	1040kg

PRICE GUIDE	
Launch price:	£10,860
Excellent:	£750,000
Good:	£500,000
Average:	£375,000
Project:	N/A

LAMBORGHINI
Espada

In 1968, Lamborghini presented a four-seater GT. Called the Espada 400GT, its styling was inspired by that of the memorable mid-engined Marzal concept car of 1966, and maintained the Marzal's expansive proportions despite being front-engined. The first Espada prototype retained the Marzal's gullwing door design too, which was abandoned for the production model. Despite its four-seater layout, the Espada was almost as agile as its two-seater sisters. A real head-turner and now it's getting fashionable. If you fancy one, be quick.

SPECIFICATIONS	
Years produced:	1968-1978 (186 in total)
Performance:	0-60mph: 6.5sec
	Top speed: 155mph
Power & torque:	325bhp/276lb ft
Engine:	Normally aspirated 3939cc V12, petrol, carburettor, 24 valves
Drivetrain:	Front-engine RWD
Structure:	Spaceframe
Transmission:	Five-speed manual/three-speed auto
Weight:	1480kg

PRICE GUIDE	
Launch price:	£10,295
Excellent:	£35,000
Good:	£25,000
Average:	£16,000
Project:	£9000

LAMBORGHINI
Jarama 400 GT

Never a popular Lamborghini, the Jarama ended up being the company's final front-engined sports car, as after that it ended up concentrating on the mid-engined Countach and Urraco. In a market in which styling counts above all else, the clumsy-looking Jarama struggled against some very elegant rivals, not least the more commodious Lamborghini Espada. As a way of getting onto the Lamborghini ownership ladder, the Jarama makes much sense – it's relatively cheap for a front-engined V12 and, although it suffers from poor build quality, it remains seriously quick.

SPECIFICATIONS

Years produced:	1970-1973 (177 in total)
Performance:	0-60mph: 7.2sec
	Top speed: 162mph
Power & torque:	350bhp/290lb ft
Engine:	Normally aspirated 3939cc V12, petrol, carburettor, 24 valves
Drivetrain:	Front-engine RWD
Structure:	Separate chassis
Transmission:	Five-speed manual
Weight:	1540kg

PRICE GUIDE

Launch price:	£9800
Excellent:	£27,500
Good:	£21,000
Average:	£14,000
Project:	£8000

LAMBORGHINI
Urraco P250/P300

The P300 was a direct answer to Ferrari's new 308 GT4, the successor to the famous Dino. The original P250 needed changing; the price was too high and the workmanship wasn't up to the desired level. The Urraco should have been a big success, but with poor build quality and limp-wristed performance in P250 form it failed to take off. The 265bhp P300 put right the latter problem, pushing the Urraco to over 160mph, but the former was a more deep-seated issue that failed to be resolved. A 2.0-litre tax-break P200 model was sold in Italy, and it's not uncommon to find one for sale now.

SPECIFICATIONS

Years produced:	1972-1979 (710 in total)
Performance:	0-60mph: 7.4sec
	Top speed: 161mph
Power & torque:	265bhp/195lb ft
Engine:	Normally aspirated 2996cc V8, petrol, carburettor, 16 valves
Drivetrain:	Mid-engine RWD
Structure:	Spaceframe
Transmission:	Five-speed manual
Weight:	1300kg

PRICE GUIDE (P300 in brackets)

Launch price:	£9975
Excellent:	£25,000 (£35,000)
Good:	£16,000 (£19,000)
Average:	£14,000 (£16,000)
Project:	£7000 (£10,000)

LAMBORGHINI
Countach LP400

Although the Miura was a tough act to follow, Lamborghini did it in style with the Countach, perhaps the most iconic bedroom poster car of all. With a dramatic wedge style, scissor doors and a *claimed* maximum speed approaching 200mph from its 375bhp V12, the Countach was a concept car for the road. It also put right many of the Miura's most serious problems, most notably its shocking aerodynamics. Cramped, noisy and impossible to see out of, the Countach is a true great – and currently undervalued compared with its forebear. For how much longer though?

SPECIFICATIONS

Years produced:	1974-1978 (150 in total)
Performance:	0-60mph: 6.8sec
	Top speed: 180mph
Power & torque:	375bhp/268lb ft
Engine:	Normally aspirated 3929cc V12, petrol, carburettor, 24 valves
Drivetrain:	Mid-engine RWD
Structure:	Spaceframe
Transmission:	Five-speed manual
Weight:	1065kg

PRICE GUIDE ('Periscopo' in brackets)

Launch price:	£17,285
Excellent:	£200,000 (£250,000)
Good:	£150,000 (£180,000)
Average:	£110,000
Project:	£90,000

LAMBORGHINI
Silhouette P300

Based on the Urraco P300, the Silhouette was an ultimately unsuccessful attempt to take on the Ferrari 308GTS. An appealing-looking car with phone-dial alloys and ultra-low profile tyres – just like a Countach – it wasn't strong enough to make the grade. It fell by the wayside when Lamborghini went through horrendous financial problems during the late 1970s, a time when Sant'Agata's model range was reduced to the Countach only. With 54 built, the Silhouette is rare and rapidly gaining desirability – but it's not as nice to drive as a 308.

SPECIFICATIONS

Years produced:	1976-1979 (52 in total)
Performance:	0-60mph: 6.8sec
	Top speed: 150mph
Power & torque:	260bhp/210lb ft
Engine:	Normally aspirated 2996cc V8, petrol, carburettor, 16 valves
Drivetrain:	Mid-engine RWD
Structure:	Spaceframe
Transmission:	Five-speed manual
Weight:	1240kg

PRICE GUIDE

Launch price:	£13,684
Excellent:	£35,000
Good:	£22,000
Average:	£15,000
Project:	£8000

LAMBORGHINI
Countach LP400S

The Countach LP400 was an astonishing machine, and although it couldn't get near its claimed 200mph, it was quicker in a straight line than in corners. Lamborghini had little development funds to rectify that situation during the '70s, but thanks to the financial 'assistance' of grand prix team owner and regular Lamborghini customer Walter Wolf, it could afford to redesign the suspension to run ultra-low profile Pirelli P7 tyres. The difference in corners was astonishing, with much higher levels of lateral grip attainable. Top speed was somewhat lower, though...

SPECIFICATIONS

Years produced:	1978-1982
Performance:	0-60mph: 6.8sec
	Top speed: 170mph
Power & torque:	375bhp/268lb ft
Engine:	Normally aspirated 3929cc V12, petrol, carburettor, 24 valves
Drivetrain:	Mid-engine RWD
Structure:	Spaceframe
Transmission:	Five-speed manual
Weight:	1200kg

PRICE GUIDE

Launch price:	N/A
Excellent:	£125,000
Good:	£80,000
Average:	£50,000
Project:	£30,000

LAMBORGHINI
Jalpa

The Jalpa was Lamborghini's last throw of the Urraco dice. The Silhouette had been out of production for two years, so it was an odd decision to revamp it for another attack on the 308. The Jalpa was usefully quicker thanks to its enlarged (by Alfieri) 3.5-litre V8 engine, but the '70s throwback styling and Airfix interior should have been a barrier to sales. However, during its nine-year production run, the Jalpa bucked the trend and sold 200 in its most successful year – making it Lamborghini's biggest-selling V8.

SPECIFICATIONS

Years produced:	1981-1988 (410 in total)
Performance:	0-60mph: 7.3sec
	Top speed: 146mph
Power & torque:	255bhp/231lb ft
Engine:	Normally aspirated 3485cc V8, petrol, carburettor, 16 valves
Drivetrain:	Mid-engine RWD
Structure:	Spaceframe
Transmission:	Five-speed manual
Weight:	1510kg

PRICE GUIDE

Launch price:	£26,001
Excellent:	£30,000
Good:	£25,000
Average:	£16,000
Project:	£9000

LAMBORGHINI
Countach LP500S

Adding the bodykit and wider tyres (and often that outrageous rear wing, which was never a factory option by the way) had the unpleasant effect of actually making the LP400S slower than the original LP400. The obvious answer was a more powerful engine, but that would have to wait until 1982, when Lamborghini's finances improved following the arrival of the Mimram family. Additional torque and lower gearing added considerable punch and, once again, placed the Countach ahead of its nemesis, the Ferrari BB. LP500S values lag behind LP400 – the nearest thing to a bargain Countach?

SPECIFICATIONS

Years produced:	1982-1985
Performance:	0-60mph: 5.6sec
	Top speed: 170mph
Power & torque:	385bhp/303lb ft
Engine:	Normally aspirated 4754cc V12, petrol, carburettor, 24 valves
Drivetrain:	Mid-engine RWD
Structure:	Spaceframe
Transmission:	Five-speed manual
Weight:	1485kg

PRICE GUIDE

Launch price:	N/A
Excellent:	£100,000
Good:	£77,500
Average:	£50,000
Project:	£30,000

LAMBORGHINI
Countach 5000QV

The Countach Quattrovalvole was built for a single purpose: to go faster than the Ferrari Testarossa. Engineering genius Giulio Alfieri created twin-cam four-valve cylinder heads, re-engineered the carburettor set-up, and allied the ensemble to a larger 5167cc block, upping maximum power by 70bhp – and making this the best Countach yet. Sales picked up and, when the 1988 Anniversary model was rolled out, they went into overdrive. By the time Countach production ended, it had become the company's longest-lived car.

SPECIFICATIONS

Years produced:	1985-1990 (610 in total)
Performance:	0-60mph: 4.8sec
	Top speed: 182mph
Power & torque:	455bhp/369lb ft
Engine:	Normally aspirated 5167cc V12, petrol, carburettor, 48 valves
Drivetrain:	Mid-engine RWD
Structure:	Spaceframe
Transmission:	Five-speed manual
Weight:	1490kg

PRICE GUIDE

Launch price:	N/A
Excellent:	£100,000
Good:	£75,000
Average:	£50,000
Project:	£30,000

LANCHESTER

THE FIRST TRULY all-British car was a Lanchester, having been cobbled together by talented engineer Frederick Lanchester. Twin-cylinder models were being produced for sale by 1900; the basic machines became more comfortable and better-engineered as automotive know-how progressed. By 1919, it was rivalling Rolls-Royce. Daimler acquired the company in 1931 and the era of 'proper' Lanchesters ended, as subsequent creations were largely badge-engineered Daimlers or BSAs. It lingered on until 1956 when Daimler's own financial woes caused it to drop the marque. Jaguar took over and used Daimler in the same way Daimler had used Lanchester.

LANCHESTER
Fourteen/Leda

Both Lanchester and Daimler were owned by BSA, giving the parent company a great excuse to experiment with badge engineering in the 1950s. Lanchester's 14 was the first version of what would become better-known as the Daimler Conquest. With a four-cylinder engine of 2.0-litres and 60bhp, it was pedestrian in both performance and looks, although the drophead coupé cut a dash. The Leda name was used abroad, to denote cars that had a steel frame instead of the wooden one of the UK cars. The last car to wear the Lanchester name.

SPECIFICATIONS

Years produced:	1951-1954 (2100 in total)
Performance:	0-60mph: N/A
	Top speed: 75mph
Power & torque:	60bhp/N/A
Engine:	Normally aspirated 1968cc four cylinder, petrol, carburettor, 8 valves
Drivetrain:	Front-engine RWD
Structure:	Separate chassis
Transmission:	Four-speed pre-selector
Weight:	1410kg

PRICE GUIDE

Launch price:	£1144
Excellent:	£6000
Good:	£4750
Average:	£3250
Project:	£1600

LANCIA

THE SON OF a soup manufacturer, Vincenzo Lancia cut his teeth at Fiat before starting his own factory in Turin in 1906. The company quickly gained a reputation for styling flair and its use of advanced technology, with vee-engines and independent suspension being its norm long before other manufacturers were brave enough to try. It also had the first production five-speed gearbox, in 1948. Sadly, its approach proved less than cost effective and, with deepening financial trouble, Fiat stepped in during 1969. The legacy of a reputation damaged by rusty Betas saw it leave the UK market in 1994, but the badge continues elsewhere on luxury cars with Fiat underpinnings.

LANCIA
Aprilia

Looking at the Aprilia's specification sheet, it's easy to see that it was lightyears ahead of its time. The features list included monocoque construction, independent suspension all-round, pillarless styling honed in the wind tunnel, and a jewel-like 1354cc V4 engine that produced enough power to ensure the Aprilia outpaced much more glamorous rivals. Three wheelbases were offered, and you could also buy coachbuilt versions. Post-war examples were upgraded with 1.5-litre engines and remained in production until 1949.

SPECIFICATIONS

Years produced:	1937-1949 (27,635 in total)
Performance:	0-60mph: N/A
	Top speed: 80mph
Power & torque:	46bhp/N/A
Engine:	Normally aspirated 1352cc V4, petrol, carburettor, 8 valves
Drivetrain:	Front-engine RWD
Structure:	Monocoque
Transmission:	Four-speed manual
Weight:	850kg

PRICE GUIDE

Launch price:	N/A
Excellent:	£16,500
Good:	£13,000
Average:	£8000
Project:	£3500

LANCIA
Aurelia Saloon

Considering the Aprilia blazed such a trail, it's scarcely believable that Lancia went and did the same with the Aurelia. The main advance was the engine – the world's first production V6; a 60-degree design developed during World War Two. It was smooth and lusty, and proved the perfect power unit for long-distance touring. In the B10 saloon it was initially available in 1754cc and 1991cc forms. The wind-cheating styling was developed with assistance from Pininfarina and still looks strikingly understated, modern and elegant today.

SPECIFICATIONS

Years produced:	1950-1958 (12,705 in total)
Performance:	0-60mph: 17.9sec
	Top speed: 91mph
Power & torque:	87bhp/118lb ft
Engine:	Normally aspirated 226cc V6, petrol, carburettor, 12 valves
Drivetrain:	Front-engine RWD
Structure:	Monocoque
Transmission:	Four-speed manual
Weight:	1232kg

PRICE GUIDE

Launch price:	£2863
Excellent:	£17,500
Good:	£14,000
Average:	£8500
Project:	£4500

LANCIA
Aurelia B20 GT

Pininfarina was responsible for building the B20 GT coupé, even though Ghia styled the bodies, which are elegantly proportioned and exquisitely detailed. Now considered to be the cars that coined the Gran Turismo epithet, the 2.0- and 2.5-litre versions were quick, smooth and effortless. Fewer than 4000 B20 GTs were built, and those that remain have risen steeply in value in recent years as demand continues to outstrip supply. In all, six series of Aurelias were built, with trim and performance upgrades being drafted in on an almost annual basis.

SPECIFICATIONS

Years produced:	1953-1958 (3424 in total)
Performance:	0-60mph: 12.3sec
	Top speed: 103mph
Power & torque:	75bhp/89lb ft
Engine:	Normally aspirated 1991cc V6, petrol, carburettor, 12 valves
Drivetrain:	Front-engine RWD
Structure:	Monocoque
Transmission:	Four-speed manual
Weight:	1194kg

PRICE GUIDE

Launch price:	£3472
Excellent:	£80,000
Good:	£50,000
Average:	£30,000
Project:	£16,000

LANCIA
Appia

Designed as an entry-level model, the Appia was unashamedly stylish and advanced. Not only was it aerodynamic but it was light, too, featuring aluminium body panels – and that made the 38bhp 1.1-litre car move along at a fair old pace. The Appia was developed constantly throughout its life, mutating into the Series 2. The styling was rejigged to provide a bigger boot and it looked good, still lightyears ahead of the opposition. These cars are almost impossible to find in the UK, especially the coachbuilt models from Vignale, Farina and Zagato.

SPECIFICATIONS

Years produced:	1953-1959 (98,006 in total)
Performance:	0-60mph: 32.5sec
	Top speed: 76mph
Power & torque:	38bhp/52lb ft
Engine:	Normally aspirated 1090cc V4, petrol, carburettor, 8 valves
Drivetrain:	Front-engine RWD
Structure:	Monocoque
Transmission:	Four-speed manual
Weight:	813kg

PRICE GUIDE

Launch price:	£1772
Excellent:	£8000
Good:	£6500
Average:	£4000
Project:	£1500

LANCIA
Aurelia B24 Spider

In 1954, to coincide with the arrival of the fourth series cars, the B24 Spider was unveiled – easily the most desirable of all the Aurelias unless you carry passengers. Although its front-end styling was similar to the B10 and B20 GT's, from the front wheels back it was radically different. The wheelbase was shortened by 203mm and Pininfarina produced the sensational coachwork. Production was limited, although many cars have survived – but with higher market values to match their elevated styling and engineering. The Spider name was rather shortlived.

SPECIFICATIONS
Years produced:	1955-1956 (240 in total)
Performance:	0-60mph: N/A
	Top speed: 115mph
Power & torque:	118bhp/127lb ft
Engine:	Normally aspirated 2451cc V6, petrol, carburettor, 12 valves
Drivetrain:	Front-engine RWD
Structure:	Monocoque
Transmission:	Four-speed manual
Weight:	1070kg

PRICE GUIDE
Launch price:	£N/A
Excellent:	£350,000
Good:	£200,000
Average:	£150,000
Project:	£120,000

LANCIA
Aurelia B24 Convertible

For the penultimate round of changes to the Aurelia, and just over a year after it first appeared, the B24 was revised. In the process it lost the Spider name, becoming the B24 Convertible. Alongside the fifth series B20 GTs, which received a sturdier transaxle, the B24 gained wind-up windows, improved seating, and a new, more conventional windscreen with opening quarter lights that proved more useful when motoring with the hood up. Because there were more Convertibles than Spiders, values are correspondingly lower.

SPECIFICATIONS
Years produced:	1957-1958 (510 in total)
Performance:	0-60mph: 12.7sec
	Top speed: 107mph
Power & torque:	110bhp/125lb ft
Engine:	Normally aspirated 2451cc V6, petrol, carburettor, 12 valves
Drivetrain:	Front-engine RWD
Structure:	Monocoque
Transmission:	Four-speed manual
Weight:	1215kg

PRICE GUIDE
Launch price:	£N/A
Excellent:	£200,000
Good:	£120,000
Average:	£90,000
Project:	£60,000

LANCIA
Flaminia 2.8

Replacing the Aurelia was never going to be easy but, with the Flaminia, Lancia managed the task with considerable style, although the two cars' production runs overlapped by a couple of years just to confuse matters. The new car heralded a new design direction, with Pininfarina going for a more angular (if conventionally beautiful) style. A new 2775cc V6 was developed for the Flaminia, and wishbone/coil-spring front suspension replaced the old car's antiquated sliding pillars. Fewer than 3500 Berlinas were produced in total and few still exist.

SPECIFICATIONS
Years produced:	1957-1970 (3424 in total)
Performance:	0-60mph: N/A
	Top speed: 121mph
Power & torque:	148bhp/165lb ft
Engine:	Normally aspirated 2775cc V6, petrol, carburettor, 12 valves
Drivetrain:	Front-engine RWD
Structure:	Monocoque
Transmission:	Four-speed manual
Weight:	1247kg

PRICE GUIDE
Launch price:	£2847
Excellent:	£7250
Good:	£6000
Average:	£3500
Project:	£1500

LANCIA
Flaminia Coupé/GT

Like the Berlina, the Flaminia Coupé was penned by Pininfarina, displaying a strong family resemblance to the four-door. Built on a shortened wheelbase that was shared with all other two-door versions, the Coupé was handsome and desirable. Again, this was not a mass-produced car – 5282 Coupés were built, excluding the Carrozzeria Touring-designed GT, which featured different styling and a two-seat cabin. The Flaminia was the last Lancia to be offered in so many coachbuilt variations. Values are high as a consequence, although not in the Aurelia league. Yet.

SPECIFICATIONS
Years produced:	1959-1967 (5282/1718 in total)
Performance:	0-60mph: 13.6sec
	Top speed: 106mph
Power & torque:	119bhp/137lb ft
Engine:	Normally aspirated 2458cc V6, petrol, carburettor, 12 valves
Drivetrain:	Front-engine RWD
Structure:	Monocoque
Transmission:	Four-speed manual
Weight:	1481kg

PRICE GUIDE
Launch price:	£3869
Excellent:	£18,500
Good:	£14,000
Average:	£7000
Project:	£3250

LANCIA
Flaminia Convertible

The Convertible was perhaps the best-looking of all the Flaminias thanks to a carefully considered roof chop of the Touring-styled coupé body. Offered with an optional hardtop and uprated 2775cc V6 engine, it remained in production until 1964 with a build total of a mere 847. The one to have is most definitely the 2.8-litre version, of which just 180 were built. However, finding one is always tough and, when you do, be prepared to pay top money for the best examples, as demand for this particularly striking car remains as strong as ever.

SPECIFICATIONS
Years produced:	1959-1967 (847 in total)
Performance:	0-60mph: N/A
	Top speed: 110mph
Power & torque:	148bhp/164lb ft
Engine:	Normally aspirated 2775cc V6, petrol, carburettor, 12 valves
Drivetrain:	Front-engine RWD
Structure:	Monocoque
Transmission:	Four-speed manual
Weight:	1360kg

PRICE GUIDE
Launch price:	N/A
Excellent:	£32,500
Good:	£25,000
Average:	£15,000
Project:	£8000

LANCIA
Flaminia Sport Zagato

The Flaminia Sport was coachbuilt by Zagato, and was almost incomparably handsome. The Sport sat on the same wheelbase as the GT and, unlike the Pininfarina and Touring cars, which were angular, the aluminium-bodied Sport was more rounded, harking back to the more timeless style of the B20 GT. It became the Super Sport in 1964, the new name reflecting the additional performance from its 2.8-litre V6. Zagato styling signatures, such as the pop-out doorhandles, were retained, although the Sport and Super Sport's styling differed significantly.

SPECIFICATIONS (Sport)
Years produced:	1960-1967 (593 in total)
Performance:	0-60mph: 12.7sec
	Top speed: 112mph
Power & torque:	119bhp/127lb ft
Engine:	Normally aspirated 2458cc V6, petrol, carburettor, 12 valves
Drivetrain:	Front-engine RWD
Structure:	Monocoque
Transmission:	Four-speed manual
Weight:	1520kg

PRICE GUIDE
Launch price:	£3888
Excellent:	£100,000
Good:	£60,000
Average:	£40,000
Project:	£20,000

LANCIA
Flavia Saloon

Like every other post-war Lancia, the Flavia was innovative compared with the class of 1960. It was the first front-wheel-drive Lancia, making the Italian company one of the earliest adopters of this transmission layout, beating BMC into the 1500cc sector by eight years. But it didn't stop there – the V4 engine was new for Lancia, as was the all-disc brake set-up. The Berlina was styled in-house, and it showed – its boxy styling doing a great job of hiding the groundbreaking technical specification under a cloud of mediocrity.

SPECIFICATIONS
Years produced:	1961-1974 (79,764 in total)
Performance:	0-60mph: 14.3sec
	Top speed: 103mph
Power & torque:	102bhp/113lb ft
Engine:	Normally aspirated 1800cc V4, petrol, carburettor, 8 valves
Drivetrain:	Front-engine FWD
Structure:	Monocoque
Transmission:	Four-speed manual
Weight:	1199kg

PRICE GUIDE
Launch price:	£2075
Excellent:	£4000
Good:	£3000
Average:	£1500
Project:	£400

LANCIA
Flavia Sport Zagato

Once again, Zagato was drafted in to create an individual-looking Sport, although for the Flavia it was more outlandish than usual. The curvaceous bodywork was a long way away from the square-rigged conventionality of the Berlina, and even the Coupé looked restrained in comparison. In lightweight form and with twin carburettors, the Sport lived up to its name, proving quick and agile on the road. Sales weren't good though, and in the wake of the Fiat takeover of Lancia in 1969, bespoke models such as this were very much off the menu.

SPECIFICATIONS
Years produced:	1962-1969
Performance:	0-60mph: 11.9sec
	Top speed: 117mph
Power & torque:	101bhp/103lb ft
Engine:	Normally aspirated 1800cc V4, petrol, carburettor, 8 valves
Drivetrain:	Front-engine FWD
Structure:	Superleggera
Transmission:	Four-speed manual
Weight:	1800kg

PRICE GUIDE
Launch price:	£2736
Excellent:	£20,000
Good:	£15,000
Average:	£9500
Project:	£3000

LANCIA
Flavia Coupé

A year after the arrival of the Flavia saloon, the eye-catching Coupé model arrived. Continuing a long tradition of co-operation with Pininfarina, its pretty two-door body style moved Lancia styling away from the classicism of the earlier models. The Coupé initially came with a 90bhp twin-carburettor version of the 1.5-litre V4, but this was uprated to 100bhp and 1.8 litres in 1963, before going to the full 126bhp and 2.0 litres in 1971. Rust has been the main enemy of these cars, although many have now been restored – and values are sure to continue rising.

SPECIFICATIONS
Years produced:	1962-1973 (26,084 in total)
Performance:	0-60mph: 13.2sec
	Top speed: 103mph
Power & torque:	91bhp/108lb ft
Engine:	Normally aspirated 1800cc V4, petrol, carburettor, 8 valves
Drivetrain:	Front-engine FWD
Structure:	Monocoque
Transmission:	Four-speed manual
Weight:	1160kg

PRICE GUIDE
Launch price:	£2275
Excellent:	£12,500
Good:	£9000
Average:	£4000
Project:	£1500

LANCIA
Fulvia Coupé

After a couple of years in production, the special variations of the Fulvia started to be released. The major news was the two-door Coupé that, like the Flavia, was distinguishable by its handsome bodywork on a shortened floorpan. It shared no external panels with the saloon. Performance was improved with a 1.2-litre 80bhp version of the engine being installed at launch, but upgraded to a 90bhp 1290cc power unit later in its life. Handling was known for its precision and neutrality, a point devastatingly proved in motor sport with the more potent HF.

SPECIFICATIONS
Years produced:	1965-1976 (139,817 in total)
Performance:	0-60mph: 15.8sec
	Top speed: 100mph
Power & torque:	80bhp/77lb ft
Engine:	Normally aspirated 1216cc V4, petrol, carburettor, 8 valves
Drivetrain:	Front-engine FWD
Structure:	Monocoque
Transmission:	Four-speed manual
Weight:	940kg

PRICE GUIDE
Launch price:	£1490
Excellent:	£10,000
Good:	£5000
Average:	£2500
Project:	£1000

LANCIA
Fulvia Coupé HF

The Fulvia's crowning achievement was to win the 1972 International Rally Championship with the HF Rallye, the competition version of the Fulvia Coupé. Powered by a tuned version of the 1298cc engine producing 87bhp, the HF was lighter than the standard Coupé, thanks to the aluminium bonnet, doors and bootlid, and Plexiglass windows. Considered too raw for the road, the HF was further developed into the Rallye 1.6 HF, a fire-breathing 1584cc version developing 115bhp. Today HFs are the most sought-after versions, with values to match.

SPECIFICATIONS
Years produced:	1965-1976 (139,817 in total)
Performance:	0-60mph: 11.9sec
	Top speed: 103mph
Power & torque:	87bhp/83lb ft
Engine:	Normally aspirated 1298cc V4, petrol, carburettor, 8 valves
Drivetrain:	Front-engine FWD
Structure:	Monocoque
Transmission:	Four-speed manual
Weight:	894kg

PRICE GUIDE
Launch price:	£1548
Excellent:	£15,000
Good:	£9500
Average:	£4750
Project:	£2500

LANCIA
Fulvia Sport Zagato

Slightly more palatable-looking than the Zagato-bodied Flavia, the aluminium Fulvia was still a challenging looker. But those concept car lines promised a great driving experience and, thankfully, the Sport Zagato lived up to its off-the-wall styling. Like the HF, the Zagato was lighter than the standard Coupé, and the power-to-weight ratio delivered by the lively V4 power units was enhanced usefully. Upgraded during its life, the Sport Zagato even picked up luxury fitments such as electric windows, a sure sign that buyers were demanding more fripperies in the 1970s.

SPECIFICATIONS
Years produced:	1968-1972
Performance:	0-60mph: 13.0sec
	Top speed: 109mph
Power & torque:	87bhp/84lb ft
Engine:	Normally aspirated 1298cc V4, petrol, carburettor, 8 valves
Drivetrain:	Front-engine FWD
Structure:	Monocoque
Transmission:	Five-speed manual
Weight:	960kg

PRICE GUIDE
Launch price:	N/A
Excellent:	£20,000
Good:	£9000
Average:	£4500
Project:	£3000

LANCIA
Beta Berlina

A gem of a saloon that was streets ahead of other family offerings when it appeared in 1972 with four-wheel disc brakes, twin-cam engine, independent suspension and a five-speed gearbox. Rust in front subframes and wings, with ferocious media hype to match, saw to the car's UK demise, despite the '76 S2 being vastly better and Lancia's introduction of a six-year anti-corrosion warranty before the troubles came to light. Most of the afflicted S1 Betas have gone to the crusher, but there are still cared-for S2s to be found.

SPECIFICATIONS
Years produced:	1972-1981 (194,914 in total)
Performance:	0-60mph: 10.5sec
	Top speed: 109mph
Power & torque:	110bhp/106lb ft
Engine:	Normally aspirated 1756cc four cylinder, petrol, carburettor, 8 valves
Drivetrain:	Front-engine FWD
Structure:	Monocoque
Transmission:	Five-speed manual
Weight:	1095kg

PRICE GUIDE
Launch price:	£1594
Excellent:	£2200
Good:	£1650
Average:	£700
Project:	£125

LANCIA
Stratos

It started life as a Bertone concept car in 1970, but the Lancia competition director Cesare Fiorio saw something in the squat little wedge that no one else did: a potential rally car. Fiorio knew that the Dino V6 engine from Ferrari was now within his grasp. A plan was hatched and, within three years, a production version was released (and 500 built), while the rally car was developed from it. From this inspired idea Lancia's domination of world rallying ensued. Road cars were hard to sell, and some languished in showrooms for up to five years. Beware imitations.

SPECIFICATIONS
Years produced:	1973-1975 (500 in total)
Performance:	0-60mph: 6.0sec
	Top speed: 143mph
Power & torque:	187bhp/166lb ft
Engine:	Normally aspirated 2419cc V6, petrol, carburettor, 12 valves
Drivetrain:	Mid-engine RWD
Structure:	Glassfibre body/tubular chassis
Transmission:	Five-speed manual
Weight:	980kg

PRICE GUIDE
Launch price:	£7000
Excellent:	£225,000
Good:	£100,000
Average:	£75,000
Project:	£50,000

LANCIA
Beta Coupé

Launched a year after the saloon it was based on, the Coupé used a 19cm shorter floorpan but still found room for adults in the rear seats. That shorter wheelbase combines well with a reduction of 90kg from the saloon's weight, creating a car that is even sharper to drive and suffers less from its lack of power-assisted steering. Engine options are the same rev-happy 1300-2000cc twin-cams as the saloon's, with Bosch fuel injection from 1981 and the addition of a supercharged version, badged Volumex, for 1983-84.

SPECIFICATIONS
Years produced:	1973-1984 (111,801 in total)
Performance:	0-60mph: 9.8sec
	Top speed: 114mph
Power & torque:	108bhp/114lb ft
Engine:	Normally aspirated 1585cc four cylinder, petrol, carburettor, 8 valves
Drivetrain:	Front-engine FWD
Structure:	Monocoque
Transmission:	Five-speed manual
Weight:	1000kg

PRICE GUIDE
Launch price:	£2153
Excellent:	£3000
Good:	£2400
Average:	£1000
Project:	£500

LANCIA
Beta Spider

In theory this is just a Beta Coupé with a clever roof, but this is Lancia so it's more complicated than that. The targa-top with folding rear window section and different window frames was designed by Pininfarina and built by Zagato, which was enough for the car to be badged Lancia Zagato in America. They also changed the tail-lights for units shared with the Bristol Beaufighter. Unusually it's a four-seater convertible. Only sold with 1600 or 2000 engines, though there's not much difference between them in performance.

SPECIFICATIONS
Years produced:	1975-1982 (9390 in total)
Performance:	0-60mph: 9.5sec
	Top speed: 115mph
Power & torque:	119bhp/129lb ft
Engine:	Normally aspirated 1995cc four cylinder, petrol, carburettor, 8 valves
Drivetrain:	Front-engine FWD
Structure:	Monocoque
Transmission:	Five-speed manual
Weight:	1048kg

PRICE GUIDE
Launch price:	£3128
Excellent:	£4000
Good:	£3200
Average:	£1600
Project:	£700

LANCIA
Montecarlo

This is actually a Beta in name only, parts shared with the rest of the range being limited to the engine block and internal door lock buttons. It's a mid-engined two-seater, originally envisaged as the Fiat X1/20 – then someone realised it could be priced higher with a Lancia badge. Only sold with a 2.0-litre engine in Europe, S1 versions had problems with locking front brakes, cured simply by removing the servo. 1980-on S2s were better in other ways too. With fine handling balance and expressive steering, these are under-rated driver's cars.

SPECIFICATIONS
Years produced:	1975-1984 (7595 in total)
Performance:	0-60mph: 8.6sec
	Top speed: 120mph
Power & torque:	118bhp/122lb ft
Engine:	Normally aspirated 1995cc four cylinder, petrol, carburettor, 8 valves
Drivetrain:	Mid-engine RWD
Structure:	Monocoque
Transmission:	Five-speed manual
Weight:	970kg

PRICE GUIDE (add £500 for Spider)
Launch price:	£5927
Excellent:	£8000
Good:	£6000
Average:	£3000
Project:	£1500

LANCIA
Gamma Berlina

If one car summed up the bitter-sweet nature of large Italian cars of the 1970s, it had to be the Gamma. Originally conceived as part of a joint venture with Citroën that never bore fruit, the Gamma ended up being developed by Lancia alone. The Gamma drove well, but its undoing was its new flat four – it leaked oil, overheated and snapped its cambelt for good measure. And then it rusted away. If you can see past the faults, there's a great car trying to escape, but there are so few survivors now that hardly any people will ever find out.

SPECIFICATIONS
Years produced:	1975-1984 (15,296 in total)
Performance:	0-60mph: N/A
	Top speed: 115mph
Power & torque:	115bhp/127lb ft
Engine:	Normally aspirated 1999cc flat four, petrol, carburettor, 8 valves
Drivetrain:	Front-engine FWD
Structure:	Monocoque
Transmission:	Five-speed manual
Weight:	1320kg

PRICE GUIDE
Launch price:	£7136
Excellent:	£3500
Good:	£1750
Average:	£900
Project:	£500

LANCIA
Beta HPE

The initials stand for High Performance Estate, created by fitting a Coupé front end and doors (with different window frames) to a saloon floorpan and finishing off with a hatchback rear section that pays homage to the Reliant Scimitar GTE. The result is a lot more stylish than it sounds, and you get the softer ride of the saloon with the lower seating position of the Coupé. In keeping with its superior intentions, only 1600 and 2000 engines were offered, with an optional 135bhp supercharged version of the 2.0-litre for the last year of production.

SPECIFICATIONS
Years produced:	1975-1985 (71,258 in total)
Performance:	0-60mph: 10.6sec
	Top speed: 116mph
Power & torque:	115bhp/130lb ft
Engine:	Normally aspirated 1995cc four cylinder, petrol, carburettor, 8 valves
Drivetrain:	Front-engine FWD
Structure:	Monocoque
Transmission:	Five-speed manual
Weight:	1060kg

PRICE GUIDE
Launch price:	£3688
Excellent:	£3500
Good:	£2500
Average:	£1250
Project:	£250

LANCIA
Gamma Coupé

The Gamma Berlina was perhaps the ultimate evolution of Pininfarina's BMC 1800 Aerodynamica concept car, first shown in 1966. The fastback saloon echoed the times perfectly yet failed to capture buyers' imaginations. However the Coupé – also styled by Pininfarina – emerged as one of the finest-looking cars of the 1970s. It might have been saddled with the same problems as the Berlina but owners have been more prepared to restore and repair than to throw away, and that's down purely to the way the Coupé looks. Buy by all means, but treat like a China doll.

SPECIFICATIONS
Years produced:	1976-1984 (6789 in total)
Performance:	0-60mph: 9.4sec
	Top speed: 120mph
Power & torque:	140bhp/154lb ft
Engine:	Normally aspirated 2484cc flat four, petrol, electronic fuel injection, 8 valves
Drivetrain:	Front-engine FWD
Structure:	Monocoque
Transmission:	Five-speed manual
Weight:	1290kg

PRICE GUIDE
Launch price:	£9186
Excellent:	£7500
Good:	£3500
Average:	£2000
Project:	£1000

LANCIA
Delta HF Turbo

In an attempt to join the 1980s hot hatch club, Lancia uprated its stylish Delta with a turbocharged version of the classic Fiat twin-cam under the bonnet. Performance was predictably rapid and, thanks to Martini stripes on all-white paintwork (for the early cars), it stood out from the crowd, too. Sales in the UK were never that rapid, thanks to the Escort XR3i and Golf GTI's dominance of the sector, but despite its obscurity the Delta HF Turbo earned itself a reputation for being fast and fun. Not the last word in finesse or refinement, but a hoot to drive.

SPECIFICATIONS

Years produced:	1984-1990
Performance:	0-60mph: 8.5sec
	Top speed: 126mph
Power & torque:	140bhp/141lb ft
Engine:	Turbocharged 1585cc four cylinder, petrol, electronic fuel injection, 8 valves
Drivetrain:	Front-engine FWD
Structure:	Monocoque
Transmission:	Five-speed manual
Weight:	1000kg

PRICE GUIDE

Launch price:	£8790
Excellent:	£3500
Good:	£2500
Average:	£1000
Project:	£350

LANCIA
Delta HF Integrale 8v

The first Integrale and, for many enthusiasts, the best. For this rally homologation special, a 2.0-litre version of the venerable Fiat twin-cam had a full-pressure turbo to deliver 185bhp. Combine this with permanent four-wheel drive and wide tyres and the ensuing super-hot hatch was fast, agile and grippy, with none of the torque steer than afflicted lesser rivals. Although part of the UK Lancia range, the Integrale was never converted to right-hand drive, so if you come across a right-hooker check to see which company carried out the conversion.

SPECIFICATIONS

Years produced:	1987-1989
Performance:	0-60mph: 6.2sec
	Top speed: 128mph
Power & torque:	185bhp/224lb ft
Engine:	Turbocharged 1995cc four cylinder, petrol, electronic fuel injection, 8 valves
Drivetrain:	Front-engine AWD
Structure:	Monocoque
Transmission:	Five-speed manual
Weight:	1267kg

PRICE GUIDE

Launch price:	£13,980
Excellent:	£10,000
Good:	£6000
Average:	£3000
Project:	£1500

LANCIA
Delta HF Integrale 16V

To keep the Integrale at the top of the heap, Lancia installed the 16-valve version of its famous twin-cam under an increasingly lumpy bonnet. With better breathing, power – in the road version – was upped to 197bhp, making the Integrale a genuinely quick car. Peakier power delivery makes the 16V more challenging to drive, but additional performance was welcome in an era of increasingly rapid GTis. Again, all cars were officially LHD, although many were done by UK dealers as official conversions, with a few retro-conversions later.

SPECIFICATIONS

Years produced:	1987-1989
Performance:	0-60mph: 5.5sec
	Top speed: 137mph
Power & torque:	197bhp/224lb ft
Engine:	Turbocharged 1995cc four cylinder, petrol, fuel injection, 16 valves
Drivetrain:	Front-engine AWD
Structure:	Monocoque
Transmission:	Five-speed manual
Weight:	1291kg

PRICE GUIDE

Launch price:	£13,980
Excellent:	£11,500
Good:	£8750
Average:	£5000
Project:	£2250

LANCIA
Thema

The Thema was the first of the joint Fiat/Alfa/Saab Type 4 cars to hit the market. The body was Giugiaro-generic, but the plush Alcantara-trimmed interior was very inviting. Pick of the range from launch was the 2.0-litre turbo, initially offered in 8-valve form. The combination of speed and serenity was an appealing one, even if the 165bhp engine resulted in ample torque steer in the wrong circumstances. Later upgraded with 16-valve engines, and facelifts improved the car little by little. Good ones can still be had for little money.

SPECIFICATIONS (ie Turbo)

Years produced:	1984-1994
Performance:	0-60mph: 7.2sec
	Top speed: 135mph
Power & torque:	165bhp/210lb ft
Engine:	Turbocharged 1995cc four cylinder, petrol, electronic fuel injection, 8 valves
Drivetrain:	Front-engine FWD
Structure:	Monocoque
Transmission:	Five-speed manual
Weight:	1150kg

PRICE GUIDE

Launch price:	£11,000
Excellent:	£2500
Good:	£1500
Average:	£750
Project:	£450

LANCIA
Thema 8.32

The Ferrari V8 that was shoehorned into Lancia's Type Four chassis was not actually assembled by Ferrari. The job of screwing it together was outsourced to Ducati engineers, and it featured a 90° crank in place of the 308's flat-planer. The epic soundtrack and moderate performance were not enough to sell it, and UK sales were dire, with just nine 8.32s officially sold. It did slightly better in Europe, but the killer for it was the Thema 16V Turbo, which was about as quick and much cheaper. Didn't have the 8.32's hand-stitched hide trim, mind.

SPECIFICATIONS

Years produced:	1988-1990 (3971 in total)
Performance:	0-60mph: 6.8sec
	Top speed: 149mph
Power & torque:	215bhp/210lb ft
Engine:	Normally aspirated 2927cc V8, petrol, electronic fuel injection, 32 valves
Drivetrain:	Front-engine FWD
Structure:	Monocoque
Transmission:	Five-speed manual
Weight:	1400kg

PRICE GUIDE

Launch price:	£40,095
Excellent:	£12,000
Good:	£7250
Average:	£3750
Project:	£1500

LAND ROVER

INITIALLY, LAND ROVER referred just to a vehicle; the original Rover off-roader launched in 1948. As the range expanded, so Land Rover became a marque in its own right, with vehicles such as the Range Rover, Defender, Freelander and Discovery sheltering under the auspices of its badge. Historically an inseparable part of Rover, the marque was sold to Ford in 2000 when owner BMW broke up the company, and it became closely connected with Jaguar during its Blue Oval days. Ford's financial troubles forced it to sell Jaguar Land Rover to Indian conglomerate Tata; with the acquisition of Land Rover came the rights to the parent Rover name as well. A revival is unlikely…

LAND ROVER
Series I

In the aftermath of World War Two, Rover's chief engineer Maurice Wilks owned a 'demobbed' Jeep and was impressed with its abilities. It wore out and, as there was no British replacement on the market, he decided to build his own. That vehicle appeared as the Land Rover in 1948, and proved so popular that demand massively outstripped supply. It went on to become an enduring success that helped keep the rest of Rover afloat during the lean years of the 1950s. Now known as the S1, these early cars are enduring classics.

SPECIFICATIONS

Years produced:	1948-1957
Performance:	0-60mph: N/A
	Top speed: 55mph
Power & torque:	50bhp/N/A
Engine:	Normally aspirated 1595cc four cylinder, petrol, carburettor, 8 valves
Drivetrain:	Front-engine AWD
Structure:	Separate chassis
Transmission:	Four-speed manual/high & low ratios
Weight:	1177kg

PRICE GUIDE

Launch price:	£450
Excellent:	£10,000
Good:	£5500
Average:	£2850
Project:	£1850

LAND ROVER
SII/SIIA

A decade after the Land Rover's launch, when it was still hugely popular, the Series II appeared. Easily identifiable by its revised styling and powered by a new 2.25-litre petrol engine, this design stayed in production – little changed – until 1990. The Series IIA that followed 18 months later was improved to include a 2.6-litre petrol engine in the LWB version, and a new 2.25-litre diesel, significantly expanding the car's appeal in export markets. Considered the ultimate DIY car, Land Rovers are revered for the ease with which you can work on them.

SPECIFICATIONS

Years produced:	1958-1971
Performance:	0-60mph: 36.1sec
	Top speed: 65mph
Power & torque:	77bhp/N/A
Engine:	Normally aspirated 2286cc four cylinder, petrol, carburettor, 8 valves
Drivetrain:	Front-engine AWD
Structure:	Separate chassis
Transmission:	Four-speed manual/high & low ratios
Weight:	1092kg

PRICE GUIDE

Launch price:	£640
Excellent:	£4250
Good:	£3000
Average:	£1400
Project:	£500

LAND ROVER
S III

Series III improvements are easy to spot thanks to the repositioned headlights (late SIIAs had them, too) and plastic radiator grille. The updated – more safety-conscious – interior and all-synchromesh gearbox acknowledged that the opposition was catching up, and the option of overdrive catered for those who needed their Land Rovers for serious on-road work. It was during Series III production that the Rover V8 engine was added to the range, initially in low-compression form to allow it to run on whatever grade of fuel its owner threw at it.

SPECIFICATIONS

Years produced:	1971-1985
Performance:	0-60mph: 29.1sec
	Top speed: 68mph
Power & torque:	70bhp/119lb ft
Engine:	Normally aspirated 2286cc four cylinder, petrol, carburettor, 8 valves
Drivetrain:	Front-engine AWD
Structure:	Separate chassis
Transmission:	Four-speed manual/high & low ratios
Weight:	1380kg

PRICE GUIDE

Launch price:	£1002
Excellent:	£4000
Good:	£3000
Average:	£1300
Project:	£400

RANGE ROVER
Classic

Instigator of the SUV and a classless conveyance, the Range Rover introduced the joys of off-roading to a whole new clienetele. Powered by Rover's ex-Buick V8 and using chassis technology similar to the Land Rover's, its off-road ability was beyond reproach, while the hose-clean interior proved just the ticket for those with an active lifestyle. Styling was so lean that the Range Rover was at home in the politest places. It became ever-more luxurious and its appeal remained undimmed during a 25-year run. Exceptional cars can name ther price.

SPECIFICATIONS

Years produced:	1970-1995
Performance:	14.2sec
	Top speed: 99mph
Power & torque:	135bhp/185lb ft
Engine:	Normally aspirated 3528cc V8, petrol, carburettor, 16 valves
Drivetrain:	Front-engine AWD
Structure:	Separate chassis
Transmission:	Four-speed manual/three-speed auto
Weight:	1760kg

PRICE GUIDE

Launch price:	£1998
Excellent:	£15,000
Good:	£3000
Average:	£1000
Project:	£500

LEA-FRANCIS

THIS BRITISH company has had a chequered existence. Its first incarnation as a car firm was in 1904 but, after a few years, it reverted to making motorcycles. Car production restarted in 1920, focusing on sports models, but the

company folded in 1937. A reborn entity bounded back but its products were never built in great numbers and, by 1954, it was all over once more for Lea-Francis. Or so it seemed. Then the controversially-styled Lynx was

shown at the 1960 British Motor Show to no interest whatsoever. Since then, the occasional Lea-Francis car has appeared, as the marque and its assets are now owned by arch-enthusiast Barrie Price.

LEA-FRANCIS
14 Saloon

As one of the original British motor industry players, the pre-war years had been good for Lea-Francis. Its competition cars had proved themselves and earned an enviable reputation with enthusiasts. After the war, the firm concentrated on saloon car production, initially with its 14hp saloon. The 14 sat very much at the upper end of the market and found fewer buyers than anticipated, but the addition of a 2.5-litre engine in 1949 widened appeal. Lea-Francis continued with this line until 1953, then abandoned car production to concentrate on other activities.

SPECIFICATIONS
Years produced: 1946-1954 (3137 in total)
Performance: 0-60mph: N/A
Top speed: 70mph
Power & torque: 55bhp/N/A
Engine: Normally aspirated 1469cc four cylinder, petrol, carburettor, 8 valves
Drivetrain: Front-engine RWD
Structure: Separate chassis
Transmission: Four-speed manual
Weight: 1270kg

PRICE GUIDE
Launch price: £951
Excellent: £8750
Good: £7250
Average: £3750
Project: £1650

LEA-FRANCIS
14hp/2.5-litre Sports

A classic English sports car powered by the saloon's 1.8-litre engine, and closely following the established template that proved so popular in export markets. The twin-cam engine was intriguing because it aped Riley's pre-war design, and delivered enough power for a top speed of 85mph. Later models gained independent front suspension and proved to be excellent-handling cars, while the 2.5-litre Sports that followed in 1950 added extra power into the mix, becoming a genuine 100mph four-seater in the process.

SPECIFICATIONS
Years produced: 1947-1953 (186 in total)
Performance: 0-60mph: 19.2sec
Top speed: 87mph
Power & torque: 87bhp/N/A
Engine: Normally aspirated 1767cc four cylinder, petrol, carburettor, 8 valves
Drivetrain: Front-engine RWD
Structure: Separate chassis
Transmission: Four-speed manual
Weight: 1016kg

PRICE GUIDE
Launch price: £1266
Excellent: £18,250
Good: £15,000
Average: £11,000
Project: £6000

LOTUS

COLIN CHAPMAN began building competition specials in 1948 and eventually expanded into selling kits to the public, forming Lotus Engineering in 1952. But it was the Seven of 1957 that really brought the small-scale manufacturer to

the attention of the masses, along with the good-looking glassfibre Elite. The Elan (1960-1973) became a benchmark for how a sports car should handle and the Esprit (1976-2004) had supercar looks and (eventually) performance.

Following Chapman's death in 1982, GM owned the marque from 1986 to 1993, Italian Romano Artioli (who also purchased Bugatti) until 1996, and it's been owned by Malaysian car-maker Proton since then.

LOTUS
Six

Intended as a street-legal weekend racer, the predecessor to the legendary Seven uses a lightweight spaceframe clothed in alloy panels (often left bare) and fitted with Ford brakes and rear axle. All were sold in kit form, so specification can vary widely from car to car. Most commonly used engines were Ford, either in sidevalve 1172cc or OHV 1500 form, though some are known to have been fitted with 1250cc MG units. In all cases the lack of weight means they provide a lot more fun and performance than you might expect.

SPECIFICATIONS
Years produced: 1953-1956 (100 in total)
Performance: 0-60mph: N/A
Top speed: 93mph
Power & torque: 36bhp/N/A
Engine: Normally aspirated 1172cc four cylinder, petrol, carburettor, 8 valves
Drivetrain: Front-engine RWD
Structure: Tub and spaceframe
Transmission: Three-speed manual
Weight: N/A (very light)

PRICE GUIDE
Launch price: £185
Excellent: £24,000
Good: £18,500
Average: £14,500
Project: £9000

LOTUS
Seven S1/S2

A legend that lives on today. Refinements over the VI it's based on include wishbone front suspension and hydraulic brakes, and that's just for starters. S1s initially sold with Ford's sidevalve engine, with later S1s and S2s offered with the 948cc BMC A-series and its four-speed 'box; from 1961 there was also the option of the 997cc Anglia engines. Don't be surprised by later upgrades though. S2s are distinguished by their glassfibre nosecones, but they also have a less complex spaceframe and revised rear axle location. Short of space for those of large frame or feet.

SPECIFICATIONS

Years produced:	1957-1968 (242/1350 in total)
Performance:	0-60mph: 17.8sec
	Top speed: 76mph
Power & torque:	40bhp/58lb ft
Engine:	Normally aspirated 1172cc four cylinder, petrol, carburettor, 8 valves
Drivetrain:	Front-engine RWD
Structure:	Tub and spaceframe
Transmission:	Three-speed manual
Weight:	457kg

PRICE GUIDE

Launch price:	£1036
Excellent:	£22,500
Good:	£17,000
Average:	£12,000
Project:	£7500

LOTUS
Super Seven

Really pushing the 'race car for the road' theme, the Super Sevens came with longer glassfibre front wings and Cosworth-tuned Ford engines of 1340, 1500 or 1600cc capacity and phenomenal performance. To rein this back, those with the larger engines came with the welcome addition of disc brakes. Many were still sold as kits, and they've always appealed to those of a tinkering nature, so expect the unexpected as far as specification goes. A dozen or so 'Super Sevens' were fitted with Lotus twin-cam engines, but only genuine ones are worth the extra these command.

SPECIFICATIONS

Years produced:	1957-1968 (500+ in total)
Performance:	0-60mph: 9.0sec
	Top speed: 102mph
Power & torque:	95bhp/103lb ft
Engine:	Normally aspirated 1498cc four cylinder, petrol, carburettor, 8 valves
Drivetrain:	Front-engine RWD
Structure:	Tub and spaceframe
Transmission:	Four-speed manual
Weight:	435kg

PRICE GUIDE

Launch price:	£1250
Excellent:	£22,500
Good:	£18,000
Average:	£13,000
Project:	£8000

LOTUS
Elite

The undoubted star of the 1957 Earl's Court Motor Show, but Lotus kept buyers waiting until the summer of 1959 to enjoy this technical marvel. Use of a chassis-less glassfibre monocoque and aluminium Coventry-Climax 1200cc 71bhp engine resulted in the incredibly light weight that made this car perform and handle so well. 1960 brought a Series II model with improved rear suspension and trim, plus the SE with its close-ratio ZF gearbox and optional breathing package for an extra 10bhp. Utterly fabulous, but noisy inside, and quite a squeeze for six-footers.

SPECIFICATIONS

Years produced:	1958-1963 (998 in total)
Performance:	0-60mph: 11.4sec
	Top speed: 112mph
Power & torque:	71bhp/77lb ft
Engine:	Normally aspirated 1216cc four cylinder, petrol, carburettor, 8 valves
Drivetrain:	Front-engine RWD
Structure:	Glassfibre monocoque
Transmission:	Four-speed manual
Weight:	660kg

PRICE GUIDE

Launch price:	£1951
Excellent:	£50,000
Good:	£35,000
Average:	£20,500
Project:	£11,000

LOTUS
Elan DHC

The lightweight sports car against whose handling all others would be measured for decades. Independent suspension on a backbone chassis was the stuff of genius, and makes the indifferent fit and finish of the glassfibre bodies almost irrelevant. Gradually improved through four series, each of which outsold the last: S2 gained larger front brake calipers; S3 (from 1966) has frames for the windows, centre-lock alloy wheels and a higher final drive ratio; S4 got a bonnet bulge to cover its twin Stromberg carbs, but reverted to Webers in late 1969. SE means 115bhp and close-ratio gearbox.

SPECIFICATIONS

Years produced:	1962-1971 (12,200 in total)
Performance:	0-60mph: 8.0sec
	Top speed: 110mph
Power & torque:	100bhp/102lb ft
Engine:	Normally aspirated 1499cc four cylinder, petrol, carburettor, 8 valves
Drivetrain:	Front-engine RWD
Structure:	Glassfibre body/backbone chassis
Transmission:	Four-speed manual
Weight:	585kg

PRICE GUIDE

Launch price:	£1499
Excellent:	£22,500
Good:	£17,500
Average:	£10,500
Project:	£5500

LOTUS
Elan S3/S4 Coupé

Hardtop version of the Elan was used to introduce the S3, and arrived the year before its soft-top brother. In line with Lotus's intention to move upmarket and justify its 'quality' prices, fit and finish was improved over the earlier Elans, and the Coupé came with a smarter dashboard and frames for the door windows to reduce wind noise. The windows themselves were now electrically operated. SE model was offered from July 1966 with 115bhp engine, standard servo brakes, a close-ratio gearbox, plus a slightly taller rear axle ratio to make things a little quieter at high speeds.

SPECIFICATIONS

Years produced:	1965-1971 (5650 in total)
Performance:	0-60mph: 8.7sec
	Top speed: 114mph
Power & torque:	105bhp/108lb ft
Engine:	Normally aspirated 1558cc four cylinder, petrol, carburettor, 8 valves
Drivetrain:	Front-engine RWD
Structure:	Glassfibre body/backbone chassis
Transmission:	Four-speed manual
Weight:	688kg

PRICE GUIDE

Launch price:	£1312
Excellent:	£18,000
Good:	£14,000
Average:	£12,000
Project:	£4500

LOTUS
Europa S1/S2

Colin Chapman's first mid-engined road car was aimed squarely at the glamorous European market, where Italians were making inroads with the layout. Based around Renault 16 running gear, all S1s went for export. They also had their glassfibre body bonded to the steel chassis, making repairs a nightmare. Europa S2s were sold in the UK from 1969, with bodies bolted to the chassis and electric windows. All but US exports came with 1470cc Renault engines, though many 1565cc units have since been transplanted from dead Renaults.

SPECIFICATIONS
Years produced:	1967-1971
Performance:	0-60mph: 9.3sec
	Top speed: 117mph
Power & torque:	78bhp/76lb ft
Engine:	Normally aspirated 1470cc four cylinder, petrol, carburettor, 8 valves
Drivetrain:	Mid-engine RWD
Structure:	Glassfibre body/backbone chassis
Transmission:	Four-speed manual
Weight:	706kg

PRICE GUIDE
Launch price:	£1996
Excellent:	£9000
Good:	£7500
Average:	£4000
Project:	£1500

LOTUS
Seven S3

Sold alongside the Super Seven, the S3 came with Ford engines in a saner state of tune, though all sizes from 1300-1600cc were available. Tuning options came from Holbay, not Cosworth for these. This is the car that was revived officially by Caterham (and unofficially by everyone else), but the 350 or so originals command a decent premium for all that heritage. Still largely sold as kits originally, which means fit and finish has always been variable, and many examples are likely to have been rebuilt several times during their life. Hard to value, but the fun factor is always the same.

SPECIFICATIONS
Years produced:	1968-1970 (1413 in total)
Performance:	0-60mph: 7.7sec
	Top speed: 99mph
Power & torque:	84bhp/96lb ft
Engine:	Normally aspirated 1598cc four cylinder, petrol, carburettor, 8 valves
Drivetrain:	Front-engine RWD
Structure:	Tub and spaceframe
Transmission:	Four-speed manual
Weight:	549kg

PRICE GUIDE
Launch price:	£775
Excellent:	£19,000
Good:	£16,000
Average:	£11,000
Project:	£7000

LOTUS
Elan Plus 2

Taking one step further away from the racetrack, Lotus widened its range to include something for buyers with young families. By stretching the Elan's chassis by a foot and widening the track, child-sized rear seats could be accommodated. This was also the first Lotus not to be sold in kit form, which at least evens out build quality. The 118bhp engine tune helps with the extra weight, and power was raised to 126bhp from 1970 for the Plus 2S/130, which is identifiable by its silver metalflake roof. Better quality trim is a feature, and from 1972 the 130-5 comes with a five-speed gearbox.

SPECIFICATIONS
Years produced:	1969-1974 (3300 in total)
Performance:	0-60mph: 8.2sec
	Top speed: 123mph
Power & torque:	118bhp/112lb ft
Engine:	Normally aspirated 1558cc four cylinder, petrol, carburettor, 8 valves
Drivetrain:	Front-engine RWD
Structure:	Glassfibre body/backbone chassis
Transmission:	Four-speed manual
Weight:	854kg

PRICE GUIDE
Launch price:	£1923
Excellent:	£17,500
Good:	£9000
Average:	£6000
Project:	£2000

LOTUS
Seven S4

The lower prices today tell you that Lotus lost the plot with the S4. In some ways it's a better car, with decent legroom at last, improved front and rear suspension and all-glassfibre bodywork over a new steel chassis. Unfortunately that all added an extra couple of hundred pounds to the weight, slightly blunting the scorching performance and handling that Sevens are all about. And that new bodywork falls somewhere between archaic special and racing beach buggy. It offers a way into Seven ownership, but you can see why Caterham went back to the S3 when it took over manufacture.

SPECIFICATIONS
Years produced:	1970-1973 (887 in total)
Performance:	0-60mph: 8.7sec
	Top speed: 116mph
Power & torque:	115bhp/108lb ft
Engine:	Normally aspirated 1598cc four cylinder, petrol, carburettor, 8 valves
Drivetrain:	Front-engine RWD
Structure:	Tub and spaceframe
Transmission:	Four-speed manual
Weight:	579kg

PRICE GUIDE
Launch price:	£1245
Excellent:	£11,500
Good:	£9000
Average:	£6500
Project:	£2500

LOTUS
Elan Sprint

Introduced to boost flagging sales, the Sprint justified its name thanks to a substantial boost in the engine department. A big-valve head with high-lift cams and a raised compression ratio raised output to 126bhp and the drivetrain was suitably toughened and braced to cope. Both coupé and roadster versions were built, with gold-painted bumpers and two-tone paint to set them apart from other Elans – single-tone paint was available as an extra-cost option. With prices approaching those of E-type Jags, only around 1000 were sold, some of the last with five-speed gearboxes.

SPECIFICATIONS
Years produced:	1971-1973
Performance:	0-60mph: 6.7sec
	Top speed: 121mph
Power & torque:	126bhp/113lb ft
Engine:	Normally aspirated 1558cc four cylinder, petrol, carburettor, 8 valves
Drivetrain:	Front-engine RWD
Structure:	Glassfibre body/backbone chassis
Transmission:	Four-speed manual
Weight:	721kg

PRICE GUIDE
Launch price:	£1706
Excellent:	£32,500
Good:	£23,500
Average:	£14,000
Project:	£7000

LOTUS
Europa Twin Cam/Special

Accusations that the Europa was underpowered were dealt with by the simple expedient of fitting the Lotus twin-cam unit, initially in 105bhp form, but with 126bhp in the Special in 1972. Most of these celebrated Lotus's grand prix success by being painted John Player Special colours. Both of these Europas still used the Renault 16 gearbox (with an improved gear linkage), though the Specials could also be had with a five-speed version from the 17TS. Visually, these twin-cam models differed from the S1/S2 by having cut-down rear 'buttresses' to improve visibility.

SPECIFICATIONS
Years produced:	1971-1975 (1580 in total)
Performance:	0-60mph: 7.7sec
	Top speed: 109mph
Power & torque:	105bhp/108lb ft
Engine:	Normally aspirated 1558cc four cylinder, petrol, carburettor, 8 valves
Drivetrain:	Front-engine RWD
Structure:	Glassfibre body/backbone chassis
Transmission:	Four-speed manual
Weight:	737kg

PRICE GUIDE
Launch price:	£1996
Excellent:	£22,500
Good:	£12,000
Average:	£8500
Project:	£3000

LOTUS
Elite

In an effort to shed its kit-car image, Lotus took a giant leap upmarket in 1974 with the Elite – a four-seater coupé with an opening glass tailgate. In concept the Elite owed much to the Reliant Scimtar GTE, even if it was less obviously a shooting brake. The all-new 2.0-litre Lotus twin-cam Type 921 first appeared in the Jensen-Healey but, by the time Lotus started selling it in its own cars, most of the teething problems had been sorted. Expanded to 2.2 litres from 1980, with the same peak power output but more torque. A Getrag five-speed gearbox was also fitted from this point.

SPECIFICATIONS
Years produced:	1974-1983 (2398 in total)
Performance:	0-60mph: 7.8sec
	Top speed: 124mph
Power & torque:	160bhp/140lb ft
Engine:	Normally aspirated 1973cc four cylinder, petrol, carburettor, 16 valves
Drivetrain:	Front-engine RWD
Structure:	Glassfibre body/backbone chassis
Transmission:	Five-speed manual
Weight:	1107kg

PRICE GUIDE
Launch price:	£5445
Excellent:	£5500
Good:	£4000
Average:	£3000
Project:	£750

LOTUS
Éclat

As the American market didn't take to the Elite's styling, it was joined the following year by the Type 76 Éclat, pretty much the same car but with the rear panels reshaped into a more familiar fastback form, also losing about 45kg in weight in the process. The Oliver Winterbottom-penned and exceptionally wedgy Éclat had more mainstream appeal even if it was less practical than the Esprit, although that could have been as much about the lower list price. Model range numbered 521, 522 and 523, with the higher the number, the higher the equipment level.

SPECIFICATIONS
Years produced:	1974-1983 (1299 in total)
Performance:	0-60mph: 7.8sec
	Top speed: 124mph
Power & torque:	160bhp/140lb ft
Engine:	Normally aspirated 1973cc four cylinder, petrol, carburettor, 16 valves
Drivetrain:	Front-engine RWD
Structure:	Glassfibre body/backbone chassis
Transmission:	Five-speed manual
Weight:	1107kg

PRICE GUIDE
Launch price:	£4995
Excellent:	£5000
Good:	£3500
Average:	£2500
Project:	£500

LOTUS
Esprit S1

Lotus turned to Giugiaro to design a flagship that gained instant pin-up status, and an appearance as a Bond car/submarine in *The Spy Who Loved Me*. Still using the established Elan system of a glassfibre body over a backbone chassis, the Esprit had its 2.0-litre twin-cam engine mid-mounted. That's a remarkably high output for an engine of such modest capacity, and placed its performance on the coat-tails of the junior supercar league. Handling was flat, grippy and nervous near the limit, but set new standards for the opposition to aim for. Reliability was – and is – a problem.

SPECIFICATIONS
Years produced:	1976-1977 (718 in total)
Performance:	0-60mph: 8.4sec
	Top speed: 135mph
Power & torque:	160bhp/140lb ft
Engine:	Normally aspirated 1973cc four cylinder, petrol, carburettor, 16 valves
Drivetrain:	Mid-engine RWD
Structure:	Glassfibre body/backbone chassis
Transmission:	Five-speed manual
Weight:	1006kg

PRICE GUIDE
Launch price:	£7883
Excellent:	£16,000
Good:	£13,000
Average:	£9000
Project:	£3500

LOTUS
Esprit S2/S2.2

The original Esprit was a standard-bearer, but it wasn't without flaws. Cooling was marginal and the interior design lacked cohesion. In an attempt to put those faults right, Lotus quickly lauched the S2. It was marked out by minor modifications that included 'ears' behind the rear side windows to improve engine airflow, Speedline alloys and Rover SD1 taillights (to replace the Fiat X1/9 originals). For the final year of production, the S2 was fitted with the 2.2-litre engine, increasing performance and driveability at no cost in fuel consumption.

SPECIFICATIONS
Years produced:	1977-1981 (1060 in total)
Performance:	0-60mph: 8.4sec
	Top speed: 135mph
Power & torque:	160bhp/140lb ft
Engine:	Normally aspirated 1973cc four cylinder, petrol, carburettor, 16 valves
Drivetrain:	Mid-engine RWD
Structure:	Separate chassis
Transmission:	Five-speed manual
Weight:	1026kg

PRICE GUIDE
Launch price:	£8500
Excellent:	£14,000
Good:	£11,000
Average:	£8000
Project:	£3000

LOTUS
Turbo Esprit

Lotus was now touching supercar territory, with a car that beat the psychological milestones of 150mph and 0-60mph in under six seconds. With almost peerless handling they could now be compared with Porsches and Ferraris. The extra 50bhp over the normal 2.2-litre Esprit comes from a Garrett T3 turbocharger, though the whole of the engine was re-engineered to cope. The first 104 were in Essex Petroleum livery. In 1985 the suspension was revised to use more Toyota and fewer Triumph parts. Shortlived HC version for 1987 gets extra 5bhp and 20lb ft of torque.

SPECIFICATIONS
Years produced:	1980-1987 (1658 in total)
Performance:	0-60mph: 5.6sec
	Top speed: 141mph
Power & torque:	215bhp/220lb ft
Engine:	Turbocharged 2174cc four cylinder, petrol, carburettor, 16 valves
Drivetrain:	Mid-engine RWD
Structure:	Glassfibre body/backbone chassis
Transmission:	Five-speed manual
Weight:	1148kg

PRICE GUIDE
Launch price:	£25,980
Excellent:	£14,500
Good:	£12,000
Average:	£8000
Project:	£3000

LOTUS
Esprit S3

Wearing most of the body, chassis and interior revisions introduced for the Turbo model the year before, the Esprit S3 also signalled a major leap forward in quality and reliability. There's a lot more sound insulation too, allegedly reducing noise levels inside by 50%. Despite the larger bumpers and air scoops, the design stays true to Giugiaro's concept. The rear wheels and tyres are larger, and lower-profile rubber is used to further sharpen the Esprit's superb handling and grip. Despite now being cheaper, experts say these are a much better bet than the S1 and S2.

SPECIFICATIONS
Years produced:	1981-1987 (767 in total)
Performance:	0-60mph: 6.5sec
	Top speed: 135mph
Power & torque:	160bhp/160lb ft
Engine:	Normally aspirated 2174cc four cylinder, petrol, carburettor, 16 valves
Drivetrain:	Mid-engine RWD
Structure:	Glassfibre body/backbone chassis
Transmission:	Five-speed manual
Weight:	1020kg

PRICE GUIDE
Launch price:	£13,461
Excellent:	£10,500
Good:	£9000
Average:	£5500
Project:	£2000

LOTUS
Excel

Thoroughly revised version of the Éclat, sold at first as the Éclat Excel to avoid the expense of putting the new car through Type Approval. Most body changes are on the rear half of the car, but the big stuff is underneath the skin with Toyota Supra five-speed transmission and brakes, plus broader, lower rear wishbones. The chassis was galvanised, too. The body was revised again in 1984 with Audi Quattro-style blisters, and from 1986 the SE version offered 180bhp, up 20bhp from the standard car. The same year the SA was launched with a ZF four-speed automatic gearbox.

SPECIFICATIONS
Years produced:	1982-1992 (2074 in total)
Performance:	0-60mph: 7.4sec
	Top speed: 128mph
Power & torque:	160bhp/160lb ft
Engine:	Normally aspirated 2174cc four cylinder, petrol, carburettor, 16 valves
Drivetrain:	Front-engine RWD
Structure:	Glassfibre body/backbone chassis
Transmission:	Five-speed manual
Weight:	1135kg

PRICE GUIDE
Launch price:	£13,787
Excellent:	£8500
Good:	£5500
Average:	£2750
Project:	£1250

LOTUS
Esprit Turbo (X180)

A subtle redesign by Peter Stevens knocked some of the sharp edges off Giugiaro's original styling, and the opportunity was also used to create more interior space. Mechanically, both normally-aspirated and Turbo versions carried on as before, with the exception of a little extra power in the lesser car to pull more weight. The Citroën SM transmission was replaced with Renault GTA units, along with outboard rear brakes. For spotters, the Turbo has flush glass covering the space between the rear buttresses, while there's none on the standard car.

SPECIFICATIONS
Years produced:	1987-1992 (3120 in total)
Performance:	0-60mph: 5.4sec
	Top speed: 150mph
Power & torque:	215bhp/220lb ft
Engine:	Turbocharged 2174cc four cylinder, petrol, fuel injection, 16 valves
Drivetrain:	Mid-engine RWD
Structure:	Glassfibre body/backbone chassis
Transmission:	Five-speed manual
Weight:	1270kg

PRICE GUIDE
Launch price:	£28,900
Excellent:	£13,250
Good:	£11,000
Average:	£8500
Project:	£5000

LOTUS
Esprit Turbo SE

For those who felt the Esprit Turbo wasn't quick enough already, the SE version breezed in during 1989. A water-to-air intercooler, which Lotus called the 'chargecooler', was introduced as part of the Lotus Type 910S engine upgrade, increasing power to 264bhp. External modifications for the SE model included a more prominent bodykit and larger rear spoiler. But the biggest news for 1989 was the additional performance, which was clearly now in the supercar league – the SE was the first production Lotus to get to 60mph in under five seconds.

SPECIFICATIONS
Years produced:	1989-1992
Performance:	0-60mph: 4.7sec
	Top speed: 167mph
Power & torque:	264bhp/260lb ft
Engine:	Turbocharged 2174cc four cylinder, petrol, fuel injection, 16 valves
Drivetrain:	Mid-engine RWD
Structure:	Glassfibre body/backbone chassis
Transmission:	Five-speed manual
Weight:	1329kg

PRICE GUIDE
Launch price:	£33,500
Excellent:	£14,250
Good:	£12,000
Average:	£9500
Project:	£5000

LOTUS
Elan M100

Conclusive proof that sports cars can be front-wheel drive, as Lotus once again leads the pack in handling technology. Almost all the first batch were turbocharged SE versions, though some 130bhp non-turbo models were sold; all use a long-lived Isuzu 1600 engine that Lotus had helped to design. Sadly, Lotus was losing money on every one of the 3855 Elans sold, so the plug was pulled after two years. When Bugatti bought Lotus in 1994 another run of 800 was made, subtly improved and using up spare engine stock. These were badged S2 and are more sought after today.

SPECIFICATIONS

Years produced:	1989-1994 (4655 in total)
Performance:	0-60mph: 6.5sec
	Top speed: 136mph
Power & torque:	165bhp/148lb ft
Engine:	Turbocharged 1588cc four cylinder, petrol, fuel injection, 16 valves
Drivetrain:	Front-engine FWD
Structure:	Monocoque with plastic panels
Transmission:	Five-speed manual
Weight:	1085kg

PRICE GUIDE

Launch price:	£19,850
Excellent:	£9000
Good:	£7000
Average:	£4000
Project:	£1000

MARCOS

THE MARCOS NAME is a contraction of the surnames of founders Jem Marsh and Frank Costin. In 1959, they came up with the novel idea of building a monocoque sports car out of plywood in Luton. Aesthetically it was a disaster, but it proved very capable in racing. In 1964 came a new and much more attractive shape, the 1800, ultimately fitted with a variety of Ford, Volvo and Triumph engines. Other models were the diminutive Mini-Marcos – using Mini components – and the Mantis, with very idiosyncratic slabby styling. Marcos went bust in 1971, but returned in 1981 to build limited numbers of cars based on its old designs. It's still going today... just about.

MARCOS
1800 GT/1500/1600

The 1800 GT was introduced to move Marcos into the MGB market, despite being available in kit form. Powered by a Volvo engine (an unusual step for a British specialist at the time) and featuring an advanced suspension layout, it was a quick and fine-handling alternative. In an attempt to widen the appeal of the GT, Ford engines replaced the expensive Volvo one, while the sophisticated semi-trailing arm/de Dion rear suspension layout of the 1800 was thrown out in favour of a simpler live axle. Good specialist back-up make it a sensible and charismatic DIY sports car.

SPECIFICATIONS (1800GT)

Years produced:	1964-1968 (99/82/192 in total)
Performance:	0-60mph: 9.1sec
	Top speed: 115mph
Power & torque:	114bhp/110lb ft
Engine:	Normally aspirated 1798cc four cylinder, petrol, carburettor, 8 valves
Drivetrain:	Front-engine RWD
Structure:	Glassfibre body/separate chassis
Transmission:	Four-speed manual with overdrive
Weight:	767kg

PRICE GUIDE (GT)

	PRICE GUIDE (GT)	1500/1600
Launch price:	£1645	£1606
Excellent:	£13,000	£8000
Good:	£10,000	£6750
Average:	£4000	£3500
Project:	£2000	£2000

MARCOS
Mini-Marcos

A cottage industry of specialists had emerged making the humble BMC Mini do things its creator Alec Issignonis had never imagined. The Mini-Marcos was one such car, combining a lightweight low-drag glassfibre monocoque with the front-wheel-drive car's drivetrain and suspension. It proved a successful combination, not only dynamically but commercially too – and when Marcos folded in 1971, the Mini-Marcos continued in various guises, and arguably inspired the Midas of the 1980s. The original has plenty of appeal, and good examples fetch strong money.

SPECIFICATIONS

Years produced:	1965-1974 (700 in total)
Performance:	0-60mph: N/A
	Top speed: 75mph
Power & torque:	34bhp/44lb ft
Engine:	Normally aspirated 848cc four cylinder, petrol, carburettor, 8 valves
Drivetrain:	Front-engine FWD
Structure:	Glassfibre monocoque
Transmission:	Four-speed manual
Weight:	483kg

PRICE GUIDE

Launch price:	£199
Excellent:	£5000
Good:	£3000
Average:	£1500
Project:	£800

MARCOS
3-litre

Marcos finally abandoned its plywood underpinnings with the 3-litre and went for a square tube chassis that cost less to build, was easier to maintain, and ultimately made it easier to sell. The 3-litre was a clear indicator that Marcos was moving upmarket and, although the Ford V6-powered car looked near-identical to its four-cylinder cousins, it offered much more performance – and therefore sales appeal. It wasn't cheap and, in moving away from its competition roots, Marcos struggled to find new buyers – especially in the wake of the cheap and plentiful Ford Capri 3000.

SPECIFICATIONS

Years produced:	1968-1972 (561 in total)
Performance:	0-60mph: 7.8sec
	Top speed: 125mph
Power & torque:	136bhp/193lb ft
Engine:	Normally aspirated 2994cc V6, petrol, carburettor, 12 valves
Drivetrain:	Front-engine RWD
Structure:	Glassfibre body/separate chassis
Transmission:	Four-speed manual with overdrive
Weight:	884kg

PRICE GUIDE

Launch price:	£2350
Excellent:	£10,000
Good:	£7500
Average:	£4750
Project:	£2500

MASERATI

INITIALLY BUILDING cars just for racing, Italian firm Maserati began to focus on road cars from 1946 with the A6/1500 model. But it was with the 3500GT of 1957 that it got serious, building a true Ferrari challenger. It continued in that vein over the next few decades with models such as the Ghibli and Bora being stand-out offerings. The latter was built while Citroën owned the firm, from 1969 to 1975. De Tomaso then took over and Maseratis were downgraded to become less exclusive machines, akin to an Italian BMW or Mercedes. The company has since moved through the hands of Fiat and Ferrari and is once again building exotic and stylish sports cars.

MASERATI
3500GT

Maserati made its name in motor racing, having produced the legendary 250F, which took Juan Manuel Fangio to championship glory in 1957. That same year the company turned its full attention to the business of building road cars, unveiling the 3500GT. With this car, Maserati evolved into a serious producer of road cars (the A6 models were always low volume semi-racers), competing strongly with Ferrari. The Touring-bodied coupé certainly looked the part and, with an Alfieri designed engine and racer-derived chassis, the 3500GT was as good to drive as it was to look at.

SPECIFICATIONS
Years produced:	1957-1964 (2000 in total)
Performance:	0-60mph: 7.6sec
	Top speed: 145mph
Power & torque:	220bhp/253lb ft
Engine:	Normally aspirated 3485cc straight six, petrol, carburettor, 12 valves
Drivetrain:	Front-engine RWD
Structure:	Monocoque
Transmission:	Four-speed manual
Weight:	1270kg

PRICE GUIDE
Launch price:	£5800
Excellent:	£90,000
Good:	£60,000
Average:	£40,000
Project:	£25,000

MASERATI
3500GT Spyder

During its seven-year production run, the 3500GT became an established member of the sporting elite, with the coupé taking the lion's share of sales. But the lighter Vignale-bodied Spider was every bit as capable as its hard-top sister, sitting on a shortened wheelbase. During its production run, it was regularly upgraded, gaining front disc brakes and Borani wire wheels in 1959 and a five-speed gearbox the following year. In 1961 the 3500GT also gained Lucas fuel injection. A handful of one-offs were also produced, and are now fabulously valuable.

SPECIFICATIONS
Years produced:	1959-1964 (227 in total)
Performance:	0-60mph: 7.6sec
	Top speed: 136mph
Power & torque:	235bhp/232lb ft
Engine:	Normally aspirated 3485cc straight six, petrol, carburettor, 12 valves
Drivetrain:	Front-engine RWD
Structure:	Separate chassis
Transmission:	Four-speed manual
Weight:	1406kg

PRICE GUIDE
Launch price:	£4450
Excellent:	£250,000
Good:	£100,000
Average:	£75,000
Project:	£40,000

MASERATI
Sebring

In essence, the Sebring was a shortened 3500GT that wore a beautiful Vignale body, styled by Giovanni Michelotti. In terms of looks, the Sebring was a perfect car for its time, although the straight-six engine was beginning to look a little outclassed compared with the latest opposition from Ferrari. But this car was designed for America, and it was style and equipment that were the prime motivators in its creation – so air conditioning and an automatic gearbox were on the options list. For the Sebring II, a 4.0-litre version of the straight six was fitted.

SPECIFICATIONS
Years produced:	1963-1969 (438 in total)
Performance:	0-60mph: 8.4sec
	Top speed: 137mph
Power & torque:	235bhp/232lb ft
Engine:	Normally aspirated 3485cc straight six, petrol, carburettor, 12 valves
Drivetrain:	Front-engine RWD
Structure:	Separate chassis
Transmission:	Five-speed manual
Weight:	1510kg

PRICE GUIDE
Launch price:	£4801
Excellent:	£60,000
Good:	£50,000
Average:	£32,500
Project:	£15,000

MASERATI
Mistral

The Frua-bodied Mistral was the last of the six-cylinder line of Maseratis that started with the 3500GT. Its name comes from the wind that blows across the south of France every year, and was the first Maserati with a wind-inspired name. The engine was a direct descendent of the 350S's, and proved lusty and long-lasting. The engine line-up was identical to the Sebring's, but few 3.5-litre versions found their way under the bonnet of the newer car. Performance was usefully improved, because the short-wheelbase Mistral weighed 200kg less than the Sebring.

SPECIFICATIONS
Years produced:	1963-1970 (948 in total)
Performance:	0-60mph: 6.9sec
	Top speed: 152mph
Power & torque:	265bhp/261lb ft
Engine:	Normally aspirated 3485cc straight six, petrol, carburettor, 12 valves
Drivetrain:	Front-engine RWD
Structure:	Tubular chassis
Transmission:	Five-speed manual
Weight:	1270kg

PRICE GUIDE
Launch price:	£5980
Excellent:	£65,000
Good:	£30,000
Average:	£17,500
Project:	£10,500

MASERATI
Mistral Spyder

Slightly happier-looking than the coupé, the Mistral Spyder bears an uncanny resemblance to the later AC 428 – both were styled by Pietro Frua. It was so close that there's some parts interchangeability between the two, a side benefit of being built in the same factory. Unusually, the Mistral was offered with either aluminium or steel bodywork, with no discernible difference in weight, though the survival rate of the former is much higher than for the latter. The final 4.0-litre Mistral was a genuinely quick car, with a top speed of over 140mph.

SPECIFICATIONS

Years produced:	1963-1970 (120 in total)
Performance:	0-60mph: 6.8sec
	Top speed: 147mph
Power & torque:	255bhp/267lb ft
Engine:	Normally aspirated 4012cc straight six, petrol, carburettor, 12 valves
Drivetrain:	Front-engine RWD
Structure:	Tubular chassis
Transmission:	Five-speed manual
Weight:	1300kg

PRICE GUIDE

Launch price:	£5980
Excellent:	£125,000
Good:	£80,000
Average:	£60,000
Project:	£35,000

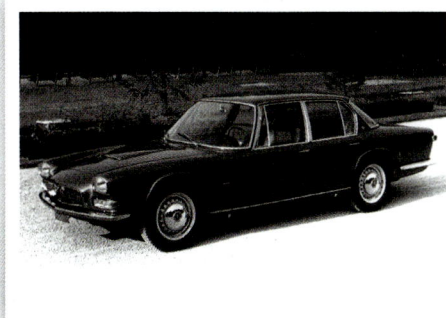

MASERATI
Quattroporte

The Quattroporte was significant for Maserati because it was the first of its cars to be powered by the new V8 engine, initially in 4.1-litre form, later 4.7. The family resemblance with the Mistral was strong, as it was also a Frua design, while underneath it was built on a sports car-like tubular frame. The platform went on to underpin a generation of Maserati sports cars, and rightly so, considering how good the Quattroporte was – and still is – to drive. There's something peculiarly Italian about being the fastest saloon in the world with an exotic-sounding name that means 'four door'.

SPECIFICATIONS

Years produced:	1963-1971 (760 in total)
Performance:	0-60mph: 8.3sec
	Top speed: 130mph
Power & torque:	260bhp/267lb ft
Engine:	Normally aspirated 4136cc V8, petrol, carburettor, 16 valves
Drivetrain:	Front-engine RWD
Structure:	Tubular chassis
Transmission:	Five-speed manual
Weight:	1728kg

PRICE GUIDE

Launch price:	£5986
Excellent:	£35,000
Good:	£25,000
Average:	£17,000
Project:	£10,000

MASERATI
Mexico

Following on from the Quattroporte in 1965, the Mexico was the next Maserati to be fitted with the new V8 engine. The four-seater coupé was styled by Vignale and, after the exuberance of the previous Frua-bodied cars, it lacked the visual drama to go with its high price. However, with the later 4.7-litre V8 fitted, it was seriously quick, with more than enough muscle to replace the Sebring. Sadly the new car failed to emulate its predecessor's sales success in the USA – a situation that hurt Maserati's finances significantly. Subtle but desirable nonetheless.

SPECIFICATIONS

Years produced:	1966-1972 (250 in total)
Performance:	0-60mph: N/A
	Top speed: 143mph
Power & torque:	260bhp/268lb ft
Engine:	Normally aspirated 4136cc V8, petrol, carburettor, 16 valves
Drivetrain:	Front-engine RWD
Structure:	Tubular chassis
Transmission:	Five-speed manual
Weight:	1651kg

PRICE GUIDE

Launch price:	£7216
Excellent:	£35,000
Good:	£20,000
Average:	£12,500
Project:	£7000

MASERATI
Ghibli

Sitting at the top of the Maserati range, and vying with the very best from Ferrari for the title 'fastest car in the world', the Ghibli is one of the finest GT cars to emerge from the 1960s. Subsequently overshadowed by the Daytona and Miura, the Ghibli combined Giorgetto Giugiaro's styling (while he was still at Ghia) with Maserati's muscle to create a genuine 170mph roadburner. The chassis engineering was beginning to look a little old hat, as it was a further variation of the Quattroporte's tubular frame – but it was effective nevertheless. Spyder prices double those of Coupé.

SPECIFICATIONS

Years produced:	1969-1974 (1274 in total)
Performance:	0-60mph: 7.5sec
	Top speed: 154mph
Power & torque:	330bhp/290lb ft
Engine:	Normally aspirated 4719cc V8, petrol, carburettor, 16 valves
Drivetrain:	Front-engine RWD
Structure:	Tubular chassis
Transmission:	Five-speed manual
Weight:	1352kg

PRICE GUIDE

Launch price:	£10,180
Excellent:	£75,000
Good:	£42,500
Average:	£25,000
Project:	£14,000

MASERATI
Indy

This was more like it: based on a shortened version of the Quattroporte's chassis, but with a wider track, the Vignale-styled Indy looked every inch the supercar it was supposed to be. Compared with the Mexico it replaced, the Indy was a huge success. The 2+2 coupé also saw a change in Maserati construction technique, as the chassis and body were now welded (instead of bolted) together, described as a unitary body. None of that mattered on the road where, in 4.7-litre form, the Indy could exceed 160mph in the right conditions, making it one of the world's fastest four-seater cars.

SPECIFICATIONS

Years produced:	1969-1974 (1136 in total)
Performance:	0-60mph: 7.2sec
	Top speed: 140mph
Power & torque:	260bhp/268lb ft
Engine:	Normally aspirated 4136cc V8, petrol, carburettor, 16 valves
Drivetrain:	Front-engine RWD
Structure:	Monocoque
Transmission:	Five-speed manual
Weight:	1651kg

PRICE GUIDE

Launch price:	£8320
Excellent:	£25,000
Good:	£17,500
Average:	£11,000
Project:	£6000

MASERATI
Bora

Considering it was a relative latecomer to the mid-engined supercar club (although it beat the Ferrari BB to the market by two years), the Maserati Bora established itself as a front-runner. Like the Ghibli, the Bora was styled by Giugiaro, who had by now gone it alone to form Ital Design, but the design studio had also devised the all-new steel unitary construction underneath it. The Bora was fitted with the Indy V8 in 4.7- or 4.9-litre form. Thanks to Maserati's association with Citroën, high pressure hydraulics powered the brakes and steering.

SPECIFICATIONS
Years produced:	1971-1978 (524 in total)
Performance:	0-60mph: 6.5sec
	Top speed: 165mph
Power & torque:	310bhp/339lb ft
Engine:	Normally aspirated 4719cc V8, petrol, carburettor, 16 valves
Drivetrain:	Mid-engine RWD
Structure:	Monocoque
Transmission:	Five-speed manual
Weight:	1550kg

PRICE GUIDE
Launch price:	£22,911
Excellent:	£60,000
Good:	£37,500
Average:	£22,500
Project:	£12,500

MASERATI
Khamsin

To show its commitment to the front-engined cause, Maserati introduced the Khamsin to sell alongside the Bora/Merak twins. Styling and body engineering was by Marcello Gandini at Bertone, and it was an arresting design. The suspension and brakes were closely related to the mid-engined cars' but the high-geared power-assisted steering was lifted from the Citroën SM, and proved remarkably successful once owners had acclimatised to it. Poor interior layout and visibility were negated by the 320bhp from its 4.9-litre Indy engine – over 150mph was possible.

SPECIFICATIONS
Years produced:	1973-1982 (421 in total)
Performance:	0-60mph: 7.1sec
	Top speed: 171mph
Power & torque:	320bhp/354lb ft
Engine:	Normally aspirated 4930cc V8, petrol, carburettor, 16 valves
Drivetrain:	Front-engine RWD
Structure:	Monocoque
Transmission:	Five-speed manual
Weight:	1530kg

PRICE GUIDE
Launch price:	£13,999
Excellent:	£45,000
Good:	£37,500
Average:	£20,000
Project:	£10,000

MASERATI
Merak

Created to fight the Ferrari 308 and Lamborghini Urraco, the Maserati Merak was a super-stylish parts-bin special that proved rather effective. The body was a lightly revised version of the Bora's (losing its flush rear window in the process), and the engine was a lightly tuned version of the Citroën SM's Maserati-designed 3.0-litre V6, boasting 190bhp. Never a light car, the Merak struggled to keep up with rivals, but the 220bhp SS version did much to make amends. Like the Bora, its values lag behind those of Lamborghini and Ferrari, making a Merak a wise investment.

SPECIFICATIONS
Years produced:	1974-1982 (1699 in total)
Performance:	0-60mph: 8.2sec
	Top speed: 135mph
Power & torque:	190bhp/188lb ft
Engine:	Normally aspirated 2965cc V6, petrol, carburettor, 16 valves
Drivetrain:	Mid-engine RWD
Structure:	Monocoque
Transmission:	Five-speed manual
Weight:	1339kg

PRICE GUIDE
Launch price:	£7996
Excellent:	£27,500
Good:	£18,500
Average:	£11,000
Project:	£4500

MASERATI
Kyalami

After De Tomaso's takeover of Maserati, badge engineering was introduced. The De Tomaso Longchamp was slightly facelifted, fitted with the Indy V8 (initially in 4.1-litre form) and re-marketed as the Maserati Kyalami. Although this version of the Ghia-styled car looked better than the original, it was not appealing enough to bring in a significant number of new buyers. Perhaps it was the price – which had taken a significant hike over the Ford-engined car it was based upon – but, more likely, there was simply no market for it in the late 1970s.

SPECIFICATIONS
Years produced:	1976-1983 (187 in total)
Performance:	0-60mph: 7.6sec
	Top speed: 147mph
Power & torque:	270bhp/289lb ft
Engine:	Normally aspirated 4136cc V8, petrol, carburettor, 16 valves
Drivetrain:	Front-engine RWD
Structure:	Monocoque
Transmission:	Five-speed manual
Weight:	1740kg

PRICE GUIDE
Launch price:	£21,996
Excellent:	£16,000
Good:	£12,500
Average:	£7000
Project:	£4000

MASERATI
Quattroporte III

Another back-to-basics offering, and none the worse for it. Where the Quattroporte II had flopped on its unconventional engineering and anodyne styling, its replacement returned to the formula that made the original car so successful – a big V8, discreet styling, and a supercar driving experience combined with additional accommodation. Sales were not as strong as they could have been, although in 4.9-litre form the Quatroporte III remained in production throughout the 1980s to be sold alongside the new Biturbo – perhaps as a reminder of greater times?

SPECIFICATIONS
Years produced:	1979-1990 (1876 in total)
Performance:	0-60mph: N/A
	Top speed: 143mph
Power & torque:	280bhp/289lb ft
Engine:	Normally aspirated 4930cc V8, petrol, carburettor, 16 valves
Drivetrain:	Front-engine RWD
Structure:	Monocoque
Transmission:	Three-speed automatic
Weight:	1900kg

PRICE GUIDE
Launch price:	£56,912
Excellent:	£13,000
Good:	£8000
Average:	£4500
Project:	£1750

MASERATI
Biturbo 220-425

lMaserati model development took a new direction in 1981. The supercar market was surrendered to Ferrari and Lamborghini as the company chased volume with its new BMW 3-Series-rivalling Biturbo. At the heart of the new car was an elegant new 28-valve four-cam 2.0-litre V6, which pushed out 180bhp thanks to its brace of turbos. The interior was plush – and its centrepiece clock was a real novelty. The Biturbo made for a novel alternative to a BMW 323i, although big sales were never forthcoming. The four-door 425, introduced in 1983, added appeal.

SPECIFICATIONS

Years produced:	1981-1994
Performance:	0-60mph: 7.2sec
	Top speed: 126mph
Power & torque:	192bhp/220lb ft
Engine:	Turbocharged 2491cc V6, petrol, carburettor, 18 valves
Drivetrain:	Front-engine RWD
Structure:	Monocoque
Transmission:	Five-speed manual
Weight:	1242kg

PRICE GUIDE

Launch price:	£28,795
Excellent:	£8000
Good:	£4600
Average:	£2250
Project:	£1000

MASERATI
Biturbo Spyder

Maserati chopped off the roof of the Biturbo to create this stylish four-seater convertible. Like the tin-topped versions it wasn't without issues and, as well as suffering from niggling build and quality issues, premature corrosion was a very real problem. Image and prices dropped massively in a short time, from which the Biturbo is only now beginning to emerge. Despite low classic values, there's a real sense of the exotic when it comes to keeping a Biturbo on the road, and restoration costs can be horrifying – especially when it comes to the engine.

SPECIFICATIONS

Years produced:	1984-1991
Performance:	0-60mph: 6.1sec
	Top speed: 140mph
Power & torque:	241bhp/246lb ft
Engine:	Turbocharged 1996cc V6, petrol, electronic fuel injection, 24 valves
Drivetrain:	Front-engine RWD
Structure:	Monocoque
Transmission:	Five-speed manual
Weight:	1251kg

PRICE GUIDE

Launch price:	N/A
Excellent:	£15,000
Good:	£8000
Average:	£4000
Project:	£2000

MATRA

MATRA – Mécanique-Aviation-Traction – was a French aerospace group that took over René Bonnet and continued making its sports car. It penned its own glassfibre design – the 530 – in 1967 as a V4 mid-engined coupé and targa model. It then jumped into bed with Simca to build the exciting Bagheera. Ironically the marque is better known for the 'lifestyle' Rancho that effectively invented the idea of rugged-looking faux off-roaders. The Renault Espace and Avantime were also built by the company, although they never carried the Matra name. The former was a runaway success, the latter a brave but total failure, which caused Matra to retreat from car-building in 2003.

MATRA
Djet V

Aerospace company Matra wasn't the first company to build the Djet, but it would go on to build a business around it. René Bonnet created the innovative car but couldn't make it pay, so Matra – which was already building the bodies – took it on to create the Matra-Bonnet Djet V. The body was light, it was powered by a tweaked Renault 8 Gordini engine, and it performed admirably thanks to a great power-to-weight ratio. The Djet proved useful in motor sport too, giving Matra the impetus it needed to front-line competition, both at Le Mans and in Formula 1.

SPECIFICATIONS

Years produced:	1965-1967 (1681 in total)
Performance:	0-60mph: 13.5sec
	Top speed: 99mph
Power & torque:	72bhp/56lb ft
Engine:	Normally aspirated 1108cc four cylinder, petrol, carburettor, 8 valves
Drivetrain:	Mid-engine RWD
Structure:	Glassfibre body/separate chassis
Transmission:	Four-speed manual
Weight:	615kg

PRICE GUIDE

Launch price:	N/A in UK
Excellent:	£10,000
Good:	£6000
Average:	£4000
Project:	N/A

MATRA
530

By the time it came to introducing a replacement for the Djet V, Matra's confidence had soared, and it decided on a car that was more unconventional. Still mid-engined and strangely styled, the 530 proved to be rather good on the road, despite using the unpromising Ford V4 engine. Construction was a steel unibody clothed in a glassfibre shell, and suspension was independent all-round. Handling was more than a match for its feeble 75bhp engine, and that would be a running theme for Matra sports cars for the coming decade. Rare and collectable for francophiles.

SPECIFICATIONS

Years produced:	1967-1973 (9609 in total)
Performance:	0-60mph: 15.6sec
	Top speed: 95mph
Power & torque:	73bhp/98lb ft
Engine:	Normally aspirated 1699cc V4, petrol, carburettor, 8 valves
Drivetrain:	Mid-engine RWD
Structure:	Steel unibody with glassfibre shell
Transmission:	Four-speed manual
Weight:	875kg

PRICE GUIDE

Launch price:	£2160
Excellent:	£6000
Good:	£4000
Average:	£2200
Project:	N/A

MATRA
Bagheera

The Matra-Simca Bagheera was one of the most innovative sports cars produced in over a decade. Featuring three-abreast seating, composite panels draped over a steel spaceframe, and mid-engined power-pack, the Bagheera was cheap, stylish and interesting. Performance never matched its looks, but the Simca-derived power units were willing enough, if unrefined, and the Bagheera could run rings around far more expensive cars. Structural corrosion has been the Bagheera's enemy, but plenty survive and back-up from the enthusiast clubs is excellent.

SPECIFICATIONS
Years produced:	1973-1980
Performance:	0-60mph: 12.3sec
	Top speed: 101mph
Power & torque:	82bhp/78lb ft
Engine:	Normally aspirated 1294cc four cylinder, petrol, carburettor, 8 valves
Drivetrain:	Mid-engine RWD
Structure:	Composite body/spaceframe
Transmission:	Four-speed manual
Weight:	885kg

PRICE GUIDE
Launch price:	£5370 (UK, 1977)
Excellent:	£4000
Good:	£3250
Average:	£2000
Project:	£600

MATRA
Murena

The Murena was a logical development of the Bagheera. It was clothed in a new aerodynamic body and, importantly, underpinned by a galvanised steel spaceframe that would prove resistant to rust. The top engine option was a 2.2-litre Talbot Tagora engine, which provided the go to match its excellent handling – something that the Bagheera had lacked. Sadly, politics between Peugeot-Talbot and Matra saw the Murena prematurely halted in 1985, by which time the innovative French company was gearing up to produce the Espace.

SPECIFICATIONS
Years produced:	1980-1983
Performance:	0-60mph: 9.2sec
	Top speed: 124mph
Power & torque:	118bhp/139lb ft
Engine:	Normally aspirated 2155cc four cylinder, petrol, carburettor, 8 valves
Drivetrain:	Mid-engine RWD
Structure:	Composite body/spaceframe
Transmission:	Five-speed manual
Weight:	1050kg

PRICE GUIDE
Launch price:	N/A in UK
Excellent:	£5000
Good:	£4000
Average:	£2500
Project:	£1000

MATRA
Rancho

Simca's 1100 VF3 van proved the unlikely starting point for Matra-Simca's pioneering Rancho. The faux off-roader was sneered at by the press, but customers loved it, and the Rancho proved to be an unlikely hit of the late '70s. Rough and tough, with big plastic bumpers, it was perfect for mean city streets, but the 1.4-litre Simca engine struggled to haul the large body on the motorway. Engines became rattly almost the moment it left the factory, and rust set in soon after – the rear section was glassfibre, so at least some of it would survive unscathed.

SPECIFICATIONS
Years produced:	1977-1984 (56,700 in total)
Performance:	0-60mph: 14.9sec
	Top speed: 89mph
Power & torque:	80bhp/89lb ft
Engine:	Normally aspirated 1442cc four cylinder, petrol, carburettor, 8 valves
Drivetrain:	Front-engine FWD
Structure:	Monocoque
Transmission:	Four-speed manual
Weight:	1130kg

PRICE GUIDE
Launch price:	£5133 (UK, 1978)
Excellent:	£2500
Good:	£1200
Average:	£800
Project:	£500

MAZDA

ALTHOUGH FOUNDED in 1920, Hiroshima's Toyo Kogyo Cork company didn't build its first car – under the Mazda name, in tribute to founder Jujiro Matsuda as well as the Zoroastrian god – until 1960. The company soon became known for its experiments in rotary engine technology, with the RX-7 its best-known and biggest-selling exponent of the type, and one of the few cars to ever make the Wankel work well. It was also applauded for the MX-5 roadster in 1989, which pioneered a renaissance for small sports cars. After operating in a partnership since 1979, Ford acquired a controlling stake in 1997, leading to several joint projects and shared resources.

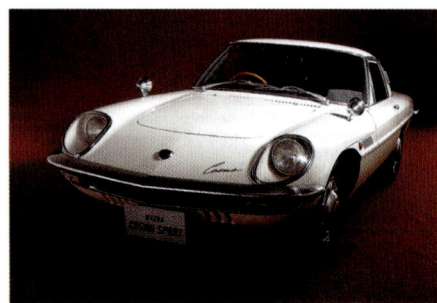

MAZDA
Cosmo 110S

The early years of the Japanese motor industry were exciting ones, so when Mazda decided to build a sports car in the mid-60s, it really went for broke. The Cosmo was powered by a Wankel engine, making it the world's first twin-rotor production car, beating the NSU Ro80 into production by months. It suffered from the usual problems associated with the rotary, such as rotor tip wear, but when it was running, the Cosmo was smooth and exciting to drive. Few made, expensive when new, and you'll pay handsomely for an original Cosmo now.

SPECIFICATIONS
Years produced:	1967-1972 (1519 in total)
Performance:	0-60mph: 9.3sec
	Top speed: 120mph
Power & torque:	108bhp/96lb ft
Engine:	Normally aspirated 1964cc twin-rotor Wankel, petrol, carburettor
Drivetrain:	Front-engine RWD
Structure:	Monocoque
Transmission:	Four-speed manual
Weight:	930kg

PRICE GUIDE
Launch price:	£2607
Excellent:	£30,000
Good:	£15,000
Average:	£9000
Project:	N/A

MAZDA
RX4/929

Mazda persisted with the Wankel more than any other manufacturer, and through diligent development managed to make it work reasonably successfully. But the 929 was the last in the line of large saloons, killed in the end by a voracious for petrol – not good in the midst of a fuel-led recession. The RX4 coupé boasts '70s Transatlantic Japanese styling that just gets better with age, but predictably there aren't many left now thanks to a proclivity for rusting. There's an active following, and rebuilds using modern components give acceptable engine life.

SPECIFICATIONS (929 Coupé)

Years produced:	1972-1979 (213,998 in total)
Performance:	0-60mph: 14.0sec
	Top speed: 92mph
Power & torque:	83bhp/99lb ft
Engine:	Normally aspirated 1769cc twin-rotor Wankel, petrol, carburettor
Drivetrain:	Front-engine RWD
Structure:	Monocoque
Transmission:	Four-speed manual
Weight:	1095kg

PRICE GUIDE (Coupe)

Launch price:	£1649
Excellent:	£4000
Good:	£2500
Average:	£1200
Project:	£900

MAZDA
323

Mazda's little 1000 – or Familia as it was known in Japan – was a popular saloon in Japan, but hardly Euro-friendly. So when it came to cooking up a replacement, Mazda's engineers developed a two-box body with hatchback rear end. As an entrant to the growing ranks of the superminis, the good-looking 323 was hardly a front-runner because it retained its predecessor's RWD underpinnings, so it was similar in concept to the Toyota Starlet and Chrysler Sunbeam. Popular down under, with enthusiasts bolting in RX-7 Wankel engines for maximum fun.

SPECIFICATIONS

Years produced:	1977-1981
Performance:	0-60mph: 18.1sec
	Top speed: 84mph
Power & torque:	45bhp/51lb ft
Engine:	Normally aspirated 985cc four cylinder, petrol, carburettor
Drivetrain:	Front-engine RWD
Structure:	Monocoque
Transmission:	Four-speed manual
Weight:	812kg

PRICE GUIDE (Coupe)

Launch price:	£1825
Excellent:	£1750
Good:	£1000
Average:	£7500
Project:	£500

MAZDA
RX-7 Series 1

This was Mazda's attempt to make the world take the rotary engine seriously. With over half-a-million sales of this first series RX-7, it clearly worked. However, the seemingly unassailable problem of the Wankel's poor economy means it could never go mainstream. The RX-7 makes the most of the engine's light weight, with perfect 50:50 weight distribution. The early version is best left to enthusiasts; from 1981 it was a better car, with an extra 10bhp, rear disc brakes, a spoiler on the back and more comprehensive equipment.

SPECIFICATIONS

Years produced:	1979-1985 (471,018 in total)
Performance:	0-60mph: 9.5sec
	Top speed: 115mph
Power & torque:	105bhp/106lb ft
Engine:	Normally aspirated 2292cc twin-rotor Wankel, petrol, carburettor
Drivetrain:	Front-engine RWD
Structure:	Monocoque
Transmission:	Five-speed manual
Weight:	980kg

PRICE GUIDE

Launch price:	£8549
Excellent:	£4000
Good:	£3000
Average:	£1600
Project:	£750

MAZDA
RX-7 Series 2

The second-generation RX-7's all-new styling stole a lot of cues from the Porsche 928 and 944 and managed to look more substantial without growing in size, and only adding 80lb in weight. It gave safer handling thanks to new rear suspension, and sharper steering with rack-and-pinion instead of recirculating ball. The revised 13A engine kicks out more power – especially in the Turbo version that became available in the UK from 1988 with up to 200bhp. The following year a convertible was added to the range, though these are harder to find.

SPECIFICATIONS

Years produced:	1986-1992 (272,027 in total)
Performance:	0-60mph: 8.5sec
	Top speed: 134mph
Power & torque:	149bhp/135lb ft
Engine:	Turbocharged 2254cc twin-rotor, petrol, electronic fuel injection
Drivetrain:	Front-engine RWD
Structure:	Monocoque
Transmission:	Five-speed manual
Weight:	1221kg

PRICE GUIDE

Launch price:	£13,995
Excellent:	£5500
Good:	£3500
Average:	£1900
Project:	£600

MAZDA
323 4WD Turbo

Look beyond the forgettable styling, and you'll find an engaging and capable '80s hot hatch masquerading as your grandmother's shopping trolley. The 323 4WD Turbo was conceived for rallying and was given its go-faster stripes by the application of an IHI turbo and prodigious boost. Handling was also incredibly well resolved, as you'd expect for a competition-bred machine. Think of it as a bargain-basement Delta Integrale and you'd be doing it a disservice, though you wouldn't be far off the mark. Few left in original condition now.

SPECIFICATIONS

Years produced:	1985-1989
Performance:	0-60mph: 7.9sec
	Top speed: 125mph
Power & torque:	150bhp/144lb ft
Engine:	Turbocharged 1597cc four cylinder, petrol, fuel injection, 16 valves
Drivetrain:	Front-engine AWD
Structure:	Monocoque
Transmission:	Five-speed manual
Weight:	1110kg

PRICE GUIDE

Launch price:	£11,750
Excellent:	£6000
Good:	£3750
Average:	£2000
Project:	£1500

MERCEDES-BENZ

MERCEDES WAS FOUNDED in 1901, named after founder Emile Jellinek's daughter, but merged with Karl Benz's 1885 firm in 1926. The combination of expertise resulted in some magnificent and stately machines prior to World War Two. After the conflict, Mercedes-Benz continued with upmarket and sporty models. The 300SL Gullwing fittingly became world-renowned and widely regarded as the first true supercar. The company forged a reputation as a maker of high quality and enduring vehicles with a touch of luxury; its 600 and S-class saloons were Rolls-Royce rivals while its long-running SL sports cars have always been successful and sought-after.

MERCEDES-BENZ
300 Cabriolet D

This convertible version of the 300 saloon was built in limited numbers and was most commonly seen with the leaders of any number of nations waving from the rear seats. Side windows and frames lower fully to make it a full convertible. A car with enormous presence, it also requires an enormous wallet should you need to undertake restoration work, though the value of a good one goes some way towards reflecting this. As with the saloons, the later the version you buy, the better equipment it will have, and the better you'll enjoy the driving experience.

SPECIFICATIONS

Years produced:	1951-1956 (707 in total)
Performance:	0-60mph: 17.0sec
	Top speed: 99mph
Power & torque:	123bhp/163lb ft
Engine:	Normally aspirated 2996cc straight six, petrol, carburettor, 12 valves
Drivetrain:	Front-engine RWD
Structure:	Separate chassis
Transmission:	Four-speed manual
Weight:	1940kg

PRICE GUIDE

Launch price:	N/A in UK
Excellent:	£125,000
Good:	£80,000
Average:	£50,000
Project:	£20,000

MERCEDES-BENZ
300A/B/C/D

Mercedes' return to the production of prestige automobiles six years after the end of WW2 resulted in this 4000lb giant. The range has since been dubbed 'Adenauer' as the car became closely associated with the German chancellor of the time, Dr Konrad Adenauer. It was built on the X-frame chassis of its pre-war counterparts, with an alloy-head straight six. Sold in the UK from 1953, and better from 1954 when a servo was added to the brakes. 1957's 300D was restyled above the waist with thinner pillars and a greater glass area.

SPECIFICATIONS

Years produced:	1951-1962 (11,430 in total)
Performance:	0-60mph: 15.0sec
	Top speed: 109mph
Power & torque:	148bhp/178lb ft
Engine:	Normally aspirated 2996cc four cylinder, petrol, carburettor, 12 valves
Drivetrain:	Front-engine RWD
Structure:	Separate chassis
Transmission:	Four-speed manual/three-speed auto
Weight:	1740kg

PRICE GUIDE

Launch price:	£3500
Excellent:	£40,000
Good:	£22,500
Average:	£10,000
Project:	£6000

MERCEDES-BENZ
300S/Sc Cabriolet/Roadster

Built on a 6in shorter 300 saloon chassis, this still-giant two-seater harked back to the 540K of Mercedes' pre-war glory days. The S was more expensive than the 300SL Gullwing in 1954, and used a predecessor of its engine. The quick way to tell the Cabriolet and Roadster apart is that the former has 'pram irons' on the side of the folding top. The Sc was introduced in 1955, the small 'c' denoting that the engine has Bosch fuel injection.

SPECIFICATIONS

Years produced:	1952-1958 (760 in total)
Performance:	0-60mph: 15.0sec
	Top speed: 109mph
Power & torque:	148bhp/178lb ft
Engine:	Normally aspirated 2996cc straight six, petrol, carburettor, 12 valves
Drivetrain:	Front-engine RWD
Structure:	Separate chassis
Transmission:	Four-speed manual
Weight:	N/A

PRICE GUIDE

Launch price:	£5529
Excellent:	£150,000
Good:	£125,000
Average:	£90,000
Project:	£65,000

MERCEDES-BENZ
180-220S Ponton

These are generally referred to by their 'Ponton' nickname, which is German for pontoon and refers to the bridge-like suspension subframe. The 180 and 190 have four-cylinder engines and were much better after 1957, when they received an overhead-cam engine in place of the old sidevalve unit. There was also a popular though underpowered 180D diesel option. 220s sit on a longer wheelbase and have six-cylinder engines, so they are worth more. These were the cars that started M-B's reputation for rugged dependability.

SPECIFICATIONS

Years produced:	1953-1962 (280,807 in total)
Performance:	0-60mph: 15.2sec
	Top speed: N/A
Power & torque:	58bhp/82lb ft
Engine:	Normally aspirated 1767cc four cylinder, petrol, carburettor, 8 valves
Drivetrain:	Front-engine RWD
Structure:	Monocoque
Transmission:	Four-speed manual
Weight:	1070kg

PRICE GUIDE

Launch price:	£1694
Excellent:	£8500
Good:	£6000
Average:	£2750
Project:	£1500

MERCEDES-BENZ
300SL Gullwing

Rarely seen but instantly recognised, this is not just a car but a true icon, generally known simply by the name Gullwing. Behind the legend is a high quality sports coupé with a racing heritage, built over a spaceframe chassis, and with the world's first production fuel-injection engine. The rest of the spec seems a little less impressive today: drum brakes, a four-speed gearbox, and swing-axle rear suspension. Most had steel bodies, but 29 were built in aluminium, for which you will have to double the prices given here.

SPECIFICATIONS
Years produced:	1954-1957 (1400 in total)
Performance:	0-60mph: 8.8sec
	Top speed: 135mph
Power & torque:	215bhp/203lb ft
Engine:	Normally aspirated 2996cc straight six, petrol, mechanical injection, 12 valves
Drivetrain:	Front-engine RWD
Structure:	Spaceframe
Transmission:	Four-speed manual
Weight:	1293kg

PRICE GUIDE
Launch price:	£4393
Excellent:	£495,000
Good:	£325,000
Average:	£250,000
Project:	£190,000

MERCEDES-BENZ
190SL Roadster

The SL tag is supposed to translate as 'sports light', but despite aluminium doors, bonnet and bootlid, the 190SL is still too heavy to do anything properly sporting with its 1.9-litre four-cylinder engine. Settle for the fact that it is a good, if not exhilarating drive, with bags of style. In fact it's just the thing for those who can't afford ten times the price for the larger 300SL. Build quality is superb, and they've survived in good enough numbers to make finding one simple enough. You may have to pay a bit more if it comes with both soft and hard tops.

SPECIFICATIONS
Years produced:	1955-1963 (25,881 in total)
Performance:	0-60mph: 13.3sec
	Top speed: 109mph
Power & torque:	104bhp/114lb ft
Engine:	Normally aspirated 1897cc four cylinder, petrol, carburettor, 8 valves
Drivetrain:	Front-engine RWD
Structure:	Steel monocoque
Transmission:	Four-speed manual
Weight:	1140kg

PRICE GUIDE
Launch price:	£2693
Excellent:	£70,000
Good:	£40,000
Average:	£22,500
Project:	£15,000

MERCEDES-BENZ
220S/SE Cabriolet

Based on the 220 Ponton saloon but on a five-inch shorter floorpan, with much prettier bodywork distinguished by really long doors. Priced roughly 75% higher than a saloon when new, they sold in small numbers. The 220S had a 100bhp six-cylinder engine with twin Solex carburettors, and was joined in 1958 by the 220SE, with the 'E' standing for fuel injection, a Bosch unit that added 15bhp – and even more to the car's already high price. They remained in production a year longer than their saloon counterparts.

SPECIFICATIONS
Years produced:	1956-1960
Performance:	0-60mph: 15.2sec
	Top speed: 101mph
Power & torque:	98bhp/119lb ft
Engine:	Normally aspirated 2195cc straight six, petrol, carburettor, 12 valves
Drivetrain:	Front-engine RWD
Structure:	Moncoque
Transmission:	Four-speed manual
Weight:	N/A

PRICE GUIDE
Launch price:	£3715
Excellent:	£85,000
Good:	£55,000
Average:	£35,000
Project:	£20,000

MERCEDES-BENZ
220S/SE Coupé

Launched a year later than the Cabriolet, the Coupé version is identical apart from the fixed roof and upright rather than slanted frames for the rear of the side window. Being based on a saloon floorpan means it's a full four-seater, and that US-influenced hardtop styling ensures plenty of headroom, even for those in the back. Built from the best materials, but before the era of rust protection so many will have suffered. Fuel-injection SE is preferred, so you may find the carburettor S version for less than the prices listed here. Both are rare in right-hand drive.

SPECIFICATIONS
Years produced:	1957-1960
Performance:	0-60mph: 17.1sec
	Top speed: 100mph
Power & torque:	98bhp/119lb ft
Engine:	Normally aspirated 2195cc straight six, petrol, carburettor, 12 valves
Drivetrain:	Front-engine RWD
Structure:	Monocoque
Transmission:	Four-speed manual
Weight:	1350kg

PRICE GUIDE
Launch price:	N/A
Excellent:	£30,000
Good:	£22,000
Average:	£14,000
Project:	£8000

MERCEDES-BENZ
300SL Roadster

The replacement for the Gullwing, the Roadster has a revised spaceframe chassis to make room for normal doors, which added 200lb to the weight. It's a softer, more relaxing car to drive than the competition-bred Gullwing. The more extensive use of chrome inside and out isn't to all tastes, but the Roadster at least enjoyed disc brakes from 1961, then got a much lighter aluminium engine block the following year, for which you'll now pay a premium. Expensive to buy, but then they cost more than a detached house in a London suburb when new.

SPECIFICATIONS
Years produced:	1957-1963 (1856 in total)
Performance:	0-60mph: 8.1sec
	Top speed: 130mph
Power & torque:	215bhp/228lb ft
Engine:	Normally aspirated 2996cc straight six, petrol, mechanical injection, 12 valves
Drivetrain:	Front-engine RWD
Structure:	Spaceframe
Transmission:	Four-speed manual
Weight:	1383kg

PRICE GUIDE
Launch price:	£4393
Excellent:	£375,000
Good:	£275,000
Average:	£200,000
Project:	£150,000

MERCEDES-BENZ
190-230 Fintail Saloon

Those tailfins that gave these cars their nickname were shamelessly tacked on to attract American buyers, and it worked: the Fintail Mercs sold extremely well, but without looking like some Pontiac pastiche. They proved handy for rallying too, with a 220SE winning the Monte Carlo rally. Low-rent models have single round headlights, with the more desirable versions treated to stacked headlamps and double-decked bumpers. Four- and six-cylinder engine are available, with diesel options for the former that sold well to taxi drivers.

SPECIFICATIONS
Years produced:	1959-1968 (966,085 in total)
Performance:	0-60mph: 12.8sec
	Top speed: 90mph
Power & torque:	90bhp/113lb ft
Engine:	Normally aspirated 1897cc four cylinder, petrol, carburettor, 8 valves
Drivetrain:	Front-engine RWD
Structure:	Monocoque
Transmission:	Four-speed manual
Weight:	1224kg

PRICE GUIDE
Launch price:	£1987
Excellent:	£8500
Good:	£5500
Average:	£2750
Project:	£1000

MERCEDES-BENZ
300SE Fintail Saloon

The range-topping 300SE gets a mention of its own as there's so much more to it. Extra chrome helps it stand out, but underneath there are real changes. Riding on self-levelling air suspension, the car also benefits from all-wheel disc brakes and has power steering as standard. That 3.0-litre straight-six is a detuned version of the engine used in the 300SL, and there was a choice of four-speed manual or automatic transmission. From 1963 there was also a 300SEL, providing more room thanks to a 4in longer wheelbase.

SPECIFICATIONS
Years produced:	1961-1965 (6748 in total)
Performance:	0-60mph: 10.9sec
	Top speed: 115mph
Power & torque:	157bhp/185lb ft
Engine:	Normally aspirated 2996cc straight six, petrol, fuel injection, 12 valves
Drivetrain:	Front-engine RWD
Structure:	Monocoque
Transmission:	Four-speed manual
Weight:	N/A

PRICE GUIDE
Launch price:	£3814
Excellent:	£11,000
Good:	£7000
Average:	£3500
Project:	£1500

MERCEDES-BENZ
220SEb Coupé/Cabriolet

The first incarnations of Paul Bracq's elegant coupé and convertible body designs which lasted over a decade and are regarded by some as Mercedes-Benz's best-looking cars of the classic era. Interior trimmings are also of the highest quality, beautifully detailed. It may not have had anything like the same performance, but you can see why these cost similar money to an Aston Martin DB4 back in 1962. Four-speed automatics were standard fitment, and you won't find many with the optional four-speed manual 'box. Add 50% for Cabrio prices.

SPECIFICATIONS
Years produced:	1961-1965 (16,902 in total)
Performance:	0-60mph: 12.8sec
	Top speed: 106mph
Power & torque:	120bhp/139lb ft
Engine:	Normally aspirated, 2195cc straight six, petrol, carburettor, 12 valves
Drivetrain:	Front-engine RWD
Structure:	Monocoque
Transmission:	Four-speed automatic
Weight:	1410kg

PRICE GUIDE
Launch price:	£4288
Excellent:	£20,000
Good:	£15,000
Average:	£8000
Project:	£4500

MERCEDES-BENZ
300SE Coupé/Cabriolet

Delivered some of the performance lacking in the 220SEb models thanks to 160bhp and then 170bhp versions of the big fuel-injection six-cylinder engine. The 300SEs also employed the self-levelling air suspension of the 300 saloons, giving them the sort of ride you would comment favourably on in a modern luxury car. With prices approaching those of Bentleys in the UK, along with a propensity for rust, there aren't a lot about. Good ones are sought after. That air suspension can also be troublesome if neglected. Again add 50% for Cabrios.

SPECIFICATIONS
Years produced:	1962-1967 (3127 in total)
Performance:	0-60mph: 10.7sec
	Top speed: 115mph
Power & torque:	167bhp/184lb ft
Engine:	Normally aspirated 2996cc straight six, petrol, fuel injection, 12 valves
Drivetrain:	Front-engine RWD
Structure:	Monocoque
Transmission:	Four-speed automatic
Weight:	1600kg

PRICE GUIDE
Launch price:	£4931
Excellent:	£24,000
Good:	£18,000
Average:	£12,000
Project:	£6000

MERCEDES-BENZ
230/250SL

In keeping with the fashion to apply generic names to Mercedes-Benz ranges to help cut through the maze of numbers, you'll find 'Pagoda' commonly attached to these sports cars, thanks to the kicked up edges to the roofline of the optional hardtop. Offering more power and performance than the 190SL it replaced, the 230SL proved its worth by winning the Spa-Sofia-Liège rally. The 250SL replaced it, but was only around for 1967. The larger engine offered no more power but extra torque, and there were only detail differences elsewhere.

SPECIFICATIONS
Years produced:	1963-1968 (19,831/5196 in total)
Performance:	0-60mph: 10.5sec
	Top speed: 124mph
Power & torque:	148bhp/145lb ft
Engine:	Normally aspirated 2308cc straight six, petrol, fuel injection, 12 valves
Drivetrain:	Front-engine RWD
Structure:	Monocoque
Transmission:	Four-speed manual/four-speed auto
Weight:	1295kg

PRICE GUIDE
Launch price:	£3595
Excellent:	£37,500
Good:	£25,000
Average:	£18,500
Project:	£8000

Nothing but the best.

Engine overhaul, bodywork repair or upholstery, our specialists face every job. Engine dynamometer and frame straightener ensure perfection down to the detail, because Kienle-restored vehicles are compared with the best - with Mercedes Benz.

photos:
GAUKLER STUDIOS
FOTO & ATELIER

KIENLE
Automobiltechnik

D-71254 Heimerdingen/Stuttgart · Max-Planck-Str. 4 · Germany
Tel. (49) 71 52/5 28 27 · Fax (49) 71 52/5 80 16
www.kienle.com · e-mail: info@kienle.com

As the leading specialist for the restoration of Mercedes-Benz vehicles we set quality standards with partial and complete restorations, repairs and maintenance for over two decades now. In addition, we own one of the world's largest spare-parts-stocks for original parts and high-quality re-manufactured parts, and prepare expert appraisals for Mercedes-Benz vehicles.

Please ask for a portrait of our company available as brochure or Video/DVD (€ 10,).

Hours of business: Weekdays 8 am - 6 pm and Saturdays 9 am - 2 pm.

text & design

Visit our large showroom with over 50 classic and exclusive cars!

MERCEDES-BENZ
600

Mercedes-Benz threw everything but the kitchen sink at this technical tour de force, designed to be bought by governments rather than mere business magnates. They weighed in at 2.5 tonnes (or more for the long-wheelbase Pullman seven-seater), and that was before bulletproof glass was added. There's air suspension, vacuum central locking, two heating and ventilation systems, and to haul it around a new 6.3-litre V8 with Bosch fuel injection. The limo stayed in production for 18 years and notched up remarkable sales for its type.

SPECIFICATIONS
Years produced:	1964-1981 (2677 in total)
Performance:	0-60mph: 9.7sec
	Top speed: 127mph
Power & torque:	247bhp/369lb ft
Engine:	Normally aspirated 6332cc V8, petrol, fuel injection, 16 valves
Drivetrain:	Front-engine RWD
Structure:	Monocoque
Transmission:	Four-speed automatic
Weight:	2475kg

PRICE GUIDE
Launch price:	£8752
Excellent:	£75,000
Good:	£40,000
Average:	£22,500
Project:	£12,500

MERCEDES-BENZ
300SE/SEL (W108/W109)

Packed with luxuries and safety items, the 300 sat comfortably at the top of the new S-class range, with the SEL – 4in longer than the standard cars – roughly twice the price of the entry-level 250S. The 300 came as standard with a four-speed automatic gearbox, later supplemented by an optional five-speed manual. All used the all-alloy 3.0-litre straight six until late 1968, when the SE was dropped and the 300SEL – confusingly for those starting to understand Mercedes-Benz nomenclature – got the 280SE's 2.8-litre engine.

SPECIFICATIONS
Years produced:	1965-1969 (7625 in total)
Performance:	0-60mph: 11.2sec
	Top speed: 115mph
Power & torque:	168bhp/184lb ft
Engine:	Normally aspirated 2996cc straight six, petrol, fuel injection, 12 valves
Drivetrain:	Front-engine RWD
Structure:	Monocoque
Transmission:	Four-speed automatic
Weight:	1575kg

PRICE GUIDE
Launch price:	£5669
Excellent:	£6500
Good:	£5000
Average:	£3000
Project:	£1250

MERCEDES-BENZ
250/280/SE Saloon

This was the dawn of the S-class, styled in a timeless if unexciting manner by Paul Bracq. Entry level was provided by the 250S with twin Solex carbs and 130bhp, with the Bosch fuel-injection 250SE offering another 20bhp and shaving two seconds off the car's 0-60mph time. In 1968 the engines were increased to 2.8-litres, still with a carburettor S and fuel-injection SE option, and the long-wheelbase bodyshell previously only offered on the top-of-the-range 300SEL came with the smaller engine as well, badged 280SEL.

SPECIFICATIONS
Years produced:	1965-1972 (325,562 in total)
Performance:	0-60mph: 11.8sec
	Top speed: 118mph
Power & torque:	148bhp/159lb ft
Engine:	Normally aspirated 2497cc straight six, petrol, fuel injection, 12 valves
Drivetrain:	Front-engine RWD
Structure:	Monocoque
Transmission:	Four-speed manual/four-speed auto
Weight:	1480kg

PRICE GUIDE
Launch price:	£2575
Excellent:	£5750
Good:	£4500
Average:	£2400
Project:	£800

MERCEDES-BENZ
250/280SE Coupé/Cabrio

With the 1965 launch of the S-class saloon, the smaller-engined versions of the Coupé and Cabriolet were improved and rationalised by being given the 2.5-litre engine from the new cars. That added 30bhp, and rear disc brakes were fitted at the same time. Two years later, when the 300SE was dropped, the 280SE replaced both that and the 250SE with its 2.8-litre 160bhp straight six, with revised fuel injection for better economy. A five-speed manual gearbox was an option from 1969. Cabriolets are worth 70% more than Coupés.

SPECIFICATIONS
Years produced:	1965-1972 (6213 in total)
Performance:	0-60mph: 11.8sec
	Top speed: 118mph
Power & torque:	148bhp/159lb ft
Engine:	Normally aspirated 2497cc straight six, petrol, fuel injection, 12 valves
Drivetrain:	Front-engine RWD
Structure:	Monocoque
Transmission:	Four-speed manual
Weight:	1480kg

PRICE GUIDE
Launch price:	£4275
Excellent:	£24,000
Good:	£18,000
Average:	£12,000
Project:	£8000

MERCEDES-BENZ
280SL

The final version of the Pagoda roadsters also turned out to be the best-selling. With the engine bored out to 2.8 litres, even with the restrictions caused by new emission controls it offered more power and torque this time, though some of the benefits were lost due to the weight the car had gained. The suspension was also retuned in favour of ride comfort, which means the 280SL doesn't have quite the same handling prowess as previous SLs. None of that has stopped it from becoming the favoured version of the range with buyers.

SPECIFICATIONS
Years produced:	1967-1971 (23,885 in total)
Performance:	0-60mph: 9.0sec
	Top speed: 124mph
Power & torque:	168bhp/177lb ft
Engine:	Normally aspirated 2778cc straight six, petrol, fuel injection, 12 valves
Drivetrain:	Front-engine RWD
Structure:	Monocoque
Transmission:	Four-speed manual/four-speed auto
Weight:	1360kg

PRICE GUIDE
Launch price:	£3850
Excellent:	£48,000
Good:	£28,000
Average:	£20,000
Project:	£8500

MERCEDES-BENZ
300SEL 6.3 (W109)

In 1968, Mercedes-Benz engineers went slightly bonkers and dropped the 6.3-litre V8 from the 600 into the long-wheelbase 300's bodyshell, keeping luxuries such as air suspension. With the engine's massive torque, the result was a muscle car in disguise, and unlike most American muscle cars it came with dual-circuit four-wheel disc brakes. This was a luxury saloon that could outpace most of the sports cars on sale at the time, though you had to cough up more than the price of a Ferrari Daytona for the pleasure.

SPECIFICATIONS
Years produced: 1967-1972 (6526 in total)
Performance: 0-60mph: 5.7sec
Top speed: 141mph
Power & torque: 247bhp/369lb ft
Engine: Normally aspirated 6332cc V8, petrol, carburettor, 16 valves
Drivetrain: Front-engine RWD
Structure: Monocoque
Transmission: Four-speed automatic
Weight: 1780kg

PRICE GUIDE
Launch price: £7743
Excellent: £20,000
Good: £10,000
Average: £6500
Project: £3500

MERCEDES-BENZ
230.6/250/280E Saloon

These saloons use the same bodyshell as the W115 cars but have six-cylinder engines, giving them the Mercedes-Benz range designation W114. At entry level is the 230.6 with 120bhp, joined at first by the 130bhp 250. The confusion begins in 1970 when the 250 is given a single-cam 2.8-litre engine, though the regular 250 continued for two years. Then a 280 joined the range, using a twin-cam 2.8-litre engine, in carburettor form, or as the 280E, with fuel injection. Only the latter came to the UK. Functional, strong, elegant, and gaining a following.

SPECIFICATIONS
Years produced: 1967-1976
Performance: 0-60mph: 12.8sec
Top speed: 112mph
Power & torque: 128bhp/147lb ft
Engine: Normally aspirated 2496cc straight six, petrol, carburettor, 12 valves
Drivetrain: Front-engine RWD
Structure: Monocoque
Transmission: Four-speed manual
Weight: 1375kg

PRICE GUIDE
Launch price: £4753
Excellent: £5500
Good: £4000
Average: £2250
Project: £600

MERCEDES-BENZ
250/280CE Coupé (W114)

Only the fuel-injection versions of these pillarless coupés came to the UK market, though carburettor versions were sold elsewhere, without the 'E' on the end of their name. They were based on the W114 saloons, retaining their length and wheelbase but with a shortened passenger compartment and a roof that was two inches lower. The 150bhp 250CE gave way to the 280CE in 1972. This later car came with the 185bhp twin-cam 2.8-litre engine. In some markets, such as the US, there was also a version of the 250 with a single-cam 2.8 engine on carbs.

SPECIFICATIONS
Years produced: 1968-1976 (21,787/11,518 in total)
Performance: 0-60mph: 8.9sec
Top speed: 118mph
Power & torque: 150bhp/174lb ft
Engine: Normally aspirated 2497cc straight six, petrol, fuel injection, 12 valves
Drivetrain: Front-engine RWD
Structure: Monocoque
Transmission: Three-speed automatic
Weight: 1360kg

PRICE GUIDE
Launch price: £3475
Excellent: £12,500
Good: £7500
Average: £3250
Project: £2000

MERCEDES-BENZ
280SE 3.5 Coupé/Cabriolet (W111)

These are the ones that everyone wants but few can afford. From late 1969 Mercedes-Benz dropped its 3.5-litre V8s into the Coupés and Cabrios to create a reassuringly expensive range-topper with 25% more power than the six-cylinder cars. Today, the SE 3.5s have become cooler than a penguin's fridge. Of course the much rarer Cabriolets take the top honours, with prices more than double those given here for Coupés.

SPECIFICATIONS
Years produced: 1969-1971 (4502 in total)
Performance: 0-60mph: 9.0sec
Top speed: 130mph
Power & torque: 197bhp/211lb ft
Engine: Normally aspirated 3499cc V8, petrol, mechanical fuel injection, 16 valves
Drivetrain: Front-engine RWD
Structure: Monocoque
Transmission: Four-speed automatic
Weight: 1570kg

PRICE GUIDE
Launch price: £5158
Excellent: £45,000
Good: £32,500
Average: £20,000
Project: £12,000

MERCEDES-BENZ
280SE 3.5/300SEL 3.5 (W108/W109)

For anyone enjoying the puzzle of the 2.8-litre 300SEL, here we have the same S-class bodies fitted with a 3.5-litre V8 to bridge the gap between the six-cylinder cars and the crazy 300SEL 6.3. So the best versions of the W108/109 S-class saloons remain something of an enigma. The 300 still has air suspension, so mechanically shy buyers might prefer a 280. There was also a 280SEL 3.5, but that seemed one choice too many and only 951 were built.

SPECIFICATIONS
Years produced: 1969-1972 (11,309/9483 in total)
Performance: 0-60mph: 8.4sec
Top speed: 115mph
Power & torque: 157bhp/185lb ft
Engine: Normally aspirated 2996cc straight six, petrol, fuel injection, 12 valves
Drivetrain: Front-engine RWD
Structure: Monocoque
Transmission: Four-speed automatic
Weight: 1673kg

PRICE GUIDE
Launch price: £5158
Excellent: £8250
Good: £6500
Average: £3400
Project: £1500

MERCEDES-BENZ
350/450SLC (C107)

Mercedes-Benz took a bit of a shortcut to creating these 2+2 coupés. In effect, what you have is an R107 roadster with 14 inches added to the wheelbase, a fixed roof and some rear seats. Of course there's a bit more to it that that, as the job was achieved while only adding 110lb to the car's weight. Launched with a 3.5-litre V8, it was joined the following year by a 4.5-litre version that outsold the smaller engine by more than two to one. Elegant and well detailed, they are considerably cheaper than the soft-tops.

SPECIFICATIONS

Years produced:	1971-1980 (13,925/31,739 in total)
Performance:	0-60mph: 9.3sec
	Top speed: 130mph
Power & torque:	217bhp/265lb ft
Engine:	Normally aspirated 4520cc V8, petrol, mechanical fuel injection, 16 valves
Drivetrain:	Front-engine RWD
Structure:	Monocoque
Transmission:	Four-speed automatic
Weight:	1630kg

PRICE GUIDE

Launch price:	£7875
Excellent:	£10,000
Good:	£6500
Average:	£3250
Project:	£1000

MERCEDES-BENZ
350/450SL (R107)

The 350SL was introduced as a replacement for the Pagoda 280SL, and once again both soft and hard tops were offered. There's more than a passing resemblance between the two cars, but the 350SL's body is three inches longer and 300lb heavier. The 450's extra litre of engine capacity didn't add much power, but torque took a big leap and allowed it to be fitted with a much taller rear axle ratio. That makes it even more of a lazy cruiser than the 350SL, but helps out on the economy front too. Nearly all were fitted with an automatic gearbox.

SPECIFICATIONS

Years produced:	1971-1980 (15,304 in total)
Performance:	0-60mph: 9.3sec
	Top speed: 126mph
Power & torque:	200bhp/211lb ft
Engine:	Normally aspirated 3499cc V8, petrol, electronic fuel injection, 16 valves
Drivetrain:	Front-engine RWD
Structure:	Monocoque
Transmission:	Four-speed manual/three-speed auto
Weight:	1545kg

PRICE GUIDE 350/450SL

Launch price:	£7395	£8598
Excellent:	£12,500	£13,500
Good:	£10,000	£10,000
Average:	£5250	£6000
Project:	£2500	£3000

MERCEDES-BENZ
280S/SE (W116)

This is the second generation of S-class cars, and the one that cemented Mercedes' reputation at the top of the saloon car pecking order. The 280s were the basic models, though not that basic, and came with a twin-cam straight six that produced either 160bhp with carbs (S) or 185bhp using fuel injection (SE). To say they led the market in safety features might sound boring, but they also had a fair turn of speed and excellent roadholding thanks to their new semi-trailing arm rear suspension. Now much cheaper than they deserve to be.

SPECIFICATIONS

Years produced:	1972-1980 (273,623 in total)
Performance:	0-60mph: 10.5sec
	Top speed: 124mph
Power & torque:	182bhp/176lb ft
Engine:	Normally aspirated 2746cc straight six, petrol, fuel injection, 12 valves
Drivetrain:	Front-engine RWD
Structure:	Monocoque
Transmission:	Four-speed manual
Weight:	1610kg

PRICE GUIDE

Launch price:	£5597
Excellent:	£5000
Good:	£3750
Average:	£2000
Project:	£750

MERCEDES-BENZ
350/450SE/SEL (W116)

Provocatively dubbed 'the best car in the world' when new, the V8-engined version of the S-class became one of the few truly deserving winners of the Car of the Year award. Its build quality and equipment level set new standards and you can still be impressed by driving one that's over 30 years old. Model numbers represent the 3.5 and 4.5-litre V8s, and there's also a 450SEL with an extra six inches in the wheelbase, mostly for the benefit of rear legroom. Good ones are still not that expensive to buy, but a poor one could quickly wither your wallet.

SPECIFICATIONS

Years produced:	1972-1980 (156,585 in total)
Performance:	0-60mph: 9.3sec
	Top speed: 130mph
Power & torque:	221bhp/279lb ft
Engine:	Normally aspirated 4520cc V8, petrol, mechanical fuel injection, 16 valves
Drivetrain:	Front-engine RWD
Structure:	Monocoque
Transmission:	Three-speed automatic
Weight:	1765kg

PRICE GUIDE

Launch price:	£6995
Excellent:	£6000
Good:	£4750
Average:	£2000
Project:	£800

MERCEDES-BENZ
450SEL 6.9 (W116)

With its all-dominating S-class cars selling so well, the range was losing the cachet of exclusivity, and Mercedes-Benz needed something extra for the image-conscious plutocrat. A 6.9-litre V8 engine did the trick, along with self-levelling oleopneumatic suspension. Reassuringly expensive, the same money would buy you two XJ-S V12s and a Lancia Beta HPE, but the 450SEL 6.9 still sold in surprising numbers. Now prices are a little closer to Earth, but you'll still need a comfortable income to meet the running costs.

SPECIFICATIONS

Years produced:	1975-1980 (7380 in total)
Performance:	0-60mph: 7.5sec
	Top speed: 140mph
Power & torque:	286bhp/405lb ft
Engine:	Normally aspirated 6834cc V8, petrol, injection, 16 valves
Drivetrain:	Front-engine RWD
Structure:	Monocoque
Transmission:	Three-speed automatic
Weight:	1935kg

PRICE GUIDE

Launch price:	£21,995
Excellent:	£20,000
Good:	£11,000
Average:	£5000
Project:	£2500

MERCEDES-BENZ
200/230E/280E (W123)

It was a case of more of the same when Mercedes-Benz came to replacing the popular stack-headlight W115 saloon. The W123 was possibly the company's high watermark when it came to build quality and longevity although, in the UK, you paid for the privilege of owning one. Base-model 200 and 200D were both flaccid, with the 230E a much better all-rounder. Twin-cam 280E is an all-purpose sporting saloon, but without the exciting dynamics associated with the rival BMW 528i. Still remarkably popular in North Africa.

SPECIFICATIONS (230E)
Years produced:	1975-1985 (2,696,915 in total)
Performance:	0-60mph: 11.5sec
	Top speed: 112mph
Power & torque:	134bhp/151lb ft
Engine:	Normally aspirated 2299cc four cylinder, petrol, injection, 8 valves
Drivetrain:	Front-engine RWD
Structure:	Monocoque
Transmission:	Four-speed manual
Weight:	1380kg

PRICE GUIDE
Launch price:	£6235
Excellent:	£6000
Good:	£4500
Average:	£2500
Project:	£600

MERCEDES-BENZ
230/280CE (C123)

Based on the W123 saloons, but with 10cm nipped out of the wheelbase, these pillarless coupés shared the same hard-wearing interior. Top of the range was the 177bhp fuel-injection 280CE, while entry level was covered by the 230C, which put out 109bhp on carbs. Some markets got the in-between 280C with 156bhp, again on carbs. Both of those were dropped in 1980 to make way for the 230CE, which not only got fuel injection but a new 2.3-litre engine to go with it. Output was now 136bhp, while the 280CE crept up to 185bhp.

SPECIFICATIONS (230CE)
Years produced:	1977-1985 (99,147 in total)
Performance:	0-60mph: 11.5sec
	Top speed: 112mph
Power & torque:	134bhp/151lb ft
Engine:	Normally aspirated 2299cc four cylinder, petrol, injection, 8 valves
Drivetrain:	Front-engine RWD
Structure:	Monocoque
Transmission:	Four-speed manual
Weight:	1380kg

PRICE GUIDE
Launch price:	£8951
Excellent:	£13,000
Good:	£7000
Average:	£4000
Project:	£2000

MERCEDES-BENZ
280/300SL (R107)

The strong-selling R107 roadsters were given a makeover in 1980. Nothing you'd really notice in the body, as this was still considered too good to mess with, but there were plenty of improvements under the skin. Main change was upgrading the standard gearbox from a four- to a five-speed manual. In September 1985 the six-cylinder twin-cam engine's capacity was increased to 3.0 litres. That only added an extra 5bhp, but the torque figure was up by 21lb ft, produced at lower revs. Both versions were good sellers that now hold their values well.

SPECIFICATIONS
Years produced:	1980-1986
Performance:	0-60mph: 9.0sec
	Top speed: 124mph
Power & torque:	185bhp/177lb ft
Engine:	Normally aspirated 2746cc straight six, petrol, injection, 12 valves
Drivetrain:	Front-engine RWD
Structure:	Monocoque
Transmission:	Four-speed automatic
Weight:	1500kg

PRICE GUIDE
Launch price:	£16,599
Excellent:	£13,000
Good:	£9000
Average:	£5500
Project:	£2500

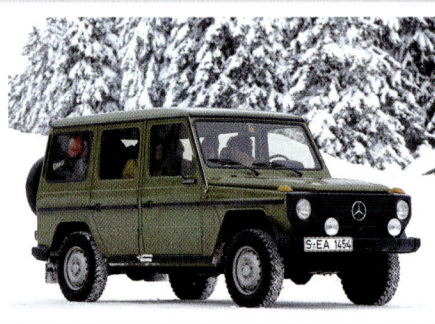

MERCEDES-BENZ
G-Wagen

More Land Rover than Range Rover, the Mercedes-Benz G-Wagen was a real beast of burden with incredible off-road ability to match. Engineered by Steyr-Daimler Puch in Austria, it was designed with military use in mind, so hardly a recipe for luxury and comfort. A high price, lack of equipment and that utilitarian style hampered sales in the UK, especially in the wake of the Mitsubishi Shogun and Isuzu Trooper. But as a classic off-roader the G-Wagen has bags of appeal, thanks to its timeless design and rugged build.

SPECIFICATIONS (230GE)
Years produced:	1979-date
Performance:	0-60mph: 15.5sec
	Top speed: 88mph
Power & torque:	125bhp/142lb ft
Engine:	Normally aspirated 2299cc four cylinder, petrol, fuel injection, 8 valves
Drivetrain:	Front-engine AWD
Structure:	Separate chassis
Transmission:	Four-speed manual
Weight:	1830kg

PRICE GUIDE
Launch price:	£14,195 (UK launch, 1981)
Excellent:	£20,000
Good:	£15,000
Average:	£3000
Project:	£1500

MERCEDES-BENZ
380/420SL (R107)

These 'junior' versions of Mercedes' V8 roadster started with the 380SL. In September 1981, after just a year in production, the engine was changed for a small-bore/long-stroke V8 of the same capacity but with a slight drop in power and a 10% improvement in fuel economy. From 1985 the capacity was increased to 4.2 litres, which at least restored power figures to their original level of 218bhp. All have automatic gearboxes, but it's the highly-regarded four-speed unit and not the three-speed used in pre-1980 SLs.

SPECIFICATIONS
Years produced:	1980-1989
Performance:	0-60mph: 7.7sec
	Top speed: 134mph
Power & torque:	245bhp/294lb ft
Engine:	Normally aspirated 4973cc V8, petrol, mechanical fuel injection, 16 valves
Drivetrain:	Front-engine RWD
Structure:	Monocoque
Transmission:	Four-speed automatic
Weight:	1605kg

PRICE GUIDE
Launch price:	£18,300
Excellent:	£11,000
Good:	£9000
Average:	£6000
Project:	£3000

MERCEDES-BENZ
380/420/500SEC (C126)

If the S-class saloon was the best car in the world during the '80s then this – built on a 4in shorter S-class floorpan – must have been the best coupé. The 380 came with 204bhp and steel wheels, with ABS only an optional extra until 1985. The 420 replaced it at the 1986 facelift, when the SE grew fatter bumpers and side skirts and was good for 218bhp. The range-topper for five years until the 560 arrived, the 500SEC came with 240bhp, electric seats, ABS and a walnut-veneered dash. Fast and comfortable, they offer a lot of car for your money.

SPECIFICATIONS
Years produced:	1981-1991
Performance:	0-60mph: 7.9sec
	Top speed: 140mph
Power & torque:	228bhp/299lb ft
Engine:	Normally aspirated 4973cc V8, petrol, injection, 16 valves
Drivetrain:	Front-engine RWD
Structure:	Monocoque
Transmission:	Four-speed automatic
Weight:	1610kg

PRICE GUIDE
Launch price:	£25,700
Excellent:	£9750
Good:	£7500
Average:	£3250
Project:	£1000

MERCEDES-BENZ
500/560SL (R107)

Expensive flagships of the SL range, though it turned out to be the best-selling model. 500SL was there from the start, standing out from lesser SLs by the addition of a fairly subtle bootlid lip spoiler. It lost a little power when retuned for economy in September 1981, gaining a taller diff' ratio at the same time, so those early cars are more sought after. The 560SL joined the 500 in 1985 but didn't displace it, merely adding power, badge one-upmanship, and a thirst for fuel. All SLs should be considered as tourers rather than sports cars.

SPECIFICATIONS
Years produced:	1982-1989
Performance:	0-60mph: 7.7sec
	Top speed: 134mph
Power & torque:	245bhp/294lb ft
Engine:	Normally aspirated 4973cc V8, petrol, injection, 16 valves
Drivetrain:	Front-engine RWD
Structure:	Monocoque
Transmission:	Four-speed automatic
Weight:	1605kg

PRICE GUIDE
Launch price:	£20,300
Excellent:	£18,000
Good:	£9750
Average:	£6500
Project:	£3500

MERCEDES-BENZ
190 (W201)

Darlings of the '80s upwardly mobile, almost two million 190s rolled out of the factory. Mercedes-Benz did an excellent job of scaling its big-car looks down into a BMW 3-series rivalling package. Largely ignored by the classic car market until recently, good examples are starting to be snapped up for what look like bargain prices. Only the Cosworth-tweaked and spoiler-clad 16V models in 2.3 and 2.5-litre form have attracted much enthusiast attention, and prices for those can be double those quoted for everyday 190s.

SPECIFICATIONS (190)
Years produced:	1982-1993 (1,874,668 in total)
Performance:	0-60mph: 13.4sec
	Top speed: 109mph
Power & torque:	88bhp/122lb ft
Engine:	Normally aspirated 1997cc four cylinder, petrol, carburettor, 8 valves
Drivetrain:	Front-engine RWD
Structure:	Monocoque
Transmission:	Five-speed manual
Weight:	1080kg

PRICE GUIDE
Launch price:	£9685
Excellent:	£3250
Good:	£2500
Average:	£1200
Project:	£400

MERCEDES-BENZ
190E 2.3/2.5-16

The '80s were an exciting time for Mercedes-Benz. It went downmarket to chase BMW, and did it in an inimitable style orchestrated by design chief Bruno Sacco. The 190E had done a great job of stealing 3-series sales, but lacked a little of that car's glamour. The 190E 2.3-16 was conceived for touring car racing and, thanks to a clever cylinder head from Cosworth, delivered ample power and torque to turn this staid-looking car into a flying machine. The 1988 2.5-litre version with 200bhp was even more exciting; Evo I and II models are worth considerably more.

SPECIFICATIONS (2.3-16)
Years produced:	1985-1993 (see above)
Performance:	0-60mph: 7.3sec
	Top speed: 144mph
Power & torque:	182bhp/173lb ft
Engine:	Normally aspirated 2299cc four cylinder, petrol, fuel injection, 16 valves
Drivetrain:	Front-engine RWD
Structure:	Monocoque
Transmission:	Five-speed manual
Weight:	1230kg

PRICE GUIDE
Launch price:	£21,045
Excellent:	£12,500
Good:	£7500
Average:	£5000
Project:	£2000

MERCEDES-BENZ
200E/300E (W124)

Replacing the W123 was a case of more of the same for Mercedes-Benz. Although the style was very much rooted in the '80s, closely mirroring the 190E, the engines and running gear were carried over from the older car. Considered by many aficionados as the final 'hewn-from-granite' Mercedes-Benzes, the W124 is a satisfying ownership proposition. There aren't many weaknesses – the engines go on forever, and the interior is strong enough to survive a nuclear attack. Rust nibbles away at the edges, and many people are finding profit in breaking rather than repair.

SPECIFICATIONS (300E Auto)
Years produced:	1985-1995 (3800 in total)
Performance:	0-60mph: 8.4sec
	Top speed: 136mph
Power & torque:	188bhp/192lb ft
Engine:	Normally aspirated 2962cc straight six, petrol, fuel injection, 12 valves
Drivetrain:	Front-engine RWD
Structure:	Monocoque
Transmission:	Five-speed manual/four-speed auto
Weight:	1470kg

PRICE GUIDE
Launch price:	£12,500
Excellent:	£4500
Good:	£2000
Average:	£1000
Project:	£500

MERCEDES-BENZ
560SEC (C126)

Quite simply the best four-seater coupé you could buy in the '80s, and there still can't be a lot to compare them with today. Mercedes-Benz created something special by taking the best of the other SECs and adding fatter tyres, flared arches and a limited-slip diff. Climate control came as standard, as did heated seats from 1988. With the aid of a mechanical/electronic fuel injection system, the 560's engine put out 20% more power than the 500SEC's. There was a price to match - by the end of the '80s these cars cost a massive £63,000.

SPECIFICATIONS

Years produced:	1985-1991
Performance:	0-60mph: 6.8sec
	Top speed: 156mph
Power & torque:	295bhp/335lb ft
Engine:	Normally aspirated 5547cc V8, petrol, injection, 16 valves
Drivetrain:	Front-engine RWD
Structure:	Monocoque
Transmission:	Four-speed automatic
Weight:	1748kg

PRICE GUIDE

Launch price:	£52,185
Excellent:	£12,000
Good:	£8500
Average:	£4000
Project:	£1750

MERCEDES-BENZ
300CE (W124)

This sleek coupé was based on a shortened saloon floorpan, in this case that of the surprisingly entertaining and almost indestructible E-class. The 300CE drives even better than it looks, and started out with a 188bhp 12-valve engine. This was joined for the 1990 model year by a 24-valve version with 231bhp. You may have to pay a little more than suggested for one of those, especially if it comes with manual transmission. Most of both versions were sold with Mercedes' tough four-speed auto, but the manual cars are the more coveted now.

SPECIFICATIONS

Years produced:	1987-1993 (19,320 in total)
Performance:	0-60mph: 8.1sec
	Top speed: 140mph
Power & torque:	177bhp/188lb ft
Engine:	Normally aspirated 2962cc straight six, petrol, injection, 12 valves
Drivetrain:	Front-engine RWD
Structure:	Monocoque
Transmission:	Five-speed manual/four-speed auto
Weight:	1390kg

PRICE GUIDE

Launch price:	£30,100
Excellent:	£5000
Good:	£3250
Average:	£1750
Project:	£1000

MERCURY

MERCURY WAS Edsel Ford's creation, intended to plug the gap between Ford and Lincoln – a middle-class offering. The name Mercury came from Roman mythology. GM's Buick division was Lincoln's target marque, and between 1945 and its death, it proved an effective foil for its rival. Although Mercury is often described as a badge-engineering exercise, it proved useful in extending the sales appeal of Ford's core platforms – such as the Mercury Cougar (below), which was based on the Ford Mustang. The marque fell as a result of the global economic crisis, as Ford rationalised its range, focusing on Lincoln. The last Mercury rolled off the line on 4 January 2011.

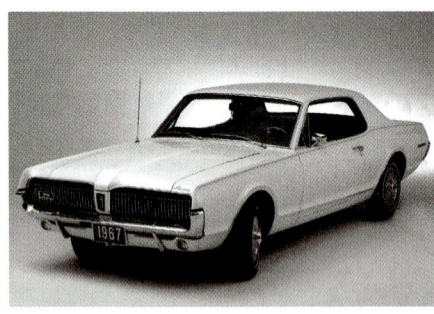

MERCURY
Cougar

The Cougar was conceived to lower the average age of the typical Lincoln-Mercury customer, and did it with some style – and a Ford Mustang platform. The 3in stretch in wheelbase and headlamps hidden behind a slatted grille were Cougar identifiers. Styling was tweaked to look more 'European', and it proved something of a hit for Ford's luxury division. The engine range was wide, with a base 200bhp 289cu in and topped by the legendary 390bhp 427. Overshadowed by the Mustang, despite a Bond cameo in *On Her Majesty's Secret Service*.

SPECIFICATIONS (289)

Years produced:	1966-1973 (614,225 in total)
Performance:	0-60mph: 8.0sec
	Top speed: 125mph
Power & torque:	275bhp/312lb ft
Engine:	Normally aspirated 4727cc V8, petrol, carburettor, 16 valves
Drivetrain:	Front-engine RWD
Structure:	Monocoque
Transmission:	Four-speed manual/three-speed auto
Weight:	1450kg

PRICE GUIDE

Launch price:	N/A in UK
Excellent:	£11,000
Good:	£8000
Average:	£6000
Project:	£3000

MESSERSCHMITT

IT'S A POPULAR myth that the Messerschmitt bubblecars used cockpits from unfinished fighters for their bodywork, although aviation experience did influence Willy Messerschmitt's globular three-wheelers. They were produced from 1953, as the company was banned from building aircraft after the war. Designed by Fritz Frend, Messerschmitts became known for their terrier-like turns of speed, especially the four-wheeled Tg500 which was fittingly known as the Tiger. The drop-off in the microcar market in the 1960s caused by the boom in small 'real' cars resulted in Messerschmitt production ending in 1964. It subsequently returned to building aircraft.

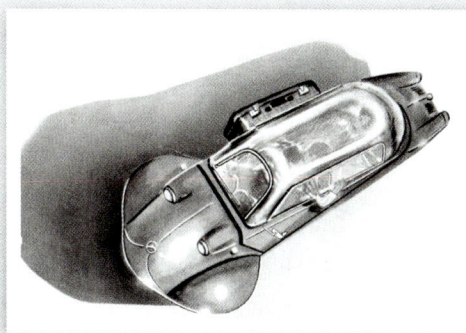

MESSERSCHMITT
KR175

The Messerschmitt KR175 (for Kabinenroller) was introduced for up-and-coming German families who needed inexpensive transport during tough times. Aircraft engineer Fritz Fend was behind the bubblecar and based it on the cockpit of a Messerschmitt plane. Initially powered by a single-cylinder engine, the lightweight machine was capable of 60mph – quite a feat considering the top speeds of standard family cars at the time. High levels of build quality and simple construction means that the survival rate is high, reflecting the cult status these cars now enjoy.

SPECIFICATIONS
Years produced:	1953-1964 (19,668 in total)
Performance:	0-60mph: N/A
	Top speed: 50 mph
Power & torque:	9bhp/N/A
Engine:	Normally aspirated 173cc two-stroke single cylinder, petrol, carburettor
Drivetrain:	Rear-engine RWD
Structure:	Tubular chassis
Transmission:	Four-speed manual
Weight:	220kg

PRICE GUIDE
Launch price:	DM 2100
Excellent:	£13,500
Good:	£10,000
Average:	£6250
Project:	£3250

MESSERSCHMITT
Tg500 Tiger

The main difference between the Tg500 and its lower-powered predecessors was the extra wheel. Now with the full complement of four, the uprated 500cc 20bhp Sachs twin-cylinder was housed in a more suitable chassis. Performance of the ultimate go-faster bubblecar was verging on the silly, with a top speed of over 75mph and a 0-60mph time of 18.7 seconds – enough to see off full-sized cars such as the Austin A30 and Morris Minor with ease. Sales were slow though, with fewer than 500 built, and that makes the Tiger highly collectable today.

SPECIFICATIONS
Years produced:	1958-1961 (320 in total)
Performance:	0-60mph: 28.1sec
	Top speed: 78 mph
Power & torque:	19.5bhp/24lb ft
Engine:	Normally aspirated 460cc two-stroke twin, petrol, carburettor,
Drivetrain:	Rear-engine RWD
Structure:	Tubular chassis, steel body
Transmission:	Four-speed manual
Weight:	370kg

PRICE GUIDE
Launch price:	DM 3650
Excellent:	£60,000
Good:	£50,000
Average:	£40,000
Project:	£30,000

MG

CECIL KIMBER WAS manager of Morris Garages in Oxford when he commissioned some sports cars to be built on a Morris chassis in 1923. Their appeal prompted more models and MG soon became one of the favourite pre-war British performance marques. In 1952, it joined BMC and introduced the much-loved MGA, then the MGB, which was produced from 1962 to 1980. After the Abingdon factory was closed, MG existed only as a badge on hot Austin saloons until the MG RV8 of 1992 announced the proper rebirth of the badge. The mid-engined MGF was an exciting return to form. Since it went into administration in 2005, MG has been Chinese-owned, first by Nanjing, then SAIC.

MG
TA/TB

The original MG Midget: a development of the PB-type, but featuring a larger body and powered by a 1292cc pushrod OHV four-cylinder engine (50bhp at 4000rpm). Twin SU carburettors and four-speed gearbox were typically sporting fitments, while hydraulic brakes and semi-elliptic springs added driver confidence. The TB, introduced in May 1939, had more of the same: larger carburettors, 54bhp at 5200rpm, and synchromesh on the top three gears. Two-seater sports, Tickford DHC and fixed-head Airline Coupé bodies were poular alternatives.

SPECIFICATIONS
Years produced:	1936-1939 (3003/379 in total)
Performance:	0-60mph: 17.6sec
	Top speed: 78mph
Power & torque:	50bhp/N/A
Engine:	Normally aspirated 1292cc four cylinder, petrol, carburettor, 8 valves
Drivetrain:	Front-engine RWD
Structure:	Separate chassis
Transmission:	Four-speed manual
Weight:	801kg

PRICE GUIDE
Launch price:	£222
Excellent:	£20,000
Good:	£17,000
Average:	£12,000
Project:	£7000

MG
WA

This was MG's attempt to move in on the luxury sports saloon market exploited by SS Jaguar, but the war intervened before many had been built. Available as a saloon or Tickford-bodied drophead coupé, there are still roughly 25 survivors of each worldwide. They turned out to be better appointed than the equivalent SS-Jaguars with lots of wood, leather and MG logos, and have better steering and road manners. They're usually snapped up quickly when they come up for sale; add 20% to the prices given for a Tickford drophead.

SPECIFICATIONS
Years produced:	1938-1939 (370 in total)
Performance:	0-60mph: N/A
	Top speed: 91mph
Power & torque:	96bhp/N/A
Engine:	Normally aspirated 2561cc straight six, petrol, carburettor, 12 valves
Drivetrain:	Front-engine RWD
Structure:	Separate chassis
Transmission:	Four-speed manual
Weight:	1232kg

PRICE GUIDE
Launch price:	£442
Excellent:	£50,000
Good:	£40,000
Average:	£30,000
Project:	£10,000

MG
TC

The first post-war MG, almost identical to TB, but with a 4in wider body and much-needed additional interior space. Easy to distinguish from the earlier car by its new instrumentation. Underneath it featured shackles instead of sliding trunnions for the front and rear springs, which had a positive effect on ride quality. Powered by the 1250cc OHV four-cylinder engine with twin SU carburettors to improve breathing (54.4bhp at 5200rpm), it had a top speed of nearly 80mph. With two-seater sports bodywork only.

SPECIFICATIONS

Years produced:	1945-1949 (10,001 in total)
Performance:	0-60mph: 27.25sec
	Top speed: 78mph
Power & torque:	54.4bhp/64lb ft
Engine:	Normally aspirated 1250cc four cylinder, petrol, carburettor, 8 valves
Drivetrain:	Front-engine RWD
Structure:	Separate chassis
Transmission:	Four-speed manual
Weight:	838kg

PRICE GUIDE

Launch price:	£526
Excellent:	£20,000
Good:	£16,500
Average:	£12,000
Project:	£7000

MG
Y-type 1.25-litre

MG's first post-war saloon car had plenty of pre-war style and panache, although it lacked genuine performance. But the good value four-seat saloon proved a mainstay in the range while the T-types continued to evolve. Its engine – the single-carburettor version of the XPAG TC's (46bhp at 4800rpm) – was shared with its open-toppped cousins. New to the saloons was independent front suspension, rack-and-pinion steering and bolt-on disc wheels. Various open and closed model variations were introduced, although few remain.

SPECIFICATIONS

Years produced:	1947-1953 (8336 in total)
Performance:	0-60mph: 27.3sec
	Top speed: 71mph
Power & torque:	46bhp/58lb ft
Engine:	Normally aspirated 1250cc four cylinder, petrol, carburettor, 8 valves
Drivetrain:	Front-engine RWD
Structure:	Separate chassis
Transmission:	Four-speed manual
Weight:	1060kg

PRICE GUIDE

Launch price:	£565
Excellent:	£7250
Good:	£6000
Average:	£3500
Project:	£1500

MG
TD

Follow-up to the much-loved TC, with most finding their way overseas during the austere years of the post-war era. The new rack-and-pinion steering and Y-Type chassis sharpened the Midget's game considerably, and increased rigidity improved durability. These cars were offered with left-hand drive, which obviously helped with the export drive. Engine-wise, it was the same story as before, with the 1250cc XPAG engine in 54bhp form putting in a fine performance, and an upgrade to 57bhp for 1950's MkII livened things up.

SPECIFICATIONS

Years produced:	1949-1953 (29,664 in total)
Performance:	0-60mph: 18.2sec
	Top speed: 78mph
Power & torque:	54bhp/64lb ft
Engine:	Normally aspirated 1250cc four cylinder, petrol, carburettor, 8 valves
Drivetrain:	Front-engine RWD
Structure:	Separate chassis
Transmission:	Four-speed manual
Weight:	876kg

PRICE GUIDE

Launch price:	£751
Excellent:	£17,500
Good:	£14,000
Average:	£10,000
Project:	£5000

MG
TF

The final flowering of the pre-war Midget concept was the TF that, like its predecessors, proved massively popular in the USA. It was a straightforward development of the TD MkII, and the TF's most obvious changes from the older car are its raked radiator grille, lowered bonnet line and faired-in headlamps. Despite this, it was looking rather old by 1953, and sales in the UK were consequently slowing. Originally powered by the TD's engine, but later 1500 (July 1954 on) had XPAG engine of 1466cc and a top speed of nearly 90mph.

SPECIFICATIONS

Years produced:	1953-1955 (9600 in total)
Performance:	0-60mph: 18.9sec
	Top speed: 81mph
Power & torque:	57bhp/65lb ft
Engine:	Normally aspirated 1250cc four cylinder, petrol, carburettor, 8 valves
Drivetrain:	Front-engine RWD
Structure:	Separate chassis
Transmission:	Four-speed manual
Weight:	916kg

PRICE GUIDE

Launch price:	£780
Excellent:	£21,000
Good:	£18,000
Average:	£13,000
Project:	£7500

MG
Magnette ZA/ZB

This post-BMC MG, designed by Gerald Palmer, was elegant, affordable and made a leap into the mainstream for MG. The chassisless saloon, based on the Wolseley 4/44, with indpendent front suspension, rack-and-pinion steering and BMC B-series power, sold well and established MG as part of BMC's badge-engineering portfolio. The 60bhp B-series engine lacked sparkle, even with twin SU carburettors, but was helped in ZB form when power was uprated to 68bhp. Varitone version had a larger rear window.

SPECIFICATIONS

Years produced:	1953-1958 (36,650 in total)
Performance:	0-60mph: 22.6sec
	Top speed: 82mph
Power & torque:	60bhp/71lb ft
Engine:	Normally aspirated 1489cc four cylinder, petrol, carburettor, 8 valves
Drivetrain:	Front-engine RWD
Structure:	Monocoque
Transmission:	Four-speed manual
Weight:	1118kg

PRICE GUIDE

Launch price:	£713
Excellent:	£6500
Good:	£5250
Average:	£2750
Project:	£1250

MG
MGA Roadster

This aerodynamic and beautiful two-seat roadster was a huge leap forward from the T-type Midgets. With twin-carburettor B-series engine, independent front suspension and rack-and-pinion steering, the differences were like night and day. Initially offered with the 1489cc four-cylinder B-Series OHV engine with 68bhp, it was uprated to a 1600 model in May 1959. Lockheed front discs made their first appearance with the larger 80bhp engine, significantly improving braking. Revered today and valued significantly ahead of the MGB.

SPECIFICATIONS
Years produced:	1955-1962 (101,000 in total)
Performance:	0-60mph: 15.6sec
	Top speed: 98mph
Power & torque:	68bhp/77lb ft
Engine:	Normally aspirated 1489cc four cylinder, petrol, carburettor, 8 valves
Drivetrain:	Front-engine RWD
Structure:	Separate chassis
Transmission:	Four-speed manual
Weight:	890kg

PRICE GUIDE
Launch price:	£894
Excellent:	£17,000
Good:	£14,000
Average:	£9000
Project:	£5500

MG
MGA Coupé

When it was launched in 1955, the beautiful MGA ushered in a new era of modernity at Abingdon – out went the pre-war cycle wings of the T-series car, and in came a slippery new body with Le Mans-inspired styling. The MGA made liberal use of the BMC parts bin, with its B-series power unit coming straight from the Morris Oxford. Performance was hardly sparkling, but quick enough to impress the Americans, who bought MGAs by the container-load. For those who wanted more performance, the Twin Cam that followed was just the ticket.

SPECIFICATIONS
Years produced:	1956-1962
Performance:	0-60mph: 15.0sec
	Top speed: 100mph
Power & torque:	72bhp/N/A
Engine:	Normally aspirated 1489cc four cylinder, petrol, carburettor, 8 valves
Drivetrain:	Front-engine RWD
Structure:	Separate chassis
Transmission:	Four-speed manual
Weight:	927kg

PRICE GUIDE
Launch price:	£894
Excellent:	£13,500
Good:	£11,000
Average:	£7000
Project:	£3500

MG
MGA Twin Cam Roadster

The trouble with the MGA was always its lack of power. Although most owners were happy with the standard 1500 and 1600cc cars, there was demand from a certain hardcore of buyers who wanted more. MG was happy to oblige and came up with the Twin Cam. Engine guru Harry Weslake design a new twin-cam head for the B-series engine, which improved breathing and top-end power. The 108bhp upgrade was enough to satisfy MGA owners with a need for speed to match the beautiful styling, although it gained a reutation for unreliability.

SPECIFICATIONS
Years produced:	1958-1960 (2111 inc Coupé in total)
Performance:	0-60mph: 9.1sec
	Top speed: 113mph
Power & torque:	108bhp/N/A
Engine:	Normally aspirated 1588cc four cylinder, petrol, carburettor, 8 valves
Drivetrain:	Front-engine RWD
Structure:	Separate chassis
Transmission:	Four-speed manual
Weight:	952kg

PRICE GUIDE
Launch price:	£1266
Excellent:	£24,000
Good:	£20,000
Average:	£12,500
Project:	£7500

MG
MGA Twin Cam Coupé

Although it's an all-time classic, the MGA Twin Cam was far from troublefree. For a start, it was an expensive engine to build, and that extra cost was passed on to the customer – a mere 2111 were sold during the late 1950s and, for those that bought one, unreliability reared its ugly head. The engine gained a reputation for piston damage, and because of this few original cars survive. Able to crack 110mph, they were fun while they lasted. Visual differences between the Twin Cam and other MGAs were kept to a minimum, making these excellent Q-cars.

SPECIFICATIONS
Years produced:	1958-1960 (see Roadster)
Performance:	0-60mph: 9.1sec
	Top speed: 113mph
Power & torque:	108bhp/105lb ft
Engine:	Normally aspirated 1588cc four cylinder, petrol, carburettor, 8 valves
Drivetrain:	Front-engine RWD
Structure:	Separate chassis
Transmission:	Four-speed manual
Weight:	952kg

PRICE GUIDE
Launch price:	£1266
Excellent:	£19,000
Good:	£15,000
Average:	£9250
Project:	£6000

MG
Magnette MkIII/IV

With a stable full of marques, BMC used its quota to the maximum with the Farina saloons. Few would have thought the staid and podgy B-series-powered car was a suitable basis for a new-age MG Magnette, but with twin carburettors and a wood-and-leather interior, it just about managed to pass it off. Later MkIVs are the ones to have with their 1622cc 68bhp engines providing just enough performance to keep up with the flow. Today, these cars are still readily available for relatively little money, and provide plenty of enjoyment.

SPECIFICATIONS
Years produced:	1959-1968 (31,104 in total)
Performance:	0-60mph: 20.6sec
	Top speed: 84mph
Power & torque:	64bhp/N/A
Engine:	Normally aspirated 1489cc four cylinder, petrol, carburettor, 8 valves
Drivetrain:	Front-engine RWD
Structure:	Monocoque
Transmission:	Four-speed manual
Weight:	1118kg

PRICE GUIDE
Launch price:	£1013
Excellent:	£3750
Good:	£3000
Average:	£1500
Project:	£500

MG
Midget MkI-III

This unit-construction sports two-seater, developed from the Austin-Healey Sprite, was MG's most successful badge-engineered model. It was initially powered by the BMC A-series 948cc, twin-carburettor, four-cylinder OHV engine, and featured a four-speed gearbox, rack-and-pinion steering and independent front suspension. A hoot to drive despite the low power output, although the arrival of the 1098cc version helped. Disc brakes were added in 1962, before the MkII of 1964 – with wind-up windows. MkIII upgunned to 1275cc.

SPECIFICATIONS
Years produced:	1961-1974 (152,158 in total)
Performance:	0-60mph: 10.8sec
	Top speed: 95mph
Power & torque:	65bhp/72lb ft
Engine:	Normally aspirated 1275cc four cylinder, petrol, carburettor, 8 valves
Drivetrain:	Front-engine RWD
Structure:	Monocoque
Transmission:	Four-speed manual
Weight:	685kg

PRICE GUIDE
Launch price:	£670
Excellent:	£5000
Good:	£4000
Average:	£2500
Project:	£900

MG
MGB Roadster MkI

Although MG found sucess with its T-type Midgets and MGA, the B took sales to a new level, eventually becoming the world's best-selling sports car until the arrival of the Datsun 240Z. A contemporary specification meant it was a delight to drive compared with its rivals, and there was plenty of power on tap, thanks to its recently upgraded 1.8-litre B-series engine. Four-speed gearbox (overdrive available), rack-and-pinion steering, independent front suspension, and disc brakes were standard fitments right from the start.

SPECIFICATIONS
Years produced:	1962-1967 (513,276 in total)
Performance:	0-60mph: 12.2sec
	Top speed: 103mph
Power & torque:	95bhp/110lb ft
Engine:	Normally aspirated 1798cc four cylinder, petrol, carburettor, 8 valves
Drivetrain:	Front-engine RWD
Structure:	Monocoque
Transmission:	Four-speed manual
Weight:	920kg

PRICE GUIDE
Launch price:	£690
Excellent:	£12,000
Good:	£9000
Average:	£6500
Project:	£2000

MG
1100/1300

The humble Austin 1100 initially seemed like an unsuitable starting point for an MG version, but as it happens, the small saloon acquitted itself very well indeed. Tenacious front-wheel-drive handling and a well-appointed interior made the MG 1100 a genuinely sporting saloon. It wasn't perfect, though – it proved difficult for mechanics to work on, and had a terrible reputation for rust, which was rightly deserved. Survival rate is low considering the huge number produced, but those that are left are not expensive to buy, and cost peanuts to run.

SPECIFICATIONS
Years produced:	1962-1971 (124,860/32,549 in total)
Performance:	0-60mph: 15.6sec
	Top speed: 78mph
Power & torque:	48bhp/60lb ft
Engine:	Normally aspirated 1098cc four cylinder, petrol, carburettor, 8 valves
Drivetrain:	Front-engine FWD
Structure:	Monocoque
Transmission:	Four-speed manual
Weight:	832kg

PRICE GUIDE
Launch price:	£949
Excellent:	£3250
Good:	£2500
Average:	£1200
Project:	£500

MG
MGB GT

It's sometimes easy to forget just how much of an impact the MGB GT made on the marketplace. That fastback roof, designed by Pininfarina, followed conventional GT styling cues but for a fraction of the price. The raised windscreen height and side windows meant that there was a realistic amount of headroom for those in the front, although rear-seat passengers didn't get such an easy ride. Underneath the glamorous new skin, the GT was pure Roadster, and that meant tidy handling and excellent performance.

SPECIFICATIONS
Years produced:	1965-1967 (21,835 in total)
Performance:	0-60mph: 13.0sec
	Top speed: 104mph
Power & torque:	97bhp/105lb ft
Engine:	Normally aspirated 1798cc four cylinder, petrol, carburettor, 8 valves
Drivetrain:	Front-engine RWD
Structure:	Monocoque
Transmission:	Four-speed manual
Weight:	1108kg

PRICE GUIDE
Launch price:	£834
Excellent:	£8500
Good:	£5000
Average:	£2500
Project:	£1200

MG
MGC

In an attempt to extend the appeal of the MGB and also plug the gap in BMC's range with the demise of the big Healeys, Abingdon's engineers came up with the bright idea of fitting a C-series engine. The power and torque figures were adequate for this GT's potential upmarket ambitions, but those looking for sporting handling would end up being disapppointed with the understeery balance. Later development (and better tyres) have tamed much of these handling indelicacies and, with proper tuning, the lumbering C-series can really deliver.

SPECIFICATIONS
Years produced:	1967-1969 (9002 in total)
Performance:	0-60mph: 10.2sec
	Top speed: 120mph
Power & torque:	145bhp/170lb ft
Engine:	Normally aspirated 2912cc straight six, petrol, carburettor, 12 valves
Drivetrain:	Front-engine RWD
Structure:	Monocoque
Transmission:	Four-speed manual with overdrive
Weight:	1116kg

PRICE GUIDE
Launch price:	£1102
Excellent:	£13,000
Good:	£9250
Average:	£6000
Project:	£2750

MG LE 50
FROM FRONTLINE DEVELOPMENTS

LIMITED EDITION · MG FIFTIETH ANNIVERSARY · 50

THE MG LE50 FROM FRONTLINE DEVELOPMENTS, a modern interpretation of a real British classic. We've taken a true icon from an era when driving had more style, then applied the very latest technology and engineering to create a motor car unlike any other.

This isn't a recreation or a rebuild. The LE50 is a brand new car from the ground up.

Inside a factory fresh MGB bodyshell, improved and enhanced to our own exacting standards, you'll find a 215bhp, 2 litre Mazda engine capable of reaching 60mph in 5 seconds and powering on to a blistering 160mph top speed, yet still returning a highly respectable 40mpg.

Supreme comfort and razor sharp handling come from our own purpose designed front and rear suspension and billet machine wheels, while we've also added a few little luxuries. Connolly hide seats hold you in the corners, Wilton carpets are underfoot, electric windows, electronic starter and a state-of-the-art sound system complete your driving pleasure.

Created to celebrate the 50th Anniversary of the birth of the MGB, the singularly exciting LE50 is available as a strictly limited edition of 50 individually numbered vehicles. So, as you'd expect, it'll go very quickly indeed.

To experience the Frontline Developments LE50 for yourself, call us on +44 (0) 1235 832632 or visit www.frontlinedevelopments.com. It's the car you've been waiting for.

LE MG 50
FRONTLINE DEVELOPMENTS

THE FUTURE OF CLASSIC MOTORING

MG
MGB MkII/III

Upgrading the evergreen MGB to MkII specification was enough to keep Abingdon busy and sales on a high. The four-speed gearbox finally received synchromesh on all forward ratios, and an optional Borg-Warner automatic gearbox became available. In 1970 the MkII was treated to a BL-style front end, which did away with the chrome grille and slats. MG fans hated the cost-constrained new style, and it was soon canned. The return to chrome ushered in the MkIII, which received a number of improvements to keep the MGB looking fresh.

SPECIFICATIONS

Years produced:	1967-1971 (310,077 in total)
Performance:	0-60mph: 13sec
	Top speed: 104mph
Power & torque:	84bhp/105lb ft
Engine:	Normally aspirated 1798cc four cylinder, petrol, carburettor, 8 valves
Drivetrain:	Front-engine RWD
Structure:	Monocoque
Transmission:	Four-speed manual
Weight:	920kg

PRICE GUIDE

Launch price:	Not known
Excellent:	£10,000
Good:	£8000
Average:	£4250
Project:	£1750

MG
MGB GT V8

The concept of a V8-engined MGB was hardly new; Ken Costello had been making a good living converting MGBs to Rover engines for some time, and even MG had a go with the Edward Turner Daimler V8 before building the MGC. When production of the C-series was cut, MG introduced its own Rover V8-engined version, just as the effects of the 1973 energy crisis were hitting hard. Although a great car, the GT V8 sold poorly, a victim of circumstance and poor marketing. Today it offers great value, but watch out for home conversions.

SPECIFICATIONS

Years produced:	1973-1976 (2591 in total)
Performance:	0-60mph: 9sec
	Top speed: 125mph
Power & torque:	137bhp/192lb ft
Engine:	Normally aspirated 3528cc V8, petrol, carburettor, 16 valves
Drivetrain:	Front-engine RWD
Structure:	Monocoque
Transmission:	Four-speed manual
Weight:	1158kg

PRICE GUIDE

Launch price:	£2294
Excellent:	£12,000
Good:	£7750
Average:	£4500
Project:	£2000

MG
MGB (rubber bumper)

North American regulations forced a raised ride height and polyurethane-covered bumpers required to withstand 5mph impacts without sustaining damage. Although condemned at the time by fans, the federalised MGB was actually a successful styling job compared with its Italian rivals. Later B-series engines in North America were reduced to a single Zenith Stromberg carb, emissions equipment and a catalyst. Now these black-bumper cars offer the best regular-use practicality and value of all the MGBs.

SPECIFICATIONS

Years produced:	1974-1980 (128,653 in total)
Performance:	0-60mph: 13.0sec
	Top speed: 104mph
Power & torque:	82bhp/104lb ft
Engine:	Normally aspirated 1798cc four cylinder, petrol, carburettor, 8 valves
Drivetrain:	Front-engine RWD
Structure:	Monocoque
Transmission:	Four-speed manual
Weight:	971kg

PRICE GUIDE

Launch price:	Not known
Excellent:	£8000
Good:	£5750
Average:	£2850
Project:	£800

MG
Metro/Metro Turbo

The first MG to appear after the closure of Abingdon in 1980 was a return to the badge-engineering ways of old. In becoming an MG in 1981, the Austin Metro received a trim upgrade and an uprated A-series engine delivering an additional 12bhp. Just over a year later, the Metro Turbo was added to the MG line-up and became a big seller. Featuring a Garrett T3 turbo, the engine was worked on by Lotus to develop 93bhp. It could have been more, but power was capped to prolong gearbox life. Most have now succumbed to rust.

SPECIFICATIONS

Years produced:	1982-1990 (37,500/21,968 in total)
Performance:	0-60mph: 9.9sec
	Top speed: 112mph
Power & torque:	93bhp/87lb ft
Engine:	Turbocharged 1275cc four cylinder, petrol, carburettor, 8 valves
Drivetrain:	Front-engine FWD
Structure:	Monocoque
Transmission:	Four-speed manual
Weight:	840kg

PRICE GUIDE

Launch price:	£4799
Excellent:	£2500
Good:	£1200
Average:	£700
Project:	£400

MG
Maestro 1600/EFi/2.0i

The early MG Maestro was fitted with a 1.6-litre R-series engine derived from the Austin Maxi's, and proved troublesome in use thanks to a hastily conceived twin-Weber carburettor set-up. 1984's shortlived 1600's S-series engine was replaced by the 2.0-litre O-series fuel-injection engine from the Montego at the end of that year. Capable and good to drive (if specified with PAS), but genuine sales success evaded the Maestro thanks to its dumpy styling and pedestrian image. One of the best hot hatches of its era, overlooked at the time.

SPECIFICATIONS (EFi)

Years produced:	1983-1991
Performance:	0-60mph: 8.5sec
	Top speed: 115mph
Power & torque:	115bhp/134lb ft
Engine:	Normally aspirated 1994cc four cylinder, petrol, electronic fuel injection, 8 valves
Drivetrain:	Front-engine FWD
Structure:	Monocoque
Transmission:	Five-speed manual
Weight:	984kg

PRICE GUIDE

Launch price:	£7279
Excellent:	£1500
Good:	£900
Average:	£700
Project:	£300

MG
Montego 2.0i/Turbo

Austin-Rover's sporting repmobile of 1984 had the potential to be a success but, once again, it proved a disappointing seller. Earliest models had a digital dashboard and voice synthesiser (like the Maestro), but the 115bhp engine failed to thrill. The same couldn't be said for 1985's 150bhp Turbo, which thanks to ample boost and an underdeveloped chassis produced vivid acceleration and matching torque steer. That was soon tamed, and the MG ended up being a fine driver. Lack of quality and rust resistance were a big problem.

SPECIFICATIONS (Turbo)

Years produced:	1984-1991
Performance:	0-60mph: 7.2sec
	Top speed: 125mph
Power & torque:	150bhp/169lb ft
Engine:	Turbocharged 1994cc four cylinder, petrol, electronic fuel injection, 8 valves
Drivetrain:	Front-engine FWD
Structure:	Monocoque
Transmission:	Five-speed manual
Weight:	1124kg

PRICE GUIDE

Launch price:	£8765
Excellent:	£1250
Good:	£900
Average:	£700
Project:	£300

MG
Maestro Turbo

After five years in production, the Montego Turbo's engine finally found its way into the Maestro and, with Tickford's help, a run of 505 was produced. Its aggressive bodykit helped add fast-lane appeal, and the tweaked chassis improved the already fine handling. Genuinely fast, with a 0-60mph time of 6.7 seconds, which saw off all rivals. Like the Montego, it can be a lively drive, but modern tyres will tame the torque steer. Like all M-cars, the Maestro suffers badly from extensive cosmetic rust, rendering restoration uneconomic.

SPECIFICATIONS

Years produced:	1988-1990 (505 in total)
Performance:	0-60mph: 6.7sec
	Top speed: 128mph
Power & torque:	150bhp/169lb ft
Engine:	Turbocharged 1994cc four cylinder, petrol, electronic fuel injection, 8 valves
Drivetrain:	Front-engine FWD
Structure:	Monocoque
Transmission:	Five-speed manual
Weight:	1094kg

PRICE GUIDE

Launch price:	£11,300
Excellent:	£3000
Good:	£1700
Average:	£1000
Project:	£700

MINI

THE FIRST BMC Minis were badged as Austins and Morrises, but, from the MkIII variant in 1969, Mini was launched as a marque in its own right, albeit solely responsible for the cars after which it was named; the original Alec Issigonis invention as well as the Clubman and Cooper variants. Largely unappreciated during the 1970s, this once most-basic of machines moved upmarket in the 1980s when it became cemented in the British national psyche. The last classic Mini was built in 2000 – after 41 years of continuous manufacture – and BMW now uses MINI as a badge for its oversized look-alikes. The popularity of these should ensure the name continues well into the future.

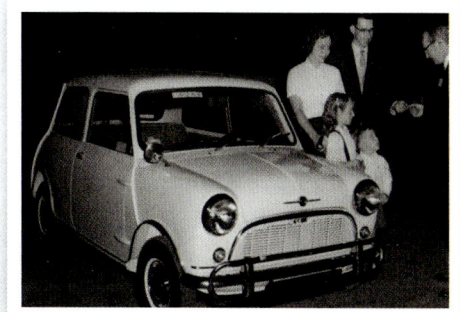

MINI
MkI

Alec Issigonis's cheap small car for BMC was innovative with its front-wheel drive and space-saving transverse engine layout but, more than that, it was incredibly entertaining to drive. The Mini had a personality that few small cars had displayed before, and it soon became a best-seller. The Austin version was initially called the Se7en, but became the Mini in 1961. The 848cc A-series engine was used throughout the life of the MkI; one significant change was the adoption of Hydrolastic suspension in place of the original rubber-cone type in 1964.

SPECIFICATIONS

Years produced:	1959-1967 (1,572,756 in total)
Performance:	0-60mph: 27.1sec
	Top speed: 72mph
Power & torque:	34bhp/33lb ft
Engine:	Normally aspirated 848cc four cylinder, petrol, carburettor, 8 valves
Drivetrain:	Front-engine RWD
Structure:	Monocoque
Transmission:	Four-speed manual
Weight:	626kg

PRICE GUIDE

Launch price:	£496
Excellent:	£4250
Good:	£3250
Average:	£1750
Project:	£850

MINI
Cooper 997/998

Mini creator Alec Issigonis was against the idea of a performance version. Fortunately, his wishes didn't prevail, and a legend was born in the 1961 Mini-Cooper, as tweaked by F1 guru John Cooper. The first cars used a 997cc twin-carb A-series; this was changed for a 998cc unit from 1964. Front disc brakes were standard and Coopers stood out thanks to their two-tone paint schemes and special grilles. Speeds of around 90mph may not have been all-out fast, but it was the Cooper's handling brilliance that turned it into such a potent rally tool.

SPECIFICATIONS

Years produced:	1961-1969 (64,224 in total)
Performance:	0-60mph: 17.2sec
	Top speed: 85mph
Power & torque:	55bhp/54lb ft
Engine:	Normally aspirated 997cc four cylinder, petrol, carburettor, 8 valves
Drivetrain:	Front-engine FWD
Structure:	Monocoque
Transmission:	Four-speed manual
Weight:	626kg

PRICE GUIDE

Launch price:	£679
Excellent:	£7500
Good:	£6000
Average:	£3000
Project:	£1250

MINI
Cooper 1071S

Cooper had more experience with A-series engines in the 1100cc racing class and put that knowledge to good use with the first Mini-Cooper S. Its enlarged 1071cc engine managed 70bhp and there were larger disc brakes to cope with its extra performance. Nothing much changed on the outside; the S looked the same as the Cooper save for 'S' badges on the bonnet and boot, and ventilated steel wheels. Inside, the upholstery was finished to more luxurious Mini Super De Luxe specification. A petite but potent rocket but even better was soon to follow...

SPECIFICATIONS
Years produced:	1963-1964 (4031 in total)
Performance:	0-60mph: 13.5sec
	Top speed: 90mph
Power & torque:	70bhp/62lb ft
Engine:	Normally aspirated 1071cc four cylinder, petrol, carburettor, 8 valves
Drivetrain:	Front-engine FWD
Structure:	Monocoque
Transmission:	Four-speed manual
Weight:	630kg

PRICE GUIDE
Launch price:	£695
Excellent:	£12,000
Good:	£9500
Average:	£5500
Project:	£2600

MINI
Cooper 970S

The reduction in engine size and power for 1964's 970S Cooper might have seemed a strange move but it was built simply as a homologation special with a short-stroke 970cc engine developing 65bhp. The specialist engine was pricey to manufacture, so BMC made it a special-order model; thus very few were sold. Aside from the engine, the mechanical specification was the same as for the 1071S. Hydrolastic suspension made an appearance three months after launch but the car itself only lasted a further seven months after this change.

SPECIFICATIONS
Years produced:	1964-1965 (963 in total)
Performance:	0-60mph: N/A
	Top speed: 92mph
Power & torque:	65bhp/N/A
Engine:	Normally aspirated 970cc four cylinder, petrol, carburettor, 8 valves
Drivetrain:	Front-engine FWD
Structure:	Monocoque
Transmission:	Four-speed manual
Weight:	630kg

PRICE GUIDE
Launch price:	£671
Excellent:	£11,000
Good:	£9000
Average:	£5500
Project:	£2750

MINI
Cooper 1275S MkI

Cooper's crowning glory was the 1275S, the MkI version of which lasted from 1964 to 1967 and won the Monte Carlo rallies in 1965 and '67. The long-stroke 1275cc A-series gave 76bhp, enough to launch the car to almost 100mph. Single-colour paint schemes were available alongside the usual two-tone ones, making these Coopers great little Q-cars, as there wasn't too much else to distinguish one from a standard Mini. Hydrolastic suspension came along in 1964, then an oil cooler and twin fuel tanks from 1966.

SPECIFICATIONS
Years produced:	1964-1967 (21,141 in total)
Performance:	0-60mph: 11.2sec
	Top speed: 96mph
Power & torque:	76bhp/79lb ft
Engine:	Normally aspirated 1275cc four cylinder, petrol, carburettor, 8 valves
Drivetrain:	Front-engine FWD
Structure:	Monocoque
Transmission:	Four-speed manual
Weight:	635kg

PRICE GUIDE
Launch price:	£756
Excellent:	£13,000
Good:	£9500
Average:	£6000
Project:	£3000

MINI
Moke

The Moke was developed as a military vehicle but the forces, er, failed to appreciate it. So, instead, BMC sold it as a fun fashion accessory. You weren't one of the in-crowd if you hadn't driven one down Carnaby Street – unless, of course, you were Patrick McGoohan in *The Prisoner*. Production switched to Australia in 1968, with a rise in engine size from 848cc to 998cc, and then 1098cc with the MkII of 1969. The Moke Californian of 1971 had a 1275cc unit. Portuguese manufacture began in 1980 and ended in 1993.

SPECIFICATIONS
Years produced:	1964-1993 (14,518 to 1968)
Performance:	0-60mph: 21.8sec
	Top speed: 65mph
Power & torque:	34bhp/N/A
Engine:	Normally aspirated 848cc four cylinder, petrol, carburettor, 8 valves
Drivetrain:	Front-engine FWD
Structure:	Monocoque
Transmission:	Four-speed manual
Weight:	406kg

PRICE GUIDE
Launch price:	£405
Excellent:	£8000
Good:	£6000
Average:	£3500
Project:	£2000

MINI
Cooper S MkII/III

The 1275cc Cooper S continued into MkII guise, with the same changes as the humbler Minis such as a reshaped grille, bigger rear window and enlarged back lights. Other Minis had dispensed with their marque names but the S continued to be available in Austin and Morris forms. The 998cc variant was dropped in 1969 but the 1275 Cooper S made it through to MkIII form with concealed door hinges and wind-up windows. It kept Hydrolastic suspension until British Leyland's agreement with Cooper was cancelled in 1971 and the model disappeared.

SPECIFICATIONS
Years produced:	1967-1971 (16,396 in total)
Performance:	0-60mph: 10.9sec
	Top speed: 96mph
Power & torque:	76bhp/79lb ft
Engine:	Normally aspirated 1275cc four cylinder, petrol, carburettor, 8 valves
Drivetrain:	Front-engine FWD
Structure:	Monocoque
Transmission:	Four-speed manual
Weight:	630kg

PRICE GUIDE
Launch price:	£631
Excellent:	£9000
Good:	£7000
Average:	£4250
Project:	£1850

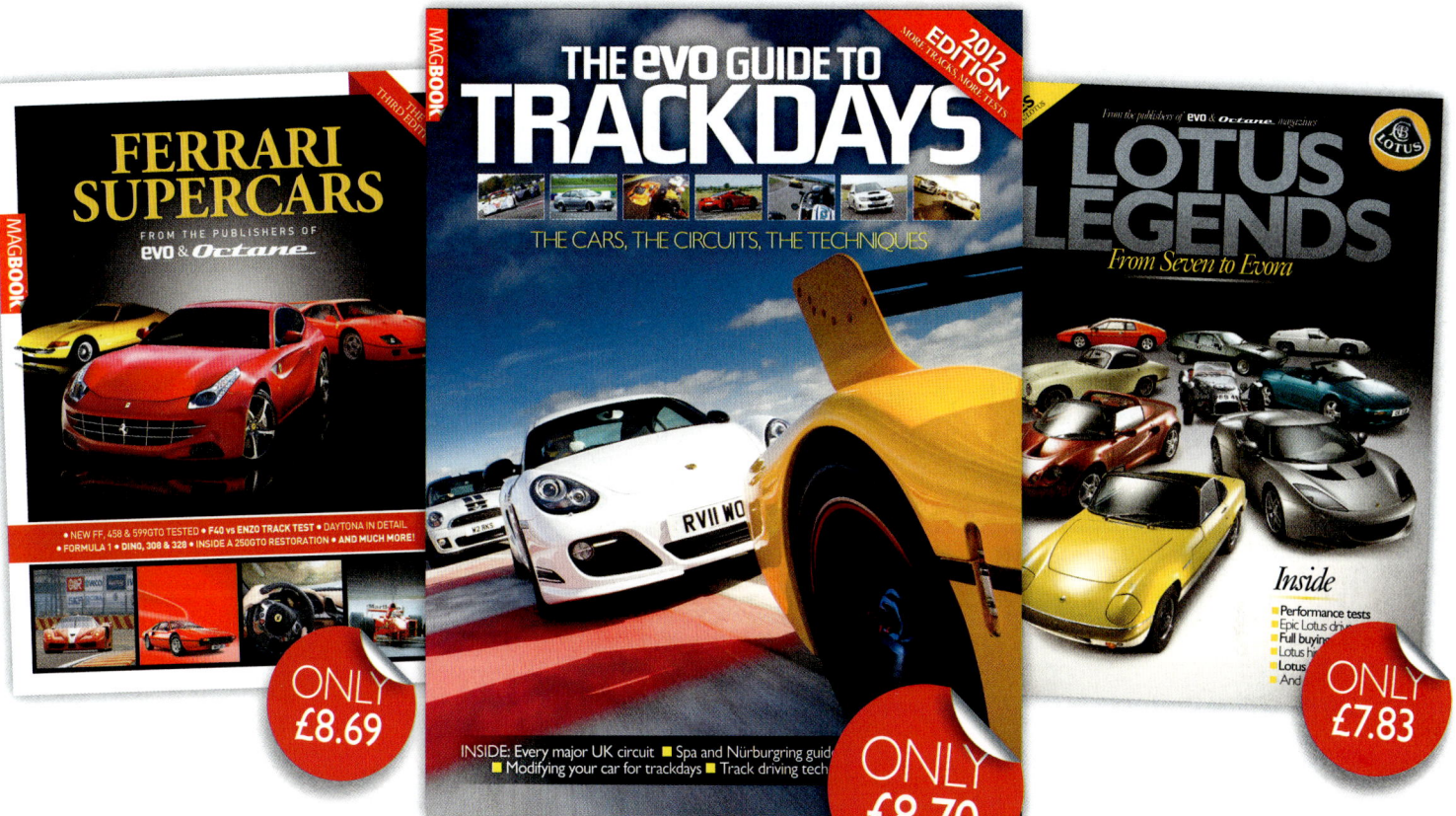

MINI
MkII-V

The short-lived MkII (1967-69) had a new grille and the option of a 998cc engine, while the MkIII (1969-76) hid the door hinges and replaced the sliding windows with wind-up ones. The old Austin and Morris badges were dropped, with the Mini now a marque in its own right. Hydrolastic suspension – more expensive to fit – was dropped in favour of the original rubber-cone type. Changes for the MkIV (1976-84) were more subtle, with alterations to the interior and subframe. The MkV took over from 1985-92, with 12in wheels and front disc brakes.

SPECIFICATIONS
Years produced:	1967-1992
Performance:	0-60mph: 27.1sec
	Top speed: 72mph
Power & torque:	39bhp/51lb ft
Engine:	Normally aspirated 998cc four cylinder, petrol, carburettor, 8 valves
Drivetrain:	Front-engine RWD
Structure:	Monocoque
Transmission:	Four-speed manual
Weight:	616kg

PRICE GUIDE
Launch price:	£509
Excellent:	£4000
Good:	£2500
Average:	£950
Project:	£300

MINI
1275GT

Seeking to save money, British Leyland replaced the Mini-Cooper with an uprated version of the Mini Clubman. However, just as the blunt-fronted Clubman lacked the character of the original Mini, so the 1275GT was a disappointment compared with the Cooper, with only a single-carburettor 1275cc engine of 59bhp. It wasn't that bad a car, with front disc brakes and more sophisticated equipment inside, and at least it stood out more than other Minis with its Rostyle wheels and decals. But it tried to supersede a legend. Tough call.

SPECIFICATIONS
Years produced:	1969-1980 (110,673 in total)
Performance:	0-60mph: 13.3sec
	Top speed: 90mph
Power & torque:	59bhp/67lb ft
Engine:	Normally aspirated 1275cc four cylinder, petrol, carburettor, 8 valves
Drivetrain:	Front-engine FWD
Structure:	Monocoque
Transmission:	Four-speed manual
Weight:	675kg

PRICE GUIDE
Launch price:	£834
Excellent:	£3500
Good:	£2500
Average:	£1275
Project:	£500

MINI
Clubman

Despite its sales success, the original Mini had never made any money for BMC. So successor British Leyland launched what it regarded as an enhanced version in 1969, which was accordingly more expensive. The Clubman had a longer, squared-off nose. The interior was enhanced with instruments now in front of the driver instead of in the centre and Hydrolastic suspension was retained until 1971. An estate was available from launch, complete with fake plastic wood trim down the sides. A cheap way into Mini ownership these days.

SPECIFICATIONS
Years produced:	1969-1982 (473,189 in total)
Performance:	0-60mph: 21.0sec
	Top speed: 75mph
Power & torque:	45bhp/55lb ft
Engine:	Normally aspirated 1098cc four cylinder, petrol, carburettor, 8 valves
Drivetrain:	Front-engine FWD
Structure:	Monocoque
Transmission:	Four-speed manual
Weight:	670kg

PRICE GUIDE
Launch price:	£720
Excellent:	£2500
Good:	£1650
Average:	£750
Project:	£250

MITSUBISHI

MITSUBISHI MOTORS

MITSUBISHI BEGAN building cars in 1917, when the Mitsubishi Shipbuilding Company introduced the Model A – Japan's first series-production car. It wasn't entirely a success, as it was handbuilt and fearsomely expensive. A mere 22 were built, before the car-building idea was chalked up to experience. Mitsubishi as we know it was created in 1934 when the company's shipbuilding and aircraft manufacturing operations were merged. The new Mitsubishi Heavy Industry company's car operations only got into the swing later, when it produced the Colt 1000 and Minica *kei car* in 1963. The company expanded quickly through the 1970s with Joint Venture partner Chrysler.

MITSUBISHI
Lancer 2000 Turbo

1980's second-generation Lancer was given a boost following the addition of a turbocharger. Initially the 1.8-litre EX Turbo pushed out 135bhp but, when it came to the UK in 1982, the Lancer Turbo had been bored out to 2.0 litres and a full 168bhp. The 4G63 engine that powered it would go on to power the legendary Evo models, and score heavily in world rallying. The chiselled '80s styling was improved drastically by the full-depth chin spoiler with reverse '2000 Turbo' badging, BMW 2002-style. Now a performance icon for lovers of Oriental classics.

SPECIFICATIONS
Years produced:	1982-1988
Performance:	0-60mph: 7.1sec
	Top speed: 124mph
Power & torque:	168bhp/181lb ft
Engine:	Turbocharged 1997cc four cylinder, petrol, fuel injection, 8 valves
Drivetrain:	Front-engine RWD
Structure:	Monocoque
Transmission:	Five-speed manual
Weight:	1052kg

PRICE GUIDE
Launch price:	£8499
Excellent:	£5000
Good:	£3750
Average:	£2500
Project:	£1750

MITSUBISHI
Starion

Considering it was Mitsubishi's first foray into the high-performance coupé market, the Starion proved incredibly popular. The turbocharged Mitsubishi not only looked good but went exceedingly well thanks to its turbocharged power unit shared with the Lancer Turbo. It was constantly developed during its eight-year life, and eventually appeared in wide-body form as well as being powered by one of the modern-era's largest four-cylinder engines - a 2.6-litre. And before you ask, the name is actually a shortened form of 'Star of Orion'.

SPECIFICATIONS (2.0)

Years produced:	1982-1989
Performance:	0-60mph: 8.3sec
	Top speed: 132mph
Power & torque:	168bhp/181lb ft
Engine:	Turbocharged 1997cc four cylinder, petrol, fuel injection, 8 valves
Drivetrain:	Front-engine RWD
Structure:	Monocoque
Transmission:	Four-speed manual
Weight:	1220kg

PRICE GUIDE

Launch price:	£11,734
Excellent:	£5500
Good:	£3000
Average:	£1750
Project:	£600

MONTEVERDI

SWITZERLAND isn't best-known for car production, but Monteverdi stands out. This performance marque was formed in 1967 by Basel garage owner Peter Monteverdi to put his Chrysler V8-engined GT cars into production. Encouraging sales made the company ambitious and it launched the mid-engined Hai as a Ferrari and Lamborghini pretender in 1970. Brave, but only two were built. Monteverdi moved to restyling existing cars, such as the Sierra (a Plymouth Volare) and the 4x4 Safari (of all things, an International Harvester Scout). The company called it a day in 1984 and ceased production, converting its factory into a car museum the following year.

MONTEVERDI
High Speed 375L/375C

Peter Monteverdi was a Swiss BMW dealer and racing driver who wanted to make an indelible mark on the luxury car market, by offering one of his own. The Frua-styled 375 was the result, which went on to sell surprisingly well despite its huge price tag. Beneath that Italianate body beat the heart of a hefty Chrysler V8, which developed up to 390bhp, all held together by a tubular chassis. The later Berlinetta model was even more potent, thanks to the fitment of a Hemi engine from the mid-engined Hai. Its 450bhp was the recipe for thrills aplenty.

SPECIFICATIONS (375S)

Years produced:	1967-1977
Performance:	0-60mph: 6.5sec
	Top speed: 162mph
Power & torque:	390bhp/481lb ft
Engine:	Normally aspirated 7206cc V8, petrol, carburettor, 16 valves
Drivetrain:	Front-engine RWD
Structure:	Tubular chassis
Transmission:	Three-speed automatic
Weight:	1600kg

PRICE GUIDE

Launch price:	£9250
Excellent:	£35,000
Good:	£22,000
Average:	£18,000
Project:	N/A

MONTEVERDI
High Speed 375/4

The Fissore-built, Frua-styled Monteverdi High Speed limousine was nothing if not extravagent. The coupé upon which it was based was hardly a compact machine, measuring 4.80m and packing 7.2 litres of Chrysler V8 power. To make a limousine, a further 50cm was added, most of which was within the wheelbase, creating a surprisingly handsome low-line saloon. During its seven-year production run, 30 were built before Monteverdi gave up bespoke vehicle manufacture in favour of modified versions of existing saloons, such as the Tiara and Sierra.

SPECIFICATIONS

Years produced:	1970-1977 (30 in total)
Performance:	0-60mph: 7.5sec
	Top speed: 145mph
Power & torque:	390bhp/481lb ft
Engine:	Normally aspirated 7206cc V8, petrol, carburettor, 16 valves
Drivetrain:	Front-engine RWD
Structure:	Tubular chassis
Transmission:	Three-speed automatic
Weight:	1755kg

PRICE GUIDE

Launch price:	N/A in UK
Excellent:	£55,000
Good:	£32,000
Average:	£21,000
Project:	N/A

MONTEVERDI
Hai 450SS/GTS

With the Lamborghini Miura and De Tomaso Mangusta setting the supercar pace with their mid-mounted engines, it was inevitable that the ambitious Peter Monteverdi would have a go at building his own version. The Fiore-styled Hai was the result. It certainly looked the part and had Miura-matching pace. Sadly, the project didn't progress beyond the second prototype car (the GTS), despite plans to build 49, leaving the Hai a fascinating might-have-been. Despite its rarity, the original Geneva Motor Show car sold in 2010 for €398,000.

SPECIFICATIONS

Years produced:	1970-1973 (2 in total)
Performance:	0-60mph: 5.5sec
	Top speed: 175mph (est)
Power & torque:	450bhp/481lb ft
Engine:	Normally aspirated 7206cc V8, petrol, carburettor, 16 valves
Drivetrain:	Mid engine RWD
Structure:	Tubular chassis
Transmission:	Three-speed automatic
Weight:	1455kg

PRICE GUIDE

Launch price:	N/A
Excellent:	£400,000
Good:	N/A
Average:	N/A
Project:	N/A

MONTEVERDI
Safari

The Safari was a clear demonstrator of what made Monteverdi's products so clever. Under the clean and handsome Euro-suit lurked an International Harvester Scout, an American off-roader rarely seen in Europe. That car was a US SUV pioneer and, along with the Range Rover, the Monteverdi did the same for Europe. The combination of luxury equipment level and automatic transmission were features that you couldn't get in the Range Rover until the early '80s. Rare outside Switzerland and, when they come up for sale, expect to pay a premium price.

SPECIFICATIONS	
Years produced:	1977-1982
Performance:	0-60mph: 13.5sec
	Top speed: 105mph
Power & torque:	150bhp/210lb ft
Engine:	Normally aspirated 5210cc V8, petrol, carburettor, 16 valves
Drivetrain:	Front-engine 4WD
Structure:	Separate body and chassis
Transmission:	Three-speed automatic
Weight:	2120kg

PRICE GUIDE	
Launch price:	N/A
Excellent:	£25,000
Good:	£20,000
Average:	£17,500
Project:	N/A

MORGAN

THE PROTOTYPE MORGAN, a three-wheeler, was constructed in 1909 in Malvern and remained in production until 1952. From 1936, Morgan moved into four-wheeled cars and showed a stubborn resistance to depart from its formula. Its handbuilt creations have very traditional pre-war-style wood-framed bodywork featuring a variety of modern engines. Its most famous model is the Plus 8, built from 1968 to 2004 with Rover's V8 engine. Still an eccentric British institution, but with more modern high-tech engineering under its new models' individual styling, Morgan seems totally immune to the whimsy of mere fashion, and remains ever-popular.

MORGAN
4/4 S1

The first post-war Morgan was similar to its pre-war cousin in styling, and almost identical underneath. The chassis was tubular, featuring Z-section side members, while the sliding pillar suspension and coil springs were just as before. For the first 4/4, a special overhead-cam Standard engine was used, mated to a Moss gearbox. It was a recipe that worked, and would continue to do so for a very long time indeed. Some of the features, such as cable brakes, remained in place but, over time, they were replaced by contemporary set-ups.

SPECIFICATIONS	
Years produced:	1945-1950 (249 in total)
Performance:	0-60mph: N/A
	Top speed: 77mph
Power & torque:	40bhp/N/A
Engine:	Normally aspirated 1267cc four cylinder, petrol, carburettor, 8 valves
Drivetrain:	Front-engine RWD
Structure:	Separate chassis
Transmission:	Four-speed manual
Weight:	721kg

PRICE GUIDE	
Launch price:	£455
Excellent:	£22,500
Good:	£17,000
Average:	£12,000
Project:	£7000

MORGAN
Plus 4

Adding four inches to the wheelbase of the 4/4 to make room for a second row of seats was a wise move, as it opened up the appeal of these vintage sports cars to those with small families. A move to hydraulically assisted brakes was a welcome move, as was the lightly restyled front end. During its 19-year run, it went through a 2.1-litre Standard Vanguard engine before moving to the Triumph TR2's. Front disc brakes were finally fitted as standard in 1961, which was a good thing, as the final TR4-engined models were genuine 100mph cars.

SPECIFICATIONS	
Years produced:	1950-1969 (3737 in total)
Performance:	0-60mph: 14.1sec
	Top speed: 85mph
Power & torque:	68bhp/113lb ft
Engine:	Normally aspirated 1991cc four cylinder, petrol, carburettor, 8 valves
Drivetrain:	Front-engine RWD
Structure:	Separate chassis
Transmission:	Four-speed manual
Weight:	838kg

PRICE GUIDE	
Launch price:	£652
Excellent:	£18,500
Good:	£15,000
Average:	£11,000
Project:	£5000

MORGAN
4/4 SII-V

After a hiatus of four years, the 4/4 was put back into production. The number of TR2 engines used in the Plus 4 models was being restricted by Triumph so Morgan turned to Ford for its cheap and readily available 1172cc sidevalve engine, to create a new entry-level model. The wheelbase of the 4/4 was standardised with the Plus 4, thus streamlining production. The Series IV received a wider, better-looking body, disc brakes and a larger Ford 1340cc engine. Despite hardly changing in style, the 4/4 remained consistently popular though the years.

SPECIFICATIONS	
Years produced:	1955-1968 (1197 in total)
Performance:	0-60mph: 29.4sec
	Top speed: 71mph
Power & torque:	36bhp/N/A
Engine:	Normally aspirated 1172cc four cylinder, petrol, carburettor, 8 valves
Drivetrain:	Front-engine RWD
Structure:	Separate chassis
Transmission:	Four-speed manual
Weight:	660kg

PRICE GUIDE	
Launch price:	£639
Excellent:	£14,000
Good:	£11,000
Average:	£8000
Project:	£5000

MOTOR WHEEL SERVICE

ESTABLISHED 85 YEARS

Renowned Worldwide for the Manufacture and Restoration of Veteran, Vintage & Classic Wire Wheels, MWS was originally established in 1927 as Motor Wheel Service and Repair Company in Shepherds Bush, London.

- We have been supplying Morgan Motor Company with original equipment wire wheels for over 30 years; we also supply Morgan knock-on centre caps (spinners).

- We supply 2½" x 19" wire wheels fitted with Avon 400 x 19 tyres as OEM for the new Morgan 3 Wheeler.

- To suit the pre-1985 Morgan 4/4 running on 5" x 15" wire wheels we recommend the new Blockley 165VR15 tyre.

- Our in-house Workshop is able to repair, restore and manufacture wire wheels, including aluminium-rim wire wheels.

- As well as supplying many types and sizes of wire wheels we are exclusive distributors for The Blockley Tyre Company's range of cross-ply tyres, road & race tubes, rim bands and their new range of radial tyres.

- Blockley Tyres are one of the few tyre manufacturers who have chosen to apply a speed rating to their cross-ply range. All Blockley radial tyres are rated at 150mph; most cross-ply tyres (except the 350 x 19 and 400 x 19) are rated at 130mph. All Blockley radial and cross-ply tyres are American DoT marked and have European 'E' marking.

- In addition to the comprehensive Blockley range we stock both radial and cross-ply tyres from manufacturers such as Avon, Dunlop, Michelin and Vredestein.

We attend several events over the year.
Please check our website or call us for details.

UK SALES
(T) 01753 549 360
(F) 01753 547 170

EXPORT SALES
(T) +44 1753 598 382
(F) +44 1753 773 443

VINTAGE & VETERAN
(T) 01753 598 380
(F) 01753 773 443

Motor Wheel Service International Ltd.
Units 1-4 Elder Way, Waterside Drive, Langley, Slough, Berkshire, SL3 6EP, UK

info@mwsint.com
www.mwsint.com

MORGAN
Plus 8

The Rover V8 engine found its way under the bonnet of a bewildering array of cars. However, Morgan's decision to buy up a stockpile of the ex-GM engines was most surprising but satisfying once it became clear just how much fun the Plus 8 actually was. It was a pragmatic move by Morgan, though, as supplies of suitable four-cylinder engines were beginning to dry up. The earliest examples made 161bhp – identical to the Rover P5 V8 – and endowed the lightweight 4/4-derived sports car with explosive acceleration and exciting handling.

SPECIFICATIONS

Years produced:	1968-1972 (482 in total)
Performance:	0-60mph: 6.7sec
	Top speed: 124mph
Power & torque:	161bhp/210lb ft
Engine:	Normally aspirated 3528cc V8, petrol, carburettor, 16 valves
Drivetrain:	Front-engine RWD
Structure:	Separate chassis
Transmission:	Four-speed manual
Weight:	839kg

PRICE GUIDE

Launch price:	£1478
Excellent:	£30,000
Good:	£25,000
Average:	£17,500
Project:	£11,000

MORGAN
4/4 1600

For increasingly affluent car buyers, the rather austere and underpowered 4/4 was looking a little out of its depth. There was nothing wrong with the way it looked, but rather the way it went. Morgan rectified this in 1968 by fitting the Ford Kent engine, boosting power to a more palatable 74bhp. The Plus 4 model was dropped, with the option of 2+2 seating being passed to the 4/4 line. It remained available in this form until 1982, when the Ford CVH used in the front-wheel-drive Escort was dropped in, improving power and economy if not refinement.

SPECIFICATIONS

Years produced:	1968-1981 (3708 in total)
Performance:	0-60mph: 9.8sec
	Top speed: 100mph
Power & torque:	74bhp/85lb ft
Engine:	Normally aspirated 1599cc four cylinder, petrol, carburettor, 8 valves
Drivetrain:	Front-engine RWD
Structure:	Separate chassis
Transmission:	Four-speed manual
Weight:	688kg

PRICE GUIDE

Launch price:	£858
Excellent:	£14,500
Good:	£12,000
Average:	£8750
Project:	£5000

MORGAN
Plus 8 (1973-86)

Morgan continued to develop the Plus 8 and, by 1973, the aluminium-engined vintage-style hot rod had the worst of its handling foibles sorted out. An all-synchromesh Rover 2000 gearbox was installed to replace the old Moss unit, a higher-output SD1-tune V8 came later and, in 1977, along with the much-needed five-speed gearbox, the option of aluminium body panels was introduced. Sales continued steadily throughout the worst of the 1970s recession, and supply was carefully managed by keeping the waiting list long, at around eight years.

SPECIFICATIONS

Years produced:	1973-1986
Performance:	0-60mph: 6.7sec
	Top speed: 124mph
Power & torque:	161bhp/210lb ft
Engine:	Normally aspirated 3528cc V8, petrol, carburettor, 16 valves
Drivetrain:	Front-engine RWD
Structure:	Separate chassis
Transmission:	Five-speed manual
Weight:	898kg

PRICE GUIDE

Launch price:	£1478
Excellent:	£25,000
Good:	£21,000
Average:	£15,000
Project:	£9000

MORGAN
Plus 8 Injection

Following the arrival of the Rover SD1 Vitesse in 1982, Morgan kept pace with developments by introducing its Lucas fuel-injection 190bhp engine into the Plus 8. Given the Morgan's interesting handling, it seemed that the last thing it needed was additional grunt, but the power hikes continued long into the 21st century, first with the 3.9-litre Range Rover V8 (still 190bhp but more torque) and then a 4.6-litre pushing out 240bhp. It was a recipe that worked, and sales remained strong through to the launch of the current Aero 8.

SPECIFICATIONS

Years produced:	1984-1990
Performance:	0-60mph: 5.6sec
	Top speed: 120mph
Power & torque:	190bhp/220lb ft
Engine:	Normally aspirated 3528cc V8, petrol, electronic fuel injection, 16 valves
Drivetrain:	Front-engine RWD
Structure:	Separate chassis
Transmission:	Five-speed manual
Weight:	839kg

PRICE GUIDE

Launch price:	£12,999
Excellent:	£22,500
Good:	£19,000
Average:	£15,000
Project:	£9000

MORGAN
Plus 4

The Plus Four made a return in 1987, initially powered by the Ford CVH, then by an optional Fiat twin-cam. Typically, these Fiat-engined cars proved lively to drive and much faster than their Ford-engined counterparts. The Plus Four name continued after the end of these 1.6-litre cars, thanks to the arrival of the 2.0-litre twin-cam Rover M16 engine, which offered 122bhp and a top speed of over 110mph. However, these four-seat Morgans never achieved the popularity of their two-seat counterparts.

SPECIFICATIONS

Years produced:	1985-2000
Performance:	0-60mph: 9.0sec
	Top speed: 112mph
Power & torque:	122bhp/127lb ft
Engine:	Normally aspirated 1995cc four cylinder, petrol, electronic fuel injection, 8 valves
Drivetrain:	Front-engine RWD
Structure:	Separate chassis
Transmission:	Five-speed manual
Weight:	848kg

PRICE GUIDE

Launch price:	£10,901
Excellent:	£17,500
Good:	£13,500
Average:	£10,000
Project:	£8000

MORRIS

BICYCLE MANUFACTURER
William Morris took the oft-trod path into building cars in 1913, with his Oxford and Cowley becoming the best-selling cars of the 1920s, and the Eight repeating the same trick the next decade. In 1948

Morris launched one of the enduring British greats, the Minor, which would continue until 1971. As part of the Nuffield Group, Morris became a major part of BMC in 1952, although many vehicles that carried its badging

also shared bodies and mechanics with other BMC members. Under British Leyland from 1968, Morris's main model was the Marina which evolved into the Ital in 1981, three years before Morris was discontinued as a marque.

MORRIS
Minor Series MM

The original Minor, complete with sidevalve engine, is a sedate performer, but delightful handling aids its progress. At first only sold as a two-door saloon or Tourer, with grille-mounted headlamps, until the four-door saloon was introduced in September 1950. These had their headlamps mounted in restyled front wings, and the change was adopted by two-doors and Tourers from January 1951. It's the early 'low lamp' Minors that attract collectors. Prices here are for low lamp saloons. Add 40% for Tourers; deduct 20% for high-headlamp MMs.

SPECIFICATIONS
Years produced: 1948-1953 (176,002 in total)
Performance: 0-60mph: 36.5sec
Top speed: 62mph
Power & torque: 27bhp/N/A
Engine: Normally aspirated 918cc four cylinder, petrol, carburettor, 8 valves
Drivetrain: Front-engine RWD
Structure: Monocoque
Transmission: Four-speed manual
Weight: 787kg

PRICE GUIDE
Launch price: £359
Excellent: £4750
Good: £3500
Average: £2000
Project: £600

MORRIS
Six

Morris's top-of-the-range early post-war offering combines the rounded body styling of the Minor/Oxford MO with the long bonnet and upright grille of pre-war offerings. It's not the most comfortable mix, but salvation lies in the straight-six engine that gives the car a decent turn of speed. The Six uses the MO's body from the screen back, but with different front door pressings and a 13in longer wheelbase. It uses cam steering, which isn't as good as the Oxford's rack-and-pinion. Not made in great numbers and survivors are rare.

SPECIFICATIONS
Years produced: 1948-1953 (12,400 in total)
Performance: 0-60mph: 22.4sec
Top speed: 83mph
Power & torque: 70bhp/100lb ft
Engine: Normally aspirated 2215cc straight six, petrol, carburettor, 12 valves
Drivetrain: Front-engine RWD
Structure: Monocoque
Transmission: Four-speed manual
Weight: 1276kg

PRICE GUIDE
Launch price: £608
Excellent: £4750
Good: £3500
Average: £1650
Project: £650

MORRIS
Oxford MO

In effect a big brother to the Minor, the Oxford promises more of everything but the extra bulk it carries means that none of it works quite as well. The 1500cc sidevalve engine, though ploddingly reliable, is rather gutless with just 41bhp, and the column-change for the four-speed gearbox borders on bearable. A wood-framed Traveller estate was introduced in 1952, pre-dating the similar Minor by a year. These have collector appeal, are now very rare and should be worth significantly more than the saloon values quoted.

SPECIFICATIONS
Years produced: 1948-1954 (159,960 in total)
Performance: 0-60mph: 31.1sec
Top speed: 71mph
Power & torque: 41bhp/67lb ft
Engine: Normally aspirated 1476cc four cylinder, petrol, carburettor, 8 valves
Drivetrain: Front-engine RWD
Structure: Monocoque
Transmission: Four-speed manual
Weight: 1092kg

PRICE GUIDE
Launch price: £505
Excellent: £3650
Good: £2500
Average: £1000
Project: £450

MORRIS
Minor Series II

Still with the charm of a split windscreen, but now powered by the A-series engine from Austin's A30. This engine only appeared in four-door models during 1952, but all models received it from February '53. Later that year the wood-framed Traveller was added to the range. From late '54 there was a new face with five horizontal grille slats, plus a new dashboard. Many of these cars have been fitted with the stronger 948cc engine from a later Minor, with no detrimental affect on their value. Add 75% for Convertible and Traveller prices.

SPECIFICATIONS
Years produced: 1952-1956 (269,838 in total)
Performance: 0-60mph: N/A
Top speed: 62mph
Power & torque: 30bhp/40lb ft
Engine: Normally aspirated 803cc four cylinder, petrol, carburettor, 8 valves
Drivetrain: Front-engine RWD
Structure: Monocoque
Transmission: Four-speed manual
Weight: 787kg

PRICE GUIDE
Launch price: £582
Excellent: £4000
Good: £2750
Average: £1300
Project: £400

MORRIS
Oxford II/III/IV

A big step forward from the Oxford MO, with an all-new body and 1500cc B-series engine. Became the Series III in October 1956 thanks to a facelift that included a more stylish fluted bonnet and finned rear wings. Drives better than it looks thanks to torsion bar front suspension and rack-and-pinion steering. Wood-framed two-door Traveller estate version of the SII/III is worth double the price of a saloon. It was replaced in 1957 by the estate-only Series IV Oxford, with an all-steel four-door body. These command about 25% more than saloons.

SPECIFICATIONS
Years produced:	1954-1960 (145,458 in total)
Performance:	0-60mph: 29.0sec
	Top speed: 73mph
Power & torque:	52bhp/78lb ft
Engine:	Normally aspirated 1489cc four cylinder, petrol, carburettor, 8 valves
Drivetrain:	Front-engine RWD
Structure:	Monocoque
Transmission:	Four-speed manual
Weight:	1067kg

PRICE GUIDE
Launch price:	£745
Excellent:	£3000
Good:	£2200
Average:	£1100
Project:	£350

MORRIS
Isis

Much like the Six it replaced, the Isis is based closely on the Oxford, but this time the front end is stretched by eight inches to make room for a single-carb version of the six-cylinder C-series engine. Mesh rather than painted slats in the grille set apart later versions, though occupants will notice the right-hand floor-change for the gearbox, to allow three-abreast seating. Updates for rarer Series II in 1956 include fluted bonnet, rear fins, and an extra 4bhp. Highly prized and hard-to-find estates worth about a third more than saloons.

SPECIFICATIONS
Years produced:	1955-1958 (12,155 in total)
Performance:	0-60mph: 17.8sec
	Top speed: 86mph
Power & torque:	86bhp/N/A
Engine:	Normally aspirated 2639cc straight six, petrol, carburettor, 12 valves
Drivetrain:	Front-engine RWD
Structure:	Monocoque
Transmission:	Four-speed manual
Weight:	1397kg

PRICE GUIDE
Launch price:	£802
Excellent:	£3750
Good:	£3000
Average:	£1600
Project:	£650

MORRIS
Minor 1000

These are the best Minors for those who want one to drive as well as to show. The larger A-series engines finally provided power to match the handling, more so after September 1962 when a 1098cc engine replaced the 948. Larger front brakes were added at the same time. The 1000s are easily distinguished by their curved one-piece windscreen and larger rear window. Convertibles were dropped in June 1969, saloon production ended in November 1970, but Travellers soldiered on until April 1971. Add 50% for Convertible/Traveller prices.

SPECIFICATIONS
Years produced:	1956-1971 (847,491 in total)
Performance:	0-60mph: 22.2sec
	Top speed: 77mph
Power & torque:	48bhp/60lb ft
Engine:	Normally aspirated 1098cc four cylinder, petrol, carburettor, 8 valves
Drivetrain:	Front-engine RWD
Structure:	Monocoque
Transmission:	Four-speed manual
Weight:	787kg

PRICE GUIDE
Launch price:	£603
Excellent:	£4500
Good:	£3500
Average:	£1750
Project:	£400

MORRIS
Marina

Replacing the much-loved Minor was never going to be easy, even if it had been with a great car. Unfortunately, Morris brought out the Marina. It was a strictly conventional machine, with much of its running gear Minor-based and therefore elderly for the era. Saloon, coupé and estate were available, with engines in 1275cc or 1798cc sizes, the latter unit from the MGB. That should have made the cars quite sporty, but handling was seriously suspect. Gradually improved until it was replaced by the Ital (really just a comprehensive facelift) in 1980.

SPECIFICATIONS (1.8TC)
Years produced:	1971-1980 (809,612 in total)
Performance:	0-60mph: 12.1sec
	Top speed: 100mph
Power & torque:	95bhp/106lb ft
Engine:	Normally aspirated 1798cc four cylinder, petrol, carburettor, 8 valves
Drivetrain:	Front-engine RWD
Structure:	Monocoque
Transmission:	Four-speed manual
Weight:	965kg

PRICE GUIDE
Launch price:	£923
Excellent:	£1750
Good:	£1100
Average:	£500
Project:	£250

MORRIS
Ital

The all-new name probably raised expectations, but it's an inescapable fact that the Ital was a disappointing end to the once-great Morris marque (a few Morris Metro vans followed, but that doesn't count). We sadly don't know Giugiaro's views on the Ital – a car that was not styled by his studios – but he can't have been flattered by the Euro-generic styling treatment that the Harris Mann studio came up with. A-plus engines were economical and the 2.0-litre O-series-powered auto could be exciting. For all the wrong reasons.

SPECIFICATIONS (1.3L)
Years produced:	1980-1984 (175,276 in total)
Performance:	0-60mph: 16.5sec
	Top speed: 91mph
Power & torque:	61bhp/69lb ft
Engine:	Normally aspirated 1275cc four cylinder, petrol, carburettor, 8 valves
Drivetrain:	Front-engine RWD
Structure:	Monocoque
Transmission:	Four-speed manual
Weight:	939kg

PRICE GUIDE
Launch price:	£5133
Excellent:	£1000
Good:	£750
Average:	£500
Project:	£250

MOSKVICH

FOUNDED IN THE 1930s, Moskvich was the car division of manufacturing giant AZLK. The name, which literally means Muscovite, refers to the car factory's original location, near the capital. Car production, using tooling purchased from Opel, started in 1947. First product was the 400, a near-clone of the 1939 Kadett, and it proved popular, honest transport that found a ready export audience thanks to its low price and solidity. The 400 was also sold into Norway, and a consignment ended up being traded for a serious quantity of herring. Moskvich ended up fading from view in 2006 after production of the Aleko hatchback halted, thanks to poor sales.

MOSKVICH
400

During the early 1970s, the Moskvich 412 was marketed in the UK as a big-value alternative to mainstream saloon rivals. And given that it boasted a list price marginally higher than a Mini's, you could see where the importer was coming from. Sadly the low price still wasn't enough to offset the rough engines, stodgy handling and high fuel consumption. The Moskvich soon picked up a poor reputation, and struggled desperately before the plug was pulled. Replaced by the Lada 1200, which was an infinitely better product – and that says it all.

SPECIFICATIONS

Years produced:	1967-1976
Performance:	0-60mph: 18.1sec
	Top speed: 90mph
Power & torque:	73bhp/81lb ft
Engine:	Normally aspirated 1479cc four cylinder, petrol, carburettor, 8 valves
Drivetrain:	Front-engine RWD
Structure:	Monocoque
Transmission:	Four-speed manual
Weight:	1080kg

PRICE GUIDE

Launch price:	£980 (launched in the UK 1972)
Excellent:	£1300
Good:	£900
Average:	£550
Project:	£300

NSU

IT WAS WITH Belgian vehicles that the Neckarsulm motorcycle and bicycle manufacturer got its start building cars in 1905 but, after some popularity, NSU ceased construction in 1929 when its factory was sold to Fiat. That was until 1957, when it re-entered the market with the compact rear-engined NSU Prinz. In 1964, it launched the world's first rotary-engined production car, the Wankel Spider, and followed it up in 1967 with the Ro80, a technological tour-de-force that was voted Car of the Year for 1968. Massice warranty claims forced NSU into the arms of Volkswagen and, after the final Ro80 was sold in April 1977, VW dropped the name so it could concentrate on Audis.

NSU
Sport Prinz Coupé

Rare and unusual today, the Sport Prinz Coupé was a good-looking marriage of Italian style and German engineering that should have done better than it did. The bodywork was styled by Scaglione and built in Italy by Bertone. Powered by the Prinz's air-cooled flat twin, the lightweight coupé was capable of 76mph, and seldom felt underpowered on the road despite its tiny engine capacity. It delighted dynamically, thanks to its quick steering and agile handling. More than 20,000 built but few left to choose from today.

SPECIFICATIONS

Years produced:	1958-1967 (20,831 in total)
Performance:	0-60mph: 27.8sec
	Top speed: 78mph
Power & torque:	30bhp/33lb ft
Engine:	Normally aspirated 598cc twin, petrol, carburettor, 4 valves
Drivetrain:	Rear-engine RWD
Structure:	Monocoque
Transmission:	Four-speed manual
Weight:	556kg

PRICE GUIDE

Launch price:	£976
Excellent:	£3000
Good:	£2250
Average:	£1400
Project:	£700

NSU
Prinz 4

When the NSU Prinz 4 arrived in 1961, it was the height of small-car fashion. Aside from the Mini, all of the important European baby cars had their engines slung out back, and many were still air-cooled. The Prinz 4 was well-built and packed with nice features – disc brakes and a slick all-synchromesh gearbox made it a pleasure to drive. However, time passed it by, and as the opposition went front-wheel drive, NSU didn't have the resources to develop a suitable replacement. The company ran out of money, and was taken over by the Volkswagen group.

SPECIFICATIONS

Years produced:	1961-1973 (576,023 in total)
Performance:	0-60mph: 27.7sec
	Top speed: 73mph
Power & torque:	30bhp/33lb ft
Engine:	Normally aspirated 598cc twin, petrol, carburettor, 4 valves
Drivetrain:	Rear-engine RWD
Structure:	Monocoque
Transmission:	Four-speed manual
Weight:	565kg

PRICE GUIDE

Launch price:	£729
Excellent:	£2000
Good:	£1500
Average:	£750
Project:	£300

NSU
Wankel Spider

For much of the 1960s, the future of the internal combustion engine remained up in the air. Felix Wankel's rotary design emerged as a credible alternative, being both smooth and compact, and it's no surprise that manufacturers were clamouring to build their own versions. The first production rotary was the NSU Wankel Spider, an open-topped variation on the Sport Prinz theme. It was a potent little car – the 497cc rotary put out 50bhp and pushed the Spider to over 100mph – but proved too expensive and unreliable for serious sales success.

SPECIFICATIONS
Years produced:	1964-1967 (2375 in total)
Performance:	0-60mph: 17.6sec
	Top speed: 92mph
Power & torque:	50bhp/70lb ft
Engine:	Normally aspirated 497cc single-rotor Wankel, petrol, carburettor
Drivetrain:	Rear-engine RWD
Structure:	Monocoque
Transmission:	Four-speed manual
Weight:	770kg

PRICE GUIDE
Launch price:	£1391
Excellent:	£6000
Good:	£4750
Average:	£3000
Project:	£1500

NSU
1000

The NSU 1000 was a larger, more civilised version of the Prinz 4. Powered by a new 1.0-litre four-cylinder air-cooled engine, the 1000 failed to make a sales impact, probably because it too closely resembled the cheaper car it was based upon. The main differences between the Prinz 4 and the 1000 were its longer wheelbase, restyled front end and plastic cooling vents – and just like its smaller brother, it was a great little car to drive. The 1000 survived the Volkswagen takeover, making it to 1973, but its replacement – the Audi 50 – shared no parts with it.

SPECIFICATIONS
Years produced:	1964-1972 (196,000 in total)
Performance:	0-60mph: 20.5sec
	Top speed: 80mph
Power & torque:	43bhp/52lb ft
Engine:	Normally aspirated 996cc four cylinder, petrol, carburettor, 8 valves
Drivetrain:	Rear-engine RWD
Structure:	Monocoque
Transmission:	Four-speed manual
Weight:	620kg

PRICE GUIDE
Launch price:	£673
Excellent:	£2000
Good:	£1500
Average:	£800
Project:	£300

NSU
Ro80

The NSU Ro80 redefined levels of expectation for buyers in the executive class. It handled beautifully, was huge inside, looked amazing and rode as well as any luxury saloon. It was crowned Car of the Year and, for a while, the Ro80 had the world at its feet. Then the problems started... Its rotary engine was silken but prone to failure, and warranty costs crippled NSU. Modern technology has conquered the rotor-tip problem, and with the correct support a Ro80 is a brilliant classic car to own. A constant reminder of what might have been.

SPECIFICATIONS
Years produced:	1966-1977 (37,204 in total)
Performance:	0-60mph: 14.2sec
	Top speed: 117mph
Power & torque:	114bhp/139lb ft
Engine:	Normally aspirated 1990cc twin-rotor Wankel, petrol, carburettor
Drivetrain:	Front-engine FWD
Structure:	Monocoque
Transmission:	Three-speed semi-automatic
Weight:	1190kg

PRICE GUIDE
Launch price:	£2249
Excellent:	£5000
Good:	£3500
Average:	£2000
Project:	£1000

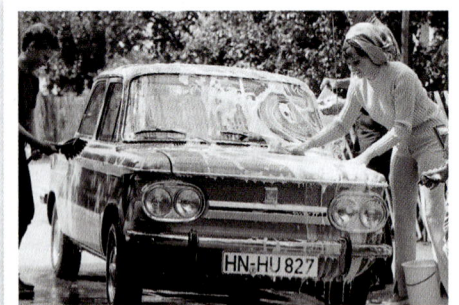

NSU
1200 TT/TTS

The NSU 1200TT proved popular with competitive drivers, and was successful in motor sport. Making the most of the basic car's lightness, the TT version was created when the engine was expanded to 1.2-litres. The excellent handling and roadholding of the 1000 it was based on were complemented by the 1200's additional power, and the TT/TTS ended up becoming Germany's answer to the Mini-Cooper and Simca 1000 Rallye. Due to their high-quality construction, a large number have survived in Germany; fewer in the UK.

SPECIFICATIONS
Years produced:	1967-1972 (63,289/2404 in total)
Performance:	0-60mph: 14.8sec
	Top speed: 96mph
Power & torque:	64bhp/65lb ft
Engine:	Normally aspirated 1172cc four cylinder, petrol, carburettor, 8 valves
Drivetrain:	Rear-engine RWD
Structure:	Monocoque
Transmission:	Four-speed manual
Weight:	650kg

PRICE GUIDE
Launch price:	£824
Excellent:	£3750
Good:	£3000
Average:	£1500
Project:	£750

OGLE

DAVID OGLE founded Ogle Associates at his home in Stevenage in England in 1954, expanding in 1959 to employ noted designer Tom Karen. First products to emerge from the company were special-bodied Minis and Daimlers, but the company diversified into production of the impressive SX1000. Ogle himself was killed driving one of his prototypes in 1962, but the company continued, with Tom Karen taking over as managing director. At this point, SX1000 production ceased, and Karen focused the company's activity as a design house. It styled a number of impressive designs, notably the Triplex GTS – which evolved into the Reliant Scimitar GTE.

OGLE
SX1000

David Ogle ventured into specialist car production in 1960, but truly came into his own when he applied his styling and engineering skills to the Mini. The SX1000 was at the vanguard of the Mini-boom that also included the Marcos and the Deep-Sanderson, and was created by mating a stumpy glassfibre body to a Mini van floorpan and kitting it out with a leather-clad interior. It was quick, too, thanks to improved aerodynamics, a kerbweight 130kg less than the donor car's, and 76bhp from the Cooper S engine. Now eligible for Goodwood.

SPECIFICATIONS

Years produced:	1961-1967 (70 in total)
Performance:	0-60mph: 9.0sec
	Top speed: 110mph
Power & torque:	76bhp/79lb ft
Engine:	Normally aspirated 1275cc four cylinder, petrol, carburettor, 8 valves
Drivetrain:	Front-engine FWD
Structure:	Monocoque
Transmission:	Four-speed manual
Weight:	500kg

PRICE GUIDE

Launch price:	N/A
Excellent:	£10,000
Good:	£8000
Average:	£6500
Project:	£3000

OPEL

OPEL, FOUNDED in 1898, built Lutzman and Darracq cars before coming out with its own. Despite its acumen, General Motors took over in 1928 to gain a foothold in the European market and, under GM leadership, Opel became the European market leader by the end of the 1930s. After the war, the Kapitan and Rekord ranges were the mainstay of Opel's catalogues, joined by the smaller Kadett in 1962. Gradually Opel's range combined with that of GM's British arm, Vauxhall. The two marques are separated by their badging, although Opel carries out the engineering, simply handing the results over to Vauxhall. The new British-developed Astra Sport Tourer is the exception.

OPEL
Kadett A/B

Opel waited until 1962 before launching its small car of the post-war era. This was the Kadett A and very successful it was too, though it was never sold in the UK. What came afterwards was even better. The Kadett B had restyled looks mated to the same chassis, but with a bigger selection of engines, ranging from 1078cc to 1897cc. As well as the saloons and estates, there was a pretty coupé that, in Rallye form, made use of the 1897cc engine with twin carburettors to give 90bhp. These are the ones that excite collectors.

SPECIFICATIONS

Years produced:	1962-1973 (2,311,389 in total)
Performance:	0-60mph: 13.8sec
	Top speed: 89mph
Power & torque:	60bhp/65lb ft
Engine:	Normally aspirated 1196cc four cylinder, petrol, carburettor, 8 valves
Drivetrain:	Front-engine RWD
Structure:	Monocoque
Transmission:	Four-speed manual
Weight:	800kg

PRICE GUIDE

Launch price:	£708
Excellent:	£3000
Good:	£2200
Average:	£1200
Project:	£400

OPEL
Rekord/Commodore D

The Commodore, launched in 1967, was an upmarket version of the Opel Rekord. Sold as a saloon or coupé, it was only available with six-cylinder engines, initially 2239cc and 2490cc units, although a 2784cc followed in 1970 and was used in the most desirable GS2800 variant, boasting 143bhp. The second-generation Commodore came on the scene in 1972, sharing its floorpan with the Vauxhall Victor FE. It upped the luxury inside, with the fuel-injection GS/E model as the flagship from 1974 up until the end of the line in 1977.

SPECIFICATIONS

Years produced:	1967-1977 (156,330 in total)
Performance:	12.1sec
	Top speed: 108mph
Power & torque:	130bhp/137lb ft
Engine:	Normally aspirated 2490cc straight six, petrol, fuel injection, 12 valves
Drivetrain:	Front-engine RWD
Structure:	Monocoque
Transmission:	Four-speed manual/three-speed auto
Weight:	1234kg

PRICE GUIDE

Launch price:	£1380
Excellent:	£4000
Good:	£3000
Average:	£1500
Project:	£500

OPEL
GT

Given Opel's General Motors heritage, nobody should have been too surprised when the GT popped up in 1968 looking like a shrunken Corvette (although it had been previously seen as a concept car at the 1965 Frankfurt Motor Show). The Kadett provided most of the underpinnings while the body was built by Brissoneau & Lotz in France. The rotating headlamps were manually operated. Most GTs ended up in the US, presumably with owners who couldn't afford to run the full-sized Corvette. Very nimble, fun, and distinctive.

SPECIFICATIONS

Years produced:	1968-1973 (103,463 in total)
Performance:	11.0sec
	Top speed: 116mph
Power & torque:	88bhp/110lb ft
Engine:	Normally aspirated 1897cc four cylinder, petrol, carburettor, 8 valves
Drivetrain:	Front-engine RWD
Structure:	Monocoque
Transmission:	Four-speed manual
Weight:	970kg

PRICE GUIDE

Launch price:	£1882
Excellent:	£8500
Good:	£6500
Average:	£4000
Project:	£1000

OPEL
Manta A

'We want a Capri!' That was the cry of most European manufacturers after Ford launched its coupé in 1969, and the Manta was Opel's attempt to get in on the act. It used the Ascona as its basis, with a new nose up front and well-proportioned coupé bodywork behind. 1584cc and 1897cc overhead-camshaft engines did service under the bonnet although mainland Europe also had the option of a 1196cc engine. A small number of turbocharged models, based on the plusher Berlinetta, was built and sold in Britain.

SPECIFICATIONS
Years produced:	1970-1975 (498,553 in total)
Performance:	0-60mph: 12.2sec
	Top speed: 105mph
Power & torque:	90bhp/108lb ft
Engine:	Normally aspirated 1897cc four cylinder, petrol, carburettor, 8 valves
Drivetrain:	Front-engine RWD
Structure:	Monocoque
Transmission:	Four-speed manual
Weight:	955kg

PRICE GUIDE
Launch price:	£1475
Excellent:	£3750
Good:	£3000
Average:	£1500
Project:	£750

OPEL
Kadett GT/E

The most appealing of all Kadetts was the Coupé, which is something of a cult car in Germany, and at the very top of the tree was the GT/E version. The fastest Kadett was distinguished by its two-tone paint and earned its stripes by using the Manta's 1.9-litre cam-in-head engine with fuel injection. Clearly it was influenced by the Group 2 rally car, right down to the Opel Team paint scheme. With 105bhp on tap, it was a genuinely quick car, and the well-damped, sharp-steering chassis was more than capable of harnessing the additional power.

SPECIFICATIONS
Years produced:	1973-1979
Performance:	0-60mph: 9.0sec
	Top speed: 110mph
Power & torque:	105bhp/110lb ft
Engine:	Normally aspirated 1897cc four cylinder, petrol, fuel injected, 8 valves
Drivetrain:	Front-engine RWD
Structure:	Monocoque
Transmission:	Four-speed manual
Weight:	915kg

PRICE GUIDE
Launch price:	£3166
Excellent:	£4000
Good:	£2500
Average:	£1500
Project:	£600

OPEL
Manta B

In 1975, the Opel Manta and its sister the Ascona were given a full make-over. Out went the Corvette-inspired curves to be replaced by a sharp new '70s suit. The Manta's handling was taut and faithful, and performance more than acceptable in fuel-injection GT/E form. The range expanded in 1978 to include a hatchback. In 1981, Opel freshened the existing car's styling with glassfibre bumpers, and introduced a new 1.8-litre engine for the cooking models. The GT/E version continued with the same 110bhp fuel-injection 2.0-litre. Rusty but trusty now.

SPECIFICATIONS (GT/E)
Years produced:	1978-1988 (603,000 in total)
Performance:	0-60mph: 8.5sec
	Top speed: 120mph
Power & torque:	110bhp/119lb ft
Engine:	Normally aspirated 1979cc four cylinder, petrol, electronic fuel injection, 8 valves
Drivetrain:	Front-engine RWD
Structure:	Monocoque
Transmission:	Five-speed manual
Weight:	1065kg

PRICE GUIDE
Launch price:	£6444 (1984)
Excellent:	£3000
Good:	£1800
Average:	£750
Project:	£400

OPEL
Senator/Monza

Opel's 1978 entrant in the executive car market was its most convincing effort yet. Based on the Senator saloon, the Monza was a good-looking and well-equipped three-door coupé that proved agile despite its bulk. Its dramatic straight-line ability – 0-60mph in 8.5 seconds, top speed of 133mph – was made possible by its six-cylinder fuel-injection engine. Variations on the theme included the ES, with a limited-slip differential to cope with all that power, and the GSE with Recaro seats, digital instrumentation and a prominent rear spoiler.

SPECIFICATIONS (Monza GS/E)
Years produced:	1978-1986 (129,644/43,500 in total)
Performance:	0-60mph: 9.3sec
	Top speed: 123mph
Power & torque:	180bhp/183lb ft
Engine:	Normally aspirated 2969cc straight six, petrol, electronic fuel injection, 12 valves
Drivetrain:	Front-engine RWD
Structure:	Monocoque
Transmission:	Four/five-speed manual
Weight:	1375kg

PRICE GUIDE
Launch price:	£9762
Excellent:	£4000
Good:	£2750
Average:	£1200
Project:	£400

PANHARD

ONE OF THE earliest French car companies, Panhard et Levassor's first vehicle was a Daimler-engined machine in 1891. Panhard then grew to become one of the most prominent manufacturers of motoring's pioneering years, marketing a wide range of models, eventually specialising in very large, very expensive and very exclusive products. One of the more notable was the Art Deco-influenced Dynamic of 1937. Post-war, Panhard altered direction completely and became known for quirky streamlined styling and air-cooled two-cylinder engines. Citroën took over in 1967 and devoted Panhard to building just military vehicles, something it still does today.

PANHARD
24 Series

'Amazing' isn't a word that troubles the French car industry as often as it might, but that superlative perfectly fits the Panhard 24. It might have been powered by a weedy two-cylinder engine but, such was its aerodynamic efficiency, the French coupé could push 100mph and deliver excellent fuel consumption. Sadly, there wasn't a market for this prescient (and expensive) car, and it contributed to Panhard's financial collapse and Citroën's takeover. A few remain in the UK, and have a keen following, even if keeping one roadworthy is challenging.

SPECIFICATIONS

Years produced:	1963-1967 (22,245 in total)
Performance:	0-60mph: 22.3sec
	Top speed: 89mph
Power & torque:	50bhp/56lb ft
Engine:	Normally aspirated 848cc two-cylinder, petrol, carburettor, 4 valves
Drivetrain:	Front-engine FWD
Structure:	Monocoque
Transmission:	Four-speed manual
Weight:	840kg

PRICE GUIDE

Launch price:	N/A in UK
Excellent:	£6500
Good:	£4000
Average:	£2500
Project:	£800

PANTHER

THE NICHE manufacturers' niche manufacturer, Panther Westwinds was founded by Robert Jankel in 1972 to build retro cars with styling inspired by 1930s greats. It even had its factory at Brooklands. Panther then branched out into such diversities as the Rio – a Triumph Dolomite repanelled and trimmed to look like a small Rolls – and the six-wheeled two-seater Panther 6 sports car. Young C Kim took over in 1980 and switched body manufacture to Korea. Much money was spent developing the ill-fated (thought stunning and advanced) mid-engined, four-wheel-drive, Cosworth-powered Solo sports coupé, and SsangYong stepped in 1988. But it was all too late and Panther folded in 1990.

PANTHER
J72

The J72 owed its looks to Jaguar's SS100, although it was more parody than replica. This being the 1970s, there was a ready market for such brash expressions of style (or lack of it), and a number of celebrities bought into British businessman Robert Jankel's dream machine. There was little sophistication to the J72, but it was very fast thanks to its Jaguar six-cylinder engines; even more so when the V12 was added in 1974. The J72 stayed in production until 1981, during which time 426 examples of this expensive vintage wannabe were constructed.

SPECIFICATIONS

Years produced:	1972-1981 (426 in total)
Performance:	0-60mph: 6.4sec
	Top speed: 114mph
Power & torque:	190bhp/200lb ft
Engine:	Normally aspirated 4235cc straight six, petrol, carburettor, 12 valves
Drivetrain:	Front-engine RWD
Structure:	Separate chassis
Transmission:	Four-speed manual with overdrive
Weight:	1136kg

PRICE GUIDE

Launch price:	£4380
Excellent:	£16,500
Good:	£12,500
Average:	£8500
Project:	£5000

PANTHER
De Ville

Clearly inspired by the Bugatti Royale, the Panther De Ville was a Jaguar V12-powered pastiche with Austin 1800 doors. It was also the most expensive car on UK price lists in its day. Much of the underpinnings came from Jaguar, as with Panther's previous efforts, making it refined and swift. It was beautifully built too, and attracted a limited and wealthy following. Available as a four- or six-door saloon and as a two-door open-top, the De Ville was the ultimate in ostentatious motoring in a dark decade. Most have survived, and are loved by doting owners.

SPECIFICATIONS

Years produced:	1974-1985 (60 in total)
Performance:	0-60mph: 12.4sec
	Top speed: 109mph
Power & torque:	190bhp/200lb ft
Engine:	Normally aspirated 4235cc straight six, petrol, carburettor, 12 valves
Drivetrain:	Front-engine RWD
Structure:	Separate chassis
Transmission:	Four-speed manual with overdrive
Weight:	1882kg

PRICE GUIDE

Launch price:	£27,000
Excellent:	£40,000
Good:	£28,000
Average:	£12,000
Project:	£9000

PANTHER
Rio

The Rio was always destined to fail. It was a good idea by Robert Jankel to launch a car that offered top-drawer luxury in a more manageable package, but the execution was spoiled by the fact that the Rio too closely resembled the car it was based on – the Triumph Dolomite. The body was re-skinned in hand-beaten aluminium, and that pushed the price up to such a degree that for the cost of a Rio Especiale you could buy a Jaguar XJ12 and still have money left over. A surprising number of the original 35 still survive, and good ones are sought after.

SPECIFICATIONS

Years produced:	1975-1977 (35 in total)
Performance:	0-60mph: 9.6sec
	Top speed: 115mph
Power & torque:	127bhp/124lb ft
Engine:	Normally aspirated 1998cc four cylinder, petrol, carburettor, 16 valves
Drivetrain:	Front-engine RWD
Structure:	Monocoque
Transmission:	Four-speed manual with overdrive
Weight:	1100kg

PRICE GUIDE

Launch price:	£5377
Excellent:	£5000
Good:	£3000
Average:	£1500
Project:	£700

PANTHER
Lima

With its Morganesque looks and Vauxhall mechanicals (Viva floorpan and Magnum 2279cc slant-four engine), the Lima was significantly cheaper than its stablemates and could even be ordered through some Vauxhall dealerships. The glassfibre bodywork surrounding MG Midget doors and windscreen made it lightweight and well-behaved, while the 108bhp on offer meant good performance, although even more was offered by 1978's turbocharged version. The MkII from 1979 had a Panther-built box-section chassis.

SPECIFICATIONS	
Years produced:	1976-1982 (897 in total)
Performance:	0-60mph: 6.7sec
	Top speed: 107mph
Power & torque:	108bhp/138lb ft
Engine:	Normally aspirated 2279cc four cylinder, petrol, carburettor, 8 valves
Drivetrain:	Front-engine RWD
Structure:	Separate chassis
Transmission:	Four-speed manual
Weight:	862kg

PRICE GUIDE	
Launch price:	£8997
Excellent:	£6250
Good:	£5000
Average:	£2250
Project:	£1250

PANTHER
Kallista

After financial troubles forced owner Robert Jankel to sell Panther, the marque ended up in the hands of a Korean conglomerate and under it the Lima evolved into the Kallista. Instead of a glassfibre body, it used aluminium over a steel chassis, and the Vauxhall mechanicals were replaced by a series of Ford engines from 1597cc four cylinder to 2935cc V6. Although production came to an end in 1990, the SsangYong Motor Company came back with a badge-engineered version of the roadster in 1992, but a mere 73 were made.

SPECIFICATIONS	
Years produced:	1982-1990
Performance:	0-60mph: 7.5sec
	Top speed: 120mph
Power & torque:	150bhp/159lb ft
Engine:	Normally aspirated 2792cc V6, petrol, fuel injection, 12 valves
Drivetrain:	Front-engine RWD
Structure:	Separate chassis
Transmission:	Five-speed manual
Weight:	965kg

PRICE GUIDE	
Launch price:	£5850
Excellent:	£7500
Good:	£6000
Average:	£3500
Project:	£1750

PEERLESS/WARWICK

NOT TO BE confused with the top-class pre-war US manufacturer, Peerless came about in 1957 when the Slough-based garage bearing the name was bought by Warwickshire hotelier James Byrnes in order to build a Triumph TR3-based GT car. The car was originally being built in London by John Gordon to designs by Bernard Rodger – and Peerless's premises were perfect for assembling it. Sadly, the project failed to gain momentum, and Rodger transferred production Wraysbury, Berkshire – and it was here that 20-50 cars were assembled under the Warwick name. The project ended in 1962, and all that remains of the Peerless marque is a pub in nearby Slough.

PEERLESS/WARWICK
GT

As an affordable GT the Peerless certainly met all of its targets. The mixture of spaceframe structure with de Dion rear axle and Triumph TR3 running gear was a wonderful set of ingredients with which to build a new sporting car. But like all such ventures, finance was always the issue, and no matter how promising the car looks and drives, if the company can't afford to develop it properly then it's likely to fail. This was the case with the Peerless GT and, although it deserved to do well, it lasted a mere three years and only 325 were made.

SPECIFICATIONS	
Years produced:	1958-1962 (325 in total)
Performance:	0-60mph: 12.8sec
	Top speed: 103mph
Power & torque:	100bhp/N/A
Engine:	Normally aspirated 1991cc four cylinder, petrol, carburettor, 8 valves
Drivetrain:	Front-engine RWD
Structure:	Spaceframe/glassfibre body
Transmission:	Four-speed manual with overdrive
Weight:	953kg

PRICE GUIDE	
Launch price:	£1498
Excellent:	£11,500
Good:	£7500
Average:	£4000
Project:	£2250

PEUGEOT

ONE OF THE world's oldest motor manufacturers: Armand Peugeot started with a steam car in 1889 and began dropping Daimler petrol engines into his chassis two years later. Racers grew Peugeot's pre-war reputation, along with some adventurous styling, but after World War Two the company's success was largely built on not being Citroën. By sticking to tried and trusted engineering, its more conservative cars were less troublesome, gaining loyal owners. Ironically, this led to Peugeot taking over Citroën in the 1970s, along with Chrysler Europe. The result was some financial strains, from which the group was rescued by the runaway success of the Peugeot 205.

PEUGEOT
203

The 203 was Peugeot's first all-new post-war design and, although it lacked the 202's idiosyncratic styling, it was a groundbreaking technical package. The alloy-headed engine and hydraulic brakes were novelties, while the independent front suspension and rack-and-pinion steering set the company's products on their way towards a reputation for dynamic pleasure. Like all Peugeots for the next 30 years, the 203 enjoyed a long production run – 12 years – and ended up donating much of its platform to its replacement. An endearing French classic.

SPECIFICATIONS
Years produced: 1948-1963 (686,628 in total)
Performance: 0-60mph: N/A
Top speed: 71mph
Power & torque: 45bhp/59lb ft
Engine: Normally aspirated 1290cc four cylinder, petrol, carburettor, 8 valves
Drivetrain: Front-engine RWD
Structure: Monocoque
Transmission: Four-speed manual
Weight: 930kg

PRICE GUIDE
Launch price: £986
Excellent: £4500
Good: £3250
Average: £1500
Project: £500

PEUGEOT
403 Saloon

Peugeot's 1950s saloon was little more than a reskin of the 203. I was larger, more luxurious, and ended up being sold alongside the older car as an upgrade for an increasingly affluent market. Pinin Farina assisted with the styling – leading to an enduring partnership – but with full-width bodywork and neat detailing, it struck a chord with the French middle classes. The popular Familiale version was innovative for offering three rows of seats, while the diesel version sold well in its home country as a rugged and reliable workhorse.

SPECIFICATIONS
Years produced: 1955-1966 (1,214,121 in total)
Performance: 0-60mph: 24.0sec
Top speed: 76mph
Power & torque: 58bhp/74lb ft
Engine: Normally aspirated 1468cc four cylinder, petrol, carburettor, 8 valves
Drivetrain: Front-engine RWD
Structure: Monocoque
Transmission: Four-speed manual
Weight: 1300kg

PRICE GUIDE
Launch price: £1129
Excellent: £3250
Good: £2250
Average: £1250
Project: £400

PEUGEOT
403 Décapotable

Pininfarina's reputation for producing stylish convertibles and coupés from family cars arguably started here. The 403 Décapotable, to give the car its correct title, shared its wheelbase and running gear with the saloon, but looked a lot more appealing. First shown at the 1956 Paris Salon, it instantly found favour with buyers. The high-compression 1.5-litre engine gave reasonable performance, but this car was always about touring. Values continue to climb, despite (or maybe due to) reruns of TV's *Columbo* – and the appearances of his unkempt example.

SPECIFICATIONS
Years produced: 1957-1961 (2050 in total)
Performance: 0-60mph: 24.0sec
Top speed: 76mph
Power & torque: 58bhp/74lb ft
Engine: Normally aspirated 1468cc four cylinder, petrol, carburettor, 8 valves
Drivetrain: Front-engine RWD
Structure: Monocoque
Transmission: Four-speed manual
Weight: 1300kg

PRICE GUIDE
Launch price: N/A in UK
Excellent: £11,000
Good: £9000
Average: £6000
Project: £2000

PEUGEOT
404 Saloon

At first glance, the Farina-styled 404 looks like a copy of BMC's and Fiat's contemporary mid-sized saloons, with 403 underpinnings. In reality, the 404 was a nicer car to drive and offered a clever design as, although it looked like a grand saloon, it was actually smaller than the car it was supposed to replace. In the end – and in good Peugeot tradition – the 404 and 403 ran concurrently for three years, before the newer car went on to sell millions worldwide. You still see a few in north Africa, thanks to solid build and simple DIY.

SPECIFICATIONS
Years produced: 1960-1978 (1,847,568 in total)
Performance: 0-60mph: 18.1sec
Top speed: 82mph
Power & torque: 68bhp/94lb ft
Engine: Normally aspirated 1618cc four cylinder, petrol, carburettor, 8 valves
Drivetrain: Front-engine RWD
Structure: Monocoque
Transmission: Four-speed manual
Weight: 1070kg

PRICE GUIDE
Launch price: £1297
Excellent: £2650
Good: £2000
Average: £1000
Project: £300

PEUGEOT
404 Cabriolet

Unlike some Peugeot/Pininfarina collaborations, the 404 Cabriolet and its coupé brother were a full rebody of an existing platform, sharing no external panels. Given such a free rein, it's not surprising that the Italian styling house came up with such a stunning car – and one that, thanks to its scarcity, is in strong demand today. Its wheelbase is shared with the saloon, so the 404 Cabriolet is a full four-seater. Power came from Peugeot's well-regarded 1.6-litre engine, and delivered excellent performance, especially in fuel injection form.

SPECIFICATIONS
Years produced: 1962-1968 (3728 in total)
Performance: 0-60mph: 12.2sec
Top speed: 92mph
Power & torque: 79bhp/100lb ft
Engine: Normally aspirated 1608cc four cylinder, petrol, carburettor, 8 valves
Drivetrain: Front-engine RWD
Structure: Monocoque
Transmission: Four-speed manual
Weight: 1030kg

PRICE GUIDE
Launch price: £2367
Excellent: £9500
Good: £7500
Average: £4250
Project: £1500

PEUGEOT
204/304 Coupé

Whereas the Peugeot 204 and 304 have been unfairly consigned to the ranks to the automotive hall of mediocrity, the coupé versions were a further Pininfarina masterclass in product maximisation. The pretty three-door fastback used a hatchback rear door, and comfortable seating for two adults plus two children, despite a wheelbase shortened by 12 inches. Surviving examples are good to drive and are likely to have been well cared for, but take care when looking for corrosion – it can strike anywhere, and often does.

SPECIFICATIONS

Years produced:	1965-1979 (42,756 in total)
Performance:	0-60mph: 18.2sec
	Top speed: 91mph
Power & torque:	53bhp/82lb ft
Engine:	Normally aspirated 1130cc four cylinder, petrol, carburettor, 8 valves
Drivetrain:	Front-engine FWD
Structure:	Monocoque
Transmission:	Four-speed manual
Weight:	838kg

PRICE GUIDE

Launch price:	£983
Excellent:	£4000
Good:	£3000
Average:	£2000
Project:	£650

PEUGEOT
204/304 Saloon

The 204 and 304 were a leap forward for Peugeot as they were the firm's first cars with transverse engines driving the front wheels. With independent rear suspension, servo-assisted brakes and anti-roll bars, the modern layout delivered surefooted handling and a comfortable ride, in true French style. The 304 was similar in concept, but with a longer front and rear, plusher interiors and a more powerful 1.3-litre engine, making it more satisfying to own. Downsides were few, but lack of glamour was one, corrosion another.

SPECIFICATIONS

Years produced:	1965-1980 (1,387,473/1,334,309 in total)
Performance:	0-60mph: 16.2sec
	Top speed: 90mph
Power & torque:	55bhp/66lb ft
Engine:	Normally aspirated 1130cc four cylinder, petrol, carburettor, 8 valves
Drivetrain:	Front-engine FWD
Structure:	Monocoque
Transmission:	Four-speed manual
Weight:	880kg

PRICE GUIDE

Launch price:	£992
Excellent:	£2500
Good:	£1750
Average:	£850
Project:	£300

PEUGEOT
204/304 Cabriolet

Unlike the Coupé, the 204 Cabriolet was never officially sold in the UK, making buying one a lengthy and involved process. But there are a few in the UK, which have quite a cult following thanks to head-turning looks and neat dynamics. The later 304, however, *did* make it here, and examples aren't too difficult to track down. The newer car's uprated engine delivered sprightly performance and excellent economy, and if you're looking for an easy-to-drive, appealing ragtop that's just a little bit different, this could be ideal for you.

SPECIFICATIONS

Years produced:	1967-1975 (18,181 in total)
Performance:	0-60mph: 14.5sec
	Top speed: 96mph
Power & torque:	74bhp/80lb ft
Engine:	Normally aspirated 1288cc four cylinder, petrol, carburettor, 8 valves
Drivetrain:	Front-engine FWD
Structure:	Monocoque
Transmission:	Four-speed manual
Weight:	895kg

PRICE GUIDE

Launch price:	£1496
Excellent:	£5250
Good:	£4000
Average:	£2200
Project:	£900

PEUGEOT
504 Saloon

Launched at the Paris Motor Show in 1968, the 504 saloon was Peugeot's flagship until the full-sized 604 arrive seven years later. The engine was mounted longitudinally, driving the rear wheels, and the combination of soft spring and damper rates with massive suspension travel made the 504 an excellent performer on poor (or non-existent) road surfaces. European 504s are a rare sight today, but they are still one of the most common forms of transport throughout Africa, due to their simplicity and reliability.

SPECIFICATIONS

Years produced:	1968-1983 (3,073,185 in total)
Performance:	0-60mph: 12.7sec
	Top speed: 106mph
Power & torque:	93bhp/124lb ft
Engine:	Normally aspirated 1971cc four cylinder, petrol, carburettor, 8 valves
Drivetrain:	Front-engine RWD
Structure:	Monocoque
Transmission:	Four-speed manual
Weight:	1175kg

PRICE GUIDE

Launch price:	£1500
Excellent:	£2500
Good:	£2000
Average:	£800
Project:	£300

PEUGEOT
504 Cabriolet

With a production run of just over 8000, and with a reputation for rust, it's a surprise just how many 504 Cabriolets have survived. Yet with such graceful styling and superb road manners, it became a classic the moment it left the production line. With fuel injection as standard, the open 504 proved fast and effective, especially the final five-speed version. It was never directly replaced, Peugeot subsequently concentrating instead on smaller convertibles. Prices here are for V6 models; four-cylinder Cabrios will be less.

SPECIFICATIONS

Years produced:	1968-1983
Performance:	0-60mph: 9.9sec
	Top speed: 105mph
Power & torque:	110bhp/131lb ft
Engine:	Normally aspirated 1971cc four cylinder, petrol, carburettor, 8 valves
Drivetrain:	Front-engine RWD
Structure:	Monocoque
Transmission:	Four-speed manual
Weight:	1165kg

PRICE GUIDE

Launch price:	£1594
Excellent:	£12,500
Good:	£10,000
Average:	£6500
Project:	£2500

PEUGEOT
504 Coupé

The same Peugeot/Pininfarina recipe used for the 404 Coupé was used once again for its replacement, which hit the road in 1969. With an all-new body on a slightly shortened 504 platform, the 504 Coupé combined the excellent road manners of this no-nonsense French saloon with a healthy dose of glamorous Italian style. The top-of-the-range version was treated to a Peugeot-Renault-Volvo V6 (which also saw service in the DeLorean DMC-12 and Alpine A310 V6) in 1974, creating easily the company's most desirable car of the period.

SPECIFICATIONS
Years produced:	1969-1983 (26,477 in total)
Performance:	0-60mph: 10.5sec
	Top speed: 111mph
Power & torque:	110bhp/131lb ft
Engine:	Normally aspirated 1971cc four cylinder, petrol, carburettor, 8 valves
Drivetrain:	Front-engine RWD
Structure:	Monocoque
Transmission:	Four-speed manual
Weight:	1165kg

PRICE GUIDE (V6 in brackets)
Launch price:	£2609
Excellent:	£6750 (£12,000)
Good:	£5000 (£10,000)
Average:	£3000 (£6000)
Project:	£1200 (£2500)

PEUGEOT
104/104Z coupé

An excellent and oft-overlooked baby motor, the Peugeot 104 combined front-wheel drive and supple suspension to prove that small cars didn't need to be a compromise. It was launched as a four-door, and would have to wait four more years to gain the hatchback its two-box body was crying out for. The 'Douvrin' engine that powered the 104 was shared with Renault and Citroën, and its underpinnings went on to find fame in the Citroën Visa, Talbot Samba and – with modifications – the Peugeot 205. Truncated Z rather like a latter-day Mini-Cooper.

SPECIFICATIONS
Years produced:	1972-1988
Performance:	0-60mph: 18.5sec
	Top speed: 86mph
Power & torque:	46bhp/54lb ft
Engine:	Normally aspirated 954cc four cylinder, petrol, carburettor, 8 valves
Drivetrain:	Front-engine FWD
Structure:	Monocoque
Transmission:	Four-speed manual
Weight:	760kg

PRICE GUIDE
Launch price:	£1194
Excellent:	£1200
Good:	£800
Average:	£550
Project:	£300

PEUGEOT
604

To look at the 604 today, it's hard to believe that so few were sold in the UK. Its Pininfarina styling appeared to all intents and purposes like a four-door Fiat 130 coupé, while the ride quality was typically Gallic-soft. Yet fail it did – and that means they're almost impossible to find now. All petrol cars were powered by the PRV V6, either carb-fed or fuel injection, and were quick, if thirsty. The 604 was the first Peugeot to be powered by a turbodiesel (80bhp from 2.3 litres still resulted in lethargic performance), but the choice of the range is a five-speed fuel-injection Ti model.

SPECIFICATIONS
Years produced:	1975-1986 (240,100 in total)
Performance:	0-60mph: 9.9sec
	Top speed: 120mph
Power & torque:	144bhp/159lb ft
Engine:	Normally aspirated 2664cc V6, petrol, fuel injection, 12 valves
Drivetrain:	Front-engine RWD
Structure:	Monocoque
Transmission:	Five-speed manual
Weight:	1475kg

PRICE GUIDE
Launch price:	£4600
Excellent:	£3000
Good:	£2200
Average:	£1200
Project:	£500

PEUGEOT
305

The 305 was another intelligent if understated Peugeot that was more accomplished to drive than its boring styling would have you believe. A long wheelbase and relaxed springing meant it was a cruiser, not a sprinter, but it could hustle along deceptively quickly. The 1.3- and 1.5-litre engines were lively and economical, too. Like fine wine, the 305 improved with age – the estate version was huge, and the facelifted models of 1983 were boosted by 205GTi power. All that held it back in the UK was the lack of a hatchback and definable image.

SPECIFICATIONS (305 SR)
Years produced:	1977-1988 (1,740,300 in total)
Performance:	0-60mph: 13.2sec
	Top speed: 97mph
Power & torque:	73bhp/86lb ft
Engine:	Normally aspirated 1472cc four cylinder, petrol, carburettor, 8 valves
Drivetrain:	Front-engine FWD
Structure:	Monocoque
Transmission:	Four-speed manual
Weight:	940kg

PRICE GUIDE
Launch price:	£2999
Excellent:	£1000
Good:	£650
Average:	£450
Project:	£250

PEUGEOT
505

Like the 504 it replaced, the 505 was one of the most recognisable and rugged saloons on the planet. The main reason for the car's success in developing countries was its ability to handle rutted and very poor road surfaces; the 505 was produced in Nigeria until 2006, although European production stopped in 1993 when it was made redundant by the smaller 405 and the larger 605. The diesel 505s were always the biggest sellers, and if you opted for the estate it could be fitted with a third row of seats, giving room for eight people.

SPECIFICATIONS
Years produced:	1979-1993
Performance:	0-60mph: 10.0sec
	Top speed: 114mph
Power & torque:	130bhp/136lb ft
Engine:	Normally aspirated 2165cc four cylinder, petrol, electronic fuel injection, 8 valves
Drivetrain:	Front-engine RWD
Structure:	Monocoque
Transmission:	Five-speed manual
Weight:	1235kg

PRICE GUIDE
Launch price:	£9595
Excellent:	£1750
Good:	£1400
Average:	£900
Project:	£300

PEUGEOT
205

The world wasn't quite ready for the 205's brilliance when it exploded onto the scene, and Fiat's less innovative Uno ended up pipping it to the Car of The Year title. Buyers rapidly cottoned on, though, and the stylish hatchback became a best-seller across Europe. On the road, the 205 distinguished itself by its keen handling and restful ride, while lightweight construction meant all models were efficient. Engine and trim options were extensive (from 954cc to 1905cc), and all models were fun to drive – even the diesels. Hot variants have the most classic appeal.

SPECIFICATIONS (205GT)

Years produced:	1983-1994
Performance:	0-60mph: 11.6sec
	Top speed: 106mph
Power & torque:	80bhp/80lb ft
Engine:	Normally aspirated 1360cc four cylinder, petrol, carburettor, 8 valves
Drivetrain:	Front-engine FWD
Structure:	Monocoque
Transmission:	Five-speed manual
Weight:	810kg

PRICE GUIDE

Launch price:	£3895
Excellent:	£1200
Good:	£800
Average:	£550
Project:	£250

PEUGEOT
205 GTi

The best hot hatch ever? Volkswagen may have started the GTi craze in 1976, but many see the 205 as king of the breed. Initially available only with a 1.6-litre engine, in 1986 the 205 received the 130bhp 1905cc unit, instantly giving more rapid acceleration and a higher top speed – although it is still hotly debated which is the better car. The 1.6 is slightly lighter and better balanced, yet the more powerful 1.9 is ultimately faster. Both variants had a reputation for lift-off oversteer – which is tamed by the fitment of modern tyres these days.

SPECIFICATIONS (1.6)

Years produced:	1984-1994
Performance:	0-60mph: 8.6sec
	Top speed: 120mph
Power & torque:	105bhp/99lb ft
Engine:	Normally aspirated 1580cc four cylinder, petrol, electronic fuel injection, 8 valves
Drivetrain:	Front-engine FWD
Structure:	Monocoque
Transmission:	Five-speed manual
Weight:	850kg

PRICE GUIDE

Launch price:	£6295
Excellent:	£6000
Good:	£3500
Average:	£1250
Project:	£500

PEUGEOT
205 T16

The Group B era is still regarded as the finest ever seen in rallying – and with the supercars built within a loose framework of rules, the manufacturers came up with some interesting packages. Peugeot's mid-engined 205 T16 was the most successful of all, winning two Group B championships, and proving convincingly that Audi's quattro was beatable. The road version was detuned to 200bhp (compared with 450bhp for the rally car), and wasn't much quicker than the GTi 1.9 in a straight line, but it was more than capable in the bends. Curiously undervalued right now.

SPECIFICATIONS

Years produced:	1985 (200 in total)
Performance:	0-60mph: 7.7sec
	Top speed: 135mph
Power & torque:	200bhp/190lb ft
Engine:	Turbocharged 1775cc four cylinder, petrol, electronic fuel injection, 16 valves
Drivetrain:	Mid-engine AWD
Structure:	Spaceframe
Transmission:	Five-speed manual
Weight:	1150kg

PRICE GUIDE

Launch price:	N/A in UK
Excellent:	£100,000
Good:	£75,000
Average:	£45,000
Project:	N/A

PEUGEOT
309 GTi

The 309 GTi arrived shortly after the mainstream model but, unlike the 205, it was available only as a 1.9. It featured uprated front and rear suspension, 15in Speedline alloy wheels and a subtle bodykit. Peugeot offered the car solely in three-door form to begin with, yet was later sold in five-door form; and in France, the exciting XU9J4 – Mi16 – engine was also offered, packing 160bhp. Always lived in the shadow of its darling smaller brother, but the 309GTi was arguably the better all-round car – a fact that enthusiasts are now waking up to.

SPECIFICATIONS

Years produced:	1987-1993
Performance:	0-60mph: 8.7sec
	Top speed: 119mph
Power & torque:	130bhp/119lb ft
Engine:	Normally aspirated 1905cc four cylinder, petrol, electronic fuel injection, 8 valves
Drivetrain:	Front-engine FWD
Structure:	Monocoque
Transmission:	Five-speed manual
Weight:	930kg

PRICE GUIDE

Launch price:	£9595
Excellent:	£2500
Good:	£1750
Average:	£950
Project:	£500

PEUGEOT
405 Mi16

The Mi16 could be one of the best performance saloons of the '80s. Its XU9J4 engine was a volume-produced, normally aspirated development of the T16 unit used in Peugeot's Group B 205 rally car. Sadly, due to cost, PSA switched to a cast-iron block in the post-1992 models. This heavier engine was also less powerful, but the torque figure was up, giving the model a more useable powerband. The 405 possessed the best suspension and steering set-up in its class, and remains a legend to this day – although finding one in good condition is becoming a challenge.

SPECIFICATIONS

Years produced:	1987-1995
Performance:	0-60mph: 8.2sec
	Top speed: 138mph
Power & torque:	160bhp/131lb ft
Engine:	Normally aspirated 1905cc four cylinder, petrol, electronic fuel injection, 16 valves
Drivetrain:	Front-engine FWD
Structure:	Monocoque
Transmission:	Five-speed manual
Weight:	1108kg

PRICE GUIDE

Launch price:	£14,995
Excellent:	£2500
Good:	£1750
Average:	£1200
Project:	£700

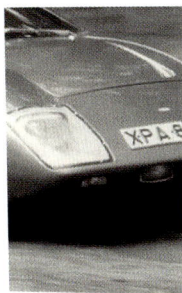

PIPER

PIPER AS A car company started out in 1967 as a maker of kits. The company was based at Campbell's Garage in Kent, which was owned by George Henrup, who had built his own Formula 3 racer, the Ettorne. After finding that motor racing was a quick way of spending large amounts of cash you don't have, he returned to running the family garage – with ambitions to build his own sports car. He and designer Tony Hilder pair joined forces, and produced the GTT (below). The company moved premises, and underwent a number of management changes, ending up trading under the name of Emmbrook Engineering, based in Lincolnshire. After 150 GTT/P2s, the operation faded away.

PIPER
GTT/P2

The Piper GTT was designed by Tony Hilder after he was commissioned by racing driver George Henrotte to create the ultimate GT. The GTT caused a sensation when it was launched, and that was enough to convince Brian Sherwood's Piper company to put the car into production in kit form, using Ford and Triumph suspension parts, with the engine choice being down to the owner. Initially the car sold well, and quite a few survive today, but Piper fell foul of the introduction of VAT and the 1973 oil crisis, and the company folded in 1975.

SPECIFICATIONS

Years produced:	1968-1975 (150 in total)
Performance:	0-60mph: N/A
	Top speed: 115mph
Power & torque:	84bhp/92lb ft
Engine:	Normally aspirated 1599cc four cylinder, petrol, carburettor, 8 valves
Drivetrain:	Front-engine RWD
Structure:	Spaceframe/glassfibre body
Transmission:	Four-speed manual
Weight:	N/A

PRICE GUIDE

Launch price:	£1435
Excellent:	£12,500
Good:	£10,000
Average:	£7000
Project:	£4000

PLYMOUTH

PLYMOUTH AUTOMOBILE was launched in 1928, as Chrysler's entry-level marque – and to fight Chevrolet and Ford. Plymouths were originally sold within Chrysler dealerships, but as the marque developed, it was increasingly marketed as a separate entity with its own showrooms. The cmarque went through many changes and probably had its best years in the 1960s, with the Barracuda and Fury – which would lead to the legendary Road Runner. Its most prolific year was 1973, with 973,000 Plymouths built, but by the late-1970s, Plymouths were merely badge-engineered versions of Chrysler, Dodge or Mitsubishi models, and in 2001 the marque was dropped.

PLYMOUTH
Barracuda

Neatly-styled Valiant saloon-based fastback that gave Plymouth an effective Mustang rival in the pony car market. Pioneering features were the wraparound back window and folding rear seats, but it wasn't until 1967, and the arrival of the reskinned and higher-powered versions, that the model really started to forge a path in the marketplace. Fastback was more popular than the notchback, yet all proved to be effective players in the musclecar market once the 330bhp 383ci small-block V8 was installed. Ignore the six cylinder if it's old school fun you're after.

SPECIFICATIONS

Years produced:	1964-1969 (c267,000 in total)
Performance:	0-60mph: 7.5sec
	Top speed: 120mph
Power & torque:	180bhp/260lb ft
Engine:	Normally aspirated 4496cc V8, petrol, carburettor, 16 valves
Drivetrain:	Front-engine RWD
Structure:	Monocoque
Transmission:	Four-speed manual
Weight:	1475kg

PRICE GUIDE

Launch price:	N/A in UK
Excellent:	£25,000
Good:	£18,000
Average:	£12,000
Project:	£8000

PLYMOUTH
Road Runner/Superbird

Among the most famous of all the American musclecars, the Road Runner and Superbird earned their legendary status even as they rolled off the production line. The Road Runner was fully backed by Warner Bros and even boasted a 'beep beep' horn, while the astonishing-looking Superbird had genuine NASCAR heritage. The Superbird was as fast as it looked – its 440ci Hemi developed 425bhp and, if you were brave, a top speed that approached 150mph. However, less-than-inspiring brakes and soft suspension mean this is not a car for British B-roads.

SPECIFICATIONS (RR 440)

Years produced:	1968-1970 (125,904/1920 in total)
Performance:	0-60mph: 7.5sec
	Top speed: 120mph
Power & torque:	330bhp/410lb ft
Engine:	Normally aspirated 7206cc V8, petrol, carburettor, 16 valves
Drivetrain:	Front-engine RWD
Structure:	Monocoque
Transmission:	Four-speed manual
Weight:	1700kg

PRICE GUIDE (Superbird in brackets)

Launch price:	N/A in UK
Excellent:	£25,000 (£120,000)
Good:	£18,000 (£80,000)
Average:	£12,000 (£50,000)
Project:	£8000 (£25,000)

PONTIAC

PONTIAC ACTUALLY started out as a sister marque for General Motors' Oakland in 1926. But the upstart soon overtook the original in terms of popularity, and by 1933, replaced it entirely. It then became Chevrolet's partner marque,

proving especially popular in Central and South America. Pontiac ended up being marketed as the performance division of General Motors, and gained popularity with the Firebird and Trans-Am models. But from those

heady years, Pontiac began to fade. In April 2009, and as a result of the group's financial problems, GM announced that it was winding-up Pontiac. The last Pontiacs were built in late 2009, and the last of those sold in 2010.

PONTIAC
Firebird/Trans Am

The Pontiac Firebird was the sister car to the popular Chevrolet Camaro, and arrived on the scene in 1967 to pick up a healthy slice of the USA car market. The 1970 models sported the more familiar shape that became something of an icon internationally thanks to countless Hollywood appearances, such as in *Hooper* and *Smokey and the Bandit*. V8 models were the ones to have, especially in Trans Am form, but as the '70s progressed power outputs continued to drop. However, by the turn of the 1980s, turbocharged versions restored some of the lost oomph.

SPECIFICATIONS (1976 Trans-Am)	
Years produced:	1970-1981 (1,061,719 in total)
Performance:	0-60mph: 8.4sec
	Top speed: 120mph
Power & torque:	200bhp/330lb ft
Engine:	Normally aspirated 7463cc V8, petrol, carburettor, 16 valves
Drivetrain:	Front-engine RWD
Structure:	Monocoque
Transmission:	Four-speed manual
Weight:	1701kg

PRICE GUIDE	
Launch price:	£8014
Excellent:	£12,000
Good:	£9000
Average:	£5000
Project:	£3000

PONTIAC
Fiero

Gutless Fiat X1/9 pastiche or advanced sports car? The Pontiac Fiero was certainly a brave experiment by General Motors that deserved to sell better than it did. It was the first American mid-engined car and the first two-seater Pontiac in over 50 years. But the sporty-looking car didn't go as well as it looked, and the 2.5-litre Iron Duke engine did its best impression of a boat anchor, although the later V6 was a massive improvement. The experiment failed – relatively speaking – and production lasted only five years and one facelift, with over 350,000 examples built.

SPECIFICATIONS	
Years produced:	1984-1988 (355,000 in total)
Performance:	0-60mph: 12.0sec
	Top speed: 97mph
Power & torque:	92bhp/134lb ft
Engine:	Normally aspirated 2471cc four cylinder, petrol, fuel injection, 8 valves
Drivetrain:	Mid-engine RWD
Structure:	Plastic body panels over steel frame
Transmission:	Five-speed manual
Weight:	1136kg

PRICE GUIDE	
Launch price:	N/A in UK
Excellent:	£3500
Good:	£2500
Average:	£1750
Project:	£1000

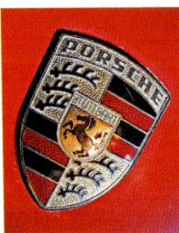

PORSCHE

FERDINAND PORSCHE would become famous for the inventing the VW Beetle but, after WW2, his son Ferry joined him in the motoring hall of fame as the man behind the first Porsche sports cars. As they were based on Volkswagens, they

had air-cooled rear engines. The 356 was followed by the iconic 911 in 1964, a long-lived legend among supercars. Later vehicles, such as the 924, 928 and 944, adopted water-cooled front-mounted engines. Porsche today is one

of the most successful of all sports car manufacturers, thanks to endless 911 evolution and a willingness to innovate. The firm also carries out research, development and design work for other companies.

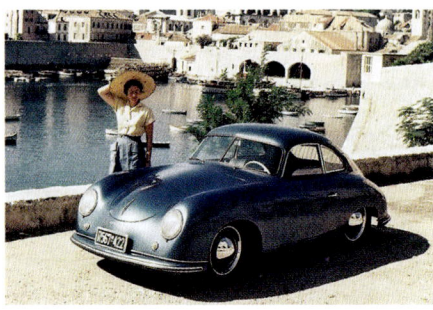

PORSCHE
356

The first 49 Porsches were built in Gmünd, Austria, and while historically important, these underpowered 1100cc cars are best left to collectors. Production proper started at Stuttgart in 1950, with steel bodies. The first year it was all coupés, then cabriolets arrived in 1951, although in sales they were usually outnumbered by coupés about 4:1. Two-piece screens were fitted until April 1952, after which they were one-piece with a bend in the centre. Engine options soon grew to 1100, 1300 and 1500. The 'S' version of the latter rated up to 72bhp, but was complex and short-lived.

SPECIFICATIONS	
Years produced:	1949-1955 (7627 in total)
Performance:	0-60mph: 17sec
	Top speed: 87mph
Power & torque:	55bhp/78lb ft
Engine:	Normally aspirated 1488cc four cylinder, petrol, carburettor, 8 valves
Drivetrain:	Rear-engine RWD
Structure:	Monocoque
Transmission:	Four-speed manual
Weight:	830kg

PRICE GUIDE	
Launch price:	£1971
Excellent:	£52,500
Good:	£30,000
Average:	£22,500
Project:	£15,000

PORSCHE
356 A/B/C

With body revisions that modernised and prettified the looks, more civilised interiors and engines increased to 1600cc (although there were still 1300s for some markets), Porsche's 356 hit the big time and sales more than doubled. 'Super' means more power, along with higher prices than those quoted here. The 356B added twin-choke carbs and some styling revisions, the most obvious being larger bumpers and front bonnet chrome. The 356C brought disc brakes at last and the lowest-powered engine was now 75bhp, up from the 60bhp of the 356B 'Normal'. Cabrios boost prices by 30%.

SPECIFICATIONS
Years produced:	1955-1965 (68,676 in total)
Performance:	0-60mph: 14.1sec
	Top speed: 102mph
Power & torque:	60bhp/81lb ft
Engine:	Normally aspirated 1582cc flat four, petrol, carburettor, 8 valves
Drivetrain:	Rear-engine RWD
Structure:	Monocoque
Transmission:	Four-speed manual
Weight:	815kg

PRICE GUIDE
Launch price:	£1891
Excellent:	£45,000
Good:	£30,000
Average:	£20,000
Project:	£10,000

PORSCHE
356 Carrera

With four gear-driven camshafts, dry-sump lubrication, twin sparkplugs and even roller-bearing crankshafts on early models, 356 Carreras are not for the faint of heart or wallet. Built with competition in mind, and producing most of their power high up in the rev range, they don't even make good road cars. However, none of that detracts from their collectibility. Even the 1500 versions will hit 120mph. The ultimate is the 2.0-litre Carrera 2, 126 of which were built starting in 1962. Be aware that this was a year before the arrival of disc brakes for these cars.

SPECIFICATIONS
Years produced:	1955-1962
Performance:	0-60mph: N/A
	Top speed: 125mph
Power & torque:	100bhp/88lb ft
Engine:	Normally aspirated 1498cc flat four, petrol, carburettor, 8 valves
Drivetrain:	Rear-engine RWD
Structure:	Monocoque
Transmission:	Four-speed manual
Weight:	850kg

PRICE GUIDE
Launch price:	N/A
Excellent:	£125,000
Good:	£80,000
Average:	£60,000
Project:	£50,000

PORSCHE
356 Speedster

Like their badges, Speedsters have become gold-plated cult classics. Much imitated by replica builders, the originals are high on many collectors' wanted lists and have been known to change hands for six-figure sums, despite nearly 3000 having been built. Most are in America, which is no surprise as that's the market they were built for. They were actually made at the suggestion of USA Porsche importer Max Hoffman, who wanted a stripped-down version of the 356 that could be driven during the week and raced at weekends, much like later Porsche Club Sports.

SPECIFICATIONS
Years produced:	1956-1956 (2910 in total)
Performance:	0-60mph: 14.5sec
	Top speed: 108mph
Power & torque:	75bhp/82lb ft
Engine:	Normally aspirated 1582cc flat four, petrol, carburettor, 8 valves
Drivetrain:	Rear-engine RWD
Structure:	Monocoque
Transmission:	Four-speed manual
Weight:	760kg

PRICE GUIDE
Launch price:	£1971
Excellent:	£100,000
Good:	£80,000
Average:	£65,000
Project:	£50,000

PORSCHE
911 2.0

As the 911 legend has grown, so desire for the pure, original, short-wheelbase version of Porsche's concept has increased with it. The flat-six engine is only a 2.0-litre, but it's a highly tuned one wearing overhead cams and two triple-choke carbs – Solexes on early cars, then Webers from early 1966. Within months of production starting, a 911 came fifth in the Monte Carlo Rally, and these models are still successfully campaigned in historic events. Semi-convertible targa version was launched in early 1967, but despite its relative rarity no price premium is attached.

SPECIFICATIONS
Years produced:	1964-1967 (10,753 in total)
Performance:	0-60mph: 8.3sec
	Top speed: 131mph
Power & torque:	130bhp/128lb ft
Engine:	Normally aspirated 1991cc flat six, petrol, carburettor, 12 valves
Drivetrain:	Rear-engine RWD
Structure:	Monocoque
Transmission:	Five-speed manual
Weight:	1080kg

PRICE GUIDE
Launch price:	£2996
Excellent:	£37,500
Good:	£25,000
Average:	£16,000
Project:	£9500

PORSCHE
912/912E

Keen to retain a slightly more affordable model in the range after production of the 356 ended, Porsche installed a 90bhp version of that car's four-cylinder engine in a 911 bodyshell, mostly featuring the optional five-speed gearbox. That sounds potentially disappointing, but with low weight and better handling than the 911, this is a fine sports car in its own right. It briefly reappeared in 1975 as the 912E, fitted with a 2.0-litre VW engine. Sold only in the US, this filled the gap between the outgoing 914-4 and Porsche's new 924. Prices are similar for either version.

SPECIFICATIONS
Years produced:	1965-1969 + 1975 (30,300/2092 in total)
Performance:	0-60mph: 11.9sec
	Top speed: 119mph
Power & torque:	90bhp/90lb ft
Engine:	Normally aspirated 1599cc flat four, petrol, carburettor, 8 valves
Drivetrain:	Rear-engine RWD
Structure:	Monocoque
Transmission:	Four-speed manual
Weight:	970kg

PRICE GUIDE
Launch price:	£2467
Excellent:	£17,500
Good:	£10,000
Average:	£6500
Project:	£3500

PORSCHE
911S

This is the hot one, ready for competition use thanks to forged alloy pistons and wheels, plus vented disc brakes. Output started at 160bhp, then grew to 170bhp with the 1969 introduction of fuel injection. The following year there was another 10bhp to go with the new 2.2-litre engine capacity, and then we finally arrived at 190bhp with the 2.4-litre 'S' for the 1972 model year. As with the slightly less sporty 911s, both coupé and targa versions were offered. Pre-1968 short-wheelbase cars are the most sought after by collectors, but the later ones are most fun.

SPECIFICATIONS
Years produced:	1966-1973 (14,841 in total)
Performance:	0-60mph: 8.0sec
	Top speed: 137mph
Power & torque:	170bhp/135lb ft
Engine:	Normally aspirated 1991cc flat six, petrol, carburettor, 12 valves
Drivetrain:	Rear-engine RWD
Structure:	Monocoque
Transmission:	Five-speed manual
Weight:	995kg

PRICE GUIDE
Launch price:	£3556
Excellent:	£65,000
Good:	£42,000
Average:	£30,000
Project:	£12,000

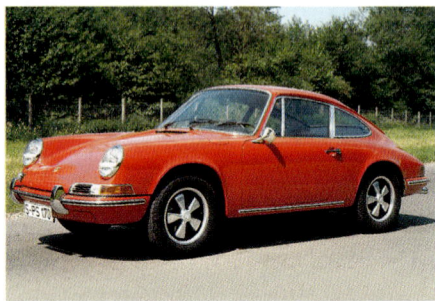

PORSCHE
911 L/T/E

From 1967 the regular 130bhp 911 was renamed 911L. This was because there was now not only the sporty 'S' version, but also an entry-level model with 110bhp called the 911T (for Touring). As standard it had a four- rather than five-speed 'box. From August 1968 the B-series body arrived with the rear wheels moved back by 61mm to lengthen the wheelbase and improve handling. At this point the 911L gained fuel injection and wider wheels and became the 140bhp 911E. For 1970 there was 2.2 litres and 125/155bhp (T/E). Two years later, capacity grew to 2.4 litres and power to 130/165bhp.

SPECIFICATIONS (2.2 T)
Years produced:	1967-1973 (62,402 in total)
Performance:	0-60mph: 7.9sec
	Top speed: 140mph
Power & torque:	125bhp/131lb ft
Engine:	Normally aspirated 2195cc six cylinder, petrol, carburettor, 12 valves
Drivetrain:	Rear-engine RWD
Structure:	Monocoque
Transmission:	Five-speed manual
Weight:	1020kg

PRICE GUIDE
Launch price:	£2745
Excellent:	£32,500
Good:	£20,000
Average:	£11,000
Project:	£7000

VW-PORSCHE
914

This was developed in conjunction with Volkswagen to replace the four-cylinder 912. The engine was borrowed from the VW 411, and it being mid- rather than rear-mounted gave the 914 excellent handling, aided by the all-independent suspension. The targa roof clipped neatly out of the way to the underside of the bootlid when you wanted fresh air. From 1973 the 1.7 was joined by a 2.0, and the following year the smaller engine capacity was raised to 1.8 litres. Low power and that VW connection haven't helped popularity, but they outrank most water-cooled Porsches.

SPECIFICATIONS
Years produced:	1969-1975 (115,646 in total)
Performance:	0-60mph: 14.8sec
	Top speed: 110mph
Power & torque:	80bhp/97lb ft
Engine:	Normally aspirated 1679cc flat four, petrol, carburettor, 8 valves
Drivetrain:	Mid-engine RWD
Structure:	Monocoque
Transmission:	Five-speed manual
Weight:	898kg

PRICE GUIDE
Launch price:	£2261
Excellent:	£10,000
Good:	£6500
Average:	£4000
Project:	£2000

VW-PORSCHE
914-6

The main difference between this and the 914-4 was its six-cylinder engine. In fact, it was the 2.0-litre flat-six from the 911, although no-one should get over-excited at the thought as, to avoid too much in-house competition, the lowest-spec version from the 911T was used, with only 110bhp. With just 3360 sold compared to over 115,000 of the 914-4, these models are also rare, though the low numbers had something to do with the price hike over their kid brother that made them 50% more expensive than an E-type. Most went to America and none was built with right-hand drive.

SPECIFICATIONS
Years produced:	1969-1972 (3360 in total)
Performance:	0-60mph: 8.3sec
	Top speed: 125mph
Power & torque:	110bhp/115lb ft
Engine:	Normally aspirated 1991cc flat six, petrol, carburettor, 12 valves
Drivetrain:	Mid-engine RWD
Structure:	Monocoque
Transmission:	Five-speed manual
Weight:	1020kg

PRICE GUIDE
Launch price:	£3475
Excellent:	£25,000
Good:	£16,000
Average:	£11,000
Project:	£7500

PORSCHE
911 Carrera 2.7 RSL/RST

To qualify Porsche for sub-3.0-litre GT racing, the firm had to build 500 of this homologation special – but it wound up selling three times that. The basis was the 2.4S, with a big-bore engine and every conceivable lightening method, from thinner steel panels to throwing away the rear seats. Really a race car you could drive on the road, it was the first 911 to have wider rear wheels than fronts; 200 RSLs were built and 1380 of the slightly softer RST (T for Touring), which actually contained a few creature comforts. Of course, the racer is more valuable, so add another 50% to our prices.

SPECIFICATIONS
Years produced:	1972-1973 (200/1380 in total)
Performance:	0-60mph: 6.1sec
	Top speed: 149mph
Power & torque:	210bhp/188lb ft
Engine:	Normally aspirated 2687cc flat six, petrol, carburettor, 12 valves
Drivetrain:	Rear-engine RWD
Structure:	Monocoque
Transmission:	Five-speed manual
Weight:	975kg

PRICE GUIDE (Lightweight in brackets)
Launch price:	£5825
Excellent:	£175,000 (£220,000)
Good:	£130,000
Average:	£90,000
Project:	£60,000

PORSCHE
911 2.7

This model represented a change in 911 ethos, with less frantic engines producing lower power but more torque. K-Jetronic injection made it more economical, while the body and wheels were wider. It heralded the start of impact bumpers as well. From August 1975 Porsche became the first manufacturer to produce hot-dip galvanised bodies, so subsequent cars were very resistant to rust, unlike earlier 911s. By now there was just the standard car and the 911S in the range; the latter having an extra 25bhp and 25% higher values in today's market.

SPECIFICATIONS
Years produced:	1973-1977
Performance:	0-60mph: 8.5sec
	Top speed: 130mph
Power & torque:	148bhp/173lb ft
Engine:	Normally aspirated 2687cc flat six, petrol, fuel injection, 12 valves
Drivetrain:	Rear-engine RWD
Structure:	Monocoque
Transmission:	Five-speed manual
Weight:	1161kg

PRICE GUIDE
Launch price:	£6249
Excellent:	£25,000
Good:	£15,000
Average:	£8500
Project:	£5000

PORSCHE
911 Carrera 2.7

The name Carrera was no longer just for racing specials but denoted the range-topping 911. It had also gone a bit soft compared to the previous 2.7 Carrera; you even got the option of a Sportomatic gearbox. They were easier cars to live with, though. The engine was in the same 210bhp state of tune, but these Carreras didn't have lightweight bodies and came fully loaded with all the equipment of the standard models, plus electric windows. Their high price limited sales compared to the other 2.7s, although that now simply makes them even more expensive.

SPECIFICATIONS
Years produced:	1974-1977 (3353 in total)
Performance:	0-60mph: 6.3sec
	Top speed: 149mph
Power & torque:	210bhp/188lb ft
Engine:	Normally aspirated 2687cc flat six, petrol, fuel injection, 12 valves
Drivetrain:	Rear-engine RWD
Structure:	Monocoque
Transmission:	Five-speed manual
Weight:	1075kg

PRICE GUIDE
Launch price:	£6993
Excellent:	£48,500
Good:	£42,500
Average:	£25,000
Project:	£15,000

PORSCHE
911 Turbo

Not just a fast car but an instant pin-up beloved of teenage boys. Having experimented with 'chargers in racing, Porsche saw turbos as the way forward for performance road cars, and the 911 Turbo was the result. With fat arches to cover the 7in and 8in rims, plus that enormous rear spoiler, the model was a trend-setter. But what really mattered was how well it went; it boasted incredible acceleration, superb grip and handling, plus enormous brakes to match. The gearbox was only a four-speed, but such was the torque that this didn't hold it back.

SPECIFICATIONS
Years produced:	1975-1977 (2873 in total)
Performance:	0-60mph: 6.1sec
	Top speed: 153mph
Power & torque:	260bhp/253lb ft
Engine:	Turbocharged 2994cc flat six, petrol, mechanical fuel injection, 12 valves
Drivetrain:	Rear-engine RWD
Structure:	Monocoque
Transmission:	Four-speed manual
Weight:	1195kg

PRICE GUIDE
Launch price:	£14,749
Excellent:	£40,000
Good:	£30,000
Average:	£25,000
Project:	£20,000

PORSCHE
924

The firm was commissioned by Volkswagen to develop the 924 project – originally conceived as a replacement for the VW-Porsche 914 – but bought the rights to the car when VW changed tack. The 924 used an Audi engine with Porsche cylinder head, and the gearbox was in unit with the rear axle to provide near-perfect 53/47 weight distribution. Build quality was to the usual superb Porsche standards, and the 924 was an instant sales success, quickly tripling the company's factory output. Best ones to buy are from 1981-on, as whole bodies were hot zinc dipped to (successfully) keep rust at bay.

SPECIFICATIONS
Years produced:	1976-1988 (122,304 in total)
Performance:	0-60mph: 9.5sec
	Top speed: 124mph
Power & torque:	125bhp/122lb ft
Engine:	Normally aspirated 1984cc four cylinder, petrol, electronic fuel injection, 8 valves
Drivetrain:	Front-engine RWD
Structure:	Monocoque
Transmission:	Five-speed manual
Weight:	1080kg

PRICE GUIDE
Launch price:	£6999
Excellent:	£3750
Good:	£2900
Average:	£1400
Project:	£475

PORSCHE
911 SC 3.0

Gaining the 3.0-litre block from the previous season's Turbo, the SC became Porsche's sole non-turbo 911, although a lengthy options list ensured enough variety. Cast alloy 15in wheels were standard, with forged 16in rims a cost extra, as was the Sport option of a Turbo rear spoiler. Power grew quickly from the original 180bhp to 188bhp for the 1980 model year, and 204bhp just 12 months later, although with improvements in economy. From 1982 the coupé and targa were joined by a cabriolet, Porsche's first full convertible since the 356. These command only a small premium.

SPECIFICATIONS
Years produced:	1978-1983
Performance:	0-60mph: 6.5sec
	Top speed: 141mph
Power & torque:	180bhp/196lb ft
Engine:	Normally aspirated 2994cc flat six, petrol, fuel injection, 12 valves
Drivetrain:	Rear-engine RWD
Structure:	Monocoque
Transmission:	Five-speed manual
Weight:	1160kg

PRICE GUIDE
Launch price:	£14,100
Excellent:	£16,000
Good:	£12,000
Average:	£8500
Project:	£5500

PORSCHE
928/S/S2

Porsche's intended replacement for the 911 may not have achieved that goal, but it wasn't for lack of performance or technological wizardry. An alloy V8 was attached to a rear-mounted gearbox, and the galvanised body had aluminium doors and bonnet plus body-coloured plastic bumpers – pretty radical for its time. The original 4.5 litres was upped to 4.7 for the 300bhp 928S in 1982. Two years later, higher compression and a new fuel-injection system raised that to 310bhp in the 928 S2, which also offered ABS as an option for the first time on a Porsche.

SPECIFICATIONS

Years produced:	1978-1987 (17,710 in total)
Performance:	0-60mph: 6.2sec
	Top speed: 158mph
Power & torque:	240bhp/257lb ft
Engine:	Normally aspirated 4474cc V8, petrol, electronic fuel injection, 16 valves
Drivetrain:	Front-engine RWD
Structure:	Monocoque
Transmission:	Five-speed manual/four-speed auto
Weight:	1468kg

PRICE GUIDE

Launch price:	£19,499
Excellent:	£8500
Good:	£6000
Average:	£3500
Project:	£1500

PORSCHE
911 Turbo 3.3

It turns out the short run of original Turbos was merely a warm-up for the main act. With an extra 300cc and an intercooler built into the rear spoiler, the 911 Turbo's power jumped by another 40bhp, putting it firmly in the supercar class. This also helped mask the previous model's turbo lag to some extent, although it seems poor by modern standards. Further development to the suspension reduced the car's power-off tail-wagging tendencies and improved safety, but the pay-off was a bone-jarring ride. A five-speed gearbox finally arrived for the 1989 model year.

SPECIFICATIONS

Years produced:	1978-1989 (21,589 in total)
Performance:	0-60mph: 5.4sec
	Top speed: 162mph
Power & torque:	300bhp/304lb ft
Engine:	Turbocharged 2994cc flat six, petrol, electronic fuel injection, 12 valves
Drivetrain:	Rear-engine RWD
Structure:	Monocoque
Transmission:	Four/five-speed manual
Weight:	1195kg

PRICE GUIDE

Launch price:	£23,200
Excellent:	£35,000
Good:	£23,000
Average:	£17,000
Project:	£10,000

PORSCHE
924 Turbo

With Porsche at the forefront of turbo technology, and the 924 chassis ripe for exploitation with more power, this car's development was inevitable. Thanks to a 45bhp power boost that raised top speed by nearly 20mph, a five-speed gearbox and uprated suspension, the 924 Turbo was very well received and more than 12,000 were sold over a five-year period. Easily identified by the row of four extra air intakes in the nose panel and NACA duct in the bonnet, they also got five- rather than four-bolt wheels and were the first 924s to use the discreet but effective rear lip spoiler.

SPECIFICATIONS

Years produced:	1979-1983 (12,385 in total)
Performance:	0-60mph: 7.7sec
	Top speed: 142mph
Power & torque:	174bhp/184lb ft
Engine:	Turbocharged 1984cc four cylinder, petrol, carburettor, 8 valves
Drivetrain:	Front-engine RWD
Structure:	Monocoque
Transmission:	Five-speed manual
Weight:	1180kg

PRICE GUIDE

Launch price:	£13,629
Excellent:	£8000
Good:	£4000
Average:	£1800
Project:	£850

PORSCHE
924 Carrera GT

This car took inspiration from prototype ideas for the forthcoming 944, which you can see in the distinctive bloated arches fabricated from flexible polyurethane. Porsche built 406 Carrera GTs to homologate the 924 for racing at Le Mans. Based on the 924 Turbo, its engine output was boosted by 40bhp thanks to an intercooler and internal modifications. The Carrera GT was sold only in red, silver or black, and just 75 right-hand-drive examples were built for the UK market. No surprise, then, that prices have been rising in recent years as its rarity and abilities are recognised.

SPECIFICATIONS

Years produced:	1980-1981 (406 in total)
Performance:	0-60mph: 6.5sec
	Top speed: 150mph
Power & torque:	207bhp/207lb ft
Engine:	Turbocharged 1984cc four cylinder, petrol, electronic fuel injection, 8 valves
Drivetrain:	Front-engine RWD
Structure:	Monocoque
Transmission:	Five-speed manual
Weight:	1179kg

PRICE GUIDE

Launch price:	£19,210
Excellent:	£30,000
Good:	£22,000
Average:	£15,000
Project:	£8000

PORSCHE
944

It shared the 924's profile, but the flared arches, wider wheels and deeper front valance turned the older car's delicacy into aggression. A 2.5-litre engine that was effectively half a 928's V8 delivered on the promise. Handling and grip were very assured, and the 944 went on to outsell even the 924, keeping Porsche afloat in the early 1990s. Interior revisions in 1985 gave it an oval dashboard and revised door panels. For 1988-'89 – the last year of 'plain' 944 production – engine capacity rose to 2.7 litres, offering little in the way of bhp but handy low-down pulling power.

SPECIFICATIONS

Years produced:	1982-1989 (117,790 in total)
Performance:	0-60mph: 8.3sec
	Top speed: 138mph
Power & torque:	163bhp/151lb ft
Engine:	Normally aspirated 2479cc four cylinder, petrol, electronic fuel injection, 8 valves
Drivetrain:	Front-engine RWD
Structure:	Monocoque
Transmission:	Five-speed manual
Weight:	1180kg

PRICE GUIDE

Launch price:	£12,999
Excellent:	£5000
Good:	£4000
Average:	£2400
Project:	£1100

PORSCHE
911 Carrera 3.2

Last of the second-generation 911s and still a viable daily driver if that's what you want. The choice of coupé, targa and cabriolet (worth perhaps £2000 more now) continued from the SC, though all now had 150mph capability. Even better, fuel economy was further improved and beat virtually everything else in this class. Could be had with either the standard or wider Turbo-look body complete with spoilers and wide wheels. Despite more drag and an extra 50kg blunting performance, this was the bigger seller. The 1987 model year got an improved five-speed gearbox.

SPECIFICATIONS
Years produced:	1984-1989 (76,473 in total)
Performance:	0-60mph: 5.6sec
	Top speed: 153mph
Power & torque:	231bhp/209lb ft
Engine:	Normally aspirated 3164cc flat six, petrol, fuel injection, 12 valves
Drivetrain:	Rear-engine RWD
Structure:	Monocoque
Transmission:	Five-speed manual
Weight:	1210kg

PRICE GUIDE
Launch price:	£23,366
Excellent:	£18,000
Good:	£13,500
Average:	£10,000
Project:	£6500

PORSCHE
924S

A master of subtlety, the 924S appealed to those who were fond of the 'Q-car' concept – there was a lot more going on than the body led you to believe. Aside from the Teledial wheels and extra 'S' on the badge at the rear, nothing gave the game away that this was virtually a 944 wearing the 924's slimline body. However, it was all there, from the new 2.5-litre overhead-cam engine to the four-wheel vented disc brakes. Engine power was raised from 150bhp to 160bhp for the 1988 model year, at the same time as Le Mans editions in black or white were offered with lowered, uprated suspension.

SPECIFICATIONS
Years produced:	1985-1988 (16,282 in total)
Performance:	0-60mph: 7.9sec
	Top speed: 136mph
Power & torque:	160bhp/155lb ft
Engine:	Normally aspirated 2479cc four cylinder, petrol, electronic fuel injection, 8 valves
Drivetrain:	Front-engine RWD
Structure:	Monocoque
Transmission:	Five-speed manual
Weight:	1164kg

PRICE GUIDE
Launch price:	£21,031
Excellent:	£4000
Good:	£3000
Average:	£1750
Project:	£900

PORSCHE
944 Turbo

As with the 924, a turbocharged version was always on the cards. Here the 2.5-litre engine was boosted by nearly 60bhp, with the clutch and gearbox uprated to suit. The chassis got thicker anti-roll bars and four-pot brake calipers, and a smoother nose panel and larger rear spoiler distinguished the model from the 944. For 1988 only, the Turbo SE was offered with 250bhp thanks to a larger turbo. The transmission was further beefed up, a limited-slip diff was standard, brakes were uprated and Koni dampers were fitted. For 1989-91 the SE specification was adopted for the normal 944 Turbo.

SPECIFICATIONS
Years produced:	1985-1991 (25,245 in total)
Performance:	0-60mph: 5.9sec
	Top speed: 152mph
Power & torque:	220bhp/243lb ft
Engine:	Turbocharged 2479cc four cylinder, petrol, electronic fuel injection, 8 valves
Drivetrain:	Front-engine RWD
Structure:	Monocoque
Transmission:	Five-speed manual
Weight:	1280kg

PRICE GUIDE
Launch price:	£25,311
Excellent:	£8500
Good:	£7000
Average:	£4500
Project:	£2400

PORSCHE
911 Carrera Club Sport

Harking back to the 1973 Carrera 2.7s, this was a stripped-out version of the 3.2, made some 100kg lighter than most by stripping out non-essentials like the rear seats, sound deadening, electric windows and even the passenger's sun visor. The engine put out the same power but revved more freely, and 300rpm higher, thanks to lightweight inlet valves and a reprogrammed ECU. Just 340 examples were made, and only 53 of those were in right-hand-drive form for the UK market. Available here in any colour you liked – as long as that was Grand Prix White with red wheel centres.

SPECIFICATIONS
Years produced:	1987-1988 (340 in total)
Performance:	0-60mph: 5.6sec
	Top speed: 149mph
Power & torque:	210bhp/188lb ft
Engine:	Normally aspirated 3164cc flat six, petrol, fuel injection, 12 valves
Drivetrain:	Rear-engine RWD
Structure:	Monocoque
Transmission:	Five-speed manual
Weight:	960kg

PRICE GUIDE
Launch price:	£34,389
Excellent:	£30,000
Good:	£25,000
Average:	£19,000
Project:	£15,000

PORSCHE
959

Conceived for the short-lived Group B motor sport formula, the 959 was Porsche's riposte to the Ferrari 288GTO. Unlike the boisterous but largely conventional Italian supercar, this was a technological tour de force with permanent four-wheel drive and twin sequential turbos. This set-up went some way to eliminating the dreaded lag which typified forced induction when the car was originally dreamed up in the early 1980s. It never really fulfilled its potential in motor sport, but established itself as a thoroughbred '80s supercar. All examples were made in left-hand-drive form.

SPECIFICATIONS
Years produced:	1987-1988 (250 in total)
Performance:	0-60mph: 3.6sec
	Top speed: 197mph
Power & torque:	444bhp/369lb ft
Engine:	Turbocharged 2849cc flat six, petrol, electronic fuel injection, 24 valves
Drivetrain:	Rear-engine AWD
Structure:	Monocoque
Transmission:	Six-speed manual
Weight:	1350kg

PRICE GUIDE
Launch price:	£155,266
Excellent:	£225,000
Good:	£150,000
Average:	£100,000
Project:	£70,000

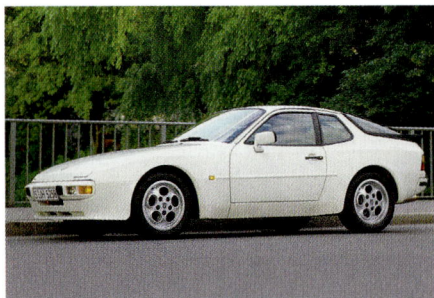

PORSCHE
944S

For those wanting more power from a 944 without the drama and cost of a Turbo, Porsche sent in the 944S to plug the gap for a couple of years. Apart from badges, it was visually the same as the 944, although the Turbo's rear undertray was added later in production. Under the bonnet, however, was the 16-valve twin-cam head developed for the 1981 924 GTP Le Mans racer. This put power output bang-slap in between the standard and Turbo 944s. Never a great seller, and the more fragile valve gear and complicated belt and chain-drive for camshafts makes them expensive to fix.

SPECIFICATIONS
Years produced:	1987-1989 (12,831 in total)
Performance:	0-60mph: 7.5sec
	Top speed: 141mph
Power & torque:	188bhp/170lb ft
Engine:	Normally aspirated 2479cc four cylinder, petrol, electronic fuel injection, 16 valves
Drivetrain:	Front-engine RWD
Structure:	Monocoque
Transmission:	Five-speed manual
Weight:	1275kg

PRICE GUIDE
Launch price:	£23,977
Excellent:	£6250
Good:	£5000
Average:	£2750
Project:	£1750

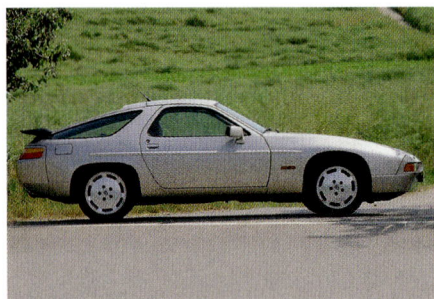

PORSCHE
928 S4

In an even greater technical tour de force than before, the V8 grew to 5.0 litres and now had twin-cam heads with four valves per cylinder. Power went up to 316bhp, but the big difference was low-end pulling power. The popular auto gearbox option was also now a Mercedes four-speed. An intelligent cooling system featured louvres in the air intake that were computer-controlled to change their angle in line with coolant temperature; when closed, they made the car more aerodynamic. Smoother front and rear bumpers lifted the looks, and there was a much larger rear spoiler.

SPECIFICATIONS
Years produced:	1987-1991 (16,213 in total)
Performance:	0-60mph: 5.7sec
	Top speed: 170mph
Power & torque:	316bhp/317lb ft
Engine:	Normally aspirated 4957cc V8, petrol, electronic fuel injection, 32 valves
Drivetrain:	Front-engine RWD
Structure:	Monocoque
Transmission:	Five-speed manual
Weight:	1538kg

PRICE GUIDE
Launch price:	£30,679
Excellent:	£10,000
Good:	£7000
Average:	£4500
Project:	£2750

PORSCHE
911 Speedster

A retro-styled homage to the 1950s 356 Speedster. Strictly a two-seater, it was all 3.2 Carrera underneath, but above the waist there was a shorter and more steeply raked screen and a hard tonneau that gave the back a bit of a hump. Weather protection was on the rudimentary side, but that didn't matter too much as the bulk of the 2000 or so produced headed to America. Also, as the car became an instant collectable, few Speedsters were pressed into daily service. That makes finding a good example pretty easy – although paying for it may be another matter.

SPECIFICATIONS
Years produced:	1988-1989 (2100 in total)
Performance:	0-60mph: 6.1sec
	Top speed: 152mph
Power & torque:	228bhp/210lb ft
Engine:	Normally aspirated 3164cc flat six, petrol, fuel injection, 12 valves
Drivetrain:	Rear-engine RWD
Structure:	Monocoque
Transmission:	Five-speed manual
Weight:	1140kg

PRICE GUIDE
Launch price:	£57,852
Excellent:	£45,000
Good:	£35,000
Average:	£26,500
Project:	£17,500

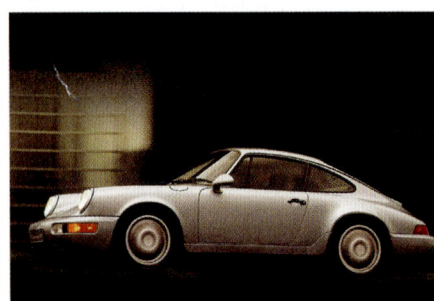

PORSCHE
911 Carrera 2/4 (964)

It looked like any other 911, but beneath that familiar body was an entirely new structure designed to meet ever-changing technical and safety requirements. With integrated bumpers and other tricks, the body was a great deal more aerodynamic, too. There was also the gadget man's dream of a rear spoiler that popped up automatically at 50mph. It was launched first in four-wheel-drive Carrera 4 form, but the rear-drive Carrera 2 released a year later was by far the best-selling version. As with past 911s, the range featured coupé, targa and cabriolet models.

SPECIFICATIONS
Years produced:	1989-1993 (55,682 in total)
Performance:	0-60mph: 5.7sec
	Top speed: 162mph
Power & torque:	246bhp/229lb ft
Engine:	Normally aspirated 3600cc flat six, petrol, fuel injection, 12 valves
Drivetrain:	Rear-engine, RWD
Structure:	Monocoque
Transmission:	Five-speed manual/automatic
Weight:	1075kg

PRICE GUIDE
Launch price:	£53,995
Excellent:	£19,000
Good:	£16,000
Average:	£12,000
Project:	£7500

PORSCHE
944 S2

For the 1989 model year the S2 replaced both standard and 'S' spec 944s. A new aluminium cylinder block employing Formula One technology allowed a capacity increase to 3.0 litres. Power was up 21bhp on the 944S, and torque took an even bigger jump. Externally the S2 adopted the lower-drag nose and tail panels from the Turbo, which along with a taller final drive ratio helped the car to hit almost 150mph. The Turbo's braking system was also adopted. For the final two years of production a cabriolet version was offered as well – add 25% for those.

SPECIFICATIONS
Years produced:	1989-1993 (19,120 in total)
Performance:	0-60mph: 6.7sec
	Top speed: 149mph
Power & torque:	208bhp/207lb ft
Engine:	Normally aspirated 2990cc four cylinder, petrol, electronic fuel injection, 16 valves
Drivetrain:	Front-engine RWD
Structure:	Monocoque
Transmission:	Five-speed manual
Weight:	1320kg

PRICE GUIDE
Launch price:	£31,304
Excellent:	£7000
Good:	£5750
Average:	£4000
Project:	£2250

RELIANT

STARTING OUT in 1935 with three-wheelers, Reliant progressed to the full picnic with its four-wheeled glassfibre Sabre sports car in 1961. However, it was for the 1968 Scimitar GTE sports estate that everybody started to take notice of the manufacturer – mainly because the idea of a fast, luxurious station wagon had never before been tried. This was the high point of Reliant's existence, as the firm was unable to come up with a suitable successor. In later years, Reliant relied more on its Robin three-wheeler (as well as the extra-wheel-endowed Kitten offshoot) for business, but this wasn't enough to sustain the company and its life as a car maker came to an end in 2002.

RELIANT
Sabre

The Reliant Sabre actually started out as a model designed as a Ford special from Ashley, to which Autocars of Israel then bought the rights. Reliant was called in to engineer the vehicle – originally called the Sabra – for production and introduction into the USA, using Ford Consul power and a ZF gearbox. Once ready, Reliant sold the car as the Sabre in the UK, where it failed to make much of an impression. The rest were sent to Israel in kit form. After a few years in production, only around 200 Sabras and Sabres were built.

SPECIFICATIONS
Years produced:	1961-1964 (208 in total)
Performance:	0-60mph: 14.4sec
	Top speed: 93mph
Power & torque:	90bhp/91lb ft
Engine:	Normally aspirated 1703cc four cylinder, petrol, carburettor, 8 valves
Drivetrain:	Front-engine RWD
Structure:	Steel chassis/glassfibre body
Transmission:	Four-speed manual
Weight:	797kg

PRICE GUIDE
Launch price:	£1165
Excellent:	£9500
Good:	£7500
Average:	£2500
Project:	£1000

RELIANT
Regal 3/25 and 3/30

Most famous for its central role in the BBC sitcom *Only Fools and Horses*, the Reliant Regal has become something of an icon in Supervan form. Until a few years ago, these hardy little three-wheelers were a common sight on British roads, which is testament to their long-lasting glassfibre bodies. The OHV 600cc (later 700cc) engine was directly related to the Austin Seven's, and was one of the first aluminium motors built in the UK. The Regal's sharp styling was a big improvement over its predecessor's, and possibly contributed to strong sales of up to 20,000 per year.

SPECIFICATIONS (3/30)
Years produced:	1962-1973 (c100,000 in total)
Performance:	0-60mph: 25.0sec
	Top speed: 75mph
Power & torque:	30bhp/34lb ft
Engine:	Normally aspirated 701cc four cylinder, petrol, carburettor, 8 valves
Drivetrain:	Front-engine RWD
Structure:	Steel chassis/glassfibre body
Transmission:	Four-speed manual
Weight:	455kg

PRICE GUIDE
Launch price:	£515
Excellent:	£2000
Good:	£1200
Average:	£650
Project:	£250

RELIANT
Scimitar SE4 coupé

Reliant's next attempt at a sports car was a lot more successful. The handsome coupé was originally designed by Ogle, and first shown on a Daimler SP250 chassis, but Reliant was so impressed with the design that it bought the rights and immediately set about putting the car into production using the Sabre Six's running gear and an all-new steel chassis. In 1964, the Scimitar went on sale and sold well. Subsequent Ford Essex V6-powered versions kept the factory busy until 1970, when it was phased out in favour of the Scimitar GTE.

SPECIFICATIONS
Years produced:	1964-1970 (1004 in total)
Performance:	0-60mph: 11.4sec
	Top speed: 117mph
Power & torque:	120bhp/140lb ft
Engine:	Normally aspirated 2553cc straight six, petrol, carburettor, 12 valves
Drivetrain:	Front-engine RWD
Structure:	Steel chassis/glassfibre body
Transmission:	Four-speed manual
Weight:	1003kg

PRICE GUIDE
Launch price:	£1292
Excellent:	£7000
Good:	£5000
Average:	£3000
Project:	£850

RELIANT
Scimitar GTE SE5

Reliant scored a major hit with the Scimitar GTE. It had been the firm's idea to ask Ogle's Tom Karen to redesign the SE4 into a sporting estate, and when the new car subsequently appeared it proved highly successful. As well as being good looking and usefully commodious, the 3.0-litre Ford V6 gave the GTE plenty of performance. The bodystyle proved such a trendsetter that other manufacturers raced to produce their own versions, with Volvo's P1800ES and Lancia's Beta HPE being the most faithful homages. Despite that, values remain low.

SPECIFICATIONS
Years produced:	1968-1975 (5127 in total)
Performance:	0-60mph: 8.9sec
	Top speed: 121mph
Power & torque:	138bhp/192lb ft
Engine:	Normally aspirated 2994cc V6, petrol, carburettor, 12 valves
Drivetrain:	Front-engine RWD
Structure:	Steel chassis/glassfibre body
Transmission:	Four-speed manual
Weight:	991kg

PRICE GUIDE
Launch price:	£1759
Excellent:	£5000
Good:	£3500
Average:	£1500
Project:	£500

RELIANT
Robin

In 1973, the Regal was replaced by the smarter Ogle-styled Robin. Aside from the improved visuals, the new car received an upgunned 850cc engine and new twin-rail chassis. Despite the massive popularity of the emergent supermini generation, the Robin sold well on account of being able to be driven on a motorcycle licence in the UK – and that was possibly its only redeeming feature for keen motorists. The ex-bikers who bought the Robin were treated to excellent fuel consumption and cheap road tax – but it's a marginal car, and the butt of many jokes.

SPECIFICATIONS

Years produced:	1973-1982
Performance:	0-60mph: 16.9sec
	Top speed: 81mph
Power & torque:	40bhp/46lb ft
Engine:	Normally aspirated 848cc four cylinder, petrol, carburettor, 8 valves
Drivetrain:	Front-engine RWD
Structure:	Steel chassis/glassfibre body
Transmission:	Four-speed manual
Weight:	495kg

PRICE GUIDE

Launch price:	£990
Excellent:	£2000
Good:	£1200
Average:	£650
Project:	£250

RELIANT
Kitten

Two years after the Robin's launch, Reliant replaced its Rebel with the Kitten. The visual similarity with the Robin was a side-effect of being closely based on the Tom Karen original – and in the Kitten's creation, Reliant produced arguably the first '70s UK supermini. In reality, the car was expensive compared with mainstream rivals, cramped and unrefined, but it was also the most economical four-wheeler money could buy. Interestingly, the Kitten is now finding favour with the engine-swap brigade, thanks to RWD. Estate version is exceptionally rare, but quite useful.

SPECIFICATIONS

Years produced:	1975-1982
Performance:	0-60mph: 18.0sec
	Top speed: 81mph
Power & torque:	40bhp/46lb ft
Engine:	Normally aspirated 848cc four cylinder, petrol, carburettor, 8 valves
Drivetrain:	Front-engine RWD
Structure:	Steel chassis/glassfibre body
Transmission:	Four-speed manual
Weight:	595kg

PRICE GUIDE

Launch price:	£990
Excellent:	£1500
Good:	£1200
Average:	£650
Project:	£250

RELIANT
Scimitar GTE SE6/a/b

The GTE formula was so right that when Reliant came to replacing the model, the job was impossible. Instead, it was made wider and given a longer wheelbase, and new chassis settings erred on the side of comfort. It continued to sell handsomely and remained Reliant's main money earner. In 1979, the 2.8-litre V6 Ford 'Cologne' engine was introduced, adding little to the mix other than continued supply. Although the GTE was later resurrected by Middlebridge, it failed to take off, and It disappeared from view in 1990.

SPECIFICATIONS (SE6b)

Years produced:	1976-1986 (4420/437 in total)
Performance:	0-60mph: 10.0sec
	Top speed: 119mph
Power & torque:	135bhp/152lb ft
Engine:	Normally aspirated 2792cc four cylinder, petrol, carburettor, 12 valves
Drivetrain:	Front-engine RWD
Structure:	Steel chassis/glassfibre body
Transmission:	Four-speed manual with overdrive
Weight:	1293kg

PRICE GUIDE

Launch price:	£10,324
Excellent:	£5500
Good:	£4000
Average:	£1750
Project:	£650

RELIANT
Scimitar GTC

This should have been another money spinner for Reliant. When it emerged in 1980, it had the market all to itself – the Stag had been dead three years. That large Triumph model had clearly provided inspiration – with its T-piece targa arrangement and removable hardtop – and, just like its fellow British marque, Reliant struggled to meet ambitious sales expectations. The main problem wasn't the product at all, as this was very good, but the fact the car was launched in the middle of a recession. By the time the economy had recovered, the GTC was old hat...

SPECIFICATIONS

Years produced:	1980-1985 (442 in total)
Performance:	0-60mph: 8.7sec
	Top speed: 114mph
Power & torque:	135bhp/152lb ft
Engine:	Normally aspirated 2792cc V6, petrol, carburettor, 12 valves
Drivetrain:	Front-engine RWD
Structure:	Steel chassis/glassfibre body
Transmission:	Four-speed manual with overdrive
Weight:	1265kg

PRICE GUIDE

Launch price:	£11,600
Excellent:	£7500
Good:	£4500
Average:	£3000
Project:	£1750

RELIANT
Scimitar SS1/SST

A brave experiment that didn't quite make the grade despite being ahead of its time. The SS1 was designed to plug the gap in the market vacated by the MGB and TR7 when they went out of production, and should have been a massive success. It was simple, cheap and fun – and handled well thanks to its all-independent suspension. However, the Michelotti styling was a mess, the Ford CVH engines were underpowered and panel fit of the glassfibre body was terrible. As a result, it never came close to selling in the numbers once envisaged.

SPECIFICATIONS

Years produced:	1984-1990
Performance:	0-60mph: 11.2sec
	Top speed: 111mph
Power & torque:	95bhp/97lb ft
Engine:	Normally aspirated 1597cc four cylinder, petrol, carburettor, 8 valves
Drivetrain:	Front-engine RWD
Structure:	Steel chassis, plastic body
Transmission:	Five-speed manual
Weight:	887kg

PRICE GUIDE

Launch price:	£6995
Excellent:	£3500
Good:	£2750
Average:	£1000
Project:	£500

RENAULT

LOUIS RENAULT'S first vehicle was knocked up in the back garden of his parents' house in 1898. It led to the formation of the self-named marque with his two brothers, with much early profit coming from taxis. However, in the interwar years Renault lost ground to rivals because of its old-fashioned engineering. Post-WW2, though, its range showed true imagination with cars like the small 4CV, utilitarian R4, stylish Floride and Caravelle, and landmark 16 of 1964 – regarded as the first modern-format hatch. Following an unsuccessful partnership with AMC in the USA, Renault is now allied with Nissan, a marriage which has benefited both in design and creativity terms.

RENAULT
4CV

With Renault's 4CV developed in secret in occupied France during the war, it's tempting to believe that this rear-engined car was influenced by certain German machines. The 4CV was launched postwar with an 18bhp 760cc four-cylinder engine, all-independent suspension plus very chic and cuddly styling. More power – albeit from a smaller 747cc engine – came in 1950, and the gradual advancements continued until 1961. Most intriguing was the R1063 Sport, with 42bhp. Not that much maybe, but in a car this light and small, more than enough to turn it into a real terrier.

SPECIFICATIONS	
Years produced:	1947-1961 (1,105,547 in total)
Performance:	0-60mph: N/A
	Top speed: 57mph
Power & torque:	19bhp/33lb ft
Engine:	Normally aspirated 760cc four cylinder, petrol, carburettor, 8 valves
Drivetrain:	Rear-engine RWD
Structure:	Monocoque
Transmission:	Three-speed manual
Weight:	560kg
PRICE GUIDE	
Launch price:	£474
Excellent:	£4250
Good:	£3250
Average:	£1750
Project:	£750

RENAULT
Dauphine

The 4CV lived on in the stylish Dauphine. Born in 1956, this was a development of the 4CV with a bigger rear engine, chassis and bodywork. It sold almost twice as many examples as the car it grew out of. Intriguing features were the Ferlec transmission – giving finger-touch changes – and Aerostable semi-pneumatic variable suspension, plus disc brakes on all four wheels from 1964. The 37-40bhp Gordini (add 50% to prices) and the 49bhp racing-striped 1093cc Rallye (not imported to UK) gave Mini-Cooper-esque performance.

SPECIFICATIONS	
Years produced:	1956-1967 (2,150,738 in total)
Performance:	0-60mph: 45.7sec
	Top speed: 70mph
Power & torque:	30bhp/43lb ft
Engine:	Normally aspirated 845cc four cylinder, petrol, carburettor, 8 valves
Drivetrain:	Rear-engine RWD
Structure:	Monocoque
Transmission:	3/4-speed manual or 3-speed auto
Weight:	650kg
PRICE GUIDE	
Launch price:	£769
Excellent:	£3250
Good:	£2500
Average:	£1200
Project:	£600

RENAULT
4

If any Renault was a true 2CV rival, then this was it. Long-lived – built from 1961 to 1992 – and utterly simple in some places yet complex in others, it was Renault's first front-wheel-drive car. Quirks included the gearlever sprouting from the dashboard – necessary because the transmission was mounted in front of the engine – plus a different wheelbase on each side. The six engines available ranged from 603cc to 1108cc, but power stayed between the limits of 23bhp and 34bhp. As well as the saloon, there was also a 4x4 and a beach car known as the Plein Air.

SPECIFICATIONS	
Years produced:	1961-1992 (8,135,424 in total)
Performance:	0-60mph: 38.1sec
	Top speed: 70mph
Power & torque:	30bhp/41lb ft
Engine:	Normally aspirated 845cc four cylinder, petrol, carburettor, 8 valves
Drivetrain:	Front-engine FWD
Structure:	Monocoque
Transmission:	Three-speed manual
Weight:	597kg
PRICE GUIDE	
Launch price:	£539
Excellent:	£2500
Good:	£1250
Average:	£600
Project:	£250

RENAULT
Caravelle

America knew the Floride as the Caravelle. Yet from 1962, the name was used in Europe for a facelifted version, available as a coupé and convertible. The shape was largely the same, although some of the over-fussy ornamentation was dispensed with and passengers in the coupé had more headroom. The 956cc engine of the Floride S was initially used, still rear-mounted, but after a year capacity was boosted to 1108cc. With 54bhp on tap, top speed rose to within a whisper of 90mph, yet Renault never managed to resolve the handling issues. Add 25% for convertibles.

SPECIFICATIONS	
Years produced:	1962-1968
Performance:	0-60mph: 17.6sec
	Top speed: 89mph
Power & torque:	54bhp/65lb ft
Engine:	Normally aspirated 1108cc four cylinder, petrol, carburettor, 8 valves
Drivetrain:	Rear-engine RWD
Structure:	Monocoque
Transmission:	Four-speed manual
Weight:	800kg
PRICE GUIDE	
Launch price:	£1168
Excellent:	£5000
Good:	£3250
Average:	£1700
Project:	£700

RENAULT
8

Renault persisted with a rear-engined layout for the 8, the successor to the Dauphine. First unveiled in 1962, it was an altogether more angular car. The 956cc engine was larger than before, suspension was independent all round, and there were disc brakes on each wheel... which certainly wasn't usual for most cars of this class at the time. They were more justified on faster, more powerful versions such as 1964's 8-1100 – also known as the 8 Major – with 1108cc, and the 8S of 1968, which could boast 53bhp and had a quad-headlamp front to show off sportier pretensions. Pay double for these.

SPECIFICATIONS

Years produced:	1964-1972 (1,316,134 in total)
Performance:	0-60mph: 16.5sec
	Top speed: 81mph
Power & torque:	45bhp/65lb ft
Engine:	Normally aspirated 1108cc four cylinder, petrol, carburettor, 8 valves
Drivetrain:	Rear-engine RWD
Structure:	Monocoque
Transmission:	Four-speed manual
Weight:	767kg

PRICE GUIDE

Launch price:	£764
Excellent:	£2750
Good:	£2200
Average:	£1100
Project:	£400

RENAULT
8 Gordini 1100/1300

When it comes to mad Renaults, the 8 Gordini takes some beating. Launched in 1964, this rear-engined car was tuned to more than 90bhp – rather more than its chassis could cope with despite the lowered suspension. The servo-assisted disc brakes at least gave it the ability to stop quickly. More madness was to follow, though, for in 1967 the engine was upped to 1255cc, giving it 103bhp and the ability to easily top the ton. Originally, Gordinis were available only in blue with white stripes; other identifiers were spotlamps and four headlamps on the 1255cc R1135 types.

SPECIFICATIONS

Years produced:	1964-1970 (12,203 in total)
Performance:	0-60mph: 12.3sec
	Top speed: 100mph
Power & torque:	95bhp/72lb ft
Engine:	Normally aspirated 1108cc four cylinder, petrol, carburettor, 8 valves
Drivetrain:	Rear-engine RWD
Structure:	Monocoque
Transmission:	Four-speed manual
Weight:	853kg

PRICE GUIDE

Launch price:	£984
Excellent:	£9000
Good:	£4500
Average:	£3000
Project:	£1500

RENAULT
16

The 16 can lay major claim to being the first modern hatchback. Its design seems to be a blueprint for much that came after it, with a lifting tailgate, two-box shape with a roomy interior, front-wheel drive, lively alloy engine and disc brakes up front. There was even what could be regarded as a hot hatch from 1973, two years before the Golf GTi popularised the genre. This was the TX with a 1647cc 93bhp engine, five-speed transmission and quad headlights. A very forward-thinking and well-behaved machine with a lot of typically French quirks to make it even more intriguing.

SPECIFICATIONS

Years produced:	1965-1979 (1,846,000 in total)
Performance:	0-60mph: 12.3sec
	Top speed: 101mph
Power & torque:	83bhp/88lb ft
Engine:	Normally aspirated 1470cc four cylinder, petrol, carburettor, 8 valves
Drivetrain:	Front-engine FWD
Structure:	Monocoque
Transmission:	Four-speed manual
Weight:	980kg

PRICE GUIDE

Launch price:	£949
Excellent:	£3500
Good:	£2250
Average:	£1000
Project:	£350

RENAULT
6

When did you last see a Renault 6? It's difficult to believe that almost two million of these forgettable hatchbacks were sold. The theory behind the 6 was simple – to turn the 4 into something more habitable, and, in doing so, add higher equipment levels and a more sober-suited bodystyle. This all combined elements of the 4 and 16, without capturing any of their charisma. Good to drive in a loping kind of way, with soft ride, door-handle cornering and a buzzy engine with little performance. Values reflect rarity, as these cars could rot for England... or France.

SPECIFICATIONS

Years produced:	1965-1979 (1,773,000 in total)
Performance:	0-60mph: 38.1sec
	Top speed: 70mph
Power & torque:	38bhp/42lb ft
Engine:	Normally aspirated 845cc four cylinder, petrol, carburettor, 8 valves
Drivetrain:	Front-engine FWD
Structure:	Monocoque
Transmission:	Four-speed manual
Weight:	750kg

PRICE GUIDE

Launch price:	£669
Excellent:	£1500
Good:	£1250
Average:	£600
Project:	£250

RENAULT
10

Renault stuck extra length onto the boot and bonnet of the 8 to create the 10. Quite what the reason for this was is unclear, and perhaps even the company didn't know, for the model lasted only three years from 1969 to 1971, and was still tagged as the 8 in some markets. However, in its homeland it was the 10, as it was in the UK. Aside from the big nose and plumper rump, changes from the 8 were minimal save for the fitment of the new five-bearing 1289cc engine (shared with the 12) at the rear to give an unremarkable top speed. Handling was better, too.

SPECIFICATIONS

Years produced:	1969-1971 (699,490 in total)
Performance:	0-60mph: 17.0sec
	Top speed: 88mph
Power & torque:	52bhp/72lb ft
Engine:	Normally aspirated 1289cc four cylinder, petrol, carburettor, 8 valves
Drivetrain:	Rear-engine RWD
Structure:	Monocoque
Transmission:	Four-speed manual
Weight:	792kg

PRICE GUIDE

Launch price:	£776
Excellent:	£2500
Good:	£1750
Average:	£900
Project:	£400

RENAULT
12

Renault's new mid-sized saloon was designed to bridge the gap between the 8/10 and the 16. The smaller car's rear-engined layout gave way to a far more orthodox (in future years) longitudinal front-driver. For a 1969 saloon, this was almost state of the art, as was the near-fastback styling, which hinted at a hatch layout. It was built in various locations, most notably in Turkey and Romania, where the Dacia pick-up version remained in production until 2006. Very few 12s survive in the UK (or France, for that matter) – rust and mechanical fragility were its weaknesses.

SPECIFICATIONS
Years produced: 1969-1980 (2,865,079 in total)
Performance: 0-60mph: 16.5sec
Top speed: 89mph
Power & torque: 54bhp/69lb ft
Engine: Normally aspirated 1289cc four cylinder, petrol, carburettor, 8 valves
Drivetrain: Front-engine FWD
Structure: Monocoque
Transmission: Four-speed manual
Weight: 840kg

PRICE GUIDE
Launch price: £870
Excellent: £1800
Good: £1250
Average: £800
Project: £350

RENAULT
15/17

After Ford unveiled the Capri in 1969, other European manufacturers launched cheap and cheerful coupés. The 15 and 17 were Renault's. Based on the chassis of the 12, the 15 was the lower-spec model with single headlamps and conventional side windows, while the 17 had four lights and louvred rear quarter glass, which gave it a strangely beguiling appearance. The range of engines encompassed 1289cc, 1565cc, 1605cc and 1647cc capacities – the latter used in the top-dog 108bhp 17 Gordini. Convertible versions were actually coupés with a full-length roll-top roof to let in the sun.

SPECIFICATIONS (15 TL)
Years produced: 1972-1978 (207,854/92,589 in total)
Performance: 0-60mph: 13.6sec
Top speed: 108mph
Power & torque: 90bhp/90lb ft
Engine: Normally aspirated 1289cc four cylinder, petrol, carburettor, 8 valves
Drivetrain: Front-engine FWD
Structure: Monocoque
Transmission: Four-speed manual
Weight: 965kg

PRICE GUIDE
Launch price: £1325
Excellent: £3000
Good: £2000
Average: £900
Project: £400

RENAULT
5

Michel Boué's legacy to the automotive world was one he would never see bear fruit, as he died months before the Renault 5 was launched. The three-door hatchback was based on the utilitarian 4, but the styling was super-chic – and when it went on sale in 1972, the 5 caused a sensation. Wraparound plastic bumpers made the car Paris-friendly, and a wide range of engines gave the driver plenty of options. Through the years the car received ever more power, and in 1979 a five-door version added even more practicality. An all-time design classic.

SPECIFICATIONS
Years produced: 1972-1984 (5,471,079 in total)
Performance: 0-60mph: 18.9sec
Top speed: 85mph
Power & torque: 42bhp/61lb ft
Engine: Normally aspirated 1289cc four cylinder, petrol, carburettor, 8 valves
Drivetrain: Front-engine, FWD
Structure: Monocoque
Transmission: Four-speed manual
Weight: 785kg

PRICE GUIDE
Launch price: £854
Excellent: £2000
Good: £1200
Average: £600
Project: £350

RENAULT
20/30

The 20/30 range was a concerted move upmarket for Renault – and, to prove the point, it was the V6-equipped 30 version that took centre stage at the launch in March 1975. PRV power marked this out as the largest-engined Renault since WW2, and gave the car excellent performance. The four-cylinder 20 arrived a few months later, and was a much more rational choice, even if it lacked any real panache. It was meant to replace the 16, but the more charismatic 1965 car remained in production for a further five years, proving that new was no better than old.

SPECIFICATIONS (30 TX)
Years produced: 1975-1984 (622,314/160,265 in total)
Performance: 0-60mph: 9.2sec
Top speed: 117mph
Power & torque: 141bhp/161lb ft
Engine: Normally aspirated 2664cc V6, petrol, fuel injection, 12 valves
Drivetrain: Front-engine FWD
Structure: Monocoque
Transmission: Five-speed manual
Weight: 1340kg

PRICE GUIDE
Launch price: £3299
Excellent: £2000
Good: £1200
Average: £750
Project: £500

RENAULT
5 Gordini/Turbo

Known as the Renault 5 Alpine in Continental Europe, the Gordini was one of the first generation hot hatches, predating the Golf GTi by a year. The car's 1397cc engine produced 93bhp, more than double the power of the standard 5. However, this was a time of rapidly expanding power figures, and the Gordini was quickly outgunned by its new-found rivals. Renault's solution to this problem, as with its F1 car, was forced induction. Bolting a Garrett T3 turbocharger on to the Gordini instantly gave the car a handy increase in power and torque.

SPECIFICATIONS (Gordini)
Years produced: 1976-1984
Performance: 0-60mph: 10.7sec
Top speed: 107mph
Power & torque: 93bhp/85lb ft
Engine: Normally aspirated 1397cc four cylinder, petrol, carburettor, 8 valves
Drivetrain: Front-engine, FWD
Structure: Monocoque
Transmission: Five-speed manual
Weight: 850kg

PRICE GUIDE
Launch price: £4149
Excellent: £3500
Good: £2500
Average: £1250
Project: £500

RENAULT
14

For its first attempt at a Golf rival, Renault decided to use a transversely-mounted Douvrin four-cylinder engine shared with the Peugeot 104. Although it made for good economic sense and fine packaging, Renault dealers and buyers weren't keen on what they saw as a half-breed. The idiosyncratic styling also soon lent itself to the unflattering name of the 'rotten pear' – which tells you all you need to know. But for all that, the 14 wasn't actually bad at all, especially in go-faster TS form, and it's an interesting curio – albeit one that is near-extinct in the UK.

SPECIFICATIONS (14 TL)

Years produced:	1976-1982 (999,093 in total)
Performance:	0-60mph: 14.1sec
	Top speed: 96mph
Power & torque:	68bhp/71lb ft
Engine:	Normally aspirated 1219cc four cylinder, petrol, carburettor, 8 valves
Drivetrain:	Front-engine FWD
Structure:	Monocoque
Transmission:	Four-speed manual
Weight:	880kg

PRICE GUIDE

Launch price:	£2562
Excellent:	£1200
Good:	£700
Average:	£500
Project:	£350

RENAULT
18/Turbo

Launched in 1978, the Renault 18 was easily the company's most conventional car in a generation. Innocuous three-box styling was modern, but clothed longitudinal power units and gearboxes that were familiar to Renault enthusiasts. Original engine choice was limited to 1.4 and 1.6 litres, but the more powerful Turbo and 2.0-litre models were added to the range to extend appeal. Surprisingly, the 18 was the first mainstream Renault to be offered with forced induction, and proved quite popular for a while. Few survive now; and even fewer are cherished.

SPECIFICATIONS (18 Turbo)

Years produced:	1978-1985
Performance:	0-60mph: 9.1sec
	Top speed: 120mph
Power & torque:	125bhp/133lb ft
Engine:	Turbocharged 1565cc four cylinder, petrol, carburettor, 8 valves
Drivetrain:	Front-engine FWD
Structure:	Monocoque
Transmission:	Five-speed manual
Weight:	1040kg

PRICE GUIDE

Launch price:	£3313
Excellent:	£1300
Good:	£700
Average:	£550
Project:	£375

RENAULT
5 Turbo/Turbo 2

The first 400 5 Turbos were built in line with Group 4 regulations with the intention of going rallying. However, this homologation special would have cost Renault too much money to put into full-scale production, as there were so many lightweight aluminium parts unique to the mid-engined rally car. That is why the firm brought out the 5 Turbo 2. This more production-friendly model shared more of its components with the front-engined Gordini Turbo. The Turbo 2 was almost as fast as the original car, but it didn't cost Renault anywhere near as much to build.

SPECIFICATIONS

Years produced:	1980-1986 (3576 in total)
Performance:	0-60mph: 6.6sec
	Top speed: 124mph
Power & torque:	160bhp/163lb ft
Engine:	Turbocharged 1397cc four cylinder, petrol, electronic fuel injection, 8 valves
Drivetrain:	Mid-engine RWD
Structure:	Steel monocoque with glassfibre panels
Transmission:	Five-speed manual
Weight:	970kg

PRICE GUIDE

Launch price:	£N/A
Excellent:	£30,000
Good:	£20,000
Average:	£15,000
Project:	£10,000

RENAULT
Fuego/Turbo

After eight years of moderate coupé sales with the 15/17, Renault needed something fresh – and despite being based on the 18 the Fuego was certainly distinctive. As the first car ever to be fitted with a PLIP, or remote central locking, it was novel, too. In 1982, after two years at the top of the sales charts in Europe, Renault introduced a 132bhp Fuego Turbo which could sprint from 0-60mph in 9.5 seconds. Wearing Turbo decals and BBS alloys, it was less than subtle, but UK sales proved surprisingly strong. British imports stopped in 1986.

SPECIFICATIONS

Years produced:	1980-1987
Performance:	0-60mph: 8.9sec
	Top speed: 120mph
Power & torque:	132bhp/147lb ft
Engine:	Turbocharged 1565cc four cylinder, petrol, carburettor, 8 valves
Drivetrain:	Front-engine FWD
Structure:	Monocoque
Transmission:	Five-speed manual
Weight:	1050kg

PRICE GUIDE

Launch price:	£8700
Excellent:	£2000
Good:	£1250
Average:	£700
Project:	£400

RENAULT
9/11 Turbo

After the 18 of four years earlier, Renault travelled a few miles further down the road of automotive conformity with the 9 and 11. However, considerable interest was added to the not especially remarkable range in 1985, when the blown engine from the 5GT Turbo was fitted. The anonymous saloon and hatchback were transformed into firebreathing Volkswagen Golf GTi chasers that torque-steered monumentally. Many gave their lives as donors for 5GT Turbos, but a few survive today. Their relative rarity is not reflected in high prices.

SPECIFICATIONS

Years produced:	1982-1989
Performance:	0-60mph: 7.9sec
	Top speed: 114mph
Power & torque:	105bhp/119lb ft
Engine:	Turbocharged 1397cc four cylinder, petrol, carburettor, 8 valves
Drivetrain:	Front-engine FWD
Structure:	Monocoque
Transmission:	Five-speed manual
Weight:	915kg

PRICE GUIDE

Launch price:	£8155
Excellent:	£1400
Good:	£950
Average:	£750
Project:	£350

RENAULT
25

Renault recruited famed designer Robert Opron, creator of the Citroën SM, to give its range a smart new look for the 1980s. His first attempt was the Fuego, which certainly looked the part, but more convincing by a mile was the 25. Top-of-the-range models boasted a digital dashboard with voice synthesiser, and all were considerably faster and more economical than their forerunner 20/30 models thanks to improved aerodynamics. Early models have rusted away, yet improved-build later models are surprisingly plentiful, if overlooked, so remain cheap.

SPECIFICATIONS

Years produced:	1984-1992 (173,685 in total)
Performance:	0-60mph: 11.1sec
	Top speed: 121mph
Power & torque:	123bhp/134lb ft
Engine:	Normally aspirated 2165cc four cylinder, petrol, fuel injection, 8 valves
Drivetrain:	Front-engine FWD
Structure:	Monocoque
Transmission:	Five-speed manual
Weight:	1200kg

PRICE GUIDE

Launch price:	£7950
Excellent:	£1600
Good:	£800
Average:	£550
Project:	£300

RENAULT
5

With 5.5 million examples sold, the original 5 was pensioned off in favour of a car that looked almost identical. But the new Gandini-styled 'Supercinq' was all-new under the skin, featuring a transverse engine for far better interior space plus MacPherson strut suspension for a taste of the conventional. Available in myriad guises, the car was consistently France's best-selling car throughout the 1980s, and the top-spec Monaco with its 1.7-litre engine and luxury kit remains a desirable car. The 5 remained in production for six years after the arrival of its replacement, the Clio.

SPECIFICATIONS

Years produced:	1984-1996 (1,109,300 in total)
Performance:	0-60mph: 18.0sec
	Top speed: 85mph
Power & torque:	44bhp/47lb ft
Engine:	Turbocharged 956cc four cylinder, petrol, carburettor, 8 valves
Drivetrain:	Front-engine FWD
Structure:	Monocoque
Transmission:	Four-speed manual
Weight:	775kg

PRICE GUIDE

Launch price:	£3450
Excellent:	£1250
Good:	£950
Average:	£750
Project:	£350

RENAULT
Espace

In reality the Espace is far from being the first MPV, but it was a massive hit for Renault and went a long way towards popularising the concept in Europe. The innovative car was developed and built by Matra, and was initially offered to Peugeot as the replacement for the Rancho. The company refused it, so Renault took it wholescale – Chrysler Alpine front end and all – and the firm has never looked back. Unfortunately, the adaptable interior wasn't well made, and the exterior panels damaged easily, so finding a minter is never easy... the perfect recipe for future classic status.

SPECIFICATIONS

Years produced:	1984-1991
Performance:	0-60mph: 12.5sec
	Top speed: 109mph
Power & torque:	106bhp/118lb ft
Engine:	Turbocharged 1995cc four cylinder, petrol, carburettor, 8 valves
Drivetrain:	Front-engine FWD
Structure:	Spaceframe
Transmission:	Five-speed manual
Weight:	1200kg

PRICE GUIDE

Launch price:	£8878
Excellent:	£1500
Good:	£850
Average:	£650
Project:	£450

RENAULT
5 GT Turbo

When the Gordini Turbo was phased out in 1984 with the arrival of the 'Supercinq', Renault had to up the ante. The GT Turbo used the same basic engine as the Gordini, but a Garrett T2 turbocharger and a few other induction system modifications raised the power to 115bhp, and again to 118bhp in 1987. This power figure on its own isn't that impressive, but the Renault 5 tipped the scales at only 820kg, giving the tiny hot hatch truly staggering acceleration – not to mention fun, rear inside wheel-lifting handling. Grab a standard example while you can.

SPECIFICATIONS

Years produced:	1985-1991
Performance:	0-60mph: 7.1sec
	Top speed: 123mph
Power & torque:	115bhp/121lb ft
Engine:	Turbocharged 1397cc four cylinder, petrol, carburettor, 8 valves
Drivetrain:	Front-engine FWD
Structure:	Monocoque
Transmission:	Five-speed manual
Weight:	820kg

PRICE GUIDE

Launch price:	£7630
Excellent:	£4000
Good:	£2750
Average:	£1650
Project:	£750

RENAULT
21 Turbo

Renault's Giugiaro-styled 21 was a pretty but forgettable repmobile. Its only technical novelty was a mixture of transverse and longitudinal engines, which betrayed the car's mixed parentage. However, when *La Regie* bolted a turbo onto the 2.0-litre model, the 21 was transformed into an entertaining sports saloon that could eat BMW 325is for breakfast. And if 175bhp doesn't sound that much these days, consider the car's 0-60mph time of 6.5 seconds, along with all the wheelspin you could ever want. Many examples are still going strong – and making good money.

SPECIFICATIONS

Years produced:	1988-1992
Performance:	0-60mph: 8.1sec
	Top speed: 141mph
Power & torque:	175bhp/199lb ft
Engine:	Turbocharged 1995cc four cylinder, petrol, fuel injection, 8 valves
Drivetrain:	Front-engine FWD
Structure:	Monocoque
Transmission:	Five-speed manual
Weight:	1190kg

PRICE GUIDE

Launch price:	£16,500
Excellent:	£3000
Good:	£1700
Average:	£950
Project:	£550

RILEY

AFTER MAINLY building tricars, Riley – established in 1898 – moved onto four wheels from 1907. As the firm matured it was responsible for some very rakish designs, and soon became a competition favourite. Unfortunately, sporting prowess was no substitute for cold, hard cash, and the ailing company was taken over by Morris to form the Nuffield Organisation. While this saved the name it ended Riley's independence, and the firm's cars became more reliant on Morris (and, from 1952, BMC) in their make-up. The last model to feature any Riley individuality was the 1953-1957 Pathfinder; after that, the models became just badge-engineered BMC variants. The Riley name was killed off in 1969.

RILEY
RMA/RME

The immediate post-war Rileys continued with their traditional method of a separate chassis and ash-frame construction. The RMA was a handsome streamlined saloon, with a lively twin-camshaft 1496cc engine giving effective performance while the independent front suspension meant effective handling as well. The RMA metamorphosed into the RME in 1952, with hydraulic brakes – one of the areas where its predecessor's had been weak – plus a larger rear window. A year before production end, wheel spats were added and the running boards dispensed with.

SPECIFICATIONS
Years produced:	1946-1955 (13,950 in total)
Performance:	0-60mph: 25.1sec
	Top speed: 81mph
Power & torque:	55bhp/76lb ft
Engine:	Normally aspirated 1496cc four cylinder, petrol, carburettor, overhead valves
Drivetrain:	Front-engine RWD
Structure:	Separate chassis
Transmission:	Four-speed manual
Weight:	1422kg

PRICE GUIDE
Launch price:	£710
Excellent:	£9000
Good:	£6500
Average:	£3750
Project:	£1750

RILEY
RMB/RMF

A step upwards from the RMA was the RMB, with its 2443cc engine offering enhanced potential. The 'B kept the same basic look as the 'A, but had a longer wheelbase and bonnet. When launched in 1946 90bhp was available, but this went up to 100bhp in 1948. By happy coincidence, this brought top speed up to 100mph as well. The RMF of 1952 was an almost identical-looking replacement with improved suspension, hydraulic brakes in place of the previous hydromechanical ones, and a larger, curved rear screen. Manufacture continued until 1953.

SPECIFICATIONS
Years produced:	1946-1953 (8959 in total)
Performance:	0-60mph: 15.2sec
	Top speed: 95mph
Power & torque:	90bhp/N/A
Engine:	Normally aspirated 2443cc four cylinder, petrol, carburettor, 8 valves
Drivetrain:	Front-engine RWD
Structure:	Separate chassis
Transmission:	Four-speed manual
Weight:	1211kg

PRICE GUIDE
Launch price:	£1125
Excellent:	£10,000
Good:	£9000
Average:	£5000
Project:	£2250

RILEY
RMC Roadster

The rarest of the RM variants, especially in Britain, was the RMC – a three-seater, two-door roadster version of the RMB. The sleek lines were even more attractive sans roof, especially with the windscreen folded flat, and the more compact interior meant a larger boot could be fitted. The engine was the same as that of the RMB – a 2443cc overhead-valve unit – and was also tuned to give 100bhp. The RMC was intended for overseas markets, with most going to North America. Only 507 were constructed up until the end of the line in 1950.

SPECIFICATIONS
Years produced:	1948-1950 (507 in total)
Performance:	0-60mph: 19.0sec
	Top speed: 98mph
Power & torque:	100bhp/N/A
Engine:	Normally aspirated 2443cc four cylinder, petrol, carburettor, 8 valves
Drivetrain:	Front-engine RWD
Structure:	Separate chassis
Transmission:	Four-speed manual
Weight:	1219kg

PRICE GUIDE
Launch price:	£1225
Excellent:	£25,000
Good:	£18,500
Average:	£12,500
Project:	£6500

RILEY
RMD Convertible

More practical than the RMC Roadster was the four-seater RMD. Introduced at the same time as the RMC, this elegant drophead coupé would turn out to be the final open-top car to wear the Riley name, aside from the specially-converted Elf convertibles of the 1960s. The RMD kept much the same lines as the RMB, so no fold-flat one-piece windscreen or enlarged boot. It did have distinctive grab irons on its hood though. Production continued one year past the RMC until 1951 but, by the end of its three-year life, only 502 had found homes.

SPECIFICATIONS
Years produced:	1948-1951 (502 in total)
Performance:	0-60mph: 15.2sec
	Top speed: 95mph
Power & torque:	100bhp/N/A
Engine:	Normally aspirated 2443cc four cylinder, petrol, carburettor, 8 valves
Drivetrain:	Front-engine RWD
Structure:	Separate chassis
Transmission:	Four-speed manual
Weight:	1239kg

PRICE GUIDE
Launch price:	£1382
Excellent:	£18,000
Good:	£14,000
Average:	£9000
Project:	£4000

RILEY
Pathfinder/2.6

The sleek Pathfinder brought Riley into the modern age, although its twin-cam four-cylinder engine was carried over from the traditional and upright RMF. Its right-hand floorshift gearstick can take some getting used to, as can the handling. Later cars got leaf rather than coil rear springs, and the improvement was clear. The 2.6 that replaced the Pathfinder was of similar style but taller, and was really a Wolseley 6/90 with a Riley grille and an extra 4bhp from its BMC C-series six-cylinder engine. Both are rare now, yet offer a large slice of 1950s British wood and leather luxury.

SPECIFICATIONS
Years produced: 1953-1958 (8959/2000 in total)
Performance: 0-60mph: 16.7sec
Top speed: 100mph
Power & torque: 110bhp/135lb ft
Engine: Normally aspirated 2443cc four cylinder, petrol, carburettor, 8 valves
Drivetrain: Front-engine RWD
Structure: Separate chassis
Transmission: Four-speed manual
Weight: 1500kg

PRICE GUIDE
Launch price: £1382
Excellent: £4500
Good: £3250
Average: £1850
Project: £750

RILEY
One-Point-Five

Originally intended as a Morris Minor successor, the One-Point-Five instead emerged in 1957 as the sassier sister to the Wolseley 1500. The shell was the same albeit with differences in trim and the front end, which sported Riley's traditional grill. It was under the bonnet where the real fun lay, though, for the BMC B-series 1489cc had an extra carburettor fitted, boosting output to 62bhp over the Wolseley's 43bhp. Coupled with Morris Minor running gear, the One-Point-Five was a nimble and entertaining car to drive. The luxurious interior also befitted the Riley image.

SPECIFICATIONS
Years produced: 1957-1965 (39,568 in total)
Performance: 0-60mph: 17.4sec
Top speed: 84mph
Power & torque: 62bhp/82lb ft
Engine: Normally aspirated 1489cc four cylinder, petrol, carburettor, 8 valves
Drivetrain: Front-engine RWD
Structure: Monocoque
Transmission: Four-speed manual
Weight: 864kg

PRICE GUIDE
Launch price: £864
Excellent: £4000
Good: £3000
Average: £1400
Project: £450

RILEY
4/68, 4/72

Or, as Shakespeare might have said, a Farina by any other name... The Riley-badged version of BMC's mid-sized Farina-penned saloons of 1959 to 1969 was arguably the most desirable, for it blended the performance and cabin luxury of its MG and Wolseley rivals respectively. The car was based on the MG Magnette, so had cut-back fins from its birth plus the same 66bhp twin-carburettor, four-cylinder engine. The 4/72 in 1961 put that figure at 68bhp; there was also a wider track, increased wheelbase and anti-roll bars to combat the body roll all Farinas suffered from.

SPECIFICATIONS
Years produced: 1959-1969 (10,940/14,151 in total)
Performance: 0-60mph: 20.6sec
Top speed: 84mph
Power & torque: 66bhp/85lb ft
Engine: Normally aspirated 1489cc four cylinder, petrol, carburettor, 8 valves
Drivetrain: Front-engine RWD
Structure: Monocoque
Transmission: Four-speed manual
Weight: 1092kg

PRICE GUIDE
Launch price: £1028
Excellent: £4500
Good: £2500
Average: £1250
Project: £350

RILEY
Elf

Continuing Riley's adventures in badge engineering was the Elf of 1961 to 1969. It looked like a Mini on steroids, with an extended rump framed by fins and an old-school Riley front end. Occupants could delight in a less spartan interior with a full-length burr walnut dash. The MkII in 1963 made use of the bigger 998cc A-series engine, Hydrolastic suspension arrived in 1964 and the MkIII introduced winding windows, better ventilation and a 'remote-control' gearbox. Despite selling well, the Elf was discontinued when British Leyland killed off Riley.

SPECIFICATIONS
Years produced: 1961-1969 (30,912 in total)
Performance: 0-60mph: 32.3sec
Top speed: 71mph
Power & torque: 34bhp/N/A
Engine: Normally aspirated 848cc four cylinder, petrol, carburettor, 8 valves
Drivetrain: Front-engine FWD
Structure: Monocoque
Transmission: Four-speed manual
Weight: 660kg

PRICE GUIDE
Launch price: £694
Excellent: £6000
Good: £4000
Average: £2500
Project: £1000

RILEY
Kestrel

The last Riley of all was the Kestrel (and subsequent 1300 upgrade). It wasn't really a Riley, though, being just a rebadged BMC 1100 with the 55bhp specification of the MG plus the now-expected individual grille and side whiskers. A walnut veneer dashboard upgraded the interior. When the 1275cc A-series was installed under the bonnet in 1967, power rose first to 65bhp, then 70bhp a year later. The car was de-named in 1968, becoming just the Riley 1300. This suggested the writing was on the wall for the marque. It was, for the car and the life of Riley ended only a year later.

SPECIFICATIONS
Years produced: 1965-1969 (21,529 in total)
Performance: 0-60mph: 18.4sec
Top speed: 85mph
Power & torque: 55bhp/62lb ft
Engine: Normally aspirated 1098cc four cylinder, petrol, carburettor, 8 valves
Drivetrain: Front-engine FWD
Structure: Monocoque
Transmission: Four-speed manual
Weight: 832kg

PRICE GUIDE
Launch price: £781
Excellent: £3000
Good: £1900
Average: £1000
Project: £500

ROCHDALE

THE BODYWORK repair business, Rochdale Motor Panels was formed in 1948 by Harry Smith and Frank Butterworth. They were both keen racers, and Specials enthusiasts, and it was inevitable that they would end up building their own. The were soon creating bespoke cars to customers' specifications, and by 1952 had abandoned aluminium in favour of glass fibre. The GT and Olympic picked up useful sales, but the company was badly affected by a factory fire in 1961. Sales continued until 1963, but by then, they had slowed – and Rochdale refocused its efforts, concentrating on making heating equipment. Continued selling cars as one-offs until 1972.

ROCHDALE
GT

Rochdale made a success of supplying bodies for the specialist auto industry. Its glassfibre shells were found adorning a number of specials – so much so that it started making complete cars. The best-selling GT (a coupé version of the Rochdale F racing body), was designed specifically to work with Ford Popular running gear. It was an advanced design, with sleek styling, a curved screen, plus ready-fitted doors and bonnet. One of the main bonuses of the coupé roof was the reduction of chassis flex – a lesson learned for subsequent models.

SPECIFICATIONS	
Years produced:	1957-1961 (1350 in total)
Performance:	0-60mph: N/A
	Top speed: N/A
Power & torque:	N/A
Engine:	Normally aspirated 1172cc four cylinder, petrol, carburettor, 8 valves
Drivetrain:	Front-engine RWD
Structure:	Separate chassis
Transmission:	Four-speed manual
Weight:	650kg

PRICE GUIDE	
Launch price:	N/A
Excellent:	£6000
Good:	£3250
Average:	£1850
Project:	£500

ROCHDALE
Olympic

When it appeared in 1960, the Olympic was only the second car to feature a glassfibre monocoque – following hot on the heels of the Lotus Elite. The Rochdale was bulbous and lacked the glamour of its rival, but it was well-engineered and handled assuredly thanks to its coil spring set-up. Production endured a critical setback following a fire at the factory a year after launch, but it picked up slowly afterwards with the car being offered in component form or as a complete package. The 1963 Olympic II moved from BMC to Ford for its running gear.

SPECIFICATIONS	
Years produced:	1960-1962 (21,529 in total)
Performance:	0-60mph: 11.9sec
	Top speed: 102 mph
Power & torque:	60 bhp/N/A
Engine:	Normally aspirated 1498cc four cylinder, petrol, carburettor, 8 valves
Drivetrain:	Front-engine RWD
Structure:	Glassfibre monocoque
Transmission:	Four-speed manual
Weight:	700 kg

PRICE GUIDE	
Launch price:	£670
Excellent:	£7500
Good:	£4750
Average:	£2500
Project:	£1000

ROLLS-ROYCE

THE PARTNERSHIP of engineer Henry Royce and rich gentleman Charles Rolls resulted in the 1906 formation of the world's most prestigious marque. The Silver Ghost was dubbed 'The best car in the world' and RR tried to stick to this creed with all subsequent models. Magnificent leviathans followed, each unstinting in their luxury and price. The postwar Silver Cloud models were perhaps the zenith of RR's accomplishments, but the succeeding Silver Shadow became a common sight because so many were built. Nationalised amid financial woes in 1971, the company was sold off again in 1973. BMW and Volkswagen competed to buy it in 1998, with BMW the eventual winner.

ROLLS-ROYCE
Silver Wraith

Rolls-Royce re-emerged after WW2 with the Silver Wraith, based on the Wraith model sold in 1939. At first it was available only for export, Great Britain having to wait until 1948 before home sales commenced. As was traditional, the Wraith was offered as a bare chassis only; it was up to the affluent owner to have a coachbuilder construct the body, with Mulliner proving the most popular option. Initially, motive power was a 4257cc straight-six engine, but this rose to 4566cc in 1951 and then jumped to 4887cc in 1954 .

SPECIFICATIONS	
Years produced:	1946-1959 (1783 in total)
Performance:	0-60mph: 16.2sec
	Top speed: 88mph
Power & torque:	N/A
Engine:	Normally aspirated 4566cc straight six, petrol, carburettor, 12 valves
Drivetrain:	Front-engine RWD
Structure:	Separate chassis
Transmission:	Four-speed automatic
Weight:	2359kg

PRICE GUIDE	
Launch price:	£4190
Excellent:	£30,000
Good:	£25,000
Average:	£15,000
Project:	£9500

ROLLS-ROYCE
Silver Dawn

Before WW2, most Rolls-Royces had been large and imposing chauffeur-driven palaces on wheels. But the world was changing, and the marque felt the need to change with it. Thus the Silver Dawn was a more compact Rolls, based on the Bentley MkVI and aimed at owners who also drove themselves. Engines were less powerful than their Bentley counterparts, and Rolls-Royce never let on the power output figures – at least not to the public. Most cars had standard Pressed Steel bodies, but there were some coachbuilt specials; some were more special than others.

SPECIFICATIONS
Years produced: 1949-1955 (761 in total)
Performance: 0-60mph: 16.2sec
Top speed: 87mph
Power & torque: N/A
Engine: Normally aspirated 4556cc straight six, petrol, carburettor, 12 valves
Drivetrain: Front-engine RWD
Structure: Separate chassis
Transmission: Four-speed automatic
Weight: 1842kg

PRICE GUIDE
Launch price: £3250
Excellent: £32,500
Good: £26,000
Average: £15,000
Project: £8500

ROLLS-ROYCE
Silver Cloud I

A new era for Rolls-Royce was ushered in with the Silver Cloud in 1955. The company started making bodies in-house, although many customers still preferred to have their favourite coachbuilder construct something special. But such was the imposing elegance of the Cloud's standard body that many buyers never felt the need to shop elsewhere. The 4887cc engine was an enlargement of that which had been used in previous models. In addition to the standard 123in wheelbase cars, a 127in limousine was offered with bodywork by Park Ward.

SPECIFICATIONS
Years produced: 1955-1959 (2359 in total)
Performance: 0-60mph: 13.0sec
Top speed: 106mph
Power & torque: N/A
Engine: Normally aspirated 4887cc straight six, petrol, carburettor, 12 valves
Drivetrain: Front-engine RWD
Structure: Separate chassis
Transmission: Four-speed automatic
Weight: 2032kg

PRICE GUIDE
Launch price: £3385
Excellent: £40,000
Good: £21,500
Average: £11,000
Project: £6500

ROLLS-ROYCE
Silver Cloud II

V8 power reached Rolls-Royce with the Silver Cloud II of 1959. The firm's new 6230cc eight cylinder brought muscle, flexibility and smoothness to this commanding heavyweight. Although the actual power figure was never revealed, it was estimated to be around 200bhp – or 25 per cent greater than in the six-cylinder Cloud. Other changes included the adoption of power-assisted steering and a new facia. The standard saloons and Park Ward limousines were now complemented by the choice of a Mulliner drophead coupé, although its price was just as fabulous as its looks.

SPECIFICATIONS
Years produced: 1959-1965 (5013 in total)
Performance: 0-60mph: 11.5sec
Top speed: 113mph
Power & torque: N/A
Engine: Normally aspirated 6230cc V8, petrol, carburettor, 16 valves
Drivetrain: Front-engine RWD
Structure: Separate chassis
Transmission: Four-speed automatic
Weight: 2109kg

PRICE GUIDE
Launch price: £5802
Excellent: £32,500
Good: £22,500
Average: £11,500
Project: £6500

ROLLS-ROYCE
Phantom V limousine

Boy, did the Phantom V need the company's new V8 engine! This ultra-luxurious leviathan weighed just under three tonnes, and the huge rear passenger compartment was made possible by the elongated 12-foot wheelbase. Everything about the Phantom was designed to pamper its occupants; aside from the acres of wood trim and leather upholstery, power steering and an automatic transmission came as standard. The styling was closely related to that of the Cloud on which the Phantom was based, with few cars being bodied by outside coachbuilders.

SPECIFICATIONS
Years produced: 1959-1968 (516 in total)
Performance: 0-60mph: 13.8sec
Top speed: 101mph
Power & torque: N/A
Engine: Normally aspirated 6223cc V8, petrol, carburettor, 16 valves
Drivetrain: Front-engine, RWD
Structure: Separate chassis
Transmission: Four-speed automatic
Weight: 2540kg

PRICE GUIDE
Launch price: £8905
Excellent: £80,000
Good: £50,000
Average: £32,500
Project: £22,500

ROLLS-ROYCE
Silver Cloud III

The adoption of the V8 engine for the Cloud II was universally regarded as an improvement. Not everybody was convinced by the 1962 facelift that created the Cloud III, though. It modernised the looks, but old-school aficionados bemoaned the loss of the traditional 'face'. However, it didn't offend the 'new money' celebrities who were now buying into the Rolls-Royce dream; John Lennon even had his Cloud III painted in a psychedelic colour scheme. A raised compression ratio resulted in more power although, predictably, how much more remained a secret.

SPECIFICATIONS
Years produced: 1962-1965 (2359 in total)
Performance: 0-60mph: 10.8sec
Top speed: 116mph
Power & torque: N/A
Engine: Normally aspirated 6230cc V8, petrol, carburettor, 16 valves
Drivetrain: Front-engine, RWD
Structure: Separate chassis
Transmission: Four-speed automatic
Weight: 2109kg

PRICE GUIDE
Launch price: £5517
Excellent: £37,500
Good: £25,000
Average: £13,500
Project: £7500

ROLLS-ROYCE
Silver Shadow

If ever there was a Rolls-Royce for the masses, then the Shadow was it. It was revolutionary for the company, with unitary construction, all-round disc brakes and self-levelling suspension. The modern lines reflected contemporary car design, yet also managed to retain Rolls-Royce's upper-class air. The 6230cc V8 rose in capacity to 6750cc in 1970, and the Shadow II fell victim to rubber-faced bumpers and a front air dam in 1977. The Silver Wraith name was used from the same year to distinguish the long-wheelbase version.

SPECIFICATIONS
Years produced:	1965-1980 (27,915 in total)
Performance:	0-60mph: 10.9sec
	Top speed: 118mph
Power & torque:	N/A
Engine:	Normally aspirated 6230cc V8, petrol, carburettor, 16 valves
Drivetrain:	Front-engine, RWD
Structure:	Monocoque
Transmission:	Three-speed automatic
Weight:	2114kg

PRICE GUIDE
Launch price:	£6670
Excellent:	£17,500
Good:	£11,000
Average:	£6250
Project:	£2000

ROLLS-ROYCE
Phantom VI Limousine

The existing Phantom metamorphosed into the even more magnificent Phantom VI in 1968, a car that Rolls-Royce would continue to build – to special order only – right up until 1992. Despite this, and its V8's capacity boost to 6750cc in 1978, it had drum brakes right until the end. However, this most stately of British limousines wasn't intended for speed, more for cruising along gently while those inside basked in the glory of being incredibly rich. During its quarter-of-a-century existence, a mere 373 were constructed, ownership reading like a 'who's who' of the global elite.

SPECIFICATIONS
Years produced:	1968-1992 (373 in total)
Performance:	0-60mph: 13.2sec
	Top speed: 112mph
Power & torque:	N/A
Engine:	Normally aspirated 6750cc V8, petrol, carburettor, 16 valves
Drivetrain:	Front-engine, RWD
Structure:	Separate chassis
Transmission:	Three-speed automatic
Weight:	2722kg

PRICE GUIDE
Launch price:	£8905
Excellent:	£90,000
Good:	£67,500
Average:	£47,500
Project:	£30,000

ROLLS-ROYCE
Corniche I

One of the few coachbuilders to create special versions of the Shadow was Mulliner Park Ward – although, as it was owned by Rolls-Royce, it was well placed to do so. Its two-door coupé and convertible had been around since 1965, but became known officially as Corniches in 1971. Britain's most expensive car at the time had the mechanical layout of the Shadow, but with even more lavish levels of equipment. Despite the saloon becoming the Shadow II a year later, the Corniche's title wasn't amended at the same time. Dropheads nowadays command a sizable premium.

SPECIFICATIONS
Years produced:	1971-1987
Performance:	0-60mph: 9.7sec
	Top speed: 126mph
Power & torque:	N/A
Engine:	Normally aspirated 6750cc V8, petrol, carburettor, 16 valves
Drivetrain:	Front-engine RWD
Structure:	Monocoque
Transmission:	Three-speed automatic
Weight:	2184kg

PRICE GUIDE
Launch price:	£11,556
Excellent:	£25,000
Good:	£17,500
Average:	£11,000
Project:	£6500

ROLLS-ROYCE
Camargue

Rolls-Royce tried to pull something special out of the bag with the Camargue, which, at £29,250 in 1975, took over from the Corniche as the UK's most expensive car. Using the Shadow platform, Italian styling house Pininfarina produced the car's razor-edged silhouette. The resemblance to its earlier Fiat 130 coupé and Ferrari GT4 2+2 designs was palpable; not quite what was expected for a flagship Rolls. The 6750cc V8 had extra (undisclosed) power, too, but in just over 10 years of production just 530 Camargues were made, including one Bentley-badged sister.

SPECIFICATIONS
Years produced:	1975-1986 (530 in total)
Performance:	0-60mph: 10.9sec
	Top speed: 118mph
Power & torque:	220bhp/330lb ft
Engine:	Normally aspirated 6750cc V8, petrol, carburettor, 16 valves
Drivetrain:	Front-engine RWD
Structure:	Monocoque
Transmission:	Three-speed automatic
Weight:	2390kg

PRICE GUIDE
Launch price:	£29,250
Excellent:	£38,000
Good:	£22,000
Average:	£14,000
Project:	£7500

ROLLS-ROYCE
Silver Spirit/Silver Spur

In 1980, Rolls-Royce pensioned off the 15-year-old Shadow and replaced it with the Silver Spirit – although the Shadow really did live on in spirit, because the new car was effectively the old one with a fresh skin. The angular body was completely new, while an update in 1989 resulted in fuel injection, more power, anti-lock brakes and a revised interior. The Silver Spur was a long-wheelbase offshoot and outlasted the short-wheelbase cars on which it was based. In 1994, the Flying Spur was added to the range, complete with Bentley-esque turbocharging.

SPECIFICATIONS
Years produced:	1980-1993
Performance:	0-60mph: 10.4sec
	Top speed: 126mph
Power & torque:	N/A
Engine:	Normally aspirated 6750cc V8, petrol, carburettor, overhead valves
Drivetrain:	Front-engine RWD
Structure:	Monocoque
Transmission:	Four-speed automatic
Weight:	2285kg

PRICE GUIDE
Launch price:	£85,609
Excellent:	£15,000
Good:	£12,000
Average:	£7000
Project:	£3750

ROLLS-ROYCE
Corniche II

The Corniche lived on beyond the Silver Shadow saloon on which it was based, and survived well into the Silver Spirit era. Although coupés were discontinued in 1982, the convertibles were updated enough for 1987 to justify a small change of name to Corniche II. Alloy and rubber bumpers replaced the chrome items and fuel injection became standard for all markets, as did ABS. Subsequent incarnations remained largely unchanged: 1989's Corniche III had colour-coded bumpers and better suspension, while the end-of-the-line Corniche S in 1995 incorporated a turbocharger.

SPECIFICATIONS

Years produced:	1987-1994 (452 in total)
Performance:	0-60mph: 17.1sec
	Top speed: 120mph
Power & torque:	215bhp/325lb ft
Engine:	Normally aspirated 6750cc V8, petrol, electronic fuel injection, 16 valves
Drivetrain:	Front-engine RWD
Structure:	Monocoque
Transmission:	Three-speed automatic
Weight:	1430kg

PRICE GUIDE

Launch price:	£115,660
Excellent:	£65,000
Good:	£50,000
Average:	£40,000
Project:	£20,000

ROVER

AFTER ROVER started car production in 1908, it was with robust, middle-class vehicles that it established itself. This image was consolidated after World War Two with models such as the P4 and P5, giving the marque its 'Auntie'

nickname. As if to rebel, Rover bit back with the radical P6 in 1963, which expanded into V8 realms in 1968 – the same year the firm became a part of British Leyland. Troubled years followed, although Rover still captured headlines with

its SD1 in 1976. It was sold to British Aerospace in 1988, and there was a national outcry when BMW took over in 1994. The loss-making firm was broken up in 2000, with MG Rover struggling until 2005 before it went into administration.

ROVER
P4 75 'Cyclops'

With the exciting new P4, Rover wiped its pre-war slate clean and presented a confident Studebaker-inspired – if rather upright – façade for the 1950s. The original P4 model shared its chassis and engines with the P3, but it appeared radically different. Its most striking feature (up to 1952) was the centrally-mounted headlight in the radiator grille – hence the car's 'Cyclops' nickname. Power was supplied by a 2.1-litre straight-six engine noted for its smoothness, and this was allied to a four-speed column-shift manual transmission.

SPECIFICATIONS

Years produced:	1949-1954 (33,267 in total)
Performance:	0-60mph: 23.1sec
	Top speed: 82mph
Power & torque:	75bhp/111lb ft
Engine:	Normally aspirated 2103cc straight six, petrol, carburettor, 12 valves
Drivetrain:	Front-engine RWD
Structure:	Separate chassis
Transmission:	Four-speed manual
Weight:	1451kg

PRICE GUIDE

Launch price:	£1106
Excellent:	£7500
Good:	£5500
Average:	£2600
Project:	£900

ROVER
P4 60/80

In 1953, the appeal of the P4 was widened considerably by the arrival of the four-cylinder model. The 2.0-litre engine was also used in the Land Rover, and after the smoothness of the straight-six it proved something of a disappointment. However, in practice it wasn't much slower than the standard car, and proved slightly more economical, too. The 60bhp engine remained in the P4 until 1959, when it made way for the more powerful 2.2-litre 80bhp engine – reason enough to re-designate the car the P4 80 in its final three seasons.

SPECIFICATIONS

Years produced:	1953-1962
Performance:	0-60mph: 19.3sec
	Top speed: 88mph
Power & torque:	60bhp/101lb ft
Engine:	Normally aspirated 1997cc four cylinder, petrol, carburettor, 8 valves
Drivetrain:	Front-engine RWD
Structure:	Separate chassis
Transmission:	Four-speed manual
Weight:	1481kg

PRICE GUIDE

Launch price:	£1163
Excellent:	£5600
Good:	£3900
Average:	£1850
Project:	£500

ROVER
P4 90/95/100/110

The six-cylinder P4 was offered in a wide variety of forms throughout its life. After its first facelift, the 2.6-litre IOE engine producing 90bhp was installed, giving it a 90mph top speed and effortless motorway cruising. However, that made way for the more powerful P4 100 in 1960. Although the engine capacities were similar, the new engine was a short-stroke version of the P5 3.0-litre, and even smoother in service. Performance was up and overdrive improved refinement at speed. All are refined, high-quality classics and currently undervalued.

SPECIFICATIONS

Years produced:	1954-1964 (60,724 in total)
Performance:	18.4sec
	Top speed: 90mph
Power & torque:	93bhp/138lb ft
Engine:	Normally aspirated 2638cc straight six, petrol, carburettor, 12 valves
Drivetrain:	Front-engine RWD
Structure:	Separate chassis
Transmission:	Four-speed manual
Weight:	1486kg

PRICE GUIDE

Launch price:	£1297
Excellent:	£7000
Good:	£4500
Average:	£2100
Project:	£600

ROVER
P4 105R/S

Top dogs in the Rover P4 range, the R and S models boasted the most power and easily topped the magic 'ton'. Introduced in 1956, the 105R and 105S shared the same engine as the 90, but had a high-compression cylinder head and twin SU carburettors to boost power to a very respectable 108bhp. The R and S designations referred to their transmissions – the 105R featured a Roverdrive automatic, while the 105S had a four-speed manual with overdrive. Both cars were luxuriously equipped, and today are in much demand among marque fans.

SPECIFICATIONS

Years produced:	1956-1959 (8755 in total)
Performance:	0-60mph: 15.9sec
	Top speed: 94mph
Power & torque:	108bhp/152lb ft
Engine:	Normally aspirated 2638cc straight six, petrol, carburettor, 12 valves
Drivetrain:	Front-engine RWD
Structure:	Separate chassis
Transmission:	Four-speed manual/auto
Weight:	1486kg

PRICE GUIDE

Launch price:	£1569
Excellent:	£7000
Good:	£5000
Average:	£2400
Project:	£650

ROVER
P5

Introduced in 1958, the Rover P5 established itself as the company's flagship, easily slotting in above the P4 105 models. In the process, it became the favoured transport of British prime ministers and royalty. The new styling had been penned by David Bache, while the monocoque body (Rover's first) had been engineered by Spen King and Gordon Bashford. Power was from a 2995cc version of the IOE that had first seen service in the P3, but which continued to deliver supreme smoothness and refinement. The cabin was predictably awash with wood and leather.

SPECIFICATIONS

Years produced:	1958-1967 (48,541 in total)
Performance:	0-60mph: 16.2sec
	Top speed: 96mph
Power & torque:	115bhp/164lb ft
Engine:	Normally aspirated 2995cc straight six, petrol, carburettor, 12 valves
Drivetrain:	Front-engine RWD
Structure:	Monocoque
Transmission:	Four-speed manual
Weight:	1613kg

PRICE GUIDE

Launch price:	£1764
Excellent:	£6000
Good:	£4500
Average:	£2200
Project:	£650

ROVER
P5B

The P5 was continuously developed during its life, first with the arrival of the more powerful 'Weslake Head' version, and then with the arrival of the handsome coupé. Nevertheless, the most exciting addition to the range came in 1967, when an ex-Buick V8 engine was squeezed under the bonnet to create the P5B. The gutsy new motor improved performance, and economy, too, while the appealing straight-six soundtrack had been replaced by a charismatic V8 rumble. For many, this was Rover's high-water mark, never to be topped.

SPECIFICATIONS

Years produced:	1967-1973 (20,600 in total)
Performance:	0-60mph: 12.4sec
	Top speed: 108mph
Power & torque:	161bhp/201lb ft
Engine:	Normally aspirated 3528cc V8, petrol, carburettor, 16 valves
Drivetrain:	Front-engine RWD
Structure:	Monocoque
Transmission:	Three-speed automatic
Weight:	1586kg

PRICE GUIDE

Launch price:	£2009
Excellent:	£8250
Good:	£6500
Average:	£2850
Project:	£800

ROVER
P6 2000/2200

In the UK the Rover and Triumph 2000 pairing created the executive car class as we know it today. Less bulky than the luxury models of old, but just as comfortable and a whole lot more economical. When it appeared the P6 was rather radical, with its skeleton structure and modern styling. The company gambled that it would appeal to traditionally conservative Rover customers, as well as attracting new ones. The bid worked, and the P6 went on to become a huge success. It was a none-too-shabby, if improbable, rally car, too.

SPECIFICATIONS

Years produced:	1963-1977 (213,890 in total)
Performance:	0-60mph: 11.9sec
	Top speed: 112mph
Power & torque:	113bhp/126lb ft
Engine:	Normally aspirated 1978cc four cylinder, petrol, carburettor, 8 valves
Drivetrain:	Front-engine RWD
Structure:	Monocoque
Transmission:	Four-speed manual
Weight:	1222kg

PRICE GUIDE

Launch price:	£1264
Excellent:	£3000
Good:	£2200
Average:	£1200
Project:	£300

ROVER
P6B 3500

Although the Rover 2000 was capable, in no way could it be described as quick. Yet with the installation of the ex-Buick V8 it became Rover's first Q-car, offering Jaguar-matching pace and poise. The P6B caught on rapidly, selling in huge numbers despite its loftier price tag than the four-cylinder models. It was initially offered in automatic guise only, but the balance was redressed in 1971 with the arrival of the more sporting, four-speed manual 3500S. Take care when buying, as clean body panels can hide many horrors beneath.

SPECIFICATIONS

Years produced:	1968-1976 (79,057 in total)
Performance:	0-60mph: 9.5sec
	Top speed: 117mph
Power & torque:	144bhp/197lb ft
Engine:	Normally aspirated 3528cc V8, petrol, carburettor, 16 valves
Drivetrain:	Front-engine RWD
Structure:	Monocoque
Transmission:	Three-speed auto/four-speed manual
Weight:	1272kg

PRICE GUIDE

Launch price:	£1801
Excellent:	£4000
Good:	£2500
Average:	£1400
Project:	£400

ROVER
SD1 3500/VDP

The SD1 was the final flowering of the Rover V8 line first masterminded by Spen King, Gordon Bashford and David Bache – although looking at its swooping Ferrari Daytona-inspired styling and BL build quality, it's hard to see the connection. Initially it sold like hot cakes, yet the shoddy quality soon started putting buyers off. The car was improved during its life, so the final models were fast, appealing and genuinely desirable, but the SD1 was always tarnished by the BL connection. Nowadays, there's excellent parts availability and club support.

SPECIFICATIONS
Years produced:	1976-1986 (303,345 in total)
Performance:	0-60mph: 8.6sec
	Top speed: 126mph
Power & torque:	155bhp/198lb ft
Engine:	Normally aspirated 3528cc V8, petrol, carburettor, 16 valves
Drivetrain:	Front-engine RWD
Structure:	Monocoque
Transmission:	Five-speed manual
Weight:	1313kg

PRICE GUIDE
Launch price:	£4750
Excellent:	£4000
Good:	£2500
Average:	£850
Project:	£350

ROVER
SD1 2000/2300/2600

As good as they are to drive, the six-cylinder Rover SD1s are always going to have two things going against them: a reputation for unreliability from their Triumph-designed engines, and the fact they are not V8-powered. And that's a shame, because the 2300 and 2600 are refined, relatively economical and punchy. The O-series-powered 2000 appeared in 1982 with the Series 2 facelift, and goes better than you might imagine, too. There's also enough room in the engine bay to climb in while servicing – and like all SD1s, that's still facilitated by plentiful parts supply.

SPECIFICATIONS
Years produced:	1977-1986 (303,345 in total)
Performance:	0-60mph: 9.5sec
	Top speed: 117mph
Power & torque:	136bhp/152lb ft
Engine:	Normally aspirated 2597cc straight six, carburettor, 12 valves
Drivetrain:	Front-engine RWD
Structure:	Monocoque
Transmission:	Five-speed manual
Weight:	1351kg

PRICE GUIDE
Launch price:	£7450
Excellent:	£2750
Good:	£1200
Average:	£550
Project:	£300

ROVER
SD1 Vitesse

Once referred to as 'the poor man's Aston Martin' by *Motor* magazine, the Vitesse remains a fast and effective bruiser of a sports saloon, despite the relatively paltry horsepower figure. Extrovert spoilers and racy trim completed the Vitesse's transformation, and, despite the SD1 having been around for six years when it first appeared, it was a surprise success for Rover. Later twin-plenum version homologation special, developed with help from Lotus, was more powerful, while TWR-prepared touring car racers won at international level.

SPECIFICATIONS
Years produced:	1982-1986
Performance:	0-60mph: 7.1sec
	Top speed: 135mph
Power & torque:	190bhp/220lb ft
Engine:	Normally aspirated 3528cc V8, petrol, electronic fuel injection, 16 valves
Drivetrain:	Front-engine RWD
Structure:	Monocoque
Transmission:	Five-speed manual
Weight:	1440kg

PRICE GUIDE
Launch price:	£14,950
Excellent:	£6000
Good:	£3500
Average:	£1650
Project:	£800

ROVER
213/216

The Viking longship had traditionally been the preserve of large cars, so when the Honda Ballade-based Rover 213 hit the market in 1984, it came as a bit of a shock. But it didn't take long for the word to get out – here was a Rover that was reliable and efficient, and within months of going on sale the 213 was selling like hot cakes. The range was extended in 1985 to include a locally-produced 1.6-litre engine, which was also available in fuel-injection form for the Vitesse version. All-round reliability was excellent, but the body suffered from horrendous rot all over. Not many left.

SPECIFICATIONS
Years produced:	1984-1990 (418,367 in total)
Performance:	0-60mph: 13.5sec
	Top speed: 104mph
Power & torque:	72bhp/82lb ft
Engine:	Normally aspirated 1342cc four cylinder, petrol, carburettor, 12 valves
Drivetrain:	Front-engine FWD
Structure:	Monocoque
Transmission:	Five-speed manual
Weight:	890kg

PRICE GUIDE
Launch price:	£5545
Excellent:	£1200
Good:	£700
Average:	£450
Project:	£250

ROVER
800 Vitesse/Sterling

As a replacement for the Rover SD1, the 800 should have hit the spot perfectly – it was sophisticated, powered by a range of multi-valve engines, and looked bang up to date. But those shiny new motors failed to deliver, and early build issues soon tarnished the car's reputation. The 2.5-litre Honda V6 was soon replaced by a torquier 2.7, and that transformed the Sterling and its new Vitesse stablemate into fast and effortless sporting saloons. Smart examples of the Honda-engined cars are now going up in value, yet there's little upward movement for the smaller fours.

SPECIFICATIONS
Years produced:	1988-1991 (49,496 827s in total)
Performance:	0-60mph: 7.7sec
	Top speed: 139mph
Power & torque:	177bhp/168lb ft
Engine:	Normally aspirated 2675cc V6, petrol, fuel injection, 24 valves
Drivetrain:	Front-engine FWD
Structure:	Monocoque
Transmission:	Five-speed manual/four-speed auto
Weight:	1427kg

PRICE GUIDE
Launch price:	£23,950
Excellent:	£2000
Good:	£1000
Average:	£550
Project:	£350

SAAB

SWEDISH AERONAUTICS firm Svenska Aeroplan Aktiebolaget thankfully shortened its name to SAAB when it started building cars in 1949. The curvaceous and aerodynamic 92 made great use of aviation principles in its design and was very advanced for its era. Subsequent developments built on the foundations of the 92 and kept much of its styling, up until the 1968 launch of the 99, which in turn grew into the 900. These cars brought Saab much acclaim thanks to their innovative use of turbocharging. Following the firm's 1980s partnership with Fiat General Motors took over in 1989, managing to destroy the marque's quirky character – and ultimately the marque itself.

SAAB
95/96 two-stroke

The Saab 96 was marketed as a new car when launched in 1960, but it was very closely related to the original two-stroke, front-wheel-drive 92 that had been around since 1949 and had proved to be a massive breakthrough in design. More than 10 years on, the 96, with its aerodynamic styling, independent suspension and tenacious roadholding, still seemed ultra-modern despite being a facelift. The 841cc two-stroke developed enough power to push the 96 to nearly 80mph. The 95 is the quirkily-styled estate version of the 96.

SPECIFICATIONS
Years produced:	1960-1968 (253,305 in total)
Performance:	0-60mph: 24.1sec
	Top speed: 79mph
Power & torque:	38bhp/60lb ft
Engine:	Normally aspirated 841cc two-stroke triple, petrol, carburettor
Drivetrain:	Front-engine FWD
Structure:	Monocoque
Transmission:	Three/four-speed manual
Weight:	803kg

PRICE GUIDE
Launch price:	£885
Excellent:	£4500
Good:	£3500
Average:	£1500
Project:	£550

SAAB
96 Sport/Monte Carlo

Introduced in 1962, the 96 Sport model was the raciest of the breed and reflected its competition breeding. The shrieking two-stroke pushed out a heady 57bhp and the model soon proved its mettle in rallying. Factory driver Erik Carlsson won the 1960, 1961 and 1962 RAC rallies in addition to the 1962 and '63 Monte Carlo classics. Three years later, the Sport was renamed Monte Carlo to reflect its top-level success. As marketing opportunities went, it was a case of too little too late, although this special edition is highly prized today.

SPECIFICATIONS
Years produced:	1962-1968 (2412/2453 in total)
Performance:	0-60mph: 19.3sec
	Top speed: 88mph
Power & torque:	57bhp/67lb ft
Engine:	Normally aspirated 841cc two-stroke triple, petrol, carburettor
Drivetrain:	Front-engine FWD
Structure:	Monocoque
Transmission:	Four-speed manual
Weight:	888kg

PRICE GUIDE
Launch price:	£1059
Excellent:	£6750
Good:	£5000
Average:	£3000
Project:	£1500

SAAB
Sonett II/III

The Sonett was an unusual addition to the Saab line-up. This Björn Karlström-penned two-seater coupé was powered initially by the 96's two-stroke, but then received Ford's V4 power unit for increased performance. The Sonett II made way for the heavily-revised, Sergio Coggiola-styled Sonett III in 1970: this retained the same centre section and, despite a more powerful 1.7-litre V4, delivered near-identical performance due to its extra heft. In 1974 the Sonett was phased out, having failed to find favour in the lucrative Stateside market.

SPECIFICATIONS
Years produced:	1967-1974 (10,236 in total)
Performance:	0-60mph: 14.4sec
	Top speed: 100mph
Power & torque:	75bhp/94lb ft
Engine:	Normally aspirated 1699cc V4, petrol, carburettor, 8 valves
Drivetrain:	Front-engine FWD
Structure:	Steel box chassis, glassfibre body
Transmission:	Four-speed manual
Weight:	810kg

PRICE GUIDE
Launch price:	£N/A in UK
Excellent:	£7000
Good:	£5500
Average:	£3500
Project:	£1250

SAAB
95/96 V4

In 1967, the two-stroke that had served so well for so long was joined by a V4. The four-stroke 1498cc Ford Taunus engine had been installed to take the 96 (and estate 95) further upmarket, but it also acted as an insurance against the threat of emissions regulations in Europe. The first V4 96s produced 55bhp – rising to 65bhp – and usefully boosted performance, with top speed climbing to over 90mph. It was in this form that the 96 remained to the end, gaining more equipment and impact-absorbing bumpers before finally being retired in 1980.

SPECIFICATIONS
Years produced:	1967-1980 (326,570/77,873 in total)
Performance:	0-60mph: 16.5sec
	Top speed: 96mph
Power & torque:	65bhp/85lb ft
Engine:	Normally aspirated 1498cc V4, petrol, carburettor, 8 valves
Drivetrain:	Front-engine FWD
Structure:	Monocoque
Transmission:	Four-speed manual
Weight:	873kg

PRICE GUIDE
Launch price:	£801
Excellent:	£3500
Good:	£2500
Average:	£1200
Project:	£450

SAAB
99

Although the 92 and 96 had done well for Saab, the firm's bosses knew that in order to retain customers, it would need to introduce a larger car. The 99 ended up being the perfect model to head the range as it was also innovative, quirky and individual. The wraparound screen and impressive aerodynamics headed up a front-wheel-drive car of commendable dynamic prowess. Its 1.7-litre engine had been developed in tandem with Triumph and UK engineering company Ricardo, although Saab developed the unit further to overcome a number of design faults.

SPECIFICATIONS
Years produced:	1968-1984 (588,643 in total)
Performance:	0-60mph: 15.2sec
	Top speed: 97mph
Power & torque:	80bhp/N/A
Engine:	Normally aspirated 1709cc four cylinder, petrol, carburettor, 8 valves
Drivetrain:	Front-engine FWD
Structure:	Monocoque
Transmission:	Four-speed manual
Weight:	925kg

PRICE GUIDE
Launch price:	£1288
Excellent:	£1750
Good:	£1250
Average:	£700
Project:	£200

SAAB
99 Turbo

During its lifetime, the 99 had received regular upgrades: first a larger version of its slant-four engine, then fuel injection to create the effective EMS sports saloon. However, in 1978, Saab created a legend – the 145bhp 99 Turbo. An early adopter of forced induction, the firm's fast but laggy 99 Turbo hit the market at just the right time – the second energy crisis of 1979 witnessed many people trading down from larger cars, and the seemingly economical new model offered all of the pace without the fuel consumption of the multi-cylinder opposition.

SPECIFICATIONS
Years produced:	1978-1981 (10,607 in total)
Performance:	0-60mph: 8.9sec
	Top speed: 121mph
Power & torque:	145bhp/174lb ft
Engine:	Turbocharged 1985cc four cylinder, petrol, electronic fuel injection, 8 valves
Drivetrain:	Front-engine FWD
Structure:	Monocoque
Transmission:	Four-speed manual
Weight:	1130kg

PRICE GUIDE
Launch price:	£7850
Excellent:	£3000
Good:	£2200
Average:	£1000
Project:	£450

SAAB
900

Saab cleverly evolved its models and augmented platforms, so when it launched the 900 in 1979 the newcomer was clearly based heavily on the decade-old 99. But given that car's continued popularity, this was no handicap. The 900 majored on safety, and its impact-absorbing bumpers, crumple zones and padded interior were touted as major selling points. It was developed through its life to keep pace with contemporary technology – and that maintained a healthy demand. Overshadowed by the Turbo, but considerably more durable due to being less stressed.

SPECIFICATIONS
Years produced:	1979-1993 (202,284 in total)
Performance:	0-60mph: 13.3sec
	Top speed: 105mph
Power & torque:	108bhp/121lb ft
Engine:	Normally aspirated 1985cc four cylinder, petrol, carburettor, 8 valve
Drivetrain:	Front-engine FWD
Structure:	Monocoque
Transmission:	Five-speed manual
Weight:	1214kg

PRICE GUIDE
Launch price:	£8675
Excellent:	£1800
Good:	£900
Average:	£600
Project:	£300

SAAB
900 Turbo

The star of the range was the 900 Turbo – earliest models pushed out 145bhp and delivered rapid and laggy performance. This was soon improved upon, first by the fitment of APC and engine management, and then with the arrival of the 175bhp 16-valve model in 1984. Three-door cars were the most popular, and have a near-cult following now – especially in Aero form. Can suffer from rust around the edges and the weak gearbox is an issue but, otherwise, the cars will take 200,000 miles, and more, in their stride. Three-door Aeros are worth a lot more than other models.

SPECIFICATIONS
Years produced:	1979-1993 (202,284 in total)
Performance:	0-60mph: 7.5sec
	Top speed: 135mph
Power & torque:	175bhp/205lb ft
Engine:	Turbocharged 1985cc four cylinder, petrol, fuel injection, 16 valves
Drivetrain:	Front-engine FWD
Structure:	Monocoque
Transmission:	Five-speed manual
Weight:	1340kg

PRICE GUIDE
Launch price:	£8675
Excellent:	£5000
Good:	£2500
Average:	£1000
Project:	£450

SAAB
9000/Turbo/Carlsson

For its first all-new car since the 99, Saab went down the collaborative route with the Italians. The 9000 was one of the 'Type 4' gang and, like its Lancia and Fiat cousins, was styled by Giorgetto Giugiaro. The engine was the familiar 2.0-litre Saab 99 unit, but mounted transversally, and the interior was ergonomically styled to make upgrading 99 owners feel right at home. Constantly improved throughout its life, the 9000 stayed on the pace right to the end of its production. Carlssons ended up with 225bhp and were 150mph flying machiines.

SPECIFICATIONS (Turbo)
Years produced:	1985-1992 (153,469 in total)
Performance:	0-60mph: 7.2sec
	Top speed: 141mph
Power & torque:	175bhp/201lb ft
Engine:	Turbocharged 1985cc four cylinder, petrol, fuel injection, 16 valves
Drivetrain:	Front-engine FWD
Structure:	Monocoque
Transmission:	Five-speed manual
Weight:	1316kg

PRICE GUIDE
Launch price:	£18,700
Excellent:	£1750
Good:	£1000
Average:	£700
Project:	£250

SEAT

SEAT STARTED life as a Fiat subsidiary in 1919, with its cars known as Fiat-Hispania. It became Seat – Sociedad Española de Automóviles de Turismo – in 1950 when the Spanish state took over. Fiat stayed very involved though, to the degree where most Seats were simply Spanish-built copies of Fiat models such as the 600, 850, 1400 and Panda (which was known as the Marbella), although there were one or two unique Seats. Fiat's involvement came to an abrupt end in 1981, leaving Volkswagen to snatch control in 1986. Since then, Seat has built its own individually-styled models, albeit using Volkswagen floorpans and engines, with its Ibiza the best-selling car in its range.

SEAT
600

The Seat Seiscientos kick-started the Spanish car industry, as a result of a tie-up between Franco's government, the Spanish banks and Fiat. It was effectively a badge-engineered Fiat 600, which ended up enjoying a long production run and becoming a Spanish legend in the process (earning the nicknames *pelotilla* and *seílla*). The 600 was an integral part of the country's post-Civil War economic boom – although, like its donor car, it was far from inspiring to drive. The Seat-only four-door was an interesting derivative. Rare in the UK.

SPECIFICATIONS
Years produced:	1957-1973 (797,350 in total)
Performance:	0-60mph: N/A
	Top speed: 66mph
Power & torque:	29bhp/40lb ft
Engine:	Normally aspirated 767cc four cylinder, petrol, carburettor, 8 valves
Drivetrain:	Rear-engine RWD
Structure:	Monocoque
Transmission:	Four-speed manual
Weight:	585kg

PRICE GUIDE
Launch price:	N/A in UK
Excellent:	£5000
Good:	£4000
Average:	£2000
Project:	£850

SEAT
133

The 133 was a strange mixture of old and new that was actually briefly imported into the UK and sold by Fiat dealerships. The floorpan, engine and gearbox were taken from the Seat 850, but the body styling was all-new, and looked like a cross between the Fiat 126 and 127. But compared with the cream of the '70s supermini crop, the 133 didn't stand a chance – and it flopped outside of its home market. In Spain, where tough import barriers had been erected and money was tight, its excellent fuel consumption and trusted mechanicals were positive selling points.

SPECIFICATIONS
Years produced:	1974-1980
Performance:	0-60mph: 18.5sec
	Top speed: 81mph
Power & torque:	39bhp/42lb ft
Engine:	Normally aspirated 903cc four cylinder, petrol, carburettor, 8 valves
Drivetrain:	Rear-engine RWD
Structure:	Monocoque
Transmission:	Four-speed manual
Weight:	780kg

PRICE GUIDE
Launch price:	N/A in UK
Excellent:	£1000
Good:	£600
Average:	£400
Project:	£250

SEAT
1200/1430 Sport

There's no doubting the Seat 1200 Sport's good looks, yet its creation was a hard-nosed business decision. The Spanish carmaker decided that it wasn't going to licence-build the Fiat 128 3P, and pledged to build its own instead. The car was known as the *Bocanegra* (Spanish for 'Black Mouth') because of its black polymer bumpers – perfect for Mediterranean driving conditions. The locally produced engine was shared with the Fiat 124, and the car's underpinnings were from the 127, so it was a real 'bitza' – but an appealing one. The body was not suited to northern climes...

SPECIFICATIONS
Years produced:	1975-1980
Performance:	0-60mph: 12.5sec
	Top speed: 102mph
Power & torque:	77bhp/82lb ft
Engine:	Normally aspirated 1438cc four cylinder, petrol, carburettor, 8 valves
Drivetrain:	Front-engine FWD
Structure:	Monocoque
Transmission:	Four-speed manual
Weight:	815kg

PRICE GUIDE
Launch price:	N/A in UK
Excellent:	£2200
Good:	£1600
Average:	£1200
Project:	£750

SEAT
Ibiza

For its first go-it-alone effort, Seat turned to the Italians and Germans to develop a convincing Fiesta-class car to sell in export markets. At first glance, the Ibiza looked the business, too – it had a smart Giugiaro-styled body and a range of System Porsche engines. Under the skin it closely resembled the Seat Ronda (itself a badge-engineered Fiat Strada), and that blessed the Ibiza with a roomy interior compared with its supermini rivals. Overall a little rough around the edges, but it was systematically improved following Volkswagen's arrival at Seat in 1986.

SPECIFICATIONS
Years produced:	1985-1993 (543,900 in total)
Performance:	0-60mph: 10.8sec
	Top speed: 115mph
Power & torque:	101bhp/94lb ft
Engine:	Normally aspirated 1461cc four cylinder, petrol, carburettor, 8 valves
Drivetrain:	Front-engine FWD
Structure:	Monocoque
Transmission:	Five-speed manual
Weight:	826kg

PRICE GUIDE
Launch price:	£4449
Excellent:	£800
Good:	£600
Average:	£450
Project:	£200

SHELBY

SHELBY THE car maker, as opposed to Shelby the racer, was created in 1961. The marque came about because Carroll Shelby heard that Bristol was no longer going to supply engines for AC – in the Ace – and thought it might be a good idea to install a V8 engine sourced in the USA instead. He approached AC with the idea, and managed to get Ford to back it, introducing the 'Shelby-AC Cobra powered by Ford' in 1962. It was a proper Anglo-American effort, with part-assembled cars being shipped to the USA, and completed in California. And a legend was born. Shelby continues to this day, with Carroll Shelby International building traditional Cobras, now based in Nevada, USA.

SHELBY
Mustang GT350

The GT350 was the brainchild of former chicken farmer and Le Mans winner Carroll Shelby. He took near-finished fastback coupés from Ford and reworked them into altogether more convincing sports cars at his California works. Chief among changes was a hike in horsepower from 271bhp to 306bhp from the existing K-code V8 engines, in addition to a weightier steering set-up and revised suspension geometry. Most appeared in Wimbledon White with blue racing stripes, the 350R edition being an off-the-peg competition version.

SPECIFICATIONS

Years produced:	1965-1967 (4117 in total)
Performance:	0-60mph: 6.7sec
	Top speed: 134mph
Power & torque:	306bhp/329lb ft
Engine:	Normally aspirated 4727cc V8, petrol, carburettor, 16 valves
Drivetrain:	Front-engine RWD
Structure:	Monocoque
Transmission:	Four-speed manual
Weight:	1265kg

PRICE GUIDE

Launch price:	£N/A
Excellent:	£125,000
Good:	£100,000
Average:	£60,000
Project:	£40,000

SIMCA

THE SOCIÉTÉ Industrielle de Mécanique et de Carrosserie Automobile was founded in France in 1935, building rebadged Fiats. This it did so well that, during the 1950s, it was able to take over a number of other manufacturers including Ford France, and put that company's V8 into production, as well as constructing its own rather distinctive designs. Chrysler, which was seeking a European toehold, took over in 1963, but it had similar problems running the marque as it suffered in the UK with Rootes. In 1970, Simca became Chrysler France, and was sold to Peugeot in 1978. It soon renamed all the models Talbot; the last Simca, a Solara, came out in 1980.

SIMCA
Aronde

The conventionally-engineered Aronde was the car that carried Simca into the world of constructors, the French firm having hitherto assembled licence-built Fiats (the Aronde retained a Fiat-conceived engine). The model proved popular in its home market, competing strongly with the Peugeot 203, and paved the way for a long line of middle-market Simcas. It was of monocoque construction with a typically soft Gallic ride. Rare even in France, especially as rust is a major enemy of these cars, so finding one won't be the work of a moment.

SPECIFICATIONS

Years produced:	1951-1964 (1,104,315 in total)
Performance:	0-60mph: 29.4sec
	Top speed: 73mph
Power & torque:	45bhp/61lb ft
Engine:	Normally aspirated 1221cc four cylinder, petrol, carburettor, 8 valves
Drivetrain:	Front-engine RWD
Structure:	Monocoque
Transmission:	Four-speed manual
Weight:	1140kg

PRICE GUIDE

Launch price:	£896
Excellent:	£2750
Good:	£1850
Average:	£1000
Project:	£500

SIMCA
Océane/Plein Ciel

Like the previous Week-End, the convertible Océane and coupé Plein Ciel are very effectively based on the frumpy Aronde saloon. Solid and dependable mechanics underneath won't set the world alight, but these delicately styled and likeable cars are pleasant to drive in an olde worlde way. More powerful engines were introduced along the way, including the charmingly named 70bhp Flash super special. Rare to the point of extinction in the UK, yet a ready following in France. Rust is a killer but the Simca Club will be happy to source you one.

SPECIFICATIONS

Years produced:	1957-1961 (11,500 in total)
Performance:	0-60mph: 18.5sec
	Top speed: 80mph
Power & torque:	56bhp/67lb ft
Engine:	Normally aspirated 1290cc four cylinder, petrol, carburettor, 8 valves
Drivetrain:	Front-engine RWD
Structure:	Monocoque
Transmission:	Four-speed manual
Weight:	1000kg

PRICE GUIDE

Launch price:	N/A in UK
Excellent:	£6500
Good:	£4750
Average:	£2800
Project:	£1500

SIMCA
1000/1200 coupé

In its desire to create a sporting version of the 1000, Simca turned to Bertone – and chief stylist Giorgetto Giugiaro – to fashion this chic coupé's outline. Under the skin, changes from the 1000 saloon were limited to the adoption of all-round disc brakes, with the donor car's robust 944cc engine/gearbox package being carried straight over. The model was upgraded to 1200S specification in 1967, by now packing an 80bhp 1204cc engine. This pert machine achieved little success outside of its homeland, due largely to its maker's near total lack of promotion.

SPECIFICATIONS
Years produced:	1963-1971
Performance:	0-60mph: 13.6sec
	Top speed: 107mph
Power & torque:	80bhp/76lb ft
Engine:	Normally aspirated 1204cc four cylinder, petrol, carburettor, 8 valves
Drivetrain:	Rear-engine RWD
Structure:	Monocoque
Transmission:	Four-speed manual
Weight:	891kg

PRICE GUIDE
Launch price:	£1493
Excellent:	£3200
Good:	£2500
Average:	£1200
Project:	£600

SIMCA
1000 GLS/Special

The Simca Mille was more than a baby car for a generation of young French families; it was a way of life. The rear-engined saloon boasted four doors, reasonable cabin space plus a large front luggage compartment. However, handling was 'interesting' due to its rearward weight bias. Later GLS and Special models had additional equipment and were powered by 1.1- and 1.3-litre engines. The improved performance made them easier to live with as a result. These cars suffer from widespread rust but are bulletproof mechanically.

SPECIFICATIONS
Years produced:	1969-1978
Performance:	0-60mph: 16.4sec
	Top speed: 88mph
Power & torque:	40bhp/47lb ft
Engine:	Normally aspirated 944cc four cylinder, petrol, carburettor, 8 valves
Drivetrain:	Rear-engine RWD
Structure:	Monocoque
Transmission:	Four-speed manual
Weight:	796kg

PRICE GUIDE
Launch price:	£758
Excellent:	£1750
Good:	£1250
Average:	£700
Project:	£400

SIMCA
1300/1301/1500/1501

After a long production run, the Simca Aronde made way for the far more modern 1300 and 1500. That Simca and Fiat were still close at the time of the new model's introduction was obvious when their cars were compared side-by-side – but the 1300/1500 was no worse for its Italian cross-pollination. Conventionally handsome, and pleasant to drive if you like a column shifter and soft ride. The 1969 facelift added a more corporate front end and integrated driving lights. Far better than its current 'forgotten' status would have you believe.

SPECIFICATIONS
Years produced:	1964-1976
Performance:	0-60mph: 13.0sec
	Top speed: 100mph
Power & torque:	81bhp/89lb ft
Engine:	Normally aspirated 1475cc four cylinder, petrol, carburettor, 8 valves
Drivetrain:	Front-engine RWD
Structure:	Monocoque
Transmission:	Four-speed manual
Weight:	1018kg

PRICE GUIDE
Launch price:	N/A
Excellent:	£1500
Good:	£1000
Average:	£700
Project:	£500

SIMCA
1100

When it arrived in 1967, the Simca 1100 was a remarkably advanced family model. Five doors, a roomy hatchback and front-wheel drive were all the ingredients for a successful mid-sized car. And in France, the 1100 certainly did the business, becoming a best-seller. Torsion bar suspension tuned for comfort and eager power units marked out the model as pleasant to drive. In the UK, its tendency towards tappet rattles and rusty bodywork marked it out unfairly as a banger before its time. Few survive as a result, and those that do are worth buttons.

SPECIFICATIONS
Years produced:	1967-1982 (2,000,000 in total)
Performance:	0-60mph: 16.7sec
	Top speed: 84mph
Power & torque:	60bhp/62lb ft
Engine:	Normally aspirated 1118cc four cylinder, petrol, carburettor, 8 valves
Drivetrain:	Front-engine FWD
Structure:	Monocoque
Transmission:	Four-speed manual
Weight:	935kg

PRICE GUIDE
Launch price:	£718
Excellent:	£1250
Good:	£850
Average:	£600
Project:	£250

SINGER

GRADUATING FROM bicycles and motorcycles, Singer built its first car in 1905, found success with the Ten in 1912, and during the 1920s rose to be Britain's third largest car maker. A certain Billy Rootes bought 50 Tens and used the profits from selling them on to start his own firm, but we'll talk about that elsewhere. The '30s recession hit Singer hard, and the firm had barely recovered when war broke out. Things were no better afterwards, and in 1955 it became another badge picked up by the Rootes empire. The cars retained their overhead-cam engines for a few years, then became Hillmans with a fancy grille and interior. Chrysler canned the marque in 1970.

SINGER
Nine Roadster/4A/4B

Inhabiting the same territory as MG's T-series, Singer's Nine Roadster used the beam axle and leaf spring suspension as found on the Ten and Twelve. It featured a vintage-looking open body with flowing wings and running boards. The 1074cc overhead-camshaft engine of 36bhp was lively enough in this wood-framed tourer, although the mechanical brakes left a lot to be desired. The 4A of 1949 changed the three-speed transmission for one with four ratios, while a year later the 4AB arrived with more compliant coil-sprung independent front suspension and better brakes.

SPECIFICATIONS
Years produced:	1939-1952 (7623 in total)
Performance:	0-60mph: 37.6sec
	Top speed: 65mph
Power & torque:	36bhp/48lb ft
Engine:	Normally aspirated 1074cc four cylinder, petrol, carburettor, 8 valves
Drivetrain:	Front-engine RWD
Structure:	Separate chassis
Transmission:	Three/four-speed manual
Weight:	840kg

PRICE GUIDE
Launch price:	£493
Excellent:	£8750
Good:	£7000
Average:	£4500
Project:	£2500

SINGER
SM1500/Hunter

For a small company like Singer the SM1500 saloon was a brave step, its blocky and slab-sided styling reflecting contemporary American trends. However, whatever the good intentions, the result was a very unappealing car with a rather plain appearance and a row of slats in place of a front grille. The 1506cc overhead-cam engine was sprightly enough, as was the 1497cc version fitted from 1951 (but which had more power). The 1954 update for the Hunter brought a more attractive and traditional look, with a proper grille but some glassfibre panels.

SPECIFICATIONS
Years produced:	1949-1956 (17,382/4772 in total)
Performance:	0-60mph: 33.7sec
	Top speed: 71mph
Power & torque:	48bhp/72lb ft
Engine:	Normally aspirated 1497cc four cylinder, petrol, carburettor, 8 valves
Drivetrain:	Front-engine RWD
Structure:	Separate chassis
Transmission:	Four-speed manual
Weight:	1184kg

PRICE GUIDE
Launch price:	£799
Excellent:	£3400
Good:	£2600
Average:	£1400
Project:	£700

SINGER
SM Roadster 4AD

The SM Roadster – a progression of the Nine Roadster – came along in 1951 to fight against MG's TD model, a car it bore rather a striking resemblance to. With an SM1500 overhead-cam engine reduced in size to 1497cc (to allow it to enter under-1500cc motor sport events), it had less power than the MG but similar performance thanks to its light weight. The battle lines were more evenly drawn from 1952, when twin carburettors became an option. With the extra carb, 58bhp was the more satisfying output. Some cars had bodies by Bertone, but these are very rare.

SPECIFICATIONS
Years produced:	1951-1955 (3440 in total)
Performance:	0-60mph: 23.6sec
	Top speed: 73mph
Power & torque:	48bhp/72lb ft
Engine:	Normally aspirated 1497cc four cylinder, petrol, carburettor, 8 valves
Drivetrain:	Front-engine RWD
Structure:	Separate chassis
Transmission:	Four-speed manual
Weight:	840kg

PRICE GUIDE
Launch price:	£724
Excellent:	£9750
Good:	£8000
Average:	£5500
Project:	£3250

SINGER
Gazelle

With the Rootes Group now in control of Singer, the marque was set to become another exercise in badge engineering, pitched between Hillman and Humber in the pecking order. However, in the new Gazelle – a plusher version of the Hillman Minx – Singer's 1497cc OHC engine was used at first, but was replaced in 1958 by Rootes' own OHV unit. Saloons, estates (rare and worth 25% more) and convertibles (pay double for those) were all available. Rootes updated the Gazelle almost every year until production ended in 1967, by which time it had a 1725cc engine and fewer curves.

SPECIFICATIONS
Years produced:	1955-1967 (83,061 in total)
Performance:	0-60mph: 21.4sec
	Top speed: 82mph
Power & torque:	53bhp/87lb ft
Engine:	Normally aspirated 1592cc four cylinder, petrol, carburettor, 8 valves
Drivetrain:	Front-engine RWD
Structure:	Monocoque
Transmission:	Four-speed manual
Weight:	1043kg

PRICE GUIDE
Launch price:	£898
Excellent:	£2650
Good:	£2000
Average:	£1000
Project:	£350

SINGER
Vogue

In Singer form, Rootes' new medium-sized family model was christened the Vogue. Originally intended as a replacement for the Gazelle, this slightly larger car kept the clan resemblance and was quite comfortably appointed inside. Powered by a 1592cc OHC engine, and due to Rootes' policy of constant change, it got front disc brakes from 1962 and a flatter roof plus changes to the window arrangement from 1964. A year later, the 1725cc engine from the Humber Sceptre found its way under the bonnet, meaning a generous jump in power to 85bhp.

SPECIFICATIONS
Years produced:	1961-1966 (47,769 in total)
Performance:	0-60mph: 14.1sec
	Top speed: 91mph
Power & torque:	85bhp/106lb ft
Engine:	Normally aspirated 1725cc four cylinder, petrol, carburettor, 8 valves
Drivetrain:	Front-engine RWD
Structure:	Monocoque
Transmission:	Four-speed manual, overdrive optional
Weight:	1092kg

PRICE GUIDE
Launch price:	£929
Excellent:	£2600
Good:	£1950
Average:	£850
Project:	£300

SINGER
Chamois

To sit alongside its mainstream Hillman Imp, Rootes also launched sportier versions. The Singer variant, from 1964, was dubbed the Chamois and followed the usual marque policy of walnut veneer inside and extra brightwork outside, including, from 1968, quad headlamps. All models had chrome grilles at the front – but these were for appearance's sake only since the Chamois was rear-engined. Still, it looked good! In 1966 a Sport version was launched. It had a 51bhp engine instead of the standard saloon's 39bhp. From 1967, there was also a pretty fastback coupé.

SPECIFICATIONS	
Years produced:	1964-1970 (97,567 in total)
Performance:	0-60mph: 25.4sec
	Top speed: 78mph
Power & torque:	39bhp/52lb ft
Engine:	Normally aspirated 875cc four cylinder, petrol, carburettor, 8 valves
Drivetrain:	Rear-engine RWD
Structure:	Monocoque
Transmission:	Four-speed manual
Weight:	711kg

PRICE GUIDE	
Launch price:	£582
Excellent:	£2100
Good:	£1600
Average:	£800
Project:	£250

SINGER
New Gazelle/Vogue

Chrysler-controlled Rootes swept aside all its old cars in the latter half of the '60s and replaced them with the new 'Arrow' range. Sadly, the boxy design wasn't too imaginative. The new Vogue was a Hillman Hunter boasting plusher touches and a touched-up nose; a year after its 1966 birth came the Gazelle. The chief differences between the two were that the Vogue had a 68bhp 1725cc engine while the Gazelle got only 61bhp from its 1496cc unit (unless it was an automatic, in which case it had the 1725cc engine). Both models were dropped in 1970, along with the Singer name.

SPECIFICATIONS	
Years produced:	1966-1970 (79,137 in total)
Performance:	0-60mph: 14.6sec
	Top speed: 90mph
Power & torque:	61bhp/81lb ft
Engine:	Normally aspirated 1496cc four cylinder, petrol, carburettor, 8 valves
Drivetrain:	Front-engine RWD
Structure:	Monocoque
Transmission:	Four-speed manual
Weight:	955kg

PRICE GUIDE	
Launch price:	£798
Excellent:	£1950
Good:	£1400
Average:	£700
Project:	£200

ŠKODA

ONCE A motoring joke because of their poor quality and cheap prices, Škodas have enjoyed a major metamorphosis in recent years under the ownership of Volkswagen. Formed in 1924 in Czechoslovakia, the firm's pre-war cars proved popular and sold well. After the war, Škoda found itself behind the Iron Curtain, which meant it concentrated on low-cost machines. During the 1960s, it moved over to building somewhat quirky rear-engined cars – at a time when many others were abandoning the layout – and continued for the next quarter of a century. VW took control in 1990, and revamped the range; Škoda today is a high-quality budget brand with a much-improved image.

ŠKODA
Felicia Convertible

The Felicia might not have been the most exciting technical package around, being based on the Octavia saloon, and it wasn't exactly quick, with just 53bhp on tap. But that didn't stop it being one of the most desirable cars produced in the Soviet Pact countries. Swing axle suspension meant that handling could be unpredictable, yet its styling largely made up for the lack of dynamic fizz. It was sold in the UK – the first Škoda to find its way over here – and was met with an apathetic response, despite its low price and overall reliability.

SPECIFICATIONS	
Years produced:	1959-1964
Performance:	0-60mph: 24.5sec
	Top speed: 85mph
Power & torque:	53bhp/55lb ft
Engine:	Normally aspirated 1089cc four cylinder, petrol, carburettor, 8 valves
Drivetrain:	Front-engine RWD
Structure:	Separate chassis
Transmission:	Four-speed manual
Weight:	863kg

PRICE GUIDE	
Launch price:	£809
Excellent:	£4000
Good:	£3250
Average:	£1750
Project:	£750

ŠKODA
Octavia

So-called because it was the eighth model line to be produced by the Czech manufacturer, the Octavia was a rugged, dependable and tough family car. Thoroughly conventional in its engineering, it was a development of the 1954 440 model. The vehicle was improved during its five-year production run, with the 50bhp 1221cc engines in the Super and TS models giving a welcome performance lift over the standard variant. Today, there are a surprising number of Octavias on the road in the UK, and they have an enthusiastic following.

SPECIFICATIONS	
Years produced:	1959-1964
Performance:	0-60mph: 29sec
	Top speed: 78mph
Power & torque:	43bhp/51lb ft
Engine:	Normally aspirated 1089cc four cylinder, petrol, carburettor, 8 valves
Drivetrain:	Front-engine RWD
Structure:	Separate chassis
Transmission:	Four-speed manual
Weight:	920kg

PRICE GUIDE	
Launch price:	£745
Excellent:	£3500
Good:	£2750
Average:	£1300
Project:	£450

ŠKODA
1000MB/1100MB

The rear-engined Škoda 1000MB represented the beginning of a very dark period in Škoda's history. It was considered a joke by many in the West, but in its home land the practical, reliable and easy-to-work-on machine had a waiting list. What is easily forgotten today is that the car, which was essentially a reskinned Renault Dauphine, was cheap to buy, cheap to run, and motorised a generation of Czechs and Slovaks. The 1000MB was one of the least expensive new motors you could purchase in the UK – and plenty of people did.

SPECIFICATIONS

Years produced:	1965-1977
Performance:	0-60mph: 30.8sec
	Top speed: 78mph
Power & torque:	48bhp/55lb ft
Engine:	Normally aspirated 988cc four cylinder, petrol, carburettor, 8 valves
Drivetrain:	Rear-engine RWD
Structure:	Monocoque
Transmission:	Four-speed manual
Weight:	787kg

PRICE GUIDE

Launch price:	£580
Excellent:	£2000
Good:	£1500
Average:	£750
Project:	£200

ŠKODA
S110R

Based on the S100 saloon, which itself was a revised 1000MB, the S110R coupé probably shouldn't have excited too many enthusiasts. Yet its introduction in the West coincided with a long rallying career that resulted in class wins on the RAC Rally on an almost annual basis. Powered by a 1107cc water-cooled four, mounted in the rear, the pretty S110R was also great value – even if its swing-axle rear suspension caused a few white knuckles on wet roundabouts. These models have a strong following on the classic scene today.

SPECIFICATIONS

Years produced:	1970-1980
Performance:	0-60mph: 17.7sec
	Top speed: 90mph
Power & torque:	52bhp/64lb ft
Engine:	Normally aspirated 1107cc four cylinder, petrol, carburettor, 8 valves
Drivetrain:	Rear-engine RWD
Structure:	Monocoque
Transmission:	Four-speed manual
Weight:	840kg

PRICE GUIDE

Launch price:	£1050
Excellent:	£4750
Good:	£3500
Average:	£1500
Project:	£500

ŠKODA
Estelle 105/120/Rapid

Škoda's MB1000 replacement was supposed to have front-wheel drive, and had the Estelle received the drivetrain it deserved, it may have been better received in the West. As it was, it ended up becoming the butt of countless bar-room jokes thanks to its total lack of desirability. In the mid-1980s, Škoda introduced a coupé version in the UK. No one expected very much of the car, least of all Škoda: marketing the Rapid strongly as the cheapest coupé in Britain was not a great message. Few examples remain, but those that do in the UK are cherished by their owners.

SPECIFICATIONS

Years produced:	1976-1991 (1,350,250 in total)
Performance:	0-60mph: 18.9sec
	Top speed: 87mph
Power & torque:	52bhp/63lb ft
Engine:	Normally aspirated 1174cc four cylinder, petrol, carburettor, 8 valves
Drivetrain:	Rear-engine RWD
Structure:	Monocoque
Transmission:	Five-speed manual
Weight:	880kg

PRICE GUIDE		Rapid
Launch price:	£1050	£3751
Excellent:	£1200	£3000
Good:	£700	£2200
Average:	£550	£1000
Project:	£200	£300

STANDARD

WHEN STANDARD was established in 1903, the word denoted quality and superiority; it was also chosen because the cars were made from standard patterns with interchangeable parts. And early cars certainly set a high standard, with the Flying models of the 1930s widely admired. Immediately postwar, it seemed Standard was on a roll; the firm bought Triumph and launched the advanced (in both engineering and looks) Vanguard. But when Leyland Motors took over in 1961, Triumph started to become the dominant partner of the pair. The marque died in 1963, as much a victim of changing language as anything else since the word 'Standard' was no longer as flattering as it had been."

STANDARD
Flying 8

Standard's smallest offering was surprisingly lively considering its 1.0-litre sidevalve engine. Built either side of WW2, the later cars lost the 'Flying' part of their name and were visually distinguished by a lack of bonnet louvres. Perhaps more significantly, they all gained a four-speed gearbox in place of the old three-speed unit. All used Bendix cable brakes, which are fine even today as long as they are set up correctly. Tourer and drophead coupé models were also offered, but these are even harder to find. When you do, expect to pay at least 50% more than for a saloon.

SPECIFICATIONS

Years produced:	1938-1948 (59,099 in total)
Performance:	0-60mph: N/A
	Top speed: 58mph
Power & torque:	28bhp/44lb ft
Engine:	Normally aspirated 1009cc four cylinder, petrol, carburettor, 8 valves
Drivetrain:	Front-engine RWD
Structure:	Separate chassis
Transmission:	Three-speed manual
Weight:	762kg

PRICE GUIDE

Launch price:	£314
Excellent:	£4250
Good:	£3250
Average:	£1500
Project:	£500

STANDARD
Flying 12 & 14/12 & 14HP

The 12 and 14 Standards were introduced in 1936, although revised in 1938 with a notchback instead of fastback appearance. After the hiatus of the war, they bounced back in 1945 with 3in-wider bodies giving more interior space. These sidevalve machines were simply engineered but robust. The 12 had a 1609cc engine while the more desirable 14 boasted 1776cc (which gave it a top speed of 70mph), but was initially for export only. The vast majority of 12s and 14s appeared as saloons, although drophead coupés and estates were also available.

SPECIFICATIONS

Years produced:	1936-1948
Performance:	0-60mph: 36.0sec
	Top speed: 65mph
Power & torque:	44bhp/69lb ft
Engine:	Normally aspirated 1609cc four cylinder, petrol, carburettor, 8 valves
Drivetrain:	Front-engine RWD
Structure:	Separate chassis
Transmission:	Four-speed manual
Weight:	1130kg

PRICE GUIDE

Launch price:	£480
Excellent:	£5000
Good:	£4000
Average:	£1750
Project:	£600

STANDARD
Vanguard I

With its modern beetle-back styling, the Vanguard replaced Standard's entire range of pre-war offerings in one go – there would be no more small cars from the marque until 1953. A full six-seater with a split windscreen, it introduced the world to the tough wet-liner four-cylinder engine that would go on to power everything from Triumph TRs to Ferguson tractors. Now-rare estate model was introduced in 1950, and all get a lower bonnet line and larger rear window from October '51. Try to find one with overdrive – it makes a big difference to fuel consumption.

SPECIFICATIONS

Years produced:	1948-1953 (184,799 in total)
Performance:	0-60mph: 22.0sec
	Top speed: 78mph
Power & torque:	68bhp/108lb ft
Engine:	Normally aspirated 2088cc four cylinder, petrol, carburettor, 8 valves
Drivetrain:	Front-engine RWD
Structure:	Separate chassis
Transmission:	Three-speed manual, optional overdrive
Weight:	1188kg

PRICE GUIDE

Launch price:	£544
Excellent:	£4000
Good:	£3000
Average:	£1400
Project:	£550

STANDARD
Vanguard II

The revised and more conventional three-box styling of the Phase II Vanguard lacked some of the character of the original, but it did provide better headroom and something in the region of 50% more luggage space. Getting in and out was easier too, as the front doors were longer. Suspension was stiffer, but the anti-roll bar had been deleted, so despite wider tyres the handling was still not a Vanguard strong point. With this car, Standard also became the first British manufacturer to offer a diesel engine (with a claimed 37mpg), although surviving examples are rare.

SPECIFICATIONS

Years produced:	1953-1955 (81,074 in total)
Performance:	0-60mph: 19.9sec
	Top speed: 80mph
Power & torque:	68bhp/108lb ft
Engine:	Normally aspirated 2088cc four cylinder, petrol, carburettor, 8 valves
Drivetrain:	Front-engine RWD
Structure:	Separate chassis
Transmission:	Three-speed manual, optional overdrive
Weight:	1270kg

PRICE GUIDE

Launch price:	£919
Excellent:	£3250
Good:	£2500
Average:	£1200
Project:	£450

STANDARD
8/10/Pennant

These were Standard's entries in the popular Minor/A30/Ford 100E market, and they were worthy rivals. The 8 came with an 803cc engine and was very basically equipped: you didn't even get winding windows until 1954, or an opening bootlid until 1957. The better-selling 10 did have these features from its inception in 1954 (except on the rare base-spec Family 10), and also a 948cc engine. The Pennant was a luxury 10 but with lengthened wings, two-tone paint, hooded headlamps and more equipment. They were outnumbered by about five-to-one by the other models.

SPECIFICATIONS

Years produced:	1953-1961 (351,727 in total)
Performance:	0-60mph: 38.3sec
	Top speed: 69mph
Power & torque:	35bhp/48lb ft
Engine:	Normally aspirated 948cc four cylinder, petrol, carburettor, 8 valves
Drivetrain:	Front-engine RWD
Structure:	Monocoque
Transmission:	Four-speed manual
Weight:	762kg

PRICE GUIDE

Launch price:	£481
Excellent:	£2400
Good:	£1800
Average:	£950
Project:	£300

STANDARD
Vanguard III

Not only was there an all-new and much lower body for the Phase III, but at last Standard did away with the separate chassis and embraced the concept of monocoque construction. As a result, the new car was lighter than its predecessors, with taller gearing that made it quicker, too. An 8in-longer wheelbase aided ride and handling, yet otherwise the running gear was pretty much as before. A curved glass windscreen in place of the old split-screen added another touch of modernity, and from 1957 an automatic gearbox option was available.

SPECIFICATIONS

Years produced:	1955-1958 (37,194 in total)
Performance:	0-60mph: 22.2sec
	Top speed: 77mph
Power & torque:	62bhp/113lb ft
Engine:	Normally aspirated 2088cc four cylinder, petrol, carburettor, 8 valves
Drivetrain:	Front-engine RWD
Structure:	Monocoque
Transmission:	Three-speed manual, optional overdrive
Weight:	1194kg

PRICE GUIDE

Launch price:	£850
Excellent:	£4000
Good:	£2250
Average:	£1000
Project:	£400

STANDARD
Vanguard Sportsman

This sporty variation on the Vanguard theme was the most distinctive car in the range. Never mind the standard two-tone paint – the main standout was that small-mouth grille that looked to have been an inspiration for the MG 1100. It was there because this was supposed to have been a new Triumph, but the company changed its plans at the last minute. The car does have a TR3 engine and bigger brakes, though. A real rarity now – the number of survivors in the UK is thought to be in single figures – hence the large price difference from other Vanguards.

SPECIFICATIONS

Years produced:	1956-1958 (901 in total)
Performance:	0-60mph: 19.2sec
	Top speed: 91mph
Power & torque:	90bhp/122lb ft
Engine:	Normally aspirated 2088cc four cylinder, petrol, carburettor, 8 valves
Drivetrain:	Front-engine RWD
Structure:	Monocoque
Transmission:	Three-speed manual
Weight:	1283kg

PRICE GUIDE

Launch price:	£1231
Excellent:	£5000
Good:	£3750
Average:	£1750
Project:	£700

STANDARD
Ensign/Ensign De Luxe

The Ensign started out as a stripped-down version of the Vanguard, lacking much of that car's chrome trim and using cheaper materials inside. It was also fitted with a small-bore engine of just 1670cc. After four-cylinder Vanguard production ended in 1961, the Ensign was revitalised as the De Luxe. That kept the cheap Ensign's grille, but had more chrome, a larger-capacity engine than the Vanguard, and all came with a four-speed floor shift. Overdrive was an option, and most cars came with disc brakes, too. Unlike the cheap Ensign, there was an estate option for the De Luxe.

SPECIFICATIONS

Years produced:	1957-1963 (18,852/2318 in total)
Performance:	0-60mph: 24.4sec
	Top speed: 78mph
Power & torque:	60bhp/91lb ft
Engine:	Normally aspirated 1670cc four cylinder, petrol, carburettor, 8 valves
Drivetrain:	Front-engine RWD
Structure:	Monocoque
Transmission:	Four-speed manual
Weight:	762kg

PRICE GUIDE

Launch price:	£900
Excellent:	£2650
Good:	£1850
Average:	£950
Project:	£350

STANDARD
Vignale/Luxury Six

That Vignale tag adds a hint of glamour, but really this is nothing more than a Vanguard Phase IV. Changes over the previous model were limited to bigger front and rear windows along with a new grille and back lights, although you also got the option of a floor-mounted gearchange. More significant changes came with 1960's Luxury Six. By then it was all over for the old four-cylinder lump, which had been replaced by the smooth twin-carb straight-six heading for the Triumph 2000. Longer rear springs improved the ride, and disc brakes were offered from 1961.

SPECIFICATIONS

Years produced:	1958-1963 (36,229 in total)
Performance:	0-60mph: 22.2sec
	Top speed: 83mph
Power & torque:	62bhp/113lb ft
Engine:	Normally aspirated 2088cc four cylinder, petrol, carburettor, 8 valves
Drivetrain:	Front-engine RWD
Structure:	Monocoque
Transmission:	Four-speed manual
Weight:	1194kg

PRICE GUIDE

Launch price:	£1021
Excellent:	£3000
Good:	£2250
Average:	£1200
Project:	£400

SUBARU

NOW A high-performance maker specialising in 4x4s, and with considerable rallying achievement to its name, Subaru's origins were very different. This division of Fuji Heavy Industry's first production car was the tiny and odd-looking 360 microcar of 1958, which stayed in production in Japan for 12 years. Exports worldwide began in the 1970s, but it wasn't until the 1980s that Subaru really started to establish itself, standing out with its permanent-four-wheel-drive passenger cars and competition exploits. The Impreza became as much a legend on the road as it was on the rally track, and remains the company's most desirable model with a massive enthusiast following.

SUBARU
360

The 360 was the first Subaru created to compete in Japan's emerging 'Kei'-class of microcars. Unlike the competition from Honda and Toyota, which were deliberately styled to resemble shrunken versions of the firms' full-scale models, the Subaru had a bug-like style all of its own. It was an interesting mixture of advanced – the independent suspension – and primitive – mechanical brakes and three-speed gearbox. Cramped, slow, utterly baffling to Europeans at the time... and yet the Subaru 360's following among enthusiasts is growing rapidly.

SPECIFICATIONS

Years produced:	1958-1971
Performance:	0-60mph: N/A
	Top speed: 59mph
Power & torque:	25bhp/30lb ft
Engine:	Normally aspirated 356cc two-stroke twin, petrol, carburettor
Drivetrain:	Rear-engine RWD
Structure:	Monocoque
Transmission:	Three-speed manual
Weight:	549kg

PRICE GUIDE

Launch price:	N/A in UK
Excellent:	£4000
Good:	£2000
Average:	£1000
Project:	N/A

SUBARU
Leone

Subaru's first official import into the UK was the mid-sized Leone saloon, although it was known simply as the 1600 in the UK. When it arrived in the mid-1970s, the flat-four-powered saloon (or estate, or coupé) stood apart from all its rivals by being offered with four-wheel-drive transmission alongside the more mainstream FWD models. And the farming set loved it for that, taking the oddball car to its collective heart. Saloons and coupés are rare in the UK as the importers concentrated on bringing in estates, but a number have subsequently been shipped in.

SPECIFICATIONS

Years produced:	1972-1981
Performance:	0-60mph: 13.0sec
	Top speed: 95mph
Power & torque:	77bhp/83lb ft
Engine:	Normally aspirated 1595cc flat-four, petrol, carburettor, 8 valves
Drivetrain:	Front-engine FWD
Structure:	Monocoque
Transmission:	Five-speed manual
Weight:	855kg

PRICE GUIDE

Launch price:	N/A
Excellent:	£3000
Good:	£2000
Average:	£850
Project:	£500

SUBARU
Leone II/1600/1800

The squarer-cut 1800GLF (as it was known in the UK) kept to the same refreshingly unconventional technical formula as before, but offered more equipment and interior room, and continued to sell well into the '80s. Subaru cleverly overlapped production of the first- and second-generation cars to maximise sales. Stand-out points in the most conservative of market sectors were a signature flat-four engine and frameless side windows. It's a shame so few survive, but the pillarless coupé (left) has picked up a good retro following in the UK.

SPECIFICATIONS

Years produced:	1979-1989
Performance:	0-60mph: 10.1sec
	Top speed: 103mph
Power & torque:	80bhp/92lb ft
Engine:	Normally aspirated 1781cc flat four, petrol, carburettor, 8 valves
Drivetrain:	Front-engine AWD
Structure:	Monocoque
Transmission:	Five-speed manual
Weight:	977kg

PRICE GUIDE

Launch price:	£4133
Excellent:	£1500
Good:	£1000
Average:	£650
Project:	£250

SUBARU
Leone III/XT

The chiselled mid-'80s Leone III expanded on Subaru's policy for sensible quirkiness, but the XT coupé was something else entirely. The wedge-shaped two-door added turbo shove to the thrumming flat-four, and was certainly quick enough. Unfortunately, that styling really was too much for most buyers to stomach, and it sold slowly. Yet for those who could live with the looks and the wacky interior, the XT rewarded with great build quality and peerless reliability. It rusted, but nowhere near as badly as its ancestors, and it now has bags of '80s retro appeal.

SPECIFICATIONS

Years produced:	1985-1989
Performance:	0-60mph: 8.7sec
	Top speed: 119mph
Power & torque:	134bhp/148lb ft
Engine:	Turbocharged 1781cc flat-four, petrol, fuel-injection, 8 valves
Drivetrain:	Front-engine AWD
Structure:	Monocoque
Transmission:	Five-speed manual
Weight:	1130kg

PRICE GUIDE

Launch price:	£12,000
Excellent:	£1750
Good:	£1100
Average:	£500
Project:	£250

SUNBEAM

FORMER CYCLE manufacturer, Wolverhampton-based Sunbeam, produced cars of great quality and sporting pedigree. It even made history with Britain's first Grand Prix win, at the 1923 French GP. However, in 1920 Sunbeam joined with Talbot and Darracq to form STD Motors Ltd, which proved an effective way to waste a lot of money. By 1935 it was bust, and the Rootes Group picked up the Sunbeam-Talbot bit to create a badge for upmarket Hillmans. The Talbot part was dropped in 1954 and Sunbeam once again became a more sporting marque, with the Rapier and Alpine. Chrysler killed off the badge in 1976, but shamefully re-used the name for its new small hatchback.

SUNBEAM
Alpine

The original Sunbeam Alpine was a stylish two-seater convertible version of the Sunbeam-Talbot 90. It shared the saloon's effective suspension set-up, but was powered by an 80bhp 2.3-litre four cylinder also used in the Humber Hawk. It was a heavy car, and didn't offer sparkling performance, yet it proved good enough to take outright victory in the 1955 Monte Carlo Rally. The Alpine was designed with the American market in mind, hence its soft ride, but failed to make the grade there. It eventually dropped out of production after just two years.

SPECIFICATIONS

Years produced:	1953-1955 (3000 in total)
Performance:	0-60mph: 18.9sec
	Top speed: 95mph
Power & torque:	80bhp/120lb ft
Engine:	Normally aspirated 2267cc four cylinder, petrol, carburettor, 8 valves
Drivetrain:	Front-engine RWD
Structure:	Separate chassis
Transmission:	Four-speed manual
Weight:	1270kg

PRICE GUIDE

Launch price:	£1269
Excellent:	£32,500
Good:	£19,500
Average:	£12,500
Project:	£8000

SUNBEAM
Rapier I-V

In design and engineering terms, the Rapier was a two-door version of the Hillman Minx. But the stylish Sunbeam was definitely that workaday car's glamorous cousin. During its production run, the Rapier went through four facelifts, starting out with 1390cc and ending up as a rapid 1592cc sporting saloon that continues to prove itself in competition. Like all Rootes Group cars of its era, build quality was good and the construction tough – and that's why so many survive today, and why the Rapier is such a popular classic choice.

SPECIFICATIONS
Years produced:	1955-1965 (76,954 in total)
Performance:	0-60mph: 21.7sec
	Top speed: 85mph
Power & torque:	63bhp/74lb ft
Engine:	Normally aspirated 1390cc four cylinder, petrol, carburettor, 8 valves
Drivetrain:	Front-engine RWD
Structure:	Monocoque
Transmission:	Four-speed manual
Weight:	1070kg

PRICE GUIDE
Launch price:	£1044
Excellent:	£5000
Good:	£4000
Average:	£1750
Project:	£700

SUNBEAM
Alpine Sports

The second car to bear the Sunbeam Alpine name was a very different proposition to its more portly predecessor. The new roadster was designed to compete with the MGA and appeal to American buyers. That meant a comfortable interior and sharp styling, but the Hillman Husky underpinnings and lack of a suitably sporting powerplant were always going to count against the Alpine. Sales were disappointing, and the final nail in the model's coffin was probably the appearance of the 1.8-litre MGB, which was a far more complete all-round package.

SPECIFICATIONS
Years produced:	1959-1968 (69,251 in total)
Performance:	0-60mph: 14.0sec
	Top speed: 98mph
Power & torque:	78bhp/74lb ft
Engine:	Normally aspirated 1494cc four cylinder, petrol, carburettor, 8 valves
Drivetrain:	Front-engine RWD
Structure:	Monocoque
Transmission:	Four-speed manual
Weight:	966kg

PRICE GUIDE
Launch price:	£972
Excellent:	£7500
Good:	£6250
Average:	£3250
Project:	£1100

SUNBEAM
Harrington Alpine GT

Made famous at the Le Mans 24 Hour race, the Harrington GT was essentially a Sunbeam Alpine GT with a swept-back hardtop that turned the roadster into a pretty, convincing-looking coupé. Of course, the reason for that shape was down to aerodynamics – and wearing the Harrington GT roof, the Sunbeam Alpine was faster down the Mulsanne Straight than it would have been with the standard steel hardtop. When the Harrington was sold as a standalone model, though, it struggled on the market and failed to dent the MGB's success.

SPECIFICATIONS
Years produced:	1961-1963 (425 in total)
Performance:	0-60mph: 12.7sec
	Top speed: 99mph
Power & torque:	93bhp/N/A
Engine:	Normally aspirated 1592cc four cylinder, petrol, carburettor, 8 valves
Drivetrain:	Front-engine RWD
Structure:	Monocoque
Transmission:	Four-speed manual
Weight:	972kg

PRICE GUIDE
Launch price:	£1225
Excellent:	£10,000
Good:	£8000
Average:	£4000
Project:	£2000

SUNBEAM
Tiger 260

Long before Ken Costello came up with the idea of stuffing an American V8 under the bonnet of a British sports car to produce the MGB GT V8, Rootes came up with the plan of fitting a 4.2-litre Ford V8 in the Sunbeam Alpine, to produce the Tiger. Sales took off in the USA far more than in the UK, where the underdeveloped suspension set-up was far more evident, but before the Tiger got into its stride the plug was pulled and the car went out of production. Why? Because Chrysler took a controlling stake in Rootes, and its own engine didn't fit in the Tiger.

SPECIFICATIONS
Years produced:	1964-1968 (7085 in total)
Performance:	0-60mph: 7.8sec
	Top speed: 117mph
Power & torque:	164bhp/258lb ft
Engine:	Normally aspirated 4261cc V8, petrol, carburettor, 16 valves
Drivetrain:	Front-engine RWD
Structure:	Monocoque
Transmission:	Four-speed manual
Weight:	1163kg

PRICE GUIDE
Launch price:	£1446
Excellent:	£32,500
Good:	£18,000
Average:	£12,000
Project:	£6000

SUNBEAM
Imp Sport

When Rootes decided to build a hot version of the Imp, it was logical to market the model as a Sunbeam, the group's most flamboyant marque. What we got was a car closely related to the original, yet thanks to the fitment of twin carburettors and wider wheels, not only was it faster in a straight line, it was more fun in the corners. Another surprising success given the dominance of the Mini-Cooper in the sector, but the Imp Sport's smooth little engine and beautifully set-up handling made it a rewarding drive for press-on drivers. Well worth seeking out now.

SPECIFICATIONS
Years produced:	1966-1976 (10,000 in total)
Performance:	0-60mph: 16.3sec
	Top speed: 90mph
Power & torque:	51bhp/52lb ft
Engine:	Normally aspirated 875cc four cylinder, petrol, carburettor, 8 valves
Drivetrain:	Rear-engine RWD
Structure:	Monocoque
Transmission:	Four-speed manual
Weight:	747kg

PRICE GUIDE
Launch price:	£665
Excellent:	£3000
Good:	£1600
Average:	£900
Project:	£300

SUNBEAM
Stiletto

Of all the Imp variants offered by the Rootes Group, the Sunbeam Stiletto remains by far the most desirable with collectors. The combination of the Hillman Californian's pretty bodyshell and Imp Sport's engine created a desirable sporting baby. Handling was further improved over the Imp Sport thanks to geometry changes to the front suspension, making this the best of the lot to drive. The jazzed-up interior with bespoke dashboard and reclining seats were further attractions, as was the ever-attractive quad-headlamp nose.

SPECIFICATIONS
Years produced:	1967-1973 (10,000 in total)
Performance:	0-60mph: 17.6sec
	Top speed: 87mph
Power & torque:	51bhp/52lb ft
Engine:	Normally aspirated 875cc four cylinder, petrol, carburettor, 8 valves
Drivetrain:	Rear-engine RWD
Structure:	Monocoque
Transmission:	Four-speed manual
Weight:	711kg

PRICE GUIDE
Launch price:	£726
Excellent:	£3000
Good:	£1800
Average:	£1150
Project:	£400

SUNBEAM
Rapier/Alpine

Although designer Roy Axe said it was pure coincidence that the Rapier looked similar to the Plymouth Barracuda, the resemblance between the half cousins was clear. Based on the Hillman Hunter, but not sharing a single panel, the Rapier (and its cheaper Alpine sister) were striking-looking cars that were well engineered, handled tidily and, in Holbay-tuned H120 form, quick. This model, which died when Chrysler rationalised the range, is overshadowed today by its earlier forebears – and rather undervalued as a consequence.

SPECIFICATIONS
Years produced:	1967-1976 (46,204 in total)
Performance:	0-60mph: 13.2sec
	Top speed: 103mph
Power & torque:	79bhp/93lb ft
Engine:	Normally aspirated 1598cc four cylinder, petrol, carburettor, 8 valves
Drivetrain:	Front-engine RWD
Structure:	Monocoque
Transmission:	Four-speed manual
Weight:	1016kg

PRICE GUIDE
Launch price:	£1200
Excellent:	£4000
Good:	£2400
Average:	£1200
Project:	£375

SUNBEAM-TALBOT
80

Introduced in 1948, the Sunbeam-Talbot 80 was the stylish entry-level model in a range that didn't fit easily within the Rootes Group. Effectively, Sunbeam-Talbots were touring versions of Humbers and Hillmans, and ended up being phased out in favour of the standalone Sunbeam. Although it was a stylish vehicle, the 80 was powered by the 1.2-litre engine also found in the Minx – a car not known for its sparkling performance. Despite that, it sold reasonably well to those looking for the style and image of the Sunbeam-Talbot 90 without the price.

SPECIFICATIONS
Years produced:	1948-1950 (3500 in total)
Performance:	0-60mph: 36.4sec
	Top speed: 73mph
Power & torque:	47bhp/61lb ft
Engine:	Normally aspirated 1185cc four cylinder, petrol, carburettor, 8 valves
Drivetrain:	Front-engine RWD
Structure:	Separate chassis
Transmission:	Four-speed manual
Weight:	1184kg

PRICE GUIDE
Launch price:	£889
Excellent:	£6000
Good:	£4000
Average:	£2250
Project:	£800

SUNBEAM-TALBOT
90

With an uninspiring suspension set-up – a beam-axle front and semi-elliptic springs all round, the Sunbeam-Talbot 90 shouldn't have been memorable to drive, and certainly not worthy of the great marque. However, its reasonably powerful 2.0-litre OHV engine produced enough grunt to allow the well set-up chassis to entertain its driver. The MkII of 1950 was a much better effort thanks to its chassis with coils and wishbone suspension – as was proved in rallying, where the car did rather well.

SPECIFICATIONS
Years produced:	1948-1954 (22,631 in total)
Performance:	0-60mph: 22.5sec
	Top speed: 80mph
Power & torque:	64bhp/101lb ft
Engine:	Normally aspirated 1944cc four cylinder, petrol, carburettor, 8 valves
Drivetrain:	Front-engine RWD
Structure:	Separate chassis
Transmission:	Four-speed manual
Weight:	1235kg

PRICE GUIDE
Launch price:	£991
Excellent:	£12,000
Good:	£6000
Average:	£2750
Project:	£1000

SUZUKI

THE SUZUKI MOTOR Company was formed in June 1954, and introduced its first car – the 360cc Suzulight – the following year, after closely studying a selection of European microcars. It proved a hit in its homeland, and was soon joined by van and pick-up versions. In 1959, it was joined by the Suzulight TL, a car styled eerily similar to BMC's Mini. The company concentrated on *kei-class* (miniature) cars well into the 1980s, producing the Fronte, Cervo and Alto – but it was the arrival of the scaled-down off-roader, the LJ80, that really opened up Suzuki to significant export success. Since then, it's grown into one of the world's leading manufacturers of small cars and off-roader.

SUZUKI
SC100GX Whizzkid

Launched as the two-cylinder Cervo in Japan in 1977, the Whizzkid started out as a coupé version of the Fronte Kei-Car, yet ended up being transformed when it came to the UK at the end of 1979 by the fitment of a 970cc four-cylinder powerplant. It was well-equipped and surprisingly sprightly, so it is no surprise that these baby racers have become something of a cult car, even if the values seldom match the interest these models generate. But with a mere 4096 imported into the UK, and rust being a killer, demand for the SC100GX Whizzkid is definitely on the rise.

SPECIFICATIONS

Years produced:	1977-1982
Performance:	0-60mph: 16.5sec
	Top speed: 85mph
Power & torque:	47bhp/61lb ft
Engine:	Normally aspirated 970cc four cylinder, petrol, carburettor, 8 valves
Drivetrain:	Rear-engine RWD
Structure:	Monocoque
Transmission:	Four-speed manual
Weight:	655kg

PRICE GUIDE

Launch price:	£3070
Excellent:	£2000
Good:	£1000
Average:	£600
Project:	£300

SWALLOW

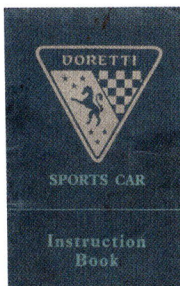

SWALLOW was born out of William Lyons' SS company. The founder of Jaguar sold his Swallow Coachbuilding Company to the Helliwell Group in 1945 with sidecar production being passed on to Tube Investments the following year. The coachbuilding company worked within the aviation business initially, but branched out into car production in 1954, with the introduction of its Triumph-based Swallow Doretti in 1954. It would prove to be the only car produced by the company – and its supply situation was made more difficult when Standard-Triumph chairman Sir John Black had a crash in one. In 1956 Swallow Coachbuilding was sold to the sidecar manufacturer Watsonian.

SWALLOW
Doretti

The Triumph TR2-based Swallow Doretti is one of the most sought-after British specials of the 1950s because of its combination of simple, elegant style and rugged TR2 mechanicals. The bodyshell had a steel inner structure with aluminium panels attached, mated to an immensely strong tubular frame chassis. The car was as good to drive as the Triumph on which it was based, and the leather-trimmed interior was well made – but its advantages over its donor weren't sufficient enough to warrant the hefty premium.

SPECIFICATIONS

Years produced:	1954-1955 (250 in total)
Performance:	0-60mph: 12.3sec
	Top speed: 100mph
Power & torque:	90bhp/117lb ft
Engine:	Normally aspirated 1991cc four cylinder, petrol, carburettor, 8 valves
Drivetrain:	Front-engine RWD
Structure:	Separate chassis
Transmission:	Four-speed manual with overdrive
Weight:	864kg

PRICE GUIDE

Launch price:	£1102
Excellent:	£25,000
Good:	£14,000
Average:	£8000
Project:	£5000

TALBOT

INITIALLY, TALBOT built French Clément cars from 1903, but it gradually moved into constructing its own machines. It became a member of the Sunbeam-Talbot-Darracq partnership in 1920 and forged a reputation as a builder of comprehensively-engineered cars with true sporting prowess. In 1935, though, the Rootes Group gained control and renamed the marque Sunbeam-Talbot. That should probably have been the end of the name in its own right, but when Peugeot took over what remained of Rootes in 1978, it decided to resurrect the badge. These 'new' Talbots included the Alpine, Horizon, Solara and Samba, but poor sales prompted Peugeot to kill off Talbot once more in 1986.

TALBOT
Solara

Chrysler had huge ambition for its European division during the early 1970s – and using the diverse Rootes and Simca ranges as a starting point, it drew up a modern-looking range of FWD hatchbacks. First off the blocks was the Alpine in 1975, which was good enough to win the European Car of The Year award. It was smart and contemporary, but the politics of its maker took over and when the Americans pulled out in 1978, the Chryslers became Talbots. The rusty, tappety Solara should have been more successful, but it really was less than the sum of its parts.

SPECIFICATIONS

Years produced:	1980-1985 (185,827 in UK)
Performance:	0-60mph: 14.6sec
	Top speed: 96mph
Power & torque:	68bhp/79lb ft
Engine:	Normally aspirated 1294cc four cylinder, petrol, carburettor, 8 valves
Drivetrain:	Front-engine FWD
Structure:	Monocoque
Transmission:	Four-speed manual
Weight:	1040kg

PRICE GUIDE

Launch price:	£3872
Excellent:	£1000
Good:	£700
Average:	£400
Project:	£250

TALBOT
Sunbeam Lotus

Chrysler commissioned Lotus to produce an effective entrant for international rallying. The Norfolk firm took a 1.6GLS shell, installed its own slant-four 2.2-litre 16-valve engine and a ZF gearbox, fitted light alloy wheels and uprated the suspension. The result proved effective in rallying, winning the 1980 RAC event. The road-going version was also quick and balanced, although it was priced higher than the comparable Vauxhall Chevette HS – and currently, values are a long way ahead of its homologation special-style opposition from Luton.

SPECIFICATIONS

Years produced:	1979-1983 (2308 in total)
Performance:	0-60mph: 7.4sec
	Top speed: 121mph
Power & torque:	150bhp/150lb ft
Engine:	Normally aspirated 2174cc four cylinder, petrol, carburettor, 16 valves
Drivetrain:	Front-engine RWD
Structure:	Monocoque
Transmission:	Five-speed manual
Weight:	960kg

PRICE GUIDE

Launch price:	£6995
Excellent:	£10,000
Good:	£6000
Average:	£3250
Project:	£1750

TALBOT
Tagora

Originally known as the Chrysler C9 project – but, thanks to the Peugeot takeover, the big Chrysler became a luxury Talbot that no-one wanted. Meanwhile, Peugeot had the 604 and Citroën's offering in the sector was the charismatic CX. When the Tagora arrived sporting a combination of Chrysler and Peugeot engineering, it underwhelmed in the marketplace. Today, beyond the 'duffer' image, the car remains pleasant to drive, and is surprisingly rapid in V6 form with 163bhp on tap. Few survive now, yet a cult following means their future is safe...

SPECIFICATIONS (SX)

Years produced:	1981-1984 (23,400 in total)
Performance:	0-60mph: 7.9sec
	Top speed: 119mph
Power & torque:	163bhp/170lb ft
Engine:	Normally aspirated 2664cc V6, petrol, carburettor, 12 valves
Drivetrain:	Front-engine RWD
Structure:	Monocoque
Transmission:	Five-speed manual
Weight:	1255kg

PRICE GUIDE

Launch price:	£7990
Excellent:	£1750
Good:	£1000
Average:	£650
Project:	£250

TALBOT
Samba

The final product of the Talbot marque was a truly Anglo-French effort, with Peugeot 104 underpinnings (on a unique wheelbase) and UK styling. Project T15 was designed to replace the shortlived Sunbeam, and was a very different beast. It had a predictable engine and model line-up, but the arrival of the cabrio in 1983 was a innovative marketing step that added some glamour to the range. The French-built Samba failed to capture the hearts of UK buyers, and despite being good to drive and economical it was overshadowed by the Metro and Fiesta.

SPECIFICATIONS

Years produced:	1981-1986
Performance:	0-60mph: 11.5sec
	Top speed: 101mph
Power & torque:	80bhp/80lb ft
Engine:	Normally aspirated 1360cc four cylinder, petrol, carburettor, 8 valves
Drivetrain:	Front-engine FWD
Structure:	Monocoque
Transmission:	Four-speed manual
Weight:	810kg

PRICE GUIDE

Launch price:	£5380
Excellent:	£3500
Good:	£1750
Average:	£1000
Project:	£450

TATRA

TATRA CAN trace its origins back to horse-drawn carriages in 1850, but when this Czechoslovakian concern started building cars from 1919, it soon became one of Europe's most imaginative car builders. After early conventionality, its products took an unorthodox turn, featuring streamlining and a rear-mounted V8 engine on 1934's T77. Post-war, under Communist control, this theme continued, and Tatra was responsible for the extraordinary T603 and T613, the latter funded by damages awarded against Volkswagen over the design of the Beetle. In 1996, by which time its designs had become outdated, Tatra withdrew from cars to concentrate on trucks.

TATRA
T603

If you were a senior Communist in any of the Eastern Bloc countries from 1956, the chances are that your vehicular possibilities included the Tatra T603. And if you had any sense of style, you'd have made a beeline straight for this Czech plutocrat with its air-cooled rear-mounted V8 and highly aerodynamic styling. it would have been a wise choice, too, as interior room was massive, the engine note was exceptional, and build quality was first rate. Most survived the Cold War and, subsequently, a great many have headed west, where they are now revered by fans.

SPECIFICATIONS

Years produced:	1955-1975 (22,422 in total)
Performance:	0-60mph: 16.0sec
	Top speed: 100mph
Power & torque:	105bhp/123lb ft
Engine:	Normally aspirated 2474cc V8, petrol, carburettor, 16 valves
Drivetrain:	Rear-engine RWD
Structure:	Monocoque
Transmission:	Four-speed manual
Weight:	1470kg

PRICE GUIDE

Launch price:	N/A in UK
Excellent:	£9000
Good:	£5500
Average:	£3000
Project:	£1750

TATRA
T613

The streamlined T603 made way for the brick-like T613 in 1974. It was styled by Vignale in Italy around the same air-cooled rear-mounted V8 engine layout, although it had been increased in capacity to 3.5 litres from the earlier 2.5. Performance was dramatically improved, although build quality slipped as the years passed by. Interestingly, the Tatra T613 was officially imported into the UK during the 1990s, but despite rocketship performance from its 4.3-litre engine, only a handful were sold and, consequently, they are cheap to buy now.

SPECIFICATIONS

Years produced:	1974-1996
Performance:	0-60mph: 11.0sec
	Top speed: 116mph
Power & torque:	165bhp/195lb ft
Engine:	Normally aspirated 3495cc V8, petrol, carburettor, 16 valves
Drivetrain:	Rear engine RWD
Structure:	Monocoque
Transmission:	Four-speed manual
Weight:	1600kg

PRICE GUIDE

Launch price:	N/A in UK
Excellent:	£5000
Good:	£3500
Average:	£2200
Project:	£1000

TOYOTA

THE FIRST TOYOTAS appeared a few years before the Second World War, but real production only got underway once the conflict was over. Early designs were American-inspired; hardly surprising as the company had started exporting its substantial Crown to that country in 1957. European sales kicked off in 1962, with the Corona and Corolla all proving big money-generators for the Japanese marque. Particularly notable models have been the sporting 2000, MR2 and Celica. Toyota now vies with GM as the world's biggest car maker, with factories around the globe. It claims its long-running Corolla to be the world's biggest-selling car, with over 30 million sold.

TOYOTA
Landcruiser

Although the Land Cruiser failed to find sales success in the UK and Europe until the 1980s and beyond, it's the 40-Series (1960-84) cars that are the most desirable, attracting a cult following – probably on the coat tails of the J-Tin (Japanese classic car) movement. Their bulletproof reliability is responsible for Land-Rover's loss of export sales over the years. Many have been imported into the UK from dry climates, but rust is still a major killer once they hit damper climes. Very cool, great to look at, ultra-dependable, and not yet expensive.

SPECIFICATIONS

Years produced:	1960-1984
Performance:	0-60mph: 11.0sec
	Top speed: 97mph
Power & torque:	135bhp/210lb ft
Engine:	Normally aspirated 4230cc straight six, petrol, carburettor, 12 valves
Drivetrain:	Front-engine AWD
Structure:	Monocoque
Transmission:	Four-speed manual
Weight:	1848kg

PRICE GUIDE

Launch price:	N/A
Excellent:	£12,000
Good:	£6500
Average:	£4000
Project:	£2000

TOYOTA
Sports 800

Considering the S800 was Toyota's first sports car, it was an impressive effort. Cast very much in the mould of the MG Midget, it was based on the Publica mini-car, and was conceived for the *Kei*-class. Its flat-twin was eager and capable of pushing the Sports 800 to almost 100mph. Unlike its rival, the Honda S800, the Toyota was no technical *tour de force*, with solid rear axle and drum brakes – but the body had been styled with particular attention to aerodynamics, and it featured a useful targa top. Never imported into the UK, but a few have subsequently made the trip.

SPECIFICATIONS

Years produced:	1965-1970 (3131 in total)
Performance:	0-60mph: 11.0sec
	Top speed: 97mph
Power & torque:	44bhp/49lb ft
Engine:	Normally aspirated 791cc twin, petrol, carburettor, four valves
Drivetrain:	Front-engine RWD
Structure:	Monocoque
Transmission:	Four-speed manual
Weight:	591kg

PRICE GUIDE

Launch price:	N/A
Excellent:	£25,000
Good:	£17,500
Average:	£8000
Project:	N/A

TOYOTA
2000GT

Thanks to its drop-dead good looks and a guest appearance in *You Only Love Twice*, the 2000GT put Toyota on the world map. Produced in a joint venture with Yamaha, the gorgeous 2000GT was offered to Toyota when Yamaha failed to excite Nissan into producing the car – and a mere 337 were built between 1967 and 1970. And that's a shame given its fantastic technical specification, which boasted a jewel-like twin-cam straight six that pumped out 150bhp to give a 135mph maximum speed. Revered as an absolute classic, and one of Japan's finest ever.

SPECIFICATIONS

Years produced:	1967-1970 (337 in total)
Performance:	0-60mph: 8.4sec
	Top speed: 137mph
Power & torque:	150bhp/129lb ft
Engine:	Normally aspirated 1988cc six cylinder, petrol, carburettor, 12 valves
Drivetrain:	Front-engine RWD
Structure:	Monocoque
Transmission:	Five-speed manual
Weight:	1125kg

PRICE GUIDE

Launch price:	N/A
Excellent:	£325,000
Good:	£175,000
Average:	£120,000
Project:	N/A

TOYOTA
Celica 1600 ST

When new, these sporting coupés were considered the dynamic inferiors of their European rivals, but considering the A20/35-generation Celica was to the Carina what the Capri was to the Cortina, they were very much the same thing. Sold in huge numbers in Japan and the USA, the Celica was a braver choice over here, although bulletproof reliability made ownership a painless experience. Rust and indifference killed most, but their chintzy mid-Atlantic styling has made these cult cars in the burgeoning Japanese car scene.

SPECIFICATIONS
Years produced: 1970-1977
Performance: 0-60mph: 11.5sec
Top speed: 104mph
Power & torque: 105bhp/101lb ft
Engine: Normally aspirated 1588cc four cylinder, petrol, carburettor, 8 valves
Drivetrain: Front-engine RWD
Structure: Monocoque
Transmission: Four-speed manual
Weight: 1100kg

PRICE GUIDE
Launch price: £1362
Excellent: £7000
Good: £4000
Average: £1750
Project: £1000

TOYOTA
Crown

The third-generation MS60 Crown was a bold leap forward stylistically. Out went conventionally boxy looks, and in their place came swooping flanks and the characteristic double-deck front lights. In the UK, the Crown was offered in saloon and estate form only, and we were denied the stylish coupé (left). Its straight-six engine was lusty and thirsty, the rest reliable and well made. Sloppy to drive compared with European rivals, but that's less of an issue now, and most cars in the UK are personal imports. A head-turner.

SPECIFICATIONS
Years produced: 1971-1974
Performance: 0-60mph: 12.5sec
Top speed: 110mph
Power & torque: 150bhp/164lb ft
Engine: Normally aspirated 2563cc straight six, petrol, carburettor, 12 valves
Drivetrain: Front-engine RWD
Structure: Monocoque
Transmission: Five-speed manual/three-speed auto
Weight: 1302kg

PRICE GUIDE
Launch price: £1362
Excellent: £4000
Good: £3000
Average: £1750
Project: £1000

TOYOTA
Celica GT

The facelifted RA25 and R28 Celicas introduced the popular liftback bodystyle (left), and provided Toyota with the perfect weapon with which to chase Capris. Referred to by many as the 'Mustang-shape' car, the GT version was genuinely quick thanks to its 124bhp twin-cam 1600. Sales were limited due to lack of badge kudos in the UK. Japanese-market cars were also treated to a mighty 2.0-litre Yamaha-headed power unit, dubbed the 18R-GU, that pushed out 134bhp. The spectre of rusty cars has long since been banished, with many cars now fully restored.

SPECIFICATIONS
Years produced: 1974-1977
Performance: 0-60mph: 8.8sec
Top speed: 120mph
Power & torque: 124bhp/113lb ft
Engine: Normally aspirated 1588cc four cylinder, petrol, carburettor, 8 valves
Drivetrain: Front-engine RWD
Structure: Monocoque
Transmission: Five-speed manual
Weight: 1116kg

PRICE GUIDE
Launch price: £2345
Excellent: £7500
Good: £5000
Average: £2750
Project: £1350

TOYOTA
Celica

Along with the Carina A40, the Celica came in for some serious updates in 1977. Sadly, whereas the saloon it was based upon became better-looking and more appealing for western tastes, the new coupé and liftbacks lost their charming mid-Atlantic good looks. But despite that, the Celica proved popular in the UK and stacked up well against the Capri and Cavalier Sportshatch. Not as highly valued as the baby 'Pony car' predecessor, though. The six-cylinder Supra version was not brought into the UK or Europe.

SPECIFICATIONS
Years produced: 1974-1977
Performance: 0-60mph: 9.5sec
Top speed: 113mph
Power & torque: 118bhp/112lb ft
Engine: Normally aspirated 1968cc four cylinder, petrol, carburettor, 8 valves
Drivetrain: Front-engine RWD
Structure: Monocoque
Transmission: Five-speed manual
Weight: 1100kg

PRICE GUIDE
Launch price: £2345
Excellent: £3500
Good: £2000
Average: £1250
Project: £850

TOYOTA
Celica Supra

Known as the Celica XX in Japan, the Celica Supra was heavily based on the Toyota Celica range. The major difference between the two was the use of a six-cylinder engine up front, which gave Toyota a direct rival to the Capri 2.8 Injection and Alfa Romeo GTV6 in Europe. The power output started out at 174bhp and rose to 178bhp. Even so, the Supra was always more of a luxury barge than a sports car. Lairy rear-wheel-drive handling made them popular in the drifting scene, but these cars are now emerging as true classics.

SPECIFICATIONS
Years produced: 1982-1985 (863,700 in total)
Performance: 0-60mph: 8.7sec
Top speed: 131mph
Power & torque: 168bhp/169lb ft
Engine: Normally aspirated 2759cc six cylinder, petrol, fuel injection, 12 valves
Drivetrain: Front-engine RWD
Structure: Monocoque
Transmission: Five-speed manual
Weight: 1265kg

PRICE GUIDE
Launch price: £9888
Excellent: £4000
Good: £2750
Average: £1400
Project: £650

TOYOTA
Corolla GT (FWD)

Although the Tercel was Europe's first FWD Toyota, it was the 1983 Corolla E80 that held the honour of being the first *popular* front-driver here. It was conservatively styled and remains pretty forgettable today, but unfairly so if the excellence of the GT is anything to go by. It's revvy and responsive, handles well and, most importantly for any '80s hot-shoe, it was considerably quicker than the market-leading Ford Escort XR3i. You'll struggle to find one in rust-free condition but, even if you do, chances are it won't be cheap – buyers have cottoned on.

SPECIFICATIONS
Years produced: 1983-1987 (3,270,000 in total)
Performance: 0-60mph: 8.7sec
Top speed: 118mph
Power & torque: 130bhp/110lb ft
Engine: Normally aspirated 1587cc four cylinder, petrol, fuel injection, 16 valves
Drivetrain: Front-engine FWD
Structure: Monocoque
Transmission: Five-speed manual
Weight: 930kg

PRICE GUIDE
Launch price: £7295
Excellent: £1400
Good: £900
Average: £550
Project: £250

TOYOTA
Corolla GT (AE86)

In 1983, there was a very confusing situation in the UK – you could buy a Corolla GT with either front- or rear-wheel drive. Both were exceptional fun. However, it's the RWD AE86 that has captured the hearts of a generation of Playstation fans, drift fanatics and club rally drivers because, with 122bhp of twin-cam power under the bonnet and RS2000-style tail-happy handling, it has become a legend in its own lifetime and values have gone stratospheric, for what is essentially a fairly humdrum Japanese coupé. Rust is an ever-present issue, but most are cherished now.

SPECIFICATIONS
Years produced: 1983-1987 (958,760 in total)
Performance: 0-60mph: 8.7sec
Top speed: 122mph
Power & torque: 122bhp/105lb ft
Engine: Normally aspirated 1587cc four cylinder, petrol, fuel injection, 16 valves
Drivetrain: Front-engine RWD
Structure: Monocoque
Transmission: Five-speed manual
Weight: 915kg

PRICE GUIDE
Launch price: £6995
Excellent: £9000
Good: £6000
Average: £3500
Project: £2000

TOYOTA
Celica GT

Toyota might have been late in adopting front-wheel drive, but it embraced the concept wholeheartedly as the '80s went on. When the Celica moved across, fans of the breed had little to fear – the outgoing model was pretty insipid, while the new one was excellent in all respects. Twin-cam power ensured performance, tidy handling made all that poke accessible and, like all Toyotas until recently, its reliability was bulletproof. Undervalued today, and the survival rate is low, as it's overshadowed by the more radical replacement from 1990. Buy, enjoy, and stock up on rust treatment.

SPECIFICATIONS
Years produced: 1985-1990
Performance: 0-60mph: 8.3sec
Top speed: 130mph
Power & torque: 148bhp/133lb ft
Engine: Normally aspirated 1998cc four cylinder, petrol, fuel injection, 16 valves
Drivetrain: Front-engine FWD
Structure: Monocoque
Transmission: Five-speed manual
Weight: 1250kg

PRICE GUIDE
Launch price: £12,000
Excellent: £2000
Good: £1200
Average: £750
Project: £350

TOYOTA
MR2 MkI

A shock to Japan and the rest of the world, Toyota brought the mid-engined MR2 to the market in 1984. No Japanese manufacturer had attempted to sell a mid-engined car before. The standard MR2 came with the 1.6 16-valve engine first seen in the Corolla GT, which gave it brisk performance. Sadly the supercharged MR2 was never officially sold in Europe, but we did get the removable roof panels and improved suspension package from that model. Like most other Toyotas, the MR2 was a very reliable car – the main thing to watch out for is rust.

SPECIFICATIONS
Years produced: 1984-1989 (166,104 in total)
Performance: 0-60mph: 7.7sec
Top speed: 116mph
Power & torque: 122bhp/105lb ft
Engine: Normally aspirated 1587cc four cylinder, petrol, electronic fuel injection, 16 valves
Drivetrain: Mid-engine RWD
Structure: Monocoque
Transmission: Five-speed manual
Weight: 1052kg

PRICE GUIDE
Launch price: £9295
Excellent: £4000
Good: £2500
Average: £1250
Project: £500

TOYOTA
Supra/Supra Turbo

This was Toyota's third incarnation of the Supra, but unlike the previous two, this 'New' Supra was not directly related to the Celica. Available with a 200bhp normally aspirated straight six at launch, the turbocharged version arrived in 1987, boasting a more impressive 232bhp. The car was very advanced, and offered (as an expensive optional extra) a clever set of electronically controlled dampers. All the gadgets in the world could not disguise its weight though, and for this reason the Supra was more grand tourer than sports car.

SPECIFICATIONS
Years produced: 1986-1993
Performance: 0-60mph: 6.9sec
Top speed: 144mph
Power & torque: 232bhp/254lb ft
Engine: Turbocharged 2954cc six cylinder, petrol, fuel injection, 24 valves
Drivetrain: Front-engine RWD
Structure: Monocoque
Transmission: Five-speed manual
Weight: 1603kg

PRICE GUIDE
Launch price: £15,299
Excellent: £3500
Good: £2500
Average: £1000
Project: £500

TRABANT

TRABANT STARTED building its infamous people's car in 1957. But its roots lay in IFA, the East German association of carmakers – Audi, DKW, Framo and Phänomen – nationalised by the new government. The first IFAs appeared in 1948, and in 1955 the F8 was renamed the Zwickau P70. In 1959, it was renamed once again to the Trabant P50, built by VEB Sachsenring Automobilwerke. Material shortages meant the first Trabants weren't built from the planned glassfibre, but resin reinforced papier-mâché – hence the subsequent jokes. By 1960, the East German car industry was rationalised into two makers, Trabant and Wartburg. And Trabant died in 1991.

TRABANT
601

Briefly Europe's most symbolic car in the aftermath of the fall of the Iron Curtain in 1989-1990, the Trabant 601's novelty soon wore off once the horrible truth emerged about how bad it was to drive. The Eastern Europeans shunned it once they had the opportunity to lay their hands on secondhand Golfs, and Duraplast-bodied Trabbies soon ended up littering scrapyards across the continent. An enthusiastic following has since emerged, and late VW-powered models are proving to be Germany's least likely Q-car – when upgraded to supercharged Polo G40 spec.

SPECIFICATIONS
Years produced: 1964-1991 (2,860,214 in total)
Performance: 0-60mph: N/A
Top speed: 62mph
Power & torque: 30bhp/35lb ft
Engine: Normally aspirated 594cc two-stroke twin, petrol, carburettor
Drivetrain: Front-engine FWD
Structure: Duraplast body/separate chassis
Transmission: Four-speed manual
Weight: 650kg

PRICE GUIDE
Launch price: N/A in UK
Excellent: £2000
Good: £700
Average: £350
Project: £250

TRIDENT

TRIDENT ORIGINATED in 1962 when chairman and managing director of TVR, Brian Hopton, wanted to find an Italian-designed body for the coil-sprung Grantura MkIII. He rejected an original proposal by Frank Costin, and went instead for Trevor Fiore's shapely design. In true British specialist car industry fashion, the car ended up in the hands of Trident, and the new marque got the car to market in 1967. The company struggled after an initial flurry of interest, and by 1973 was effectively bankrupt. A reorganisation saw continued production from 1976 (after stopping in 1975), based on an ambitious export plan – but by 1978, Trident was finished.

TRIDENT
Clipper

The Trident Clipper is one of those fascinating British nearly-cars that could have conquered the world. Could have... It started life as a TVR prototype, but when the Blackpool company was declared bankrupt, the Fissore-styled Clipper project was picked up by Suffolk company Trident. It was blindingly quick with Detroit muscle under the bonnet, but the lengthened Triumph TR6 chassis that underpinned the whole ensemble wasn't really good enough. Basically a handsome British sports car, its styling was constantly tinkered with, but sales were elusive.

SPECIFICATIONS
Years produced: 1968-1977 (135 in total)
Performance: 0-60mph: 5.0sec
Top speed: 145mph
Power & torque: 270bhp/312lb ft
Engine: Normally aspirated 4727cc V8, petrol, carburettor, 16 valves
Drivetrain: Front-engine RWD
Structure: Glassfibre body/separate chassis
Transmission: Four-speed manual
Weight: 1200kg

PRICE GUIDE
Launch price: £2400
Excellent: £35,000
Good: £17,500
Average: £8000
Project: £5000

TRIDENT
Venturer V6/Tycoon

An attempt to find more sales for Trident resulted in Ford V6 power being installed and a new name. It was the same car in essence, with the same all-independent suspension set-up, but with 138bhp instead of 270bhp, making it a much tamer beast. Tycoon was a similar car again, but with Triumph 2500 power. Production halted in 1974, revived in 1976 with a fully Federalised version. Problem was, the required impact bumpers and joke ride height made it look plain silly. The concept was revived – in a way – by the TVR Tasmin in 1980.

SPECIFICATIONS
Years produced: 1967-1977
Performance: 0-60mph: 9.2sec
Top speed: 120mph
Power & torque: 138bhp/192lb ft
Engine: Normally aspirated 2994cc V6, petrol, carburettor, 12 valves
Drivetrain: Front-engine RWD
Structure: Glassfibre body/separate chassis
Transmission: Four-speed manual
Weight: 1090kg

PRICE GUIDE
Launch price: £2400
Excellent: £15,000
Good: £10,000
Average: £6000
Project: £3000

TRIUMPH

TRIUMPH CONCENTRATED on motorcycles until its first car in 1923. The motorbike arm was sold off in 1936 after financial struggles largely due to over-concentration on sporting models. After entering receivership in 1939, it was rescued by Standard and soon began to eclipse its saviour with the TR sports cars and, from 1959, the Herald saloon. That became the basis for the Spitfire and six-cylinder Vitesse and GT6. Triumph became part of Leyland Motors in 1961, and British Leyland in 1968, its notables of that era being the Stag and Dolomite Sprint. The marque disappeared in 1984; for the final three years its sole product was the Acclaim, a thinly disguised Honda Ballade.

TRIUMPH
1800/2000 Roadster

It's impossible to write this without mentioning the *Bergerac* connection, especially as so many that come up for sale claim to have appeared in the Jersey-based TV detective series. There's reasonable evidence to suggest that five cars did, but don't pay a premium for one without checking its provenance. There were 1800 and 2000 versions, the former using a Triumph unit with a four-speed 'box, the latter adopting more powerful Standard Vanguard running gear, though that means you only get a three-speed gearbox. Stiffer chassis and better brakes make up for it, though.

SPECIFICATIONS
Years produced:	1946-1949 (2501/2000 in total)
Performance:	0-60mph: 24.8sec
	Top speed: 77mph
Power & torque:	68bhp/108lb ft
Engine:	Normally aspirated 2088cc four cylinder, petrol, carburettor, 8 valves
Drivetrain:	Front-engine RWD
Structure:	Separate chassis
Transmission:	Three-speed manual
Weight:	1283kg

PRICE GUIDE
Launch price:	£991
Excellent:	£20,000
Good:	£14,000
Average:	£9000
Project:	£4500

TRIUMPH
1800/2000/Renown

Proper coachbuilt cars in the great British tradition, with sharp-edged aluminium bodies on an ash frame, mounted on a steel chassis. The 1800s use a Triumph four-cylinder engine and four-speed gearbox (column-change, as all versions would be) and transverse-leaf front suspension. The 2000 was only produced during 1949 and had switched to the Standard 2088cc engine and three-speed gearbox. The Renown used the same body mounted on a lengthened Standard Vanguard chassis, complete with its coil spring front suspension. From 1952 this was lengthened by three inches.

SPECIFICATIONS
Years produced:	1946-1954 (4000/2000/9301 in total)
Performance:	0-60mph: 25.1sec
	Top speed: 75mph
Power & torque:	68bhp/108lb ft
Engine:	Normally aspirated 2088cc four cylinder, petrol, carburettor, 8 valves
Drivetrain:	Front-engine RWD
Structure:	Separate chassis
Transmission:	Three-speed manual with overdrive
Weight:	1283kg

PRICE GUIDE
Launch price:	£889
Excellent:	£6750
Good:	£5750
Average:	£2750
Project:	£1250

TRIUMPH
Mayflower

A peculiar little car with shrunken Rolls-Royce styling that doesn't quite fit the short wheelbase. It is, however, roomy and comfortable, and assembled from good-quality materials. As long as you are in no real hurry, the unique-to-this-model aluminium-headed 1247cc sidevalve engine has enough torque to make decent progress, though its maximum speed is just over 60mph. It is very economical though, and enthusiastic club back-up is there to keep it on the road. Just as when it was new, this makes an intriguing alternative to a Minor or Austin Devon.

SPECIFICATIONS
Years produced:	1949-1953 (34,000 in total)
Performance:	0-60mph: N/A
	Top speed: 63mph
Power & torque:	38bhp/58lb ft
Engine:	Normally aspirated 1247cc four cylinder, petrol, carburettor, 8 valves
Drivetrain:	Front-engine RWD
Structure:	Separate chassis
Transmission:	Three-speed manual
Weight:	914kg

PRICE GUIDE
Launch price:	£480
Excellent:	£3500
Good:	£2750
Average:	£1200
Project:	£600

TRIUMPH
TR2

Did Triumph know what it was starting? The TR2 practically defined the new wave of British sports cars that came along in the '50s: quick, basic, admirably strong with, under the bonnet, a well-proven engine from a saloon car with an extra carburettor bolted on. Instantly distinguished from later cars by its deeply recessed grille, the TR2 will easily pass 100mph, won rallies in its day, and is still popular for classic rallying. A strong seller, it could be worth hanging out for one built after October 1954. These got shorter doors so you could at last get out next to kerbs.

SPECIFICATIONS
Years produced:	1953-1955 (8628 in total)
Performance:	0-60mph: 11.9sec
	Top speed: 103mph
Power & torque:	90bhp/117lb ft
Engine:	Normally aspirated 1991cc four cylinder, petrol, carburettor, 8 valves
Drivetrain:	Front-engine RWD
Structure:	Separate chassis
Transmission:	Four-speed with overdrive
Weight:	838kg

PRICE GUIDE
Launch price:	£787
Excellent:	£25,000
Good:	£14,250
Average:	£8500
Project:	£5000

TRIUMPH
TR3/3A

The TR3 had been in production for almost a year before it gained its great claim to automotive fame. In September 1956 this became the first production car to be fitted as standard with front disc brakes, beating the Jaguar XK150 by four months. Eggcrate grille marks it out over the TR2, and it gained an extra 5bhp thanks to larger carbs. Sales were even better, and 90% were exported. The 3A is easily distinguished by its full-width grille and headlamps that were recessed further into the front panel. Public demand brought the welcome addition of external doorhandles.

SPECIFICATIONS
Years produced:	1955-1961 (13,377/58,236 in total)
Performance:	0-60mph: 11.4sec
	Top speed: 106mph
Power & torque:	100bhp/117lb ft
Engine:	Normally aspirated 1991cc four cylinder, petrol, carburettor, 8 valves
Drivetrain:	Front-engine RWD
Structure:	Separate chassis
Transmission:	Four-speed manual with overdrive
Weight:	902kg

PRICE GUIDE
Launch price:	£976
Excellent:	£25,000
Good:	£13,750
Average:	£8250
Project:	£6000

TRIUMPH
Herald

One of the new small family-car stars of the 1959 Motor Show, the Herald was a bit more upmarket than the Mini and Anglia. All that really held it back was the lack of power from its 948cc engine, even in the twin-carb form used in the convertible launched in 1960 (worth a 25% premium) and soon offered as an option for the saloon. There was also a Herald S launched in 1961, but don't go thinking that stands for Sport. It was actually a stripped-out budget model that continued for some time after the 1200 arrived and, though rarer, is the least valuable of the range.

SPECIFICATIONS
Years produced:	1959-1964 (76,860 in total)
Performance:	0-60mph: 31.1sec
	Top speed: 71mph
Power & torque:	35bhp/41lb ft
Engine:	Normally aspirated 948cc four cylinder, petrol, carburettor, 8 valves
Drivetrain:	Front-engine RWD
Structure:	Separate chassis
Transmission:	Four-speed manual
Weight:	870kg

PRICE GUIDE
Launch price:	£702
Excellent:	£2500
Good:	£1650
Average:	£850
Project:	£350

TRIUMPH
Herald Coupé

By a couple of weeks, this was actually the first Herald model to become available, and was what Michelotti's Herald prototype had looked like. Initially all Coupés were sold with a twin-carb version of the 948cc engine, though this was increased to a single-carb 1147cc along with the rest of the range in 1961. Front disc brakes became optional just before the engine swap. All but very early cars had strengthening ribs on the hardtop behind the side windows. Though undoubtedly pretty and sought after today, the Coupé proved a poor seller and was discontinued in 1964.

SPECIFICATIONS
Years produced:	1959-1964 (20,472 in total)
Performance:	0-60mph: 23.6sec
	Top speed: 77mph
Power & torque:	39bhp/41lb ft
Engine:	Normally aspirated 948cc four cylinder, petrol, carburettor, 8 valves
Drivetrain:	Front-engine RWD
Structure:	Separate chassis
Transmission:	Four-speed manual
Weight:	749kg

PRICE GUIDE
Launch price:	£731
Excellent:	£3000
Good:	£2400
Average:	£1600
Project:	£650

TRIUMPH
Italia

The Italia was a very successful attempt – stylistically – to turn the very capable Triumph TR3A convertible into a fixed head coupe. Styled by Giovanni Michelotti, who had pretty much defined Triumph's corporate style during the '50s, and built up from rolling chassis at *carrozzeria* Vignale, the Italia was short-lived and now in serious demand. The Italia was never officially imported into the UK, the majority remaining in their home country, but a few have been personally imported since. Production quality isn't all it should be, but that adds to the charm.

SPECIFICATIONS
Years produced:	1959-1963 (329 in total)
Performance:	0-60mph: 12.0 secs
	Top speed: 110mph
Power & torque:	100bhp / 117lb ft
Engine:	Normally aspirated 1991cc in-line four, petrol, carburettor, 8 valves
Drivetrain:	Front-engine RWD
Bodyframe:	Chassis and separate body
Transmission:	Four-speed manual with overdrive
Weight:	975kg

PRICE GUIDE
Launch price:	N/A
Excellent:	£40,000
Good:	£25,000
Average:	£15,000
Project:	N/A

TRIUMPH
TR4/4A

Michelotti's radically restyled body on a widened TR3A chassis so frightened American dealers that they ordered another 3000-odd TR3As for 1962 instead. Everyone else took well to the sharp modern lines, though there were a few purist mutterings about it having gone soft, what with the wind-up windows and face-level air vents (it was the first British car to have them). Other benefits included rack-and-pinion steering, all-synchro gearbox and an extra 150cc in engine capacity. From 1964 the TR4A was more of the same, but with independent rear suspension.

SPECIFICATIONS
Years produced:	1961-1967 (40,253/28,465 in total)
Performance:	0-60mph: 11.4sec
	Top speed: 109mph
Power & torque:	104bhp/132lb ft
Engine:	Normally aspirated 2138cc four cylinder, petrol, carburettor, 8 valves
Drivetrain:	Front-engine RWD
Structure:	Separate chassis
Transmission:	Four-speed manual with overdrive
Weight:	1016kg

PRICE GUIDE
Launch price:	£968
Excellent:	£20,000
Good:	£12,000
Average:	£7250
Project:	£3750

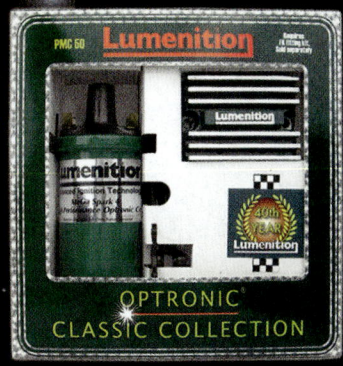

TRIUMPH
Herald 1200

The backbone ordinary model that was easily the Herald range's best-seller and continued almost to the end of production. The 1147cc engine produced less power than the smaller twin-carb engine it replaced, but gave much better torque figures, so it always felt more powerful. A higher axle ratio was fitted for easier cruising and this time there's an estate version as well as a convertible. Either of those can command up to 50% more than the saloon. Fittings were more luxurious than earlier Heralds and disc brakes were an option worth looking out for now.

SPECIFICATIONS

Years produced:	1961-1970 (284,256 in total)
Performance:	0-60mph: 28.6sec
	Top speed: 74mph
Power & torque:	39bhp/51lb ft
Engine:	Normally aspirated 948cc four cylinder, petrol, carburettor, 8 valves
Drivetrain:	Front-engine RWD
Structure:	Separate chassis
Transmission:	Four-speed manual
Weight:	800kg

PRICE GUIDE

Launch price:	£708
Excellent:	£2400
Good:	£1600
Average:	£825
Project:	£300

TRIUMPH
Vitesse 1600

Largely a Herald with an extra two cylinders, twin headlamps and a beefed-up chassis, all of which can be considered improvements. Though by far the most numerous Vitesses from a production point of view, the classic car movement came too late to save many and the 1600 is now the hardest to find. The small-bore engine was never used in this capacity in another Triumph. Overdrive was an optional extra worth paying more for now, on which subject there was a convertible version for which you should budget an extra 35% over the saloon prices quoted here.

SPECIFICATIONS

Years produced:	1962-1966 (31,278 in total)
Performance:	0-60mph: 17.6sec
	Top speed: 91mph
Power & torque:	70bhp/92lb ft
Engine:	Normally aspirated 1596cc six cylinder, petrol, carburettor, 12 valves
Drivetrain:	Front-engine RWD
Structure:	Separate chassis
Transmission:	Four-speed manual with overdrive
Weight:	909kg

PRICE GUIDE

Launch price:	£839
Excellent:	£4000
Good:	£2500
Average:	£1250
Project:	£550

TRIUMPH
Spitfire 4/MkII

Inspired by the success of the Frogeye Sprite, and Triumph's firm belief that it could build something better, the Spitfire was born in 1962, after the Frogeye had gone, but in time to tackle the MG Midget head-to-head. With similar performance and the benefit of independent rear suspension it fulfilled that task with great success. Overdrive became an option from October '63, and was something else the Midget never got. The MkII arrived in March 1965 with a new grille and improved interior, but there was an extra 4bhp thanks to a new cam and tubular exhaust manifold.

SPECIFICATIONS

Years produced:	1962-1967 (45,753/37,409 in total)
Performance:	0-60mph: 15.5sec
	Top speed: 92mph
Power & torque:	67bhp/67lb ft
Engine:	Normally aspirated 1147cc four cylinder, petrol, carburettor, 8 valves
Drivetrain:	Front-engine RWD
Structure:	Separate chassis
Transmission:	Four-speed manual with overdrive
Weight:	711kg

PRICE GUIDE

Launch price:	£730
Excellent:	£5000
Good:	£3500
Average:	£2000
Project:	£900

TRIUMPH
Herald 12/50

Best thought of as a GT version of the Herald 1200, the 12/50 has become the most popular saloon version as it combines the prettier looks of the early cars with almost the performance of the blander Herald 13/60 that replaced it. A higher compression ratio and other tweaks took power from 39 to 51bhp, disc brakes were standard, as was a Webasto folding sunroof. A fine-barred aluminium grille and '12/50' badges were the only other external giveaways, though you also got a padded dashtop. Perhaps due to the sunroof, Triumph never built a convertible version.

SPECIFICATIONS

Years produced:	1963-1967 (54,807 in total)
Performance:	0-60mph: 25.2sec
	Top speed: 78mph
Power & torque:	51bhp/63lb ft
Engine:	Normally aspirated 1147cc four cylinder, petrol, carburettor, 8 valves
Drivetrain:	Front-engine RWD
Structure:	Separate chassis
Transmission:	Four-speed manual
Weight:	841kg

PRICE GUIDE

Launch price:	£635
Excellent:	£2800
Good:	£2100
Average:	£1000
Project:	£450

TRIUMPH
2000

The demise of the Standard brand saw the Vanguard's replacement wearing a Triumph badge – and bearing no relation to its predecessor apart from the 2.0-litre engine that was passed on. Michelotti's styling took a brave leap into the 1960s, and Triumph now had a credible Rover 2000 rival with all-independent suspension in what would become known as the executive saloon class. A MkII arrived in 1969 with more of an edge to the styling, and longer bonnet and boot. Relatively few estates were built, but they make a practical and interesting classic if you can find one.

SPECIFICATIONS

Years produced:	1963-1977 (219,816 in total)
Performance:	0-60mph: 14.9sec
	Top speed: 96mph
Power & torque:	84bhp/100lb ft
Engine:	Normally aspirated 1998cc six cylinder, petrol, carburettor, 12 valves
Drivetrain:	Front-engine RWD
Structure:	Monocoque
Transmission:	Four-speed manual with overdrive
Weight:	1188kg

PRICE GUIDE

Launch price:	£1412
Excellent:	£2600
Good:	£1900
Average:	£850
Project:	£250

TRIUMPH
1300/1500 FWD

This small, well-appointed front-wheel-drive saloon was another radical departure for Triumph that it subsequently retreated from. Engine is the same as the Herald 13/60's, but it was joined in 1967 by a twin-carb version in the sportier 1300TC. That got an extra 14bhp, plus a brake servo to help cope with it. Both were replaced by the 1500 in 1970, an elegant restyle that saw the car grow seven inches in length and acquire twin headlamps. Wood trim and deep carpets added to the attractions, but its days were numbered as Triumph already had a rear-wheel-drive alternative.

SPECIFICATIONS
Years produced:	1965-1973
Performance:	0-60mph: 15.9sec
	Top speed: 93mph
Power & torque:	75bhp/75lb ft
Engine:	Normally aspirated 1296cc four cylinder, petrol, carburettor, 8 valves
Drivetrain:	Front-engine FWD
Structure:	Monocoque
Transmission:	Four-speed manual
Weight:	914kg

PRICE GUIDE
Launch price:	£874
Excellent:	£2000
Good:	£1200
Average:	£600
Project:	£250

TRIUMPH
Vitesse 2-litre MkI

The whole world loves a small car with more power than is strictly good for it, and that pretty well sums up why a Vitesse costs so much more than a Herald. The Vitesse is much more of a success now than when it was new, and outsold by the Herald by nearly ten-to-one. The 2-litre was an inevitable development of the 1600, as the larger engine was already in use in other Triumphs. As well as taller gearing and wider wheels, the 2-litre was also treated to larger front brake discs. The suspension was left unchanged, and that power can overstretch its abilities.

SPECIFICATIONS
Years produced:	1966-1968 (10,830 in total)
Performance:	0-60mph: 12.6sec
	Top speed: 95mph
Power & torque:	95bhp/117lb ft
Engine:	Normally aspirated 1998cc six cylinder, petrol, carburettor, 12 valves
Drivetrain:	Front-engine RWD
Structure:	Separate chassis
Transmission:	Four-speed manual with overdrive
Weight:	946kg

PRICE GUIDE
Launch price:	£839
Excellent:	£4000
Good:	£2650
Average:	£1350
Project:	£550

TRIUMPH
TR5/TR250

In the search for greater power and refinement, Triumph dropped a long-stroke version of its six-cylinder engine into the TR4A body and created the 2.5-litre TR5. Most of the world got the 150bhp Lucas fuel-injection engine. America was different. To get around emissions regulations Triumph sent them a twin-carb version with just 104bhp and called it the TR250. It sounds like a terrible idea, but these outsold the TR5 by almost three-to-one. It's not unusual to find examples repatriated to the UK and fitted with the injection engine from the much-less-valuable TR6.

SPECIFICATIONS
Years produced:	1967-1968 (2947 in total)
Performance:	0-60mph: 8.8sec
	Top speed: 120mph
Power & torque:	150bhp/164lb ft
Engine:	Normally aspirated 2498cc six cylinder, petrol, carburettor, 12 valves
Drivetrain:	Front-engine RWD
Structure:	Separate chassis
Transmission:	Four-speed with overdrive
Weight:	1029kg

PRICE GUIDE
Launch price:	£1212
Excellent:	£27,500
Good:	£20,000
Average:	£12,000
Project:	£6500

TRIUMPH
Spitfire MkIII

Instantly recognisable by the raised front bumper (by nine inches) that adds a hint of Lotus Elan, the MkIII Spitfire may count as the only car in history to have its looks improved by trying to meet American regulations. The soft-top is also much improved, in both looks and ease of operation. But the best change lies under the bonnet: a 1296cc engine with an eight-port cylinder head based on the FWD Triumph 1300 unit. This adds up to a 12% power increase (with better economy), so a stronger clutch and larger brake calipers join the party, along with stiffer front springs.

SPECIFICATIONS
Years produced:	1967-1970 (65,320 in total)
Performance:	0-60mph: 14.5sec
	Top speed: 95mph
Power & torque:	75bhp/75lb ft
Engine:	Normally aspirated 1296cc four cylinder, petrol, carburettor, 8 valves
Drivetrain:	Front-engine RWD
Structure:	Separate chassis
Transmission:	Four-speed with overdrive
Weight:	749kg

PRICE GUIDE
Launch price:	£717
Excellent:	£4500
Good:	£4000
Average:	£2250
Project:	£1000

TRIUMPH
Herald 13/60

The final and most powerful Herald got a single-carb version of the 1300 engine. That makes it the most useable of the range, and you'll usually find it in any magazine's list of the top ten starter classics, as they combine driveability with ease of maintenance. There's a new dashboard and more space for rear passengers, but the most noticeable change is to a single-headlamp version of the Vitesse's front end and bonnet. Saloon production ended in 1970, with convertibles and estates lasting another year. Both can be worth 50% more than saloons.

SPECIFICATIONS
Years produced:	1967-1971 (82,650 in total)
Performance:	0-60mph: 17.7sec
	Top speed: 84mph
Power & torque:	58bhp/73lb ft
Engine:	Normally aspirated 1296cc four cylinder, petrol, carburettor, 8 valves
Drivetrain:	Front-engine RWD
Structure:	Separate chassis
Transmission:	Four-speed manual
Weight:	838kg

PRICE GUIDE
Launch price:	£700
Excellent:	£3500
Good:	£1700
Average:	£900
Project:	£400

TRIUMPH
GT6 MkI/II

Conceived as a Spitfire GT, with the same four-cylinder running gear, it was quickly discovered that the extra weight of the fastback resulted in less performance. The solution was the six-cylinder Triumph 2000 engine, also creating an instant rival for the newly launched MGB GT. An E-type-like bonnet bulge completed the visual move upmarket. Great in a straight line, but that extra power highlights the deficiencies of the MkI's swing-axle rear suspension – lift-off oversteer means they must be driven with respect. Improved suspension makes the MkII a much better car.

SPECIFICATIONS
Years produced:	1968-1970 (15,818/12,066 in total)
Performance:	0-60mph: 10.0sec
	Top speed: 107mph
Power & torque:	104bhp/117lb ft
Engine:	Normally aspirated 1998cc six cylinder, petrol, carburettor, 12 valves
Drivetrain:	Front-engine RWD
Structure:	Separate chassis
Transmission:	Four-speed manual with overdrive
Weight:	864kg

PRICE GUIDE
Launch price:	£1125
Excellent:	£7500
Good:	£5000
Average:	£2750
Project:	£900

TRIUMPH
Vitesse 2-Litre MkII

Engine revisions left the capacity unchanged for the MkII Vitesse, but power was up by almost 10%. Thankfully this time Triumph saw fit to revise the rear suspension with lower wishbones, making the handling safer near the limit. Visually, a three-bar grille is the instant giveaway that you're looking at a MkII. It was a poor seller as people were attracted to more modern cars like the identically priced Hillman Hunter (how times change). Convertibles are worth a 50% premium, but make sure you buy a real one. The commission plate should have the code 'CV' on it.

SPECIFICATIONS
Years produced:	1968-1971 (9121 in total)
Performance:	0-60mph: 11.3sec
	Top speed: 100mph
Power & torque:	95bhp/115lb ft
Engine:	Normally aspirated 1998cc six cylinder, petrol, carburettor, 12 valves
Drivetrain:	Front-engine RWD
Structure:	Separate chassis
Transmission:	Four-speed manual
Weight:	927kg

PRICE GUIDE
Launch price:	£951
Excellent:	£4250
Good:	£3000
Average:	£1500
Project:	£650

TRIUMPH
TR6

It might look like a new car but all Triumph did was ask Karmann to reshape the front and rear panelwork in a more modern style. The doors and windscreen are still TR4. Wider wheels are now more commonly steel with chrome trim rings, and the seats have a bit more padding, but under the bonnet things continued as with the TR5/TR250, with fuel injection and 150bhp for most of the world and 104bhp with carbs for the US, where most were sold. That differential was reduced in 1972 when the injection cars' output was cut to 125bhp to aid refinement, and US cars were re-rated at 106bhp.

SPECIFICATIONS
Years produced:	1968-1976 (91,850 in total)
Performance:	0-60mph: 8.2sec
	Top speed: 119mph
Power & torque:	150bhp/164lb ft
Engine:	Normally aspirated 2498cc six cylinder, petrol, carburettor, 12 valves
Drivetrain:	Front-engine RWD
Structure:	Separate chassis
Transmission:	Four-speed manual with overdrive
Weight:	1122kg

PRICE GUIDE
Launch price:	£1334
Excellent:	£15,000
Good:	£11,000
Average:	£6500
Project:	£3250

TRIUMPH
2.5PI/2500TC/2500S

Think Triumph 2000 with TR5 engine, which made this Britain's first family car to be fitted with fuel injection. After little over a year it got the MkII bodyshell, but neither had the best reputation for reliability – mostly fuel-injection problems, though you can expect those to have been sorted out by now. This led Triumph back to using carburettors again in 1974 for the 2500TC, which had 99bhp, lower spec, and was cheaper than the 2.5PI. Then in 1975 the 2500S fully replaced the PI with a 106bhp carburettor engine, stiffer suspension and Stag alloys. This is the one to have.

SPECIFICATIONS
Years produced:	1968-1977 (47,455 in total)
Performance:	0-60mph: 11.5sec
	Top speed: 106mph
Power & torque:	132bhp/153lb ft
Engine:	Normally aspirated 2498cc six cylinder, petrol, carburettor, 12 valves
Drivetrain:	Front-engine RWD
Structure:	Monocoque
Transmission:	Four-speed manual with overdrive
Weight:	1252kg

PRICE GUIDE
Launch price:	£1595
Excellent:	£4000
Good:	£2400
Average:	£1250
Project:	£300

TRIUMPH
GT6 MkIII

Visual changes were made in line with the MkIV Spitfire, though if anything they are more successful on the GT6, whose fastback styling suits the new cut-off tail. At the front, the bonnet bulge remains, in a flatter and wider form. Rear side windows are reprofiled for a cleaner look. There was no significant change to the 2.0-litre power unit, but switching to the DIN standard of power measurement drops quoted output from 104bhp to 98bhp. The rear axle was changed to the cheaper Spitfire system for 1973 – but you won't notice the difference.

SPECIFICATIONS
Years produced:	1970-1973 (13,042 in total)
Performance:	0-60mph: 10sec
	Top speed: 112mph
Power & torque:	104bhp/117lb ft
Engine:	Normally aspirated 1998cc six cylinder, petrol, carburettor, 12 valves
Drivetrain:	Front-engine RWD
Structure:	Separate chassis
Transmission:	Four-speed manual with overdrive
Weight:	921kg

PRICE GUIDE
Launch price:	£1287
Excellent:	£7500
Good:	£5500
Average:	£3000
Project:	£1000

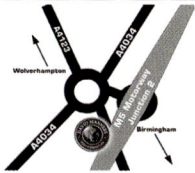

TRIUMPH
Spitfire MkIV

Michelotti restyled the Spitfire for the 1970s using many cues from the recently launched Stag – only the sills and doorskins were carried over from the MkIII. A change to 'swing-spring' rear suspension made a vast difference to roadholding. The engine is often said to have been detuned from MkIII spec, but in fact only the system of measuring output changed – from SAE to DIN – so the drop from 75bhp to 63bhp was not a real one. The MkIV was slower though, thanks to both extra weight and the taller gearing fitted to improve economy.

SPECIFICATIONS

Years produced:	1970-1974 (70,021 in total)
Performance:	0-60mph: 16.2sec
	Top speed: 90mph
Power & torque:	63bhp/69lb ft
Engine:	Normally aspirated 1296cc four cylinder, petrol, carburettor, 8 valves
Drivetrain:	Front-engine RWD
Structure:	Separate chassis
Transmission:	Four-speed manual with overdrive
Weight:	779kg

PRICE GUIDE

Launch price:	£985
Excellent:	£4000
Good:	£3400
Average:	£1850
Project:	£750

TRIUMPH
Stag

Triumph's four-seat V8 tourer stumbled at the hurdles marked 'development budget' and 'build quality.' The good news is that all the teething troubles are now well known and a large proportion of surviving Stags have been put together properly, with specialist knowledge. That leaves us free to describe it as a stylish, strong and refined grand tourer that's simple and cheap to maintain and has one of the best exhaust notes this side of a street rod event. Common with a three-speed auto, but the manual/overdrive version is preferred, not just because it uses less fuel.

SPECIFICATIONS

Years produced:	1970-1977 (25,939 in total)
Performance:	0-60mph: 9.7sec
	Top speed: 117mph
Power & torque:	145bhp/170lb ft
Engine:	Normally aspirated 2997cc V8, petrol, carburettor, 16 valves
Drivetrain:	Front-engine RWD
Structure:	Monocoque
Transmission:	Four-speed manual with overdrive
Weight:	1273kg

PRICE GUIDE

Launch price:	£1996
Excellent:	£15,000
Good:	£10,000
Average:	£5000
Project:	£2250

TRIUMPH
Toledo/1500TC/Dolomite

Are you sitting comfortably? The Toledo was a 1300cc rear-wheel-drive car that used the front-wheel-drive 1500's body with a shorter nose and tail, but was launched at the same time. These rear-drive underpinning were used in the 1500's replacement, the 1500TC, in 1973. That got the 1500's full-length body. Both were renamed Dolomite in 1976, when you could have either 1300 or 1500 engines and rectangular headlamps, or, for driveway one-upmanship, the 1500HL with twin headlamps, more gauges and a better standard of trim. An excellent starter classic.

SPECIFICATIONS

Years produced:	1970-1981 (220,017 in total)
Performance:	0-60mph: 14.2sec
	Top speed: 91mph
Power & torque:	71bhp/84lb ft
Engine:	Normally aspirated 1493cc four cylinder, petrol, carburettor, 8 valves
Drivetrain:	Front-engine RWD
Structure:	Monocoque
Transmission:	Four-speed manual
Weight:	980kg

PRICE GUIDE

Launch price:	£2441
Excellent:	£2000
Good:	£1250
Average:	£700
Project:	£200

TRIUMPH
Dolomite 1850

A woefully under-rated sporting saloon that was a genuine BMW contender in its day, but has come to be overshadowed by the Sprint. In essence it's a 1500TC fitted with an 1854cc version of the overhead-cam slant-four engine Triumph had been building for the Saab 99. Wishbone front suspension and live rear axle was all very conventional, but tightened up for the 1850 it created a sweet-handling and friendly machine that could be driven hard. Plusher 1850HL from 1976, and from 1973 all could be had with automatic transmission or manual with overdrive.

SPECIFICATIONS

Years produced:	1972-1980 (79,010 in total)
Performance:	0-60mph: 11.6sec
	Top speed: 100mph
Power & torque:	91bhp/105lb ft
Engine:	Normally aspirated 1854cc four cylinder, petrol, carburettor, 8 valves
Drivetrain:	Front-engine RWD
Structure:	Monocoque
Transmission:	Four-speed manual with overdrive
Weight:	965kg

PRICE GUIDE

Launch price:	£1399
Excellent:	£2250
Good:	£1500
Average:	£850
Project:	£250

TRIUMPH
Dolomite Sprint

With a strong background in touring car racing winning it the accolade of BL's most successful competition car of the 1970s, by rights the Dolomite Sprint should be valued as highly as its old rivals: Alfa GTV, BMW 2002tii or Escort RS2000. But it's not, which must make it a bargain. Those others may all be two-doors, but the Dolly is the only one with a 16-valve head. Well equipped as standard, they come with plenty of wood trim and tinted glass plus that most 1970s of items, a vinyl roof. Overdrive too, from May 1975. With around 400 UK survivors, choice is good.

SPECIFICATIONS

Years produced:	1973-1980 (22,941 in total)
Performance:	0-60mph: 8.7sec
	Top speed: 115mph
Power & torque:	127bhp/124lb ft
Engine:	Normally aspirated 1998cc four cylinder, petrol, carburettor, 16 valves
Drivetrain:	Front-engine RWD
Structure:	Monocoque
Transmission:	Four-speed manual with overdrive
Weight:	1004kg

PRICE GUIDE

Launch price:	£1740
Excellent:	£6000
Good:	£4000
Average:	£2000
Project:	£500

TRIUMPH
Spitfire 1500

Aside from the very obvious Spitfire 1500 decals on the nose and tail, you'd need to be a devout anorak-wearer to spot the external differences between this and a MkIV. Silver rather than black wheel centres are probably the most obvious. The real change comes under the bonnet. The new capacity came from a longer-stroke crankshaft which rather blunted the engine's will to rev, and made life tougher for the crank bearings, but it punches out a lot more mid-range power and the taller gearing it allowed made the Spitfire a genuine 100mph car at last.

SPECIFICATIONS

Years produced:	1974-1980 (91,137 in total)
Performance:	0-60mph: 13.2sec
	Top speed: 100mph
Power & torque:	71bhp/82lb ft
Engine:	Normally aspirated 1493cc four cylinder, petrol, carburettor, 8 valves
Drivetrain:	Front-engine RWD
Structure:	Separate chassis
Transmission:	Four-speed with overdrive
Weight:	794kg

PRICE GUIDE

Launch price:	£1360
Excellent:	£4400
Good:	£3500
Average:	£2000
Project:	£750

TRIUMPH
TR7

After the TR6 this was a disappointment for purists, having gained a roof but lost two cylinders, 500cc and independent rear suspension. It really wasn't a true TR, until the convertible version arrived in 1979 – those initials simply meant Triumph Roadster. But for all the criticism over these points and the still controversial 'wedge' styling, it sold faster than the TR6 ever had. It's a much easier car to live with too, driving more like a two-seater saloon than a sports car. It's also by far the cheapest way to join the ranks of Triumph TR ownership.

SPECIFICATIONS

Years produced:	1975-1981 (112,375 in total)
Performance:	0-60mph: 9.1sec
	Top speed: 109mph
Power & torque:	105bhp/119lb ft
Engine:	Normally aspirated 1998cc four cylinder, petrol, carburettor, 8 valves
Drivetrain:	Front-engine RWD
Structure:	Monocoque
Transmission:	4/5-speed manual or 3-speed auto
Weight:	1000kg

PRICE GUIDE

Launch price:	£3000
Excellent:	£3000
Good:	£2000
Average:	£1000
Project:	£400

TRIUMPH
TR8

This was the car the TR7 should have been – it was designed to accept the Rover V8 engine from the outset. Sadly it arrived too late, was in production for less than two years and nearly all were left-hand drive examples for the US market. A handful of UK cars escaped into the wild – many more have since been created on a DIY basis (you can buy a kit from Rimmer Bros). Some price guides carry an entry for these conversions. There are few other differences apart from bigger brakes, radiator and modified crossmember. They might not be original, but are probably the best bet for UK buyers.

SPECIFICATIONS

Years produced:	1979-1981 (2722 in total)
Performance:	0-60mph: 8.4sec
	Top speed: 120mph
Power & torque:	137bhp/168lb ft
Engine:	Normally aspirated 3528cc V8, petrol, mechanical fuel injection, 16 valves
Drivetrain:	Front-engine RWD
Structure:	Monocoque
Transmission:	Five-speed manual
Weight:	1163kg

PRICE GUIDE

Launch price:	£N/A
Excellent:	£11,000
Good:	£9750
Average:	£6000
Project:	£3000

TRIUMPH
Acclaim

The Triumph Acclaim was significant in so many ways that it's difficult to understand why it has such a rough ride in the classic press. It proved that the BL workers could screw together a car as well as their Japanese counterparts; it was the first Anglo-Japanese production car; and it was the final Triumph ever made. Honda running gear made it pleasant to drive and reliable like no other BL car of the time, but it was too cramped for European families, and soon proved itself as a rampant ruster. Cheap to buy, and still reliable. Look out for luxury Avon Turbo models.

SPECIFICATIONS

Years produced:	1981-1984 (133,625 in total)
Performance:	0-60mph: 13.5sec
	Top speed: 92mph
Power & torque:	72bhp/80lb ft
Engine:	Normally aspirated 1335cc four cylinder, petrol, carburettor, 8 valves
Drivetrain:	Front-engine FWD
Structure:	Monocoque
Transmission:	Five-speed manual
Weight:	880kg

PRICE GUIDE

Launch price:	£4688
Excellent:	£1400
Good:	£900
Average:	£400
Project:	£250

TURNER

JOHN TURNER Sports Cars was created in 1949 to build specials and racing engines. His 500cc Formula 3 engine proved effective, and would have starred in the Egyptian-made Phoenix sports car, had it survived the Suez Crisis. In 1954, Turner moved into the production of his own cars from his factory near Wolverhampton, and the first sports car was available either with 803cc BMC A-Series power, or Coventry-Climax for competition use. The cars were developed throughout the 1960s, after picking up the nickname 'Tatty Turner' in racing circles. Despite its apparent sales success (600 cars were sold), the company went into liquidation in 1966, and production ceased.

TURNER
803/950 Sports

Jack Turner started out making specials, but such was the quality of his work that others would ask him to make cars for them. Before he knew it, he'd become a car constructor. The 803 and 950 Sports were powered by Austin A30 and A35 A-series engines, and suspension was by torsion bars and trailing arms. It was a simple but effective recipe that appeared a while before the Austin-Healey Sprite. BMC ended up refusing to supply parts directly, pushing up the price of the final product but, like all Turners, it was available in kit form.

SPECIFICATIONS

Years produced:	1955-1959 (260 in total)
Performance:	0-60mph: 12.0sec
	Top speed: 94mph
Power & torque:	34bhp/50lb ft
Engine:	Normally aspirated 803cc four cylinder, petrol, carburettor, 8 valves
Drivetrain:	Front-engine RWD
Structure:	Spaceframe
Transmission:	Four-speed manual
Weight:	560kg

PRICE GUIDE

Launch price:	£789
Excellent:	£6000
Good:	£4500
Average:	£2750
Project:	£1000

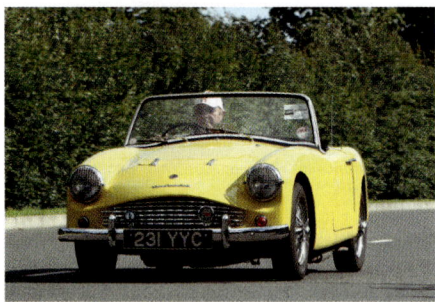

TURNER
Climax

All Turners shared the same ingredients as the original 803 Sports and, from the 950 Sports onwards, the excellent Climax FWA and 1220cc 90bhp FWE engines were made an optional extra to create the Turner-Climax. Considering it was a low-volume special, the Turner-Climax was very well finished, and drove every bit as well as the Austin-Healey Sprite that it was often compared with. In truth, the special car was far quicker, but because it cost at least a third more than its BMC rival, sales were slow.

SPECIFICATIONS

Years produced:	1959-1966
Performance:	0-60mph: 12.8sec
	Top speed: 99mph
Power & torque:	85bhp/75lb ft
Engine:	Normally aspirated 1216cc four cylinder, petrol, carburettor, 8 valves
Drivetrain:	Front-engine RWD
Structure:	Spaceframe
Transmission:	Four-speed manual
Weight:	600kg

PRICE GUIDE

Launch price:	£N/A
Excellent:	£12,000
Good:	£10,000
Average:	£6250
Project:	£3000

TVR

TVR GREW OUT of Trevcar Motors, run by young engineer Trevor Wilkinson, who was persuaded to truncate his idea to badge the cars 'Trevors.' The first was sold in 1949, and the firm soon settled on the glassfibre body over steel frame that would form the structure of all TVRs. After several changes of management Wilkinson left in 1962. Martin Lilley bought the company in 1965 and revitalised it. However, its Tasmin 'wedge' range strained finances and in 1981 the company was sold to Peter Wheeler, who turned TVR into a serious car maker, even producing its own engines. He sold out to Nikolay Smolensky in 2004, who struggled and stopped production two years later.

TVR
Grantura I-1800S

Trevor Wilkinson's company started out like so many other sports car manufacturers in the UK – marrying lightweight special bodies with tried-and-tested mechanicals to produce affordable kit cars that could be enjoyed by many. What set TVR apart was its staying power, and most of that was down to the appeal of early models like the Grantura, and the sheer number of permutations you could buy it in – with engines ranging from the 1172cc Ford Popular engine to the 1798cc twin-carburettor MGB engine, there was bound to be a TVR for you.

SPECIFICATIONS

Years produced:	1958-1967 (800 approx in total)
Performance:	0-60mph: 10.0sec
	Top speed: 111mph
Power & torque:	95bhp/N/A
Engine:	Normally aspirated 1799cc four cylinder, petrol, carburettor, 8 valves
Drivetrain:	Front-engine RWD
Structure:	Glassfibre body/separate chassis
Transmission:	Four-speed manual
Weight:	864kg

PRICE GUIDE

Launch price:	£1426
Excellent:	£15,000
Good:	£8000
Average:	£4500
Project:	£2750

TVR
Griffith V8

American racing driver Jack Griffith approached TVR with a proposal to produce a V8-engined Grantura for competition. TVR agreed and supplied Grantura bodies and chassis for Griffith to fit 4727cc Ford V8s into. These cars were badged as the Griffith in the USA and were offered with either a manual or automatic gearbox. Performance was predictably swift. Some models could top 150mph and hit 60mph in around six seconds. They were overpowered – and only remained in production for a couple of years. A great idea for the future, though.

SPECIFICATIONS

Years produced:	1963-1965 (300 in total)
Performance:	0-60mph: 6.9sec
	Top speed: 140mph
Power & torque:	195bhp/282lb ft
Engine:	Normally aspirated 4727cc V8, petrol, carburettor, 16 valves
Drivetrain:	Front-engine RWD
Structure:	Glassfibre body/separate chassis
Transmission:	Four-speed manual
Weight:	922kg

PRICE GUIDE

Launch price:	£1620
Excellent:	£35,000
Good:	£20,000
Average:	£15,000
Project:	£9000

TVR
Vixen S1-S4

Early Vixens were really just Granturas with a Cortina GT engine in place of the old MGB unit. The improved S2 from October 1968 came with a longer wheelbase - and longer doors to go with it. It is easily distinguishable by its Cortina MkII tail-lights. A year later the S3 brought further upgrades, including a Capri-spec engine, cast alloy wheels, and grilles to cover the engine bay cooling vents. To use up old bodies, 23 Vixen S4s were built on the new M-series chassis. Quite quick, but with a hard ride and quite twitchy handling.

SPECIFICATIONS
Years produced:	1967-1973 (746 in total)
Performance:	0-60mph: 10.5sec
	Top speed: 109mph
Power & torque:	88bhp/96lb ft
Engine:	Normally aspirated 1599cc four cylinder, petrol, carburettor, 8 valves
Drivetrain:	Front-engine RWD
Structure:	Spaceframe
Transmission:	Four-speed manual
Weight:	762kg

PRICE GUIDE
Launch price:	£1387
Excellent:	£15,000
Good:	£5000
Average:	£3250
Project:	£1500

TVR
Tuscan V6/V8/V8 SE

Here's a car that probably deserves greater respect and collector interest than it currently receives, especially with such low build numbers. And if the Tuscan looks rather like the Vixen, that's because in effect it is one, but fitted with a selection of US Ford V8s (like the Griffith), and with two body widths – although the UK only saw two wide-bodied Tuscan V8s. Capri-engined V6 Tuscan was a precursor for the mainstream TVR range of the 1970s. Quality was vastly improved over early cars, but can be hard to find these days. Worth the effort.

SPECIFICATIONS (V6)
Years produced:	1969-1971 (174 in total)
Performance:	0-60mph: 8.3sec
	Top speed: 125mph
Power & torque:	128bhp/173lb ft
Engine:	Normally aspirated 2994cc V6, petrol, carburettor, 12 valves
Drivetrain:	Front-engine RWD
Structure:	Spaceframe
Transmission:	Four-speed manual with overdrive
Weight:	907kg

PRICE GUIDE
Launch price:	£1930
Excellent:	£15,000
Good:	£5500
Average:	£3500
Project:	£2000

TVR
2500/3000M

The need for two different engines in the Tuscan's replacement was due to the UK market's 3.0-litre Ford V6 not meeting US emissions standards. So cars heading that way were fitted with the already-approved TR6 engine, with carburettors and smog gear, and quite a few bhp less than the fuel-injection versions the UK was used to. Though most of those went to America, a few found British homes, but 3000Ms are what you will mostly find. Thanks to the TR6's demise, 2500M production ended in 1977. The 3000M soldiered on for another two years.

SPECIFICATIONS
Years produced:	1971-1979 (947/654 in total)
Performance:	0-60mph: 7.7sec
	Top speed: 124mph
Power & torque:	86bhp/92lb ft
Engine:	Normally aspirated 1599cc six cylinder, petrol, carburettor, 12 valves
Drivetrain:	Front-engine RWD
Structure:	Spaceframe
Transmission:	Four-speed manual
Weight:	925kg

PRICE GUIDE
Launch price:	£2170
Excellent:	£8000
Good:	£5500
Average:	£3750
Project:	£2000

TVR
1600M

Cleverly restyled from the waist down, the M-series TVRs (the M is for TVR boss Martin Lilley) were wider and nine inches longer, mostly in the nose, and built on a dynamically improved, stronger and better protected chassis. Still using the Capri GT 'Kent' engine, the 1600M was a poor seller compared with its more powerful brethren and was dropped in 1973 after less than a year on sale, but reintroduced with a mild restyle and bigger alloys in 1975 in the wake of an energy crisis. The return of such concerns once again makes the 1600M an interesting alternative.

SPECIFICATIONS
Years produced:	1972-1977 (148 in total)
Performance:	0-60mph: 10.4sec
	Top speed: 106mph
Power & torque:	86bhp/92lb ft
Engine:	Normally aspirated 1599cc four cylinder, petrol, carburettor, 8 valves
Drivetrain:	Front-engine RWD
Structure:	Spaceframe
Transmission:	Four-speed manual
Weight:	910kg

PRICE GUIDE
Launch price:	£1886
Excellent:	£7000
Good:	£4750
Average:	£3000
Project:	£1750

TVR
Taimar

Sold alongside the 3000M for three years, the Taimar finally answered a long-asked question of TVRs and provided proper external access to the boot via a large hatchback. A vast improvement compared with leaning over the seats. This added a mere 9kg in extra weight, and otherwise the cars were identical. Their appeal was obvious and, despite a price premium, the Taimar was a strong seller. Of special note is the Taimar Turbo, of which around 30 were built. Alongside a handful of 3000Ms, these were the first British production cars to be turbocharged. Prices are commensurately higher.

SPECIFICATIONS
Years produced:	1976-1979 (395 in total)
Performance:	0-60mph: 7.7sec
	Top speed: 121mph
Power & torque:	142bhp/174lb ft
Engine:	Normally aspirated 2994cc V6, petrol, carburettor, 12 valves
Drivetrain:	Front-engine RWD
Structure:	Spaceframe
Transmission:	Four-speed manual
Weight:	1025kg

PRICE GUIDE
Launch price:	£4260
Excellent:	£8000
Good:	£5250
Average:	£3750
Project:	£2250

TVR
3000S

Soft-top version of the 3000M, called simply Convertible at the time, but it was no simple roof-chop. In fact not much more than the chassis, engine and bonnet are shared. The windscreen is new, and the roof detaches completely to stow in the boot. Removing the side windows leaves cutaways in the doors at comfortable elbow height. Even the dashboard joins in the game, with centrally-mounted instruments. Underneath, all Convertibles got a much stronger XJ6 rear axle as supplies of the TR6 unit used in the 3000M had dried up.

SPECIFICATIONS
Years produced:	1978-1979 (258 in total)
Performance:	0-60mph: 7.7sec
	Top speed: 125mph
Power & torque:	142bhp/174lb ft
Engine:	Normally aspirated 2994cc V6, petrol, carburettor, 12 valves
Drivetrain:	Front-engine RWD
Structure:	Spaceframe
Transmission:	Four-speed manual
Weight:	1098kg

PRICE GUIDE
Launch price:	£6390
Excellent:	£10,000
Good:	£8000
Average:	£5000
Project:	£3000

TVR
Tasmin/280i

All change for the 1980s as TVR adopts radical new wedge-shaped bodies from the pen of former Lotus designer Oliver Winterbottom. Launched as a two-seater coupé, the range expanded with a 2+2 and convertible in 1981. The former was shortlived but, when it was dropped, the larger body, without rear seats, was used for the coupé. Engine was from Ford again: the Cologne V6 from the Capri 2.8i. A five-speed gearbox was introduced in 1983; the following year the Tasmin was rebadged 280i. There was a Pinto-powered Tasmin 200 for a short time; not popular.

SPECIFICATIONS
Years produced:	1980-1988
Performance:	0-60mph: 9.7sec
	Top speed: 134mph
Power & torque:	150bhp/150lb ft
Engine:	Normally aspirated 2792cc V6, petrol, electronic fuel injection, 12 valves
Drivetrain:	Front-engine RWD
Structure:	Spaceframe
Transmission:	Five-speed manual
Weight:	1143kg

PRICE GUIDE
Launch price:	£15,540
Excellent:	£6000
Good:	£4000
Average:	£2250
Project:	£1250

TVR
350i

The arrival of Peter Wheeler at the helm of TVR brought excitement to the marque. He started by bolting a Rover V8 into the Tasmin (it was known as the Tasmin V8 at first, then simplified to 350i). Tubular exhaust manifolds turned up the volume to what would become a TVR trademark, while the much lighter engine, along with revisions to the suspension, brought a significant handling improvement. There was a Series II version from 1985 with larger rear lights and no bonnet vents. Perhaps surprisingly there's only around a 10% premium for the convertible.

SPECIFICATIONS
Years produced:	1983-1986
Performance:	0-60mph: 6.5sec
	Top speed: 134mph
Power & torque:	197bhp/220lb ft
Engine:	Normally aspirated 3528cc V8, petrol, electronic fuel injection, 16 valves
Drivetrain:	Front-engine RWD
Structure:	Spaceframe
Transmission:	Five-speed manual
Weight:	1004kg

PRICE GUIDE
Launch price:	£16,975
Excellent:	£7000
Good:	£4750
Average:	£2750
Project:	£1500

TVR
390/420SE

With the Rover V8 bored out to 3.9 litres and expertly fiddled with by racer Andy Rouse to extract serious horsepower, TVR's wedge really staked its claim as a performance car. To prevent it being too much of a handful, the rear axle received a TorSen limited-slip differential, ducts were added for brake cooling, and the aerodynamics were tweaked to keep the wheels in better touch with the tarmac. The result was raved about in the press, but 390SE sales were restricted by it being more expensive than a Lotus Esprit, without the heritage. All models were convertibles.

SPECIFICATIONS
Years produced:	1985-1988
Performance:	0-60mph: 4.9sec
	Top speed: 144mph
Power & torque:	275bhp/270lb ft
Engine:	Normally aspirated 3905cc V8, petrol, mechanical fuel injection, 16 valves
Drivetrain:	Front-engine RWD
Structure:	Spaceframe
Transmission:	Five-speed manual
Weight:	1107kg

PRICE GUIDE
Launch price:	£19,700
Excellent:	£9500
Good:	£6250
Average:	£4250
Project:	£2500

TVR
420/450 SEAC

The AC on the end stands for Aramid Composite, which translates to mean a body created using carbonfibre and Kevlar to shave off a lot of weight. The racing version cemented TVR's bad-boy image: it was banned for being too fast, a marketing man's dream ticket. Around 40 of the 300bhp 420SEACs were built, along with 17 of the 450 version, which added 25bhp. The huge rear wing does nothing for the car's appearance, but an awful lot for high-speed stability. Rumours abound of upgraded SEs, so make sure you buy the real thing.

SPECIFICATIONS
Years produced:	1986-1988 (40/17 in total)
Performance:	0-60mph: 5.0sec
	Top speed: 165mph
Power & torque:	300bhp/290lb ft
Engine:	Normally aspirated 4228cc V8, petrol, carburettor, 16 valves
Drivetrain:	Front-engine RWD
Structure:	Spaceframe
Transmission:	Five-speed manual
Weight:	1130kg

PRICE GUIDE
Launch price:	£31,000
Excellent:	£40,000
Good:	£20,000
Average:	£10,000
Project:	£6000

TVR
S1-S3

The Convertible S range was introduced as an entry-level traditional sports car, specifically aimed at those who thought TVRs had grown too fast and too expensive. Pitched 30% cheaper than the 350i, they found a ready market. Early versions used the same Ford 2.8-litre Cologne V6 as the 280i, but this was replaced from 1988 in the S2 by Ford's new 2.9-litre Granada V6. For 1990, the S3 got a better interior and four-inch longer doors for easier access. There were also around 40 S4Cs – basically a V8S with the V6 engine fitted.

SPECIFICATIONS

Years produced:	1986-1994
Performance:	0-60mph: 7.6sec
	Top speed: 128mph
Power & torque:	160bhp/162lb ft
Engine:	Normally aspirated 2792cc V6, petrol, electronic fuel injection, 12 valves
Drivetrain:	Front-engine RWD
Structure:	Spaceframe
Transmission:	Five-speed manual
Weight:	987kg

PRICE GUIDE

Launch price:	£12,995
Excellent:	£8000
Good:	£5500
Average:	£3500
Project:	£1600

TVR
400/450SE

These bigger-engined TVRs succeeded the 390/420SE and were, in effect, glassfibre versions of the lightweight SEAC cars, aimed at those with a little less money and a little more sanity. Not that they were that much slower, as you can see from the figures. They can prove to be quite a handful on a wet road too, so it's not a bad idea to check the car and its history for past accident damage. Interiors were improved, with better seats and materials, and more curves. TVRs were getting away from the hint of kit-car that had affected their earlier offerings.

SPECIFICATIONS

Years produced:	1988-1991
Performance:	0-60mph: 5.0sec
	Top speed: 150mph
Power & torque:	275bhp/270lb ft
Engine:	Normally aspirated 3998cc V8, petrol, carburettor, 16 valves
Drivetrain:	Front-engine RWD
Structure:	Spaceframe
Transmission:	Five-speed manual
Weight:	1150kg

PRICE GUIDE

Launch price:	£24,995
Excellent:	£15,000
Good:	£8500
Average:	£6000
Project:	£4000

VANDEN PLAS

EARLY IN ITS life, Vanden Plas built coachwork mainly for Bentley. But in 1946 it was bought by Austin, which used the firm to build its luxury Princess model. The cachet of the name prompted Austin – now part of the British Motor Corporation – to set Vanden Plas up as a separate marque in 1960. A series of large and well-appointed machines followed, although the offshoot also produced its own version of small machines based on BMC's 1100/1300 range and British Leyland's Allegro. The latter was not an aesthetic success. After its London plant closed in 1979, Vanden Plas became a mere trim level on certain Austins, Rovers and Jaguars.

VANDEN PLAS
Princess 4-Litre Limo

What had been the Austin A135 Princess in 1952 became a Vanden Plas model in 1957, the prestigious badge being regarded as a way of making it seem even more upmarket. This cut-price Rolls-Royce had much to recommend it, becoming a particular favourite of mayors and successful businessman across Britain. Its 3993cc six-cylinder 122bhp engine made it a capable cruiser, and it could be had in three body styles; saloon, six-seater limousine or landaulette. An offshoot was the Princess IV of 1956, an expensive grand touring version intended to compete with Jaguar.

SPECIFICATIONS

Years produced:	1957-1968 (3344 in total)
Performance:	0-60mph: 26.0sec
	Top speed: 75mph
Power & torque:	120bhp/185lb ft
Engine:	Normally aspirated 3990cc six cylinder, petrol, carburettor, 12 valves
Drivetrain:	Front-engine RWD
Structure:	Separate chassis
Transmission:	Four-speed manual/three-speed auto
Weight:	2121kg

PRICE GUIDE

Launch price:	£3047
Excellent:	£7500
Good:	£6000
Average:	£4000
Project:	£2000

VANDEN PLAS
3-Litre

Farina styling reached Vanden Plas in 1959 with the 3-Litre model. The VP was top dog of the trio that also included the Austin Westminster and Wolseley 6/99. It was packed with even more wood and leather and offered silent refinement from its extensive soundproofing, which successfully drowned the burble of the six-cylinder 2912cc C-series engine. The MkII of 1961 gave more power – 120bhp – and the ability to sail past 100mph at last, plus a four-speed floor-mounted transmission. As well as the standard saloon, a touring limousine could also be specified.

SPECIFICATIONS

Years produced:	1959-1964 (12,703 in total)
Performance:	0-60mph: 17.9sec
	Top speed: 97mph
Power & torque:	108bhp/165lb ft
Engine:	Normally aspirated 2912cc six cylinder, petrol, carburettor, 12 valves
Drivetrain:	Front-engine RWD
Structure:	Monocoque
Transmission:	Three-speed manual
Weight:	1530kg

PRICE GUIDE

Launch price:	£1396
Excellent:	£6000
Good:	£4000
Average:	£1800
Project:	£500

VANDEN PLAS
Princess 1100/1300

BMC badge engineering ran amok with the 1100 and 1300 range, but the flagship Vanden Plas Princess was quite a superior machine. For its size, it managed to pack in a lot of luxury. All the trimming was done at the Vanden Plas factory in London and, as well as all the expected wood and leather touches, VP also fitted extra sound deadening and picnic tables for rear seat passengers. The initial 1098cc engine gave 55bhp, which rose to 65bhp with the MkII of 1967 (but only after BMC upgraded it from single- to twin-carb in 1968). Probably the most desirable of all BMC 1100s.

SPECIFICATIONS

Years produced:	1963-1974 (43,741 in total)
Performance:	0-60mph: 21.1sec
	Top speed: 85mph
Power & torque:	55bhp/60lb ft
Engine:	Normally aspirated 1098cc four cylinder, petrol, carburettor, 8 valves
Drivetrain:	Front-engine FWD
Structure:	Monocoque
Transmission:	Four-speed manual
Weight:	832kg

PRICE GUIDE

Launch price:	£895
Excellent:	£3500
Good:	£2500
Average:	£1350
Project:	£400

VANDEN PLAS
4-Litre R

A brief encounter between Rolls-Royce and BMC led to the Vanden Plas 4-Litre R of 1964. The 'R' of the name was shorthand for the 3909cc Rolls-Royce six-cylinder engine under the bonnet of a modified 3-Litre bodyshell. The 175bhp of the all-alloy unit meant an easy car to drive – even without the extra refinement from the Borg Warner automatic transmission, power steering and servo-assisted front disc brakes. There was even more wood and leather inside than in the 3-Litre cars. Rolls-Royce even considered building its own version as a Bentley.

SPECIFICATIONS

Years produced:	1964-1968 (6999 in total)
Performance:	0-60mph: 12.7sec
	Top speed: 106mph
Power & torque:	175bhp/218lb ft
Engine:	Normally aspirated 3909cc six cylinder, petrol, carburettor, 12 valves
Drivetrain:	Front-engine RWD
Structure:	Monocoque
Transmission:	Three-speed automatic
Weight:	1575kg

PRICE GUIDE

Launch price:	£1994
Excellent:	£7000
Good:	£4000
Average:	£2000
Project:	£600

VANDEN PLAS
1500/1750

Yes, it's an Allegro. With a faux-Bentley grille and a rather pretentious air. When the Allegro superseded the 1300 range, it seemed only logical that a posh version would follow to satisfy British Leyland devotees who prized luxury motoring in a small package. The disproportionate grille did little for the Allegro's already inelegant looks but it had a great interior. Those picnic tables were there, alongside the walnut veneer and hide. Most cars had 1485cc ohc engines of 68bhp but in the final couple of years there was a 90bhp 1748cc unit, only mated to automatic transmission.

SPECIFICATIONS

Years produced:	1974-1980 (11,840 in total)
Performance:	0-60mph: 16.7sec
	Top speed: 90mph
Power & torque:	69bhp/77lb ft
Engine:	Normally aspirated 1485cc four cylinder, petrol, carburettor, 8 valves
Drivetrain:	Front-engine FWD
Structure:	Monocoque
Transmission:	Five-speed manual
Weight:	850kg

PRICE GUIDE

Launch price:	£1951
Excellent:	£2000
Good:	£1300
Average:	£600
Project:	£300

VAUXHALL

BUILDING ITS FIRST car in 1903, Vauxhall Ironworks started out as a manufacturer of mostly sports and touring cars, and became Vauxhall Motors in 1907. However, the takeover by General Motors in 1925 saw it head more profitably for the mass market that was starting to grow.

In 1932 the milestone Cadet became the first British car with a synchromesh gearbox. Another first came in 1938 with unitary construction for the Vauxhall 10.

Subsequent rationalisation gradually pushed Vauxhall closer to its German counterpart Opel and, after Viva production ended in 1979, all subsequent Vauxhalls were in effect little more than rebadged Opels.

VAUXHALL
Velox/Cresta E

Moving upmarket from the Wyvern were Vauxhall's Velox and Cresta, six-cylinder models with considerably enhanced creature comforts. Launched in 1951, the monocoque-construction Velox had a 2275cc engine and Chevrolet-inspired looks, with a significant amount of chrome on its body. After one year, a 2262cc engine made an appearance; although smaller in capacity, it had more power (from 58bhp to 64 or 69bhp). The Cresta joined the line-up in 1954 as an even more prestigious model; from the outside it could be distinguished by its two-tone paint.

SPECIFICATIONS

Years produced:	1951-1957 (251,800 in total)
Performance:	0-60mph: 20.9sec
	Top speed: 80mph
Power & torque:	58bhp/106lb ft
Engine:	Normally aspirated 2275cc six cylinder, petrol, carburettor, 12 valves
Drivetrain:	Front-engine RWD
Structure:	Monocoque
Transmission:	Three-speed manual
Weight:	1021kg

PRICE GUIDE

Launch price:	£803
Excellent:	£5250
Good:	£4000
Average:	£2000
Project:	£800

VAUXHALL
Wyvern E

Along with the closely-related Velox and Cresta, the Wyvern EIX was the first completely new post-war Vauxhall. The 1442cc engine was carried over from the previous Wyvern but the bodywork was thoroughly modern and very American in its look, with a lot of flashy chrome up-front and a curved windscreen, something unusual for the era. The increased weight of the new styling blunted performance so, from 1952, a 1507cc engine was fitted. This increased power from 35bhp to 40 or 48bhp. Aside from tweaks to its exterior, the Wyvern continued in this form until 1957.

SPECIFICATIONS

Years produced:	1951-1957 (5315 in total)
Performance:	0-60mph: 37.2sec
	Top speed: 71mph
Power & torque:	35bhp/68lb ft
Engine:	Normally aspirated 1442cc four cylinder, petrol, carburettor, 8 valves
Drivetrain:	Front-engine RWD
Structure:	Monocoque
Transmission:	Three-speed manual
Weight:	1001kg

PRICE GUIDE

Launch price:	£495
Excellent:	£4000
Good:	£3000
Average:	£1500
Project:	£500

VAUXHALL
Velox/Cresta PA

British restraint went completely out of the window with the Velox and Cresta of 1957. Flamboyant American design was wholeheartedly embraced, with fins, a dogleg wraparound windscreen, two-tone paint schemes (on the Cresta) and cascades of chrome. The 2262cc six-cylinder engine was shared by both, so the Cresta only stood out from the cheaper Velox by its greater levels of luxury and equipment inside. In 1960, engine size went up to 2651cc and front disc brakes became available to cope with the extra power; the fins also grew in stature.

SPECIFICATIONS

Years produced:	1957-1962 (173,759 in total)
Performance:	0-60mph: 18.0sec
	Top speed: 87mph
Power & torque:	83bhp/124lb ft
Engine:	Normally aspirated 2651cc six cylinder, petrol, carburettor, 12 valves
Drivetrain:	Front-engine RWD
Structure:	Monocoque
Transmission:	Three-speed manual
Weight:	1193kg

PRICE GUIDE

Launch price:	£984
Excellent:	£5500
Good:	£4500
Average:	£2250
Project:	£850

VAUXHALL
Victor FB

More restrained and sensible styling marked the 1961-64 FB Victor incarnation, albeit still with leanings across the Atlantic. But the new look was neat, handsome and inoffensive and helped make this mid-sized family car one of Vauxhall's big successes of the 1960s. Four-door saloons and five-door estates were available, with the first cars (1961-63) sporting the same 1507cc engine as the F-type, but those from September 1963 until the end of production had a 1595cc engine of 58.5bhp, and front disc brakes were also adopted.

SPECIFICATIONS

Years produced:	1961-1964 (328,640 in total)
Performance:	0-60mph: 22.6sec
	Top speed: 76mph
Power & torque:	55bhp/80lb ft
Engine:	Normally aspirated 1507cc four cylinder, petrol, carburettor, 8 valves
Drivetrain:	Front-engine RWD
Structure:	Monocoque
Transmission:	Three-speed manual
Weight:	953kg

PRICE GUIDE

Launch price:	£574
Excellent:	£3250
Good:	£2400
Average:	£1100
Project:	£400

VAUXHALL
VX4/90 FB

As well as the standard Victor FB there was, for the first time, a performance-oriented version of the type, dubbed the VX4/90. Twin carburettors and a high-compression 1507cc engine boosted power from 50bhp to 71bhp, while a floor-mounted transmission and servo front disc brakes allowed the sporty Vauxhall driver to make the most of this extra potential. Spotters could recognise a VX4/90 by its contrasting colour side stripe and a vertical bar grille. When a 1595cc engine was fitted in 1963, power rose to 74bhp, with a wood-panelled dash to make up for this meagre increase.

SPECIFICATIONS

Years produced:	1961-1964
Performance:	0-60mph: 16.4sec
	Top speed: 90mph
Power & torque:	71bhp/92lb ft
Engine:	Normally aspirated 1508cc four cylinder, petrol, carburettor, 8 valves
Drivetrain:	Front-engine RWD
Structure:	Monocoque
Transmission:	Three-speed manual
Weight:	990kg

PRICE GUIDE

Launch price:	£674
Excellent:	£3750
Good:	£3000
Average:	£1350
Project:	£550

VAUXHALL
Velox/Cresta PB

Vauxhall toned things down for the 1962-65 PB generation of Velox and Cresta. There was still a US influence and imposing size, but with a more British flavour. Front disc brakes were standard but the traditional three-speed column-mounted transmission persisted; there was also a three-speed Hydramatic automatic which changed to a two-speed Powerglide in 1965. Futuristic names were then all the rage of course. Initially, the 2651cc six-cylinder engine was carried over from the PA, but this jumped to 3294cc in 1964, its 115bhp providing a much-needed shot of adrenalin.

SPECIFICATIONS

Years produced:	1962-1965 (87,047 in total)
Performance:	0-60mph: 19.5sec
	Top speed: 92mph
Power & torque:	95bhp/149lb ft
Engine:	Normally aspirated 2651cc six cylinder, petrol, carburettor, 12 valves
Drivetrain:	Front-engine RWD
Structure:	Monocoque
Transmission:	Three-speed manual or auto
Weight:	1220kg

PRICE GUIDE

Launch price:	£805
Excellent:	£3000
Good:	£2250
Average:	£1100
Project:	£350

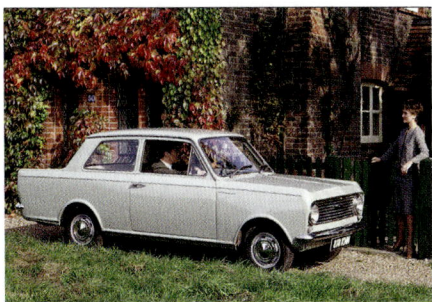

VAUXHALL
Viva HA

The British small-car market was swelled in 1963 by the belated entry of Vauxhall with its Viva HA. Stylistically it was nothing to get excited about; the angular looks were bland by comparison with rivals. However, the mechanical package was neat enough with a four-speed all-synchromesh gearbox, sharp rack-and-pinion steering and front disc brakes as an option. The more desirable variants – the De Luxe and the SL90 – boasted 54bhp from their 1057cc engines, but the Viva's main claim to fame was in being the first UK car with acrylic lacquer paint. Not memorable.

SPECIFICATIONS
Years produced:	1963-1966 (309,538 in total)
Performance:	0-60mph: 19.6sec
	Top speed: 78mph
Power & torque:	44bhp/56lb ft
Engine:	Normally aspirated 1057cc four cylinder, petrol, carburettor, 8 valves
Drivetrain:	Front-engine RWD
Structure:	Monocoque
Transmission:	Four-speed manual
Weight:	709kg

PRICE GUIDE
Launch price:	£578
Excellent:	£1750
Good:	£1400
Average:	£600
Project:	£150

VAUXHALL
Victor FC 101

Marketed as the 101, the third incarnation of Victor was a spacious car with a number of novel design features such as curved side windows, ridged wing tops and front indicators/sidelights incorporated in the bumper. The 1594cc engine was carried over from the preceding type, although there was more power for the FC. As before, the VX4/90 did duty as the racier model, with twin carburettors, higher compression, enhanced suspension and more instrumentation inside, as well as a wood-panelled dashboard. This extra appeal means 25% can be added onto standard FC prices.

SPECIFICATIONS
Years produced:	1964-1967 (219,814 in total)
Performance:	0-60mph: 17.1sec
	Top speed: 85mph
Power & torque:	60bhp/86lb ft
Engine:	Normally aspirated 1594cc four cylinder, petrol, carburettor, 8 valves
Drivetrain:	Front-engine RWD
Structure:	Monocoque
Transmission:	Four-speed manual
Weight:	1086kg

PRICE GUIDE
Launch price:	£655
Excellent:	£2400
Good:	£1750
Average:	£750
Project:	£250

VAUXHALL
Cresta PC/Viscount

The PC was only available with a 3294cc six-cylinder engine. At first, the Cresta De Luxe, with its four headlamps and extra brightwork, did service as the most luxurious model, but then came the 1966 Viscount with its vinyl roof, power steering and windows, plus those essential plush touches of wood and leather inside. Most Viscounts came with automatic transmission, which was improved considerably once the two-speed Powerglide gearbox was ditched in favour of a General Motors three-speeder.

SPECIFICATIONS
Years produced:	1965-1972 (66,937 in total)
Performance:	0-60mph: 12.6sec
	Top speed: 97mph
Power & torque:	123bhp/175lb ft
Engine:	Normally aspirated 3294cc six cylinder, petrol, carburettor, 12 valves
Drivetrain:	Front-engine RWD
Structure:	Monocoque
Transmission:	Two/three-speed automatic
Weight:	1179kg

PRICE GUIDE
Launch price:	£956
Excellent:	£2500
Good:	£1800
Average:	£950
Project:	£250

VAUXHALL
Viva HB

The Viva got more attractive and trendy in HB form. Not only was it larger, but it also featured distinctive 'Coke bottle' side styling, one of the first UK cars to do so. Aside from the engine, an enlarged (to 1159cc) version of the HA unit, little was carried over from the previous model. The suspension was totally new and quite advanced, resulting in impressive handling. This could be better enjoyed in the high compression SL90, with 59.5bhp. When the Viva started to lag behind its rivals in the late 1960s, the overhead-cam 1599cc engine from the Victor was added to the mix.

SPECIFICATIONS
Years produced:	1966-1970 (566,391 in total)
Performance:	0-60mph: 19.7sec
	Top speed: 80mph
Power & torque:	47bhp/62lb ft
Engine:	Normally aspirated 1159cc four cylinder, petrol, carburettor, 8 valves
Drivetrain:	Front-engine RWD
Structure:	Monocoque
Transmission:	Four-speed manual
Weight:	777kg

PRICE GUIDE
Launch price:	£508
Excellent:	£1650
Good:	£1200
Average:	£500
Project:	£100

VAUXHALL
Viva Brabham HB

If BMC could do it with Cooper and Ford with Lotus, then why shouldn't Vauxhall do it with Brabham? That was the thinking behind 1967's Brabham HB Viva, developed with world racing champion Jack Brabham. The hotted-up 1159cc engine had twin Stromberg carburettors, reworked exhaust manifolds and an uprated camshaft, combining to give 69bhp. Interior trim was improved, and the bodywork embellished with stripes running from the bonnet and around the front wings to the doors. Nice! It was in production for just a year before being replaced by the Viva 1600.

SPECIFICATIONS
Years produced:	1967-1968
Performance:	0-60mph: 14.4sec
	Top speed: 90mph
Power & torque:	68bhp/66lb ft
Engine:	Normally aspirated 1159cc four cylinder, petrol, carburettor, 8 valves
Drivetrain:	Front-engine RWD
Structure:	Monocoque
Transmission:	Four-speed manual
Weight:	777kg

PRICE GUIDE
Launch price:	£690
Excellent:	£4000
Good:	£2750
Average:	£1750
Project:	£750

VAUXHALL
Victor FD

The FD Victor's 'Coke bottle' kink on its rear doors reflected contemporary American trends, just as previous Victors before it had done. Thus the looks were bold and brash, with quad-headlamp styling and the continuation (on some models) of the three-speed column-mounted gearchange and front bench seating that Vauxhall had persisted with for years. Two new hemispherical-head overhead-cam engines of 1599cc and 1975cc were introduced, with servo-assisted front brakes for the latter. The VX4/90 was the sporty model, with twin carburettors, overdrive and Rostyle wheels.

SPECIFICATIONS

Years produced:	1967-1972 (198,085 in total)
Performance:	0-60mph: 14.0sec
	Top speed: 95mph
Power & torque:	83bhp/90lb ft
Engine:	Normally aspirated 1599cc four cylinder, petrol, carburettor, 8 valves
Drivetrain:	Front-engine RWD
Structure:	Monocoque
Transmission:	Four-speed manual/three-speed auto
Weight:	1066kg

PRICE GUIDE

Launch price:	£819
Excellent:	£2250
Good:	£1600
Average:	£600
Project:	£150

VAUXHALL
Viva GT

The Viva Brabham was a half-hearted effort at injecting some vigour into the HB range but the same couldn't be said of the 1968 Viva GT. This was a storming machine that gave the Viva a heady degree of sportiness that was absent before. To achieve this, Vauxhall dropped in the 1975cc engine from the Victor, adorned with twin carburettors and mated with a close-ratio gearbox. This unleashed 104 horses, giving 100mph. The suspension was uprated, while bonnet scoops, a black grille and contrasting bonnet made it look the part. Vauxhall's equivalent of the Lotus Cortina.

SPECIFICATIONS

Years produced:	1968-1970 (4606 in total)
Performance:	0-60mph: 11.4sec
	Top speed: 100mph
Power & torque:	104bhp/117lb ft
Engine:	Normally aspirated 1975cc four cylinder, petrol, carburettor, 8 valves
Drivetrain:	Front-engine RWD
Structure:	Monocoque
Transmission:	Four-speed manual
Weight:	925kg

PRICE GUIDE

Launch price:	£1062
Excellent:	£3500
Good:	£2500
Average:	£1600
Project:	£600

VAUXHALL
Ventora FD/FE

Vauxhall continued its obsession with the letter 'V' in 1968, with the launch of the Ventora. It wasn't a new car though, just the amalgam of two existing machines; the Victor FD and the Cresta PC. The body was taken from the former, the 3294cc six-cylinder 123bhp engine came from the latter, while enhanced trim levels raised the car above normal Victor standards of comfort and equipment. The car continued as an FE model from 1972, using the same engine with the same level of power. Slightly bizarrely, estate versions were badged as Victor 3300s rather than Ventoras until 1973.

SPECIFICATIONS

Years produced:	1970-1975 (25,185 in total)
Performance:	0-60mph: 12.1sec
	Top speed: 107mph
Power & torque:	123bhp/176lb ft
Engine:	Normally aspirated 3294cc six cylinder, petrol, carburettor, 12 valves
Drivetrain:	Front-engine RWD
Structure:	Monocoque
Transmission:	Four-speed manual
Weight:	1124kg

PRICE GUIDE

Launch price:	£1102
Excellent:	£2100
Good:	£1600
Average:	£675
Project:	£175

VAUXHALL
Viva HC

Little changed underneath the Viva HC when it appeared in 1970, for the engines and platform were carried over from the HB. However, the bodies – available as saloons, estates and coupés – were restyled for the new decade, adopting a square-cut style (on the saloons) more reminiscent of the HA than the HB. Within a few years, a range of new engines was introduced; 1256cc, 1759cc and 2279cc. To make the higher-powered cars stand out, they were badged as Magnums from 1973, and the coupés were known by this name for just over a year as well.

SPECIFICATIONS

Years produced:	1970-1979 (640,863 in total)
Performance:	0-60mph: 20.6sec
	Top speed: 78mph
Power & torque:	60bhp/87lb ft
Engine:	Normally aspirated 1159cc four cylinder, petrol, carburettor, 8 valves
Drivetrain:	Front-engine RWD
Structure:	Monocoque
Transmission:	Four-speed manual
Weight:	817kg

PRICE GUIDE

Launch price:	£783
Excellent:	£1400
Good:	£1000
Average:	£450
Project:	£100

VAUXHALL
Firenza

The success of Ford's Capri prompted other manufacturers to offer similar models. The Firenza coupé was Vauxhall's effort, launched in 1971. It bore a family resemblance to the Viva HC it was based on, but had more rounded fastback styling; arguably, it was a more attractive creation than the Capri. Engines ranged from an insipid 1159cc to a rather enjoyable 1975cc, but changes in 1972 introduced 1256cc, 1759cc units, as well as the thoroughly entertaining 2279cc powerhouse of 110bhp. In 1973, the coupés became known as Magnums instead.

SPECIFICATIONS

Years produced:	1971-1973 (18,352 in total)
Performance:	0-60mph: 22.0sec
	Top speed: 84mph
Power & torque:	62bhp/65lb ft
Engine:	Normally aspirated 1159cc four cylinder, petrol, carburettor, 8 valves
Drivetrain:	Front-engine RWD
Structure:	Monocoque
Transmission:	Four-speed manual
Weight:	856kg

PRICE GUIDE

Launch price:	£1017
Excellent:	£1850
Good:	£1400
Average:	£700
Project:	£150

VAUXHALL
Victor FE/VX1800/2300

British Vauxhalls started to lose their individuality with the Victor FE of 1972, for this car also shared some of its underpinnings with the Opel Rekord, albeit with different suspension and engines. The latter were 1759cc and 2279cc four-cylinder overhead-cam units, giving these mid-sized models effective performance, while front disc brakes meant they stopped well too. The sportier Rostyle wheel-decorated variant was known as the VX4/90 and managed 116bhp from its twin-carb 2.3-litre engine. From 1976, the cars became known as VX1800s or VX2300s.

SPECIFICATIONS
Years produced:	1972-1978 (80,610 in total)
Performance:	0-60mph: 12.4sec
	Top speed: 97mph
Power & torque:	110bhp/138lb ft
Engine:	Normally aspirated 2279cc four cylinder, petrol, carburettor, 8 valves
Drivetrain:	Front-engine RWD
Structure:	Monocoque
Transmission:	Four-speed manual
Weight:	1178kg

PRICE GUIDE
Launch price:	£1299
Excellent:	£2000
Good:	£1350
Average:	£500
Project:	£100

VAUXHALL
Firenza Droopsnoot

The Firenza departed even further from the standard Viva HC formula with the unveiling of the Firenza HP – nicknamed the Droopsnoot – in 1973. This was the HC coupé body with a glassfibre nosecone and injected with 131bhp courtesy of its tweaked 2279cc engine. The streamlined front was more than just show as top speed was raised to 120mph, yet the car wasn't a success. Just 204 had been built by the time it was dropped in 1975, against estimates of 1000 a year. Resourcefully, Vauxhall then used the left-over noses on 197 HC estate cars, dubbed Sportshatches.

SPECIFICATIONS
Years produced:	1973-1975 (204 in total)
Performance:	0-60mph: 9.4sec
	Top speed: 120mph
Power & torque:	131bhp/145lb ft
Engine:	Normally aspirated 2279cc four cylinder, petrol, carburettor, 8 valves
Drivetrain:	Front-engine RWD
Structure:	Monocoque
Transmission:	Five-speed manual
Weight:	1015kg

PRICE GUIDE
Launch price:	£2625
Excellent:	£5000
Good:	£4000
Average:	£2000
Project:	£850

VAUXHALL
Chevette

When launched in 1975, the Chevette combined the GM T-Car platform that had proved so successful in Germany as the Opel Kadett, and the willing Viva engine/transmission package. It was a very competent small car that was offered in saloon, hatchback and estate car form. The 'droopsnoot' styling proved to be a Vauxhall styling signature for a decade, and set them apart from their German counterparts. Easy to drive and a tidy handler, the Chevette proved popular enough to stay in production until 1984 – long after it was supposed to have been replaced by the Astra.

SPECIFICATIONS
Years produced:	1975-1984 (415,608 in total)
Performance:	0-60mph: 15.5sec
	Top speed: 90mph
Power & torque:	56bhp/66lb ft
Engine:	Normally aspirated 1256cc four cylinder, petrol, carburettor, 8 valves
Drivetrain:	Front-engine RWD
Structure:	Monocoque
Transmission:	Four-speed manual
Weight:	860kg

PRICE GUIDE
Launch price:	£1650
Excellent:	£1200
Good:	£750
Average:	£500
Project:	£200

VAUXHALL
Cavalier/Sportshatch

The Cavalier proved to be a major turning point for Vauxhall – the Opel Ascona-based saloon proved the perfect weapon for the Luton manufacturer to go Cortina fighting. Like the Chevette, it was well-engineered, handled well and was great on the motorway, but the larger car also had the benefit of being offered with an engine range spanning 1.3 to 2.0 litres. Luton-built cars were more prone to corrosion than their Belgian counterparts, but all were leagues ahead of earlier models – even if it was at the expense of their 'Britishness'.

SPECIFICATIONS (1.6GL)
Years produced:	1975-1981 (238,980 in total)
Performance:	0-60mph: 13.0sec
	Top speed: 100mph
Power & torque:	75bhp/85lb ft
Engine:	Normally aspirated 1584cc four cylinder, petrol, carburettor, 8 valves
Drivetrain:	Front-engine RWD
Structure:	Monocoque
Transmission:	Four-speed manual
Weight:	980kg

PRICE GUIDE
Launch price:	£2749
Excellent:	£1500
Good:	£800
Average:	£450
Project:	£250

VAUXHALL
Chevette 2300HS

The Chevette, of course, was pure family car. The HS and HSR versions were very different beasts though. Built for rally homologation purposes, road versions went on sale in 1978, equipped with a 2279cc twin-cam engine and Getrag five-speed transmission. With 135bhp on tap and the potential for 117mph, this put it head-to-head with Ford's RS Escorts. Front and rear spoilers and wide alloy wheels marked it out from the Chevette herd. The HSR Evolution in 1979 went the whole hog with flared wheelarches and a bodykit, plus 150bhp. Double the prices shown for one of those.

SPECIFICATIONS
Years produced:	1976-1980 (450 in total)
Performance:	0-60mph: 8.8sec
	Top speed: 117mph
Power & torque:	135bhp/134lb ft
Engine:	Normally aspirated 2279cc four cylinder, petrol, carburettor, 16 valves
Drivetrain:	Front-engine RWD
Structure:	Monocoque
Transmission:	Five-speed manual
Weight:	970kg

PRICE GUIDE
Launch price:	£5107
Excellent:	£6500
Good:	£5000
Average:	£2750
Project:	£1500

VAUXHALL
Carlton/Viceroy

The rapid Opelisation of Vauxhall continued apace throughout the 1970s and, with the arrival of the Carlton – a rebranded Opel Rekord – in 1978, it heralded the end of the long-lived Victor range. The 2.0-litre saloon was solidly engineered and competent to drive, but lacked the glamour to take the fight to the Ford Granada and Rover SD1. Six-cylinder Viceroy model (the UK-badged Opel Commodore) followed in 1980, and proved even less popular. Find either now, and you'll be rewarded with a prime slice of German solidity, with a dash of Luton homeliness.

SPECIFICATIONS (2000)
Years produced:	1978-1986 (86,000 in total)
Performance:	0-60mph: 12.3sec
	Top speed: 104mph
Power & torque:	100bhp/109lb ft
Engine:	Normally aspirated 1979cc four cylinder, petrol, carburettor, 8 valves
Drivetrain:	Front-engine RWD
Structure:	Monocoque
Transmission:	Four-speed manual
Weight:	1120kg

PRICE GUIDE
Launch price:	£6496
Excellent:	£1800
Good:	£1100
Average:	£600
Project:	£200

VAUXHALL
Royale

Topping off the Vauxhall tree in the late-1970s were the Royale saloons and coupés, Anglicised versions of Opel's Senator and Monza models. Aside from the front grille and badges, they were identical to their Opel counterparts and were even built in Germany. The saloons were four-door, coupés had two and a hatchback. The 2784cc six-cylinder engine gave a reassuring 138bhp, but the big bruiser was 1980's 2969cc fuel-injection version, with a dramatic rise in power to 180bhp and, with it, the ability to top 130mph. Less kudos than an Opel but still sought after.

SPECIFICATIONS (2.8)
Years produced:	1978-1982 (7119 in total)
Performance:	0-60mph: 11.4sec
	Top speed: 118mph
Power & torque:	140bhp/161lb ft
Engine:	Normally aspirated 2784cc six cylinder, petrol, carburettor, 12 valves
Drivetrain:	Front-engine RWD
Structure:	Monocoque
Transmission:	Four-speed manual
Weight:	1370kg

PRICE GUIDE
Launch price:	£8248
Excellent:	£2650
Good:	£2000
Average:	£1000
Project:	£350

VAUXHALL
Cavalier Mk2 SRi/130

When the Cavalier Mk2 arrived in August 1981, it marked the point when the mantle of the UK's favourite repmobile passed from Dagenham to Luton. Underneath its conservative styling was an up-to-the-minute FWD platform that proved durable and reliable, and resulted in a fine driver's car. When the 115bhp 1.8-litre engine was installed, the Cav was turned into a real wolf in sheep's clothing, and the ultimate overtaking lane tool. The 1987 SRi 130 was even quicker, and more desirable. Rare now, in demand, and excellent value for money.

SPECIFICATIONS
Years produced:	1981-1988 (806,359 in total)
Performance:	0-60mph: 9.1sec
	Top speed: 115mph
Power & torque:	115bhp/111lb ft
Engine:	Normally aspirated 1796cc four cylinder, petrol, fuel injection, 8 valves
Drivetrain:	Front-engine FWD
Structure:	Monocoque
Transmission:	Five-speed manual
Weight:	1060kg

PRICE GUIDE
Launch price:	£6588
Excellent:	£2000
Good:	£1000
Average:	£600
Project:	£250

VAUXHALL
Astra GTE Mk1

Vauxhall was a late entrant to the hot-hatch market, but when it finally arrived, it headed straight to the head of the pile. The Astra was always a great-handling car, but when fitted with wide, low-profile tyres and the excellent 115bhp 1.8-litre 'Family Two' engine, it was transformed into a flying machine. The GTE arrived in 1983, and within a few months received a close-ratio gearbox – yet, not long after, it made way for the aerodynamic Mk2 version. Not many survive now, and rust claimed many. Not surprisingly, values are ahead of the newer car.

SPECIFICATIONS
Years produced:	1983-1984
Performance:	0-60mph: 8.7sec
	Top speed: 118mph
Power & torque:	115bhp/111lb ft
Engine:	Normally aspirated 1796cc four cylinder, petrol, fuel injection, 8 valves
Drivetrain:	Front-engine FWD
Structure:	Monocoque
Transmission:	Five-speed manual
Weight:	930kg

PRICE GUIDE
Launch price:	£6412
Excellent:	£4000
Good:	£2200
Average:	£800
Project:	£450

VAUXHALL
Astra GTE/16V Mk2

During the hot-hatch wars of the 1980s, the Astra GTE was usually a pace-setter. The original 115bhp car boasted a top speed of 126mph, but this was soon upped when the 130bhp 2.0-litre arrived in 1987. But less than two years later, the ultimate Astra arrived – the 150bhp GTE 16V, which used its red-top twin-cam to power way beyond 130mph. The rivals could only sit and watch. But straight-line speed wasn't everything – the 16V's road manners lacked breeding, and a combination of torque-steer and poor traction meant it was often difficult to make the most of its power.

SPECIFICATIONS
Years produced:	1984-1991
Performance:	0-60mph: 6.9sec
	Top speed: 135mph
Power & torque:	150bhp/144lb ft
Engine:	Normally aspirated 1998cc four cylinder, petrol, fuel injection, 16 valves
Drivetrain:	Front-engine FWD
Structure:	Monocoque
Transmission:	Five-speed manual
Weight:	1007kg

PRICE GUIDE
Launch price:	£9499
Excellent:	£3500
Good:	£1800
Average:	£600
Project:	£300

VAUXHALL
Carlton GSi 3000

The 1986 Vauxhall Carlton/Opel Omega was an impressive leap into the 1980s. The slippery new car boasted an Audi-beating drag co-efficient of 0.28, and a well-sorted RWD chassis that challenged BMW's overall ability. But it was a little dull – until the good men at GM shoehorned in the Senator's 3.0-litre straight six. With 177bhp on tap, the bespoiled GSi was capable of topping 135mph, and doing it all day long. The best was to come in 1990, though, when the 24V version was installed, producing Luton's first genuine BMW 535i-baiter in the process.

SPECIFICATIONS
Years produced:	1986-1994 (241,041 in total)
Performance:	0-60mph: 8.2sec
	Top speed: 134mph
Power & torque:	177bhp/177lb ft
Engine:	Normally aspirated 2969cc six cylinder, petrol, electronic fuel injection, 12 valves
Drivetrain:	Front-engine RWD
Structure:	Monocoque
Transmission:	Five-speed manual
Weight:	1370kg

PRICE GUIDE
Launch price:	£16,999
Excellent:	£2500
Good:	£1500
Average:	£750
Project:	£350

VAUXHALL
Senator

And here it was, the ultimate Vauxhall for the ultimate businessman in a hurry. The Senator might have been pure Carlton under the skin, but the imposing new body with cheesegrater grille gave it a presence all of its own. So, it's no wonder that traffic police took the big Vauxhall to their bosom, happy that they'd finally found a replacement for their ageing Rover SD1s. Digital dashboards were an acquired taste, and the 2.5-litre model was a little sluggish. Pick of the range is the 200bhp 24V model that, in manual form, will hit 150mph given a long enough run.

SPECIFICATIONS
Years produced:	1987-1994 (33,125 in total)
Performance:	0-60mph: 9.3sec
	Top speed: 132mph
Power & torque:	177bhp/177lb ft
Engine:	Normally aspirated 2969cc six cylinder, petrol, electronic fuel injection, 12 valves
Drivetrain:	Front-engine RWD
Structure:	Monocoque
Transmission:	Five-speed manual/four-speed auto
Weight:	1530kg

PRICE GUIDE
Launch price:	£14,830
Excellent:	£2000
Good:	£1200
Average:	£650
Project:	£250

VOLKSWAGEN

Revolutionise Your Ride Polybush®

THE BEETLE, as designed in 1938, was simply known as the Volkswagen ('people's car'); the company set up to produce it also adopted the same name. The durable simplicity of Volkswagen's products – the Beetle and the Type 2 bus/van/camper series especially – made the marque phenomenally successful across the globe. It took until the mid-1970s for VW's reliance on the Beetle to end, but it enjoyed similar universal acclaim with the handsome Golf replacement. Subsequent models have enjoyed similar glory. Volkswagen today is a large conglomerate, owning Audi, Skoda, Seat, Bentley, Bugatti and Lamborghini, with a reputation for quality and reliability.

VOLKSWAGEN
Beetle (split-screen)

Adolf Hitler had the idea for the 'Volkswagen' (People's Car) and Ferdinand Porsche designed it, for the purposes of getting Nazi Germany mobile. Who would have thought that from such a troubled birth, the Beetle would go on to conquer the world? After the war, the British army restarted production and gradually the car started to grow more refined, finding itself exported globally. The original split-rear window models were built until 1953 and featured an 1131cc rear-mounted air-cooled engine of just 25bhp. A simple, charming and ruggedly reliable motoring legend.

SPECIFICATIONS
Years produced:	1946-1953
Performance:	0-60mph: N/A
	Top speed: 62mph
Power & torque:	24bhp/49lb ft
Engine:	Normally aspirated 1131cc flat four, petrol, carburettor, 8 valves
Drivetrain:	Rear-engine RWD
Structure:	Separate chassis
Transmission:	Four-speed manual
Weight:	749kg

PRICE GUIDE
Launch price:	£690
Excellent:	£17,500
Good:	£9000
Average:	£6000
Project:	£4000

VOLKSWAGEN
Beetle (Oval)

Poor visibility was always an issue with the original Beetle and its split back window. Volkswagen addressed this in March 1953 when the screen was replaced by a larger single-piece oval one. This important change coincided with the beginning of sales in the UK, and all but the very first of the 'Oval Beetles' benefitted from the first increase in engine size since 1945 when an 1192cc unit added 5bhp. With 30bhp to play with now, 66mph was possible... not much on paper but, of course, a Beetle could happily cruise at that speed all day. Add 25% for Cabriolet prices.

SPECIFICATIONS
Years produced:	1953-1957
Performance:	0-60mph: 47.6sec
	Top speed: 66mph
Power & torque:	24.5bhp/49lb ft
Engine:	Normally aspirated 1131cc flat four, petrol, carburettor, 8 valves
Drivetrain:	Rear-engine RWD
Structure:	Separate chassis
Transmission:	Four-speed manual
Weight:	711kg

PRICE GUIDE
Launch price:	£690
Excellent:	£12,000
Good:	£7500
Average:	£4750
Project:	£3000

VOLKSWAGEN
Kombi/Camper

The initial idea for a VW-based van was in 1947, but it wasn't until 1950 that the officially designated Type 2 appeared. Many different variants were available but the most popular and numerous were the Kombi (Kombinationskraftwagen – a windowed combination of passenger and cargo vehicle, usually referred to as a 'bus') and the Camper. Westfalia created most of the latter. They were nicknamed 'Split' or 'Splittie' due to their divided windscreen, and VW updated the mechanical side of the vehicles constantly while leaving their looks mostly untouched... at least until 1968.

SPECIFICATIONS
Years produced:	1950-1968
Performance:	0-60mph: N/A
	Top speed: 65mph
Power & torque:	30bhp/56lb ft
Engine:	Normally aspirated 1192cc flat four, petrol, carburettor, 8 valves
Drivetrain:	Rear-engine RWD
Structure:	Separate chassis
Transmission:	Four-speed manual
Weight:	1105kg

PRICE GUIDE
Launch price:	N/A
Excellent:	£35,000
Good:	£20,000
Average:	£10,000
Project:	£5000

VOLKSWAGEN
Karmann-Ghia Coupé

With the Beetle so easy to put different bodies on – after all, this was how Porsche started out – it was almost inevitable that Volkswagen would come up with a sports car. Actually, it was coachbuilder Karmann which had the idea and VW jumped at the chance when it saw the pretty coupé body that Ghia designed. The public liked it too, and this sleeker Beetle sold well. However, it was a sheep in wolf's clothing, for its underpinnings were pure Beetle, with anaemic performance. The original 1192cc engine was increased in stages up to 1584cc by 1974.

SPECIFICATIONS
Years produced:	1955-1974 (364,401 in total)
Performance:	0-60mph: 26.5sec
	Top speed: 77mph
Power & torque:	30bhp/56lb ft
Engine:	Normally aspirated 1192cc flat four, petrol, carburettor, 8 valves
Drivetrain:	Rear-engine RWD
Structure:	Separate chassis
Transmission:	Four-speed manual
Weight:	730kg

PRICE GUIDE
Launch price:	£1235
Excellent:	£9000
Good:	£7000
Average:	£5000
Project:	£2500

VOLKSWAGEN
Beetle 1200/1300

For the 1200, Volkswagen finally fitted a proper rectangular back window to the Beetle, almost twice the size of what had been there before. With a bigger windscreen too, visibility was much improved. The basic car was constantly updated in detail until 1968 when it was thoroughly revised again. New headlamps and thicker bumpers were fitted, and uprated safety kit appeared inside. Mechanical changes included – at last – 12-volt electrics and dual-circuit brakes, plus a fuel tank that didn't have to be filled by via the front boot. Building continued in Mexico until 2003.

SPECIFICATIONS
Years produced:	1957-1978
Performance:	0-60mph: 32.1sec
	Top speed: 72mph
Power & torque:	40bhp/65lb ft
Engine:	Normally aspirated 1192cc flat four, petrol, carburettor, 8 valves
Drivetrain:	Rear-engine RWD
Structure:	Separate chassis
Transmission:	Four-speed manual
Weight:	739kg

PRICE GUIDE
Launch price:	£617
Excellent:	£5000
Good:	£3500
Average:	£1900
Project:	£900

VOLKSWAGEN
Karmann-Ghia Convertible

After the hardtop version of the Karmann-Ghia proved such a success, Volkswagen and Karmann didn't take long to come up with a convertible version. It was unveiled in late 1957 to much the same level of appreciation as its tin-lid sister. Extra strengthening made the convertible heavier and therefore slower than the coupé, but that didn't matter to those who admired this fresh-air fashion statement; America loved it, of course. The car started life with a rear-mounted air-cooled 1192cc engine, which gradually increased in size through 1285cc and 1493cc to 1584cc.

SPECIFICATIONS
Years produced:	1958-1974 (80,899 in total)
Performance:	0-60mph: 27.0sec
	Top speed: 80mph
Power & torque:	39bhp/68lb ft
Engine:	Normally aspirated 1285cc flat four, petrol, carburettor, 8 valves
Drivetrain:	Rear-engine RWD
Structure:	Separate chassis
Transmission:	Four-speed manual
Weight:	830kg

PRICE GUIDE
Launch price:	£1196
Excellent:	£11,000
Good:	£9000
Average:	£6250
Project:	£3500

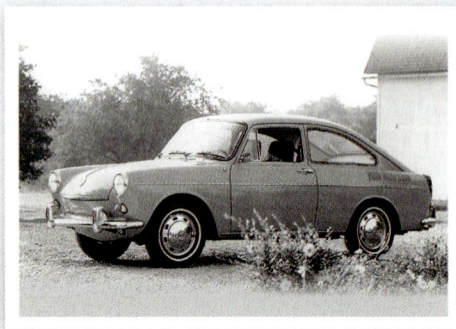

VOLKSWAGEN
1500/1600 Type 3

The Type 3 was a spin-off from the Beetle, intended to address some of its perceived shortcomings of being old-fashioned, cramped and having poor luggage capacity. And it was a more modern-looking machine, with extra space inside and a boot front and rear. Initially available as a two-door saloon with a 1493cc engine, a two-door estate – known as the Variant – came along in 1962, with a fastback saloon in 1965. By this time there was also a 1584cc engine. All are highly prized these days by air-cooled VW modifiers.

SPECIFICATIONS
Years produced:	1961-1973 (1,813,600 in total)
Performance:	0-60mph: 25.3sec
	Top speed: 78mph
Power & torque:	44bhp/72lb ft
Engine:	Normally aspirated 1493cc flat four, petrol, carburettor, 8 valves
Drivetrain:	Rear-engine RWD
Structure:	Separate chassis
Transmission:	Four-speed manual
Weight:	860kg

PRICE GUIDE
Launch price:	£998
Excellent:	£5000
Good:	£4250
Average:	£2000
Project:	£650

VOLKSWAGEN
Karmann-Ghia Type 34

From 1961, there was another Karmann-Ghia coupé alongside the more familiar type. An offshoot of VW's Type 3, Ghia styled the vaguely BMW-ish machine while coachbuilder Karmann built it. Although less pretty than its stablemate, it was still very attractive and the wider floorpan and 1493cc engine gave it more practicality and performance too. However, it was never a big seller, even when a 1584cc engine of 54bhp was added, along with front disc brakes, in 1965. A high price, thirst for fuel and not being sold in the USA were the main reasons for this.

SPECIFICATIONS
Years produced: 1962-1969 (42,563 in total)
Performance: 0-60mph: 21.3sec
Top speed: 85mph
Power & torque: 65bhp/87lb ft
Engine: Normally aspirated 1585cc flat four, petrol, carburettor, 8 valves
Drivetrain: Rear-engine RWD
Structure: Separate chassis
Transmission: Four-speed manual
Weight: 920kg

PRICE GUIDE
Launch price: £1330
Excellent: £8000
Good: £5500
Average: £3250
Project: £1750

VOLKSWAGEN
411/412

One of the main issues with Volkswagen's passenger cars of the 1960s was that none had four doors. The 411 of 1968 changed all this; it managed to squeeze all the requisite doors onto a Beetle chassis (with a wheelbase stretched by 4in) but kept the faith with the rear-engined layout. However, at the front were MacPherson struts and disc brakes, meaning the 411 was a better-behaved machine than the Beetle. The 1679cc engine received fuel injection in 1969 and the gawky styling was reworked in 1972 for the 412. A 1795cc engine was adopted in 1973.

SPECIFICATIONS
Years produced: 1968-1974 (367,728 in total)
Performance: 0-60mph: 16.8sec
Top speed: 96mph
Power & torque: 80bhp/97lb ft
Engine: Normally aspirated 1679cc flat four, petrol, electronic fuel injection, 8 valves
Drivetrain: Rear-engine RWD
Structure: Separate chassis
Transmission: Four-speed manual
Weight: 1030kg

PRICE GUIDE
Launch price: £1290
Excellent: £3750
Good: £2250
Average: £1000
Project: £500

VOLKSWAGEN
Beetle 1302/1303

Although they looked the same as previous models, the 1302 and 1303 'Super' Beetles were the most radical reworks of the car during its long life. MacPherson strut front suspension was adopted, which allowed more front boot space and improved handling. The struts also allowed front disc brakes to be fitted. The 1303, from 1972, had a more safety-conscious padded dashboard and wraparound windscreen, plus bigger tail lights. Engines were the usual air-cooled units of 1285cc and 44bhp, and 1584cc and 50bhp. Not quite as liked as other Bugs.

SPECIFICATIONS
Years produced: 1970-1975
Performance: 0-60mph: 18.3sec
Top speed: 81mph
Power & torque: 50bhp/78lb ft
Engine: Normally aspirated 1584cc flat four, petrol, carburettor, 8 valves
Drivetrain: Rear-engine RWD
Structure: Separate chassis
Transmission: Four-speed manual
Weight: 870kg

PRICE GUIDE
Launch price: £875
Excellent: £4500
Good: £2750
Average: £1600
Project: £600

VOLKSWAGEN
K70

Often overlooked in VW history, the K70 remains significant in Volkswagen's history for being its first FWD car – even if it was going to be an NSU. The boxy saloon was designed to be the Ro80's smaller brother, but weeks before its launch, VW pulled the plug on NSU, and took the car for itself. The fact that Wolfsburg desperately needed a new generation of models to replace the Beetle-derived cars had absolutely nothing to do with its decision... It was a poor seller but, in the classic market, the K70 has picked up a small yet enthusiastic following.

SPECIFICATIONS
Years produced: 1970-1974 (211,127 in total)
Performance: 0-60mph: 13.5sec
Top speed: 104mph
Power & torque: 75bhp/91lb ft
Engine: Normally aspirated 1605cc four cylinder, petrol, carburettor, 8 valves
Drivetrain: Front-engine FWD
Structure: Monocoque
Transmission: Four-speed manual
Weight: 1015kg

PRICE GUIDE
Launch price: £1570
Excellent: £2000
Good: £1000
Average: £750
Project: £450

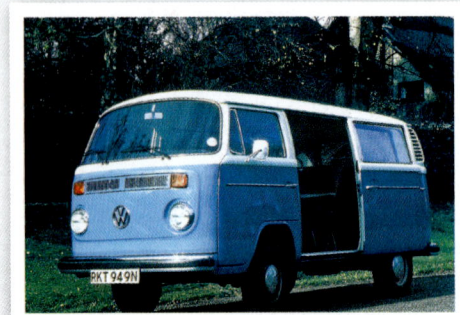

VOLKSWAGEN
Camper

In 1968, the second generation of Type 2 (some might say, belatedly) had thoroughly modernised looks with a single-piece windscreen, which earned the model the nickname of the 'Bay Window.' Although with less character to its styling, this version was easier to drive with improved suspension and larger engines; at introduction there was a 1584cc unit with a 1679cc one from 1971, when disc brakes also appeared. By the time European assembly came to an end in 1978, the Camper sported a 1970cc engine. Endowed with 70bhp, it was almost fast.

SPECIFICATIONS
Years produced: 1968-1979
Performance: 0-60mph: N/A
Top speed: 75mph
Power & torque: 70bhp/90lb ft
Engine: Normally aspirated 1970cc flat four, petrol, carburettor, 8 valves
Drivetrain: Rear-engine RWD
Structure: Separate chassis
Transmission: Four-speed manual
Weight: 1105kg

PRICE GUIDE
Launch price: £N/A
Excellent: £15,000
Good: £7000
Average: £3500
Project: £1500

VOLKSWAGEN
Passat MkI

Volkswagen's *real* FWD future started here. After the K70 false start, the Audi-engineered Passat proved to be the perfect product at the right time. Although VW's big sellers were the smaller cars in its range, the Passat offered the perfect upgrade path, as it looked and felt so familiar to drive. Its EA827 1.6-litre was a revelation, being smooth, revvy and powerful – providing the mainstay for VW's mid-range models for generations to come. A little clinical compared with rivals, yet more than capable of entertaining. But it had a serious capacity for rusting.

SPECIFICATIONS
Years produced:	1973-1980 (2,000,000 in total)
Performance:	0-60mph: 11.0sec
	Top speed: 104mph
Power & torque:	75bhp/70lb ft
Engine:	Normally aspirated 1588cc four cylinder, petrol, carburettor, 8 valves
Drivetrain:	Front-engine FWD
Structure:	Monocoque
Transmission:	Four-speed manual
Weight:	855kg

PRICE GUIDE
Launch price:	£1495
Excellent:	£2000
Good:	£900
Average:	£550
Project:	£250

VOLKSWAGEN
Polo MkI

Like the Passat, this Volkswagen started life as an Audi. Yes, forget the 1990s A3 or A2, the first small Audi was actually the 50, which begat the Polo in 1976. It was a great supermini, too, especially when one considers the lack of experience the company had with small cars. Great build, a functional interior, and stylish Bertone bodywork made these cars practically irresistible to small-car buyers in Germany. Some would say the Polo is perhaps a little too rational compared with the fabulous Renault 5 and Fiat 127, but sometimes it's good to be sensible.

SPECIFICATIONS
Years produced:	1975-1981 (1,200,000 in total)
Performance:	0-60mph: 16.0sec
	Top speed: 90mph
Power & torque:	40bhp/55lb ft
Engine:	Normally aspirated 1043cc four cylinder, petrol, carburettor, 8 valves
Drivetrain:	Front-engine FWD
Structure:	Monocoque
Transmission:	Four-speed manual
Weight:	700kg

PRICE GUIDE
Launch price:	£1798
Excellent:	£2000
Good:	£1100
Average:	£650
Project:	£250

VOLKSWAGEN
Scirocco MkI

The first in Volkswagen's new front-wheel-drive generation, the Scirocco emerged as a smart and desirable Capri alternative. Styled by Giorgetto Giugiaro and engineered by Audi, it was a major departure for the Wolfsburg company that previewed the ultra-successful Golf's front-wheel drive platform. In injection form (it shared its engine with the Golf GTI), it was quick and flighty, and handled in a tidy fashion. Cramped interior was not such a problem for coupé buyers, but rot-prone body would prove to be a major bugbear a few years down the line. An all-time classic.

SPECIFICATIONS (GLi)
Years produced:	1973-1988 (504,200)
Performance:	0-60mph: 8.5sec
	Top speed: 113mph
Power & torque:	110bhp/96lb ft
Engine:	Normally aspirated 1588cc four cylinder, petrol, electronic fuel injection, 8 valves
Drivetrain:	Front-engine FWD
Structure:	Monocoque
Transmission:	Four-speed manual
Weight:	865kg

PRICE GUIDE
Launch price:	£1995
Excellent:	£4000
Good:	£2000
Average:	£800
Project:	£300

VOLKSWAGEN
Golf Mk1/GTI

Having scored such huge global success with the Beetle, Volkswagen then annoyed its rivals by repeating the same trick with its small hatchback Golf. This Giugiaro-designed masterpiece was exactly the right car at the right time, but it was in GTI form, from 1975, that it was most impressive. The car that first earned the term 'hot hatch' used a Bosch fuel-injection 1588cc engine to pump 110bhp through its front wheels and the tight and nimble handling meant all this could be used to the max. A 1781cc engine and quad headlamps marked out 1982's 1800 model.

SPECIFICATIONS
Years produced:	1976-1984 (600,000 in total)
Performance:	0-60mph: 8.7sec
	Top speed: 112mph
Power & torque:	110bhp/96lb ft
Engine:	Normally aspirated 1588cc four cylinder, petrol, electronic fuel injection, 8 valves
Drivetrain:	Front-engine FWD
Structure:	Monocoque
Transmission:	Four-speed manual
Weight:	830kg

PRICE GUIDE
Launch price:	£3707
Excellent:	£6000
Good:	£3000
Average:	£1700
Project:	£650

VOLKSWAGEN
Golf Cabriolet

The MkI Cabriolet was a latecomer to the Golf scene, not seeing the light of day until 1979. However, it would far outlast the saloon on which it was based. Built by Karmann, the four-seater Cabriolet had body strengthening, a transverse roll bar and enhanced trim. Earlier cars had manually-operated hoods but they eventually graduated to powered operation. The GTI equivalent was known as the GLi until 1984 but proved slower and less rigid than the hatch. Because of the high costs of building a MkII version, the roofless MkI continued through until 1993.

SPECIFICATIONS
Years produced:	1979-1993 (400,871 in total)
Performance:	0-60mph: 14.2sec
	Top speed: 94mph
Power & torque:	54bhp/71lb ft
Engine:	Normally aspirated 1272cc four cylinder, petrol, carburettor, 8 valves
Drivetrain:	Front-engine FWD
Structure:	Monocoque
Transmission:	Four-speed manual
Weight:	845kg

PRICE GUIDE
Launch price:	£6985
Excellent:	£4000
Good:	£3000
Average:	£1500
Project:	£500

VOLKSWAGEN
Passat/Santana GX5

The 1980 Passat retained much of the earlier car's engineering, but was clothed in a larger, more maturely styled body. Offered in three-box saloon form – and called the Santana in the UK – as well hatchback and estate guises, there was a version for everyone. The most interesting model by far was the Santana GX5, which was powered by Audi's warbling five-pot in 1.9-litre form. Pretty much a forgotten entity today, though, and if you find one, it's unlikely to have been cared for. But bag a GX5 for a bargain price, and enjoy the Quattro fantasy.

SPECIFICATIONS (GX5)
Years produced:	1980-1988 (1,978,200 in total)
Performance:	0-60mph: 9.5sec
	Top speed: 113mph
Power & torque:	115bhp/122lb ft
Engine:	Normally aspirated 1921cc five cylinder, petrol, carburettor, 10 valves
Drivetrain:	Front-engine FWD
Structure:	Monocoque
Transmission:	Five-speed manual
Weight:	1085kg

PRICE GUIDE
Launch price:	£5315
Excellent:	£1200
Good:	£800
Average:	£550
Project:	£250

VOLKSWAGEN
Polo/Polo Coupé

The 1981 Polo was effectively a rebody of the original car – but where the older car was elegant and delicate, the newer car was practical and rational. Fans have long since been calling it the 'breadvan' and, with that vertical tailgate, it's easy to see why. The older car's look came back in 1983 when the Coupé arrived, with its sloping rear end. More power arrived, although this was no GTi in miniature, whatever VW might have told you. After the facelift in 1991, the mad-cap supercharged G40 was added to the range, and that really did earn its cult status.

SPECIFICATIONS
Years produced:	1981-1995 (2,200,000 in total)
Performance:	0-60mph: 12.5sec
	Top speed: 95mph
Power & torque:	55bhp/71lb ft
Engine:	Normally aspirated 1272cc four cylinder, petrol, carburettor, 8 valves
Drivetrain:	Front-engine FWD
Structure:	Monocoque
Transmission:	Four-speed manual
Weight:	740kg

PRICE GUIDE
Launch price:	£3799
Excellent:	£1500
Good:	£900
Average:	£450
Project:	£250

VOLKSWAGEN
Scirocco MkII

Volkswagen went in-house for the second-generation Scirocco, and many would say that without its delicate Italian styling, it lost a fair chunk of appeal. But what the new car lost in style, it gained in practicality – and pace. It benefited from the rising power of the Golf GTi – initially its 112bhp 1.8-litre 8-valve, and then the 136bhp 16-valve engines. So equipped, the Scirocco was a flying machine. Eventually replaced by the Corrado (which was planned to be called Scirocco), and now overlooked compared with what came before and after. Still fun to drive, but watch out for rust!

SPECIFICATIONS
Years produced:	1982-1992 (340,700 in total)
Performance:	0-60mph: 9.1sec
	Top speed: 120mph
Power & torque:	112bhp/113lb ft
Engine:	Normally aspirated 1781cc four cylinder, petrol, electronic fuel injection, 8 valves
Drivetrain:	Front-engine FWD
Structure:	Monocoque
Transmission:	Five-speed manual
Weight:	920kg

PRICE GUIDE
Launch price:	£5424
Excellent:	£2500
Good:	£1800
Average:	£800
Project:	£300

VOLKSWAGEN
Golf Mk2/GTI/GTI 16V

Volkswagen's update of the Giugiaro-penned original was an improvement over the 1974 original in every way. It was roomier, easier to service, more rust resistant and generally faster. However, it also didn't look as good – not that this dented sales in the slightest. GTI used carry-over 1.8-litre engine, but lacked a little fizz of the original. That was restored by the arrival of the 16V in 1986, which pushed power to 136bhp and dropped the 0-60mph time to under 8 seconds. The classiest and most complete hot hatch of its era, and that's reflected by its popularity today.

SPECIFICATIONS
Years produced:	1983-1992 (6,300,000 in total)
Performance:	0-60mph: 8.5sec
	Top speed: 115mph
Power & torque:	112bhp/113lb ft
Engine:	Normally aspirated 1781cc four cylinder, petrol, electronic fuel injection, 8 valves
Drivetrain:	Front-engine FWD
Structure:	Monocoque
Transmission:	Five-speed manual
Weight:	907kg

PRICE GUIDE
Launch price:	£7800
Excellent:	£5000
Good:	£2200
Average:	£800
Project:	£400

VOLKSWAGEN
Corrado 16V/G60

Volkswagen's 1988 replacement for the Scirocco successfully updated its predecessor's three-door hatchback style with a brooding and imposing persona. Closely related to the Golf Mk2, it debuted with a 1781cc engine. Topping the range initially was the G60, a supercharged monster of 158bhp that took just 7.8 seconds to reach 60mph and ultimately reached 140mph. And then came the VR6 version, a 187bhp fire-breather that encroached on supercar territory, with a maximum speed of 143mph and the dash from zero to 60mph taking a mere 6.2 seconds.

SPECIFICATIONS
Years produced:	1988-1993
Performance:	0-60mph: 7.8sec
	Top speed: 140mph
Power & torque:	160bhp/166lb ft
Engine:	Supercharged 1781cc four cylinder, petrol, electronic fuel injection, 8 valves
Drivetrain:	Front-engine FWD
Structure:	Monocoque
Transmission:	Five-speed manual
Weight:	1115kg

PRICE GUIDE
Launch price:	£19,907
Excellent:	£5500
Good:	£4250
Average:	£2500
Project:	£1250

VOLVO

FOR MUCH OF its life, Volvo – derived from the Latin for 'I roll' – has been a byword for safety and solidity. Its first car left the Swedish factory in 1927, and all proved tough in more hospitable climates than the Arctic environment it was designed for. Volvo also placed great store in passenger protection. Its robust, no-nonsense approach was exemplified by the 140 and 240-series, which kept the same basic style from 1967 to 1993, but still sold in huge volumes across the globe. Volvos started to become sexier from the 1990s onwards and moved upmarket under Ford ownership from 1998. The company was bought by Chinese car manufacturer Geely in 2010.

VOLVO
121/122S/131/132

The 120-series brought Volvo cars to Britain as well as raising the marque's profile elsewhere. Rugged and reliable, with handsome but traditional looks, the 120's unburstable reputation put it in the same category as the Beetle on the worldwide stage. The 121 was the lower-specification four-door machine with less powerful engines, 122S versions had better performance and equipment levels, and were initially intended for export only. Two-door cars (131 and 132) outlived the four-door, as Volvo discontinued the more useful car to make way for the 140-series cars.

SPECIFICATIONS	
Years produced:	1955-1970
Performance:	0-60mph: 17sec
	Top speed: 85mph
Power & torque:	66bhp/76lb ft
Engine:	Normally aspirated 1582cc four cylinder, petrol, carburettor, 8 valves
Drivetrain:	Front-engine RWD
Structure:	Monocoque
Transmission:	Four-speed manual
Weight:	1000kg

PRICE GUIDE	
Launch price:	£1197
Excellent:	£4300
Good:	£3500
Average:	£1800
Project:	£750

VOLVO
PV544

Volvo's first model to be exported in any great numbers was the PV444 of 1947. When the time came to replace it, in 1958, Volvo simply modified the curvaceous and sturdy bodyshell slightly – with bigger front and rear windows – and dubbed the new model the PV544 (to signify that this *personvagn* could now seat five instead of four). Two engines were used; a 1584cc unit and, from 1960, a 1778cc one. Sport models boasted twin carburettors and extra levels of equipment. The PV was meant to be superseded by the 120 but lasted seven years alongside it.

SPECIFICATIONS	
Years produced:	1959-1965
Performance:	0-60mph: 19sec
	Top speed: 87mph
Power & torque:	66bhp/86lb ft
Engine:	Normally aspirated 1584cc four cylinder, petrol, carburettor, 8 valves
Drivetrain:	Front-engine RWD
Structure:	Monocoque
Transmission:	Four-speed manual
Weight:	940kg

PRICE GUIDE	
Launch price:	£N/A in UK
Excellent:	£5600
Good:	£4250
Average:	£2500
Project:	£900

VOLVO
P1800/S/E

Volvo gets racy! Or at least looked it. The P1800, designed by Frua and launched in 1960, was a startling-looking creation and British eyebrows were raised when Roger Moore drove one in *The Saint*. But that sweptback glamour disguised little more than 120 mechanicals, which gave reasonable enough performance but fell short of being exhilarating. Post-1963, the name was changed to 1800S as power increased to 108 and 115bhp. A bit more wolf and less sheepish was the fuel-injection 1800E of 1969 to 1972; its 130bhp gave performance that went with the looks.

SPECIFICATIONS	
Years produced:	1961-1972
Performance:	0-60mph: 13.2sec
	Top speed: 104mph
Power & torque:	115bhp/108lb ft
Engine:	Normally aspirated 1780cc four cylinder, petrol, carburettor, 8 valves
Drivetrain:	Front-engine RWD
Structure:	Monocoque
Transmission:	Four-speed manual
Weight:	1070kg

PRICE GUIDE	
Launch price:	£1836
Excellent:	£9000
Good:	£7500
Average:	£3750
Project:	£1500

VOLVO
122 B18

In 1961, Volvo gave the 120-series cars more power to cope with their heavyweight engineering. The B18 engine was a fresh design, which would soon earn a reputation for longevity. Sized at 1778cc, it provided the single-carburettor 121 with 75 or 85bhp, while 122 cars, with their twin carburettors, enjoyed fruitier 90, 95 and 100bhp outputs. Even more power and performance was supplied courtesy of the B20 engine. This was a bored-out version of the B18 with a capacity of 1998cc, and resulted in the most powerful 120 of all, the 1968-1970 122S with 115bhp and 100mph potential.

SPECIFICATIONS (122S)	
Years produced:	1962-1967
Performance:	0-60mph: 13.8sec
	Top speed: 104mph
Power & torque:	115bhp/112lb ft
Engine:	Normally aspirated 1778cc four cylinder, petrol, carburettor, 8 valves
Drivetrain:	Front-engine RWD
Structure:	Monocoque
Transmission:	Four-speed manual
Weight:	1090kg

PRICE GUIDE	
Launch price:	£1022
Excellent:	£4850
Good:	£4000
Average:	£2000
Project:	£750

VOLVO
123GT

Thanks to their inherent strength and reliability, Amazons proved natural rally cars. To capitalise on this, Volvo gave the go-faster world of 1966 the 123GT. Its twin-carburettor 1778cc engine came from the more sporty 1800S coupé and it had servo-assisted front disc brakes and bumper-mounted spotlamps while, inside, the driver could revel in his special steering wheel and dash-mounted rev counter. Only available as a two-door, this Swedish grand tourer proved a potent tool. British tuner Ruddspeed offered a package to boost power to an entertaining 132bhp.

SPECIFICATIONS

Years produced:	1967-1968
Performance:	0-60mph: 12.5sec
	Top speed: 109mph
Power & torque:	115bhp/107lb ft
Engine:	Normally aspirated 1778cc four cylinder, petrol, carburettor, 8 valves
Drivetrain:	Front-engine RWD
Structure:	Monocoque
Transmission:	Four-speed manual
Weight:	1050kg

PRICE GUIDE

Launch price:	£1372
Excellent:	£6000
Good:	£4750
Average:	£2750
Project:	£1200

VOLVO
144/145/142

Volvo's reputation for safety first, style second started in earnest with the 140-series. These big and boxy cars, built from 1967 to 1974, were uncompromising in their looks but thoroughly protected their occupants. The third figure of the model designation denoted the number of doors; thus the 142 had two, the 144 had four, and the 145 was the five-door estate. At first, the 1778cc engine was all that was available, albeit with twin carburettors on the S models, but 1986cc engines became standard in 1968. Best was the 1970s GL, with fuel injection and leather upholstery.

SPECIFICATIONS

Years produced:	1967-1974
Performance:	0-60mph: 10.1sec
	Top speed: 106mph
Power & torque:	124bhp/123lb ft
Engine:	Normally aspirated 1986cc four cylinder, petrol, mechanical fuel injection, 8 valve
Drivetrain:	Front-engine RWD
Structure:	Monocoque
Transmission:	Four-speed manual
Weight:	1290kg

PRICE GUIDE

Launch price:	£1354
Excellent:	£1850
Good:	£1400
Average:	£700
Project:	£200

VOLVO
164

Seeking to enter the luxury realms of Jaguar and Mercedes-Benz, Volvo unveiled the 164 in 1968. It was based on the 140-series, with a longer body and a 2978cc six-cylinder engine lurking behind its much grander grille, plus generous equipment. With the TE, owners got leather, air conditioning and power steering. The cars started with 145bhp, but that rose to 175bhp when fuel injection arrived in 1971. The fitment of built-in foglamps from 1969 was a very Jaguar touch, but the 164 failed to appeal as much as the prettier Jags it wanted to emulate, despite the better build quality.

SPECIFICATIONS

Years produced:	1968-1975
Performance:	0-60mph: 11sec
	Top speed: 110mph
Power & torque:	145bhp/163lb ft
Engine:	Normally aspirated 2978cc six cylinder, petrol, carburettor, 12 valves
Drivetrain:	Front-engine RWD
Structure:	Monocoque
Transmission:	Four-speed manual
Weight:	1320kg

PRICE GUIDE

Launch price:	£1791
Excellent:	£2100
Good:	£1600
Average:	£850
Project:	£300

VOLVO
1800ES

One of the most intriguing of all Volvos appeared in 1971, with the 1800ES. Cast in the mould of Reliant's Scimitar GTE, this was the 1800 given an estate rear as a way of updating its dated appearance for the 1970s. It was a gamble that worked, for this idiosyncratic load-lugger proved very popular, despite its nickname of 'Snow White's hearse'. The 130bhp fuel-injection engine still gave good performance – 115mph was possible for the boutique shopper in a hurry – while the trademark frameless glass hatchback was a theme that Volvo would return to again.

SPECIFICATIONS

Years produced:	1971-1973 (8077 in total)
Performance:	0-60mph: 9.7sec
	Top speed: 112mph
Power & torque:	130bhp/123lb ft
Engine:	Normally aspirated 1986cc four cylinder, petrol, carburettor, 8 valves
Drivetrain:	Front-engine RWD
Structure:	Monocoque
Transmission:	Four-speed manual
Weight:	1130kg

PRICE GUIDE

Launch price:	£2650
Excellent:	£8250
Good:	£7000
Average:	£3250
Project:	£1250

VOLVO
264/265

Alongside the four-cylinder 240-series cars, Volvo weighed in with six-cylinder variants using the same bodyshell. The 264 saloon was launched at the same time; the 265 estate followed a year later. Both used the brand new 2664cc V6 engine developed with Peugeot and Renault; a smooth and mighty motor especially in 140bhp fuel-injection form. This went up to 2849cc in 1981, which added an extra 14bhp. Flagship was the 264TE, a Bertone-built stretched limousine, complete with a telephone and a fridge. As ABBA used one, it must have been special!

SPECIFICATIONS

Years produced:	1974-1979 (169,127 in total)
Performance:	0-60mph: 12.7sec
	Top speed: 108mph
Power & torque:	148bhp/161lb ft
Engine:	Normally aspirated 2664cc V6, petrol, electronic fuel injection, 12 valves
Drivetrain:	Front-engine RWD
Structure:	Monocoque
Transmission:	Four-speed manual with overdrive
Weight:	1456kg

PRICE GUIDE

Launch price:	£3799
Excellent:	£1800
Good:	£1400
Average:	£600
Project:	£200

VOLVO
244/245

The Flying Brick, Swedish Tank... nicknames for Volvo's Lego-like 244/245 were hardly complimentary. But what this tough-mobile lacked in style, it more than made up for in safety and sales. The cars – the 244 was the four-door saloon, the 245 the estate – were based on the 140. However, the fronts were re-engineered for MacPherson strut suspension and a new nose. Aside from Volvo's existing 1986cc engine, a new overhead-cam 2127cc unit featured; this rose to 2315cc in 1978. The last were built in 1993; as durable in lifespan as they were in quality and strength.

SPECIFICATIONS

Years produced:	1974-1993 (3,000,000+ in total)
Performance:	0-60mph: 11.4sec
	Top speed: 106mph
Power & torque:	123bhp/125lb ft
Engine:	Normally aspirated 2127cc four cylinder, petrol, electronic fuel injection, 8 valves
Drivetrain:	Front-engine RWD
Structure:	Monocoque
Transmission:	Four-speed manual with overdrive
Weight:	1404kg

PRICE GUIDE

Launch price:	£2155
Excellent:	£1750
Good:	£1300
Average:	£600
Project:	£175

VOLVO
340/360

The Volvo 300 actually started life as DAF's P900 project, a car that was supposed to replace the quirky 66 model. The Dutch company needed help to get it into production, and in the end Volvo ended up buying a majority stake and rebranding it. Known as the 343, the new small Volvo retained DAF's Variomatic transmission (a manual came later), mounted at the rear. Sales were slow initially, but picked up throughout the 1980s, the 340 eventually becoming a UK top ten seller. Younger classic car fans are drawn to its RWD layout and low running costs.

SPECIFICATIONS

Years produced:	1976-1991 (1,086,405 in total)
Performance:	0-60mph: 13.5sec
	Top speed: 104mph
Power & torque:	70bhp/79lb ft
Engine:	Normally aspirated 1397cc four cylinder, petrol, carburettor, 8 valves
Drivetrain:	Front-engine RWD
Structure:	Monocoque
Transmission:	Variomatic CVT
Weight:	943kg

PRICE GUIDE

Launch price:	£3455
Excellent:	£1800
Good:	£750
Average:	£450
Project:	£275

VOLVO
262C

The 262C was a wild card in the Volvo pack, as an attempt to build a luxury coupé. It was distinctive, although the lowered black-vinyl clad roof with swept-back and chunky rear pillars plonked on top of a 260 lower body gave a distinctly tank-like appearance, but the sumptuous leather-bound interior certainly pampered its occupants. Engines were the same as the standard 260's; thus a 140bhp 2664cc V6 at first, followed by a 155bhp 2849cc V6 towards the end of production. Definitely mean and moody but not all that magnificent, although Volvo aficionados adore them.

SPECIFICATIONS

Years produced:	1978-1981 (5622 in total)
Performance:	0-60mph: 11.1sec
	Top speed: 109mph
Power & torque:	148bhp/161lb ft
Engine:	Normally aspirated 2664cc V6, petrol, electronic fuel injection, 12 valves
Drivetrain:	Front-engine RWD
Structure:	Monocoque
Transmission:	Three-speed automatic
Weight:	1450kg

PRICE GUIDE

Launch price:	£13,000
Excellent:	£4500
Good:	£2750
Average:	£1400
Project:	£600

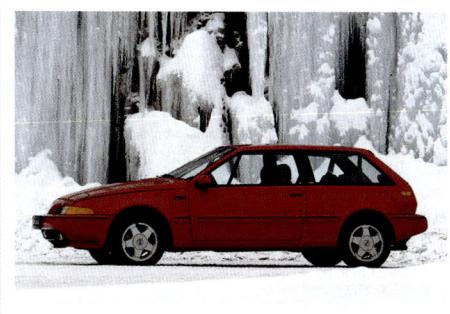

VOLVO
480 ES/Turbo

As a belated successor to the 1800ES, the quirky 480ES echoed its predecessor's frameless glass hatchback but, from the front, looked like no Volvo before. The design was a dramatic and sleek wedge with pop-up headlamps and a tiny Volvo-badged grille hiding under the front bumper. Front-wheel drive was a first for the marque and there were faddish features such as door pillar-mounted locks and an electronic information centre. 1721cc and 1998cc engines featured and there was a turbocharged version from 1989. An oddball in the Volvo canon but an intriguing creation.

SPECIFICATIONS

Years produced:	1986-1995 (80,463 in total)
Performance:	0-60mph: 8.6sec
	Top speed: 124mph
Power & torque:	120bhp/129lb ft
Engine:	Turbocharged 1721cc four cylinder, petrol, electronic fuel injection, 8 valves
Drivetrain:	Front-engine FWD
Structure:	Monocoque
Transmission:	Five-speed manual
Weight:	900kg

PRICE GUIDE

Launch price:	£10,850
Excellent:	£1250
Good:	£1000
Average:	£500
Project:	£200

WARTBURG

THE WARTBURG NAME dates back to 1898, but had been long-dead when the East German VEB Automobilwerk Eisenach revived it for its new range of upper-middle class saloons in 1956. The first Wartburg was an updated version of the IFA F9, now powered by a three-cylinder two-stroke engine driving the front wheels. The equally advanced 353 arrived in 1965, and proved reasonably successful in export markets well into the 1970s. However, Wartburg found itself starved of funds, and couldn't replace its ageing two-stroke engine. The company stagnated, and only became competitive again late in 1988. Too late: Wartburg died in 1991. Its factory is now owned by Opel.

WARTBURG
353/Knight

Despite being based on a pre-war DKW design, the Wartburg 353 was still an advanced car when it hit the market in 1965. Front-wheel drive and aerodynamically efficient (if boxy) styling meant 80mph from a mere 49bhp. It became a big hit in East Germany where it became the professionals' car of choice, but was soon left behind by the western opposition thanks to drum brakes and that smoky two-stroke. Sold in the UK at a very low price until 1974, but continued in East Germany until 1988. Two-stroke engine made way for VW power.

SPECIFICATIONS

Years produced:	1965-1988
Performance:	0-60mph: 20.0sec
	Top speed: 80mph
Power & torque:	49bhp/72lb ft
Engine:	Normally aspirated 993cc two-stroke three cylinder, carburettor, 6 valves
Drivetrain:	Front-engine FWD
Structure:	Monocoque
Transmission:	Four-speed manual
Weight:	960kg

PRICE GUIDE

Launch price:	£N/A
Excellent:	£1800
Good:	£1000
Average:	£650
Project:	£400

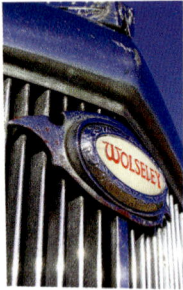

WOLSELEY

THE WOLSELEY SHEEP Shearing Company decided to experiment with cars in 1895 and brought in Herbert Austin as designer. He left in 1906 to start his own company, but Wolseley persisted until 1927, when it went bankrupt and was purchased by William Morris. He positioned Wolseley as a luxury marque, and many boasted Wolseley's lively overhead-cam engine during the 1930s to mark them out from the Morris cars they were based on. Post-war rationalisation reduced most of the marque's output to better-equipped Austins or Morrises; there was even a Mini variant called the Hornet. The Wolseley illuminated grille badge was extinguished forever in 1975.

WOLSELEY
18/85

The 18/85 was really a large pre-war Wolseley that re-emerged after the end of hostilities. Practically identical to the 14/60, it justified its higher price by having a bigger 2322cc six-cylinder engine. With 85bhp available, performance was good and it became well-known as a police car. A novel feature was the 'Nightpass' lights, an anti-dazzle, dipped head and driving lamp arrangement. The 18/85's bulletproof reputation was well-justified; one managed to break the London to Cape Town record despite falling 30ft off a bridge in the Congo. Now that's build quality.

SPECIFICATIONS

Years produced:	1938-1948 (8213 in total)
Performance:	0-60mph: 25.4sec
	Top speed: 75mph
Power & torque:	85bhp/99lb ft
Engine:	Normally aspirated 2322cc six cylinder, petrol, carburettor, 12 valves
Drivetrain:	Front-engine RWD
Structure:	Separate chassis
Transmission:	Four-speed manual
Weight:	1422kg

PRICE GUIDE

Launch price:	£680
Excellent:	£5250
Good:	£4000
Average:	£2000
Project:	£750

WOLSELEY
Eight

At first glance, the Wolseley Eight of 1946 looked like nothing more than a Morris Eight with a Wolseley bonnet and grille transplant. However, it was more than just that, for a smoother 918cc overhead-valve engine of 33bhp was installed in place of the pedestrian 30bhp sidevalve engine of the Morris. A four-speed transmission and hydraulic brakes also featured. A plusher wood and leather interior helped to raise the Wolseley above its humbler Morris sibling and make any passengers feel they were in something a bit special.

SPECIFICATIONS

Years produced:	1946-1948 (5344 in total)
Performance:	0-60mph: N/A
	Top speed: 63mph
Power & torque:	33bhp/45lb ft
Engine:	Normally aspirated 918cc four cylinder, petrol, carburettor, 8 valves
Drivetrain:	Front-engine RWD
Structure:	Separate chassis
Transmission:	Four-speed manual
Weight:	864kg

PRICE GUIDE

Launch price:	£416
Excellent:	£3600
Good:	£2800
Average:	£1400
Project:	£600

WOLSELEY
4/50

The Nuffield Organisation introduced greater levels of rationalisation after World War Two, and Wolseley was one of the marques that lost its individuality as a result. The 4/50, of 1948, was to all intents and purposes a Morris Oxford MO wearing traditional Wolseley identity tags. Thus the more stately Wolseley grille was installed, with interior fitments upgraded to suit middle-class sensibilities. The Wolseley also junked the Morris sidevalve engine and had its own 1476cc overhead-cam four-cylinder of 51bhp instead. Handling wasn't a strong point.

SPECIFICATIONS

Years produced:	1948-1953 (8925 in total)
Performance:	0-60mph: 31.6sec
	Top speed: 74mph
Power & torque:	51bhp/72lb ft
Engine:	Normally aspirated 1476cc four cylinder, petrol, carburettor, 8 valves
Drivetrain:	Front-engine RWD
Structure:	Monocoque
Transmission:	Four-speed manual
Weight:	1181kg

PRICE GUIDE

Launch price:	£704
Excellent:	£3650
Good:	£2850
Average:	£1400
Project:	£600

WOLSELEY
6/80

While the closely related Wolseley 4/50 was a Morris Oxford MO in drag, the 6/80 was a Morris Six in an evening dress with a Pinocchio nose. The prominent snout was needed to accommodate the hefty 2215cc six-cylinder engine which offered more power than its Morris equivalent (72bhp versus 66bhp) thanks to an extra carburettor. The engineering – independent front suspension and unitary construction – was also modern for its day. Obviously, as befitted a Wolseley, the cabin featured sufficient wood and leather to justify its illuminated grille badge and higher price tag.

SPECIFICATIONS
Years produced:	1948-1954 (25,281 in total)
Performance:	0-60mph: 27.8sec
	Top speed: 81mph
Power & torque:	72bhp/102lb ft
Engine:	Normally aspirated 2215cc six cylinder, petrol, carburettor, 12 valves
Drivetrain:	Front-engine RWD
Structure:	Monocoque
Transmission:	Four-speed manual
Weight:	1308kg

PRICE GUIDE
Launch price:	£767
Excellent:	£4400
Good:	£3500
Average:	£1800
Project:	£700

WOLSELEY
4/44, 15/50

This time, it was the Wolseley that was built before any other badge-engineering took place; the equivalent MG Magnette ZA didn't appear for a year after the 4/44's 1952 birth. The Wolseley focused more on opulence than performance, with just a single carburettor for its MG-derived 1250cc overhead valve engine. Nevertheless, its handling was adept thanks to the independent front suspension and rack-and-pinion steering and the sleek lines gave it a rakish persona. In 1956, it was upgraded into the 15/50; identical in looks but with a 1489cc B-series engine.

SPECIFICATIONS
Years produced:	1953-1958 (42,198 in total)
Performance:	0-60mph: 24.3sec
	Top speed: 78mph
Power & torque:	50bhp/78lb ft
Engine:	Normally aspirated 1250cc four cylinder, petrol, carburettor, 8 valves
Drivetrain:	Front-engine RWD
Structure:	Monocoque
Transmission:	Four-speed manual
Weight:	1118kg

PRICE GUIDE
Launch price:	£997
Excellent:	£3750
Good:	£3000
Average:	£1400
Project:	£500

WOLSELEY
6/90 Saloon

Riley introduced its Pathfinder in 1953, Wolseley followed suit in 1954 with the visually-similar 6/90. Aside from minor trim, the two cars looked one and the same. However, the Wolseley boasted two extra cylinders from its 2.6-litre six-pot C-series engine, borrowed from the Austin Westminster. This gave 95bhp as well as 90mph. The Series II of 1956 brought in semi-elliptic rear suspension and a floor-mounted gearchange, but only lasted a year before the Series III added a larger rear window and servo-assisted brakes. Overall, an elegant large saloon.

SPECIFICATIONS
Years produced:	1954-1959 (11,852 in total)
Performance:	0-60mph: 18.1sec
	Top speed: 94mph
Power & torque:	95bhp/133lb ft
Engine:	Normally aspirated 2639cc six cylinder, petrol, carburettor, 12 valves
Drivetrain:	Front-engine RWD
Structure:	Monocoque
Transmission:	Four-speed manual
Weight:	1492kg

PRICE GUIDE
Launch price:	£1064
Excellent:	£3850
Good:	£3000
Average:	£1450
Project:	£500

WOLSELEY
1500

After the Morris Minor replacement project was aborted, the resultant small car became the Riley 1.5 and Wolseley 1500 in 1957. The Minor's floorpan and suspension were retained, but with a new, well-rounded and smart-looking body. The Wolseley was the comfortable cruiser of the pair and thus gave a lower 43bhp from its single-carburettor BMC B-series 1489cc engine. The 1960 MkII hid its bonnet and boot hinges, while the 1961 MkIII had lowered suspension, new tail lamps and tweaks to the grille. Quite a characterful small classic today.

SPECIFICATIONS
Years produced:	1957-1965 (100,722 in total)
Performance:	0-60mph: 24.4sec
	Top speed: 78mph
Power & torque:	43bhp/71lb ft
Engine:	Normally aspirated 1489cc four cylinder, petrol, carburettor, 8 valves
Drivetrain:	Front-engine RWD
Structure:	Monocoque
Transmission:	Four-speed manual
Weight:	1129kg

PRICE GUIDE
Launch price:	£759
Excellent:	£3500
Good:	£2750
Average:	£1250
Project:	£400

WOLSELEY
6/99, 6/110

The sharp lines of the BMC Farina range worked well on the large Wolseley 6/99 and 6/110. Sharing the same engine and bodyshell as the Austin Westminster and the Vanden Plas 3-Litre, the 6/99 was a prestigious machine with its big 2912cc C-series engine giving a lazy but smooth 103bhp. All the extra Wolseley trim and interior touches were in place to pamper occupants. In 1961, a revamp saw the car become the 6/110, with more power (120bhp) and improved handling from a Panhard rod rear end and power-assisted steering.

SPECIFICATIONS (6/99)
Years produced:	1959-1968 (37,209 in total)
Performance:	0-60mph: 14.4sec
	Top speed: 98mph
Power & torque:	103bhp/158lb ft
Engine:	Normally aspirated 2912cc six cylinder, petrol, carburettor, 12 valves
Drivetrain:	Front-engine RWD
Structure:	Monocoque
Transmission:	Three-speed manual
Weight:	1530kg

PRICE GUIDE
Launch price:	£1255
Excellent:	£4750
Good:	£4000
Average:	£2000
Project:	£600

WOLSELEY
15/60, 16/60

BMC badge engineering ran riot with the fintastic family-sized Farinas; there were Austin, Morris, MG, Wolseley and Riley versions. Wolseley, as usual, performed the luxury duties, which meant a higher quality cabin of hide and walnut and the trademark grille. So as not to detract from the MG and Riley versions, it shared the 52bhp single-carburettor 1489cc engine of the Austin and Morris machines. In 1961, the type metamorphosised into the 16/60, with a 1622cc engine of 61bhp, anti-roll bars to rein in the excessive body roll and cut-down fins.

SPECIFICATIONS

Years produced:	1959-1971 (87,661 in total)
Performance:	0-60mph: 24.3sec
	Top speed: 77mph
Power & torque:	52bhp/82lb ft
Engine:	Normally aspirated 1489cc four cylinder, petrol, carburettor, 8 valves
Drivetrain:	Front-engine RWD
Structure:	Monocoque
Transmission:	Four-speed manual
Weight:	1118kg

PRICE GUIDE

Launch price:	£991
Excellent:	£3000
Good:	£2250
Average:	£1000
Project:	£350

WOLSELEY
Hornet

With the Mini a big success, BMC decided to extend its appeal even further in 1961 with the Wolseley Hornet, sister model to the Riley Elf. This was a far less utilitarian version than the original though. So there was a rather flamboyant chrome-laden front, a larger boot framed by small fins, and a three-instrument dashboard surrounded by wood veneer. In 1963, the MkIII Hornet introduced the 998cc A-series engine to the Mini for the first time and Hydrolastic suspension replaced the bouncy rubber-cone type. The MkIII of 1966 had winding windows and improved ventilation.

SPECIFICATIONS

Years produced:	1961-1969 (28,455 in total)
Performance:	0-60mph: 32.3sec
	Top speed: 71mph
Power & torque:	34bhp/44lb ft
Engine:	Normally aspirated 848cc four cylin, petrol, carburettor, 8 valves
Drivetrain:	Front-engine FWD
Structure:	Monocoque
Transmission:	Four-speed manual
Weight:	624kg

PRICE GUIDE

Launch price:	£672
Excellent:	£3400
Good:	£2650
Average:	£1400
Project:	£450

WOLSELEY
1100/1300

BMC badge engineering was rife with the popular 1100/1300 range. The Wolseley was a comparative latecomer to the stable, not being launched until 1965, three years after the first-born Morris. Mechanically it played with the same 55bhp as the Riley and MG versions and also had the option of attractive two-tone paintwork. The 1300 appeared in 1967 with a 1275cc engine instead of 1098cc. This had an all-synchromesh manual gearbox and offered 70bhp thanks to twin carburettors. Autos stuck with the less powerful single-carb version.

SPECIFICATIONS

Years produced:	1965-1973 (44,867 in total)
Performance:	0-60mph: 18.4sec
	Top speed: 85mph
Power & torque:	55bhp/61lb ft
Engine:	Normally aspirated 1098cc four cylinder, petrol, carburettor, 8 valves
Drivetrain:	Front-engine FWD
Structure:	Monocoque
Transmission:	Four-speed manual
Weight:	832kg

PRICE GUIDE

Launch price:	£754
Excellent:	£2400
Good:	£1750
Average:	£850
Project:	£200

WOLSELEY
18/85, Six

Top of the Landcrab tree was the Wolseley 18/85, introduced in 1967. This ultimate enlargement of the Issigonis front-wheel-drive theme begun with the Mini was a capacious car and, in Wolseley form, offered a lot to please class-conscious customers with leather, wood and high-quality carpeting. Naturally there was the usual Wolseley grille with its trademark illuminated centre-badge. The 18/85S of 1969 had 96bhp to the standard car's 85bhp. Four cylinders grew to six in 1972 with the fitment of a silky-smooth 2227cc overhead-cam engine.

SPECIFICATIONS (18/85)

Years produced:	1967-1975 (35,597 in total)
Performance:	0-60mph: 17.1sec
	Top speed: 90mph
Power & torque:	85bhp/99lb ft
Engine:	Normally aspirated 1798cc four cylinder, petrol, carburettor, 8 valves
Drivetrain:	Front-engine FWD
Structure:	Monocoque
Transmission:	Four-speed manual
Weight:	1155kg

PRICE GUIDE

Launch price:	£1040
Excellent:	£2600
Good:	£1850
Average:	£1000
Project:	£250

WOLSELEY
18-22 Series saloon

The 1975 Six was the final Wolseley to be built. Designed by Harris Mann, the car that would forever become known as The Wedge was the upmarket version of its Austin and Morris lookalikes, available only with the 2227cc six-cylinder engine (its humbler siblings were available with four cylinders). At the front was a shrunken version of the traditional Wolseley grille and lit-up badge, the distinctive shape of the car dictating no room for anything larger. After just six months, the entire range was de-badged and the cars renamed as Princesses.

SPECIFICATIONS

Years produced:	1975-1975 (3800 in total)
Performance:	0-60mph: 13.5sec
	Top speed: 104mph
Power & torque:	110bhp/125lb ft
Engine:	Normally aspirated 2227cc six cylinder, petrol, carburettor, 12 valves
Drivetrain:	Front-engine FWD
Structure:	Monocoque
Transmission:	Four-speed manual
Weight:	1215kg

PRICE GUIDE

Launch price:	£2838
Excellent:	£2500
Good:	£1500
Average:	£650
Project:	£15